Lady Gregory was born in 1852 at Roxborough, the large Galway estate of the Anglo-Irish Persse family. Although she received little formal education, she eventually learned four languages and read widely in literature, history and philosophy. In 1880 Augusta Persse married Sir William Gregory, a former governor of Ceylon and the owner of Coole Park. The Gregorys travelled in Europe and the East while maintaining a home in London, where their son Robert was born in 1881. After Sir William's death in 1892, Lady Gregory returned to Coole Park, gradually creating the cultural milieu that attracted other writers and intellectuals such as Douglas Hyde, George Moore, John Synge and W. B. Yeats. Lady Gregory was a founder and director of the Abbey Theatre in Dublin, which opened in 1904, and one of its major playwrights. In the course of her career she wrote some forty plays including *Spreading the News*, *The Rising of the Moon* and *The Workhouse Ward*. She took a leading role in resisting efforts to censor Synge's *Playboy of the Western World* and Bernard Shaw's *Shewing-up of Blanco Posnet*. Gregory published two volumes of Irish saga and romance, *Cuchulain of Muirthemne* and *Gods and Fighting Men*, six volumes of folklore and translations, a history of the Abbey Theatre and a biography of her nephew, the art-collector Hugh Lane. Her autobiography, *Seventy Years*, and her journals were published posthumously. Lady Gregory's life was marred by personal tragedy: widowed at thirty-nine, she lost her only son, Robert, in the First World War. In 1927 she was forced to negotiate the sale of Coole Park, which had been home to her beloved grandchildren, but she managed to live there until her death in 1932.

Lucy McDiarmid is the author of *Saving Civilization: Yeats, Eliot and Auden between the Wars* (1984) and *Auden's Apologies for Poetry* (1990), and co-editor of the forthcoming *High and Low Moderns: Literature and Culture 1889–1939*. A fellow of the John Simon Guggenheim Memorial Foundation (1993–4), she received her Ph.D. from Harvard University and has taught at the University of Maryland

Baltimore County, Princeton and Villanova University, where she is Professor of English. She has lectured widely in Ireland and the United States and has published many articles on modern Irish culture; she is currently completing *The Irish Art of Controversy*.

Maureen Waters is the author of *The Comic Irishman*; her essays and reviews appear in *Eire-Ireland*, *Études Irlandaises*, *The Canadian Journal of Irish Studies*, the *Irish Literary Supplement* and the *Irish University Review*. She has a doctorate from Columbia University and is Associate Professor of English at Queens College, City University of New York. Her most recent work is *Crossing Highbridge*, a memoir of Irish America.

# LADY GREGORY

## *Selected Writings*

EDITED WITH AN INTRODUCTION
BY LUCY McDIARMID AND MAUREEN WATERS

PENGUIN BOOKS

## PENGUIN BOOKS

Published by the Penguin Group
Penguin Books Ltd, 27 Wrights Lane, London w8 5tz, England
Penguin Books USA Inc., 375 Hudson Street, New York, New York 10014, USA
Penguin Books Australia Ltd, Ringwood, Victoria, Australia
Penguin Books Canada Ltd, 10 Alcorn Avenue, Toronto, Ontario, Canada m4v 3b2
Penguin Books (NZ) Ltd, 182–190 Wairau Road, Auckland 10, New Zealand

Penguin Books Ltd, Registered Offices: Harmondsworth, Middlesex, England

This edition first published 1995
1 3 5 7 9 10 8 6 4 2

Typeset by Datix International Limited, Bungay, Suffolk
Printed in England by Clays Ltd, St Ives plc
Set in 10/12.75 pt Monophoto Baskerville

# CONTENTS

# CONTENTS

# ACKNOWLEDGEMENTS

The editors are grateful to the following people for advice, expertise and help of various kinds: James Pethica for his generosity and patience in answering our many questions about Lady Gregory; Derek Mahon for support and friendship throughout our work on this project; Paul Keegan, Susan Piquemal and Donna Poppy at Penguin; our fellow scholars in Irish Studies Angela Bourke, Elizabeth Butler Cullingford, Michael Durkan, Nicholas Grene, Dan H. Laurence, Catherine McKenna, James MacKillop, Maureen Murphy, Philip O'Leary, Patrick Sheeran and Mary Helen Thuente; the Staff of the Berg Collection of the New York Public Library; the administration of Villanova University; and our families: Harris Savin, Emily Savin, Katharine Savin and Lucy Schneider; David Kleinbard and Lee Oser.

# INTRODUCTION

I had been told how to find Biddy Early's house 'beyond the little humpy bridge', and I walked on till I came to it, a poor cottage enough, high up on a mass of rock by the roadside. There was only a little girl in the house, but her mother came in afterwards and told me that Biddy Early had died about twenty years before . . . When I got back at nightfall to the lodge in the woods I found many of the neighbours gathered there, wanting to hear news of 'the Tulla Woman' and to know for certain if she was dead. I think as time goes on her fame will grow and some of the myths that always hang in the air will gather round her, for I think the first thing I was told of her was, 'There used surely to be enchanters in the old time, magicians and freemasons. Old Biddy Early's power came from the same thing.' (p. 58)[1]

When Lady Gregory made her 1897 pilgrimage to Feakle, in Clare, she found stories clustering around Biddy Early, a healer who had cured many of the people who told the stories and had outlived three or four husbands. She was remembered with respect and affection, her cures still cited – cold oranges, dandelions and salt, holy water, a glass of whiskey, advice to take a different road home, or to catch a hen, or to spit on and bless a horse – and her words still quoted: 'It's a thing you never should do, to beat a child that breaks a cup or a jug' (p. 61). Whatever the source of Biddy Early's gift, she posed a threat to the local power structure, and the anxious interferences of priests and doctors figure as often in the tales as the little green bottles that held the cures. Lady Gregory was given an unopened bottle handed to someone years ago by Biddy Early; she placed it, still unopened, on a shelf in her storeroom.

Some of those 'myths that always hang in the air' have gathered around Lady Gregory too. The house, Coole Park, in Co. Galway, has been gone since 1941, but the words remain, in the many volumes of the Coole Edition and in uncollected and unpublished writings. Lady Gregory was one of the most important writers of the period when Irish writing achieved international prominence and one of the most important presences on the cultural scene in the period when cultural nationalism flourished. She collected 'visions and beliefs' on the Aran Islands and in the western counties; she found and translated poems by the blind Irish-speaking poet Raftery; she retranslated Irish saga and romance for a modern readership; and during the Black and Tan Terror she published in an English journal her witness of atrocities in Galway. At Coole she set up a branch of the Gaelic League; for the English readers of *Cornhill Magazine* she wrote about the 'Felons of Our Land'; and for the Irish readers of *An Claidheamh Soluis* she wrote about Raftery and about the Irish language movement.[2] One of the founders of the Abbey Theatre, she made it famous in Ireland, England and America. Listening, talking, recording, reading, writing, translating, publishing, fund-raising, reviewing, she kept Irish culture in circulation.

For over sixty years Lady Gregory has been a part of Irish memory and literary tradition, as much contested as every aspect of Irish culture, and defended, condemned, anthologized or ignored, depending on which book one reads. Any Lady Gregory is someone's construction, as she herself knew well. But she has figured in recent Irish cultural debate only as a playwright and Abbey Theatre director, although her folklore collections, journals and translations constitute equally important parts of her life's work; as close kin to the male writers of the Literary Revival, although her autobiography, plays and poems show the difference her gender made; as the denizen of a Big House, although it was Coole woods she loved most; and as a cautious political moderate, although she was a nationalist and a republican. Not to settle any contemporary debate, but rather to present to it a more complex Lady Gregory, to resituate her and focus attention on her time, place and gender, we offer selections from the many genres of her writings.

# Biography

Isabella Augusta Persse was born at Roxborough, Co. Galway, in 1852, one of the thirteen children of Dudley and Frances Persse; there were three older children as well from Dudley's first marriage. The Persses were members of the Anglo-Irish ruling class whose estate, originally acquired in the seventeenth century, had grown to encompass thousands of well-stocked acres. The first Persse landlord was a Church of Ireland clergyman, and the Persses remained firmly Protestant despite links through intermarriage with Gaelic Catholic and Jacobite Ireland.

Augusta Persse was born following the Great Famine of 1846–51, which struck hardest in the west of Ireland, leaving approximately a million people dead of starvation and disease and forcing another million to emigrate. The Persses were among those who benefited economically from the consolidation of small holdings abandoned by famine victims. Augusta Persse thus grew up in a prosperous household, but one shadowed by a catastrophe that eroded the political and social order supporting a small colonial class against the disenfranchised majority.

In *Seventy Years* Lady Gregory observes that at Roxborough sons were privileged but daughters received little formal education and a great deal of discipline under the censorious eye of their beautiful mother, referred to as 'the Mistress'. Augusta was summarily denied access to whatever person or activity met with parental disapproval; she was not allowed the pleasure of horse-riding or, on a more serious level, of reading Shakespeare's plays before she was eighteen. Daughters were expected to marry well, and if they were plain, like Augusta, they were expected to submit to a life of service to others. Apart from schooling in French and good manners, the Persse daughters were prepared for adult life by weekly Bible lessons that inspired in Augusta a strong religious faith, though in later life she no longer assumed that Protestantism was the only route to God. Reflecting on the powerful effect of those lessons, Lady Gregory noted that they gave her an appreciation of poetic language and prepared her 'to understand and recognize the beauty of our Irish dialect'.[3] Under the influence of her Irish-speaking nurse, Mary Sheridan, this youngest Persse daughter eventually rebelled against the attitudes of her class by purchasing Irish books and patriotic ballads at a bookshop in Loughrea. Her sympathy with the dispossessed native Irish and a commitment to the Victorian ideal of service seem to have been established at an early age.

In 1880 Augusta Persse's marriage to Sir William Gregory, sixty-three, a former governor of Ceylon and the owner of nearby Coole Park, drew her into a larger, sophisticated world. Remembering the pleasurable surprise of this turn of events, she observed wryly that her mother always believed Sir William had proposed 'as a kind of compliment to herself' (p. 28). With her husband, Lady Gregory travelled in Europe, India and the Near East; abroad and in London, she became acquainted with a wide circle of powerful and gifted English people – Robert Browning, Tennyson, the Gladstones, Lord Dufferin – some of whom she later enlisted in Irish causes. She began to read more widely in English and American literature; having earlier learned enough Italian to enjoy Dante, she now studied German through a translation of Shakespeare. In spite of some initial shyness – she was afraid to ask for the salt at her first dinner party – Lady Gregory discovered a talent for conversation and for friendship, nurtured throughout her life by prodigious letter-writing. The Gregorys' only child, Robert, was born in 1881 in London, signalling his impending arrival during a luncheon party over which Lady Gregory continued to preside with characteristic presence of mind until the last guest departed.

Despite a practical marriage and considerable respect for propriety, Lady Gregory was attracted to unconventional men. For nearly a year beginning in August 1882, she was passionately involved with the English poet Wilfrid Scawen Blunt, a romantic Byronic figure and an active anti-imperialist to whom she wrote a number of poems. Their intimacy (according to Blunt) grew out of their joint efforts to influence British public opinion about the Egyptian nationalist known as Arabi Bey and to save his life.[4] Later, at the height of her professional success in 1912, she had a brief affair with John Quinn, the American patron of Irish art and lawyer who defended the Abbey players when they were arrested in Philadelphia. Through correspondence and occasional visits Lady Gregory maintained close friendships with both men for the rest of their lives. Blunt and Lady Gregory were avid diarists as well as poets; Lady Gregory and Quinn shared an interest in Irish painting, especially that of John Butler Yeats, whom they both supported.

After Sir William's death in 1892, Lady Gregory returned to the heavily mortaged, neglected estate at Coole, though she lived intermittently in London for several more years while Robert attended Harrow. In 1894 she decided that she enjoyed 'the free and silent life here', where she had 'elbow room to write and liberty of thought which had been denied me of late'.[5] Despite a limited income that required personal frugality, she replanted woods and gardens, gradually freed the estate from debt, and began the more profound process of transforming Coole into the vital cultural milieu that was to attract all the major artists of the Irish Revival: John Synge, Douglas Hyde, George Moore, Sean O'Casey and W. B. Yeats.

The creation of Coole as a cultural centre began with the construction of the Gregory legacy. In 1894 she edited her husband's autobiography, testifying fully to his liberal political views and cosmopolitanism. This work was followed in 1897 by an edition of the letters of Sir William's grandfather, who had been under-secretary for Ireland between 1821 and 1831. 'I would like to leave a good memory and not a "monument of champagne bottles",' she wrote at this time, expressing a conscious will to separate herself and her family from the appalling record of the Anglo-Irish as a class.[6]

Reading more in Irish history and politics and generally looking about her in the west of Ireland, Lady Gregory in the 1890s could not fail to appreciate the vast changes taking place in the structure of rural society. As a consequence of the alliance between the Parnellites and the Land League in the 1880s, a period of agrarian violence that was particularly bad in Galway and Kerry, ownership was gradually being transferred from the landlords to the tenant farmers. These were changes whose inevitability and appropriateness she acknowledged. She was, as she wrote, 'thankful that we landowners have been given even a little time to prepare and to work while it is day. It is necessary that as democracy gains power, our power should go; and God knows how many of our ancestors and forerunners have eaten sour grapes and we must not repine if our teeth are set on edge.'[7]

Continuing the task of restoring and managing Coole and coming to know the local people more intimately intensified those opinions and encouraged Lady Gregory to move into the public arena. Her administrative abilities were put to use in promoting the weaving and embroidery industry of the nuns at Gort Convent. Then, more ambitiously, in support of Horace Plunkett's co-operative farm movement, she helped to organize meetings encouraging modernization and securing better prices for small farmers. In 1897 she met Douglas Hyde, and began a long and fruitful collaboration in gathering folk material, establishing a branch of the Gaelic League at Coole and writing plays in Irish. Of these efforts she observed 'with a little pride that when Michael Collins and Eamon de Valera[8] were in their short jackets going to school or marching from it, I was spending time and money and energy in bringing back the Irish among my own people'.[9]

Lady Gregory met Yeats in 1894 at a party in London; she was a particular admirer of his prose, and reading the Sligo legends in *The Celtic Twilight* made her 'jealous for Galway'. Gathering folk material was an important focus of their early relationship when Yeats first visited Coole in 1896. In 1897, during the first of twenty extended summer visits, Lady Gregory and Yeats began formulating plans for a national theatre that would 'show that Ireland is not the home of buffoonery and of easy sentiment, as it has been represented, but the home of an ancient idealism'.[10] Their efforts led first to the Irish Literary Theatre, which produced Yeats's *Countess Cathleen* and Edward Martyn's *The Heather Field* in 1899. Subsequent work by Moore, Martyn, Alice Milligan and Hyde appeared in 1900 and 1901. In 1902 *Kathleen ni Houlihan* by Lady Gregory and Yeats was presented by the Irish

National Theatre Company, directed by Frank and Willie Fay. Talented actors as well as directors who had trained Irish players, the Fays joined Lady Gregory and Yeats in 1903 to form the Irish National Theatre Society. On 27 December 1904 the Abbey Theatre, subsidized by the English heiress Annie Horniman, opened with a double bill offering Yeats's *On Baile's Strand* and Gregory's *Spreading the News*. Lady Gregory was the patentee and one of the directors, along with Yeats and Synge.

Primarily through her work at the Abbey and the publicity generated by the theatre's many controversial productions, Lady Gregory became a public figure. She developed a close friendship with Bernard Shaw, whose *Shewing-up of Blanco Posnet* was produced at the Abbey in 1909 in defiance of English censorship and viceregal threats. Touring in England and America with the Abbey players during the period 1911–13, Lady Gregory was interviewed at each port of call and spoke frequently on Irish subjects. Although there were violent protests over *The Playboy* and her life was threatened (in Chicago she received a letter emblazoned with a pistol and coffin), she succeeded in making an international audience more aware of Irish writers. Theodore Roosevelt, who regretted that he could not annex Ireland as a new state (it was 'too far off'), was one of her fans: he believed that American artists could learn from the Abbey's example by focusing on native subjects instead of turning to Europe for inspiration.[11]

Lady Gregory used her formidable gifts to publish in a variety of literary genres. Her continuing interest in native culture led to the publication of two collections of Irish saga and romance, *Cuchulain of Muirthemne* (1902) and *Gods and Fighting Men* (1904), and six books of folk material and translations; all these became important resources for contemporary writers. She also wrote a history of the Abbey, *Our Irish Theatre* (1913), and a biography, *Hugh Lane's Life and Achievement* (1921). Her autobiography, *Seventy Years*, and her journals were published after her death.

Lady Gregory's life was marred by personal tragedies that to a certain extent reflected the conflicting ties of the Anglo-Irish gentry. Widowed at thirty-nine, she lost her only son Robert, a member of the Royal Flying Corps, during the First World War when he was accidentally shot down over Italy in 1918. His wife Margaret was more fortunate as the only survivor of five people when a car was ambushed by Irish soldiers in Galway in 1921. Several of Lady Gregory's nephews died during the Great War, among them a favourite, Hugh Lane. After he was lost with the *Lusitania* in 1915, she battled unsuccessfully for the rest of her life against the Trustees of the National Gallery in London for the return to Ireland of his collection of Impressionist paintings. Lady Gregory underwent three operations for breast cancer and saw her birthplace, Roxborough, destroyed in the Civil War.

Despite these tragedies and the pressures of a crowded professional life, Lady Gregory derived great joy from her three grandchildren, Richard, Anne and Catherine, who spent many of their early years at Coole. Her journals record her delight in 'the chicks', who seem always to have been 'cheery' and occupied with bicycles, squirrels, horses, boats, and apples – when they were not eavesdropping on famous guests. Anne Gregory's memoir *Me and Nu: Childhood at Coole* is a tribute, in return, to her devoted grandmother. In 1927 Gregory was forced to negotiate the sale of the estate (held in trust for Robert, then for Richard) to the Ministry of Lands and Agriculture. By renting back the house and gardens, she none the less managed to live at Coole until her death in 1932, supporting herself in part by royalties from the sale of her books. The house was torn down in 1941, but the famous beech tree, etched with the initials of literary friends, remains. In 1992, in belated recognition of her achievements, the Irish government opened a visitors' centre at Coole Park.

## Lady Gregory and Yeats

'Willie read me pages from his proofs of his new book – [*A Vision*],' Lady Gregory noted in her journal in September 1925. 'He told me my division, 24, was a "very good one", but I don't know that I like being classed as a "certain friend" ... with Queen Victoria!! So do we appear to our friends. But I don't

think she could have written *Seven Short Plays*' (p. 499). Lady
Gregory's succinct refutation of this tiresome stereotype deserves
greater visibility. If she had not been slightly put off by *A Vision*
('some chapters quite unintelligible to me') she might have verified
that her category was not quite so good as Yeats suggested: how
could anyone who knew Lady Gregory have put her in a phase
where 'there is . . . no intellectual curiosity'?[12]

From the moment in 1897 when Lady Gregory and Yeats put
their names to the proposal for an Irish national theatre, her
reputation has been entangled with his, and her image with his
representations of her – as Duchess of Urbino, as Queen Victoria,
as frail old woman. She is not alone in this fate: Maud Gonne
took matters into her own hands with her autobiography *Servant
of the Queen*, and Irish history makes it clear that Constance
Gore-Booth Markievicz[13] did not spend her days in 'ignorant
goodwill'. Dorothy Wellesley's insistence on her autonomy fills
the space between the letters to Yeats in her edition of their
correspondence: 'W. B. Y. is for ever trying to revise my poems.
We have quarrelled about this.' When she wanted to annotate his
revisions ('. . . this line was altered by W. B. Y.') he insisted, 'No!
it has always been done in a company of poets . . . Lady Gregory
wrote the end of my "Deirdre" on my fundamental mass.'[14]

Like Maud Gonne, Lady Gregory speaks out against Yeats's
construction of her image, though her counter-assertions are
more casual and more diffuse, occurring here and there in works
not published in her lifetime, such as her journals and letters. She
never published a book, or a memoir, or even a play with the
explicit purpose of denying the self that Yeats publicized; but the
denials are there. Her emphatic resistance to another Yeatsian
representation may be found in the journal entry for 11 March
1924. She had spent a hectic few days, leaving Coole to go to
Dublin 'by early train', giving hot tea and a clean handkerchief
to a consumptive young man on the train; visiting a friend in
Baggot Street Hospital; watching *Juno and the Paycock* at the
Abbey two nights in a row and chatting with Sean O'Casey;
giving one of her famous tea-and-barmbrack parties on the
Abbey stage, where she also entertained an American journalist;

returning to Baggot Street Hospital; having tea with Douglas Hyde; and conferring with Lennox Robinson about her *Story Brought by Brigit*. It was after this flurry of artistic and eleemosynary activity that Yeats (who had recently received the Nobel Prize) put in her hands 'the typed article on his visit to Sweden in which he describes me as "An old woman sinking into the infirmities of age" – (not even fighting against them!)' (p. 487).

In spite of Lady Gregory's feeling that 'this description would send down my market value, and be considered to mean I had gone silly', and Yeats's promise to remove it, the phrase remains in all editions of 'The Bounty of Sweden' (revised only to 'the infirmity of age'). Just as, earlier, it had been important for Yeats to think of Lady Gregory as the Duchess of Urbino, so in the 1920s it was important for him to think of her as the feeble old woman she was not. She did not live to read Yeats's poem 'Beautiful Lofty Things' (1937), in which for literary effect he aged her ten years; 'her eightieth winter approaching' describing an event of 1922. Her parenthetic comment ('not even fighting against them!') should be read in the light of some of her last words: only seven hours before she died, Lady Gregory refused to go to bed, because ' "that would be giving in" '.[15]

Imagining a Lady Gregory independent of Yeatsian influence or myths is especially difficult because cultural nationalism grew and thrived in collectivities – leagues, societies, associations; all the linguistic, dramatic and athletic energies that kept the national movement alive at the turn of the century formed themselves into group enterprises. In the heyday of the Literary Revival, Yeats, Lady Gregory, George Moore, Edward Martyn and Douglas Hyde were always involved in one collaboration or another. Lady Gregory enjoyed work in 'the company of poets' and a year before her death was imagining an historical pageant about the 1916 Rising that someone like James Stephens (she thought) could complete: 'Perhaps if I could write out suggestions some one or two of our young poets & writers might take it up' (p. 523).

But the myth of a lonely, bored widow waiting to have her talents awakened is contradicted by any bibliography of her

writings: before she ever met Yeats she had published a long
article in *The Times* ('Arabi and His Household'), at least eleven
other pieces in periodicals, a pamphlet (*A Phantom's Pilgrimage; or
Home Ruin*, 1893) and an edition of her husband's autobiography,
and she had written other pieces (such as *An Emigrant's Notebook*)
that she did not publish.[16] Her publications before 1894, however
modest, indicate that she was already a writer. And the Coole
Edition of her works shows her achievements in areas where her
authority exceeds Yeats's, such as folklore and translation.

Because the Yeatsian constructions of Lady Gregory de-sexual-
ize her, readers used to these and other stereotypes will be
surprised to discover a hidden discourse of sexuality in her writing.
Gregory's excellent proto-feminist lyric 'Alas! a woman may not
love!', an explicit complaint against the emotional limitations of a
patriarchal society, dates from the pre-Yeatsian time of her life
(1886). The most sustained writings of this period are the sonnets
she handed Blunt at the end of their affair in 1883 – sonnets
'improved' by Blunt and later published, with her permission,
under his name. The publication of both versions of the sonnets
to Blunt, and recent commentary on the manuscript drafts of
*Grania*, show that feminist scholarship has much material to draw
on. And the publication of the poems she wrote to Blunt while he
was in Galway Gaol (1888) reveal a Lady Gregory persisting in
the transgressive love she allegedly gave up in the last of the
sonnets.[17]

In its mixture of nationalist fervour and literary activity, the
relationship with Blunt certainly anticipates that with Yeats.
Lady Gregory's willingness to let men publish her work under
their names had already manifested itself in the 1880s; she also
wrote a letter signed by her husband to the *Spectator* in 1892. So
impressed was Blunt with Lady Gregory's talents – and so accus-
tomed to her earlier habits of collaboration – that he assumed she
had written 'Easter 1916' and had allowed Yeats to publish it as
his own.[18] But the literary entanglements with Yeats were more
numerous, more complex, and longer-lasting by far than those
with Blunt. In folklore as in other areas, projects merged and
then separated. The core of *Visions and Beliefs in the West of Ireland*,

for instance, remained stories collected by Lady Gregory, but the inspiration for collecting many of them had come from Yeats, and at one point he was an equal collaborator. The volume as published includes 'two essays and notes' by Yeats. And as Colin Smythe puts it, 'Lady Gregory's hand was quietly in much that was published by Yeats in periodicals.'[19] She also had a hand in *The Pot of Broth*, *The King's Threshold*, *Deirdre*, *On Baile's Strand*, the prose version of *The Hour-Glass* and *The Unicorn from the Stars*.

The most notorious of many Gregory–Yeats collaborations remains *Kathleen ni Houlihan*, notorious because Lady Gregory's authorship, suppressed by her at the time, was also suppressed by Yeats and minimized or trivialized by other commentators. Yeats's memorable rhetorical question, 'Did that play of mine send out / Certain men the English shot?' has been criticized for its arrogant notion of the poet's possible role in the Easter Rising; yet it deserves more interrogation for its claims to sole authorship. In acknowledgement of Lady Gregory's indisputable co-authorship, definitively established in James Pethica's study of the manuscripts, we have printed the play in this volume, using her preferred spelling of 'Kathleen'.[20] The selections from the journals include Lady Gregory's account of the occasion in 1919 when she played the title role at the Abbey because the actress Maire Walker was unable to get to Dublin for the scheduled production. Of Lady Gregory's performance Yeats 'said coldly that it was "very nice, but if I had rehearsed you it would have been much better"'. She played the part for three nights, each time, in her own opinion, 'better and with more confidence'.

Yet the importance of recognizing Lady Gregory's separateness from Yeats should not obscure their intimacy and their awareness that each made a profound and fundamental change in the other's life. The literary and financial exchanges, the expectations of loyalty, the minor quarrels and irritations – all these are lacking in the many close relationships Lady Gregory had with literary men who were not collaborators, such as Shaw or John Quinn.[21] Her relationship with Yeats began in mutual need: he needed folklore, which she showed an unusual gift for collecting; whereas she needed a direction for her gifts and a way into the

Irish cultural movement. Whether Lady Gregory asked Yeats if he could 'set her to some work for our intellectual movement' as he entered the library at Coole the first time (as he recalled) or in a walk from Lissatumna to Ballylee (as she recalled), the question was put in what was surely one of their first moments alone.[22] In a famous phrase in 'Estrangement' Yeats called Lady Gregory 'mother, friend, sister and brother', and she certainly thought of him as a family member. Yeats sat at the head of her dining table even after Robert Gregory had attained his majority, he continued to occupy the other master bedroom at Coole after Robert had married, and he attended Lady Gregory in her last illness. He was family. Talking in the library at Coole the day Lady Gregory died, Margaret Gregory Gough, Robert's widow, said to Yeats, 'Yes it is your home too that is broken up.'[23]

## Folklore

Although Yeats accompanied Lady Gregory on many occasions when she collected stories in Galway and Clare, he tended to stand in the cottage doorway while she went inside, questioning and listening to the people. Lady Gregory was a natural folklorist: her genius for remembering direct speech makes her an excellent source of lore and anecdote as well as of 'visions and beliefs'. She could catch the pomposity in the language of government officials as well as the Irish–English of the country. All her life she recorded the stories people told her, at dinner parties in Dublin and London, in cottages in the west, on the Aran Islands, or in her own house.

On 27 August 1924, for instance, one of Lady Gregory's tenants, Patrick Niland, came to Coole in need of money. She had given him five shillings the week before,

> but he looked so tired I sent for bread and butter and a couple of glasses of port and put half a crown in my pocket and promised him some firing *before* he told me a little story: 'There was a poor woman had nothing in the house, nothing for herself and her children, and she went to ask charity from four women that were

in rich houses. And she came back empty and when she was sitting in the house and had nothing to give the children there was a man came in and he asked her what ailed her. And when she told him he said, "Go open that chest you have in the room." And she said there was nothing in it. But when she opened it she found it was full of every sort of thing. And the man said, "From this day you will never be in want, but as to those four women that refused you, before a twelve-month they will come begging to your door." And so they did before the twelve-month was over. But as to her, she had full and plenty from that out, and she had three daughters in America that helped her. For the man who came to tell her that was an angel from God' (p. 491).

It has been suggested that Lady Gregory, in all her years of folklore-collecting, never heard any 'bad landlord' stories, but perhaps this one qualifies. Its ambiguities are considerable: is it a veiled threat, the curse visited on the uncharitable? Is it a thank you, because Lady Gregory, like the 'angel', has given to the poor; or perhaps a thank you on the surface and a threat just beneath the surface? Or is it, as Gregory's own 'Ragged Man' predicts at the end of *The Rising of the Moon*, a wishful glimpse of that future time 'when the small rise up and the big fall down . . . when we all change places at the Rising of the Moon'? Lady Gregory herself makes no comment on the story, offering only the words of 'Old Niland'. The complexity of the situation is reflected in the complexity of Niland's story, a poor tired working man's obviously mixed feelings about begging at the door of the rich woman in her rich house, wishing instead that a divine messenger would tell him 'from this day you will never be in want', and that prosperous American children existed to share their wealth.

The episode is paradigmatic, because it shows how the nature of folkloric material can be determined and shaped by the context of the exchange; and it shows the fidelity of the recorder. No doubt Lady Gregory felt the tensions at work in the story, but she writes them down without comment. It may be that a quantitative analysis of all Irish folk stories from T. Crofton Croker onwards would show that Gregory did in fact hear fewer 'bad landlord' tales than the average; but then, Croker probably collected fewer stories about female healers or the pains of childbirth than Lady Gregory did. The gender, class, age and general demeanour of the listener will always affect the folkloric exchange in some way, but the sheer quantity of stories Lady Gregory collected, from many of the same sources over the years, indicates that people were willing to talk to her at great length and often.

For Henry Glassie, Lady Gregory is 'one of the first great modern folklorists'. On collecting trips she 'listened closely and recorded with precision' and thus performed the first 'duty' of a folklorist in an age before technological aids to memory, recording 'folktales exactly and lovingly in the words of their narrators'.[24] To assume, as even an admirer like Brinsley MacNamara once did, that 'she had been industriously plied with folklore specially invented for her visits, and all of which she had innocently accepted', is to exhibit the deep prejudice based on gender and class that has made so many people critical of Lady Gregory's achievements.[25] If, as Dan Ben-Amos has argued, folklore is 'artistic communication in small groups', a process of exchange rather than a particular kind of content, then there could no more be an 'invented' folklore than there could be an 'invented' dream: all are expressive narratives that emerge from the context of a specific exchange.[26]

In her many years of travelling, listening, transcribing and publishing, Lady Gregory did what the first modern government of an independent Ireland did: she gave value to the stories, to the mind and imagination of Irish country people. The establishment of the Irish Folklore Commission in 1935 transformed into an official state project what Lady Gregory had done on her own years earlier. And listening, as she did, beginning in the 1890s, she retrieved what the Free State folklorists could never have gotten, memories of historical figures then in the process of becoming legendary.

The stories of Biddy Early's practices and techniques, and the many direct quotations from her, show a woman whose success at curing many sorts of physical and mental ailments made the priests and doctors think her fraudulent and dangerous. In one story a 'bad landlord', Dr Murphy, unable to evict Biddy Early, hauls her off to court, '"Faeries and all," he said, for he brought the bottle along with her. So she was put out, but Murphy had cause to remember it, for he was living in a house by himself, and one night it caught fire and was burned down, and all that was left of him was one foot that was found in a corner of the walls' (p. 69). Like Patrick Niland's story of the beggar and the angel, this tale also encodes the revenge of the 'small' on the 'big', though here the mysterious, subversive aura around Biddy Early adds another dimension to the economic distinction.

Although Lady Gregory shared some of Yeats's interest in the mystic and international aspects of folklore, her own was grounded in the national and the local: the stories 'Wandering Mary' told about her encounters with British soldiers during the Terror Lady Gregory considered no less significant than those she collected about Saints Brigit, Columcille and Patrick. Well before 'oral history' became fashionable, Gregory recorded stories about Irish national figures like Daniel O'Connell, and about the Famine, the Great War and the Terror. She made distinctions of genre – such as that between *The Kiltartan History Book* and *The Kiltartan Wonder Book* – but not distinctions of value. Of the *History Book* she wrote, 'I might perhaps have better named the little book Myths in the Making.'[27] If there is such a thing as a line demarcating 'legend' from 'oral history', or 'oral history' from some purportedly more factual kind, Lady Gregory would not have acknowledged its usefulness, because Kiltartan history was defined and validated through the stories told by the people of Kiltartan.

Like all her literary activities, Gregory's folklore-collecting shaped her own intellectual and artistic development at the same time as it made a contribution to Irish culture. Her long hours of listening served her well in play-writing: many people wondered how Yeats could have written the early conversations in *Kathleen ni Houlihan*, because his own play *Countess Cathleen* made it quite clear that he had no knack for country speech. But of course the answer is that he had not written them. Lady Gregory's sense of the spoken idiom also went directly into the conversation of the Fool and the Blind Man in the revised version of Yeats's *On*

*Baile's Strand*, not to mention the many plays entirely her own that are written in the speech of the people she knew.

## Saga and Romance

By 1900 Lady Gregory had conceived the idea of putting together a collection of tales centred on Cuchulain, hero of the Ulster saga the *Táin Bó Cuailnge* (*The Táin*), the earliest redactions of which date from the eighth century. Her expressed intention was to produce a work comparable in style and literary merit to Malory's *Morte D'Arthur*. In preparing *Cuchulain of Muirthemne* and then *Gods and Fighting Men*, Gregory used sources at the British Museum, the Royal Irish Academy and the National Library in Dublin, relying heavily on nineteenth-century printed versions of the Middle Irish texts; these editions provided translations, though the language tended to be stilted and archaic. Lady Gregory was concerned with producing an accessible, readable text.

Sometimes, as in the case of *The Tain*, she had to piece together several versions to produce a coherent tale. She consulted linguists and scholars such as Eoin MacNeill, Kuno Meyer and her cousin Standish Hayes O'Grady; and she worked with Sean Conolly, a language teacher from Aran, to ensure that her translations had the quality of living speech. Her radical solution to the problem of style was to use the Kiltartan dialect, the Irish English of local Galway people. In doing so, she was validating a language system long regarded as inferior to standard English: 'I was the first to use the Irish idiom, as it is spoken to any large extent and with belief in it.'[28] She was particularly pleased about her influence on Synge, referring in *Our Irish Theatre* to his telling Yeats that Kiltartanese was 'the dialect he had been trying to master'.[29] She observes that although Douglas Hyde had used Irish–English in his translations, he had eventually given up this usage under pressure from publishers – a pressure Lady Gregory adamantly resisted, even when she could find no Irish publisher willing to take her manuscript. In making this claim to originality, she underestimated the influence of Hyde and of nineteenth-century novelists like William Carleton and Gerald Griffin. But in an important sense she was right: despite some faulty constructions, she helped to validate for a new and wider audience a language that had been viewed with contempt by commentators as disparate as Swift and Carlyle.

While Yeats hailed *Cuchulain of Muirthemne* as 'the best book that has come out of Ireland in my time' and made immediate use of it in *On Baile's Strand*, others (including Joyce, who lampooned Gregory in *Ulysses*) have been less complimentary.[30] *Cuchulain of Muirthemne* and *Gods and Fighting Men* have been criticized for bowdlerizing the original tales and suppressing grotesquely violent, sexual and 'vulgar' elements. Kuno Meyer, for instance, objected that Lady Gregory eliminated from 'The Wooing of Etain' a description of the heroine's naked body, offering instead a passage about her embroidered clothing. Seeking a popular audience, she was undoubtedly constrained by Victorian standards and rules of censorship, as were most male writers of the time. She was also reacting against the influence of Professors Robert Atkinson and John Pentland Mahaffy at Trinity College, Dublin, who insisted that Irish literature was 'almost intolerably low in tone' and that it lacked idealism and imagination.[31] Concerned as well with lending support to Douglas Hyde's efforts to introduce Irish into the school curriculum, she responded by emphasizing the heroic, the tragic and the hauntingly beautiful details of the saga material, such as the singing of the enchanted children of Lir.

Other translation projects involved collaboration: the most unusual arrangement, according to George Moore in *Hail and Farewell*, was one proposed for *Diarmuid and Grania*. In his satiric memoir Moore describes Yeats's waking him in the middle of the night with an enthusiastic response to Moore's own earlier proposal to write the play in French: 'Lady Gregory will translate your text into English. Taidgh O'Donoghue will translate the English text into Irish, and Lady Gregory will translate the Irish text into English.' Yeats would then 'put style upon it'. Moore claims he actually went to France to begin writing ('une caverne.

Grania est couchée sur une peau d'ours . . .') before admitting his folly.[32]

## Play-writing

At Coole the collaborative process was usually more fruitful. Not only Lady Gregory and Yeats but also Martyn, Hyde, Moore and George Russell (AE) worked together, reading, translating and revising one another's scripts. Synge tended to work independently, but he helped Gregory with *Kincora*. Synge, Yeats and AE wrote different versions of the story of Deirdre, and Synge's version was completed after his death by Gregory and Yeats. Lady Gregory, who enjoyed the collaborative process, also provided the story-line and the conclusion to Hyde's *An Pósadh* (*The Marriage*), and their joint work on *The Poorhouse* was rewritten by her as *The Workhouse Ward*.

In *Our Irish Theatre* (1913) Lady Gregory explains that her play-writing career developed as she began writing dialogue 'when wanted'; just as she became a fund-raiser, critic and theatre-manager (Shaw called her 'the charwoman of the Abbey') because there was 'no one else to do it at the time'.[33] Characteristically speaking of herself as working for Ireland or the Irish people, she rarely sounds the direct note of egotism, even in her journals. Such modesty may strike the reader as disingenuous. Like many Victorian women, Lady Gregory had been taught to suppress any impulse toward self-aggrandizement, or at least to conceal that impulse. In *Our Irish Theatre*, however, the emphasis given to her role in the struggles over *The Playboy of the Western World* and Shaw's *Blanco Posnet* reveals how much she enjoyed stage-centre, fighting off the philistines, lecturing and giving interviews to the press. She especially liked America, writing to Shaw in January 1912, 'It is a great excitement seeing a new country at my time of life, and since Philadelphia I feel any romantic adventure possible!'[34] (The romantic adventure with Quinn occurred at this time.) Lady Gregory was well aware of her power and competence, but her personal satisfaction was genuinely grounded in convictions about the larger cultural value of her work.

Like Yeats, Hyde and Synge, she began by making folk materials central to her dramatic work, and they remained central throughout her career. Occasionally this aspect of Abbey productions has been condemned as either an exoticizing of peasant life or a parochialism that forfeited opportunities for growth, rejecting experimental plays such as O'Casey's *Silver Tassie* and Denis Johnston's *The Old Lady Says 'No'*. No doubt there are grounds for these criticisms, but the original Abbey directors effectively completed a process that began with Congreve and Goldsmith and gathered momentum in the nineteenth century with plays such as Samuel Lover's *Rory O'More* and the Irish plays of Dion Boucicault. Rejecting the traditional double plot structure that had consigned the rustics, or the 'downstairs' people, to comic relief, they placed the historically marginalized figures of Irish country people at the centre of the new drama. Although the Abbey directors have been criticized for their 'Ascendancy' character, their strategy here challenged colonial attitudes.

Using folk materials soon involved Lady Gregory, far more than Yeats or Synge, in an effort to dramatize Irish history. By turning to the expressly historic, however, Lady Gregory directly engaged the political despite her preference for 'staying out of politics'. In a series of full-length plays – *Kincora, Dervorgilla, The White Cockade* – she tackled critical turning-points in the nation's history: 'For to have a real success and to come into the life of the country, one must touch a real and eternal emotion, and history comes only next to religion in our country' (p. 533). Her one-act plays are more successful because they are tautly constructed and more firmly grounded in the local and personal, particularly in the seductive, tragic tensions between men and women. Their powerful nationalist and militant tone, denouncing the English, sympathizing with the rebels of 1798, with Jacobites and Fenians, was an important reason for Annie Horniman's suspicion of Abbey policies and her dislike of Lady Gregory. The two women had conflicting views even on the price of tickets, with Lady Gregory holding out for the sixpenny seats and thus for a more democratic idea of audience.[35]

*Kathleen ni Houlihan*, written with Yeats, draws on Irish history and poetic form in commemorating the Rising of 1798. The original inspiration, according to Yeats, was his 'dream almost as distinct as a vision, of a cottage where there was well-being and firelight and talk of a marriage, and into the midst of that cottage there came an old woman in a long cloak. She was Ireland herself' (p. 534). This revelation has ample precedent in the *aisling* poetry of the seventeenth and eighteenth centuries, in which a poet calls upon Spanish and French aristocrats to aid his captive nation figured as a helpless, beautiful woman. In developing a scenario and writing dialogue together, Lady Gregory and Yeats also drew on the folk tradition of the *cailleach*, the hag associated with the sovereignty of Ireland who appears in such nineteenth-century ballads as the *Shan Van Vocht*. Lady Gregory's and Yeats's adaptation of this material, in which the vision of Kathleen inspires a young Mayo farmer to leave home and fight for her, is consistent with the populist ideals of contemporary nationalist organizations. With Maud Gonne in the title role, the first production of *Kathleen ni Houlihan* in 1902 made a powerful political statement that reverberated in the years that followed.

According to Lady Gregory, *The Gaol Gate* (1906) developed out of events close at hand, among them an incident of local terrorism: 'An agent was fired at on the road from Athenry, and some men were taken up on suspicion. One of them was a young carpenter from my old home, and in a little time a rumour was put about that he had informed against the others in Galway gaol' (p. 537). Out of this episode she wrote a play that fused Christian iconography with republican ideals: 'It was not a little thing for him to die, and he protecting his neighbour!' Lady Gregory's configuration of two women grieving for son and husband recalls the women at the tomb of Christ. But in a provocative departure from the biblical story, the two Marys of Galway inscribe the death of the male victim with meaning: they will 'make a great praise' for Denis Cahel and 'tell it out in the streets for the people to hear', thereby defeating official efforts to obliterate him from the communal memory.

*The Rising of the Moon* (1907) was based on a story told by

Mary Sheridan, the nurse who encouraged Gregory's initial interest in Fenian Ireland. Here the rebel is a shrewd, complicated figure who deftly outmanoeuvres the police sergeant hunting for him. At the climactic moment of their conversation, as the rebel sings the ballad of 'old Granuaile', the sergeant acknowledges their common allegiance to an Ireland represented as a captive woman. During the Anglo-Irish War, which exposed critical divisions among the local police, a performance in Tipperary was forbidden because the play was thought too 'seditious'.[36]

Lady Gregory's nationalism was expressed publicly and unequivocally in her plays, but her feminism tended to be disguised. She created vital and articulate women characters, but only *Grania* offers a sustained and explicit feminist perspective. No doubt because of the frankly sexual character of its heroine, *Grania* (published 1910) was never produced at the Abbey. In this three-act play, based on a well-known Middle Irish tale, the heroine casts off a disappointing lover, Diarmuid, and then sets the terms by which she will return to the community whose laws she violated by running away with him in the first place. Here Lady Gregory seems determined to revise the romantic stereotype of women as helpless victims of fate. Grania believes she is entitled to a full sexual life: 'Why should I be a widow always that went so long a maid?' She not only demands to be heard, she demands a share in, and transformation of, the male power structure. And she is willing to risk public humiliation, tantamount to death in early Irish society, to secure those demands. Her ultimate position, rejecting orthodox patterns of behaviour, is exactly the reverse of that taken by the heroine in the Yeats–Moore version of the tale (*Diarmuid and Grania*, 1901) or by Pegeen Mike in Synge's *Playboy*, who would rather see her lover hanged than be laughed at, herself, by the people of Mayo.

Although Lady Gregory wrote, collaborated on or translated into Kiltartanese some forty plays, including four by Molière, she thought that if she was remembered as a writer, it would be mainly for her comedies. In the first years of the theatre movement these one-act plays were a staple feature of Abbey production at home and on tour, and many remain as vivid and witty as ever.

Spare and well crafted, they reflect both Lady Gregory's humorous regard for her fellow creatures and a profound interest in the way language can spin free of its context to generate new meanings.

The inhabitants of her fictive world of Cloon are reminiscent of Sholem Aleichem's fools of Chelm, though they are probably not on such intimate terms with God. Typical country villagers, shop-keepers, small farmers and pensioners, they seem unaware of history or the nation at large, though the local butcher does not hesitate to exploit English soldiers 'that devour all sorts'. Unlike earlier playwrights who romanticized Ireland, such as Edmund Falconer (whose *Eileen Oge* appeared in 1871), Lady Gregory offers little in the way of local colour and little of the sheer physical energy that usually propels comedy. What is dynamic is the conversation, in its distinctive rhythmic patterns: 'And if it was for any sort of a fine handsome woman, but for a little fistful of a woman like Kitty Keary, that's not four feet high hardly, and not three teeth in her head unless she got new ones!' (p. 326).

Lady Gregory's characters escape poverty and melancholy through fantastical arguments and stories, competing and collaborating with one another in the scripting of an event, and so invest their lives with pleasurable drama and importance. In *Spreading the News* a casual misunderstanding develops into a tale of violence and adultery in which the innocent Bartley Fallon is assumed to have murdered a neighbour and run off to America with the victim's wife. In *Hyacinth Halvey* a man's reputation for piety is so absurdly exaggerated that even robbing the church does not enable him to escape the burden of respectability. In this play, as in *Spreading the News*, efforts of the authorities to comprehend, or 'improve', the inhabitants of Cloon are continually thwarted. In *The Workhouse Ward* two witty, cantankerous old men, McInerney and Miskell, battle for the right to interpret their lives together and to show off their rhetorical skill. This contest of wit draws on the classic pattern of bardic 'contention' found, for example, in *Cúirt an Mheán-Oíche* (*The Midnight Court*) by Brian Merriman. In *Poets and Dreamers* Lady Gregory presents an account of just such a 'contention' between the poets Raftery and Callinan, who were rivals in the late eighteenth and early nineteenth centuries and whose merits were the subject of yet another 'contention' among her Galway storytellers. The high point of the exchange between McInerney and Miskell, a vision of plenty, draws upon a poem by Raftery, Lady Gregory's champion, to whom she thus attributes the last word: 'Ploughing and seed-sowing, blossom at Christmas time, the cuckoo speaking through the dark days of the year! . . . Age will go from me and I will be young again. Geese and turkeys for the hundreds and drink for the whole world!'

In a note to *Workhouse Ward* Lady Gregory refers to the Irish saying 'It is better to be quarrelling than to be lonesome.' But there is much more than companionship at stake here: all of these plays, like *Grania* and *The Gaol Gate*, are ultimately concerned with questions of representation: who is speaking for whom? Whose version of truth will have the stronger claim? Lady Gregory saw clearly the relation between discursive power and political power. In her lecture 'Laughter in Ireland' she anticipates post-colonial theory in her analysis of the way nineteenth-century comic fiction and drama were used to debase and disenfranchise the Irish peasant to please an English audience:

> They wanted, and got what they wanted, Mickey Free, Handy Andy, the butt, the blunderer, the inferior, who to them symbolise Ireland, whose mistakes would make them feel comfortably superior, over which they would comfortably laugh. (p. 291)

By using dialect rather than standard English for all her characters, high and low, Lady Gregory eliminated the invidious contrast of earlier comedy, such as Lover's *Handy Andy*.

## *The Journals*

Lady Gregory's most momentous representation of Irish people did not occur on the stage of the Abbey but in the pages of the *Nation*.[37] During the worst period of the Black and Tan Terror in Gort, in the autumn, winter and spring of 1920–21, she transcribed into her journal a kind of horrible folklore, all the stories of assault, robbery, torture, rape and murder told her by the people who came to her door – neighbours, doctors, priests, everyone. Published in a periodical read by the English liberal public, Lady Gregory's diaries became a witness to atrocity and an urgent, activist record of outrages and massacre. The selections used initials instead of names, and were signed 'An Irish Land-lord' – though, as Elizabeth Coxhead points out, anyone who 'knew Lady Gregory's style could have had no difficulty in identifying the writer, but doubtless this did not include any officer of the Black and Tans'.[38]

Those who persist in thinking of Lady Gregory as a moderate, lukewarm nationalist cannot have read these passages or have known of her desperate attempts to enlist the sympathy and help of friends in England. She wrote to Shaw, 'begging him to come over to Coole and examine into these Black and Tan horrors'. But 'What would be the use? What need have we of witnesses?' he wrote back, arguing plausibly that the British government distorted the news and would claim that the 'burnings and slaughterings . . . are all the work of Sinn Feiners disguised in the uniforms they have stolen'.[39]

Because Lady Gregory kept almost daily records, readers of these passages experience the Terror as it unfolds: the Loughnane boys are missing; someone thinks he has seen one of them; their bodies are found but are not recognizable because 'the flesh was as if torn off the bones'; the bodies are identified: they had been 'dragged after lorries' and drowned. Lady Gregory is told, 'Those boys were winnowing at their mother's house when they were taken . . .' Gradually more stories emerge: 'after the older was beaten, the younger took his part and they beat him too and the mother looking on' (p. 455).

As Lady Gregory describes it, the death of Eileen Quinn, wife of her tenant Malachi Quinn, appears more terrible by far than the poeticized alliterative 'mother murdered at her door' who, in Yeats's 'Nineteen Hundred and Nineteen', crawls 'in her own blood' while the soldiers who killed her 'go scot-free'. Yeats, we learn from the journals, was in England receiving the news in letters from Gregory, not living in the midst of it as she was. Mrs Quinn, only one among many such victims, was sitting in front of her own house, holding her youngest child, pregnant with her next, when she was shot. 'You could take up the three little children in your arms together,' Lady Gregory was told. The official 'inquiry' and the bureaucratic indifference, the distress and later madness of Malachi Quinn, complete the story less picturesquely, but more compellingly, than the 'insolent fiend' and peacock feathers of Yeats's poem.

For those who know nothing of Lady Gregory but the Protestant dowager and Abbey director of recent literary history, the journals offer a remarkable vision of a woman's life lived in a time of political upheaval. Scenes of her three grandchildren and their activities at Coole – learning Irish geography, feeding squirrels, enjoying birthday parties – occur in frequent juxtaposition to news of critical events in Irish history. The likes of Michael Collins, de Valera and Edward Carson appear almost as regularly as Richard, Anne and Catherine Gregory, and great worldly events are presented as they penetrate the rural and the domestic. 'I was getting ready for church,' Gregory notes in her journal, Sunday, 8 January 1922,

> when Anne came up to say the telegraph boy was coming and was calling out that the Treaty is ratified ... The little boy had fallen off his bicycle with excitement on the avenue and had shouted the news to the maids coming from Mass and they had cheered. He said, 'This is the first time I ever was sent with a message, and I brought the best message that ever was brought!' and I gave him a shilling in addition to his apples ... We met a motor lorry leaving Gort in charge of one soldier and I said to Guy, 'There is the army in retreat!' (p. 471)

The details of the first post-colonial moments in the west of Ireland, set down in all their randomness by Lady Gregory, offer much of value to cultural historians: the Treaty announced to the world it will alter forever, the society of Big Houses and long avenues, tenants and servants, visible in all Lady Gregory's details – the 'gentry' going to the Protestant church, 'the maids coming from Mass', Lady Gregory's shilling tip for the little boy and the gift of apples – and the ironic tone of her observation about the army, retreating from the people it had terrorized. The passage shows a world where oral and written forms of commun- ication join in 'spreading the news'; where the content of every telegram is common knowledge by the time it reaches the person it was sent to, and has already acquired a distinctive spin; and where the grand sweep of international politics, the partial col- lapse of empire and the decisive compromises of ministers are manifest in the smallest consequences, a motor lorry 'in charge of one soldier' and a boy falling off his bicycle.

A careful reader of the complete journals will see the continu- ation of some of the rituals of Anglo-Irish life even as the class is in decline, as well as Lady Gregory's own attempts to 'de-anglicize' that life: her objections to the singing of 'God Save the King' in church, for instance, or her substitution of Irish names for English ones during the prayer for 'those appointed for the government of this land'. Moving of necessity in the urban Anglo-Irish circles of her Abbey patrons, Gregory in 1924 attended a gathering at Lady Ardilaun's that felt like a 'sort of *ancien régime* party, a lament for banished society', at which a Mr Stoney regrets the absence of officers at the Barracks: 'Now who is there for our daughters to dance with?' (p. 494). Talking and visiting in the country and in the city, balancing on the hyphen between Anglo and Irish, Gregory recorded the lore and stories of many Irelands between 1916 and 1932. The Lady Ardilauns were soon to be as extinct as the Biddy Earlys.


## A New Lady Gregory

On the day of the battle of Almhuin, Brigit was seen over the men of Leinster, and Columcille was seen over the Ua Neill; and it was the men of Leinster won that battle.


The tutelary role of Brigit, her regional loyalty and protective concern for her people, bear a strong resemblance to Lady

Gregory's feelings about Galway. Its place-names echo throughout her writings: 'tell it out in the streets for the people to hear,
Denis Cahel from Slieve Echtge is dead,' chants the old mother
Mary Cahel in *The Gaol Gate*. 'It was Denis Cahel from Daire-
caol that died in the place of his neighbour! . . . I will go through
Gort and Kilbecanty and Druimdarod and Daroda.' Reading
Yeats's *Celtic Twilight* with its Sligo lore, Lady Gregory was
'jealous for Galway'. Some of that local feeling found a place
in their first major collaboration: 'yellow-haired Donough',
Dhonncha Ban, is identified by Kathleen ni Houlihan as a man
'that was hanged in Galway', as Lady Gregory was informed,
though elsewhere he is associated with Mayo. During the Terror,
perhaps more than any other time, when she collected and
publicized all the atrocities she was told of, Lady Gregory took
on a protective role, as if charged with the care not only of Coole
but of an entire region. Students of Irish culture may find it impossible to distinguish this moral responsibility from a lingering
feudal responsibility for her tenants, though the argument
could be made that Lady Gregory's republicanism grew out
of a feudal sense of obligation. Whatever its origin, Lady
Gregory's feeling about Galway was not metropolitan pastoral
nostalgia but the rural person's passion for the land of a particular
place.

So deep was Lady Gregory's identification with her own county
that in a spontaneous meditation during her 1926 operation for
breast cancer she imagined herself the river that ran through her
childhood home in Roxborough:

> . . . the dip of the stream underground, rising later to join its sunlit
> branch; a rushing current again, passing by Ravahasey, Caherlin-
> ney, Poll na Sionnach, Eserkelly, Castleboy, bridges again and
> then through thickets of laurel, beside a forsaken garden – (A sting
> of pain here from the knife, but I only make a face and hear a
> voice say 'put in another drop') . . . and for a moment I think of
> the river that has bounded my second phase of life rising in the
> park at Coole, flowing under the high poplars on its steep bank,
> vanishing under rocks that nature has made a bridge; then flowing
> on again till it widens into the lake. But before I had come to its

disappearance under the rocks at Inchy only to appear again as it mixes into Galway Bay, the Surgeon told me the knife had done its work. And presently the flow of warm blood was stopped with straps and bandages . . . (p. 508)

Like the Celts for whom rivers were female deities, Lady Gregory, feeling the 'flow of warm blood' over her body, thinks of herself as water flowing in the midst of land. Joining in autobiographical reverie rivers and lands not in fact geographically contiguous, reliving her life in sensuous topographical detail, Lady Gregory finds hidden sources of vitality as the surgeon cuts into her flesh. Her body is like the Paps of Anu in Kerry, or the *cailleach* of whom Nuala Ní Dhomhnaill has written, or its most famous literary source, 'The Old Woman of Beare', which Lady Gregory translated: 'The flood-wave and the second ebb-tide; they have all come as far as me, the way that I know them well . . . what used to be on the flood-tide is all on the ebb today!' (p. 150).[40]

Passages such as the meditation, along with the many Galwegian references, suggest the value of considering Lady Gregory in connection with the Irish literary traditions of *dinnseanchas*, or place-lore. Newly available writing by Lady Gregory will also suggest other approaches. Her poem 'Alas! a woman may not love!' and her sonnets to Blunt show the value of seeing her in the context of women's writing, although she took pains in her journals to dissociate her work from that of other women, such as Emily Lawless. Nevertheless, her choice of Grania, Gormleith and Dervorgilla as heroines, and her determination to seek out Biddy Early's house and hear about her cures, reveal a need to find precursors, to define a tradition of strong, unconventional Irish women to place herself in. Her preference was for the native Irish or Gaelic women, though she might have found a predecessor also in Charlotte Brooke, the eighteenth-century editor and translator of *Reliques of Irish Poetry: Consisting of Heroic Poems, Odes, Elegies and Songs* . . . (1789). As the 'first mediator of importance between the Irish-Gaelic and the Anglo-Irish literary traditions', Brooke flourished in the tradition of Patriot antiquarianism that (according to Joseph Leerssen) anticipated cultural nationalism.[41]

New ways of placing Lady Gregory in Irish literary and cultural traditions are necessary because so long as she is considered, as she always has been, in the company of the male Revivalists – Yeats, Hyde, Synge, Moore – she will be seen as the duchess who says yes or the old lady who says no. She will, moreover, be implicated in the alleged political subtexts of her colleagues, without consideration of her quite distinct opinions. Many contemporary critics insist on Lady Gregory's membership in an Anglo-Irish cultural élite who were 'conscious . . . of the threat to their social standing from the increasingly self-assured and powerful majority', and who therefore 'sought to popularize the stark outlines of politics, class and sectarianism in the benign glow of culture'.[42] Lady Gregory and other writers of the Irish Literary Revival, argues Terence Brown, depict 'an ancient Ireland, heroic and self-sacrificially magnificent, in which unity of culture was manifest in a pagan, mythic, rural paradise'.[43]

Even the most casual reading of Lady Gregory's work reveals the inaccuracy of this image. If anything, she romanticized the rebel tradition and its associated symbols, many of them deriving from the 1798 Rising: the speech from the dock, for instance, and the belief that 'A felon's cap's the noblest crown / An Irish head can wear.' Her 1900 essay 'The Felons of Our Land', her collaboration on *Kathleen ni Houlihan*, her play *The Rising of the Moon*, her lifelong interest in prison literature from John Mitchel's *Jail Journal* through Frank Gallagher's *Days of Fear*, her 1923 litany of martyrs *An Old Woman Remembers*, and countless comments in her journals, essays and introductions, all show a Fenian Lady Gregory. No wonder her nephew Desmond Shawe-Taylor was warned not to visit her because 'Your Aunt Augusta is hand in glove with the rebels.'[44] To say that in her work a 'prelapsarian Ireland knows nothing of the political and sectarian strife of the modern' is to ignore the greater part of Lady Gregory's work, which contains so many Irelands as to defy such crude simplification.[45] And although she did indeed begin with an idealized notion of Irish rebels, by the time she published her detailed accounts of the Terror, no one could accuse her of romanticizing.

Lady Gregory might then be seen as doing the cultural work not of the landed elite but of the women political activists who were her contemporaries, women like Maud Gonne, Constance Markievicz, Kathleen Clarke – the women of Inghinidhe na hÉireann, whose patron saint was Brigit, or Cumann na mBan. Like Lady Gregory, they found their public voices not in a feminist movement but in a rebel one.[46] Although Lady Gregory did not enjoy close friendships with these women, the connection was one she recognized and acknowledged: in her journals she recalls meeting Markievicz once late at night after 'hard hours' work at the Abbey. I felt tired and jaded in the tram. And then she got in, tired and jaded also from some drilling of her "Fianna", and I felt drawn to her . . . We were each working for what we believed would help Ireland' (p. 511).

Lady Gregory will, we hope, be understood anew in all these traditions and contexts. The greatest error would be to insist on a static or an unambiguous Lady Gregory. The complexities of her life and work defy the easy categories that those who study Ireland, or women, or both, occasionally indulge in. She gave token respect to the patriarchy of the Anglo-Irish but her political unconscious was matriarchal; she lived in Big Houses most of her life but never owned land; in her youth she was presented to Queen Victoria but in her old age she supported the Republicans in the Civil War; the black-clad widow, one of the few remaining parishioners of the little Protestant church in Gort, enjoyed, at age fifty-nine, an affair with a younger man; the powerful 'Old Lady' of the Abbey never publicly asserted her co-authorship of *Kathleen ni Houlihan*; and with what diffidence and trepidation did that author, almost sixty-seven years old, appear on the stage of the Abbey in the title role of her most famous play. As time goes on, she wrote of Biddy Early, 'her fame will grow and some of the myths that always hang in the air will gather round her': for Lady Gregory, it is now time to clear the air.

# Notes

1. All parenthetical page references are to the Penguin *Selected Writings of Lady Gregory*. Publication details about Lady Gregory's works can be found in the Bibliography section.

2. 'The Felons of Our Land', *Cornhill Magazine*, May 1900, pp. 622–34; 'The Language Movement in Ireland', the *Speaker*, 12 August 1899, pp. 151–2, reprinted in part in *An Claidheamh Soluis*, 19 August 1899, p. 365; 'Raftery, The Poet of the Poor', *An Claidheamh Soluis*, 14 October 1899, pp. 488–9.

3. *Memoirs*, typescript draft, vol. I, dated 21 October 1918, p. 5. Berg Collection, New York Public Library.

4. See Elizabeth Longford, 'Lady Gregory and Wilfrid Scawen Blunt', *Lady Gregory, Fifty Years After*, ed. Ann Saddlemyer and Colin Smythe (Gerrards Cross, Bucks.: Colin Smythe Ltd, 1987), p. 90.

5. *Seventy Years, 1852–1922*, p. 267.

6. *Seventy Years, 1852–1922*, p. 284.

7. *Seventy Years, 1852–1922*, p. 284.

8. See Glossary.

9. *Seventy Years, 1852–1922*, pp. 321–2.

10. *Our Irish Theatre*, p. 20.

11. *Seventy Years, 1852–1922*, p. 455.

12. Yeats, *A Vision* (London: T. Werner Laurie, 1925), p. 103.

13. See Glossary.

14. *Letters on Poetry from W. B. Yeats to Dorothy Wellesley* (London: Oxford University Press, 1940; rpt. 1964), p. 46.

15. W. B. Yeats, 'The Death of Lady Gregory', *The Journals. Volume II, 21 February 1925–9 May 1932*, p. 637.

16. See Colin Smythe, 'Lady Gregory's Contributions to Periodicals: A Checklist' in *Lady Gregory, Fifty Years After*, ed. Ann Saddlemyer and Colin Smythe (Gerrards Cross, Bucks.: Colin Smythe Ltd, 1987), pp. 322–45.

17. For the poems written to Blunt while he was imprisoned, see James Mitchell, 'The Imprisonment of Wilfrid Scawen Blunt in Galway: Cause and Consequence', *Journal of the Galway Archaeological Society* (46, 1994), pp. 91–5.

18. Elizabeth Longford, 'Lady Gregory and Wilfrid Scawen Blunt', p. 95.

19. Colin Smythe, 'Lady Gregory's Contributions to Periodicals: A Checklist', p. 322.

20. James Pethica, ' "Our Kathleen": Yeats's Collaboration with Lady Gregory in the Writing of *Cathleen ni Houlihan*', *Yeats Annual 6*, ed. Warwick Gould (London: Macmillan, 1988), pp. 3–31.

21. See James Pethica, 'Patronage and Creative Exchange: Yeats, Lady Gregory and the Economy of Indebtedness', *Yeats and Women*, ed. Deirdre Toomey (London: Macmillan, 1992), pp. 60–94.

22. James Pethica, 'Introduction', *Lady Gregory's Diaries 1892–1902*, p. xxiv.

23. W. B. Yeats, 'The Death of Lady Gregory', p. 634.

24. Henry Glassie, 'Introduction', *Irish Folktales* (New York: Pantheon, 1985), pp. 24, 21.

25. 'At the Abbey Theatre', *Lady Gregory, Fifty Years After*, p. 29.

26. Dan Ben-Amos, 'Toward a Definition of Folklore in Context', *Toward New Perspectives in Folklore*, eds. Americo Paredes and Richard Bauman (Austin, Texas: University of Texas Press, 1972), p. 13.

27. 'Notes', *The Kiltartan Books* (*The Kiltartan Poetry Book, The Kiltartan History Book, The Kiltartan Wonder Book*), p. 148.

28. *Our Irish Theatre*, p. 147.

29. *Our Irish Theatre*, p. 75.

30. W. B. Yeats, 'Preface', *Cuchulain of Muirthemne*, p. 11.

31. *Seventy Years, 1852–1922*, pp. 391–3.

32. George Moore, *Hail and Farewell*, ed. Richard Allen Cave (Gerrards Cross, Bucks.: Colin Smythe Ltd, 1976), pp. 247–55.

33. *Our Irish Theatre*, p. 53.

34. *Shaw, Lady Gregory and the Abbey: A Correspondence and a Record*, ed. Dan H. Laurence and Nicholas Grene (Gerrards Cross, Bucks.: Colin Smythe Ltd, 1993), p. 68.

35. Adrian Frazier, *Behind the Scenes: Yeats, Horniman, and the Struggle for the Abbey Theatre* (Berkeley: University of California Press, 1990), p. 174, n. 62.

36. *The Journals. Volume I. 10 October 1916–24 February 1925*, p. 115.

37. 'A Week in Ireland', *Nation*, 16 October 1920, pp. 63–4; 'Another Week in Ireland', *Nation*, 23 October 1920, pp. 123–4; ' "Murder by the Throat" – Mr Lloyd George', *Nation*, 13 November 1920, pp. 215–6; 'A Third Week in Ireland', *Nation*, 4 December 1920, p. 333; 'A Fourth Week in Ireland', *Nation*, 18 December 1920, pp. 413–14.

38. Elizabeth Coxhead, *Lady Gregory: A Literary Portrait* (London: Secker & Warburg, 1961, 1966), p. 174.

39. *Shaw, Lady Gregory and the Abbey: A Correspondence and a Record*, p. 154.

40. Nuala Ní Dhomhnaill, 'Cailleach', *Pharoah's Daughter* (Oldcastle, Co. Meath: The Gallery Press, 1990), pp. 134–7.

41. Joseph Th. Leerssen, *Mere Irish & Fíor-Ghael: Studies in the Idea of Irish Nationality, Its Development and Literary expression Prior to the Nineteenth Century* (Amsterdam/Philadelphia: John Benjamins Publishing Co., 1986), pp. 422, 426.

42. Terence Brown, 'Cultural Nationalism 1880–1930', *The Field Day Anthology of Irish Writing*, vol. II, eds. Seamus Deane et al. (Derry: Field Day Publications, 1991), p. 517.

43. Terence Brown, 'Cultural Nationalism 1880–1930', p. 518.

44. Desmond Shawe-Taylor, 'A Woman Young and Old', *New Yorker*, 19 July 1976, p. 95.

45. Terence Brown, 'Cultural Nationalism 1880–1930', p. 518.

46. See Carol Coulter, *The Hidden Tradition: Feminism, Women and Nationalism in Ireland* (Cork: Cork University Press, 1993).

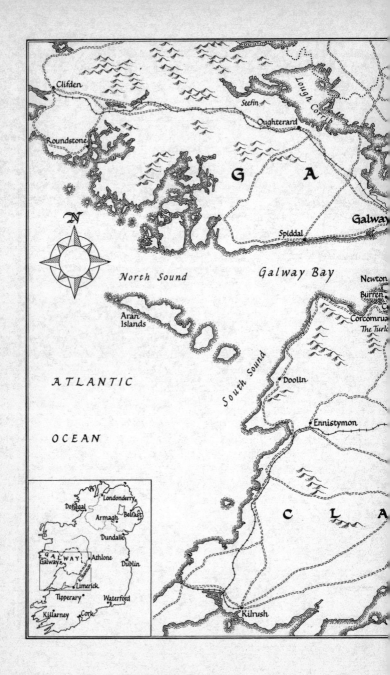

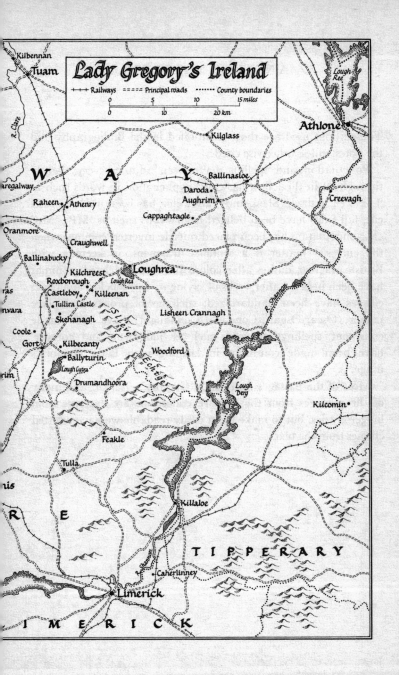

# Lady Gregory's Ireland

Railways +++++  Principal roads =====  County boundaries ••••••

0        5        10        15 miles
0        10        20 km

Kilbennan
Tuam
Kilglass
Athlone
Lough Ree
Ballinasloe
W   A   Y
Creevagh
Daroda
Aughrim
aregalway
Raheen   Athenry
Cappaghtagle
Oranmore
Craughwell
Ballinabucky
Kilchreest
Loughrea
Lough Rea
Roxborough
Castleboy   Killeenan
nvara
Tullira Castle
Lisheen Crannagh
R. Shannon
Skehanagh
Coole
Kilbecanty
Woodford
Gort
Ballyturin
Lough Cutra
Drumandhoora
Lough Derg
Kilcomin
Feakle
Tulla
Killaloe
is
T   I   P   P   E   R   A   R   Y
R   E
Shannon
Caherlinney
Limerick
I   M   E   R   I   C   K
Sliev
Echtge

# A NOTE ON THE TEXTS

The editions used are those mentioned in the Bibliography and the notes, unless otherwise cited.

Punctuation and spelling have been adjusted very slightly throughout in the following ways: hyphenation in words such as 'folklore', 'today', 'Black and Tans', etc., has been made consistent; full stops have been deleted from words such as 'MP', 'Mr', etc.; punctuation has been placed outside inverted commas when the enclosed matter is a sentence fragment, in keeping with British practice; dashes after colons have been deleted; commas have been inserted after verbs of saying or doing before dialogue; ellipses have been standardized; spellings of proper and place names (Oscar/Osgar; Connacht/Connaught) have been made consistent; spellings in words such as 'judgment' and 'forever' have been made consistent in keeping with Lady Gregory's usage.

Most of the passages from Lady Gregory's *Journals* and many of the passages from the folklore collections are excerpts from longer entries, but to make them easily readable we have omitted ellipses from the text.

# AUTOBIOGRAPHY

# from *Seventy Years*

## The First Decades

If the children at Coole should ever read this account of their grandmother as a child, although they might easily enough think of her learning lessons (for that is what she is doing to this day), they would find it very hard to think of her as of their own age, lightfooted, running along that hillside of Slieve Echtge they can see a glimpse of from the upper windows of the house. So I think it will be best to tell this part of her life just as if she were one of the children of fancy they read about in their story books.

At the midnight hour between the fourteenth and fifteenth of March 1852, the planet Jupiter, so astrologers say, being in mid heaven, a little girl was born at Roxborough that is in Connacht. She was the fifth daughter of her mother, and there were two stepdaughters also in the house. And although her mother had four sons of her own, besides a stepson, [this birth made the numbers even, and] she liked boys better than girls and wished for more sons than daughters, and so was sorry this was not a boy. Yet when, according to the old nurse's story, this little-welcomed girl had nearly gone out with but a breath of the world's air, being laid aside and forgotten for a while in the quilt of covering when the mother said that she would have been sorry for such a loss, because the other children would have been disappointed at not having a new baby to play with. And anyway she was the last girl in the family; there came four brothers after that. And so with eight boys to their five daughters, their mother had to be satisfied.

When the christening day came and the big china bowl was carried to the church and back again, to be used instead of the white basin there that was not without some cracks, the youngest daughter of the house was weighted with a many syllabled 'Isabella Augusta', borrowed from a never to be seen godmother, a Miss Brown of Bath.

The reason of this little girl's story being told, now written by

3

her later self, is that her passing out of sight is in the course of nature not far off, and she knows that according to the fashion of the time, there is a trade in such things as the life history of anyone whose name has gone far enough or has been held in enough repute to bring as many buyers as will pay for the making of the book. And her name has come to be thus known, chiefly she thinks through her having written eleven short plays, and in a lesser degree through some longer ones; and by her translations and arrangement of many of the old stories and legends of Ireland, and even through other writings that are to her mind of less value, not having in them a record of the old vanished world, but of the visible world of today, and in this lower place she thinks this book now to be written will of necessity stand. And yet, if written it must be, she will herself take the burden and not expect another to do well what she thinks can not be done supremely well, or put the task on some friend dear to her, or leave it to some indifferent scribe. And indeed it is not as herself but as another that she must write of that early self, so far away does it seem to her now, though standing clearer in the memory than the self maybe, some score or more years later, when the outline grows confused by the tangled interests and associations that have caught it into their nest. And if she does not always put down her own errors and mistakes it is not because she does not know and is not sorry for them. And she thanks God that she has been able to work so long, and above all that anything she has done that is worth the doing has been in Ireland and through Ireland, and for Ireland's sake.

For it was her happy fortune to have been cradled there, never indeed leaving the county of Galway that was her birthplace, save for crossing the border into Clare now and again, when the heather was in bloom on the Munster side as well as on the Connacht side of a dividing stream, until taken on a visit to Dublin in that fifteenth year that is between childhood and girlhood, purple hilltops there also calling from the untrodden land. And she was happy in being in the care of old Mary Sheridan, the seventh of her nurselings in the house.

It was but yesterday, November 1921, she told her little granddaughters, when they read in their history book of the war with Napoleon, how that old nurse had been as a child in a theatre where all the people had of a sudden stood up and shouted because news had come of the landing of the French at Killala – 'she told me she remembered it, and that happened a hundred and twenty-three years ago'. 'And does that make you one-hundred and twenty-three years old grandmamma?' they asked. They themselves, or the elder, may have some faint recollection of the rising of 1916, but they will not either of them forget the shots so often heard last winter, fired by the passing Black and Tans[1] on their devastating round, even less the ambush last May when their mother was the sole survivor of a carful of five!

Mary Sheridan had lived also in the family of Hamilton Rowan[2] the rebel, and would tell of his escape in a boat and his uneasiness lest the boatmen should recognise him, for there was a reward upon his head; and how they had indeed recognised him, but had told him that he was safe with them whatever might be the offered reward. She told also when once she had come with her children to the room where he was breakfasting, a sudden anger had seized him as he read the newspaper, and he had flung a knife that slashed the face of a portrait of Lord Norbury, the Judge, that hung upon the wall. And once on the hall door steps the little girl had wondered to see her, that proud old nurse that seldom so condescended, in eager converse with a white-haired woman, a wandering beggar, and listening, learned that woman also had a memory of that rising and that landing of the French.

Sometimes, not very often, nurse Sheridan would be persuaded by the half dozen younger children to 'tell a story'. And it would not be of the people of today, but of horses wearing silver bells [that must be stuffed with wool before the captive Princess could escape from the witch who held her;], or of a wolf that swallowed whole and alive the goat's six little kids [but falling asleep after the meal was cut open by a wise seventh hidden in the clock case, and who while the six leaped away safe and sound put stones in their places, so that going to drink, the weight overbalanced the wolf, and he fell into the river and was drowned;], or of the Hairy

Girl who became beautiful when that enchantment had been broken and who lived in a castle guarded by cats, one, the most terrible, bearing the name Maol-Wall; so that one at least of the hearers remembers being afraid to cross the dusky passage from the boys' to the girls' nursery, while trembling from the thought of those monsters, beyond nature terrible.

That was up at the top of the house under the sloping roof of what was said to have been the first house slated in the county. Downstairs, the stories worth listening to, that made their lodging in the mind, had come from the Eastern world, the wonderful histories of the flood and the Tower of Babel, and David and the Giant, and Jonah who was swallowed by the Great Fish. For the Bible was read through and through at family prayers from year's end to year's end, and what better food for the imagination could be given? A chapter of the Old Testament in the morning, at evening prayer a chapter of the New; how happy when near the last cover of the book came the vision of precious stones in the New Jerusalem, and of the Tree of Life that bore twelve manner of fruit.

These teachings were perhaps to be of more lasting worth to one young pupil than the schoolroom tasks from Mangnall's *Questions* and Abbot's *Astronomy* and Pinnock's *Greece* and *Little Arthur's History of England*, or any set by what appears in memory's panorama as a procession of amiable incompetent governesses. A little French was learned, and many scales and exercises on the piano made music seem for many a day a hard enemy. At reading the little girl was slow, and she blushed as she stumbled through her verses at a Bible Class held for a while by a Wesleyan Minister. Memory became a more efficiently trained servant through the accident of a long poem, written but rejected for the Newdigate prize at Oxford, having found its way to a bookstall, where her brothers' tutor bought it. And that his couple of pence might not run all to waste, he gave this *Destruction of Nineveh*, telling of God's vengeance long delayed and fiery wrath descending low with arm uplifted high to his boy pupils' little sister to learn by heart. For it is likely those many pages of blank verse may have been of more use in strengthening her memory than would have been a poem on some more winning subject and holding sweeter sounds. The Mother, 'The Mistress', as she was called by all, children as well as servants [as it seems,], did not consider book learning as of any great benefit to girls; for sometimes a new governess asking for new lesson books would be told to wait until the girls could answer all of Mangnall's questions, and of course they never could. Religion and courtesy, and holding themselves straight, these were to her mind the three things needful. French perhaps also, for her grandmother had been a Huguenot. She was less indulgent to the girls than to the boys, and for all the large expenditure and the plenty, even luxury, in food, she would not willingly allow a fire to be lighted in the schoolroom until the dahlias had been cut down by the frost. She set an example in courtesy, having fine manners inherited perhaps from that French ancestress Frances Algoin, whose little book – *Frances Algoin her Book – 1st January 1724/5* – is on the table where these lines are written; and so taught by example as well as precept. In her long life she was never seen to appear impatient with the dullness or ill-manners of a guest, and she would always defend the absent against the criticisms of her flock. It was but the other day that some acquaintance was told by a French tutor whose wandering spirit had led him in his early life to Roxborough to teach the younger boys for a while, how when he arrived at night, a frightened stranger, after a nine miles' drive along a dreary road, a tall lady in black velvet and diamonds had come to the open hall door and welcomed him to Ireland with a friendliness he had remembered through half a hundred years. He may not remember that she gave thought to his soul's welfare also, and although he had declared himself a Protestant, was one day overheard giving him instruction in his own language, on the errors of Rome, translating from the open book of *Revelations* the words 'Babylon est tombée, tombée, tombée.'

It was during the long evenings in the drawing-room that the little girl's love of reading began. All the family and many of the household, but not the old nurse or other Catholic servants, gathered there for family prayers. After they were over, a silver urn was brought in and the Mistress made tea at a table at the end of the room, where tutor and governess and children might sit for a while. There was no conversation during the evening in which all might join. The Master's wheeled chair was beside the fire. The Mistress had her place near; the elder brothers when at home, and the elder sisters had their easy chairs; the younger boys escaped to a more lively part of the house. There was silence except when the musical sister played on the piano, or the Mistress read extracts with approval from the leading articles of *The Times*. The two youngest daughters occupied two high-backed chairs on the fireless side of the round table in the middle of the room. One, intelligent beyond her years and sociable, would listen to any scraps of talk and sometimes even herself look at a newspaper. The youngest, very shy and quiet except when with the younger boys, would open one or other of the few books that lay on the table, arranged like the spokes of a wheel, the lamp in the centre its hub. The book best remembered is *Lalla Rookh*,[3] for although its text was forbidden as 'not fit for little girls', each engraved illustration had some lines of the poem under it, and the broken context gave it mystery:

> Ah turn not from me that dear face!
> Am I not thine, thine own loved bride,
> The one, the chosen one whose place
> In life or death is by thy side!

What romance in those lines, with the picture of the plague-stricken lover and the pale turbaned girl bending over him, did not this awaken! And there was one page dreaded yet opened in spite of trembling, the unveiled face of the hideous Prophet of Khorassan. There were two or three *Books of Beauty* also [the fairest of these beauties to the childish mind a lovely Irish-born Princess of Capua, whose sorrowful eyes seem to mourn ceaselessly for her native land]. And when no one was looking a page would be opened, a frontispiece showing 'The Marchioness of London-derry and her child', and two little cheeks would glow with pride and shyness because the elder sisters had been heard to say that the child in the picture was 'like Augusta'; and this was the only flattery she had to bring to mind in those early days, in that overflowing plain-speaking household. But when there were dinner parties, and these not only at the great winter shooting parties but in summertime, there was a greater evening joy to be found. For then the centre table was covered with a cloth of velvet pile, and a few carefully kept books in handsome bindings were brought out and laid upon it, chief among them a large volume of English ballads, a never failing treasury of delight. And of these the one most stirring was *Chevy Chase*, not only from its own simplicity and high matter and the unforgettable dauntlessness of him who seemed its greatest hero –

> For Witherington my heart is woe,
> I write in doleful dumps,
> For when his legs were hewn away
> He fought upon his stumps.

But because this Persse household claimed descent from these Persses of the ballad; a Duke of Northumberland had been a guest at Roxborough; another part of the property in the county bore the Border name of Newcastle; while over the hills in a fold of Slieve Echtge, where wild deer ran in the woods, the Irish names of yet another Daroda, Dairebrian, Druim-da-rod had been long overlaid with the less lovely yet still romantic name of Chevy Chase. That ballad book, and some poems of Wordsworth's on shining paper, with gilded edges, and the *Books of Beauty*, and a Shakespeare in small print, in red morocco [(but the time had not come for opening that)] were taken away by the elder sister when she married, yet were not quite out of reach, for they adorned another drawing-room table on a neighbouring estate, Castle Taylor, but some five or six miles to the north west.

The eldest brother was but seldom at home. He had been wounded in the Crimean War; there was a tradition, it could hardly be a recollection, of his eldest sister having fainted in the manner that belonged to that generation, when the news came, and fallen from a little beadworked stool in the drawing-room that used to hurt the bare elbows of the child that sometimes knelt at it for family prayers. He was brave; his name is given in

Kinglake's story of the storming of the Alma, and there was a coloured print at Roxborough representing him (or so it was said, and it was a good likeness), with words that justified a tradition that he had killed in that battle seven Russians. He himself was but a tradition in those early days, for some quarrel or coolness with his father had kept him away. Then there was a reconciliation and he came back for a while. He was very quiet in manner, very kind, very handsome, with fair hair and beard and blue eyes. One of the young stepbrothers was learning music, and one evening when he played among his little tunes, 'Partant pour la Syrie', the soldier came across the room very much moved and put a sovereign into his hand. He had so often heard that air that was composed by Louis Napoleon's mother, Queen Hortense, played in those Crimean Camps.

As for gaieties, there were not any for the children especially, and so not ever having been known were never missed; it was delight sufficient to act as audience at an occasional servants' ball, or at the great dance in the barn that followed and crowned each year's sheep-shearing. McDonough, the piper, whose father had learned strange tunes among the Sidhe,[4] who had so bewitched the pipes that 'they would play of themselves when thrown up into the rafters', would sit with a colleague high on a corn bin; his name has now passed into folklore as one who had but to 'squeeze the pipes' at that festival to bring golden sovereigns rattling into his plate on the barn floor. And even the days of the shearing were a long delight, the chasing with long crooks of the sheep, the packing of the immense sacks of wool, the taste of the shearers' oaten bread. In the winter the great days were those when the house was filled with county friends, owners of neighbouring estates, for the three days' shooting at home, and [it might be] a fourth at Chevy Chase. The children of the house would trot after the procession of guests and keepers and beaters from the covers by the river through Eserkelly and Cahirlinny to Moneen Pollah, and even across Castleboy to Kynadife [though the Echtge hillsides were too steep for the little limbs,], and would nibble at the sandwiches carried out and eaten standing according to the hardy custom of those days. And so a lasting picture remains of the Master taking aim and never missing from his tall white horse Ehren Breitstein (a name turned by the stable-keepers to Iron Brightside), and the straight shooting of the county lords, Clonbrock like the fowler in the Arabian tale, finding the loss of one eye no impediment to his skill; his son Gerald, blue-eyed, with golden curls and Grecian features, the very type and model of a young man's beauty. Dunkellin, stout, brown-haired, with humorous prominent eyes, eyes so short-sighted that he had walked into the enemy's lines in the Crimea believing them to be British lines – 'the Russian officers were very kind', he wrote to W. H. Gregory (his fellow MP for the county), 'even offering to lend me money, I could not help thinking how many a Galway landlord would have been glad to exchange places with me'. He was looked on with wondering interest by at least one of those following children. For she had heard one of the grown-up people quote some lines concerning him, from a paper that had in itself a mysterious sound, *The Owl*: 'Where can the heir of Clanricarde be? Eating, or hunting with a double T?'

And another had said, 'That means ratting', and so she having never heard of the Parliamentary term for a change of mind or conscience [or (outside the Bible) of the cave of Adullam[5]], gazed astonished at a man who in her imagination turned at some times from this fine aristocratic covert shooting to that stable occupation of killing rats. And with a yet greater amazement did she witness the skill with which his father, the ancient and ghostlike Marquis of Clanricarde, was used to turn aside during a lull in the beaters' noisy cries to blow his nose with his fingers. It was told that he had so much admired one of the daughters of the house of an older generation [(one who would tell of a holiday from lessons given her on the day the bells rang for the victory of Waterloo)] as to leave the Portumna bonfires for his coming of age and drive the twenty miles across the county to finish the great day in her company. But he married a Canning's daughter, and she a Lord Clanmorris, after whose death she turned to religion, and was only kept back, as we were told, from joining the Plymouth Brethren by a fear that her favourite velvet would be brought into the common possession of goods. But the friendship between the old Marquis and her brother, Dudley Persse, was not broken. Charles Lever[6] tells of their hunting together and that Clanricarde once seeing his companion disappear over a wall that had hidden a steep drop called out, 'What's on the other side, Dudley?' and the answer came from below, 'I am, thank God.' Clear in memory also are the feasts of the four evenings, all the countryside coming in turn to dinner; the children watching from some nook the procession of guests walk arm in arm across the hall; listening to the buzz of conversation that would rise into a sudden loudness each time the door was opened for service [(a puzzling repetition as it seemed of a phrase above the hubbub 'that's just what I was going to say')]; the artfully arranged dishes left down on the hall tables for a few moments as they were carried out, perhaps not Mrs Glasse's Desert Island of cake with gravel walks of shot comfits, yet a tempting prey to little pilferers, a jelly nest containing eggs of blanc-mange, a tower of spun sugar, its head hidden in clouds of thickened cream. Then the procession of ladies alone; after that the buzz of voices continuing, rising even louder in the one room, while those in the other grew fainter and more languid until the coming of the men. Sometimes, not often, there was a little music; once a daughter of the family doctor had the courage to send next day a messenger for a roll of songs brought by her, but, humiliation, not asked for.

Religion was taught by the Mistress. The children were questioned after morning prayers on the Old Testament chapter that had been read. They stood round the dining-room fire, and were sometimes told they must not come nearer to it than the edge of the hearthrug, but this law can not have been severely enforced, for one child at least can remember the smooth touch of the marble of the chimney piece jamb against which she used to lean, longing to grow to the level of its shelf; and at length, on tiptoe and triumphant, being able to see in the mirror above it her forehead at least and eyes. In the evening they were sometimes examined from a card beginning: 'What sin have I this day committed in thought, word and deed?' But that was soon given up, perhaps because they were more prone to remind each other of the faults to be confessed than to tell out of their own; and this sometimes led to a scuffle, and most often on the Sunday evening after the idleness of the day. For if they were told, 'This is Sunday Sabbath Day; That is why we must not play,' the boys would whisper, 'This is Sunday Sabbath night; That is why we'll have a fight.' The theology was very definite, and although repeated rumours and then authoritative statements of geologists at last forced the Mistress to give up the six days creation of the world in favour of six periods, she refused other concessions. And a certain summer evening is remembered [most likely a Sunday evening, for she would then try to turn the conversation to more or less biblical subjects], when the children coming in to dessert found her reproving with some heat a guest, a young Mr Browne, a cousin of Lord O.[7] [They did not hear him say anything at all, but it must have been] for saying that possibly only a part and not the whole of the world had been drowned in Noah's time. Later, when he had been called out into the quiet air by the sons of the house, she continued her argument, saying she had but lately read in some sermon book that to give up belief in any one fact given in the Bible was the same thing as to reject the Bible altogether. And the Master murmured in sympathy, 'And I thought he seemed a quiet sort of young chap.' But he was never invited to visit the house again.

It was a pleasant walk to the friendly little Killinane Church across wide Castleboy, the estate won through long lawsuits,[8] with its river and trees and sloping lawns. Neighbours from two or three houses came there, and there was a customary chatting at the door after service (though the children were in agreement with an early saying of the elder brother, 'I hate the nasty how d'ye do's'). In yet remembered days a troop of village girls used to come and sing in the choir, Catholics some of them, but tempted by the drive in an open carriage provided by Lord Guillamore's son, old Archdeacon O'Grady, not as it seems aiming at their conversion, but at their support of the scanty Protestant voices in the hymns. But with his death they ceased to come. He was the last incumbent before Disestablishment[9] struck out Church livings as a provision for younger brothers. [The son of a Lord Guillamore he was liberal and kindly; proud of showing the figs that ripened on his garden walls and the red-blossomed rhododendrons, rare in that limestone soil, growing indeed in peat, for which rumour said he had dug pits to a depth of eighteen feet. The clerk was the Kilchreest schoolmaster, Mr Bateman, a Wesleyan, very severe with the cane. When now and again his pastor came on a visit a Wesleyan service would be held in the schoolroom, and perhaps through courtesy the 'Church of England' congregation as it then was, would attend. He led the singing in church until with the new Archdeacon, Burkett, a harmonium was provided. A blanket was also provided to keep it from damp during the week, but one cold winter day the old sexton, Murphy, carried it away to cover his own limbs and it never came back, and the notes of the harmonium grew very hoarse. Old Murphy used, as the sermon was about to begin, to bring in an armful of sticks gathered under the trees and put them in the stove, poking the fire till it crackled. There were large square pews, well cushioned, with high hassocks on which a child could stand and watch pheasants and rabbits picking or nibbling on the grass-grown graves. An elder brother, whose training at the Bar had given him respect for law and order, told the old sexton on a visit home that the tall nettles in the churchyard were unseemly and should be done away with. But he was indignant and cried out 'And what would the Master say if I was to cut them before the young pheasants are reared?']

The children were sometimes taken to Sunday School at Kilchreest and they were allowed to go out of doors on Sunday but not to play or work in the garden or put a hand to any occupation; but this was not much to grumble at, with all the wide demesne around them, and the river with its wild fowl, and its reeds.

The 'Monday books', as the children used to call them, were all hidden away on the Saturday night, and in their places would be found Mrs Sherwood's *Stories on the Church Catechism*, which had its attractive chapters, and her *Henry Milner* which was dull, and *Ministering Children* which laid in at least one little reader the foundations of philanthropy. And if, when that lasting delight *The Fairchild Family* was read aloud, she blushed under the meaning looks of the others when the misdeeds of that villain of the piece, 'Miss Augusta' Noble, were held up to odium, she loved (as do at this day her grandchildren) Master Henry's fall into the tub of pig's wash, and the greediness of Mr Crosbie, and all the consequences of hunting the farmer's pig in the lane. The elders were not so well off; there were some sermons for them, and *Doing and Suffering*, the story of an invalid girl who had died, and a *Life* of Hedley Vicars [a stepdaughter, Maria, had been given one Christmas the *Life* of Dr Kitto, but a few weeks later the Mistress took up a new book, an unusual intruder, and asked where it had come from, and in the silence Arabella, a little pitcher always ready of speech, said, 'Maria got it in exchange for the *Life* of Dr Kitto.' And it is hard to say which was in deeper disgrace, Maria with the authorities or Arabella with the elder sisters.]

Sometimes in the evening a story would be read to them from a Sunday magazine or religious paper [but they came to know the form of these and would prophesy, when the good poor boy was taken into the merchant's office, that he would marry the merchant's daughter in the end].

Dr Cumming's prophecies were now and then brought to the drawing-room to eke out the Sunday Books, but they were usually kept in the Mistress's dressing-room. He had proved in them by various calculations that the Emperor Louis Napoleon was the beast of the Revelations [the Roman letters of his name coming through some calculations to], the mystic number 666. He was to begin the war that would only end with Armageddon, and the end of the world was very near. [Those who accepted these interpretations would find signs of this approaching end in 'Wars and Rumours of Wars' as they looked through the newspapers, though this was in the peaceful times, after the Crimean and the American Civil War.] But after France's pre-destined Emperor had rushed to his own Armageddon against Prussia, the Mistress became less confident, although she would still refuse to buy some new dress or spend money on such things as furniture because the end of the world might soon be here and turn all to dust.

It was not only that tale of the landing of the French at Killala that led the youngest daughter of the house to her country's history. She would often finger the lichen-grown letters cut on a stone of the bridge near the avenue gates 'Erected by William Persse Colonel of the Roxborough Volunteers in the year 1782 in memory of Ireland's Emancipation from foreign Jurisdiction'; when those Volunteers had gained for at least a while the freedom of the Irish Parliament to make its own laws. So it came about that she would bring out the sixpences, earned if memory held good, by repeating on the Sunday evenings Bible verses learned during the week; and standing on tiptoe at the counter of the little Loughrea book-shop would purchase one by one the paper covered collections of national ballads, *The Harp of Tara*, *The Irish Song Book*, and the like. It was perhaps because of the old bookseller calling attention to this by saying in his shop one day, 'I look to Miss Augusta to buy all my Fenian books,' that led to a birthday present of *The Spirit of the Nation*,[10] a shilling copy, bound in green cloth, from the sister next in age to her, with Dr Johnson's sarcasm written in it 'Patriotism is the last refuge of a Scoundrel.' It is not likely that the idea of her having any thoughts of sympathies different from their own had ever entered the mind of any of the elders of the house.

Childhood had thus slipped away, and it was perhaps some fifteen years after that midnight arrival in the world when religion in that Evangelical form in which it had always been set before the child, drove all other thoughts from the mind of the growing child. The theology taught had been that of the hymn 'There is a dreadful hell, With everlasting pains', 'Where sinners must with devils dwell in darkness, fire and chains'. To escape it even if you had been absolutely sinless would be impossible, and were it possible there would still be the guilt of Adam's disobedience, for which as one of his descendants, you were responsible; there was no escape except being washed in the Blood of the Lamb, and that could not be unless you were converted, unless you believed while still in this earthly life; there was no place for repentance, no Purgatory. It was before Disestablishment, and the difficult Athanasian Creed was still given out two or three times in the year by the Archdeacon 'which faith except everyone keep whole and undefiled, without doubt he shall perish everlastingly'. And to this others besides the Clerk would give a whole hearted 'Amen'.

So it was no wonder that she was troubled. Was she a believer? Lacking it, what must she do to be saved? What was the wall between her and heaven; the closed door between her and Christ? She would break it open by prayer; she would earn its unclosing by a blameless day. But belief, like Queen Vashti, was shy and would not come to order, and before the day was over a moment's forgetfulness of this high task would seem a crime, and prayer itself a vanity. The matter must be fought out alone, it is not in a large and critical family that such a secret of the heart could be made common property. The restlessness of the mind increased. Then of a sudden one morning in the cottage on Lough Corrib her father had taken as a fishing lodge, she rose up from her bed at peace with God. All doubts and all fears had gone, she was one of His children, His angels were her friends. The ballads, and poems and patriotic songs had become as ashes; His word, the Bible was her only book. She need no longer strive to do His will, it was her delight to do it. She was a little ashamed of this ecstasy, a little shy, unwilling to have it known. [Yet it came to be accepted, without words, little by little, that she was not as it were quite in the same world as the others, that it was by a different table of values that she lived. 'I am not like Augusta who grew into religion from her childhood,' one married sister wrote, long after to another, Adelaide Lane.] She was very happy.

For what might have been a long time the Bible and religious books, the only ones of which there were a plenty in the house, satisfied her. Then she began to discriminate. George Herbert's poems, given to a brother as a school prize, stayed more comfortably in the mind than the hymns of doctrine held to in the first fervour, as did the monk's vision of the jewel-decked city, the sardius and amethyst of the New Jerusalem. The sermon books gave way to à Kempis's *Imitation of Christ*. As to novels, she had been taught to consider them food unfit for the use of Christ's flock; and indeed the daughters of the house were forbidden to read even the Waverleys until they attained the age of eighteen. And for this she was afterwards grateful, for coming later they never won her heart and all her romantic sympathies were kept for Ireland.

Although the books that had lain on the table at stated times, the *Ballads* and the yet unopened Shakespeare, had been taken away, the centre table was not quite unfurnished. Each Christmas a box of books would arrive to be chosen from, children's books chiefly, and religious ones, the *Sunday at Home*, the *Leisure Hour*. But from one of these boxes an elder sister, Gertrude, saying frankly she did not care for reading but would choose the biggest, took and laid on the drawing-room table the two volumes of Chambers' *Encyclopaedia of English Literature*.

That was to the younger sister the breaking of a new day, the discovering of a new world. She looked forward to those evening hours when she could read those volumes, first straight through, then over and over, a page here and there, till some of the poems given were known almost off by heart. The Bible had its appointed hours but was no longer everything, it may be its own beauty of words and imagination had spoiled her for common books; or she had become aware that there was other beauty and other poetry that might come near it, and had learned to know under what names this might be found. She knew now what to ask for at Christmas or from a brother in good humour, for the boys had more money in their pockets than the girls, given for the shooting of mischievous pests, and they were glad to give the sister who was their companion and favourite a share in this now and again, and would let her make her own choice. In this way there came into her possession by degrees Scott's poems, and Tennyson's (the Pre-Raphaelite edition), and even the excitement of each new volume of his as it came out, Scott, Burns, Montaigne, Matthew Arnold's essays, and Clough and Hood and Keats; and above and beyond all, most enduring of joys, Malory's *Morte D'Arthur*.

Yet the distinctly religious life lasted through all her early girlhood, although it leaned perhaps more by degrees to the practical, the philanthropic, than to the spiritual side, for she gave up a good deal of her time to works of charity, taking the poorest village on the estate, Illerton at the foot of Slieve Echtge, as her especial care; going day after day the couple of miles on foot with food and comforts, saving her pocket money for such purposes, she visited the sick and clothed the children, and tended the dying. These visits of charity sometimes brought her under suspicion of wishing to turn those she succoured from the Catholic faith, for that was the fashion of the day among those zealous Protestants, who were possessed with the same assurance held by zealous Catholics, that their own faith was the only one that had its correspondence fixed with Heaven, that travelled the path to that door. The eldest stepdaughter had given her energy to this cause of leading those who were astray to that path, and the children had one day been awed by hearing the account of an actual hand to hand struggle between her and the parish priest, each holding on to one arm of a disputed child. She had married and gone to England, and perhaps lost there some illusions as to the infallibility of Protestant piety, for there is memory of a letter read at the breakfast table, telling of a negro cook she and her husband had found praying on the English sands for a good master, and so had engaged him and then of a later letter of disappointment that he had turned out to be a rogue. Then the eldest daughter at home had taken up the same work, holding her own, it is said, in written arguments with the priests. She believed it was her duty, her mission, to turn the people to the written word of God in the Bible free from the interpretation of their church, and in this belief she was never shaken to her life's end, but continued her work with a gallant heart, though her youngest sister carries in her memory a word said to her with some emotion: 'I sometimes think how happy you are not to feel called to this business as I do. It is a heavy task.' For as if by some imperceptible change the daughters of the family, after her, showed little or no interest in that side of the religious life. And as to the youngest; she did not 'feel called to this business' of controversy, but was for a time held in suspicion especially by a priest who believed that in her work of visiting and helping the poor in his flock she must have some hidden aim. But he found and confessed later that this was not so; and she was told that in later days he was sad at having shown a discourtesy to one who had now been joined in marriage with a man who had been so good a member for the County, so trusted by Catholics, so liberal and so kind.

There was no formal 'coming out' at ball or races for this youngest of the Miss Persses. There were not many gaieties near at hand, and she had no mind for such amusements, from no actual belief perhaps that such frivolity was wrong, although religion as she had learned it did not lend its countenance to such, but rather because of the saving of money for the poor. Hunting might have been a temptation, had it not been forbidden to girls at Roxborough, for the impulse towards the gay exercise of youth took her riding with the brothers she had been used to follow at their other sports, over many stone walls across country, sometimes with an occasional pack of harriers, and once, only once, with the foxhounds, when a triumphant run ended on the very lawn of Roxborough in full sight of her astonished father. It may be she would have been more tempted by dress and society had she nursed any expectation of being admired. But the Mistress, disappointed in a birthday prayer that she might grow not only in wisdom but in stature, made her aware, and this was true enough, that she was not to think herself the equal of her sisters, all tall, handsome, and one at least beautiful. Yet going to stay at cousins' houses she gained more confidence, especially in finding that her hands which because of winter chilblains she had grown up in a habit of hiding whenever a table made it possible were now, that disfigurement being outgrown, even admired.

Guests in the meanwhile with a respect for letters were not quite unknown, one of these having leave to borrow from the Galway College Library, and bringing a yet greater joy by some poems written out in a manuscript book, some at least of these, never as it happens since met with, keeping still their place in the reader's memory as,

> With reverend tread,
> And uncovered head,
> Pass by the dome gate,
> Where buried lie,
> The men of July,
> And the dog howls desolate.

And once a wild undergraduate of Trinity College brought on

a visit by a wild son of the house, would drift, coming back at evening from sports or races, to the youngest sister's side, and would talk of what she cared for, and enter into the enthusiasms that then possessed her. For she had but lately, having attained the freedom of her eighteenth year, bought a Shakespeare, green, the Globe edition, rebound later when some pages were all but worn away. And finding all new to her, even the very stories of the plays, she felt the joys of an explorer; and leaving no page unread, learned even the sonnets at her dressing-table, repeating them aloud on the mountain side. In those evenings she would be full of the day's discoveries, and where could she have found better sympathy than in one who, for all his wild ways, was Dowden's[11] favourite pupil and the first man in literature of his year? Alas that the caution of elders interrupted that companionship, those delightful conversations in which one or the other of the great poets or writers was ever a third. There was an abrupt banishment, a sudden silence. It was not until years had passed that she came to know that he had written to her, and that the letter had been opened by the authorities, the Church itself being represented by the Archdeacon of the time. But as she was told, the broken seal had but disclosed a friendly note giving the authorship of a once discussed quotation. Her heart had not been wounded nor had her hand trembled at the parting, and if she has now and again blushed at the recollection, it is with shame for herself and yet more for Dowden's favourite pupil, that the line whose authorship they could not recognise was 'Among the faithless faithful only he.'

But the study of the great dramatist went on unabated, and if her acquaintance with his splendid sentences was of necessity less than long intimacy had given her with those of another Book, it was the German translations of Shakespeare and of the Bible that were from familiarity her best text books when she set out to teach herself the German language.

Then while in her early twenties there came a sudden change, and being given the charge of an elder brother whose health had failed, she left the large household, the comradeship of the boys, the great plenty, the fireside comfort, the winter shooting parties, the wide demesne, the hillsides where she had often started the wild deer as she climbed to look at the shadowy mountain tops of Connemara beyond the shining Atlantic Bay, for a quiet hotel on the Riviera, monotonous walks beside the invalid's chair, or drives on the dusty roads; the companionship of one that she had never intimately known, so much was he her elder, and whose turn for satire had increased the shy tremors of her early days. And as she saw it, Cannes was not France, it had no history, no national life, no language but a patois, few inhabitants save an organised English society, seeking health, or the mild gaieties of the seventies.

But with the springtime in each of these three (four?) years there came what made up for all, a few weeks of Italy; the journey through olive groves to the palaces of Genoa, or across the yet untunnelled Alps to Lombardy, to the Lakes, to Tuscany. And having begun to learn its language, and to know a little of the grammar, with the audacity of the young she began to read Dante, at first with the help of a French translation, and then, making her own, she wrote it out to the very end of the Purgatorio and the triple stars. And the beautiful sound of the language was added to the other unbounded joys of those blossoming Italian Aprils, the freedom of cities, the glory of the arts, the triumphant beauty of Dante's Florence above all.

There had not been much of the education of sorrows in the home at Roxborough. No heavy grief had come until, after those foreign winters had begun, the death of the dear Cornish sister Gertrude, and soon after that the death of old Mary Sheridan. Then in the autumn of 1878 a younger brother fell ill with pleurisy; it was before the day of trained nurses, and his younger sister was with him night and day. One day at lunch-time going to the dining-room for something needed for him she heard one of those at the table say that during the night the cry of the banshee had been heard; and although looking on such tales as idle, anxiety about her brother made her feel a sudden dread. In the evening he was still very ill, and towards midnight he had fallen asleep, when she heard voices and a stir in the house and going to the staircase saw a group of the servants, and [asked them not to make any noise.] one among them came up the stairs to her and said, 'The Master is dead.'

To those of his children still living under the roof, it seemed as if all had been shattered around them. Roxborough had been such a hive of life, with its stables full of horses, its kennels full of sporting dogs, Gordon setters, retrievers, greyhounds – the deer-hound had been long done away with; the sawmill with its carpenters and engineers and turners; the gamekeepers and trappers; the long array of labourers coming each morning to their work; the garden so well tilled, so full, at this September time, of grapes and melons and peaches and apples, inexhaustible fruit. Must they leave it all? Where should they go? For the eldest son, the stepbrother, was now lord of all and was impatient to take possession.

\* \* \*

The Mistress took a house in Dublin to be a home for herself and those of her children who might need it. The immediate change meant less to the youngest daughter than to the others, for she went for the third time with the invalid to the South of France.

# Marriage

In the third winter abroad a visitor to Cannes came sometimes and talked with me and read to me from little manuscript books into which from time to time he had copied prose or poetry he cared for. And on our way back to Ireland that spring we stayed for a few days in London at 3 St George's Place as guests of Sir William Gregory.

My husband's *Autobiography* has told the story of his life and I will but quote from some chapters written by his old friend, the Hon. Frank Lawley, in his *Racing Life of Lord George Bentinck* (1892). Mr Lawley tells that he was brought up in the society of Dublin Castle, in the house of his grandfather, the Rt Hon. William Gregory, then Under-Secretary, of whom it was said, from his great influence and experience that 'Gregory was the dry nurse of young English Statesmen.'

'In 1842 young Mr William Gregory was invited to stand for Dublin in opposition to Lord Morpeth who was vigorously supported by O'Connell.[1] It would have been difficult for a young man, not yet twenty-five, to encounter a more formidable opponent. The seat for Dublin was of no slight importance, and the Whigs were extremely anxious to wrest it from the Tories. On the nomination day O'Connell, then Lord Mayor of Dublin, was so pleased with the plucky way in which his youthful antagonist had stood up to him that he exclaimed, "Young man, may I shake you by the hand? Your speech has so gratified me that if you will but whisper REPEAL,[2] only *whisper* it mind you, Daniel O'Connell will be the first man at the polling booth to vote for you tomorrow." The mystic word was not whispered, or uttered, but from that time O'Connell and Gregory were always the best of friends. Sir William was returned by a triumphant majority.'

He says also, 'Few men have ever lived whose experience was more diversified; he was a man of ready sympathy to whom *quicquid agunt homines*[3] was full of interest. He had known everybody who was anybody, for even as a Harrow[4] lad he was intimate with illustrious Harrovians like Sir Robert Peel, Lord Palmerston, Lord Aberdeen, and Sir James Graham. He knew the Turf and all its intricacies as well as Scott's William of Deloraine knew the passes and fords of the Scottish Border. Although not more than twenty-two years old when accompanied by the Earl of Winchelsea and other undergraduates he rode on a series of hacks strewn along the road, from Christ Church to Epsom and back to see his first Derby, he was at once admitted to the best society in the United Kingdom and soon became a prominent pillar of the English Turf. He was on the most intimate terms of friendship with Lord George Bentinck, the noble owner of Crucifix, Miss Elis and Gafer . . . I have long regretted that he could never be prevailed upon to write a history of the "Sport of Kings". He was the only man of my acquaintance possessed of the literary ability and also of the keen insight into character requisite to enable him to draw correct pen portraits of heroes of the Turf who are to the present generation mere *homines umbrae*[5] . . .

'During the last thirty years of his life, however, politics, litera-ture and art engaged his attention to such a degree that . . . he had no time or inclination for composing a work *de longue haleine*[6] on the pursuits of his youth.

'Fortunately for himself, Sir William Gregory's active connec-tion with the Turf as an owner of racehorses ceased for ever in the spring of 1855. Under all circumstances and all conditions he never ceased to be an industrious worker, and his Catholic taste for the classics, for literature of all kinds and for art in particular, was well known to his many friends. The dissolution of 1857 gave him an opportunity of returning to Parliament as Liberal member for his native county of Galway . . . Upon domestic subjects, especially upon those connected with Ireland, with the British Museum, the National Gallery and matters of art and taste he was a frequent speaker. He was appointed a Trustee of the National Gallery by Mr Disraeli, and sworn as a member of the Privy Council for Ireland in 1871 under Gladstone's first adminis-tration . . . In 1872 he was appointed Governor of Ceylon. At last "the hour and the man had both come" . . . It has often been remarked that the best Colonial Governors come from Ireland; and of those who have served her Majesty within my recollection none was ever more successful than Sir William Gregory.'

I had first seen him [(though he always declared he had seen me as a child and had said to my mother 'that is the prettiest of all your daughters')] at a cricket match at Roxborough. There was a long table in the dining-room where guests were being given lunch, and I came in and went from chair to chair seeing that their wants were supplied. Sir William came late, was brought in and put in almost the only place left empty, it was at the head of the table. I, as I came to him, a stranger, for he had but just returned from his five years' government of Ceylon, felt a little shy, most likely I blushed as was then my habit. I think I must have been looking rather nice, for later when someone told my still unmarried sister that I, who have made so good a marriage, lived so quietly and had dressed so simply, she answered that on the day that had such an influence on my fate I had worn a Paris dress [(bought at the Bon Marché on my way home)] and a Mrs Heath hat. I kept the hat for many years, a black and white straw with bunches of corn ears and poppies. Anyhow, Sir William greeted me with all his great charm of manner, and I sat next him for a while, glad of an opportunity of talking about Ceylon, as one of my brothers thought of going there. After lunch also we walked and talked for a good deal of the afternoon. (It is but the other day I read in Sir Horace Rumbold's *Recollections of a Diplomatist* that they had made a journey together with him and that 'the hours pass quickly in Gregory's company'.)

[A little later we were at dinner one evening, when a message came from a neighbour's house with a note asking if I would come over and stay the night 'to meet two agreeable men, Edward O'Brien and William Gregory'. The summer evening was still bright and a brother offered to drive over and I had a pleasant evening there. It was not until long afterwards that our hostess – his cousin – explained that sudden invitation. It was just before dinner that he had spoken of me in a way that made her certain he liked me; and she had sent her messenger at once.]

Very soon after that he wrote to ask me, with my elder brother Richard, to dine and sleep at Coole. He took us for a drive, my first through the woods I was to know so well and that Yeats has made known to so many as 'The Seven Woods':

Shan-walla where a willow-bordered pond
Gathers the wild duck from the winter dawn;
Shady Kyle-dortha; sunnier Kyle-na-no,
Where many hundred squirrels are as happy
As though they had been hidden by green boughs
Where old age cannot find them; Pairc-na-lee,
Where hazel and ash and privet blind the paths;
Dim Pairc-na-carraig, where the wild bees fling
Their sudden fragrances on the green air;
Dim Pairc-na-tarav, where enchanted eyes
Have seen immortal, mild, proud shadows walk;
Dim Inchy wood, that hides badger and fox
And marten-cat, and borders that old wood
Wise Biddy Early called the wicked wood;
Seven odours, seven murmurs, seven woods . . .

The lake that touched on woodlands is often in his poems also, and its wild swans that come and go.

We drove also to the pool where the river rises and dips again under rocks, beside which Colman, the Saint, who has left his name and his blessing on so many wells of healing, was born.

The plain white house has little changed through the years. It was not the first time that I had seen it, for one day in my childhood I had been taken there, in old Mrs Gregory's time. We had walked in the garden, where she showed us a mulberry tree covered with fruit – and did not offer us any. When I came here the summer after my marriage I thought, 'Now I shall be able to taste mulberries.' But alas! the tree was dying, and had no fruit. I have planted others over and over again and some failed and one at least is flourishing now, but has not yet begun to bear. But the memory of that disappointment, those untasted berries, has made me always careful to give children, rich or poor, some little pleasant thing to eat or take away whenever they come, so that my poor little great-niece, Vera Shawe-Taylor, said once as I took her to rummage in the store room, 'It is always Christmas in this house.'

[And I remember that an old barrister, my brother's friend, a lover of literature and art, who had helped me in those years of nursing, giving me books, Pope's *Iliad* and *Odyssey*, with the Flaxman illustrations; and Milton's *Prose*, and above all Jarvis's translation of *Don Quixote*, had once driven to Coole, at that time empty, and coming back spoke of it as a house showing a fine intellectual tradition, of the library with its rich collection of books, and had said with what seemed a flight of fantasy, 'That is the only house I have seen in the county that would make a right setting for you.']

There had always been a certain distinction about Coole, [and about its owner when representing the county in Parliament or when there were echoes of his doings in London or Ceylon. And his mother spent her winters abroad, in the South of France, not then so common a harbour as it became; there were occasional guests, some of high rank, and she openly said there were very few neighbours she could associate with. My mother she was kind enough to make an exception, and the Shawe-Taylors and the Goughs. Her early and brilliant married life at the Under-Secretary's Lodge in the Phoenix Park and the distinction of her son were the excuse for this. But my sister at Castle Taylor, and I, and Lady Layard and I, used sometimes to say to one another, 'How is it that our predecessors managed to give themselves airs, and we have never managed to do so?']

[My brother, asked after our return from that visit how we had got on, had said rather discontentedly, that our host had 'talked more to Augusta than to me'. He had showed us his Ceylon treasures, and had given me a pearl ring. That did not mean much, for he was ever a giver of presents – a quoter of 'les petits cadeaux entretiennent l'amitié'[7] – and my mother, never quite sure he had not married me as a compliment to her, used to show us, and gave me later, an embroidered Maltese shawl he had once brought her from the Mediterranean.]

[I think it must have been about this time that (as he told me afterwards) he had, in making his will, directed I should be given my choice of any six books from the Coole Library. I have often wondered what they would have been. Johnson's *Dictionary*, that fine edition, would probably then, as it would certainly now, have been one of them, I have so often used it since I have been here. And Evelyn's *Silva* perhaps, and Lord Berners' *Froissart*. There are more valuable books than these, but I was not mercenary at that time.]

Yet Roxborough with its romance of river and hillsides came for a long time first in my imagination. It was not until my child's birth that I began really to care for Coole, looking before as well as after. And that love has grown through the long years of widowed life, when the woods especially became my occupation and delight. [Only yesterday, 23 October 1918, the little grandchildren, Anne and Catherine, walked with me in these woods through the afternoon, or rather ran and hid and rushed out again so happily through the autumn coloured larch and the shining silvers and the nut thickets, and I saw that these would be a romantic memory to them hereafter. It was for my son I was yet planting there a year ago.]

After that visit [and that pearl ring,] I did not seem to meet Sir William often; I think only at Cannes and during that week in London. And on his last day at Cannes he had called three times to see me, and three times the porter, Henri, had told him I was out, as porters do. I had got to like him very much. He cared for the things I cared for, he could teach me and help me so much. But although at that time I cannot say the thought of marriage did not occur to me – I lived in too large and irreverent a family for that detachment of mind – yet it did not fit into the life that seemed planned out for me. The winter after my father's death I seemed more bound than ever to the invalid. The doctors told me when we went abroad that he was losing ground, and it was possible he would not even live to arrive at Cannes. But he lived to come back to the next summer to Roxborough. It was there that he weakened, and one night when I was alone with him he died.

My half-brother, Dudley, who had succeeded, then needed my care and Algernon, that brother who had taken over the management of the estate, had gone through a hard and anxious time and was glad of my help. We planned to keep the herdsmen when going with sheep and cattle to Ballinasloe Fair from the public houses, and sent a cricket tent to be pitched outside the town with arrangements for cooking and a store of food. It served the purpose well, and I hoped to get a manager and send our 'temperance tent' to other fairs and assemblies. Then we found our labourers were paying very high prices for food at the Kilchreest shops, and we got supplies of tea and sugar, flour, and bacon and opened a shop at the Steward's Lodge on Friday afternoons when their wages were paid. It was a great boon. The wives came to buy their goods and were astonished to find how far their money went, and how good were the purchases. Miss Samuella, the Archdeacon's sister, took me to task and said I was injuring the respectable Protestant shopkeepers of Kilchreest. But when I asked her where she got her own supplies, she confessed from Dublin; so I felt she had no right to object. [I hoped to get in other goods by degrees.]

Once, during this time, my mother had a visit from Sir William in Dublin, and he spoke to her with some indignation of the life I was kept to, a life of self-sacrifice he thought it. I did not feel it so. My heart was in Roxborough, the fields, the hills, the villages. I still found opportunity in the mornings and on our drives to see and help some of the poor people. The Gort doctor had told Sir William of meeting me at that time at the bedside of a dying boy, whom I had to visit every day because he would only take nourishment from my hand. I had to look after the housekeeping also, for there were still some of the old servants who were used to the old wasteful times, the lavish killing of beasts, the masses of meat for all in the house and yard and stables, the beer barrels, the large household, and all this had to be changed and brought within bounds.

About Christmas time Algernon went for a two days' shoot at Coole where he found I think Gerald Dillon, Lord Crofton, John Blakeney and one of the Grevilles, Lord Warwick's brother. He came back pleased with the good woodcock shoot, and the good dinners and the pleasant company. He brought with him a book Sir William had given him for me to read. He was half sarcastic. I don't think he, or the others, yet believed that I could really enjoy reading. A little time afterwards, Sir William came to lunch one day to say goodbye, as he was going abroad for the rest of the winter. He looked ill and was, I thought, depressed, and when he said goodbye I felt sad and lonely. [I used to say to myself that when one is sad one should try to make things happier for someone else, and so when I went for my usual drive with Dudley I stopped at the Kilchreest Dispensary – it was the day on which the doctor from Loughrea attended – and gave or promised help to some of the patients. Then I settled down to my usual life. I was reading in the evenings *The Stones of Venice*, which I had unexpectedly found in the Castle Taylor bookshelves, though it seemed without much prospect of ever seeing Venice itself.]

One morning soon afterwards, when I opened the postbag before morning prayers, which I read as had been the habit, to a dwindled household, there was a letter for me, from Sir William, and chancing to turn it over, I saw it was sealed, which was unusual. The servants were waiting and I read the chapter and the prayer. Then I opened the letter. It was written from London, and in it he asked me to marry him.

I felt extraordinarily happy and serene, happy in the thought of being with him, of serving him, of learning from him. And I was happy also in the thought of not leaving the country, the neighbourhood that I loved, for it was but a drive of seven miles to Coole, in the next barony, the next parish.

Then came a difficulty. I had said in my answer to him I could not leave Roxborough until there was someone to take my place there. I could not walk out of the door leaving the two brothers who needed me. But a very simple solution was found. An uncle's widow and her daughter were looking for a new home. It was a benefit to them to go for a while to Roxborough.

All my family were pleased, some of them astonished; feeling perhaps as an old neighbour did, saying to Algernon after church at Killinane, 'How did that little thing get the big man?' The boys were pleased to think of all the shootings that would run together; Castle Taylor, adjoining the Roxborough property; Coole woods but separated by a fence from the Shawe-Taylors' woods of Garrylands. One of them hoped that the last unmarried sister would marry Edward Martyn of Tillyra, because then they could shoot the whole countryside without a break. (She did marry in the county afterwards and have her shooting parties [afterwards], but they were at Moyne Park to the north of the county and not marching with the home boundaries.) And old Rick Burke, the steward, who had given me fourpenny bits at the Customs Gap at Eserkelly Fair in my childhood, took off his hat with a great sweep whenever he met me. But Dudley was sad. He had become used to my care. And I saw tears in Algernon's eyes one day when a tenant coming to the office on business and saying, 'So you're going to join with the Gregorys,' said also, 'What at all will you do? You will never get so good a helper.'

According to our wish we were not given wedding presents [there had been several marriages in the county just then, and I think all our friends were pleased] but my elder brother [however,] gave me a phaeton which is still in existence. It was quite smart in its beginning when we chose it in London, but as little round tubs came into fashion it seemed from year to year to grow longer and longer and went out of fashion. It was very useful later in my lonely life. I drove in it every year to Galway with Robert in his holidays to stay the night with my mother who had moved there. And, drawn by the pony, Shamrock, I went many a time to Chevy in the mountains or to Duras by the sea, to visit old Count de Basterot; and once across the mountains and through two unbridged rivers to see the place where Biddy Early, the witch doctor, had made her prophecies and cures.

So an announcement in *The Times* (1880) said:
'On the 4th March, by special licence, at St Matthias Church, Dublin, the Rt Hon. Sir William Gregory of Coole Park, Co. Galway, and 3 St George's Place, Hyde Park Corner, to Augusta, daughter of the late Dudley Persse, Esq., D.L., of Roxborough, Co. Galway.'

I wore a grey hat and grey travelling dress and [I had been so long in mourning for my father and for Richard, I did not like to change to colours. But I have always been rather sorry I did not, however quiet the wedding, wear white, with wreath and veil. I feel it was a break of tradition, something missed out of my life;

or perhaps, I should like to remember myself in bride's attire. I did not feel like that at the time. Indeed, I had lived so simple and so self-forgetting a life for so long I gave little thought to clothes.] that wedding dress is seen in a photograph taken at Constantinople, with a little black bonnet my husband liked very much; a bonnet such as is never seen in these days, except on a charwoman in an omnibus. For years afterwards, whenever I looked at that photograph, the strings, like my phaeton, seemed to have grown longer. For strings went first, shorter and shorter, until by a gradual transition akin to the casting of claws by a crab, the bonnet became a toque.

We stayed but a short while in London, some of my own part of it under the dressmakers, for there had been but little opportunity before my marriage for these, and there was hospitality before us in the cities we were about to visit, Rome and Athens and Constantinople. And there was the Queen's drawing-room to be attended, and I am glad this was not put off.

It happened one night, long after, that I was alone in a box at a New York theatre, and my mind, entangled in some business of the day, had strayed between Act and Act. And when the curtain went up again, it seemed to me as if some thirty years had melted away, for I saw before me the Throne Room at Buckingham Palace, as I had first seen it, and the fine ladies with trains and veils, wearing plumes of feathers as I had worn them, curtseying or bending to kiss the Queen's hand as I as a bride had kissed it. And there in the background stood a figure as I had seen it, dominating as it seemed all the rest, a diamond star glittering from his black velvet; an unforgettable Eastern face. And there came back the memory of a momentary disappointment when my husband, having to hurry away to meet some members of the Arundel Society who wished to consult him about some lately uncovered frescoes at Rome, had been sorry he could not wait to make me known to Disraeli; for although never his follower in politics there had always been friendliness between them, even at one time intimacy, and no doubt, according to his habit, he would have greeted his friend's bride with some finely phrased compliment. And it happened there never was opportunity again that year, and in the next year he died. And this disappointment, long forgotten, came back with sudden sharpness in that sudden sight of Mr Arless on the stage.

Rome, Athens, Constantinople, a wonderful wedding journey. In Rome the pictures and statues and churches were too many and too confusing for a short visit. I was rather bewildered by it all. There are too many ages huddling on one another in Rome – 'the exhaustless scattered fragmentary city' as it is called by Goethe.

[The other day and since I wrote those last words, I met the daughter of one who had been an attaché at the Embassy at Rome. His name brought back to me of a sudden my arrival there, my confusion and bewilderment in sightseeing. It happened that he had come to Rome for the first time on the same day as I. He, like me, was being asked 'Have you seen St Peter's' or told he must see the Vatican Galleries or the Capitol or it might be the frescoes at the Baths of Caracalla. Our ignorance brought about sympathy we found it comforting to confess it to each other, and to talk of the trivial things of the day.]

My first real dinner party was a sudden entering into society after my quiet years. Sir Augustus Paget coming out from church on our first Sunday asked us to dine at the Embassy to meet the Crown Princess of Prussia, Princess Royal of England.

I wrote, 'it was a small dinner at a round table, the guests were the Duc de Ripaldo, the Duchess Massimo, Gay Paget very lovely, two or three of the Embassy people, and the Princess Royal of England, Crown Princess of Prussia'. I did not feel shy, I liked the flowers and the lighted rooms. I was dressed in white satin and old lace, a dress made to represent the one I should have worn on March 4th, and Lady Paget and the Duchess were also in white and in that matter I felt at ease [though I had not then put into words my axiom as to dress, that it should be such as to make one feel at ease in whatever company you are in. The Princess wore a black barège or some such material, almost high. She was a striking figure at the reception afterwards with her dark intellectual face and royal air, receiving the Roman ladies with their fine dresses and jewels. I don't know if she noticed them, but when I was presented to her she had touched the bracelet I was wearing, one made of replicas of old Greek coins, and asked to see it more closely, and had recognised each, giving the name of its city.]

My first ball also was at the Embassy, it was in honour of that royal guest, and in honour of her the Roman Princesses had brought out their tiaras from bankers' strong rooms. Of my few balls it was the most dazzling and glittering and brilliant; those at Buckingham Palace were more formal and less opulent. One at Government House, Calcutta, was a more beautiful sight, with its spacious whiteness of background, the rich colours of the native dresses.

On another day to be remembered we went to the Pope's reception at the Vatican and received his blessing, which he gave very solemnly. To us, indeed, he had given a special word and smile, because of the service my husband had done in Ceylon to his Church there, and because also of the gratitude of the priests and bishops in Ireland. I remember the pallid, fleshless face, dark eyes glowing as if with a fire that was consuming the wasted body. I had brought rosaries with me that I might give them to some of the devout old women at home, when they had received Leo the Tenth's blessing.

Athens looked very tranquil, lovely and serene after the confusion of Roman streets and ruins, the low white marble temples were in harmony with the low violet hills. In the fields scarlet poppies were in flower. The ships in the harbour were decorated with flags for the Greek Easter. My husband had been a good friend of Greece in his Parliamentary days and so we received kindness from Tricoupis, the Prime Minister, and his sister, Sophie. Professor Rousopolis showed us the Antiquities; and Dr Schliemann entertained us at his house, and gave me a 'whorl' from the ruins of Troy.

I forgot whether it was before or after this that the almost tragic event happened of Schliemann being blackballed for the Athenaeum Club. He was in London when his name was coming up, and saw no harm in offering a tip, in Southern fashion, to, I think, the Head Porter who reported the offer to the Committee

with as much indignation as that with which he had rejected it.
By rule or pedantry, Schliemann was excluded and he went away
very sore of heart from England and bequeathed the collection he
had intended for the British Museum to, I think, Berlin.

Through the Ionian Isles to Constantinople; some pleasant
weeks at the British Embassy; my beginning of a long and happy
friendship with the Layards.

London again, and a short London season, dinners, receptions,
the Marlborough House Garden Party, the Queen's Ball, the
friendly faces of my husband's friends.

Then home to Coole; Gort is decorated, Priest and Archdeacon
to welcome us, a bonfire at the gate, an arch with Cead Mile
Failthe,[8] goodwill everywhere.

The education through books was now in the background,
another education was begun.

# The Changing Ireland

I think it was in 1896 that I suddenly became aware of the change that had come about in Ireland in those first years after Parnell's death. My twelve years of married life had been the years of the Land War, tenant struggling to gain a lasting possession for his children, landlord to keep that which had been in trust to him for his. All the passion of Ireland seemed to be thrown into that fight, it obscured the vision beyond it of the rebuilding of a nation. Then, at last, had come the breaking of Parnell's power and his death, the quarrel among his followers that pushed politics into the background, and with the loss of that dominance of his, there came a birth of new hope and interests, as it were, a setting free of the imagination. First among the builders of the new Ireland I had already set the name of Douglas Hyde, the founder of the Gaelic League, when I saw last year (May 1922) that Michael Collins had thus written of that League under the title of 'The Greatest Event' and 'It restored the language to its place in the reverence of the people. It revived Gaelic culture; while being non-political it was, by its very nature, intensely national ... Irish history will recognise in the birth of the Gaelic League in 1893 the most important event of the nineteenth century but in the whole history of our nation. It did more than any other movement to restore the national pride, honour and self-respect. Through the medium of the past it linked the people with the past and led them to look to a future that would be a noble continuation of it.' I think he has not said too much, and that the small beginning, in Galway first of all, and then other Irish-speaking places, the bringing together of the people to give the songs and poems, old and new, kept in their memory, led to the discovery, the disclosure, of folk-learning, of folk-poetry of ancient tradition, to an upsetting of the table of values, to an extraordinary excitement. The imagination of Ireland had found a new homing place. Douglas Hyde's vision, as he founded that League had been one of those 'solid announcements' of the poets that, while looked on as dreams, come true.

37

Horace Plunkett was another of those first builders. He had led that unloosed imagination to practical uses, like the farmer in the old folk-tale who set his sons to dig in search of a treasure to be found in the field, he urged the better cultivation of the soil, the better management of dairies, of farms; above all, he brought about that friendliness and strength that comes from working together, rather than in isolation. He began that co-operative farming that England and America have not been too proud to take a lesson from. Yeats, on the other hand, forming a Literary Society, speaking on literature, had called for the freedom of the individual from the long tradition of patriotic poetry of propagandist writing, which to criticise was to lay a hand upon the sacred Ark. He would never have any truce with a poet who was content with less than the perfect form, whatever national cause he might be trying to serve.

These were the men I was happy enough to meet after I had tried here and there in my lonely months to find work to do for my country. I did not find it in a moment. As usual in my parochial way, working at what was close at hand, I was brought through Gort Convent into connection with the 'Irish Industries'. I had taught the nuns or their pupils to embroider with linen thread upon linen in the old Portuguese style, and when they had made some very charming blinds and counterpanes they asked me to take them to the London sale, together with hand-woven flannel and linen, and even 'tennis dresses' made from a distant view of some tennis parties seen from the convent windows. My letters telling of having slept on the eve of a sale 'with a pyramid of parcels in the middle of my room . . .' And at the sale the 'tennis dresses' recalling those of the wives in the Noah's Arks in our childhood lay despised till Lady Fingall slipped them one by one over her own dress and sold them off triumphantly.

But I didn't like the sales; I didn't think they 'brought dignity to Ireland'. I was not sorry when a break-down in the convent on the business side set me free.

I went on with my quiet life. In the February of 1895 I wrote to E.L.:[1] 'The garden is like Italy, warm sunshine and many flowers out, wallflowers, grape hyacinths, violets and in the woods, primroses. I did a little ornamental planting yesterday, putting out copper beeches and laburnums raised from seed in my own nursery. I hope, if there are ever grandchildren, they will be grateful some day. Our people are paying rents and paying very well, and a policeman who came from Gort in the holidays to cut the boys' hair said he was glad of the distraction, as they have absolutely nothing to do about here now.' And then in August: 'Paul Bourget and his wife have been at Duras, de Basterot brought them over one day to lunch. Bourget was interested in oriental things but most of all in a photograph of Parnell, the last taken of him, which I had put in a frame, writing at the back the words of an old ballad –

> Oh, I hae dream'd a dreary dream
> Beyond the Isle of Skye:
> I saw a dead man win a fight
> And I think that man was I.

He held it to his breast and walked about the house with it, struck by the tragedy of the dying face. Edward Martyn had also poets with him, Arthur Symons,[2] and W. B. Yeats, who is full of charm and the Celtic revival. I have been collecting fairy-lore since his visit and am surprised to find how full of it are the minds of the people, and how strong the belief in the invisible world around us.' I remember the first day Edward and his mother brought them out to lunch with me, I showed Yeats a letter from Bret Harte, to whom I had sent his *Celtic Twilight*, and saying, 'I am reading it during my only really intelligent and lucid intervals – in bed, at night! Then I have time and leisure to enjoy what I am reading, and it is, after all, not a bad thing to drop off to sleep with the fairies! I think I am particularly delighted with a certain Mr Montgomery who doubts the alleged fact of his wife's ghostly reappearance on earth, on the grounds that "she would not show herself to Mrs Kelly! She with respectable people to appear to!" This seems to me to add another sting to death! Let us hope that we may all live such a life in this world that we shall be able to reappear in it hereafter to the most respectable people, and in the best society.'

The Sligo legends in that little book made me jealous for Galway, and the gathering of legend among my own neighbours became a chief interest and a great part of my work for many years to come. The gathering was for the most part mine, but as it had been begun so it was continued under Yeats's direction so to speak, so far as the lore of vision was concerned. The folk-history and folk-tales and poems came later and made a foundation for many of my plays; I found suggestion, inspiration, and the means of expression there. Is there not a tale of a King and his Court who went through the world looking for a wonder worker, a saint or healer, they believed to be living in some far place; and it was when they had returned after years of the vain pursuit they found he had sat all the while hidden under the rags of a beggar they had seen daily sitting at the door. And I know that even as a child my heart would feel oppressed at some rare moments with emotion, as I saw the snipe rise sidelong from the rushy marsh, sunset reflected in its pools, or the wild deer among the purple heather of the hills from which I looked on distant mountain and sea. That feeling came again and again in later years, when some olive-belted hill, or lovely southern plain that well satisfied the eye, filled the heart with a hunger, a pain of longing, I knew not for what. I know now it was the artist's desire to capture, to express, the perfect. And although fulfillment has fallen far, far short of vision, I know how barren one side of my life would have been without that poetry of the soil, those words and dreams and cadences of the people that helped me to give some echoed expression to that dragging driving force.

But folklore was only one among Yeats's interests at that time. He was tumbling now and again into politics. He wrote to me from Manchester in that autumn of 1897, 'We had a long and exhausting political meeting this morning and will have another tonight . . . Miss Gonne and I went to the picture gallery after the meeting to see a Rossetti that is there . . . This is a very feeble letter, the sort of thing one writes when one is ten years old. It is a fine day. How are you? A tree has fallen into the pond. I have a new canary, and etc. You know the style. But I have been chairman of a noisy meeting for three hours and am very done up. I have a speech to prepare for tonight. Everything went smoothly this morning in spite of anonymous letters warning us to have a bodyguard at the door. Perhaps the disturbance waits for tonight. I find the infinite triviality of politics more trying than ever. We tear each other's character to pieces for things that don't matter to anybody.'

And I had written in that summer, 'One evening Hanlon brought me in some trout he had caught at the Natural Bridge, and as next day was Friday, I drove over to Tillyra to offer them to Mrs Martyn. There I found W. B. Yeats just arrived from Dublin, white, haggard, voiceless, fresh from the Jubilee riots[3] which he had been in the thick of, having been led into them as escort to Miss Gonne. However, he had by main force and lock and key kept her from reaching the mob when it had come into collision with the police. Black flags had been distributed and windows broken. It was not a very dignified proceeding and he himself disapproved of it, not because of respect for the Queen for he thinks it was right to make some protest against the unhappy misgovernment and misfortunes of Ireland during her reign, but that he thinks that the impulse should come from the people themselves and not be thrust on them from above. Some episodes were amusing. He heard "cheers for the French" and then some men cried "and boo for the Germans", and another said: "Why do you boo the Germans, don't you know they're the worst enemies of England now?" "Are they so?" said the other, "then hi for them!" And going into the Theosophist Society afterwards he saw a tall Theosophist, whom he had last seen lying on his face on a hillside striving after unearthly visions, sitting in triumph with a thick stick by his side, with which he had just knocked down a policeman; somebody whispered to Yeats, "We saw him carried away to the hospital."'

But even my growing friendship with Yeats did not bring me into that National struggle in which he had a hand, although my feeling against Home Rule had gradually been changing. It is hard to say how the change of mind came. There was preparation for it in my husband's liberal views (though he, too, had cried out against Gladstone's proposals), and in my friendship with

Wilfrid Blunt, and my always friendly and affectionate intercourse with the people. Perhaps also in that work on the *Letter-Box* which had given me a more intimate knowledge of Irish history. But I felt less and less interest in politics as other interests came in. I had soon laid down a formula for myself, 'Not working for Home Rule, but preparing for it', and this, by adding dignity to the country through our work. But it is hard to keep quite clear.

And in the summer of 1897, I wrote: 'I have been a little in disgrace myself about the Jubilee. George Gough had ordered a bonfire to be lighted at Lough Cutra, and then had written to all the neighbours calling on them to do the same. I refused on the ground of the Queen's neglect of the country. (The Prince told Sir William in Ceylon she had even prevented him from coming when he wished to.) W. Shawe-Taylor wrote and refused on the ground of turf being dear. Edward Martyn wrote that he had no turf himself but he hoped those of his tenants who had bogs might see their way to lighting bonfires. George Gough was sadly grieved by my refusal. On Sunday his wife asked me if I had received a "dreadful letter" from him. I said, "No, it was only a wail over a lost soul." In the end the As and Zs (who have English wives) lighted bonfires but the people did not go near them, or take any notice. Next night, St John's Eve, the mountains alight with fires and the people in crowds around them.'

Yeats came over to Coole several times. It was then that we had begun making our plans for a theatre. And in the next year at the end of July, a week before the holidays, W. B. Yeats came to stay with me, the first of many visits, bringing his friend, George Russell ('A.E.'). He had told me he had described him as 'Michael Robartes' in *Rosa Alchemica*, and when one Monday morning I had a letter saying that they would be with me by lunch-time I looked at the passage and read 'with his wild red hair, fierce eyes and sensitive lips and rough clothing, Michael Robartes looks something between a peasant, a saint and a debauchee', so I was rather apprehensive and went down to meet them feeling quite shy, but to my relief found a quiet gentleman, perfectly simple and composed. Yeats told me that eight years ago he was the most promising student in the Dublin Art schools, but one day he came and said, as well as I understand, that the will is the only thing given us in this life as absolutely our own, and that we should allow no weakening of it, and that Art, which he cared for so much, would, he believed, weaken his will. And so he went into Pim's shop as cashier, and has been there ever since, and Pim says he is the best cashier he has ever had.

He works till six in the evening, had £60 a year, out of which he not only supports himself, but helps others poorer than himself. He edits *The Theosophist*, writing a great part and has formed a little band of mystics believing, I think, in universal brotherhood and reincarnation. Yeats says his poems are not so good now as when they were dictated by the spirits, he only paints now on the white-washed wall of his lodgings, as he is sure it will be all white-washed out when he leaves it, and to paint anything that lasts would be 'a bond upon his soul'. He signed his poems Æ, but the publishers insisted on separating the letters, a great grievance to the writer, who says that the diphthong exactly by its sound expressed the mood of his soul . . . He said one evening, 'This life bores me, I am waiting for a higher one.' His *Homeward Songs by the Way* have gone into a second edition here and have a great sale in America. On Saturday afternoon and Sunday, his only holidays, he goes to the Wicklow hills and wanders there, sometimes lying down and seeing visions of the old Celtic Gods; of these he has done some beautiful pastel drawings; the first afternoon I took the two poets across the lake to the cromlech, and there they sat until A.E. saw a purple druid appear.[4] Next day we went to Burren hills to Corcomroe, a grey day but it pleased them, and we heard fairy-lore from a young man there.

W.B.Y. had written to me before they came. Rosses Point: 'George Russell has made drawings since he came here of quite a number of supernatural beings. The resemblance between the things seen by him at certain places and the things seen there at a different time by a cousin of mine has been very curious. They have met, however, and so, as we say, "may have got things out of each other's sphere", although they did not talk about them'.

1922. Yeats said the other day: 'Do you remember that I brought Russell to the old castle of Balinamantane, where old

Mrs Sheridan has told us about seeing a drawbridge across the river there, and ladies looking out from the windows, but A.E. hated to be put to see anyone else's ghosts and wandered about in a discontented silence. Presently I said, "Don't you see anything, Russell?" and he replied, "Oh, yes, I do, but they are a low lot." '

One evening they talked about Shelley. Yeats is writing his essays on him, and A.E. says, 'It will make people angry to be told he had a meaning because what people go to poetry for is to escape from conviction.' Yeats said, 'Shelley was not a political reformer, but a prophet with the eternal vision that is never welcome, for people want reformation, not revelation, which offers nothing but itself,' A.E. doesn't like *The Water of the Wondrous Isles*, which Yeats delights in; he says it is wallpaper, a mere decoration, and that it is an imitation of Malory. Yeats says it is no more imitation than Rossetti is imitator of early Italian pictures, the individual soul comes through, and that there could be no art at all without tradition. A.E. doesn't like Swinburne, says, 'There is nothing but words; nothing behind, while Wordsworth had faith behind him.'

And as to their acquaintances, Yeats declared George Russell was always looking about for a clothes-horse on which to hang his superfluous ideals and would rend to pieces those to whom he gave any praise; 'A. has good ideas but is long-winded, and getting at them is like laying out an old-fashioned tea service.' 'B. is rather an overwhelming patron of a society. He is like the elephant that when he had put his foot on the old partridge, said, "Never mind, I will be a father to the young birds!" ' 'C. has a formula and one always gets tired of people with a formula. You know what they will say on every occasion. Bernard Shaw has a formula, but he knows it, and takes as much pains to hide it, as a dog burying a bone.' 'D. will be a very good sort of wife for E. A nice kind sort of woman, who will always be ready to take up an idea that has just died.' 'F. as curator of a gallery – a sort of man whose knowledge exists to give courage to his ignorance.' 'G. has the genius for the inexpedient.' 'H. is ponderous in the chair and getting him to propose a resolution is like setting a whole army to peel a potato.'

Mr Russell left in a few days, having to go back to his cash office but Mr Yeats stayed for two months – a most charming companion, never out of humour, gentle, interested in all that went on, liking to do his work in the library in the midst of the coming and going. Then if I was typing in the drawing-room suddenly bursting in with some great new idea, and when it was expounded, laughing and saying: 'I treat you as my father says, as an anvil to beat out my ideas on.' We searched for folklore. I gave him all I had collected, and took him about looking for more, and whoever came to the door, fisherwoman or beggar or farmer, I would talk to on the subject, and if I found the stories worth having would call him down that he might have them first hand. His healthiness, both of mind and body, increased while with us, so that he wrote afterwards: 'My days at Coole passed like a dream – a dream of peace.'

'Standish O'Grady[5] came to stay with us, but during dinner the first evening he had a telegram calling him away as Revising Barrister to Belfast. He had mistaken the time by a month. He is a fine writer. He is now a little over-excited on the financial movement. Next day, after his early start, another of my best countrymen arrived, Horace Plunkett. He is working himself to death in his agricultural organisation movement but he is doing a great work in Ireland, teaching the farmers to get over their suspicion of each other, and to manage their own affairs. We had asked the farmers to meet him, but it was a fine day after long rain, and very few came, we had to call our workmen and even F.'s driver to fill the background, but he came and talked to them, explaining the methods with so much courtesy and earnestness, that he won their hearts. His quiet manner, with so much enthusiasm underneath, strikes one very much and he was a pleasant guest, played cricket with Robert and talked with Yeats. Edward Martyn stayed with us for his visit, and will help his co-operative work. I saw Mr Plunkett off in the morning, taking him to the convent on the way to the station. He saw the work being done there and promised a loom for the weaving.'

And some months later I wrote, 'Sitting idle, the shopkeepers are,' old O. says, 'for the people are getting the worth of their money in manure and seed from the Organisation. And before this the shopkeepers had to work hard to spend all the fortune they were making.'

Horace Plunkett is quite with the Celtic movement, asked E.M. and Yeats to the Agricultural Organisation dinner and made Yeats speak – a charming little speech, he said, 'like a rose leaf falling among a lot of agricultural implements'. And he has been very kind about the theatre and went to see the Attorney General on its behalf, and to see me about it in one day over here. And he has taken George Russell out of Pim's and made him an organiser of rural banks.

As to the work that has held me through so many years. I need say but little here. I have given its history in *Our Irish Theatre*. I tell how in this year, 1898,[6] Edward Martyn having written a play, *Maeve*, lent it to Count de Basterot, and I read it while staying with him on the sea coast at Duras, and admired it very much. And then one day, when E. Martyn and Yeats had come to spend a day with the old Count, and rain came on, I had a talk with Yeats as we had tea together in the steward's office, and the idea came to us that if *Maeve* could be acted in Dublin instead of London, or Germany as E.M. thought of, and with Yeats's *Countess Cathleen*, it might lead to a theatre in which plays by Irish writers might be given in Ireland. It would help to get rid of the stage Irishman, and help to restore dignity to Ireland. This seaside talk was the practical beginning of all that led to the Abbey Theatre, to the dramatic movement.

Twenty-five years have passed since that talk by the seaside, that planning of a Theatre where Irish plays could be performed in Ireland. I have told in my book of the building, the difficulties, of the generosity of friends, the attacks of enemies, the battle with the Castle, with the Crowd – so I will not repeat it here.

The Abbey Theatre still endures. Through that quarter of a century it has won and held a good name. William Peel has said in public that it 'has revolutionised other theatres and will be spoken of in a hundred years to come'. Theodore Roosevelt, that it has 'not only made an extraordinary contribution to the sum of Irish literary and artistic achievement, it has done more for the drama than has been accomplished by any other nation of recent years'. C. E. Montague praising its method of acting says that actors 'come at an effect of spiritual austerity. They contrive to reach past most of the futilities; they take a fresh clear hold on their craft in its elements'. Ford Madox Hueffer says, 'I don't think there is anything like it in the world.' And many people ask in other words the question in the Aran Fisherman's song, 'What way has your little curragh come to land when the big ships have gone away?'

When I was asked that question in America sometimes by students of a University – as that of Pennsylvania for an instance, I said I thought one reason of our success was a rule that had been forced on us, of limitation. A clause had been forced into our licence by the jealousy of other Dublin theatres limiting us outside foreign masterpieces to Irish plays. We had less than half a dozen plays with which to begin our enterprise, two by Mr Martyn and two by Mr Yeats. Without that clause we might have been tempted for convenience sake to borrow from England, but with it came the necessity to encourage every attempt to welcome every writer who showed he had the dramatic idea. My own comedies were written simply because at the time comedy was so much needed.

'And then,' I said, 'necessity put upon us the limitation of expense. Managers are slow to put on new work unless they are sure of a big return because of the heavy cost of staging that is expected. We had by necessity to use the same cottage scene for a dozen or so of the peasant plays, and our set of hangings, our kilts and fillets for heroic ones. I have seen "The Faery Child" in Mr Yeats's *Land of Heart's Desire* dancing across the stage in a dress I had myself made some time before for Synge's *Deirdre of the Sorrows*. So a new play even of Kings and Queens did not rob us of many pounds. A roll of dyed sacking and a stencil will furnish a palace wall. And as to Irish subjects, I must myself be grateful for that limitation, and so may we all. Our windows should be open to Heaven, but the floor of the house of *our own* earth. Every work that we take up in that home we should be able to work out by the light above us and not be ashamed of the work. I believe it is in what is closest to us we find our best inspiration. Whitman has told us that, and so has Turguenieff when he says of his country, Russia, "She can do without everyone of us, but not one of us can do without her. Woe to him who thinks he can, and woe twofold to him who actually does without her! The Cosmopolitan is a nonentity, without nationality is no art nor truth, nor life, nor anything. You cannot have an ideal face without an individual expression; only a vulgar face can be without it." Synge had done no good work till he came back to his own country. It was there he found all he wanted. Fable, emotion, style. Whatever I myself have written that is, as our people would say, "worth while" has come from my own surroundings, my own parish, my own home.'

And when the students, who had been very patient, asked me for some rule of choice as to the plays they put on, I said that in the Abbey Theatre we had chosen nothing that we had not hoped to revive from time to time, thus keeping out plays of merely passing interest. And I said, 'We have some plays on our list that reach so high a standard we should feel it unfitting to put vulgarity in their company.' And then I told them how in my husband's Oxford days a dealer had tried to persuade him to buy a beautiful line engraving of Leonardo da Vinci's 'Madonna of the Rocks' and he had refused, saying, 'I like the picture in my room.' But the dealer said, 'I will lend you the picture for a month, sir; it will drive the others out.' And sure enough before the month was over that picture had driven away the prizefighters and ballet dancers, and he bought others of the same beauty to put with it, and all now hang together at my home. 'And so,' I said, 'put on your stage some one play at least of the highest quality, even if you must borrow it from the great masters, and test every play you choose afterwards by asking if it is worth to claim comradeship with this. We want to have a base of reality, and an apex of beauty. I think we have even in our roughest comedies some quality of imagination or fantasy or some sincerity of purpose that makes them fitting to be given in the same season at least with Yeats's *King's Threshold* or Hyde's *Nativity* or Synge's *Riders to the Sea*. Are not the story of the procession of beasts into the Ark and of Jonah swallowed by the great fish bound within the same cover as the Revelation of St John the Divine?'

But it is hard to lay down fixed rules, and often when I was asked how to make a theatre, I would say 'by beginning to make it'. I was talking once to Bernard Shaw about a new manager, an untried one, and he said, 'He'll learn. You and Yeats knew nothing about the Theatre when you began, and you've done it better than anyone.'

And then another enriching influence came into my life. 'Dr Douglas Hyde came one day to Tillyra, where I was staying, pushing along a broken bicycle, because instead of coming to the station by train, as had been expected, he had got out at Craughwell to look for folklore. That afternoon I took him to the cromlech at Crannagh, and he talked in Irish with Fahey, who to my pride came out with legends of Finn and the Fianna. Hyde was full of enthusiasm and Irish. I was able to find for him later some manuscripts containing Irish poems, from a man who had left Galway a year ago, and whom I traced at last to a butcher's shop in Oranmore.' . . . I have written elsewhere how once in my childhood I had been eager to learn Irish, I thought to get leave to take lessons from an old Scripture-reader who spent a part of his time in the parish of Killinane, teaching such scholars as he could find to read their own language in the hope that they might turn to the only book then being printed in Irish, the Bible. But my asking, timid with the fear of mockery, was unheeded. Yet I missed by a little an opportunity that might have made me a real Irish scholar, and not as I am, imperfect, stumbling. For a kinsman learned in the language, Standish Hayes O'Grady, the translator of the wonderful *Silva Gaedelica*, had been sometimes a guest in the house, and would still have been welcomed there but that my mother, who had a great dislike to the marriage of cousins, had fancied he was taking a liking to one of my elder sisters; and with that suspicion the 'winged nymph, Opportunity' had passed from my reach.

This same Standish Hayes O'Grady had refused, Yeats tells me, to join the Irish Literary Society or the Gaelic League, declaring them both Fenian organisations. But yet he was so little

English that he boasted to me near his life's end, that though he had lived forty years in England, he had never made an English friend.

After my marriage I had bought a grammar and worked at it for a while with the help of a gardener. But it was difficult, and my teacher was languid, suspecting it may be some hidden mockery, for those were the days before Irish had become the fashion.

But in 1897 I had written after Yeats's first visit and A.E.'s and Horace Plunkett's, and the beginning of our Theatre projects, 'The result of this little national literary stir was that Robert near the end of the holidays said he wanted to learn Irish. We tried in vain for a teacher, many speak but none know the grammar, so we began with a primer and mastered the first exercises, taking them out to Mike to get the pronunciation right. But the partridge shooting interfered at the end. Robert's first chance (which he owed to the Jubilee extra week) was also his last. He was pretty successful, getting a good many birds at Coole but making his biggest bag at Tillyra. The Birch boys had come at the end very glad to find themselves back again.'

But I went on working and learning, and I found the task far easier than when I had first taken up a grammar. 'For that young priest Eugene O'Growney (I have still a little Gaelic League badge sent to me by him), sent from Ireland to look for health in California, had used the short span of life left to him in writing simple lessons in Irish grammar that made at least the first steps easy.'

I was given renewed enthusiasm by that meeting with the Founder of 'the Gaelic League, one in the first three of our "Mighty Men". And a little later I was spending ten days very pleasantly at Spiddal with the Morrises. Fine weather had come at last, a sort of Indian summer; the Atlantic was beautiful . . . I ran down when I could to the school and had an Irish lesson and gathered some folk-stories . . . Then Yeats came and I arranged an interview with a witch doctor for him, of which he will doubtless give an account. I stirred up the master of the school to collect folk-stories, and offered a prize for stories written down in either English or Irish . . . The school children have already sent me eleven . . .'

And again, 'I spent a day or two at Spiddal, the Leckys there. I had a talk with Lecky[7] about compulsory purchase, which he thinks likely, though from his usual balancing mind, it is hard to say if he approves or not (I have heard his Athenaeum friends complain that it is very hard to get him to give a definite opinion on anything they ask him). At dinner I had a fight for the Irish language. Lord Morris says he never spoke against its being taught in the schools, for he never heard any proposal at all made for it at the board – if he had he would only have laughed at such an absurd craze. Lecky, defending his Trinity Professors, sneered at me for calling Irish a modern language. I said, "Yes, just in the same way as modern Greek"; and Lady Morris told him it is spoken all round Spiddal; and I told him the people's songs are still composed in it, which disturbed him. Lord M. gave some Irish phrases, which luckily I understood, so I came pretty well out of it.'

And later, 'I went to Galway with W.B.Y. to support the Gaelic movement, very glad we went, for none of the "classes" were there to support it unless priests can so be called.'

Grealey, the young schoolmaster, gave a recitation with great vigour, and as Daly, the other master, was giving the next, W.B.Y. asked Grealey what they were all about and he said: 'Both poems are called "Thoughts on Ireland", my one tells how the Sassanachs[8] murdered us a while ago.' Very characteristic 'Thoughts on Ireland'!

In a letter written to Lady Layard in the Christmas holidays of 1898/9 I said, 'they have passed very cheerily so far. Douglas Hyde, LL.D., an Irish scholar, was here for a week, spent the days shooting with the boys, and I captured old men with songs and stories for him to interview in the evenings; and we have started a branch of the Gaelic League. Miss Borthwick, the Irish scholar who had been giving me lessons in London, is staying here and has classes every afternoon at the gate lodge, about eight girls and thirty to forty young men alternately, some walking as far as three miles to attend. They get on very quickly, knowing the spoken language; it is just the reading and grammatical construction they have to learn; a splendid educational help to say the least, and they will be able to appreciate in the end the dignity and beauty of our own literature ... The Theatre project has now been announced, and I hope all will go well with it.'

We had done other things besides the classes for the language: 'On Thursday I took lunch to the boys who were shooting at Inchy, and in the afternoon had a meeting at Kiltartan school, Dr Fahey in the chair, and a branch of the Gaelic League was formed ... Dr Hyde made a very eloquent speech in Irish, not that I understood it, but it roused the people. Then he made one in English in which he drew attention to the inferiority of the vocabulary of the English peasant to that of the Irish. All very good, except that he came a little too near what may be taken for politics in saying, "Let English go their road and let us go ours, and God forbid their road should ever be our road."'

And then I wrote of a great climax, the first performance as I believe of a Punch and Judy show in Irish! 'On Friday the Christmas tree, very hard work, a holy day, and the boys went off to shoot Tillyra and took the Mikes (keeper and steward), so I could get no help but Murty's to set up the Punch and Judy show. And when I proposed to decorate the tree I was told it was still in the woods! However, John Rourke appeared and dug up a small silver fir, to be planted again. We had a good many children, over a hundred, more than usual at Christmas; however, provisions and presents held out, some of the latter, Italian pottery, I had brought home from Venice. The Punch and Judy, a great success, first Wyndham Birch and my niece, Frances, did it in English, and then Dr Hyde and Miss Borthwick in Irish, and this brought down the house; his chastising of the baby was much applauded – the children's own chastisement had probably been accompanied by the same words. He made only the "peeler" speak English, and said the *páistín*[9] has fallen out of the window of itself ... A success, but very tiring, twenty-five guests in the breakfast-room afterwards to tea. Old Diveney says "that gentlemen has very good Irish, only his tongue is a little hard and sharp because he's Englified. But I am a common labourer and so I speak flat." On Saturday – the boys to the bogs, but didn't get much, but R. and D.H. got a pheasant and two woodcocks when they got back.

'On Sunday. After lunch I took D.H. across the lake to Fahey's and left him there but he didn't get much except my story of Usheen and says mine was just as good in English and very accurate. Fahey says, "Father Fahey has good Irish but he's that talented the people can't well understand it." He also says they can't understand more than half what he said in English. Miss Borthwick found about sixty pupils at the gate house.

'At the Convent. Sister Frances tells me that last year £2 was sent for the poor, after their appeal, with a letter written in a strange language. They puzzled over it, and thought the signature was a Turkish one, so the Reverend Mother thought it must be a gift from the Sultan, sent through the Turkish Ambassador in Paris and wrote to thank him (the Ambassador) (for it has never been forgotten that the Sultan sent money in the Famine years "And that is what the Queen never did"). His Secretary wrote back to say His Excellency knew nothing of it. Then they took the letter to Dr Fahey who burst out laughing, for it was written in Irish! They have begun teaching the little boys their prayers in Irish!

'Tommy Hynes came last night and D.H. got some songs from him, the best was by Raftery, "Mary Hynes of Ballylee"; and there was "Mary Brown" and "Raftery and death", too long to be all taken down. Miss Borthwick had thirty young men at her class and they got through fifty pages! The boys shot the bogs and got a nice mixed bag.'

29 January (1899). 'The holidays over, all gone, "Fade an la gan Cloinne Uisnigh" (It is long the day without the sons of Usnach). The workmen have made a bond only to speak Irish when together, and John Burke knows the first book by heart and has sent for the second; and Mike says, "There isn't a child you'll meet on the road now, but will say 'God save you' in Irish."' It was also in that year, 1899, there is an entry – 28 June – J. M. Synge came from Aran.

And so I found my work in Ireland and could claim comrade-ship with other workers. The threads of new interests began to be woven into the pattern of my life. The theatre, the folk-legends, the language. And as to this last, I sometimes think with a little pride that when Michael Collins and Eamon de Valera were in their short jackets going to school or marching from it, I was spending time and money and energy in bringing back the Irish among my own people.

# FOLKLORE AND TRANSLATIONS
## FROM THE IRISH

# from *Visions and Beliefs*

## from 'Seers and Healers'

### BIDDY EARLY

In talking to the people I often heard the name of Biddy Early, and I began to gather many stories of her, some calling her a healer and some a witch. Some said she had died a long time ago, and some that she was still living. I was sure after a while that she was dead, but was told that her house was still standing, and was on the other side of Slieve Echtge, between Feakle and Tulla. So one day I set out and drove Shamrock, my pony, to a shooting lodge built by my grandfather in a fold of the mountains, and where I had sometimes, when a young girl, stayed with my brothers when they were shooting the wild deer that came and sheltered in the woods. It had like other places on our estate a border name brought over from Northumberland, but though we called it Chevy Chase the people spoke of its woods and outskirts as Daire-caol, the Narrow Oak Wood, and Daroda, the Two Roads, and Druim-da-rod, their Ridge. I stayed the night in the low thatched house, setting out next day for Feakle 'eight strong miles over the mountain'. It was a wild road, and the pony had to splash his way through two unbridged rivers, swollen with the summer rains. The red mud of the road, the purple heather and foxglove, the brown bogs were a contrast to the grey rocks and walls of Burren and Aidhne, and there were many low hills, brown when near, misty blue in the distance; then the Golden Mountain, Slieve nan-Or, 'where the last great battle will be fought before the end of the world'. Then I was out of Connacht into Clare, the brown turning to green pasture as I drove by Raftery's Lough Greine.

I put up my pony at a little inn. There were portraits of John Dillon and Michael Davitt hanging in the parlour, and the landlady told me Parnell's likeness had been with them, until the priest had told her he didn't think well of her hanging it there.[1]

There was also on the wall, in a frame, a warrant for the arrest of one of her sons, signed by, I think, Lord Cowper, in the days of the Land War. 'He got half a year in gaol the same year Parnell did. He got sick there, and though he lived for some years the doctor said when he died the illness he got in gaol had to do with his death.'

I had been told how to find Biddy Early's house 'beyond the little humpy bridge', and I walked on till I came to it, a poor cottage enough, high up on a mass of rock by the roadside. There was only a little girl in the house, but her mother came in afterwards and told me that Biddy Early had died about twenty years before, and that after they had come to live in the house they had been 'annoyed for a while' by people coming to look for her. She had sent them away, telling them Biddy Early was dead, though a friendly priest had said to her, 'Why didn't you let on you were her and make something out of them?' She told me some of the stories I give below, and showed me the shed where the healer had consulted with her invisible friends. I had already been given by an old patient of hers a 'bottle' prepared for the cure, but which she had been afraid to use. It lies still unopened on a shelf in my store room. When I got back at nightfall to the lodge in the woods I found many of the neighbours gathered there, wanting to hear news of 'the Tulla Woman' and to know for certain if she was dead. I think as time goes on her fame will grow and some of the myths that always hang in the air will gather round her, for I think the first thing I was told of her was, 'There used surely to be enchanters in the old time, magicians and freemasons. Old Biddy Early's power came from the same thing.'

*An Old Woman in the Lodge Kitchen says:*

Do you remember the time John Kevin beyond went to see Biddy Early, for his wife, she was sick at the time. And Biddy Early knew everything, and that there was a forth[2] behind her house, and she said, 'Your wife is too fond of going out late at night.'

*Mrs Kearns:*

Did I know anyone that was taken by them? Well, I never knew one that was brought back again. Himself went one time to Biddy Early for his uncle, Donohue, that was sick, and he found her there and her fingers all covered with big gold rings, and she gave him a bottle, and she said: 'Go in no house on your way home, or stop nowhere, or you'll lose it.' But going home he had a thirst on him and he came to a public-house, and he wouldn't go in, but he stopped and bid the boy bring him out a drink. But a little farther on the road the horse got a fall, and the bottle was broke.

*Mrs Cregan:*

It's I was with this woman here to Biddy Early. And when she saw me, she knew it was for my husband I came, and she looked in her bottle and she said, 'It's nothing put upon him by my people that's wrong with him.' And she bid me give him cold oranges and some other things – herbs. He got better after.

*Daniel Curtin:*

Did I ever hear of Biddy Early? There's not a man in this countryside over forty year old that hasn't been with her some time or other. There's a man living in that house over there was sick one time, and he went to her, and she cured him, but says she, 'You'll have to lose something, and don't fret after it.' So he had a grey mare and she was going to foal, and one morning when he went out he saw that the foal was born, and was lying dead by the side of the wall. So he remembered what she said to him and he didn't fret.

There was one Dillane in Kinvara, Sir William knew him well, and he went to her one time for a cure. And Father Andrew came to the house and was mad with him for going, and says he, 'You take the cure out of the hands of God.' And Mrs Dillane said, 'Your Reverence, none of us can do that.' 'Well,' says Father Andrew, 'then I'll see what the devil can do and I'll send my horse tomorrow, that has a sore in his leg this long time, and try will she be able to cure him.'

So next day he sent a man with his horse, and when he got to Biddy Early's house she came out, and she told him every word that Father Andrew had said, and she cured the sore. So after that, he left the people alone; but before it, he'd be dressed in a frieze coat and a riding whip in his hand, driving away the people from going to her.

She had four or five husbands, and they all died of drink one after another. Maybe twenty or thirty people would be there in the day looking for cures, and every one of them would bring a bottle of whiskey. Wild cards they all were, or they wouldn't have married her. She'd help too to bring the butter back. Always on the first of May, it used to be taken, and maybe what would be taken from one man would be conveyed to another.

*Mr McCabe:*

Biddy Early? Not far from this she lived, above at Feakle. I got cured by her myself one time. Look at this thumb – I got it hurted one time, and I went out into the field after and was ploughing all the day, I was that greedy for work. And when I went in I had to lie on the bed with the pain of it, and it swelled and the arm with it, to the size of a horse's thigh. I stopped two or three days in the bed with the pain of it, and then my wife went to see Biddy Early and told her about it, and she came home and the next day it burst, and you never seen anything like all the stuff that came away from it. A good bit after I went to her myself, where it wasn't quite healed, and she said, 'You'd have lost it altogether if your wife hadn't been so quick to come.' She brought me into a small room, and said holy words and sprinkled holy water and told me to believe. The priests were against her, but they were wrong. How could that be evil doing that was all charity and kindness and healing?

She was a decent-looking woman, no different from any other woman of the country. The boy she was married to at the time was lying drunk in the bed. There were side-cars and common cars and gentry and country people at the door, just like Gort market, and dinner for all that came, and everyone would bring her something, but she didn't care what it was. Rich farmers would bring her the whole side of a pig. Myself, I brought a bottle of whiskey and a shilling's worth of bread, and a quarter of sugar and a quarter pound of tea. She was very rich, for there wasn't a farmer but would give her the grass of a couple of bullocks or a filly. She had the full of a field of fillies if they'd all been gathered together. She left no children, and there's no doubt at all that the reason of her being able to do cures was that she was *away* seven years. She didn't tell me about it but she spoke of it to others.

When I was coming away I met a party of country people on a cart from Limerick, and they asked where was her house, and I told them: 'Go on to the cross, and turn to the left, and follow the straight road till you come to the little humpy bridge, and soon after that you'll come to the house.'

But the priests would be mad if they knew that I told anyone the way.

She died about twelve year ago; I didn't go to the wake myself, or the funeral, but I heard that her death was natural.

No, Mrs Early is no relation to Biddy Early – the nuns asked her the same thing when she was married. A cousin of hers had her hand cut with a jug that was broke, and she went up to her and when she got there, Biddy Early said: 'It's a thing you never should do, to beat a child that breaks a cup or a jug.' And sure enough it was a child that broke it, and she beat her for doing it. But cures she did sure enough.

*Bartley Coen:*
There was a neighbour of my own, Andrew Dennehy:
I was knocked up by him one night to go to the house, because he said *they* were calling to him. But when they got there, there was nothing to be found. But some see these things, and some can't. It's against our creed to believe in them. And the priests won't let on that they believe in them themselves, but they are more in dread of going about at night than any of us. They were against Biddy Early too. There was a man I knew living near the sea, and he set out to go to her one time. And on his way he went into his brother-in-law's house, and the priest came in there, and

bid him not to go on. 'Well, Father,' says he, 'cure me yourself if you won't let me go to her to be cured.' And when the priest wouldn't do that (for the priests can do many cures if they like to), he went on to her. And the minute he came in, 'Well,' says she, 'you made a great fight for me on the way.' For though it's against our creed to believe it, she could hear any earthly thing that was said in every part, miles off. But she had two red eyes, and some used to say, 'If she can cure so much, why can't she cure her own eyes?'

No, she wasn't *away* herself. It is said it was from a son of her own she got the knowledge, a little chap that was astray. And one day when he was lying sick in the bed he said: 'There's such and such a woman has a hen down in the pot, and if I had the soup of the hen, I think it would cure me.' So the mother went to the house, and when she got there, sure enough, there was a hen in the pot on the fire. But she was ashamed to tell what she came for, and she let on to have only come for a visit, and so she sat down. But presently in the heat of the talking she told what the little chap had said. 'Well,' says the woman, 'take the soup and welcome, and the hen too if it will do him any good.' So she brought them with her, and when the boy saw the soup, 'It can't cure me,' says he, 'for no earthly thing can do that. But since I see how kind and how willing you are, and did your best for me, I'll leave you a way of living.' And so he did, and taught her all she knew. That's what's said at any rate.

*The Little Girl of Biddy Early's House:*
The people do be full of stories of all the cures she did. Once after we came to live here a carload of people came, and asked was Biddy Early here, and my mother said she was dead. When she told the priest he said she had a right to shake a bottle and say she was her, and get something from them. It was by the bottle she did all, to shake it, and she'd see everything when she looked in it. Sometimes she'd give a bottle of some cure to people that came, but if she'd say to them, 'You'll never bring it home,' break it they should on the way home, with all the care they'd take of it.

She was as good, and better, to the poor as to the rich. Any poor person passing the road, she'd call in and give a cup of tea or a glass of whiskey to, and bread and what they wanted.

She had a big chest within in that room, and it full of pounds of tea and bottles of wine and of whiskey and of claret, and all things in the world. One time she called in a man that was passing and gave him a glass of whiskey, and then she said to him, 'The road you were going home by, don't go by it.' So he asked why not, and she took the bottle – a long-shaped bottle it was – and looked into it, holding it up, and then she bid him look through it, and he'd see what would happen him. But her husband said, 'Don't show it to him, it might give him a fright he wouldn't get over.' So she only said, 'Well, go home by another road.' And so he did and got home safe, for in the bottle she had seen a party of men that wouldn't have let him pass alive. She got the rites of the Church when she died, but first she had to break the bottle.

It was from her brother that she got the power, when she had to go to the workhouse, and he came back, and gave her the way of doing the cures.

*The Blacksmith I met near Tulla:*
I know you to be a respectable lady and an honourable one because I know your brothers, meeting them as I do at the fair of Scariff. No fair it would be if they weren't there. I knew Biddy Early well, a nice fresh-looking woman she was. It's to her the people used to be flocking, to the door and even to the window, and if they'd come late in the day, they'd have no chance of getting to her, they'd have to take lodgings for the night in the town. She was a great woman. If any of the men that came into the house had a drop too much drink taken, she'd turn them out if they said an unruly word. And if any of them were fighting or disputing or going to law, she'd say, 'Be at one, and ye can rule the world.' The priests were against her and used to be taking the cloaks and the baskets from the country people to keep them back from going to her.

I never went to her myself – for you should know that no ill or harm ever comes to a blacksmith.

*An Old Midwife:*

Tell me now is there anything wrong about you or your son that you went to that house? I went there but once myself, when my little girl that was married was bad, after her second baby being born. I went to the house and told her about it, and she took the bottle and shook it and looked in it, and then she turned and said something to himself [her husband] that I didn't hear – and she just waved her hand to me like that, and bid me go home, for she would take nothing from me. But himself came out and told that what she was after seeing in the bottle was my little girl, and the coffin standing beside her. So I went home, and sure enough on the tenth day after, she was dead.

*The Spinning-Woman:*

Biddy Early was a witch, wherever she got it. There was a priest at Feakle spoke against her one time, and soon after he was passing near her house and she put something on the horse so that he made a bolt into the river and stopped there in the middle, and wouldn't go back or forward. Some people from the neighbourhood went to her, and she told them all about the whole place, and that one time there was a great battle about the castle, and that there is a passage going from here to the forth beyond on Dromore Hill, and to another place that's near Maher's house. And she said that there is a cure for all sicknesses hidden between the two wheels of Ballylee mill. And how did she know that there was a mill here at all? Witchcraft wherever she got it; away she may have been in a trance. She had a son, and one time he went to the hurling beyond at some place in Tipperary, and none could stand against him; he was like a deer.

I went to Biddy Early one time myself, about my little boy that's now in America that was lying sick in the house. But on the way to her I met a sergeant of police and he asked where was I going, and when I told him, he said, to joke with me, 'Biddy Early's dead.' 'May the devil die with her,' says I. Well, when I got to the house, what do you think, if she didn't know that, and what I said. And she was vexed and at the first, she would do nothing for me. I had a pound for her here in my bosom. But when I held it out she wouldn't take it, but she turned the rings on her fingers, for she had a ring for every one, and she said, 'A shilling for this one, sixpence for another one.' But all she told me was that the boy was nervous, and so he was, she was right in that, and that he'd get well, and so he did.

There was a man beyond in Cloon, was walking near the gate the same day and his little boy with him, and he turned his foot and hurt it, and she knew that. She told me she slept in Ballylee mill last night, and that there was a cure for all things in the world between the two wheels there. Surely she was *away* herself, and as to her son, she brought him back with her, and for eight or nine year he lay in the bed in the house. And he'd never stir so long as she was in it, but no sooner was she gone away anywhere than he'd be out down the village among the people, and then back again before she'd get to the house.

She had three husbands, I saw one of them when I was there, but I knew by the look of him he wouldn't live long. One man I know went to her and she sent him on to a woman at Kilrush – one of her own sort, and they helped one another. She said to some woman I knew: 'If you have a bowl broke or a plate throw it out of the door, and don't make any attempt to mend it, it vexes *them*.'

*Mrs Locke:*

It was my son was thatching Heniff's house when he got the touch, and he came back with a pain in his back and in his shoulders, and took to the bed. And a few nights after that I was asleep, and the little girl came and woke me and said, 'There's none of us can sleep, with all the cars and carriages rattling round the house.' But though I woke and heard her say that, I fell into a sound sleep again and never woke till morning. And one night there came two taps at the window, one after another, and we all heard it and no one there. And at last I sent the eldest boy to Biddy Early and he found her in the house. She was then married to her fourth man. And she said he came a day too soon and would do nothing for him. And he had to walk away in the rain. And the next day he went back and she said, 'Three days later and you'd have been too late.' And she gave him two bottles, the one he was to bring to a boundary water and to fill it up, and that was to be rubbed to the back, and the other was to drink. And the minute he got them he began to get well, and he left the bed and could walk, but he was always delicate. When we rubbed his back we saw a black mark, like the bite of a dog, and as to his face, it was as white as a sheet.

I have the bottle here yet, though it's thirty year ago I got it. She bid the boy to bring whatever was left of it to a river, and to pour it away with the running water. But when he got well I did nothing with it, and said nothing about it – and here it is now for you to see. I never let on to Father Folan that I went to her, but one time the Bishop came, MacInerny. I knew he was a rough man, and I went to him and made my confession, and I said, 'Do what you like with me, but I'd walk the world for my son when he was sick.' And all he said was, 'It would have been no wonder if the two feet had been cut off from the messenger.' And he said no more and put nothing on me.

There was a boy I saw went to Biddy Early, and she gave him a bottle and told him to mind he did not lose it in the crossing of some road. And when he came to the place it was broke.

Often I heard of Biddy Early, and I knew of a little girl was sick and the brother went to Biddy Early to ask would she get well. And she said, 'They have a place ready for her, room for her they have.' So he knew she would die, and so she did.

The priests can do things too, the same way as she could, for there was one Mr Lyne was dying, a Protestant, and the priest went in and baptised him a Catholic before he died, and he said to the people after, 'He's all right now, in another world.' And it was more than the baptising made him sure of that.

*An Old Man from Kinvara:*
My wife is paralysed these thirty-six years, and the neighbours said she'd get well if the child died, for she got it after her confinement, all in a minute. But the child died in a year and eleven months, and she got no better. And then they said she'd get taken after twenty-one years, but that passed, and she's

just the same way. And she's as good a Christian as any all the time.

I went to Biddy Early one time about her. She was a very old woman, all shaky, and the crankiest woman I ever saw. And the husband was a fine young man, and he lying in the bed. It was a man from Kinvara half-paralysed I brought with me, and she would do nothing for him at first, and then the husband bid her do what she could. So she took the bottle and shook it and looked in it, and she said what was in him was none of her business. And I had work to get him a lodging that night in Feakle, for the priests had all the people warned against letting any one in that had been to her. She wouldn't take the whiskey I brought, but the husband and myself, we opened it and drank it between us.

She gave me a bottle for my wife, but when I got to the workhouse, where I had to put her in the hospital, they wouldn't let me through the gate for they heard where I had been. So I had to hide the bottle for a night by a wall, on the grass, and I sent my brother's wife to find it, and to bring it to her in the morning into the workhouse. But it did her no good, and Biddy Early told her after it was because I didn't bring it straight to her, but had left it on the ground for the night.

Biddy Early beat all women. No one could touch her. I knew a girl, a friend of my own, at Burren and she was sick a long while and the doctors could do nothing for her, and the priests read over her but they could do nothing. And at last the husband went to Biddy Early and she said, 'I can't cure her, and the woman that can cure her lives in the village with her.' So he went home and told this and the women of the village came into the house and said, 'God bless her,' all except one, and nothing would make her come into the house. But they watched her, and one night when a lot of them were sitting round the fire smoking, she let a spit fall on the floor. So they gathered that up (with respects to you), and brought it in to the sick woman and rubbed it to her, and she got well. It might have done as well if they brought a bit of her petticoat and burned it and rubbed the ashes on her. But there's something strange about spits, and if you spit on a child or a beast it's as good as if you'd say, 'God bless it.'

*John Curtin:*

I was with Biddy Early one time for my brother. She was out away in Ennis when we got to the house, and her husband that she called Tommy. And the kitchen was full of people waiting for her to come in. So then she came, and the day was rainy, and she was wet, and she went over to the fire, and began to take off her clothes, and to dry them, and then she said to her husband: 'Tommy, get the bottle and give them all a drop.' So he got the bottle and gave a drink to everyone. But my brother was in behind the door, and he missed him and when he came back to the fire she said: 'You have missed out the man that has the best heart of them all, and there he is, behind the door.' And when my brother came out she said, 'Give us a verse of a song,' and he said, 'I'm no songster,' but she said, 'I know well that you are, and a good dancer as well.' She cured him and his wife after.

There was a neighbour of mine went to her too, and she said: 'The first time you got the touch was the day you had brought a cart of turf from that bog at Ballinabucky to Scahanagh. And when you were in the road you got it, and you had to lie down on the creel of turf till you got to the public road.' And she told him that he had a pane of glass broke in his window and that was true enough. She must have been away walking with the faeries every night or how did she know that, or where the village of Scahanagh was?

Mrs Kenny has been twice to Biddy Early. Once for her brother who was ill, and light-headed and sent to Galway. And Biddy Early shook the bottle twice, and she said, 'It is none of my business, and it's a heavy cold that settled in his head. And she would not take the shilling. A red, red woman she was.

*Mary Glyn:*

I am a Clare woman, but the last fifty years I spent in Connacht. Near Feakle I lived, but I only saw Biddy Early once, the time she was brought to the committee and to the courthouse. She lived in a little house near Feakle that time, and her landlord was Dr Murphy in Limerick, and he sent men to evict her and to pull the house down, and she held them in the door and said: 'Whoever will be the first to put a bar to the house, he'll remember it.' And then a man put his bar in between two stones, and if he did, he turned and got a fall someway and he broke the thigh. After that Dr Murphy brought her to the court, 'Faeries and all,' he said, for he brought the bottle along with her. So she was put out, but Murphy had cause to remember it, for he was living in a house by himself, and one night it caught fire and was burned down, and all that was left of him was one foot that was found in a corner of the walls. She had four husbands, and the priest wouldn't marry her to the last one, and it was by the teacher that she was married. She was a good-looking woman, but like another, the day I saw her. My husband went to her the time Johnny, my little boy, was dying. He had a great pain in his temple, and she said: 'He has enough in him to kill a hundred; but if he lives till Monday, come and tell me.' But he was dead before that. And she said, 'If you came to me before this, I'd not have let you stop in that house you're in.' But Johnny died; and there was a blush over his face when he was going, and after that I couldn't look at him, but those that saw him said that *he* wasn't in it. I never saw him since, but often and often the father would go out thinking he might see him. But I know well he wouldn't like to come back and to see me fretting for him.

We left the house after that and came here. A travelling woman that came in to see me one time in that house said, 'This is a fine airy house,' and she said that three times, and then she said, 'But in that corner of it you'll lose your son,' and so it happened, and I wish now that I had minded what she said. A man and his family went into that house after, and the first summer they were in it, he and his sons were putting up a stack of hay in the field with pitchforks, and the pitchfork in his hand turned some way into his stomach and he died.

It is Biddy Early had the great name, but the priests were against her. There went a priest one time to stop her, and when he came near the door the horse fell that was in his car. Biddy Early came out then and bid him to give three spits on the horse, and he did that, and it rose up then and there. It was himself had put the evil eye on it. 'It was yourself did it, you bodach,'[3] she said to the priest. And he said, 'You may do what you like from this out, and I will not meddle with you again.'

## MRS SHERIDAN

Mrs Sheridan, as I call her, was wrinkled and half blind, and had gone barefoot through her lifetime. She was old, for she had once met Raftery, the Gaelic poet, at a dance, and he died before the famine of '47. She must have been comely then, for he had said to her: 'Well planed you are; the carpenter that planed you knew his trade'; and she was ready of reply and answered him back, 'Better than you know yours,' for his fiddle had two or three broken strings. And then he had spoken of a neighbour in some way that vexed her father, and he would let him speak no more with her. And she had carried a regret for this through her long life, for she said: 'If it wasn't for him speaking as he did, and my father getting vexed, he might have made words about me like he did for Mary Hynes and for Mary Brown.' She had never been to school she told me, because her father could not pay the penny a week it would have cost. She had never travelled many miles from the parish of her birth, and I am sure had never seen pictures except the sacred ones on chapel walls; and yet she could tell of a Cromwellian castle built up and of a drawbridge and of long-faced, fair-haired women, and of the yet earlier round house and saffron dress of the heroic times, I do not know whether by direct vision, or whether as Myers wrote: 'It may even be that a World-soul is personally conscious of all its past, and that individual souls, as they enter into deeper con-sciousness enter into something which is at once reminiscence and actuality . . . Past facts were known to men on earth, not from memory only but by written record; and these may be records, of what kind we know not, which persist in the spiritual world. Our retrocognitions seem often a recovery of isolated fragments of thought and feeling, pebbles still hard and rounded amid the indecipherable sands over which the mighty waters are "rolling evermore".'

She had never heard of the great mystic Jacob Behman, and yet when an unearthly visitor told her the country of youth is not far from the place where we live, she had come near to his root idea that 'the world standeth in Heaven and Heaven in the World, and are in one another as day and night.'

*I was told by Mrs Sheridan:*
There was a woman, Mrs Keevan, killed near the big tree at Raheen, and her husband was after that with Biddy Early, and she said it was not the woman that had died at all, but a cow that died and was put in her place. All my life I've seen *them* and enough of them. One day I was with Tom Mannion by the big hole near his house, and we saw a man and a woman come from it, and a great troop of children, little boys they seemed to be, and they went through the gate into Coole, and ran away and threw him from it. And he asked to be brought to my house, for he wouldn't stop where he was; 'for' says he, 'the woman of this house gave me no drink and showed me no kindness, and she'll be repaid for that.' And sure enough within the year she got the dropsy and died. And he was carried out of the door backwards, but the mother brought him to her own house and wouldn't let him come to mine, and 'twas as well, for I wouldn't refuse him, but I don't want to be annoyed with *them* any more than I am.

Did you know Mrs Byrne that lived in Doolin? Swept she was after her child was born. And near a year after I saw her coming down the road near the old castle. 'Is that you, Mary?' I said to her, 'and is it to see me you are coming?' But she went on. It was in May when *they* are all changing.[4] There was a priest, Father Waters, told me one time that he was after burying a boy, one Fahy, in Kilbecanty churchyard. And he was passing by the place again in the evening, and there he saw a great fire burning, but whether it was of turf or of sticks he couldn't tell, and there was the boy he had buried sitting in the middle of it.

I know that I used to be away among them myself, but how they brought me I don't know, but when I'd come back, I'd be cross with the husband and with all. I believe when I was with them I was cross that they wouldn't let me go, and that's why they didn't keep me altogether, they didn't like cross people to be with them. The husband would ask me where I was, and why I stopped so long away, but I think he knew I was *taken* and it fretted him, but he never spoke much about it. But my mother knew it well, but she'd try to hide it. The neighbours would come in and ask where was I, and she'd say I was sick in the bed – for whatever was put there in place of me would have the head in under the bed-clothes. And when a neighbour would bring me in a drink of milk, my mother would put it by and say, 'leave her now, maybe she'll drink it tomorrow.' And maybe in a day or two I'd meet someone and he'd say, 'Why wouldn't you speak to me when I went into the house to see you?' And I was a young fresh woman at that time. Where they brought me to I don't know, or how I got there, but I'd be in a very big house, and it round, the walls far away that you'd hardly see them, and a great many people all round about. I saw there neighbours and friends that I knew, and they in their own clothing and with their own appearance, but they wouldn't speak to me nor I to them, and when I'd met them again I'd never say to them that I saw them there. But the others had striped clothes of all colours, and long faces, and they'd be talking and laughing and moving about. What language had they? Irish of course, what else would they talk?

And there was one woman of them, very tall and with a long face, standing in the middle, taller than any one you ever saw in this world, and a tall stick in her hand; she was the mistress. She had a high yellow thing on her head, not hair, her hair was turned back under it, and she had a long yellow cloak down to her feet and hanging down behind. Had she anything like that in the picture in her hand? [a crown of gold balls or apples.] It was not on her head, it was lower down here about the body, and shining, and a thing [a brooch] like that in the picture, but down hanging low like the other. And that picture you have there in your hand, I saw no one like it, but I saw a picture like it hanging on the wall. It was a very big place and very grand, and a long table set out, but I didn't want to stop there and I began crying to go home. And she touched me here in the breast with her stick, she was vexed to see me wanting to go away. They never brought me away since. Grand food they'd offer me and wine, but I never would touch it, and sometimes I'd have to give the breast to a child.

Himself died, but it was *they* took him from me. It was in the night and he lying beside me, and I woke and heard him move, and I thought I heard some one with him. And I put out my hand and what I touched was an iron hand, like knitting needles it felt. And I heard the bones of his neck crack, and he gave a sort of a choked laugh, and I got out of the bed and struck a light and I saw nothing, but I thought I saw some one go through the door. And I called to Bridget and she didn't come, and I called again and she came and she said she struck a light when she heard the noise and was coming, and someone came and struck the light from her hand. And when we looked in the bed, himself was lying dead and not a mark on him.

Yes, the Sidhe sing, and they have pipers among them, a bag on each side and a pipe to the mouth, I think I never told you of one I saw.

I was passing a field near Kiltartan one time when I was a girl, where there was a little lisheen,[5] and a field of wheat, and when I was passing I heard a piper beginning to play, and I couldn't but begin to dance, it was such a good tune; and there was a boy standing there, and he began to dance too. And then my father came by, and he asked why were we dancing, and no one playing for us. And I said there was, and I began to search through the wheat for the piper, but I couldn't find him, and I heard a voice saying, 'You'll see me yet, and it will be in a town.' Well, one Christmas eve I was in Gort and my husband with me, and that night at Gort I heard the same tune beginning again – the grandest I ever heard – and I couldn't but begin to dance. And Glynn the chair-maker heard it too, and he began to dance with me in the street, and my man thought I had gone mad, and the people gathered round us, for they could see or hear nothing. But I saw the piper well, and he had plaid clothes, blue and white, and he said, 'Didn't I tell you that when I saw you again it would be in a town?'

I never saw fire go up in the air, but in the wood beyond the tree at Raheen I used often to see like a door open at night, and the light shining through it, just as it might shine through the house door, with the candle and the fire inside, if it would be left open.

Many of *them* I have seen – they are like ourselves only wearing bracket clothes,[6] and their bodies are not so strong or so thick as ours, and their eyes are more shining than our eyes. I don't see many of them here, but Coole is alive with them, as plenty as grass; I often go awhile and sit inside the gate there. I saw them make up a house one time near the natural bridge, and I saw them coming over the gap twice near the chapel, a lot of little boys, and two men and a woman, and they had old talk and young talk. One of them came in here twice, and I gave him a bit of bread, but he said, 'There's salt in it' and he put it away.

When Annie Rivers died the other day, there were two funerals in it, a big funeral with a new coffin and another that was in front of them, men walking, the handsomest I ever saw, and they with black clothes about their body. I was out there looking at them, and there was a cow in the road, and I said, Take care would you drive away the cow. And one of them said, 'No fear of that, we have plenty of cows *on the other side of the wall*.' But no one could see them but myself. I often saw them and it was they took the sight of my eyes from me. And Annie Rivers was not in the grand coffin, she was with *them* a good while before the funeral.

That time I saw the two funerals at Rivers's that I was telling you about, I heard Annie call to those that were with her, 'You might as well let me have Bartley; it would be better for the two castles to meet.' And since then the mother is uneasy about Bartley, and he fell on the floor one day and I know well he is *gone* since the day Annie was buried. And I saw others at the funeral, and some that you knew well among them. And look now, you should send a coat to some poor person, and your own friends among the dead will be covered, for you could see the skin here. [She made a gesture passing her hand down each arm, exactly the same gesture as old Mary Glynn of Slieve Echtge had made yesterday when she said, 'Have you a coat you could send me, for my arms are bare?' and I had promised her one.]

## OLD DERUANE

Old Deruane lived in the middle island of Aran, Inishmaan, where I have stayed more than once. He was one of the evening visitors to the cottage I stayed in, when the fishers had come home and had eaten, and the fire was stirred and flashed on the dried mackerel and conger eels hanging over the wide hearth, and the little vessel of cod oil had a fresh wick put in it and lighted. The men would sit in a half-circle on the floor, passing the lighted pipe from one to another; the women would find some work with yarn or wheel. The talk often turned on the fallen angels or the dead, for the dwellers in those islands have not been moulded in that dogma which while making belief in the after-life an essential, makes belief in the shadow-visit of a spirit yearning after those it loved a vanity, a failing of the great essential, common sense, and sets down one who believes in such things as what Burton calls in his Anatomy 'a melancholy dizzard'.

This is a story was going about twenty years ago. There was a curate in the island, and one day he got a call to the other island for the next day. And in the evening he told the servant maid that attended him to clean his boots good and very good, for he'd be meeting good people where he was going. And she said, 'I will, Holy Father, and if you'll give me your hand and word to marry me for nothing, I'll clean them grand.' And he said, 'I will; whenever you get a comrade I'll marry you for nothing, I give you my hand and word.' So she had the boots grand for him in the morning. Well, she got a sickness after, and after seven months going by, she was buried. And six months after that, the curate was in his parlour one night and the moon shining, and he saw a boy and a girl outside the house, and they came to the window, and he knew it was the servant girl that was buried. And she said, 'I have a comrade now, and I came for you to marry us as you gave your word.' And he said, 'I'll hold to my word since I gave it,' and he married them then and there, and they went away again.

## from 'Away'

*Mrs Feeney:*

When one is taken, the body is taken as well as the spirit, and some good-for-nothing thing left in its place. What they take them for is to work for them, and to do things they can't do themselves. You might notice it's always the good they take. That's why when we see a child good for nothing we say, 'Ah, you little faery.'

There was a man lost his wife and a hag was put in her place, and she came back and told him to come out at night where she'd be riding with the rest, and to throw something belonging to her after her – he'd know her by her being on a white horse. And so he did and got her back again. And when they were going home he said, 'I'll have the life of that old hag that was put in your place.' But when they got to the house, she was out of it before him, and was never heard of again.

There was a man telling me it was in a house where the woman was after a youngster, and she died, that is, we'll call it died, but she was *taken*, that the husband saw her coming back to give the breast to the child and to wash it. And the second night he got hold of her and held her until morning, and when the cock crowed she sat down again and stayed; they had no more power over her.

*A Hillside Woman:*

Surely there are many taken; my own sister that lived in the house beyond, and her husband and her three children, all in one year. Strong they were and handsome and good – the best – and that's the sort that are taken. They got in the priest when first it came on the husband, and soon after a fine cow died and a calf. But he didn't begrudge that if he'd get his health, but it didn't save him after. Sure Father Andrews in Kilbrennan said not long ago in the chapel that no one had gone to *heaven* for the last ten years.

But whatever life God has granted them, when it's at an end

go they must, whether they're among them or not. And they'd sooner be among them than to go to Purgatory.

There was a little one of my own taken. Till he was a year old he was the stoutest and the best and the finest of all my children, and then he began to pine till he wasn't thicker than that straw; but he lived for about four years.

How did it come on him? I know that well. He was the grandest ever you saw, and I proud of him, and I brought him to a ball in his house and he was able to drink punch. And I was stopped one day at a house beyond, and a neighbouring woman came in with her child and she says, 'If he's not the stoutest he's the longest,' and she took off her apron and the string to measure them both. I had no right to let her do that but I thought no harm at the time. But it was from that night he began to screech and from that time he did no good. He'd get stronger through the winter, and about the Pentecost, in the month of May, he'd always fall back again, for that's the time they're at the worst.

I didn't have the priest in. It does them no good, but harm, to have a priest take notice of them when they're like that.

It was in the month of May at the Pentecost he went at last. He was always pining, but I didn't think he'd go so soon. At the end of the bed he was lying with the others, and he called to me and put up his arms. But I didn't want to take too much notice of him or to have him always after me, so I only put down my foot to where he was. And he began to pick straws out of the bed and to throw them over the little sister beside him, till he had thrown as much as would thatch a goose. And when I got up, there he was dead, and the little sister asleep beside him all covered with straws.

### from 'Herbs, Charms and Wise Women'

There is a saying in Irish, 'An old woman without learning, it is she will be doing charms'; and I have told in *Poets and Dreamers* of old Bridget Ruane who came and gave me my first knowledge of the healing power of certain plants, some it seemed having a natural and some a mysterious power. And I said that she had died last winter, and we may be sure that among the green herbs that cover her grave there are some that are good for every bone in the body and that are very good for a sore heart.

As to the book she told me of that had come from the unseen and was written in Irish, I think of Mrs Sheridan's answer when I asked in what language the strange unearthly people she had been among had talked: 'Irish of course – what else would they talk?' And I remember also that when Blake told Crabb Robinson of the intercourse he had had with Voltaire and was asked in what tongue Voltaire spoke he said, 'To my sensations it was English. It was like the touch of a musical key. He touched it probably in French, but to my ear it became English.'

*I was told by her:*

There is a Saint at the Oratory in London, but I don't know his name, and a girl heard of him in London, and he sent her back to Gort, and he said, 'There's a woman there that will cure you,' and she came to me, and I cured her in two days. And if you could find out the name of that Saint through the Press, he'd tell me his remedies, and all the world would be cured. For I can't do all cures though there are a great many I can do. I cured Pat Carty when the doctor couldn't do it, and a woman in Gort that was paralysed and her two sons that were stretched. For I can bring back the dead with the same herbs our Lord was brought back with – the *slanlus* and the *garblus*.[7] But there are some things I can't do. I can't help any one that has got a stroke from the Queen or the Fool of the Forth.

I know a woman that saw the Queen one time, and she said she looked like any Christian. I never heard of any that saw the Fool but one woman that was walking near Gort, and she called out, 'There's the Fool of the Forth coming after me.' So her friends that were with her called out though they could see nothing, and I suppose he went away at that for she got no harm. He was like a big strong man, and half-naked – that's all she said about him.

It was my brother got the knowledge of cures from a book that was thrown down before him on the road. What language was it written in? What language would it be but Irish. Maybe it was God gave it to him, and maybe it was the *other people*. He was a fine strong man, and he weighed twenty-five stone – and he went to England, and then he cured all the world, so that the doctors had no way of living. So one time he got on a ship to go to America, and the doctors had bad men engaged to shipwreck him out of the ship; he wasn't drowned but he was broken to pieces on the rocks, and the book was lost along with him. But he taught me a good deal out of it. So I know all herbs, and I do a good many cures, and I have brought a great many children home, home to the world – and never lost one, or one of the women that bore them. I was never away myself, but I am a cousin of Saggarton, and his uncle was away for twenty-one years.

This is *dwareen* (knapweed) and what you have to do with this is to put it down, with other herbs, and with a bit of three-penny sugar, and to boil it and to drink it for pains in the bones, and don't be afraid but it will cure you. Sure the Lord put it in the world for curing.

And this is *corn-corn* (small aromatic tansy); it's very good for the heart – boiled like the others.

This is *atair-talam* (wild camomile), the father of all herbs – the father of the ground. This is very hard to pull, and when you go for it, you must have a black-handled knife.

And this is *camal-buide* (loosestrife) that will keep all bad things away.

This is *fearaban* (water buttercup) and it's good for every bone of your body.

This is *dub-cosac* (lichen), that's good for the heart, very good for a sore heart.

*Mrs Quaid:*
Monday is a good day for pulling herbs, or Tuesday, not Sunday. A Sunday cure is no cure. The *cosac* (lichen) is good for the heart, there was Mineog in Gort, one time his heart was wore to a silk thread, and it cured him. The *slanugad* (ribgrass) is very good,

and it will take away lumps. You must go down when it's growing on the scraws,[8] and pull it with three pulls, and mind would the wind change when you are pulling it or your head will be gone. Warm it on the tongs when you bring it and put it on the lump. The *lus-mor* (mullein) is the only one that's good to bring back children that are away. But what's better than that is to save what's in the craw of a cock you'll kill on St Martin's Eve and put it by and dry it, and give it to the child that's away.

There's something in green flax I know, for my mother often told me about one night she was spinning flax, before she was married and she was up late. And a man of the faeries came in. She had no right to be sitting up so late, they don't like that. And he told her to go to bed, for he wanted to kill her, and he couldn't touch her while she was handling the flax. And every time he'd tell her to go to bed, she'd give him some answer, and she'd go on pulling a thread of the flax, or mending a broken one, for she was wise, and she knew that at the crowing of the cock he'd have to go. So at last the cock crowed, and he was gone, and she was safe then, for the cock is blessed.

*Mrs Ward:*

As to the *lus-mor*, whatever way the wind is blowing when you begin to cut it, if it changes while you're cutting it, you'll lose your mind. And if you're paid for cutting it, you can do it when you like, but if not *they* mightn't like it. I knew a woman was cutting it one time, and a voice, an enchanted voice, called out, 'Don't cut that if you're not paid, or you'll be sorry.' But if you put a bit of this with every other herb you drink, you'll live for ever. My grandmother used to put a bit with everything she took, and she lived to be over a hundred.

*An Old Man on the Beach:*

I wouldn't give into those things, but I'll tell you what happened to a son of my own. He was as fine and as stout a boy as ever you saw, and one day he was out with me, and a letter came and told of the death of someone's child that was in America, and all the island gathered to hear it read. And all the people were pressing to each other there. And when we were coming home, he had a bit of a kippeen in his hand, and getting over a wall he fell, and some way the kippeen[9] went in at his throat, where it had a sharp point and hurt the palate of his mouth, and he got paralysed from the waist up.

There was a woman over in Spiddal, and my wife gave me no ease till I went to her, and she gave me some herb for him. He got better after, and there's no man in the island stronger and stouter than what he is but he never got back the use of his left hand, but the strength he has in the other hand is equal to what another man would have in two. Did the woman in Spiddal say what gave him the touch? Oh well, she said all sorts of things. But I wouldn't like to meddle too much with such as her, for it's by witchcraft I believe it's done. There was a woman of the same sort over in Roundstone, and I knew a man went to her about his wife, and first she said the sickness had nothing to do with *her* business, but he said he came too far to bring back an answer like that. So she went into a little room, and he heard her call on the name of all the devils. So he cried out that that was enough, and she came out then and made the sign of the Cross, but he wouldn't stop in it.

But a priest told me that there was a woman in France used to cure all the dumb that came to her, and that it was a great loss and a great pity when she died.

*Old Heffernan:*

The best herb-doctor I ever knew was Conolly up at Ballyturn. He knew every herb that grew in the earth. It was said that he was away with the faeries one time, and when I knew him he had the two thumbs turned in, and it was said that was the sign they left on him. I had a lump on the thigh one time and my father went to him, and he gave him an herb for it but he told him not to come into the house by the door the wind would be blowing in at. They thought it was the evil I had, that is given by *them* by a touch, and that is why he said about the wind, for if it was the evil, there would be a worm in it, and if it smelled the herb that was brought in at the door, it might change to another place. I don't know what the herb was, but I would have been dead if I had it on another hour, it burned so much, and I had to get the lump lanced after, for it wasn't the evil I had.

Conolly cured many a one. Jack Hall that fell into a pot of water they were after boiling potatoes in, had the skin scalded off him and that Doctor Lynch could do nothing for, he cured.

He boiled down herbs with a bit of lard, and after that was rubbed on three times, he was well.

And Pat Cahel that was deaf, he cured with the *rib-mas-seala*, that herb in the potatoes that milk comes out of. His wife was against him doing the cures, she thought that it would fall on herself. And anyway, she died before him. But Connor at Oldtown gave up doing cures, and his stock began to die, and he couldn't keep a pig, and all he had wasted away till he began to do them again; and his son does cures now, but I think it's more with charms than with herbs.

*Mrs West:*

Dandelion is good for the heart, and when Father Prendergast was curate here, he had it rooted up in all the fields about, to drink it, and see what a fine man he is. *Garblus*; how did you hear of that? That is the herb for things that have to do with the faeries. And when you'd drink it for anything of that sort, if it doesn't cure you, it will kill you then and there. There was a fine young man I used to know and he got his death on the head of a pig that came at himself and another man at the gate of Ramore, and that never left them, but was at them all the time till they came to a stream of water. And when he got home, he took to his bed with a headache, and at last he was brought a drink of the *garblus* and no sooner did he drink it than he was dead. I remember him well. Biddy Early didn't use herbs, but let people say what they like, she was a sure woman. There is something in flax, for no priest would anoint you without a bit of tow. And if a woman that was carrying was to put a basket of green flax on her back, the child would go from her, and if a mare that was in foal had a load of flax put on her, the foal would go the same way.

*Mrs Allen:*

I don't believe in faeries myself, I really don't. But all the people in Kildare believe in them, and I'll tell you what I saw there one time myself. There was a man had a splendid big white horse, and he was leading him along the road, and a woman, a next-door neighbour, got up on the wall and looked at him. And the horse fell down on his knees and began to shiver, and you'd think buckets of water were poured over him. And they led him home, but he was fit for nothing, and everyone was sorry for the poor man, and him being worth ninety pounds. And they sent to the Curragh and to every place for vets, but not one could do anything at all. And at last they sent up in to the mountains for a faery doctor, and he went into the stable and shut the door, and whatever he did there no one knows, but when he came out he said that the horse would get up on the ninth day, and be as well as ever. And so he did sure enough, but whether he kept well, I don't know, for the man that owned him sold him the first minute he could. And they say that while the faery doctor was in the stable, the woman came to ask what was he doing, and he called from inside, 'Keep her away, keep her away.' And a priest had lodgings in the house at the same time, and when the faery doctor saw him coming, 'Let me out of this,' says he, and away with him as fast as he could. And all this I saw happen, but whether the horse only got a chill or not I don't know.

*James Mangan:*

My mother learned cures from an Ulster woman, for the Ulster women are the best for cures; but I don't know the half of them, and what I know I wouldn't like to be talking about or doing, unless it might be for my own family. There's a cure she had for the yellow jaundice; and it's a long way from Ennistymon to Creevagh, but I saw a man come all that way to her, and he fainted when he sat down in the chair, he was so far gone. But she gave him a drink of it, and he came in a second time and she gave it again, and he didn't come a third time for he didn't want it. But I don't mind if I tell you the cure and it is this: take a bit of the dirt of a dog that has been eating bones and meat, and put it on top of an oven till it's as fine as powder and as white as flour, and then pound it up, and put it in a glass of whiskey, in a bottle, and if a man is not too far gone with jaundice, that will cure him.

There was one Carthy at Imlough did great cures with charms and his son can do them yet. He uses no herbs, but he'll go down on his knees and he'll say some words into a bit of unsalted butter, and what words he says, no one knows. There was a big man I know had a sore on his leg and the doctor couldn't cure him, and Doctor Moran said a bit of the bone would have to come out. So at last he went to Jim Carthy and he told him to bring him a bit of unsalted butter the next Monday, or Thursday, or Saturday, for there's a difference in days. And he would have to come three time, or if it was a bad case, he'd have to come nine times.

But I think it was after the third time that he got well, and now he is one of the head men in Persse's Distillery in Galway.

*A Slieve Echtge Woman:*
The wild parsnip is good for gravel, and for heartbeat there's nothing so good as dandelion. There was a woman I knew used to boil it down, and she'd throw out what was left on the grass. And there was a fleet of turkeys about the house and they used to be picking it up. And at Christmas they killed one of them, and when it was cut open they found a new heart growing in it with the dint of the dandelion.

My father went one time to a woman at Ennis, not Biddy Early, but one of her sort, to ask her about three sheep he had lost.

And she told him the very place they were brought to, a long path through the stones near Kinvara. And there he found the skins, and he heard that the man that brought them away had them sold to a butcher in Loughrea. So he followed him there, and brought the police, and they found him − a poor-looking little man, but he had £60 within in his box.

There was another man up near Ballylee could tell these things too. When Jack Fahy lost his wool, he went to him, and next morning there were the fleeces at his door.

Those that are *away* know these things. There was a brother of my own took to it for seven years – and we at school. And no one could beat him at the hurling and the games. But I wouldn't like to be mixed with that myself.

There was one Moyra Colum was a great one for doing cures. She was called one time to see some sick person, and the man that came for her put her up behind him, on the horse. And some youngsters began to be humbugging him, and humbugging is always bad. And there was a young horse in the field where the youngsters were and it began to gallop, and it fell over a stump and lay on the ground kicking as if in a fit. And then Moyra Colum said, 'Let me get down, for I have pity for the horse.' And she got down and went into the field, and she picked a blade of a herb and put it to the horse's mouth and in one minute it got up well.

The herbs they cure with, there's some that's natural, and you could pick them at all times of the day; there's a very good cure for the yellow jaundice I have myself, and I offered it to a woman in Ballygrah the other day, but some people are so taken up with pride and with conceit they won't believe that to cure that sickness you must take what comes from your own nature. She's dead since of it, I hear. But I'll tell you the cure, the way you'll know it. If you are attending a funeral, pick out a few little worms from the earth that's thrown up out of the grave, few or many, twenty or thirty if you like. And when you go home, boil them down in a sup of new milk and let it get cold; and believe me, that will cure the sickness.

There's one woman I knew used to take a bit of tape when you'd go to her, and she'd measure it over her thumb like this; and when she had it measured she'd know what was the matter with you.

## Mrs Quaid:

There was a girl in a house near this was pining away, and a travelling woman came to the house and she told the mother to bring the girl across to the graveyard that's near the house before sunrise and to pick some of the grass that's growing over the remains. And so she did, and the girl got well. But the mother told me that when the woman had told her that, she vanished away, all in a minute, and was seen no more.

I have a charm myself for the headache, I cured many with it. I used to put on a ribbon from the back of the head over the mouth, and another from the top of the head under the chin and then to press my hand on it, and I'd give them great relief and I'd say the charm. But one time I read in the Scriptures that the use of charms is forbidden, so I had it on my conscience, and the next time I went to confession I asked the priest was it any harm for me to use it, and I said it to him in Irish. And in English it means 'Charm of St Peter, Charm of St Paul, an angel brought it from Rome. The similitude of Christ, suffering death, and all suffering goes with Him and into the flax.' And the priest didn't say if I might use it or not, so I went on with it, for I didn't like to turn away so many suffering people coming to me.

I know a charm a woman from the North gave to Tom Mangan's mother, she used to cure ulcers with it and cancers. It was with unsalted butter it was used, but I don't know what the words were.

*John Phelan:*

If you cut a hazel rod and bring it with you, and turn it round about now and again, no bad thing can hurt you. And a cure can be made for bad eyes from the ivy that grows on a white-thorn bush. I know a boy had an ulcer on his eye and it was cured by that.

*Kevin Ralph:*

I went to Macklin near Loughrea myself one time, when I had an ulcer here in my neck. But when I got to him and asked for the charm, he answered me in Irish, 'The Soggarth[10] said to me, any man that will use charms to do cures with will be damned.' I persuaded him to do it after, but I never felt that it did me much good. Because he took no care to do it well after the priest saying that of him. But there's some will only let it be said in an outhouse if there's a cure to be done in the house.

*A Woman in County Limerick:*

It is twenty year ago I got a pain in my side, that I could not stoop; and I tried Siegel's Syrup and a plaster and a black blister from the doctor, and every sort of thing and they did me no good. And there came in a man one day, a farmer I knew, and he said, 'It's a fool you are not to go to a woman living within two miles of you that would cure you – a woman that does charms.' So I went to her nine times, three days I should go and three stop away, and she would pass her hand over me, and would make me hold on to the branch of an apple tree up high, that I would hang from it, and she would be swinging me as you would swing a child. And she laid me on the grass and passed her hands over me, and what she said over me I don't know. And at the end of the nine visits I was cured, and the pain left me. At the time she died I wanted to go lay her out but my husband would not let me go. He said if I was seen going in, the neighbours would say she had left me her cures and would be calling me a witch. She said it was from an old man she got the charm that used to be called a wizard. My father knew him, and said he could bring away the wheat and bring it back again, and that he could turn the four winds of heaven to blow upon your house till they would knock it.

*A Munster Midwife:*

Is it true a part of the pain can be put on the man? It is to be sure, but it would be the most pity in the world to do it; it is a thing I never did, for the man would never be the better of it, and it would not take any of the pain off the woman. And shouldn't we have pity upon men, that have enough troubles of their own to go through?

*Mrs Hollaran:*

Did I know the pain could be put on a man? Sure I seen my own mother that was a midwife do it. He was such a Molly of an old man, and he had no compassion at all on his wife. He was as if making out she had no pain at all. So my mother gave her a drink, and with that he was on the floor and around the floor crying and roaring. 'The devil take you,' says he, and the pain upon him; but while he had it, it went away from his wife. It did him no harm after, and my mother would not have done it but for him being so covetous. He wanted to make out that she wasn't sick.

*Mrs Stephens:*

At childbirth there are some of the old women are able to put a part of the pain upon the man, or any man. There was a woman in labour near Oran, and there were two policemen out walking that night, and one of them went into the house to light his pipe. There were two or three women in it, and the sick woman stretched beyond them, and one of them offered him a drink of the tea she had been using, and he didn't want it but he took a drink of it, and then he took a coal off the hearth and put it on his pipe to light it and went out to his comrade. And no sooner was he there than he began to roar and to catch hold of his belly and he fell down by the roadside roaring. But the other knew something of what happened, and he took the pipe, and it having a coal on it, and he put it on top of the wall and fired a shot of the gun at it and broke it; and with that the man got well of the pain and stood up again.

No woman that is carrying should go to the house where another woman is in labour; if she does, that woman's pain will come on her along with her own pain when her time comes.

A child to come with the spring tide, it will have luck.


## From 'Banshees and Warnings'

*A Herd:*

Crying for those that are going to die you'd hear of often enough. And when my own wife was dying, the night she went I was sitting by the fire, and I heard a noise like the blow of a flail on the door outside. And I went to see what it was, but there was nothing there. But I was not in any way frightened and wouldn't be if she came back in a vision, but glad to see her I would be.

*A Connemara Woman:*

One night the clock in my room struck six and it had not struck for years, and two nights after – on Christmas night – it struck six again, and afterwards I heard that my sister in America had died just at that hour. So now I have taken the weights off the clock, that I wouldn't hear it again.

*Pat. Linskey:*
Well, the time my own wife died I had sent her into Cloon to get some things from the market, and I was alone in the house with the dog. And what do you think but he started up and went out to the hill outside the house, and there he stood a while howling, and it was the very next day my wife died.

Another time I had shut the house door at night and fastened it, and in the morning it was standing wide open. And as I knew by the dates afterwards that was the very night my brother died in India.

Sure I told Stephen Green that, when he buried his mother in England, and his father lying in Kilmacdaugh. 'You should never separate,' says I, 'in death a couple that were together in life, for sure as fate, the one'll come to look for the other.'

And when there's one of them passing in the air you might get a blast of holy wind you wouldn't be the better of for a long time.

*A Woman near Loughrea:*
There are houses in Cloon, and Geary's is one of them, where if the people sit up too late the warning comes; it comes as a knocking at the door. Eleven o'clock, that is the hour. It is likely it is some that lived in the house are wanting it for themselves at the time. And there is a house near the Darcys' where, as soon as the potatoes are strained from the pot, they must put a plateful ready and leave it for the night, and milk and the fire on the hearth, and there is not a bit left at morning. Some poor souls that come in, looking for warmth and for food.

## from 'The Unquiet Dead'

*Mrs Casey:*
Near the strand there were two little girls went out to gather cow-dung. And they sat down beside a bush to rest themselves

and there they heard a groan coming from under the ground. So they ran home as fast as they could. And they were told when they went again to bring a man with them.

So the next time they went they brought a man with them, and they hadn't been sitting there long when they heard the saddest groan that ever you heard. So the man bent down and asked what was it. And a voice from below said, 'Let someone shave me and get me out of this, for I was never shaved after dying.' So the man went away, and the next day he brought soap and all that was needful and there he found a body lying laid out on the grass. So he shaved it, and with that wings came and carried it up to high heaven.

*A Connemara Man:*

There was a man had come back from Boston, and one day he was out in the bay, going towards Aran with £3 worth of cable he was after getting from McDonagh's store in Galway. And he was steering the boat, and there were two turf-boats along with him, and all in a minute they saw he was gone, swept off the boat with a wave and it a dead calm.

And they saw him come up once, straight up as if he was pushed, and then he was brought down again and rose no more.

And it was some time after that a friend of his in Boston, and that was coming home to this place, was in a crowd of people out there. And he saw him coming to him and he said, 'I heard that you were drowned,' and the man said, 'I am not dead, but I was brought here, and when you go home, bring these three guineas to McDonagh in Galway for it's owned him for the cable I got from him.' And he put the three guineas in his hand and vanished away.

*An Old Army Man:*

I have seen hell myself. I had a sight of it one time in a vision. It had a very high wall around it, all of metal, and an archway in the wall, and a straight walk into it, just like what would be leading into a gentleman's orchard, but the edges were not trimmed with box but with red-hot metal. And inside the wall there were cross walks, and I'm not sure what there was to the right, but to the left there was five great furnaces and they full of souls kept there with great chains. So I turned short and went away; and in turning I looked again at the wall and I could see no end to it.

And another time I saw purgatory. It seemed to be in a level place and no walls around it, but it all one bright blaze, and the souls standing in it. And they suffer near as much as in hell, only there are no devils with them there, and they have the hope of heaven.

And I heard a call to me from there, 'Help me to come out of this!' And when I looked it was a man I used to know in the army, an Irishman and from this country, and I believe him to be a descendant of King O'Connor of Athenry. So I stretched out my hand first but then I called out, 'I'd be burned in the flames before I could get within three yards of you.' So then he said, 'Well, help me with your prayers,' and so I do.

## from 'Appearances'

When I had begun my search for folklore, the first to tell me he himself had seen the Sidhe was an old, perhaps half-crazed man I will call Michael Barrett (for I do not give the real names either of those who are living or who have left living relatives). I had one day asked an old woman who had been spinning wool for me, to be made into frieze by our weavers, if she had ever seen the faery host. She said, 'I never saw them myself nor I don't think much of them; it is God that takes us or leaves us as He will. But a neighbouring man was standing in my door last night, and there's no day of the year he doesn't hear them or feel them.

'It's in his head I think it does be, and when he stood in the door last night I said, "The wind does be always in my ears and the sound of it never stops," to make him think it was the same with him. But he said, "I hear them singing and making music all the time, and one of them's after bringing out a little flute, and it's on it he's playing to them." Sure he has half his chimney pulled down, where they used to be sitting and singing to him day and night. But those that are born in the daytime never have power to see or hear them all their life.'

Another neighbour talked to me of him and said, 'One night he was walking across the bog, and a lurcher, a bastard hound, with him. And something ran across the path in the shape of a white cat, and the lurcher went after him, and Barrett went home and to bed and left the door open for the lurcher to come in. And in the morning they found it there, lying under the table, and it paralysed and not able to stir. But after a few months it got better, and one night they were crossing the bog again and the same thing ran across their path, and this time in the form of a deer. But the dog wouldn't follow it again, but shrank behind Barrett until such time as it had passed by.'

My spinning woman, coming another time with chickens to sell, said, 'Barrett is after telling me this morning that they were never so bad as these last two nights. "Friday fine-day" is what they say now, in Irish, and he got no sleep till he threatened to throw dirty water over them. The poor man, they do say they are mostly in his head now, but sure he was a fine fresh man twenty years ago, the night he saw them all linked in two lots, like slips of girls walking together. And it was that very same day that Hession's little girl got a touch from them. She was as fine a little girl as ever you saw, and her mother sent her into Gort to do a message. And on the road she met a red-haired woman, with long wisps of hair as bright as silver, and she said, "Where are you going and who are you?" "I'm going to Gort on a message," says she, "and I'm Mrs Hession's daughter of such a place." Well, she came home, and that very night she got a pain in her thigh, with respects to you, and she and her mother have half the world walked since then, trying to get relief for her; but never a bit better did she ever get. And no doubt at all but that's the very same day Michael Barrett saw *them* in the field near Hession's house.'

I asked Mr Yeats to come with me to see the old man, and we walked up the long narrow lane, from which we could see Slieve Echtge and the Burren hills, the little cabin with its broken chimney where Michael Barrett told us of those that had disturbed his rest. This was the first time we went together to enquire into the Hierarchy of the Sidhe, of which by degrees we have gathered so much traditional and original knowledge.

As to old Barrett, I saw him from time to time, and he told me he was still 'tormented', and that 'there is one that sat and sang b-b-b all the night' till a few evenings before he had got a bit of rag and tied it to a long stick, and hit at him when he came, and drove him out with the rest. And in the next spring I heard he was ill, and that 'on Saturday he had been told by three he was to die'. When I visited him I found him better, and he said that since the warning on Saturday they had left him alone 'and the children that used to be playing about with them have gone to some other place; found the house too cold for them maybe'. That was the last time I saw him; I am glad I had been able to help him to more warmth and comfort before the end.

I asked the old man's brother, a labourer, what he thought of Michael's visions, but he made little of them. 'Old he is, and it's all in the brain the things he does be talking of. If it was a *young* man told us of them we might believe him, but as to him, we pay no attention to what he says at all. Those things are passed away, and you – I beg your pardon for using that word – a person – hears no more of them.

'John Casey saw queer things? So he might. Them that travel by night, why wouldn't they see queer things? But they'd see nothing if they went to their bed quiet and regular.

'Lydon that had the contract for the schoolhouse, we didn't mind much what he said happened him the night he slept there alone, and in the morning he couldn't stir across the floor from the place where he was. But who knows? Maybe he had too much drink taken before he went to bed. It was no wonder in the old times if there was signs and the like where murder had been. But that's come to an end, and time for it.

'There's another man, one Doran, has the same dreams and thoughts as my brother, and he leaves pieces of silver on the wall; and when they're took – it's the faeries! But myself I believe it's the boys do be watching him.

'No, these things are gone from the world, and there's not the same dread of death there used to be. When we die we go to judgment, and the places we'll get there, they won't be the same as what we had here. The charitable, the kind-hearted, lady or gentleman, who'd have a chance if they didn't? But the tyrants and schemers, what chance will there be for the like of them?

'You will have a good place there, Barrett, you and John Farrell. You have done your work better than most of us through all your life, and it's likely you'll be above us there.

'I did my work all my life, fair and honest every day; and now that I'm old, I'll keep on the same track to the last. Like a horse that might be racing at Galway racecourse or another, there might be eight leaps or ten leaps he might be frightened at; but when he's once over the last leap there's no fear of him. Why would he fail then, with the winning post so near at hand?'

*I was told by a Gatekeeper:*
One night at the house below it was just getting dark, and a man came in the gate and to the door and came in and fell down on a chair. And when I saw him shaking and his face so white, I thought it was the *fear gortha* (the hungry grass) he had walked on, and I called to the wife to give him something to eat. But he would take nothing but a cup of water with salt in it, and when he got better he told us that when he was passing the big tree a man and a woman came out and came along with him. They didn't speak but they walked on each side of him, and then the woman seemed to go away, but the man's step was with him till he came in at the gate.

Niland that met the coach that time and saw them other times, he told me that there were two sets among them. The one handsome and tall and like the gentry; the others more like ourselves, he said, and short and wide, and the body starting out in front, and wide belts about their waists. Only the women he saw, and they were wearing white caps with borders, and their hair in curls over the forehead and check aprons and plaid shawls. They are the spiteful ones that would do you a mischief, and others that are like the gentry would do nothing but to laugh and criticise you.

94

One night myself I was outside Loughrea on the road, about one o'clock in the morning and the moon was shining. And I saw a lady, a true lady she was, dressed in a sort of a ball dress, white and short in the skirt, and off the shoulders. And she had long stockings and dancing shoes with short uppers. And she had a long thin face, and a cap on her head with frills, and every one of the frills was the breadth of my six fingers. As to flowers or such things, I didn't notice, for I was more fixed in looking at the cap. I suppose they wore them at balls in some ancient times. I followed her a bit, and then she cross the road to Johnny Flanigan the joiner's house, that had a gate with piers. And I went across after her, to have a better view, and when she got to the pier she shrank into it and there was nothing left.

*Mike Martin:*

They are of the same size as we are. People only call them diminutive because they are made so when they're sent on certain errands.

There was a man of Ardrahan used to see many things. But he lost his eyesight after. It often happens that those that see these things lose their earthly sight.

The coach and four is seen by many. It appears in different forms, but there is always the same woman in it. Handsome I believe she is, and white; and there she will always be seen till the end of the world.

It's best to be neighbourly with them anyway – best to be neighbourly.

There was a woman woke one night and she saw two women by the fire, and they came over and tried to take away her baby. But she held him and she nudged her husband with her arm, but he was fast asleep. And they tried him again, and all she could do wouldn't waken the husband, but still she had the baby tight, and she called out a curse in the devil's name. So then they went away, for they don't like cursing.

One night coming home from Madden's where I was making frames with him, I began to tremble and to shake, but I could see nothing. And at night there came a knocking at the window, and the dog I had that would fight any dog in Ireland began to shrink to the wall and wouldn't come out. And I looked out the door and saw him. Little clothes he had on, but on his head a quarter cap, and a sort of a bawneen about him.[11] And I would have followed him, but the rest wouldn't let me.

## from 'Forths and Sheoguey Places'

*Steve Simon:*

I don't know did I draw down to you before, your ladyship, the greatest wonder ever I saw in my life?

I was passing by the forth at Corcomroe, coming back from some shopping I had done in Belharbour, and I saw twelve of the finest horses ever I saw, and riders on them racing round the forth. Many a race I saw since I lived in this world, but never a race like that, for tipping and tugging and welting the horses; the jockeys in coloured clothes, striped and blue, and little blue caps on them, and a lady in the front of them on a bayish horse and wearing a scarlet jacket.

I told what I saw the same evening to an old woman living near and she said, 'Whatever you saw keep it secret, or some harm will come upon you.' There was another thing I saw besides the riders. There were crowds and crowds of people, standing as we would against walls or on a stage, and taking a view. They were shouting, but the men racing on the horses said nothing at all. Never a race like that one, with the swiftness and the welting and fine horses that were in it.

What clothing had these people? They had coats on them, and on their back there were pictures, pictures in the form of people. Shields I think they were. Anyway there were pictures on them. Striped the coats were, and a sort of scollop on them the same as that screen in the window (a blind with Celtic design). They had little blue caps, such as wore them, but some had nothing on the head at all; and they had blue slippers – those I saw of them – but I was afeared to take more than a side view except of the racers.

## from 'Monsters and Sheoguey Beasts'

The Dragon that was the monster of the early world now appears only in the traditional folk-tales, where the hero, a new Perseus, fights for the life of the Princess who looks on crying at the brink of the sea, bound to a silver chair, while the Dragon is 'put in a way he will eat no more kings' daughters'. In the stories of today he has shrunk to eel or worm, for the persons and properties of the folklore of all countries keep being transformed or remade in the imagination, so that once in New England on the eve of George Washington's birthday, the decorated shop windows set me wondering whether the cherry tree itself might not be a remaking of the red-berried dragon guarded rowan of the Celtic tales, or it may be of a yet more ancient apple. I ventured to hint at this in a lecture at Philadelphia, and next day one of the audience wrote me that he had looked through all the early biographies of Washington, and either the first three or the first three editions of the earliest – I have mislaid the letter – never mention the cherry tree at all.

The monstrous beasts told of today recall the visions of Mael-dune on his strange dream-voyage, where he saw the beast that was like a horse and that had 'legs of a hound with rough sharp nails', and the fiery pigs that fed on golden fruit, and the cat that with one flaming leap turned a thief to a heap of ashes; for the folk-tales of the world have long roots, and there is nothing new save their reblossoming.

*By others:*
The worst form a monster can take is a cow or a pig. But as to a lamb, you may always be sure a lamb is honest.

A pig is the worst shape they can take. I wouldn't like to meet anything in the shape of a pig in the night.

No, I saw nothing myself, I'm not one of those that can see such things; but I heard of a man that went with the others on rent day, and because he could pay no rent but only made excuses, the landlord didn't ask him in to get a drink with the others. So as he was coming home by himself in the dark, there was something on the road before him, and he gave it a hit with the toe of his boot, and it let a squeal. So then he said to it, 'Come in here to my house, for I'm not asked to drink with them; I'll give drink and food to you.' So it came in, and the next morning he found by the door a barrel full of wine and another full of gold, and he never knew a day's want after that.

# from *Poets and Dreamers*

## Raftery

### [ I ]

One winter afternoon as I sat by the fire in a ward of Gort
Workhouse, I listened to two old women arguing about the
merits of two rival poets they had seen and heard in their
childhood.

One old woman, who was from Kilchreest, said: 'Raftery
hadn't a stim[1] of sight; and he travelled the whole nation; and he
was the best poet that ever was, and the best fiddler. It was
always at my father's house, opposite the big tree, that he used to
stop when he was in Kilchreest. I often saw him; but I didn't take
much notice of him then, being a child; it was after that I used to
hear so much about him. Though he was blind, he could serve
himself with his knife and fork as well as any man with his sight. I
remember the way he used to cut the meat – across, like this.
Callinan was nothing to him.'

The other old woman, who was from Craughwell, said: 'Callinan was a great deal better than him; and he could make songs
in English as well as in Irish; Raftery would run from where
Callinan was. And he was a nice respectable man, too, with cows
and sheep, and a kind man. *He* would never put anything that
wasn't nice into a poem, and *he* would never run anyone down;
but if you were the worst in the world, he'd make you the best in
it; and when his wife lost her beetle, he made a song of fifteen
verses about it.'

'Well,' the Kilchreest old woman admitted, 'Raftery would run
people down; he was someway bitter; and if he had anything
against a person, he'd give him a great lacerating. But there were
more for him than for Callinan; some used to say Callinan's songs
were too long.'

'I tell you,' said the other, 'Callinan was a nice man and a nice
neighbour. Raftery wasn't fit to put beside him. Callinan was a

man that would go out of his own back door, and make a poem about the four quarters of the earth. I tell you, you would stand in the snow to listen to Callinan!' But, just then, a bedridden old woman suddenly sat up and began to sing Raftery's 'Bridget Vesach' as long as her breath lasted; so the last word was for him after all.

Raftery died over sixty years ago; but there are many old people still living, besides those two old women, who have seen him, and who keep his songs in their memory. What they tell of him shows how closely he was in the old tradition of the bards, the wandering poets of two thousand years or more. His satire, his praises, his competitions with other poets were the dread and the pride of many Galway and Mayo parishes. And now the songs that he never wrote down, being blind, are known, if not as our people say, 'all over the world', at least in all places where Irish is spoken.

Raftery's satires, as I have heard them repeated by the country people, do not seem, even in their rhymed original – he only composed in Irish – to have the 'sharp spur' of some of his predecessors, such as O'Higinn, whose tongue was cut out by men from Sligo, who had suffered from it, or O'Daly, who criticised the poverty of the Irish chiefs in the sixteenth century until the servant of one of them stuck a knife into his throat. Yet they were much dreaded. 'He was very sharp with anyone that didn't please him,' I have been told; 'and no one would like to be put in his songs.' And though it is said of his songs in praise of his friends that 'whoever he praised was well praised', it was thought safer that one's own name should not appear in them. The man at whose house he died said to me: 'He used often to come and stop with us, but he never made a verse about us; my father wouldn't have liked that. Someway it doesn't bring luck.' And another man says: 'My father often told me about Raftery. He was someway gifted, and people were afraid of him. I was often told by men that gave him a lift in their car when they overtook him now and again, that if he asked their name, they wouldn't give it, for fear he might put it in a song.' And another man says: 'There was a friend of my father's was driving his car on the road one day, and he saw Raftery, but he didn't let on to see him. But when he was passing, Raftery said: "There was never a soldier marching but would get his billet. But the rabbit has an enemy in the ferret"; so then the man said in a hurry, "Oh, Mr Raftery, I never knew it was you: won't you get up and take a seat in the car?"' A girl in whose praise he had made a song, Mary Hynes, of Ballylee, died young, and had a troubled life; and one of her neighbours says of her: 'No one that has a song made about them will ever live long'; and another says: 'She got a great tossing up and down; and at last she died in the middle of a bog.' They tell, too, of a bush that he once took shelter under from the rain, and how he 'praised it first; and then when it let the rain down, he dispraised it, and it withered up, and never put out leaf or branch after'. I have seen his poem on the bush in a manuscript book, carefully written in the beautiful Irish character, and the great treasure of a stonecutter's cottage. This is the form of the curse: 'I pronounce ugliness upon you. That bloom or leaf may never grow on you, but the flame of the mountain fires and of bonfires be upon you. That you may get your punishment from Oscar's flail, to hack and to bruise you with the big sledge of a forge.'

There are some other verses made by him that have been less legendary in their effect. The story is: 'It was Anthony Daly, a carpenter, was hanged at Seefin. It was the two Z's got him put away. He was brought before a judge in Galway, and accused of being a Captain of Whiteboys,[2] and it was sworn against him that he fired at Mr X. He was a one-eyed man; and he said: "If I did, though I have but one eye, I would have hit him" – for he was a very good shot; and he asked that some object should be put up, and he would show the judge that he would hit it, but he said nothing else. Some were afraid he'd give up the names of the other Whiteboys; but he did not. There was a gallows put up at Seefin; and he was brought there sitting on his coffin in a cart. There were people all the way along the road, and they were calling on him to break through the crowd, and they'd save him; and some of the soldiers were Irish, and they called back that if he did they'd only fire their guns in the air; but he made no attempt, but went to the gallows quiet enough. There was a man in Gort was telling me he saw it, planting potatoes he was at Seefin that day. It was in the year 1820; and Raftery was there at the hanging, and he made a song about it. The first verse of the song said: "Wasn't that the good tree, that wouldn't let any branch that was on it fall to the ground?" He meant by that he didn't give up the names of the other Whiteboys. And at the end he called down judgment from God on the two Z's, and, if not on them, on their children. And they that had land and farms in all parts, lost it after; and all they had vanished; and the most of their children died – only two left, one a friar, and the other living in the town.' And quite lately I have been told by another neighbour, in corroboration, that a girl of the Z family married into a family near his home the other day, and was coldly received; and when my neighbour asked one of the family why this was, he was told that 'those of her people that went so high ought to have gone higher' – meaning that they themselves ought to have been on the gallows; and then he knew that Raftery's curse was still having its effect. And he had also heard that the grass had never grown again at Seefin.

This is a part of the song:

'The evening of Friday of the Crucifixion, the Gael was under the mercy of the Gall. It was as heavy the same day as when the only Son of Mary was on the tree. I have hope in the Son of God, my grief! and it is of no use for me; and it was Conall and his wife hung Daly, and may they be paid for it!

'But oh! young woman, while I live, I put death on the village where you will be; plague and death on it; and may the flood rise over it; that much is no sin at all, O bright God; and I pray with longing it may fall on the man that hung Daly; that left his people and his children crying.

'O stretch out your limbs! The air is murky overhead; there is darkness on the sun, and the fish do not leap in the water; there is no dew on the grass, and the birds do not sing sweetly. With sorrow after you, Daly, till death, there never will be fruit on the trees.

'And that is the true man, that didn't humble himself or lower himself to the Gall; Anthony Daly, O Son of God! He was that with us always, without a lie. But he died a good Irishman; and he never bowed the head to any man; and it was with false swearing that Daly was hung, and with the strength of the Gall.

'If I were a clerk – kind, light, cheerful with the pen – it is I would write your ways in clear Irish on a flag above your head. A thousand and eight hundred and sixteen, and four put to that, from the coming of the Son of God, to the death of Daly at the Castle of Seefin.'

I have heard, and have also seen in manuscript, a terrible list of curses that he hurled at the head of another poet, Seaghan Burke. But these were, I think, looked on as a mere professional display, and do not seem to have any ill effect.

Here are some of them:

'That God may perish you on the mountainside, without a priest, bishop or clerk. Seven years may you be senseless and without wit, going from door to door as an unfortunate creature.

'May you have a mouth that will go back to your ear, and may your lips be turned back like gums; that your legs may lose feeling from the knee down, your eyes lose their sight, and your hands lose their strength.

'Deformity and lameness and corruption upon you; flight and defeat and the hatred of your kin. That shivering fever may stretch you nine times, and that particularly at the time of Easter ("because", it is explained, "it was at Easter time our Lord was put to death, and it is the time He can best hear the curses of the poor").

'May a sore heart and cold flesh be upon you; may there be no marrow or moisture in your bones. That clay may never be put over your coffin-boards, but wind and a sharp blast on you from the north.

'Baldness and nakedness come upon you, judgment from above, and the curses of the crowd. May dragon's gall and poison mixed through it be your best drink at the hour of death.'

Sometimes he left a scathing verse on a place where he was not well treated, as: 'Oranmore without merriment. A little town in scarce fields – a broken little town, with its back to the water, and with women that have no understanding.'

He did not spare persons any more than places, especially if they were well-to-do, for his gentleness was for the poor. An old woman who remembers him says: 'He didn't care much about big houses. Just if they were people he liked, and that he was friendly with them, he would be kind enough to go in and see them.' A Mr Burke, who met him going from his house, asked how he had fared, and he said in a scornful verse:

> Potatoes that were softer than the fog,
> And with neither butter nor meat,
> And milk that was sourer than apples in harvest –
> That's what Raftery got from Burke of Kilfinn.

'And Mr Burke begged him to rhyme no more, but to come back, and he would be well taken care of.' I am told of another house he abused and that is now deserted: 'Frenchforth of the soot, that was wedded to the smoke, that is all that remains of the property . . . There were some of them on mules, and some of them unruly, and the biggest of them were smaller than asses, and the master cracking them with a stick'; 'but he went no further than that, because he remembered the good treatment used to be there in former times, and he wouldn't have said that much if it wasn't for the servants that vexed him.' A satire, that is remembered in Aran, was made with the better intention of helping a barefooted girl, who had been kept waiting a long time for a pair of shoes she had ordered. Raftery came, and sat down before the shoe-maker's house and began:

> 'A young little girl without sense, the ground tearing her feet, is not satisfied yet by the lying Peter Glynn. Peter Glynn, the liar, in his little house by the side of the road, is without the strength in his arms to slip together a pair of brogues.'

'And, before he had finished the lines, Peter Glynn ran out and called to him to stop, and he set at work on the shoes then and there.' He even ventured to poke a little satire at a priest sometimes. 'He went into the chapel at Kilchreest one time, and there was some cabbage after being stolen from a garden, and the priest was speaking about it. Raftery was at the bottom of the chapel, and at last he called out in verse: "What a lot of talk about cabbage! If there was meat with it, it would feed the whole parish!" The priest didn't mind, but afterwards he came down, and said: "Where is the cabbage man?" and asked him to make some more verses about it; but whether he did or not I don't know.' And another time, I am told: 'A priest wanted to teach him the rite of lay baptism; for there were scattered houses a priest might take a long time getting to, away from the roads, and certain persons were authorised to give the rite. So the priest put his hat in Raftery's hand, and told him the words to say; but it is what he said: "I baptise you without either foot or hand, without salt or tow, beer or drink. Your father was a ram and your mother was a sheep, and your like never came to be baptised before." He was put under a curse, too, one time by a priest, and he made a song about him; but he said he put his frock out of the bargain, and it was only the priest's own body he would speak about. And the priest let him alone after that.' And an old basket-maker, who had told me some of these things, said at the end: 'That is why the poets had to be banished before in the time of St Columcille.[3] Sure no one could stand the satire of them.'

## [ II ]

Irish history having been forbidden in schools, has been, to a great extent, learned from Raftery's poems by the people of Mayo, where he was born, and of Galway, where he spent his later years. It is hard to say where history ends in them and religion and politics begin; for history, religion and politics grow on one stem in Ireland, an eternal trefoil. 'He was a great historian,' it is said; 'for every book he'd get hold of, he'd get it read out to him.' And a neighbour tells me: 'He used to stop with my uncle that was a hedge schoolmaster in those times in Ballylee, and that was very fond of drink; and when he was drunk, he'd take his clothes off, and run naked through the country. But at evening he'd open the school; and the neighbours that would be working all day would gather in to him, and he'd teach them through the night; and there Raftery would be in the middle of them.' His chief historical poem is the 'Talk with the Bush', of over three hundred lines. Many of the people can repeat it, or a part of it, and some possess it in manuscript. The bush, a forerunner of the 'Talking Oak' or the 'Father of the Forest', gives it recollections, which go back to the times of the Firbolgs,[4] the Tuatha De Danann, 'without heart, without humanity'; the Sons of the Gael; the heroic Fianna, who 'would never put more than one man to fight against one'; Cuchulain[5] 'of the Grey Sword, that broke every gap'; till at last it comes to 'O'Rourke's wife that brought a blow to Ireland': for it was on her account the English were first called in. Then come the crimes of the English, made redder by the crime of Martin Luther. Henry VIII 'turned his back on God and denied his first wife'. Elizabeth 'routed the bishops and the Irish Church. James and Charles laid sharp scourges on Ireland . . . Then Cromwell and his hosts swept through Ireland, cutting before him all he could. He gave estates and lands to Cromwellians, and he put those that had a right to them on mountains.' Whenever he brings history into his poems, the same strings are touched. 'At the great judgment, Cromwell will be hiding, and O'Neill in the corner. And I think if William can manage it at all, he won't stand his ground against Sarsfield.'[6] And a moral often comes at the end, such as: 'Don't be without courage, but join together; God is stronger than the Cromwellians, and the cards may turn yet.'

For Raftery had lived through the '98 Rebellion, and the struggle for Catholic Emancipation; and he saw the Tithe War, and the Repeal movement; and it is natural that his poems, like those of the poets before him, should reflect the desire of his people for 'the mayntenance of their own lewde libertye', that had troubled Spenser in his time.

Here are some verses from his '*Cuis da ple*', 'Cause to plead', composed at the time of the Tithe War:

'The two provinces of Munster are afoot, and will not stop till tithes are overthrown, and rents accordingly; and if help were given them, and we to stand by Ireland, the English guard would be feeble, and every gap made easy. The Gall (English) will be on their back without ever returning again; and the Orangemen bruised in the borders of every town, a judge and jury in the courthouse for the Catholics, England dead, and the crown upon the Gael . . .

'There is many a fine man at this time sentenced, from Cork to Ennis and the town of Roscrea, and fair-haired boys wandering and departing from the streets of Kilkenny to Bantry Bay. But the cards will turn, and we'll have a good hand: the trump shall stand on the board we play at . . . Let ye have courage. It is a fine story I have. Ye shall gain the day in every quarter from the Sassanach. Strike ye the board, and the cards will be coming to you. Drink out of hand now a health to Raftery: it is he would put success for you on the *Cuis da ple*.'

This is part of another song:

'I have a hope in Christ that a gap will be opened again for us . . . The day is not far off, the Gall will be stretched without anyone to cry after them; but with us there will be a bonfire lighted up on high . . . The music of the world entirely, and Orpheus playing along with it. I'd sooner than all that, the Sassanach to be cut down.'

But with all this, he had plenty of common sense, and an old man at Ballylee tells me: 'One time there were a sort of nightwalkers – Moonlighters as we'd call them now, Ribbonmen[7] they were then – making some plan against the government; and they asked Raftery to come to their meeting. And he went; but what he said was this, in a verse, that they should look at the English government, and think of all the soldiers it had, and all the police – no, there were no police in those days, but gaugers and such like – and they should think how full up England was of guns and arms, so that it could put down Buonaparty; and that it had conquered Spain, and took Gibraltar from it; and the same in America, fighting for twenty-one years. And he asked them what they had to fight with against all those guns and arms? – nothing but a stump of a stick that they might cut down below in the wood. So he bid them give up their nightwalking, and come out and agitate in the daylight.'

I have been told – but I do not know if it is true – that he was once sent to Galway Gaol for three months for a song he made against the Protestant Church, 'saying it was like a wall slipping, where it wasn't built solid'.

## [ III ]

When, at the beginning of the seventeenth century, the poets O'Lewy and O'Clery and their supporters held a 'Contention', the results were written down in a volume containing 7,000 lines. I think the greater number of the 'Contentions' between Raftery and his fellow poets were never written down; but the country people still discuss them with all the eagerness of partisans. An old man from Athenry says: 'Raftery travelled Ireland, challenging all the poets of that time. There were hundreds of country poets in those days, and a welcome for them all. Raftery had enough to do to beat them, but he was the best; his poetry was the gift of God, and his poems are sung as far away as Limerick and Dublin.' There is a story of his knocking at a door one night, when he was looking for the house of a poet he had heard of and wanted to challenge, and saying: 'I am a poet seeking shelter'; and a girl answered him from within with a verse, saying he must be a blind man to be out so late looking for shelter; and then he knew it was the house he was looking for. And it is said that the daughter of another poet he was on his way to see in Clare, gave him such a sharp answer when he met her outside the house that he turned back and would not contend with her father at all. And he is said to have 'hunted another poet, Daly – hunted him all through Ireland'. But these other poets do not seem to have left a great name. There was a Connemara poet, Sweeny, that was put under a curse by the priests 'because he used to make so much fun at the wakes'; and in one of Raftery's poems he thanks Sweeny for having come to his help in some dispute; and there was 'one John Burke, who was a good poet, too; he and Raftery would meet at fairs and weddings, and be trying which would put down the other', I am told of an 'attack' they made on each other one day on the fair green of Cappaghtagle. Burke said:

'After all your walk of land and callows, Burke is before you at the fair of Cappagh.' And Raftery said: 'You are not Burke but a breed of *scatties*,[8] That's all over the country gathering *praties*;[9] When I'm at the table filling glasses, You are in the corner with your feet in the ashes.' Then Burke said: 'Raftery a poet, and he with bracked (speckled) shins, And he playing music with catgut; Raftery the poet, and his back to the wall, And he playing music for empty pockets. There's no one cares for his music at all, but he does be always craving money.' For he was sometimes accused of love of money; 'he wouldn't play for empty pockets, and he'd make the plate rattle at the end of a dance'.

But his most serious rival in his own part of the country was Callinan, the well-to-do farmer who lived near Craughwell, of whom the old women in the workhouse spoke. I have heard some of Callinan's poems and songs; but I do not find the imaginative power of Raftery in them. He seems, in distinction to him, to be the poet of the domestic affections, of the settled classes. His songs have melody and good sentiments; and they are often accompanied by a rhymed English version, made by his brother, a lesser poet. The favourite among them is a song on a wooden beetle, lost by his wife when washing clothes at the river. She is made to lament the loss of 'so good a servant' in a sort of allegory; and then its journey is traced from the river to the sea. An old man gives me a little memory of him: 'I saw Callinan one time when we went to dig potatoes for him at his own place, the other side of Craughwell. We went into the house for dinner; and we were in a hurry, and he was sitting by the hearth talking all the time; for he was a great talker, so that the veins of his neck swelled up. And he was telling us about the song he made about his own Missus when she was washing by the river. He was up to eighty years at that time.' And there are accounts of the making of some of his songs that show his kindly disposition and amiability. 'One time there was a baby in the house, and there was a dance going on near, and Mrs Callinan was a young woman; and she said she'd go for a bit to the dance-house; and she bid Callinan rock the cradle till she'd come back. But she never came back till morning, and there he was rocking the cradle still; and he had a song composed while she was away about the time of a man's life, and the hours of the day, and the seasons of the year; how when a man is young he is strong, and then he grows old and passes away, and goes to the feast of the Saviour; and about the day, how bright the morning is, and the birds singing; and a man goes out to work, and he comes in tired out, and sits by the fire to talk with his neighbour; and the night comes on, and he says his prayers, and thinks of the feast of the Saviour; and about the seasons, the spring so nice, and the summer for work; and autumn brings the harvest, and winter brings Christmas, the feast of the Saviour. In Irish and English he made that.' And this is another story: 'A carpenter made a plough for Callinan one time, and when it came, it was the worst ever made; and he said to his brother: "I'll make a song that will cut him down altogether." But his brother said: "Do not, for if you cut him down, it will take his means of living from him, but make a song in his praise." And he did so, for he wouldn't like to do him any harm.' I have asked if he made any love-songs, and was told of one he had made 'about a girl he met going to a bog. He praised herself first, and then he said, he had information as well that she had fifty gold guineas saved up.'

His having been well off seems to make his poetic merit the greater in the eyes of farmers; for one says: 'He was as good a poet, for he had a plough and horses and a good way of living, and never sang in any public-house; but Raftery had no way of living but to go round and to mark some house to go to, and then all the neighbours would gather in to hear him.' Another says: 'Raftery was the best poet, for he had nothing else to do, and laid his mind to it; but Callinan was a strong farmer, and had other things to think of'; and another says: 'Callinan was very apt: it was all Raftery could do to beat him'; and another sums up by saying: 'The both of them was great.' But a supporter of Raftery says: 'He was the best; he put his words so strong and stiff, following one another.'

I had been often told, by supporters of either side, that there was one contest between the two, at which Callinan 'made Raftery cry tears down'; and I wondered how it was that his wit had so far betrayed him. It has been explained to me lately. Raftery had made a long poem, 'The Hunt', in which he puts 'a Writer' in the place of the fox, and calls on all the gentlemen of Galway and Mayo, and even on 'Sarsfield from Limerick', to come and hunt him through their respective neighbourhoods with a pack of hounds. It contains many verses; and he seems to have improvised others in the different places where he sang it. In the written copy I have seen, Burke is the 'Writer' who is thus hunted. But he probably put in the name of any other rival from time to time. This is the story: 'He and the Callinans were sometimes vexed with one another, but they'd make friends after; but there was one day he was put down by them. There was a funeral going on at Killeenan, and Raftery was there; and he was asked into the corpse-house afterwards, and the people asked him for the song about Callinan and he began hunting him all through the country, and the people were laughing and making him go on; but Callinan's brother had come in, and was listening to him, and Raftery didn't see him, being blind; and he brought him to Killeenan at last, and he said: "Where can the rogue go now, unless he'll swim the turlough?" And at that Callinan's brother stood up and said, "Who is it you are calling a rogue?" And Raftery tried to laugh it off, and he said, "You mustn't expect poetry and truth to go together." But Callinan said: "I'll give you poetry that's truth as well"; and he began to say off some verses his brother had made on Raftery; and Raftery was choked up that time, and hadn't a word.' This story is corroborated by an eye-witness who said to me: 'It was in this house he was on the night Callinan made him cry. My father was away at the time; if he had been there, he never would have let Callinan come into the house unknown to Raftery.' I have not heard all of Callinan's poem, but this is part of it:

'He left the County Mayo; he was hunted up from the country of the brothons' (thick bed-coverings, then made in Mayo) 'without any for the night, nor any shift for bedding, but with an old yellow blanket with a thousand patches; he had a black trouser down to the ground with two hundred holes and forty pieces; he had long legs like the shank of a pipe, and a long great coat, for it is many the dab he put in his pocket. His coat was greasy, and it was no wonder, and an old grey hat as grey as snuff as it was many the day it was in the dunghill.'

It is said that 'Raftery could have answered that song better, but he had no back here; and Callinan was well-to-do, and had so many of his family and so many friends.' But others say there were some allusions in it to the poverty of his home, that had become known through a servant girl from Raftery's birth-place. But I think even Callinan's friends are sorry now that Raftery was ever made to 'cry tears down'.

## [ IV ]

A man near Oranmore says: 'There used to be great talk of the Fianna; and everyone had the poems about them till Raftery came, and he put them out. For when the people got Raftery's songs in their heads, they could think of nothing else: his songs put out everything else. I remember when I was a boy of ten, I was so taken up with his rhymes and songs, I had them all off. And I heard he was coming one night to a stage he had below there where he used to come now and again. And I begged my father to bring me with him that night, and he did; but whatever happened, Raftery didn't come that time, and the next year he died.'

But it is hard to judge of the quality of Raftery's poems. Some of them have probably been lost altogether. There are already different versions of those written out in manuscript books, and of these books many have disappeared or been destroyed, and some have been taken to America by emigrants. It is said that when he was on his deathbed, he was very sorry that his songs had not all been taken down; and that he dictated one he composed there to a young man who wrote it down in Irish, but could not read his own writing when he had done, and that vexed Raftery; and then a man came in, and he asked him to take down all his songs, and he could have them for himself; but he said, 'If I did, I'd always be called Raftery,' and he went out again.

I hear the people say now and then: 'If he had had education, he would have been the greatest poet in the world.' I cannot but be sorry that his education went so far as it did, for 'he used to carry a book about with him – a Pantheon – about the heathen gods and goddesses; and whoever he'd get that was able to read, he'd get him to read it to him, and then he'd keep them in his mind, and use them as he wanted them'. If he had been born a few decades later, he would have been caught, like other poets of the time, in the formulas of English verse. As it was, both his love poems and his religious poems were caught in the formulas imported from Greece and from Rome; and any formula must make a veil between the prophet who has been on the mountain top, and the people who are waiting at its foot for his message. The dreams of beauty that formed themselves in the mind of the blind poet become flat and vapid when he embodies them in the well-worn names of Helen and Venus. The truths of God that he strove in his last years, as he says, 'to have written in the book of the people', left those unkindled whose ears were already wearied with the well-known words 'the keys of Heaven', 'penance, fasts and alms', to whom it was an old tale to hear of hell as a furnace, and the grave as a dish for worms. When he gets away from the formulas, he has often a fine line on death or on judgment; the cheeks of the dead are 'cold as the snow that is at the back of the sun'; the careless – those who 'go out looking at their sheep on Sunday instead of going to Mass' – are warned that 'on the side of the hill of the tears there will be Ochone!'[10]

His love songs are many; and they were not always thought to bring ill luck; for I am told of a girl 'that was not handsome at all, but ugly, that he made a song about her for civility; for she used to be in a house where he used to lodge, and the song got her a husband; and there is a son of hers living now down in Clare-Galway'. And an old woman tells me, with a sigh of regret for what might have been, that she saw Raftery one time at a dance, and he spoke to her and said: 'Well planed you are; the carpenter that planed you knew his trade.' 'And I said: "Better than you know yours"; for there were two or three of the strings of his fiddle broke. And then he said something about O'Meara, that lived near us; and my father got vexed at what he said, and would let him speak no more with me. And if it wasn't for him speaking about O'Meara, and my father getting vexed, he might have made words about me like he did for Mary Hynes and for Mary Brown.'

'Bridget Vesach', which I have heard in many cottages, as well as from the old woman in Gort Workhouse, begins: 'I would wed courteous Bridget without coat, shoe, or shirt. Treasure of my heart, if it were possible for me, I would fast for you nine meals, without food, without drink, without any share of anything, on an island of Lough Erne, with desire for you and me to be together till we should settle our case ... My heart started with trouble, and I was frightened nine times that morning that I heard you were not to be found ... I would sooner be stretched by you with nothing under us but heather and rushes, than be listening to the cuckoos that are stirring at the break of day ... I am in grief and in sorrow since you slipped from me across the mearings.'

Another love poem, 'Mairin Stanton', shows his habit of mixing comparisons drawn from the classics with those drawn from nature:

'There's a bright flower by the side of the road, and she beats Deirdre in the beauty of her voice; or I might say Helen, Queen of the Greeks, she for whose sake hundreds died at Troy.

'There is light and brightness in her as in those others; her little mouth is as sweet as the cuckoo on the branch. You would not find a mind like hers in any woman since the pearl died that was in Ballylee.

'To see under the sky a woman settled like her walking on the road on a fine sunny day, the light flashing from the whiteness of her breast, would give sight to a man without eyes.

'There is the love of hundreds in her face, and there is the promise of the evening star. If she had been living in the time of the gods, it is not Venus that would have had the apple.

'Her hair falls down below her knees, waving and winding to the mouth of her shoes; her locks spread out wide and pale like dew, they leave a brightness on the road behind her.

'She is the girl that has been taught the nicest of all whose eyes still open to the sun; and if the estate of Lord Lucan belonged to me, on the strength of my cause this jewel would be mine.

'Her slender lime-white shape, her face like flowers, her neck, her cheek, and her amber hair; Virgil, Cicero and Homer could tell of nothing like her; she is like the dew in the time of harvest.

'If you could see this plant moving or dancing, you could not but love the flower of the branch. If I cannot get a hundred words with Mairin Stanton, I do not think my life will last long.

'She said "Good morrow" early and pleasantly; she drank my health, and gave me a stool, and it not in the corner. At the time that I am ready to go on my way I will stay talking and talking with her.'

The 'pearl that was at Ballylee' was poor Mary Hynes, of whom I have already spoken. His song on her is very popular; 'a great song, so that her name is sung through the three parishes'. She must have been beautiful, for many who knew her still speak of her beauty, of her long, shining hair, and the 'little blushes in her cheeks'. An old woman says: 'I never can think of her but I'll get a trembling, she was so nice; and if she was to begin talking, she'd keep you laughing till daybreak.' But others say: 'It was the poet that made her so handsome'; or, 'whatever she was, he made twice as much of it.' I give one or two verses of the song:

'There was no part of Ireland I did not travel: from the rivers to the tops of the mountains, to the edge of Lough Greine, whose mouth is hidden; but I saw no beauty but was behind hers.

'Her hair was shining, and her brows were shining too; her face was like herself, her mouth pleasant and sweet. She is the pride, and I give her the branch. She is the shining flower of Ballylee.'

Even many miles from Ballylee, if the *posin glégeal* – the 'shining flower' – is spoken of, it is always known that it is Mary Hynes who is meant.

Raftery is said to have spent the last seven years of his life praying and making religious songs, because death had told him in a vision that he had only seven years to live. His own account of the vision was given me by the man at whose house he died. 'I heard him telling my father one time, that he was sick in Galway, and there was a mug beside the bed, and in the night he heard a noise, and he thought it was the cat was on the table, and that she'd upset the mug; and he put his hand out, and what he felt was the bones and the thinness of death. And his sight came to him, and he saw where his wrapper was hanging on the wall. And death said he had come to bring him away, or else one of the neighbours that lived in such a house. And after they had talked a while, he said he would give him a certain time before he'd come for him again, and he went away. And in the morning when his wife came in, he asked where did she hang his wrapper the night before, and she told him it was in such a place, and that was the very place he saw it, so he knew he had had his sight. And then he sent to the house that had been spoken of to know how was the man of it, and word came back that he was dead. I remember when he was dying, a friend of his, one Cooney, came in to see him, and said: 'Well, Raftery, the time is not up yet that death gave you to live.' And he said: 'The Church and myself have it made out that it was not death that was there, but the devil that came to tempt me.'

His description of death in his poem on the 'Vision' is vivid and unconventional:

'I had a vision in my sleep last night, between sleeping and waking, a figure standing beside me, thin, miserable, sad and sorrowful; the shadow of night upon his face, the tracks of the tears down his cheeks. His ribs were bending like the bottom of a riddle; his nose thin, that it would go through a cambric needle; his shoulders hard and sharp, that they would cut tobacco; his head dark and bushy like the top of a hill; and there is nothing I can liken his fingers to. His poor bones without any kind of covering; a withered rod in his hand, and he looking in my face. It is not worth my while to be talking about him; I questioned him in the name of God.'

A long conversation follows; Raftery addresses him:

'"Whatever harbour you came from last night, move up to me and speak if you can." Death answers: "Put away Hebrew, Greek and Latin, French, and the three sorts of English, and I will speak to you sweetly in Irish, the language that you found your verses in. I am death that has hidden hundreds: Hannibal, Pompey,

Julius Caesar; I was in the way with Queen Helen. I made Hector fall, that conquered the Greeks, and Conchubar, that was king of Ireland; Cuchulain and Goll, Oscar and Diarmuid, and Oisin, that lived after the Fenians; and the children of Usnach that brought away Deirdre from Conchubar;" at a touch from me they all fell." But Raftery answers: "O high Prince, without height, without followers, without dwelling, without strength, without hands, without force, without state: all in the world wouldn't make me believe it, that you'd be able to put down the half of them."'

But death speaks solemnly to him then, and warns him that:

'"Life is not a thing that you get a lease of; there will be stones and a sod over you yet. Your ears that were so quick to hear everything will be closed, deaf, without sound without hearing; your tongue that was so sweet to make verses will be without a word in the same way . . . Whatever store of money or wealth you have, and the great coat up about your ears, death will snap you away from the middle of it."'

And the poem ends at last with the story of the Passion and a prayer for mercy.

He was always ready to confess his sins with the passionate exaggeration of St Paul or of Bunyan. In his 'Talk with the Bush', when a flood is threatened, he says:

'I was thinking, and no blame to me, that my lease of life wouldn't be long, and that it was bad work my hands had left after them; to be committing sins since I was a child, swearing big oaths and blaspheming. I never think to go to Mass. Confession at Christmas I wouldn't ask to go to. I would laugh at my neighbour's downfall, and I'd make nothing of breaking the Ten Commandments. Gambling and drinking and all sorts of pleasures that would come across me, I'd have my hand in them.'

The poem known as his 'Repentance' is in the same strain. It is said to have been composed one time he went to confession to Father Bartley Kilkelly, and he refused him absolution because he was too much after women and drink. And that night he made up his 'Repentance' and the next day he went again, and Father Pat Burke, the curate, was with Father Bartley, and he said: 'Well, Raftery, what have you composed of late?' and he said: 'This is what I composed,' and he said the Repentance. And then Father Bartley said to the curate: 'You may give him absolution, where he has his repentance made before the world.'

It is one of the finest of his poems. It begins:

> 'O King, who art in heaven, . . . I scream to Thee again and again aloud, For it is Thy grace I am hoping for.
>
> 'I am in age, and my shape is withered; many a day I have been going astray . . . When I was young, my deeds were evil; I delighted greatly in quarrels and rows. I liked much better to be playing or drinking on a Sunday morning than to be going to Mass . . . I was given to great oaths, and I did not let lust or drunkenness pass me by . . . The day has stolen away, and I have not raised the hedge until the crop in which Thou didst take delight is destroyed . . . I am a worthless stake in a corner of a hedge, or I am like a boat that has lost its rudder, that would be broken against a rock in the sea, and that would be drowned in the cold waves.'

But in spite of this self-denunciation, people who knew him say 'there was no harm in him'; though it is added: 'but as to a drop of drink, he was fond of that to the end'. And in another mood, in his 'Argument with Whiskey', he claims, as an excuse for this weakness, the desire for companionship felt by a wanderer. 'And the world knows it's not for love of what I drink, but for love of the people that do be near me.' And he has always a confident belief in final absolution: 'I pray to you to hear me, O Son of God; as you created the moon, the sun, the stars, it is no task or trouble for you to ready me.'

There are some fine verses in a poem made at the time of an outbreak of cholera:

> 'Look at him who was yesterday swift and strong, who would leap stone wall, ditch and gap, who was in the evening walking the street, and is going under the clay on the morrow.
>
> 'Death is quicker than the wave of drowning or than any horse, however fast, on the racecourse. He would strike a goal against the crowd; and no sooner is he there than he is on guard before us.
>
> 'He is changing, hindering, rushing, starting, unloosed; the day

is no better to him than the night; when a person thinks there is no fear of him, there he is on the spot laid low with keening.[12]

'Death is a robber who heaps together kings, high princes, and country lords; he brings with him the great, the young, and the wise, gripping them by the throat before all the people.

'It is a pity for him who is tempted with the temptations of the world; and the store that will go with him is so weak, and his lease of life no better if he were to live for a thousand years, than just as if he had slipped over on a visit and back again.

'When you are going to lie down, don't be dumb. Bare your knee and bruise the ground. Think of all the deeds that you put by you, and that you are travelling towards the meadow of the dead.'

Some of his poems of places, usually places in Mayo, the only ones he had ever looked on – for smallpox took his sight away in his childhood – have much charm. 'Cnocin Saibhir', 'the Plentiful Little Hill', must have sounded like a dream of Tir-Nan-Oge[13] to many a poor farmer in a sodden-thatched cottage:

'After the Christmas, with the help of Christ, I will never stop if I am alive; I will go to the sharp-edged little hill; for it is a fine place, without fog falling; a blessed place that the sun shines on, and the wind doesn't rise there or any thing of the sort.

'And if you were a year there, you would get no rest, only sitting up at night and eternally drinking.

'The lamb and the sheep are there; the cow and the calf are there; fine lands are there without heath and without bog. Ploughing and seed-sowing in the right month, and plough and harrow prepared and ready; the rent that is called for there, they have means to pay it. There is oats and flax and large-eared barley . . . There are beautiful valleys with good growth in them, and hay. Rods grow there, and bushes and tufts, white fields are there, and respect for trees; shade and shelter from wind and rain; priests and friars reading their book; spending and getting is there, and nothing scarce.'

In another song in the same manner on 'Cilleaden', he says:

'I leave it in my will that my heart rises as the wind rises, or as the fog scatters, when I think upon Carra and the two towns below it, on the two-mile bush, and on the plains of Mayo . . . And if I were standing in the middle of my people, age would go from me, and I would be young again.'

He writes of friends that he has made in Galway as well as in Mayo, a weaver, a carpenter, a priest at Kilcolgan who is 'the good Christian, the clean wheat of the Gael, the generous messenger, the standing tree of the clergy'. Some of his eulogies both on persons and places are somewhat spoiled by grotesque exaggeration. Even Cilleaden has not only all sorts of native fishes, 'as plenty as turf', and all sorts of native trees, but is endowed with 'tortoises', with 'logwood and mahogany'. His country weaver must not only have frieze and linen in his loom, but satin and cambric. A carpenter near Ardrahan, Seaghan Conroy, is praised with more simplicity for his 'quick, lucky work', and for the pleasure he takes in it. 'I never met his master; the trade was in his nature'; and he gives a long list of all the things he could make: 'doors and all that would be wanted for a big house'; mills and ploughs and spinning-wheels 'nicely finished with a clean chisel'; 'all sorts of things for the living, and a coffin for the dead'. And with all this 'he cares little for money, but to spend, as he earns, decently. And if he was up for nine nights, you wouldn't see the sign of a drop on him.'

Another of his more simple poems is what Spenser would call an 'elegie or friend's passion' on a player on fiddle or pipes; Thomas O'Daly, that gives him a touch of kinship with the poets who have mourned their Astrophel, their Lycidas, their Adonais, their Thyrsis. This is how I have been helped to put it into English by a young working farmer, sitting by a turf fire one evening, when his day in the fields was over:

'It was Thomas O'Daly that roused up young people and scattered them, and since death played on him, may God give him grace. The country is all sorrowful, always talking, since their man of sport died that would win the goal in all parts with his music.

'The swans on the water are nine times blacker than a blackberry since the man died from us that had pleasantness on the top of his fingers. His two grey eyes were like the dew of the morning that lies on the grass. And since he was laid in the grave, the cold is getting the upper hand.

'If you travel the five provinces, you would not find his equal for countenance or behaviour, for his equal never walked on land or grass. High King of Nature, you who have all powers in yourself, he that wasn't narrow-hearted, give him shelter in heaven for it.

'He was the beautiful branch. In every quarter that he ever knew he would scatter his fill and not gather. He would spend the estate of the Dalys, their beer and their wine. And that he may be sitting in the chair of grace, in the middle of Paradise.

'A sorrowful story on death, it's he is the ugly chief that did treachery, that didn't give him credit, O strong God, for a little time.

'There are young women, and not without reason, sorry and heart-broken and withered, since he was left at the church. Their hair thrown down and hanging, turned grey on their head.

'No flower in any garden, and the leaves of the trees have leave to cry, and they falling on the ground. There is no green flower on the tops of the tufts, since there did a boarded coffin go on Daly.

'There is sorrow on the men of mirth, a clouding over the day, and no trout swim in the river. Orpheus on the harp, he lifted up everyone out of their habits; and he that stole what Argus was watching the time he took away Io; Apollo, as we read, gave them teaching, and Daly was better than all these musicians.

'A hundred wouldn't be able to put together his actions and his deeds and his many good works. And Raftery says this much for Daly, because he liked him.'

Though his praises are usually all for the poor, for the people, he has left one beautiful lament for a landowner:

'There's no dew or grass on Cluan Leathan. The cuckoo is not to be seen on the furze; the leaves are withering and the trees complaining of the cold. There is no sun or moon in the air or in the sky, or no light in the stars coming down, with the stretching of O'Kelly in the grave.

'My grief to tell it! he to be laid low; the man that did not bring grief or trouble on any heart, that would give help to those that were down.

'No light on the day like there was; the fruits not growing; no children on the breast; there's no return in the grain; the plants don't blossom as they used since O'Kelly with the fair hair went away; he that used to forgive us a great share of the rent.

'Since the children of Usnach and Deirdre went to the grave and Cuchulain, who, as the stories tell us, would gain victory in every step he would take; since he died, such a story never came of sorrow or defeat; since the Gael were sold at Aughrim, and since Owen Roe[14] died, the Branch.'

## [ V ]

His life was always the wandering, homeless life of the old bards. After Cromwell's time, as the houses they went to grew poorer, they had added music to their verse-making; and Raftery's little fiddle helped to make him welcome in the Ireland which was, in spite of many sorrows, as merry and light-hearted up to the time of the great famine as England had been up to the time of the Puritans. 'He had no place of his own,' I am told, 'but to be walking the country. He did well to die before the bad years came. He used to play at Kiltartan cross for the dancing of a Sunday evening. And when he'd come to any place, the people would gather and he'd give them a dance; for there was three times as many people in the world then as what there is now. The people would never have let him want; but as to money, what could he do with it, and he with no place of his own? An old woman near Craughwell says: 'He used to come here often; it was like home to him. He wouldn't have a dance then; my father liked better to be sitting listening to his talk and his stories; only when we'd come in, he'd take the fiddle and say: "Now we must give the youngsters a tune." And an old man, who is still lamenting the fall in prices after the Battle of Waterloo, remembers having seen him 'one time at a shebeen[15] house that used to be down there in Clonerle. He was playing the fiddle, and there used to be two couples at a time dancing; and they would put two halfpence in the plate, and Raftery would rattle them and say: "It's good for the two sorts to be together," and there would be great laughing.' And it is also said 'there was a welcome before him in every house he'd come to; and wherever he went, they'd think the time too short he would be with them.' There is a story I often hear told about the marriage near Cappaghtagle of a poor servant boy and girl, 'that was only a marriage and not a wedding, till Raftery chanced to come in; and he made it one. There wasn't a bit but bread and herrings in the house; but he made a great song about the grand feast they had, and he put every sort of thing into the song – all the beef that was in Ireland; and went to the Claddagh,[16] and didn't leave a fish in the sea. And there was no one at all at it; but he brought all the *bacach*[17] and poor men in Ireland, and gave them a pound each. He went to bed after, without them giving him a drop to drink; but he didn't mind that when they hadn't got it to give.'

The wandering, unrestrained life was probably to his mind; and I do not think there is a word of discontent or complaint in any of his verses, though he was always poor, and must often have known hardship. In the 'Talk with the Bush', he describes in his whimsical, exaggerated way, a wetting, which must have been one of very many.

'It chanced that I was travelling and the rain was heavy; stepped aside, and not without reason, till I'd get a wall or a bush that would shelter me.

'I didn't meet at the side of a gap only an old, withered miserable bush by the side of the wall, and it bent with the west wind. I stepped under it, and it was a wet place; torrents of rain coming down from all quarters, east and west and straight downwards; its equal I couldn't see, unless it is seeds winnowed through a riddle. It was sharp, angry, fierce, and stormy, like a deer running and racing past me. The storm was drowning the country, and my case was pitiful, and I suffering without cause.

'An hour and a quarter it was raining; there isn't a drop that fell but would fill a quart and put a heap on it afterwards; there's not a wheat or rape mill in the neighbourhood but it would set going in the middle of a field.'

At last relief comes:

'It was shortly then the rain grew weak, the sun shone, and the wind rose. I moved on, and I smothered and drowned in wet, till I came to a little house, and there was a welcome before me. Many quarts of water I squeezed from my skirt and my cape. I hung my hat on a nail, and I lying in a sweet flowery bed. But I was up again in a little while. We began sports and pleasures; and it was with pride we spent the night.'

But there is a verse in his 'Argument with Whiskey' that seems to have a wistful thought in it, perhaps of the settled home of his rival, Callinan:

'Cattle is a nice thing for a man to have, and his share of land to reap wheat and barley. Money in the chest, and a fire in the evening time; and to be able to give shelter to a man on his road; a hat and shoes in the fashion – I think, indeed, that would be much better than to be going from place to place drinking *uisge beatha*.'[18]

And there is a little sadness in the verses he made in some house, when a stranger asked who he was:

'I am Raftery the poet, full of hope and love; with eyes without light, with gentleness without misery.

'Going west on my journey with the light of my heart; weak and tired to the end of my road.

'I am now, and my back to a wall, playing music to empty pockets.'

'He was a thin man,' I am told by one who knew him, 'not very tall, with a long frieze coat and corduroy trousers. He was very strong; and he told my father there was never any man he wrestled with but he could throw him, and that he could lie on his back and throw up a bag with four hundred of wheat in it, and take it up again. He couldn't see a stim; but he would walk all the roads, and give the right turn, without ever touching the wall. My father was wondering at him one time they were out together; and he said: "Wait till we come to the turn to Athenry, and don't tell me of it, and see if I don't make it out right." And sure enough, when they came to it, he gave the right turn, and just in the middle.' This is explained by what another man tells me: 'There was a blind piper with him one time in Gort, and they set out together to go to Ballylee, and it was late, and they couldn't find the stile that led down there, near Early's house. And they would have stopped there till somebody would come by, but Raftery said he'd go back to Gort and step it again; and so he did, turned back a mile to Gort, and started from there. He counted every step that he stepped out; and when he got to the stile, he stopped straight before it.' And I was told also there used to be a flagstone put beside the bog-holes to leap from, and Raftery would leap as well as any man. He would count his steps back from the flag, and take a run and alight on the other side.

## [ VI ]

His knowledge and his poetic gift are often supposed to have been given to him by the invisible powers, who grow visible to those who have lost their earthly sight. An old woman who had often danced to his music, said: 'When he went to his rest at night, it's then he'd make the songs in the turn of a hand, and you would wonder in the morning where he got them.' And a man who 'was too much taken up with sport and hurling when he was a boy to think much about him' says: 'He got the gift. It's said he was asked which would he choose, music or the talk. If he chose music, he would have been the greatest musician in the world; but he chose the talk, and so he was a great poet. Where could he have found all the words he put in his songs if it wasn't for that?' An old woman, who is more orthodox, says: 'I often used to see him when I was a little child, in my father's house at Corker. He'd often come in there, and here to Coole House he used to come as well. He couldn't see a stim, and that is why he had such great knowledge. God gave it to him. And his songs have gone all through the world; and he had a voice that was like the wind.'

Legends are already growing up about his death. It has been said that 'he knew the very day his time would be up; and he went to Galway, and brought a plank to the house he was stopping at, and he put it in the loft; and he told the people of the house his time was come, and bid them make a coffin for him with the plank – and he was dead before morning'. And another story says he died alone in an empty house, and that flames were seen about the house all night; and 'the flames were the angels waking him'. But many told me he had died in the house of a man near Craughwell; and one autumn day I went there to look for it, and the first person I asked was able to tell me that the house where Raftery had died was the other side of Craughwell, a mile and a half away. It was a warm, hazy day; and as I walked along the flat, deserted road that Raftery had often walked, I could see few landmarks – only a few more grey rocks, or a few more stunted hazel bushes in one stone-walled field than in another. At last I came to a thatched cottage; and when I saw an old man sitting outside it, with hat and coat of the old fashion, I felt sure it was he who had been with Raftery at the last. He was ready to talk about him, and told me how he had come there to die. 'I was a young chap at that time. It must have been in the year 1835, for my father died in '36, and I think it was a year before him that Raftery died. What did he die of? Of weakness. He had been bet up in Galway with some fit of sickness he had; and then he came to gather a little money about the country, and when he got here he was bet up again. He wasn't an old man – only about seventy years. He was in the bed for about a fortnight. When he got bad, my father said it was best get a priest for him; but the parish priest was away. But we saw Father Nagle passing the road, and I went out and brought him in, and he gave him absolution, and anointed him. He had no pain; only his feet were cold, and the boys used to be warming a stone in the fire and putting it to them in the bed. My mother wanted to send to Galway, where his wife and his daughter and his son were stopping, so that they would come and care him; but he wouldn't have them. Someway he didn't think they treated him well.'

I had been told that the priest had refused him absolution when he was dying, until he forgave some enemy; and that he had said afterwards, 'If I forgave him with my mouth, I didn't with my heart'; but this was not true. 'Father Nagle made no delay in anointing him; but there was a carpenter down the road there he said too much to, and annoyed him one time; and the carpenter had a touch of the poet too, and was a great singer, and he came out and beat him, and broke his fiddle; and I remember when he was dying, the priest bringing in the carpenter, and making them forgive one another, and shake hands; and the carpenter said: "If two brothers were to have a falling out, they'd forgive one another – and why wouldn't we?'' He was buried in Killeenan; it wasn't a very big funeral, but all the people of the village came to it. He used often to come and stop with us . . . It was of a Christmas Eve he died; and he had always said that, if God had a hand in it, it was of a Christmas Day he'd die.'

I went to Killeenan to look for his grave. There is nothing to mark it; but two old men who had been at his funeral pointed it out to me. There is a ruined church in the graveyard, which is crowded; 'there are people killing one another now to get a place in it'. I was asked into a house close by; and its owner said with almost a touch of jealousy: 'I think it was coming in here Raftery was the time he died; but he got bet up, and turned in at the house below. It was of a Christmas Eve he died, and that shows he was blessed; there's a blessing on them that die at Christmas. It was at night he was buried, for Christmas Day no work could be done, but my father and a few others made a little gathering to pay for a coffin, and it was made by a man in the village on St Stephen's Day; and then he was brought here, and the people from the villages followed him, for they all had a wish for Raftery. But night was coming on when they got here; and in digging the grave there was a big stone in it, and the boys thought they would put him in a barn and take the night out of him. But my mother – the Lord have mercy on her – had a great veneration for Raftery; and she sent out two mould candles lighted; for in those days the women used to have their own mould, and to make their own candles for Christmas. And we held the candles there where the grave is, near the gable end of the church; and my brother went down in the grave and got the stone out, and we buried him. And there was a sharp breeze blowing at the time, but it never quenched the candles or moved the flame of them, and that shows that the Lord had a hand in him.'

He and all the neighbours were glad to hear that there is soon to be a stone over the grave. 'He is worthy of it; he is well worthy of it,' they kept saying. A man who was digging sand by the roadside took me to his house, and his wife showed me a little book, in which the 'Repentance' and other poems had been put down for her, in phonetic Irish, by a beggar who had once stayed in the house. 'Many who go to America hear Raftery's songs sung out there,' they told me with pride.

As I went back along the silent road, there was suddenly a sound of horses and a rushing and waving about me, and I found myself in the midst of the County Galway Fox Hounds, coming back from cub-hunting. The English MFH and his wife rode by; and I wondered if they had ever heard of the poet whose last road this had been. Most likely not; for it is only among the people that his name has been kept in remembrance.

There is still a peasant poet here and there, making songs in the 'sweet Irish tongue', in which death spoke to Raftery; and I think these will be held in greater honour as the time of awakening goes on. But the nineteenth century has been a time of swift change in many countries; and in looking back on that century in Ireland, there seem to have been two great landslips – the breaking of the continuity of the social life of the people by the famine, and the breaking of the continuity of their intellectual life by the shoving out of the language. It seems as if there were no place left now for the wandering versemaker, and that Raftery may have closed the long procession that had moved unbroken during so many centuries, on its journey to 'the meadow of the dead'.

1900

It was after I had written this that I went to see Raftery's birth-place, Cilleaden, in the County Mayo.

A cousin of his came to see me, and some other men, but none of them remembered him; but they were very proud of his song on Cilleaden, which 'is all through the world'. An old woman told me she had heard it in a tramcar in America; and an old man said: 'I was coming back from England one time, and there were a lot of Irish-speaking boys from Galway on board. There was one of them sick all through the night, but he was well in the morning; and the others came round him and asked him for a song, and the song he gave was "Cilleaden".'

They did not seem to know many of his other songs, except the 'Repentance', which someone remembered having seen sold as a ballad, with the English on one side and the Irish on the other. And one man told me: 'The first song Raftery wrote was about a hat that was stole from a man that was working in that middle field beyond. When the man was digging, he used to put his hat on a stick in the field to frighten away the crows; and Raftery got someone to bring away the hat, to make fun of the man. And then he made a song, making out it was the fairies had taken it; and he made the man follow them to Cruachmaa, and from that to Roscommon, and tell all that happened him there.'

And one of them told me: 'He was six years old when the smallpox took his sight from him; and he was marked very little by the pox, only three or four little marks – it seemed to settle in his eyes. His father was a cottier – there were many here in those times. His mother was a Brennan. There are cousins of his living yet; but in the schools they are Englished into Rochford.'

A young man said he had been told Raftery was born in some place beyond, at the foot of the mountain, but the others were very indignant; one got very angry, and said: 'Don't I know where he was born, and my father was the one age with him, and they sisters' sons; and isn't Michael Conroy there below his cousin? and it's up in that field was the house he was born in, so don't be trying to bring him away to the mountain.'

I went to see the birth-place, a very green field, with two thorn bushes, growing close together by a stone. The field is called 'Sean Straid' – the old street – for a few cottages had stood there. A man who lives close by told me he had dug up a blackened stone just there, and a stone into which a bar had been let, to hang a pot on; and that may have been the very hearth where Raftery had sat as a child.

I found one old man who remembered him. 'He used to come to my father's house often, mostly from Easter to Whitsuntide, when the cakes were made, and there would be music and dancing. He used to play the fiddle for Frank Taafe that lived here, when he would be going out riding, and the horse used to prance when he heard it. And he made verses against one

Seaghan Bradach, that used to be paid thirteen pence for every head of cattle he found straying in the Jordan's fields, and used to drive them in himself. There was another poet called Devine that praised Seaghan Bradach; and a verse was made against him again by a woman-poet that lived here at the time.

There is a stone over Raftery's grave now, and the people about Killeenan gather there on Sunday in August every year to do honour to his memory. This year they established a *Feis*;[19] and there were prizes given for traditional singing, and for old poems repeated, and old stories told, all in the Irish tongue.

And the *Craoibhhin Aoibhin*[20] is printing week by week all of Raftery's poems that can be found, with translations, and we shall soon have them in a book.

And he has written a little play, having Raftery for its subject; and at a Galway Feis this year he himself acted, and took the blind poet's part; and he will act it many times again, *le congnamh De* – with the help of God.

1902

# West Irish Ballads

It was only a few years ago, when Douglas Hyde published his literal translations of Connacht Love Songs, that I realised that, while I had thought poetry was all but dead in Ireland, the people about me had been keeping up the lyrical tradition that existed in Ireland before Chaucer lived. While I had been looking in the columns of Nationalist newspapers for some word of poetic promise, they had been singing songs of love and sorrow in the language that has been pushed nearer and nearer to the western seaboard – the edge of the world. 'Eyes have we, but we see not; ears have we, but we do not understand.' It does not comfort me to think how many besides myself, having spent a lifetime in Ireland, must make this confession.

The ballads to be gathered now are a very few out of the great mass of traditional poetry that was swept away during the last century in the merciless sweeping away of the Irish tongue, and of all that was bound up with it, by England's will, by Ireland's need, by official pedantry.

To give an idea of the ballads of today, I will not quote from the translations of Douglas Hyde or of Dr Sigerson already published. I will rather give a few of the more homely ballads, sung and composed by the people, and, as far as I know, not hitherto translated.

Those I have heard since I have begun to look for them in the cottages, are, for the most part, sad; but not long ago I heard a girl sing a merry one, in a mocking tone, about a boy on the mountain, who neglected the girls of his village to run after a strange girl from Galway; and the girls of the village were vexed, and they made a song about him; and he went to Galway after her, and there she laughed at him, and said he had never gone to school or to the priest, and she would have nothing to do with him. So then he went back to the village, and asked the smith's daughter to marry him; but she said she would not, and that he might go back to the strange girl from Galway. Another song I have heard was a lament over a boy and girl who had run away to America, and on the way the ship went down. And when they were going down, they began to be sorry they were not married; and to say that if the priest had been at home when they went away, they would have been married; but they hoped that when they were drowned, it would be the same with them as if they were married. And I heard another lament that had been made for three boys that had lately been drowned in Galway Bay. It is the mother who is making it; and she tells how she lost her husband the father of her three boys. And then she married again, and they went to sea and were drowned; and she wouldn't mind about the others so much, but it is the eldest boy, Peter, she is grieving for. And I have heard one song that had a great many verses, and was about 'a poet that is dying, and he confessing his sins'.

The first ballad I give deals with sorrow and defeat and death; for sorrow is never far from song in Ireland; and the names best praised and kept in memory are of those –

> Lonely antagonists of destiny
> That went down scornful under many spears;
> Who soon as we are born are straight our friends,
> And live in simple music, country songs,
> And mournful ballads by the winter fire.

In this simple lament, the type of a great many, only the first name of the young man it was made for is given: 'Fair-haired Donough'. It is likely the people of his own place know still to what family he belonged; but I have not heard it sung, and only know that he was 'some Connachtman that was hanged in Galway'. And it is clear it was for some political crime he was hanged, by the suggestion that if he had been tried nearer his own home, 'in the place he had a right to be', the issue would have been different, and by the allusion to the Gall, the English:

It was bound fast here you saw him, and you wondered to see him,
Our fair-haired Donough, and he after being condemned;
There was a little white cap on him in place of a hat,
And a hempen rope in the place of a neckcloth.

I am after walking here all through the night,
Like a young lamb in a great flock of sheep;

My breast open, my hair loosened out,
And how did I find my brother but stretched before me!

The first place I cried my fill was at the top of the lake;
The second place was at the foot of the gallows;
The third place was at the head of your dead body
Among the Gall, and my own head as if cut in two.

If you were with me in the place you had a right to be,
Down in Sligo or down in Ballinrobe,
It is the gallows would be broken, it is the rope would be cut,
And fair-haired Donough going home by the path.

O fair-haired Donough, it is not the gallows was fit for you;
But to be going to the barn, to be threshing out the straw;
To be turning the plough to the right hand and to the left,
To be putting the red side of the soil uppermost.

O fair-haired Donough, O dear brother,
It is well I know who it was took you away from me;
Drinking from the cup, putting a light to the pipe,
And walking in the dew in the cover of the night.

O Michael Malley, O scourge of misfortune!
My brother was no calf of a vagabond cow;
But a well-shaped boy on a height or a hillside,
To knock a low pleasant sound out of a hurling-stick.

And fair-haired Donough, is not that the pity,
You that would carry well a spur or a boot;
I would put clothes in the fashion on you from cloth that would
    be lasting;
I would send you out like a gentleman's son.

O Michael Malley, may your sons never be in one another's
    company;
May your daughters never ask a marriage portion of you;
The two ends of the table are empty, the house is filled,
And fair-haired Donough, my brother, is stretched out.

There is a marriage portion coming home from Donough,

But it is not cattle nor sheep nor horses;
But tobacco and pipes and white candles,
And it will not be begrudged to them that will use it.

A very pathetic touch is given by the idea of the 'marriage portion', the provision for the wake, being brought home for the dead boy.

But it is chiefly in Aran, and on the opposite Connemara coast, that Irish ballads are still being made as well as sung. The little rock islands of Aran are fit strongholds for the threatened language, breakwaters of Europe, taking as they do the first onset of the ocean 'that hath no limits nearer than America'. The fisher-folk go out in their canvas curraghs[21] to win a living from the Atlantic, or painfully carry loads of sand and seaweed to make the likeness of an earth-plot on the bare rock. The Irish coast seems far away; the setting sun very near. When a sea-fog blots out the mainland for a day, a feeling grows that the island may have slipped anchor, and have drifted into unfamiliar seas. The fisher-folk are not the only dwellers upon the islands; they are the home, the chosen resting-place, of 'the Others', the Fairies, the Fallen Angels, the mighty Sidhe. From here they sweep across the sea, invisible or taking at pleasure the form of a cloud, of a full-rigged ship, of a company of policemen, of a flock of gulls. Sometimes they only play with mortals; sometimes they help them. But often, often, the fatal touch is given to the first-born child, or to the young man in his strength, or the girl in her beauty, or the young mother in her pride; and the call is heard to leave the familiar fireside life for the whirling, vain, unresting life of the irresistible host.

It is, perhaps, because of the very mistiness and dreaminess of their surroundings, the almost unearthly silences, the fantasy of story and of legend that lie about them, that the people of Aran and the Galway coast almost shrink from idealism in their fireside songs, and choose rather to dwell upon the slight incidents of daily life. It is in the songs of the greener plains that the depths of passion and heights of idealism have been reached.

It is at weddings that songs are most in use – even the saddest not being thought out of place; and at the evening gathering in one cottage or another, while the pipe, lighted at the turf-fire, is passed from hand to hand. Here is one that is a great favourite, though very simple, and somewhat rugged in metre; for it touches on the chief events of an islander's life – emigration, loss of life by sea, the land jealousy. It is called 'a sorrowful song that Bridget O'Malley made'; and she tells in it of her troubles at the Boston factory, of her lasting sorrow for her drowned brothers and her as lasting anger against her sister's husband.

'Do you remember, neighbours, the day I left the white strand? I did not find anyone to give me advice, or to tell me not to go. But with the help of God, as I have my health, and the help of the King of Grace, whichever State I will go to, I will never turn back again.

'Do you remember, girls, that day long ago when I was sick, and when the priest said, and the doctor, that with care I would come through? I got up after; I went to work at the factory, until Sullivan wrote a letter that put me down a step.

'And Bab O'Donnell rose up and put a shawl about her. She went to the office till she got work for me to do; there was never a woman I was with that would not shake hands with me; now I am at work again, and no thanks to Sullivan.

'It is a great shame to look down on Ireland, and I think myself it is not right; for the potatoes are growing in the gardens there, and the women milking the cows. That is not the way in Boston, but you may earn it or leave it there; and if the man earns a dollar, the woman will be out drinking it.

'My curse on the curragh, and my blessings on the boats; my curse on that hooker that did the treachery; for it was she snapped away my four brothers from me; the best they were that ever could be found. But what does Kelly care, so long as he himself is in their place?

'My grief on you my brothers that did not come again to land; I would have put a boarded coffin on you out of the hand of the carpenter; the young women of the village would have keened you, and your people and your friends; and is it not Bridget O'Malley you left miserable in the world?

'It is very lonely after Pat and Tom I am, and in great trouble for them, to say nothing of my fair-haired Martin that was drowned long ago; I have no sister, and I have no other brother, no mother; my father weak and bent down; and, O God, what wonder for him!

'My curse on my sister's husband; for it was he made the boat; my own curse again on himself and on his tribe. He married my sister on me, and he sent my brothers to death on me; and he came himself into the farm that belonged to my father and my mother!'

A Connemara schoolmaster tells me: 'At Killery Bay one time, I went into a house where there was an old man that had just lost his son by drowning. And he was sitting over the fire with his head in his hands, making a lament. I remember one verse of it that said: "My curse on the man that made the boat, that he did not tell me there was death lurking in it." I asked afterwards what the meaning of that was, and they said there is a certain board in every boat that the maker gives three blows of his hammer on, after he is done making it. And he knows someway by the sound of the blows if anyone will lose his life in that boat.' It is likely Bridget O'Malley had this idea in her mind when she made her lament.

Another little emigration song, very simple and charming, tells of the return of a brother from America. He finds his pretty brown sister, his 'cailin deas donn', gathering rushes in a field, but she does not know him; and after they have exchanged words of greeting, he asks where her brother is, and she says 'beyond the sea'; then he asks if she would know him again, and she says she would surely; and he asks by what sign, and she tells of a mark on his white neck. When she finds it is her brother who is there and speaking to her, she cries out, 'Kill me on the moment,' meaning that she is ready to die with joy.

This is the lament of a woman whose bridegroom was drowned as he was rowing the priest home, on the wedding day:

'I am widow and maid, and I very young; did you hear my great grief, that my treasure was drowned? If I had been in the boat that day, and my hand on the rope, my word to you, O'Reilly, it is I would have saved you sorrow.

'Do you remember the day the street was full of riders, and of priests and brothers, and all talking of the wedding feast? The fiddle was there in the middle, and the harp answering to it; and twelve mannerly women to bring my love to his bed.

'But you were of those three that went across to Kilcomin, ferrying Father Peter, who was three-and-eighty years old; if you came back within a month itself, I would be well content; but is it not a pity I to be lonely, and my first love in the waves?

'I would not begrudge you, O'Reilly, to be kinsman to a king; white bright courts around you, and you lying at your ease; a quiet, well-learned lady to be settling out your pillow; but it is a great thing you to die from me when I had given you my love entirely.

'It is no wonder a broken heart to be with your father and your mother; the white-breasted mother that crooned you, and you a baby; your wedded wife, O thousand treasures, that never set out your bed; and the day you went to Trabawn, how well it failed you to come home.

'Your eyes are with the eels, and your lips with the crabs; and your two white hands under the sharp rule of the salmon. Five pounds I would give to him that would find my true love. Ochone! it is you are a sharp grief to young Mary ni-Curtain!'

Some men and women who were drowned in the river Corrib, on their way to a fair at Galway, in the year 1820, have still their names kept green in a ballad:

'Mary Ruane, that you would stand in a fair to look at, the best-dressed woman in the place; John Cosgrave, the best a woman ever reared; your mother thought that if a hundred were drowned, your swimming would take the sway; but the boat went down, and when I got up early on Friday, I heard the keening and the clapping of women's hands, with the women that were drowsy and tired after the night there, without doing anything but laying out the dead.'

There are laments for other things besides death. A man taken up 'not for sheep-stealing or any crime, but just for making a drop of *poteen*',[22] tells of his hardships in Galway gaol. A lover who has enlisted because he cannot get the girl he loves – 'a pity I not be going to Galway with my heart's love on my arm' – tells of his hardships in the army: 'The first day I enlisted I was well pleased and satisfied; the second day I was vexed and tormented;

and the third day I would have given a pound if I had it to get my pardon.' And I have heard a song 'made by a woman out of her wits, that lost her husband and married again, and her three sons enlisted', who cannot forgive herself for having driven them from home. 'If it was in Ballinakill I had your bones, I would not be half so much tormented after you; but you to be standing in the army of the Gall, and getting nothing after it but the bit in your mouth.'

Here is a song of daily life, in which a girl laments the wandering and covetous appetite of her cow:

> 'It is following after the white cow I spent last night; and, indeed, all I got by it was the bones of an old goose. Do you hear me, Michael Taylor? Give word to your uncle John that, unless he can lay his hand on her, Nancy will lose her wits.
>
> 'It's what she is wanting, is the three islands of Aran for herself; Brisberg, that is in Maimen, and the glens of Maam Cross; all round about Oughterard, and the hills that are below it; John Blake's farm where she often does be bellowing; and as far as Ballinamuca, where the long grass is growing; and it's in the wood of Barna she'd want to spend her life.
>
> 'And when I was sore with walking through the dark hours of the night, it's the coastguard came crying after her, and he maybe with a bit of her in his mouth.'

The little sarcastic hit at the coastguard, who may himself have stolen the cow he joins in the search for, is characteristic of Aran humour. The comic song, as we know it, is unknown on the islands; the nearest to it I have heard there is about the awkward meeting of two suitors, a carpenter and a country lad, at their sweetheart's house, and of the clever management of her mother, who promised to give her to the one who sang the best song, and how the country lad won her.

Douglas Hyde, who is almost a folk-poet, the people have taken so many of his songs to their heart, has caught this sarcastic touch in his 'love' song:

> '"O sweet queen, to whom I gave my love; O dear queen, the flower of fine women; listen to my keening, and look on my case; as you are the woman I desire, free me from death."

'He speaks so humbly, humble entirely. Without mercy or pity she looks on him with contempt. She puts mispleading in her cold answer; there is a drop of poison in every quiet word:

'"O man, wanting sense, put from you your share of love; it is bold you are entirely to say such a thing as that; you will not get hate from me; you will not get love from me; you will not get anything at all, good or bad, for ever."

'I was myself the same night at the house of drink; and I saw the man, and he under the table. Laid down by the strength of wine, and without a twist in him itself; it was she did that much with the talk of her mouth.'

There is another that I thought was meant to provoke laughter, the lament of a girl for her 'beautiful comb' that had been carried off by her lover, whom she had refused to marry, 'until we take a little more out of our youth', and invites instead to 'come with me to Eochaill reaping the yellow harvest.' Then he steals the comb, and the mother gives her wise advice how to get it back:

'He will go this road tomorrow, and let you welcome him; settle down a wooden chair in the middle of the house; snatch the hat from him, and do not give him any ease until you get back the beautiful comb that was high on the back of your head.'

But an Aran man has told me: 'No, this is a very serious song; it was meant to praise the girl, and to tell what a loss she had in the comb.'

I am told that the song that makes most mirth in Aran is 'The Carrageen'; the day-dream of an old woman, too old to carry out her purpose, of all she will buy when she has gathered a harvest of the Carrageen moss, used by invalids:

'If I had two oars and a little boat of my own, I would go pulling the Carrageen; I would dry it up in the sun; I would bring a load of it to Galway; it would go away in the train, to pay the rent to Robinson, and what is over would be my own.

'It is long I am hearing talk of the Carrageen, and I never knew what it was. If I spent the last spring-tide at it, and I to take care of myself, I would buy a gown and a long cloak and a wide little shawl; that, and a dress cap, with frills on every side like feathers.'

'(This is what the Calleac[23] said, that was over a hundred years old:)

'"I lost the last spring-tide with it, and I went into sharp danger. I did not know what the Carrageen was, or anything at all like it; but I will have tobacco from this out, if I lose the half of my fingers!"'

This is a little song addressed by a fisherman to his little boat, his curragh-cin:

'There goes my curragh-cin, it is she will get the prize; she will be tonight in America, and back again with the tide . . .

'I put pins of oak in her, and oars of red pine; and I made her ready for sailing; for she is the six-oared curragh-cin that never gave heed to the storm; and it is she will be coming to land, when the sailing boats will be lost.

'There was a man came from England to buy my little boat from me; he offered me twenty guineas for her; there were many looking on. If he would offer me as much again, and a guinea over and above, he would not get my curragh-cin till she goes out and kills the shark.'

For a shark will sometimes flounder into the fishing-nets and tear his way out; and even a whale is sometimes seen. I remember an Aran man beginning some story he was telling me with: 'I was going down that path one time, with the priest and a few others; for a whale had come ashore, and the jawbones of it were wanted, to make the piers of a gate.'

As for the love-songs of our coast and island people, they seem to be for the most part a little artificial in method, a little strained in metaphor, perhaps so giving rise to the Scotch Gaelic saying: 'as loveless as an Irishman'. Love of country, *tirgradh*, is I think the real passion; and bound up with it are love of home, of family, love of God. Constancy and affection in marriage are the rule; yet marriage 'for love' is all but unknown; marriage is a matter of commonsense arrangement between the heads of famil- ies. As Mr Yeats puts it, the countryman's 'dream has never been entangled by reality'. However this may be, my Aran friends tell me: 'The people do not care for love-songs; they would rather have any others.'

Yet I have just seen some love-songs, taken down the other day by a Kinvara man from a Connemara man, that have some charming lines:

> 'Going over the hills after parting from the store of my heart, there is a mist on them and the darkness of night.'
>
> 'It is my sharp grief, my thousand treasures, my road not to be to the door of your house; it is with you I wore out my shoes from the beginning of my youth until now.'
>
> 'It is not sorry I would be if there was the length of a year in the day, and the leaves of the trees dropping honey; I myself on the side where the blossoms are falling, my love beside me, and a little green branch in her hand.'
>
> 'She goes by me like a little breeze of the wind.'

And this line that in a country of separations is already, they tell me, 'passing into a proverb':

> 'It is far from one another our rising is every day.'

But the tradition of classical allusions, brought in some centuries ago, joined to the exaggeration that has been the breath of Irish poets, from the time Naoise called Deirdre 'a woman brighter than the sun', has brought monotony into most of the love-songs.

The ideal country girl, with her dew-grey eye and long amber hair, is always likened to Venus, to Juno, to Deirdre. 'I think she is nine times nicer than Deirdre,' says Raftery, 'or I may say Helen, the affliction of the Greeks'; and he writes of another country girl, that she is 'beyond Venus, in spite of all Homer wrote on her appearance, and Cassandra also, and Io that bewitched Mars; beyond Minerva, and Juno, the king's wife'; and he wishes 'they might be brought face to face with her, that they might be confused':

> 'She comes to me like a star through the mist; her hair is golden and goes down to her shoes; her breast is the colour of white sugar, or like bleached bone on the card-table; her neck is whiter than the froth of the flood, or the swan coming from swimming . . . If France and Spain belonged to me, I'd give it up to be along with you.'

And he gives 'a thousand praises to God, that I didn't lose my wits on account of her'. Raftery puts distinction into each one of his songs; but when lesser poets, echoing the voices of so many generations, bring in the same goddesses, and the same exaggerations, and the same amber hair, monotony brings weariness at last.

There is an Aran song, 'Brigid na Casad', that has more originality than is usual:

'Brigid's kiss was sweeter than the whole of the waters of Lough Erne; or the first wheaten flour, worked with fresh honey into dough; there are streams of bees' honey on every part of the mountain, there is brown sugar thrown on all you take, Brigid, in your hand.

'It is not more likely for water to change than for the mind of a woman; and is it not a young man without courage will not run the chance nine times? It's not nicer than you the swan is when he comes to the shore swimming; it's not nicer than you the thrush is, and he singing from tree to tree.'

And here is another, homely in the extreme in the beginning, and suddenly rising to wild exaggeration:

'Late on the evening of last Monday, and it raining, I chanced to come into Seagan's and I sat down. It is there I saw her near me in the corner of the hearth; and her laugh was better to me than to have her eyes down; her hair was shining like the wool of a sheep, and brighter than the swan swimming. It is then I asked who owned her, and it is with Frank Conneely she was.

'It is a good house belongs to Frank Conneely, the people say that do be going to it; plenty of whiskey and punch going round, and food without stint for a man to get; and it is what I think the girl is learned, for she has knowledge of books and of the pen, and a schoolmaster coming to teach her every day.

'The troop is on the sea, sailing eternally, and looking always, always on my Nora Ban. Is it not a great sin, she to be on a bare mountain, and not to be dressed in white silk, and the King of the French coming to the island for her, from France or from Germany?

'Is it not nice the jewel looked at the races and at the church in Barna? She took the sway there as far as the big town. Is she not the nice flower with the white breast, the comeliness of a woman? and the sun of summer pleased with her, shining on her at every side, and hundreds of men in love with her.

'It is I would like to run through the hills with her, and to go the roads with her; and it is I would put a cloak around my Nora Ban.'

The very *naïveté*, the simplicity of these ballads, made one feel that the peasants who make and sing them may be trembling on the edge of a great discovery; and that some day – perhaps very soon – one born among them will put their half-articulate, eternal sorrows and laments and yearnings into words that will be their expression for ever, as was done for the Hebrew people when the sorrow of exile was put into the hundred and thirty-seventh Psalm, and the sorrow of death into the lament for Saul and Jonathan, and the yearning of love into what was once known as 'the ballad of ballads', the Song of Solomon.

I have one ballad at least to give, that shows, even in my prose translation, how near that day may be, if the language that holds the soul of our West Irish people can be saved from the 'West Briton'[24] destroyer. There are some verses in it that attain to the intensity of great poetry, though I think less by the creation of one than by the selection of many minds; the peasants who have sung or recited their songs from one generation to another, having instinctively sifted away by degrees what was trivial, and kept only what was real, for it is in this way the foundations of literature are laid. I first heard of this ballad from the South; but when I showed it to an Aran man, he said it was well known there, and that his mother had often sung it to him when he was a child. It is called 'The Grief of a Girl's Heart':

'O Donall og,[25] if you go across the sea, bring myself with you and do not forget it; and you will have a sweetheart for fair days and market days, and the daughter of the King of Greece beside you at night.

'It is late last night the dog was speaking of you; the snipe was speaking of you in her deep marsh. It is you are the lonely bird through the woods; and that you may be without a mate until you find me.

'You promised me, and you said a lie to me, that you would be before me where the sheep are flocked; I gave a whistle and three hundred cries to you, and I found nothing there but a bleating lamb.

'You promised me a thing that was hard for you, a ship of gold under a silver mast; twelve towns with a market in all of them, and a fine white court by the side of the sea.

'You promised me a thing that is not possible, that you would give me gloves of the skin of a fish; that you would give me shoes of the skin of a bird; and a suit of the dearest silk in Ireland.

'O Donall og, it is I would be better to you than a high, proud, spendthrift lady: I would milk the cow; I would bring help to you; and if you were hard pressed, I would strike a blow for you.

'O, ochone, and it's not with hunger or with wanting food, or drink, or sleep, that I am growing thin, and my life is shortened; but it is the love of a young man has withered me away.

'It is early in the morning that I saw him coming, going along the road on the back of a horse; he did not come to me; he made nothing of me; and it is on my way home that I cried my fill.

'When I go by myself to the Well of Loneliness, I sit down and I go through my trouble; when I see the world and do not see my boy, he that has an amber shade in his hair.

'It was on that Sunday I gave my love to you; the Sunday that is last before Easter Sunday. And myself on my knees reading the Passion; and my two eyes giving love to you for ever.

'O, aya! my mother, give myself to him; and give him all that you have in the world; get out yourself to ask for alms, and do not come back and forward looking for me.

'My mother said to me not to be talking with you today, or tomorrow, or on the Sunday; it was a bad time she took for telling me that; it was shutting the door after the house was robbed.

'My heart is as black as the blackness of the sloe, or as the black coal that is on the smith's forge; or as the sole of a shoe left in white halls; it was you put that darkness over my life.

'You have taken the east from me; you have taken the west from me; you have taken what is before me and what is behind me; you have taken the moon, you have taken the sun from me; and my fear is great that you have taken God from me!'

1901

# from *A Book of Saints and Wonders*

## from 'Brigit, the Mother of the Gael'

### BRIGIT HELPS THE MOTHER OF GOD

There was a poor man, and a poor woman, living in an ancient place in Ireland, a sort of a wilderness. The man used to be wishing for a son that would be a help to him with the work, but the woman used to say nothing, because she was good. They had a baby at last, but it was a girl, and the man was sorry and he said, 'We will always be poor now.' But the woman said, for it was showed to her at that time, 'This child will be the Mother of God.' The girl grew up in that ancient place, and one day she was sitting at the door, and our Saviour sent One to her that said, 'Would you wish to be the Mother of God?' 'I would wish it,' said she. And on the minute, as she said that, the Saviour went into her as a child. The Messenger took her with him then, and he put beautiful clothing on her, and she turned to be so beautiful that all the people followed them, crowding to see the two beautiful people that were passing by. They met then with Brigit, and the Mother of God said to her, 'What can we do to make these crowds leave following us?' 'I will do that for you,' said Brigit, 'for I will show them a greater wonder.' She went into a house then and brought out a harrow and held it up over her head, and every one of the pins gave out a flame like a candle; and all the people turned back to look at the shining harrow that was such a great wonder. And it is because of that the harrow is blessed since that time. The Mother of God asked her then what would she do for her as a reward. 'Put my day before your own day,' said Brigit. So she did that, and Saint Brigit's day is kept before her own day ever since. And there are some say Brigit fostered the Holy Child, and kept an account of every drop of blood he lost through his lifetime, and anyway she was always going about with the Mother of God.

144

## THE FIRST OF FEBRUARY

And from that time to this the housekeepers have a rhyme to say on Saint Brigit's day, bidding them to bring out a firkin of butter and to divide it among the working boys. For she was good always, and it was her desire to feed the poor, to do away with every hardship, to be gentle to every misery. And it is on her day the first of the birds begin to make their nests, and the blessed Crosses are made with straw and are put up in the thatch; for the death of the year is done with and the birthday of the year is come. And it is what the Gael of Scotland say in a verse:

'Brigit put her finger in the river on the feast day of Brigit, and away went the hatching-mother of the cold.

'She washed the palms of her hands in the river on the day of the feast of Patrick, and away went the birth-mother of the cold.'

## HER CARE FOR LEINSTER

On the day of the battle of Almhuin, Brigit was seen over the men of Leinster, and Columcille was seen over the Ua Neill; and it was the men of Leinster won that battle. And a long time after that again, when Strongbow[1] that had brought great trouble into Ireland and that was promised the kingdom of Leinster was near his end, he cried out from his bed that he saw Brigit of the Gael, and that it was she herself was bringing him to his death.

## SHE REMEMBERS THE POOR

But if Brigit belonged to the east, it is not in the west she is forgotten, and the people of Burren and of Corcomruadh and Kinvara go every year to her blessed well that is near the sea, praying and remembering her. And in that well there is a little fish that is seen every seven years, and whoever sees that fish is cured of every disease. And there is a woman living yet that is poor and old and that saw that blessed fish, and this is the way she tells the story: 'I had a pearl in my eye one time, and I went to Saint Brigit's well on the cliffs. Scores of people there were in it, looking for cures, and some got them and some did not get them. And I went down the four steps to the well and I was looking into it, and I saw a little fish no longer than your finger coming from a stone under the water. Three spots it had on the one side and three on the other side, red spots and a little green with the red, and it was very civil coming hither to me and very pleasant wagging its tail. And it stopped and looked up at me and gave three wags of its back, and walked off again and went in under the stone.

'And I said to a woman that was near me that I saw the little fish, and she began to call out and to say there were many coming with cars and with horses for a month past and none of them saw it at all. And she proved me, asking had it spots, and I said it had, three on the one side and three on the other side. "That is it," she said. And within three days I had the sight of my eye again. It was surely Saint Brigit I saw that time; who else would it be? And you would know by the look of it that it was no common fish. Very civil it was, and nice and loughy, and no one else saw it at all. Did I say more prayers than the rest? Not a prayer. I was young in those days. I suppose she took a liking to me, maybe because of my name being Brigit the same as her own.'

## from 'Blessed Patrick of the Bells'

### PATRICK AND CASCORACH THE MUSICIAN

One time the King of Ulster went up with Caoilte to a great liss[2] that was called Foradh-na-Feinne, the Resting-place of the Fianna. And when they were there they saw coming towards them a young man that was wearing a beautiful green cloak having in it a silver brooch; a shirt of yellow silk next his skin he had; a coat of soft satin, and a harp from his neck. 'Where do you come from and who are you yourself?' said the King. 'I come from the South from the Hill of Bodb Dearg son of the

Dagda,' said he; 'and I am Cascorach, son of Cainchen that is poet to the Tuatha de Danaan and I am the makings of a poet myself. And it is what I am come for now,' he said, 'to get true knowledge and the stories of the Fianna and their great deeds from Caoilte son of Ronan.' With that he took his harp and made music for them till he had put them all into their sleep. 'Well Caoilte my soul,' he said then, 'what answer will you give me?' 'I will give you all you are asking,' said Caoilte, 'if you have skill and understanding to learn all the Fianna did of arms and of bravery. And it was a great fighting-man used to be in this place,' he said, 'that was Finn, son of Cumhal, and it is great riches and great wages you would have got from him for your music; although this day the place is empty.' And he made this lament:

'The Resting-place of the Fianna is bare tonight where Finn of the naked sword used to be; through the death of the king that was without gloom, wide Almhuin is deserted;

'The high company are not living; Finn the very prince is not alive; no armies to be seen, no captains with the King of the Fianna.

'They are all gone, the people of Finn, they that used to be going from valley to valley; it is a pity the life I have now, to be left after Diarmuid and Conan, after Goll son of Morna from the plain.

'It is the truth I am telling you; all that I say is true; it is great our losses were there beyond. They are gone, the armies and the hundreds; it is a pity I myself not to have found death; they are all gone now; they used to be together from border to border.'

Then Caoilte brought to mind the loss of the heroes and of the great companies he used to be going among, and he cried miserably, sorrowfully, till all his breast was wet with him. He set out after that and Cascorach with him and they went up by hills and rocks to the top of green-grassed Slieve Fuad, to the rowan tree of the Meadow of the Two Stags and to the place where the men of Ulster left their chariots after the last battle of the War for the Bull of Cuailgne. And Patrick was there before him, having with him three times fifty bishops and three times fifty priests and three times fifty deacons and three times fifty singers of psalms. And they sat down there, and Patrick kept his Hours with praising the Maker of the world. Then he gave a welcome to Caoilte. 'Well, my soul,' he said, 'who is that well-looking dark-eyebrowed curly-headed young man that is with you, having a harp with him?' 'He is Cascorach son of the musician of the Tuatha De Danaan, that is come to find news and knowledge of the Fianna from me.' 'It is a good road he has chosen,' said Patrick. 'And O Caoilte,' he said, 'it is great good you yourself have waited for, the time of belief and of saints and of holiness, and to be in friendship with the King of Heaven and earth. And play to us now Cascorach,' he said, 'till we hear your music and your skill.' 'I will do that,' said Cascorach; 'and I never was better pleased, holy Clerk, to do it for any man than for yourself.' He took his harp then and readied it, and played a strain of music, and the clerks had never heard the like of that music for sweetness, unless it might be the praises of the King of Heaven sung according to the Rule. And they all fell into their sleep listening to the continuous music of the Sidhe. And when Cascorach had made an end of playing, he asked a reward of Patrick. 'What reward are you asking, my soul?' said Patrick. 'Heaven for myself,' said he, 'for that is the reward is best; and good luck to go with my art and with all that will follow it after me.' 'I give you heaven,' said Patrick, 'and I give this to your art, it to be one of the three arts by which a man can find profit to the last in Ireland. And however great the grudgingness a man of your art may meet with, let him but make his music, and no one will begrudge him anything. And that they may have all happiness,' he said, 'so long as they are not slothful in their trade.' After that Cascorach put back his harp in its covering. 'That was good music you gave us,' said Brogan the scribe. 'It was good indeed,' said Patrick; 'and but for a taste of the music of the Sidhe that was in it I never heard anything nearer to the music of heaven.' 'If there is music in heaven why should it not be on earth?' said Brogan. 'And so it is not right to banish it away.' 'I do not say we should banish it,' said Patrick, 'but only that we should not hold to it out of measure.'

## from 'Great Wonders of the Olden Time'

### THE OLD WOMAN OF BEARE

Digdi was the name of the Old Woman of Beare. It is of Corca Dubhne she was and she had her youth seven times over, and every man that had lived with her died of old age, and her grandsons and great-grandsons were tribes and races. And through a hundred years she wore upon her head the veil Cuimire had blessed. Then age and weakness came upon her and it is what she said:

'Ebb-tide to me as to the sea; old age brings me reproach; I used to wear a shift that was always new; today I have not even a cast one.

'It is riches you are loving, it is not men; it was men we loved in the time we were living.

'There were dear men on whose plains we used to be driving; it is good the time we passed with them; it is little we were broken afterwards.

'When my arms are seen it is long and thin they are; once they used to be fondling, they used to be around great kings.

'The young girls give a welcome to Beltaine[3] when it comes to them; sorrow is more fitting for me, an old pitiful hag.

'I have no pleasant talk; no sheep are killed for my wedding; it is little but my hair is grey; it is many colours I had over it when I used to be drinking good ale.

'I have no envy against the old, but only against women; I myself am spent with old age, while women's heads are still yellow.

'The stone of the kings on Feman; the chair of Ronan in Bregia; it is long since storms have wrecked them, they are old mouldering gravestones.

'The wave of the great sea is speaking; the winter is striking us with it; I do not look to welcome today Fermuid son of Mugh.

'I know what they are doing; they are rowing through the reeds of the ford of Alma; it is cold is the place where they sleep.

'The summer of youth where we were has been spent along with its harvest; winter age that drowns everyone, its beginning has come upon me.

'It is beautiful was my green cloak, my king liked to see it on me; it is noble was the man that stirred it; he put wool on it when it was bare.

'Amen, great is the pity, every acorn has to drop. After feasting with shining candles, to be in the darkness of a prayer-house.

'I was once living with kings, drinking mead and wine; today I am drinking whey-water among withered old women.

'There are three floods that come up to the dun[4] of Ard-Ruide: a flood of fighting-men, a flood of horses, a flood of the hounds of Lugaidh's Son.[5]

'The flood-wave and the two swift ebb-tides; what the flood-wave brings you in, the ebb-wave sweeps out of your hand.

'The flood-wave and the second ebb-tide; they have all come as far as me, the way that I know them well.

'The flood-tide will not reach to the silence of my kitchen; though many are my company in the darkness, a hand has been laid upon them all.

'My flood-tide! It is well I have kept my knowledge. It is Jesus Son of Mary keeps me happy at the ebb-tide.

'It is far is the island of the great sea where the flood reaches after the ebb; I do not look for flood to reach to me after the ebb-tide.

'There is hardly a little place I can know again when I see it; what used to be on the flood-tide is all on the ebb today!'

# from *The Kiltartan Poetry Book*

## Raftery's Praise of Mary Hynes

Going to Mass by the will of God, the day came wet and the wind rose; I met Mary Hynes at the cross of Kiltartan, and I fell in love with her there and then.

I spoke to her kind and mannerly, as by report was her own way; and she said, 'Raftery my mind is easy; you may come today to Ballylee.'

When I heard her offer I did not linger; when her talk went to my heart my heart rose. We had only to go across the three fields; we had daylight with us to Ballylee.

The table was laid with glasses and a quart measure; she had fair hair and she sitting beside me; and she said, 'Drink, Raftery, and a hundred welcomes; there is a strong cellar in Ballylee.'

O star of light and O sun in harvest; O amber hair, O my share of the world! Will you come with me on the Sunday, till we agree together before all the people?

I would not begrudge you a song every Sunday evening; punch on the table or wine if you would drink it. But O King of Glory, dry the roads before me till I find the way to Ballylee.

There is sweet air on the side of the hill, when you are looking down upon Ballylee; when you are walking in the valley picking nuts and blackberries, there is music of the birds in it and music of the Sidhe.

What is the worth of greatness till you have the light of the flower of the branch that is by your side? There is no good to deny it or to try and hide it; she is the sun in the heavens who wounded my heart.

There was no part in Ireland I did not travel, from the rivers to the tops of the mountains; to the edge of Lough Greine whose mouth is hidden, and I saw no beauty but was behind hers.

Her hair was shining and her brows were shining too; her face was like herself, her mouth pleasant and sweet; She is the pride and I give her the branch; she is the shining flower of Ballylee.

It is Mary Hynes, the calm and easy woman, has beauty in her mind and in her face. If a hundred clerks were gathered together they could not write down a half of her ways.

## His Praise of the Little Hill and the Plains of Mayo

After the Christmas, with the help of Christ, I will never stop if I am alive; I will go to the sharp-edged little hill; for it is a fine place without fog falling; a blessed place that the sun shines on, and the wind doesn't rise there or anything of the sort.

And if you were a year there you would get no rest, only sitting up at night and forever drinking.

The lamb and the sheep are there; the cow and the calf are there, fine lands are there without heath and without bog. Ploughing and seeding in the right month, plough and harrow prepared and ready; the rent that is called for there, they have means to pay it. There is oats and flax and large-eared barley. There are beautiful valleys with good growth in them and hay. Rods grow there, and bushes and tufts, white fields are there and respect for trees; shade and shelter from wind and rain; priests and friars reading their book; spending and getting is there, and nothing scarce.

I leave it in my will that my heart rises as the wind rises, and as the fog scatters, when I think upon Carra and the two towns below it, on the two-mile bush and on the plains of Mayo. And if I were standing in the middle of my people, age would go from me and I would be young again.

## His Answer When Some Stranger Asked Who He Was

I am Raftery the poet, full of hope and love; my eyes without light, my gentleness without misery. Going west on my journey with the light of my heart; weak and tired to the end of my road.

I am now, and my back to a wall, playing music to empty pockets.

## A Blessing on Patrick Sarsfield[1]

O Patrick Sarsfield, health be to you, since you went to France and your camps were loosened; making your sighs along with the king, and you left poor Ireland and the Gael defeated – Och ochone! O Patrick Sarsfield, it is a man with God you are; and blessed is the earth you ever walked on. The blessing of the bright sun and the moon upon you, since you took the day from the hands of King William – Och ochone!

O Patrick Sarsfield, the prayer of every person with you; my own prayer and the prayer of the Son of Mary with you, since you took the narrow ford going through Biorra, and since at Cuilenn O'Cuanac you won Limerick – Och ochone!

I will go up on the mountain alone; and I will come hither from it again. It is there I saw the camp of the Gael, the poor troop thinned, not keeping with one another – Och ochone!

My five hundred healths to you, halls of Limerick, and to the beautiful troop was in our company; it is bonfires we used to have and playing-cards, and the word of God was often with us – Och ochone!

There were many soldiers glad and happy, that were going the way through seven weeks; but now they are stretched down in Aughrim – Och ochone!

They put the first breaking on us at the bridge of the Boyne; the second breaking on the bridge of Slaine; the third breaking in Aughrim of O'Kelly; and O sweet Ireland, my five hundred healths to you – Och ochone!

O'Kelly has manuring for his land, that is not sand or dung, but ready soldiers doing bravery with pikes, that were left in Aughrim stretched in ridges – Och ochone!

Who is that beyond on the hill, Ben Edair? I a poor soldier with King James. I was last year in arms and in dress, but this year I am asking alms – Och ochone!

## An Aran Maid's Wedding

I am widow and maid, and I very young; did you hear my great grief, that my treasure was drowned? If I had been in the boat that day, and my hand on the rope, my word to you, O'Reilly, it is I would have saved you sorrow.

Do you remember the day the street was full of riders, and of priests and brothers, and all talking of the wedding feast? The fiddle was there in the middle, and the harp answering to it; and twelve mannerly women to bring my love to his bed.

But you were of those three that went across to Kilcomin, ferrying Father Peter, who was three-and-eighty years old; if you came back within a month itself, I would be well content; but is it not a pity I to be lonely, and my first love in the waves?

I would not begrudge you, O'Reilly, to be kinsman to a king; white bright courts around you, and you lying at your ease; a quiet, well-learned lady to be settling out your pillow; but it is a great thing you to die from me when I had given you my love entirely.

It is no wonder a broken heart to be with your father and your mother; the white-breasted mother that crooned you, and you a baby; your wedded wife, O thousand treasures, that never set out your bed; and the day you went to Trabawn, how well it failed you to come home.

Your eyes are with the eels, and your lips with the crabs; and your two white hands under the sharp rule of the salmon. Five pounds I would give to him that would find my true love. Ochone! it is you are a sharp grief to young Mary ni-Curtain!


## A Poem Written in Time of Trouble by an Irish Priest Who Had Taken Orders in France

My thoughts, my grief! are without strength
My spirit is journeying towards death

My eyes are as a frozen sea
My tears my daily food;
There is nothing in life but only misery.
My poor heart is torn
And my thoughts are sharp wounds within me,
Mourning the miserable state of Ireland.

Misfortune has come upon us all together
The poor, the rich, the weak and the strong
The great lord by whom hundreds were maintained
The powerful strong man, and the man that holds the plough;
And the cross laid on the bare shoulder of every man.

Our feasts are without any voice of priests
And none at them but women lamenting
Tearing their hair with troubled minds
Keening miserably after the Fenians.

The pipes of our organs are broken
Our harps have lost their strings that were tuned
That might have made the great lamentations of Ireland.
Until the strong men come back across the sea
There is no help for us but bitter crying,
Screams, and beating of hands, and calling out.

I do not know of anything under the sky
That is friendly or favourable to the Gael
But only the sea that our need brings us to,
Or the wind that blows to the harbour
The ship that is bearing us away from Ireland;
And there is reason that these are reconciled with us,
For we increase the sea with our tears
And the wandering wind with our sighs.


## The Heart of the Wood

My hope and my love, we will go for a while into the wood,
scattering the dew, where we will see the trout, we will see the

blackbird on its nest; the deer and the buck calling, the little bird that is sweetest singing on the branches; the cuckoo on the top of the fresh green; and death will never come near us for ever in the sweet wood.

## Her Lament for His Death

Then when Grania was certain of Diarmuid's death she gave out a long very pitiful cry that was heard through the whole place, and her women and her people came to her, and asked what ailed her to give a cry like that. And she told them how Diarmuid had come to his death by the Boar of Beinn Gulbain in the hunt Finn had made. When her people heard that, they gave three great heavy cries in the same way, that were heard in the clouds and the waste places of the sky. And then Grania bade the five hundred that she had for household to go to Beinn Gulbain for the body of Diarmuid, and when they were bringing it back, she went out to meet them, and they put down the body of Diarmuid, and it is what she said: I am your wife, beautiful Diarmuid, the man I would do no hurt to; it is sorrowful I am after you tonight.

I am looking at the hawk and the hound my secret love used to be hunting with; she that loved the three, let her be put in the grave with Diarmuid.

Let us be glad tonight, let us make all welcome tonight, let us be open-handed tonight, since we are sitting by the body of a king.

And O Diarmuid, she said, it is a hard bed Finn has given you, to be lying on the stones and to be wet with the rain. Ochone! she said, your blue eyes to be without sight, you that were friendly and generous and pursuing. O love! O Diarmuid! it is a pity it is he sent you to your death.

You were a champion of the men of Ireland, their prop in the middle of the fight; you were the head of every battle; your ways were glad and pleasant.

It is sorrowful I am, without mirth, without light, but only sadness and grief and long dying; your harp used to be sweet to me, it wakened my heart to gladness. Now my courage is fallen down, I not to hear you but to be always remembering your ways. Och! my grief is going through me.

A thousand curses on the day when Grania gave you her love, that put Finn of the princes from his wits; it is a sorrowful story your death is today.

You were the man was best of the Fenians, beautiful Diarmuid, that women loved. It is dark your dwelling-place is under the sod, it is mournful and cold your bed is; it is pleasant your laugh was today; you were my happiness, Diarmuid.

# from *The Kiltartan History Book*

## Usheen[1] in Tir-Nan-Oge

Usheen was the last of the Fianna and the greatest of them. It's he was brought away to Tir-Nan-Oge, that place where you'd stop for a thousand years and be as young as the first day you went. Out hunting they were, and there was a deer came before them very often, and they would follow it with the hounds, and it would always make for the sea, and there was a rock a little way out in the water, and it would leap on to that, and they wouldn't follow it. So one day they were going to hunt, they put Usheen out on the rock first, the way he could catch a hold of the deer and be there before it. So they found it and followed it, and when it jumped on to the rock Usheen got a hold of it. But it went down into the sea and brought him with it to some enchanted place underground that was called Tir-Nan-Oge, and there he stopped a very long time, but he thought it was only a few days he was in it. It is in that direction, to the west he was brought, and it was to the Clare coast he came back. And in that place you wouldn't feel the time passing, and he saw the beauty of heaven and kept his youth there a thousand years. It is a fine place, and everything that is good is in it. And if anyone is sent there with a message he will want to stop in it, and twenty years of it will seem to him like one half-hour. But as to where Tir-Nan-Oge is, it is in every place, all about us.

## His Return to Ireland

Well, when he thought he had been a twelvemonth there, he began to wish to see the strong men again, his brothers; and he asked whoever was in authority in that place to give him a horse and to let him go. And they told him his brothers were all dead, but he wouldn't believe it. So they gave him a horse, but they bade him not to get off it or to touch the ground while he would be away; and they put him back in his own country. And when he went back to his old place, there was nothing left of the houses but broken walls, and they covered with moss; and all his friends and brothers were dead, with the length of time that had passed. And where his own home used to be he saw the stone trough standing that used to be full of water, and where they used to be putting their hands in and washing themselves. And when he saw it he had such a wish and such a feeling for it that he forgot what he was told and got off the horse. And in a minute it was as if all the years came on him, and he was lying there on the ground, a very old man and all his strength gone.

## Usheen and Patrick

It was before the Flood those strong men lived here, Finn and Usheen and others; and they lived longer than people do now, three or four hundred years. Usheen lived the longest of all, because of all those years he was away in a trance. He was saved after that by Saint Patrick. But all the others are said to be in hell because they cared nothing about God. For if one of us has a field of oats or of barley ripening in the sun we'll say, 'Thanks be to God.' But if they had a field of oats or of barley ripening, they'd be thankful to one another or to themselves, for they thought themselves to be as much as God. Did he have much trouble to convert him? Not at all; he was as blind as that floor.

## The Arguments

It was after Usheen fell from his horse, Saint Patrick began to instruct and to convert him. And he asked where all his companions were, and Goll the champion of Ireland. And it is what Saint Patrick said that God had them all shut up in hell with the devil. And Usheen said, 'If I could see them I would draw them out of that, and the devil with them and his whole forge.' And Saint Patrick told him about Adam and Eve and how they were turned out and lost for eating the forbidden fruit, an apple he called it. And Usheen said, 'Although God has all my friends shut up in hell, if I knew fruit was so scarce with him, and he to think so much of it, I'd have sent him seven cartloads of it.' It was very decent of Usheen to say that; he always had a very decent name for those sort of things. And Usheen said another thing to Patrick. He said, 'Don't the blackbird and the thrush whistle very well, and don't they make their nests very nice, and they never got any instruction or teaching from God?' And what Saint Patrick answered to that I don't know. It was not long after that Saint Patrick got him converted, and as soon as he converted him he was in such a hurry not to lose a minute but to baptise him at once, that he struck down his spear on his foot without seeing it, and pinned him by the instep to the ground. And when he saw a stream of blood coming from the instep he said, 'Why did you make no sign when the spear struck you?' And Usheen said, 'I thought it was part of the rite of baptism. And I wouldn't begrudge a little drop of blood to God Almighty.' He died soon after that and was saved, because he showed such patience. But all his friends are in hell; but when they lived angels used to come sometimes to see them and to talk with them; they were so nice and so respectable.

## Elizabeth

Queen Elizabeth was awful. She was a very lustful woman. Beyond everything she was. When she came to the turn she dyed her hair red, and whatever man she had to do with, she sent him to the block in the morning, that he would be able to tell nothing. She had an awful temper. She would throw a knife from the table at the waiting ladies, and if anything vexed her she would maybe work upon the floor. A thousand dresses she left after her. Very superstitious she was. Sure after her death they found a card, the ace of hearts, nailed to her chair under the seat. She thought she would never die while she had it there. And she bought a bracelet from an old woman out in Wales that was over a hundred years. It was superstition made her do that, and they found it after her death tied about her neck.

## Emmet's Dress

It was a pity to hang so fine a man. I was looking at his picture a while ago, and his dress, very nice, knee breeches and a collar turned over, they dressed very nice in those days. But now you'll see a man having a thing stiff the same as a washboard in front of him, and one button in it, and you wouldn't know has he a soutane under it or anything at all. It is likely the linen Emmet was wearing was made at home, for I remember the days when every house had flax sowed in the garden.

## The Tinker

O'Connell[2] was a great man. I never saw him, but I heard of his name. One time I saw his picture in a paper, where they were giving out meal, where Mrs Gaynor's is, and I kissed the picture of him. They were laughing at me for doing that, but I had heard of his good name. There was some poor man, a tinker, asked help of him one time in Dublin, and he said, 'I will put you in a place where you will get some good thing.' So he brought him to a lodging in a very grand house and put him in it. And in the morning he began to make saucepans, and he was making them there, and the shopkeeper that owned the house was mad at him to be doing that, and making saucepans in so grand a house, and he wanted to get him out of it, and he gave him a good sum of money to go out. He went back and told that to O'Connell, and O'Connell said, 'Didn't I tell you I would put you in the way to get some good thing?'

## A Present

There was a gentleman sent him a present one time, and he bade
a little lad to bring it to him. Shut up in a box it was, and he
bade the boy to give it to himself, and not to open the box. So the
little lad brought it to O'Connell to give it to him. 'Let you open
it yourself,' says O'Connell. So he opened it, and whatever was in
it blew up and made an end of the boy, and it would have been
the same with O'Connell if he had opened it.

## His Strategy

O'Connell was a grand man; the best within the walls of the
world. He never led anyone astray. Did you hear that one time
he turned the shoes on his horses? There were bad members
following him. I cannot say who they were, for I will not tell
what I don't know. He got a smith to turn the shoes, and when
they came upon his track, he went east and they went west.
Parnell was no bad man, but Dan O'Connell's name went up
higher in praises.

## The Man Who was Going to be Hanged

I saw O'Connell in Galway one time, and I couldn't get anear
him. All the nations of the world were gathered there to see him.
There were a great many he hung and a great many he got off
from death, the dear man. He went into a town one time, and
into a hotel, and he asked for his dinner. And he had a frieze
dress, for he was very simple, and always a clerk along with him.
And when the dinner was served to him, 'Is there no one here,'
says he, 'to sit along with me; for it is seldom I ever dined without
company.' 'If you think myself good enough to sit with you,' says
the man of the hotel, 'I will do it.' So the two of them sat to the
dinner together, and O'Connell asked was there any news in the

town. 'There is,' says the hotel man, 'there is a man to be hung tomorrow.' 'Oh, my!' says O'Connell, 'what was it he did to deserve that?' 'Himself and another that had been out fowling,' says he, 'and they came in here and they began to dispute, and the one of them killed the other, and he will be hung tomorrow.' 'He will not,' says O'Connell. 'I tell you he will,' says the other, 'for the Judge is come to give the sentence.' Well, O'Connell kept to it that he would not, and they made a bet, and the hotel man bet all he had on the man being hung. In the morning O'Connell was in no hurry out of bed, and when the two of them walked into the Court, the Judge was after giving the sentence, and the man was to be hung. '*Maisead*,'[3] says the judge when he saw O'Connell, 'I wish you had been here a half-an-hour ago, where there is a man going to be hung.' 'He is not,' says O'Connell. 'He is,' says the judge. 'If he is,' says O'Connell, 'that one will never let anyone go living out of his hotel, and he making money out of the hanging.' 'What do you mean saying that?' says the judge. Then O'Connell took the instrument out of his pocket where it was written down all the hotelkeeper had put on the hanging. And when the judge saw that, he set the man free, and he was not hanged.

## The Cup of the Sassanach

He was over in England one time, and he was brought to a party, and tea was made ready and cups. And as they were sitting at the table, a servant girl that was in it, and that was Irish, came to O'Connell and she said, 'Do you understand Irish, O'Connell?' It is in Irish she said that, and he answered her in Irish, 'I understand it.' 'Have a care,' says she, 'for there is in your cup what would poison the whole nation!' 'If that is true, girl, you will get a good fortune,' said he. It was in Irish they said all that, and the people that were in it had no ears. Then O'Connell quenched the candle, and he changed his cup for the cup of the man that was next him. And it was not long till the man fell dead. They were always trying to kill O'Connell, because he was a good man. The Sassanach it was were against him. Terrible wicked they were, and God save us, I believe they are every bit as wicked yet!

## A Grand Man

Is that O'Connell's picture up there? He is a grand man. Did I ever tell you of the way he saved the man that stole a horse? He came to a town and there was a man to be tried for stealing a horse, and the wife came to O'Connell asking him to get him off. And he said to the wife, 'There is but one way to get him off, and that is for yourself to join with the man that is against him, in swearing he did steal the horse.' So in Court the woman got up and said it was true he did steal it. Then O'Connell said to the Judge, 'It's easy to see this woman and the man that accused him are great with one another, and they had a plan made up to hang the husband and to banish him out of the world.' And the Judge thought the same thing; so the husband was let off. Wasn't O'Connell a good man to think of that?

## The Thousand Fishers

O'Connell came to Galway one time, and he sent for all the trades to come out with the sign of their trade in their hand, and he would see which was the best. And there came ten hundred fishers, having all white flannel clothes and black hats and white scarves about them, and he gave the sway to them. It wasn't a year after that, the half of them were lost, going through the fogs at Newfoundland, where they went for a better way of living.

IRISH SAGA AND ROMANCE

# from *Cuchulain of Muirthemne*

## Fate of the Sons of Usnach

Now it was one Fedlimid, son of Doll, was harper to King Conchubar, and he had but one child, and this is the story of her birth.

Cathbad, the Druid, was at Fedlimid's house one day. 'Have you got knowledge of the future?' said Fedlimid. 'I have a little,' said Cathbad. 'What is it you are wanting to know?' 'I was not asking to know anything,' said Fedlimid, 'but if you know of anything that may be going to happen to me, it is as well for you to tell me.'

Cathbad went out of the house for a while, and when he came back he said: 'Had you ever any children?' 'I never had,' said Fedlimid, 'and the wife I have had none, and we have no hope ever to have any; there is no one with us but only myself and my wife.' 'That puts wonder on me,' said Cathbad, 'for I see by Druid signs that it is on account of a daughter belonging to you, that more blood will be shed than ever was shed in Ireland since time and race began. And great heroes and bright candles of the Gael will lose their lives because of her.' 'Is that the foretelling you have made for me?' said Fedlimid, and there was anger on him, for he thought the Druid was mocking him; 'if that is all you can say, you can keep it for yourself; it is little I think of your share of knowledge.' 'For all that,' said Cathbad, 'I am certain of its truth, for I can see it all clearly in my own mind.'

The Druid went away, but he was not long gone when Fedlimid's wife was found to be with child. And as her time went on, his vexation went on growing, that he had not asked more questions of Cathbad, at the time he was talking to him, and he was under a smouldering care by day and by night, for it is what he was thinking, that neither his own sense and understanding, or the share of friends he had, would be able to save him, or to make a back against the world, if this misfortune should come upon him, that would bring such great shedding of blood upon the earth; and it is the thought that came, that if this child should be born, what he had to do was to put her far away, where no eye would see her, and no ear hear word of her.

The time of the delivery of Fedlimid's wife came on, and it was a girl-child she gave birth to. Fedlimid did not allow any living person to come to the house or to see his wife, but himself alone.

But just after the child was born, Cathbad, the Druid, came in again, and there was shame on Fedlimid when he saw him, and when he remembered how he would not believe his words. But the Druid looked at the child and he said:

'Let Deirdre be her name; harm will come through her.
'She will be fair, comely, bright-haired; heroes will fight for her, and kings go seeking for her.'

And then he took the child in his arms, and it is what he said:
'O Deirdre, on whose account many shall weep, on whose account many women shall be envious, there will be trouble on Ulster for your sake, O fair daughter of Fedlimid.

'Many will be jealous of your face, O flame of beauty; for your sake heroes shall go to exile. For your sake deeds of anger shall be done in Emain; there is harm in your face, for it will bring banishment and death on the sons of kings.

'In your fate, O beautiful child, are wounds, and ill-doings, and shedding of blood.

'You will have a little grave apart to yourself; you will be a tale of wonder forever, Deirdre.'

Cathbad went away then, and he sent Levarcham, daughter of Aedh, to the house; and Fedlimid asked her would she take the venture of bringing up the child, far away where no eye would see her, and no ear hear of her. Levarcham said she would do that, and that she would do her best to keep her the way he wished.

So Fedlimid got his men, and brought them away with him to a mountain, wide and waste, and there he bade them to make a little house, by the side of a round green hillock, and to make a garden of apple trees behind it, with a wall about it. And he bade them put a roof of green sods over the house, the way a little company might live in it, without notice being taken of them.

Then he sent Levarcham and the child there, that no eye might see, and no ear hear of Deirdre. He put all in good order before them, and he gave them provisions, and he told Levarcham that food and all she wanted would be sent from year to year as long as she lived.

And so Deirdre and her foster-mother lived in the lonely place among the hills without the knowledge or the notice of any strange person, until Deirdre was fourteen years of age. And Deirdre grew straight and clean like a rush on the bog, and she was comely beyond comparison of all the women of the world, and her movements were like the swan on the wave, or the deer on the hill. She was the young girl of the greatest beauty and of the gentlest nature of all the women of Ireland.

Levarcham, that had charge of her, used to be giving Deirdre every knowledge and skill that she had herself. There was not a blade of grass growing from root, or a bird singing in the wood, or a star shining from heaven, but Deirdre had the name of it. But there was one thing she would not have her know, she would not let her have friendship with any living person of the rest of the world outside their own house.

But one dark night of winter, with black clouds overhead, a hunter came walking the hills, and it is what happened, he missed the track of the hunt, and lost his way and his comrades.

And a heaviness came upon him, and he lay down on the side of the green hillock by Deirdre's house. He was weak with hunger and going, and perished with cold, and a deep sleep came upon him. While he was lying there a dream came to the hunter, and he thought that he was near the warmth of a house of the Sidhe, and the Sidhe inside making music, and he called out in his dream, 'If there is any one inside, let them bring me in, in the name of the Sun and the Moon.' Deirdre heard the voice, and she said to Levarcham, 'Mother, mother, what is that?' But Levarcham said, 'It is nothing that matters; it is the birds of the air gone astray, and trying to find one another. But let them go back to the branches of the wood.' Another troubled dream came on the hunter, and he cried out a second time. 'What is that?' asked Deirdre again. 'It is nothing that matters,' said Levarcham. 'The birds of the air are looking for one another; let them go past to the branches of the wood.' Then a third dream came to the hunter, and he cried out a third time, if there was any one in the hill to let him in for the sake of the Elements, for he was perished with cold and overcome with hunger. 'Oh! what is that, Levarcham?' said Deirdre. 'There is nothing there for you to see, my child, but only the birds of the air, and they lost to one another, but let them go past us to the branches of the wood. There is no place or shelter for them here tonight.' 'Oh, mother,' said Deirdre, 'the bird asked to come in for the sake of the Sun and the Moon, and it is what you yourself told me, that anything that is asked like that, it is right for us to give it. If you will not let in the bird that is perished with cold and overcome with hunger, I myself will let it in.' So Deirdre rose up and drew the bolt from the leaf of the door, and let in the hunter. She put a seat in the place for sitting, food in the place for eating, and drink in the place for drinking, for the man who had come into the house. 'Come now and eat food, for you are in want of it,' said Deirdre. 'Indeed it is I was in want of food and drink and warmth when I came into this house; but by my word, I have forgotten that since I saw yourself,' said the hunter. 'How little you are able to curb your tongue,' said Levarcham. 'It is not a great thing for you to keep your tongue quiet when you get the shelter of a house and the warmth of a hearth on a dark winter night.' 'That is so,' said the hunter, 'I may do that much, to keep my mouth shut; but I swear by the oath my people swear by, if some others of the people of the world saw this great beauty that is hidden away here, they would not leave her long with you.' 'What people are those?' said Deirdre. 'I will tell you that,' said the hunter; 'they are Naoise, son of Usnach, and Ainnle and Ardan, his two brothers.' 'What is the appearance of these men, if we should ever see them?' said Deirdre. 'This is the appearance that is on those three men,' said the hunter: 'the colour of the raven is on their hair, their skin is like the swan on the wave, their cheeks like the blood of the speckled red calf, and their swiftness and their leap are like the salmon of the stream and like the deer of the grey mountain; and the head and shoulders of Naoise are above all the other men of Ireland.' 'However they may be,' said Levarcham, 'get you out from here, and take another road; and by my word, little is my thankfulness to yourself, or to her that let you in.' 'You need not send him out for telling me that,' said Deirdre, 'for as to those three men, I myself saw them last night in a dream, and they hunting upon a hill.'

The hunter went away, but in a little time after he began to think to himself how Conchubar, High King of Ulster, was used to lie down at night and to rise up in the morning by himself, without a wife or any one to speak to; and that if he could see this great beauty it was likely he would bring her home to Emain, and that he himself would get the goodwill of the king for telling him there was such a queen to be found on the face of the world.

So he went straight to King Conchubar at Emain Macha,[1] and he sent word in to the king that he had news for him, if he would hear it. The king sent for him to come in. 'What is the reason of your journey?' he said. 'It is what I have to tell you, King,' said the hunter, 'that I have seen the greatest beauty that ever was born in Ireland, and I am come to tell you of it.'

'Who is this great beauty, and in what place is she to be seen, when she was never seen before you saw her, if you did see her?' 'I did see her, indeed,' said the hunter, 'but no other man can see her, unless he knows from me the place where she is living.' 'Will you bring me to the place where she is, and you will have a good reward?' said the king. 'I will bring you there,' said the hunter. 'Let you stay with my household tonight,' said Conchubar, 'and I myself and my people will go with you early on the morning of tomorrow.' 'I will stay,' said the hunter, and he stayed that night in the household of King Conchubar.

Then Conchubar sent to Fergus and to the other chief men of Ulster, and he told them of what he was about to do. Though it was early when the songs and the music of the birds began in the woods, it was earlier yet when Conchubar, king of Ulster, rose up with his little company of near friends, in the fresh spring morning of the fresh and pleasant month of May, and the dew was heavy on every bush and flower as they went out towards the green hill where Deirdre was living.

But many a young man of them that had a light glad, leaping step when they set out, had but a tired, slow, failing step before the end, because of the length and the roughness of the way. 'It is down there below,' said the hunter, 'in the house in that valley, the woman is living, but I myself will not go nearer it than this.'

Conchubar and his troop went down then to the green hillock where Deirdre was, and they knocked at the door of the house. Levarcham called out that neither answer nor opening would be given to any one at all, and that she did not want disturbance put on herself or her house. 'Open,' said Conchubar, 'in the name of the High King of Ulster.' When Levarcham heard Conchubar's voice, she knew there was no use trying to keep Deirdre out of sight any longer, and she rose up in haste and let in the king, and as many of his people as could follow him.

When the king saw Deirdre before him, he thought in himself that he never saw in the course of the day, or in the dreams of the night, a creature so beautiful and he gave her his full heart's weight of love there and then. It is what he did; he put Deirdre up on the shoulders of his men, and she herself and Levarcham were brought away to Emain Macha.

With the love that Conchubar had for Deirdre, he wanted to marry her with no delay, but when her leave was asked, she would not give it, for she was young yet, and she had no knowledge of the duties of a wife, or the ways of a king's house. And when Conchubar was pressing her hard, she asked him to give her a delay of a year and a day. He said he would give her that, though it was hard for him, if she would give him her certain promise to marry him at the year's end. She did that, and Conchubar got a woman teacher for her, and nice, fine, pleasant, modest maidens to be with her at her lying down and at her rising up, to be companions to her. And Deirdre grew wise in the works of a young girl, and in the understanding of a woman; and if any one at all looked at her face, whatever colour she was before that, she would blush crimson red. And it is what Conchubar thought, that he never saw with the eyes of his body a creature that pleased him so well.

One day Deirdre and her companions were out on a hill near Emain Macha, looking around them in the pleasant sunshine, and they saw three men walking together. Deirdre was looking at the men and wondering at them, and when they came near, she remembered the talk of the hunter, and the three men she saw in her dream, and she thought to herself that these were the three sons of Usnach, and that this was Naoise, that had his head and shoulders above all the men of Ireland. The three brothers went by without turning their eyes at all upon the young girls on the hillside, and they were singing as they went, and whoever heard the low singing of the sons of Usnach, it was enchantment and music to them, and every cow that was being milked and heard it, gave two thirds more of milk. And it is what happened, that love for Naoise came into the heart of Deirdre, so that she could not but follow him. She gathered up her skirt and went after the three men that had gone past the foot of the hill, leaving her companions there after her.

But Ainnle and Ardan had heard talk of the young girl that was at Conchubar's Court, and it is what they thought, that if Naoise their brother would see her, it is for himself he would have her, for she was not yet married to the king. So when they saw Deidre coming after them, they said to one another to hasten their steps, for they had a long road to travel, and the dusk of night coming on. They did so, and Deirdre saw it, and she cried out after them, 'Naoise, son of Usnach, are you going to leave me?' 'What cry was that came to my ears, that it is not well for me to answer, and not easy for me to refuse?' said Naoise. 'It was nothing but the cry of Conchubar's wild ducks,' said his brothers; 'but let us quicken our steps and hasten our feet, for we have a long road to travel, and the dusk of the evening coming on.' They did so, and they were widening the distance between themselves and her. Then Deirdre cried, 'Naoise! Naoise! son of Usnach, are you going to leave me?' 'What cry was it that came to my ears and struck my heart, that it is not well for me to answer, or easy for me to refuse?' said Naoise. 'Nothing but the cry of Conchubar's wild geese,' said his brothers; 'but let us quicken our steps and hasten our feet, the darkness of night is coming on.' They did so, and were widening the distance between themselves and her. Then Deirdre cried the third time, 'Naoise! Naoise! Naoise! son of Usnach, are you going to leave me?' 'What sharp, clear cry was that, the sweetest that ever came to my ears, and the sharpest that ever struck my heart, of all the cries I ever heard,' said Naoise. 'What is it but the scream of Conchubar's lake swans,' said his brothers. 'That was the third cry of some person beyond there,' said Naoise, 'and I swear by my hand of valour,' he said, 'I will go no further until I see where the cry comes from.' So Naoise turned back and met Deirdre, and Deirdre and Naoise kissed one another three times, and she gave a kiss to each of his brothers. And with the confusion that was on her, a blaze of red fire came upon her, and her colour came and went as quickly as the aspen by the stream. And it is what Naoise thought to himself, that he never saw a woman so beautiful in his life; and he gave Deirdre, there and then, the love that he never gave to living thing, to vision, or to creature, but to herself alone.

Then he lifted her high on his shoulder, and he said to his brothers to hasten their steps; and they hastened them.

'Harm will come of this,' said the young men. 'Although there should harm come,' said Naoise, 'I am willing to be in disgrace while I live. We will go with her to another province, and there is not in Ireland a king who will not give us a welcome.' So they called their people, and that night they set out with three times fifty men, and three times fifty women, and three times fifty greyhounds, and Deirdre in their midst.

They were a long time after that shifting from one place to another all around Ireland, from Essruadh in the south, to Beinn Etair in the east again, and it is often they were in danger of being destroyed by Conchubar's devices. And one time the Druids raised a wood before them, but Naoise and his brothers cut their way through it. But at last they got out of Ulster and sailed to the country of Alban, and settled in a lonely place; and when hunting on the mountains failed them, they fell upon the cattle of the men of Alban, so that these gathered together to make an end of them. But the sons of Usnach called to the king of Scotland, and he took them into his friendship, and they gave him their help when he went out into battles or to war.

But all this time they had never spoken to the king of Deirdre, and they kept her with themselves, not to let any one see her, for they were afraid they might get their death on account of her, she being so beautiful.

But it chanced very early one morning, the king's steward came to visit them, and he found his way into the house where Naoise and Deirdre were, and there he saw them asleep beside one another. He went back then to the king, and he said: 'Up to this time there has never been found a woman that would be a fitting wife for you; but there is a woman on the shore of Loch Ness now, is well worthy of you, king of the East. And what you have to do is to make an end of Naoise, for it is of his wife I am speaking.' 'I will not do that,' said the king; 'but go to her,' he said, 'and bid her to come and see me secretly.' The steward brought her that message, but Deirdre sent him away, and all that he had said to her, she told it to Naoise afterwards. Then when she would not come to him, the king sent the sons of Usnach into every hard fight, hoping they would get their death, but they won every battle, and came back safe again. And after a while they went to Loch Eitche, near the sea, and they were left to themselves there for a while in peace and quietness. And they settled and made a dwelling house for themselves by the side of Loch Ness, and they could kill the salmon of the stream from out their own door, and the deer of the grey hills from out their window. But when Naoise went to the court of the king, his clothes were splendid among the great men of the army of Scotland, a cloak of bright purple, rightly shaped, with a fringe of bright gold; a coat of satin with fifty hooks of silver; a brooch on which were a hundred polished gems; a gold-hilted sword in his hand, two blue-green spears of bright points, a dagger with the colour of yellow gold on it, and a hilt of silver. But the two children they had, Gaiar and Aebgreine, they gave into the care of Manannan, Son of the Sea. And he cared them well in Emhain of the Apple Trees, and he brought Bobaras the poet to give learning to Gaiar. And Aebgreine of the Sunny Face he gave in marriage afterwards to Rinn, son of Eochaidh Juil of the Land of Promise.

*

Now it happened after a time that a very great feast was made by Conchubar, in Emain Macha, for all the great among his nobles, so that the whole company were easy and pleasant together. The musicians stood up to play their songs and to give poems, and they gave out the branches of relationship and of kindred. These are the names of the poets that were in Emain at the time, Cathbad, the Druid, son of Conall, son of Rudraige; Geanann of the Bright Face, son of Cathbad; Ferceirtne, and Geanann Black-Knee, and many others, and Sencha, son of Ailell.

They were all drinking and making merry until Conchubar, the king, raised his voice and spoke aloud, and it is what he said: 'I desire to know from you, did you ever see a better house than this house of Emain, or a hearth better than my hearth in any place you were ever in?' 'We did not,' they said. 'If that is so,' said Conchubar, 'do you know of anything at all that is wanting to you?' 'We know of nothing,' said they. 'That is not so with me,' said Conchubar. 'I know of a great want that is on you, the want of the three best candles of the Gael, the three noble sons of Usnach, that ought not to be away from us for the sake of any woman in the world, Naoise, Ainnle and Ardan; for surely they are the sons of a king, and they would defend the High Kingship against the best men of Ireland.' 'If we had dared,' said they, 'it is long ago we would have said it, and more than that, the province of Ulster would be equal to any other province in Ireland, if there was no Ulsterman in it but those three alone, for it is lions they are in hardness and in bravery.' 'If that is so,' said Conchubar, 'let us send word by a messenger to Alban, and to the dwelling-place of the sons of Usnach, to ask them back again.' 'Who will go there with the message?' said they all. 'I cannot know that,' said Conchubar, 'for there is *geasa*, that is bonds, on Naoise not to come back with any man only one of the three, Conall Cearnach, or Fergus, or Cuchulain, and I will know now,' said he, 'which one of those three loves me best.' Then he called Conall to one side, and he asked him, 'What would you do with me if I should send you for the sons of Usnach, and if they were destroyed through me – a thing I do not mean to do?' 'As I am not going to undertake it,' said Conall,

'I will say that it is not one alone I would kill, but any Ulsterman I would lay hold of that had harmed them would get shortening of life from me and the sorrow of death.' 'I see well,' said Conchubar, 'you are no friend of mine,' and he put Conall away from him. Then he called Cuchulain to him, and asked him the same as he did the other. 'I give my word, as I am not going,' said Cuchulain, 'if you want that of me, and that you think to kill them when they come, it is not one person alone that would die for it, but every Ulsterman I could lay hold of would get shortening of life from me and the sorrow of death.' 'I see well,' said Conchubar, 'that you are no friend of mine.' And he put Cuchulain from him. And then he called Fergus to him, and asked him the same question, and Fergus said, 'Whatever may happen, I promise your blood will be safe from me, but besides yourself there is no Ulsterman that would try to harm them, and that I would lay hold of, but I would give him shortening of life and the sorrow of death.' 'I see well,' said Conchubar, 'it is yourself must go for them, and it is tomorrow you must set out, for it is with you they will come, and when you are coming back to us westward, I put you under bonds to go first to the fort of Borach, son of Cainte, and give me your word now that as soon as you get there, you will send on the sons of Usnach to Emain, whether it be day or night at the time.' After that the two of them went in together, and Fergus told all the company how it was under his charge they were to be put.

Then Conchubar went to Borach and asked had he a feast ready prepared for him. 'I have,' said Borach, 'but although I was able to make it ready, I was not able to bring it to Emain.' 'If that is so,' said Conchubar, 'give it to Fergus when he comes back to Ireland, for it is *geasa* on him not to refuse your feast.' Borach promised he would do that, and so they wore away that night.

So Fergus set out in the morning, and he brought no guard nor helpers with him, but himself and his two sons, Fair-Haired Iollan, and Rough-Red Buinne, and Cuillean, the shield-bearer, and the shield itself. They went on till they got to the dwelling-place of the sons of Usnach, and to Loch Eitche in Alba. It is how the sons of Usnach lived; they had three houses, and the house where they made ready the food, it is not there they would eat it, and the house where they would eat it, it is not there they would sleep.

When Fergus came to the harbour he let a great shout out of him. And it is how Naoise and Deirdre were, they had a chess-board between them, and they playing on it. Naoise heard the shout, and he said, 'That is the shout of a man of Ireland.' 'It is not, but the cry of a man of Alban,' said Deirdre. She knew at the first it was Fergus gave the shout, but she denied it. Then Fergus let another shout out of him. 'That is an Irish shout,' said Naoise again. 'It is not, indeed,' said Deirdre, 'let us go on playing.' Then Fergus gave the third shout, and the sons of Usnach knew this time it was the shout of Fergus, and Naoise said to Ardan to go out and meet him. Then Deirdre told him that she herself knew at the first shout that it was Fergus. 'Why did you deny it, then, Queen?' said Naoise. 'Because of a vision I saw last night,' said Deirdre. 'Three birds I saw coming to us from Emain Macha, and three drops of honey in their mouths, and they left them with us, and three drops of our blood they brought away with them.' 'What meaning do you put on that, Queen?' said Naoise. 'It is,' said Deirdre. 'Fergus that is coming to us with a message of peace from Conchubar, for honey is not sweeter than a message of peace sent by a lying man.' 'Let that pass,' said Naoise. 'Is there anything in it but troubled sleep and the melancholy of woman? And it is a long time Fergus is in the harbour. Rise up, Ardan, to be before him, and bring him with you here.' And Ardan went down to meet him, and gave a fond kiss to himself and to his two sons. And it is what he said: 'My love to you, dear comrades.' After that he asked news of Ireland, and they gave it to him, and then they came to where Naoise and Ainnle and Deirdre were, and they kissed Fergus and his two sons, and they asked news of Ireland from them. 'It is the best news I have for you,' said Fergus, 'that Conchubar, king of Ulster, has sworn by the earth beneath him, by the high heaven above him, and by the sun that travels to the west, that he will have no rest by day nor sleep by night, if the sons of Usnach, his own foster-brothers, will not come back to the land of their home and the country of their birth; and he has sent us to ask you there.' 'It is better for them to stop here,' said Deirdre, 'for they have a greater sway in Scotland than Conchubar himself has in Ireland.' 'One's own country is better than any other thing,' said Fergus, 'for no man can have any pleasure, however great his good luck and his way of living, if he does not see his own country every day.' 'That is true,' said Naoise, 'for Ireland is dearer to myself than Alban, though I would get more in Alban than in Ireland.' 'It will be safe for you to come with me,' said Fergus. 'It will be safe indeed,' said Naoise, 'and we will go with you to Ireland; and though there were no trouble beneath the sun, but a man to be far from his own land, there is little delight in peace and a long sleep to a man that is an exile. It is a pity for the man that is an exile; it is little his honour, it is great his grief, for it is he will have his share of wandering.'

It was not with Deirdre's will Naoise said that, and she was greatly against going with Fergus. And she said: 'I had a dream last night of the three sons of Usnach, and they bound and put in the grave by Conchubar of the Red Branch.' But Naoise said: 'Lay down your dream, Deirdre, on the heights of the hills, lay down your dream on the sailors of the sea, lay down your dream on the rough grey stones, for we will give peace and we will get it from the king of the world and from Conchubar.' But Deirdre spoke again, and it is what she said: 'There is the howling of dogs in my ears; a vision of the night is before my eyes, I see Fergus away from us, I see Conchubar without mercy in his dun; I see Naoise without strength in battle; I see Ainnle without his loud-sounding shield; I see Ardan without shield or breastplate, and the Hill of Atha without delight; I see Conchubar asking for blood; I see Fergus caught with hidden lies; I see Deirdre crying with tears, I see Deirdre crying with tears.'

'A thing that is unpleasing to me, and that I would never give in to,' said Fergus, 'is to listen to the howling of dogs, and to the dreams of women; and since Conchubar, the High King, has sent a message of friendship, it would not be right for you to refuse it.' 'It would not be right indeed,' said Naoise, 'and we will go with you tomorrow.' And Fergus gave his word, and he said, 'If all the men of Ireland were against you, it would not profit them, for neither shield nor sword or a helmet itself would be any help or protection to them against you, and I myself to be with you.' 'That is true,' said Naoise, 'and we will go with you to Ireland.'

They spent the night there until morning, and then they went where the ships were, and they went on the sea, and a good many of their people with them, and Deirdre looked back on the land of Alban, and it is what she said: 'My love to you, O land to the east, and it goes ill with me to leave you; for it is pleasant are your bays and your harbours and your wide flowery plains and your green-sided hills; and little need, was there for us to leave you.' And she made this complaint:

'Dear to me is that land, that land to the east, Alban, with its wonders; I would not have come from it hither but that I came with Naoise.

'Dear to me, Dun Fiodhaigh and Dun Fionn; dear is the dun above them; dear to me Inis Droignach, dear to me Dun Suibhne.

'O Coill Cuan! Ochone! Coil Cuan! where Ainnle used to come. My grief! it was short I thought his stay there with Naoise in Western Alban. Glen Laoi, O Glen Laoi, where I used to sleep under soft coverings; fish and venison and badger's flesh, that was my portion in Glen Laoi.

'Glen Masan, my grief! Glen Masan! high its hart's-tongue, bright its stalks; we were rocked to pleasant sleep over the wooded harbour of Masan.

'Glen Archan, my grief! Glen Archan, the straight valley of the pleasant ridge; never was there a young man more light-hearted than my Naoise used to be in Glen Archan.

'Glen Eitche, my grief! Glen Eitche, it was there I built my first house; beautiful were the woods on our rising; the home of the sun is Glen Eitche.

'Glen-da-Rua, my grief! Glen-da-Rua, my love to every man that belongs to it; sweet is the voice of the cuckoo on the bending branch on the hill above Glen-da-Rua.

'Dear to me is Droighin over the fierce strand, dear are its waters over the clean sand; I would never have come out from it at all but that I came with my beloved!'

After she had made that complaint they came to Dun Borach,

and Borach gave three fond kisses to Fergus and to the sons of Usnach along with him. It was then Borach said he had a feast laid out for Fergus, and that it was *geasa* for him to leave it until he would have eaten it. But Fergus reddened with anger from head to foot, and it is what he said: 'It is a bad thing you have done, Borach, laying out a feast for me, and Conchubar to have made me give my word that as soon as I would come to Ireland, whether it would be by day or in the night-time, I would send on the sons of Usnach to Emain Macha.' 'I hold you under bonds,' said Borach, 'to stop and use the feast.'

Then Fergus asked Naoise what should he do about the feast. 'You must choose,' said Deirdre, 'whether you will forsake the children of Usnach or the feast, and it would be better for you to refuse the feast than to forsake the sons of Usnach.' 'I will not forsake them,' said he, 'for I will send my two sons, Fair-Haired Iollan and Rough-Red Buinne, with them to Emain Macha.' 'On my word,' said Naoise, 'that is a great deal to do for us; for up to this no other person ever protected us but ourselves.' And he went out of the place in great anger; and Ainnle, and Ardan, and Deirdre, and the two sons of Fergus followed him, and they left Fergus dark and sorrowful after them. But for all that, Fergus was full sure that if all the provinces of Ireland would go into one council, they would not consent to break the pledge he had given.

As for the sons of Usnach, they went on their way by every short road, and Deirdre said to them, 'I will give you a good advice, Sons of Usnach, though you may not follow it.' 'What is that advice, Queen?' said Naoise. 'It is,' said she, 'to go to Rechrainn, between Ireland and Scotland, and to wait there until Fergus has done with the feast; and that will be the keeping of his word to Fergus, and it will be the lengthening of your lives to you.' 'We will not follow that advice,' said Naoise; and the children of Fergus said it was little trust she had in them, when she thought they would not protect her, though their hands might not be so strong as the hands of the sons of Usnach; and besides that, Fergus had given them his word. 'Alas! it is sorrow came on us with the word of Fergus,' said Deirdre, 'and he to forsake us for a feast,' and she made this complaint:

'It is grief to me that ever I came from the east on the word of the unthinking son of Rogh. It is only lamentations I will make. Och! it is very sorrowful my heart is!

'My heart is heaped up with sorrow; it is tonight my great hurt is. My grief! my dear companions, the end of your days is come.'

And it is what Naoise answered her: 'Do not say that in your haste, Deirdre, more beautiful than the sun. Fergus would never have come for us eastward to bring us back to be destroyed.

And Deirdre said, 'My grief! I think it too far for you, beautiful sons of Usnach, to have come from Alban of the rough grass; it is lasting will be its lifelong sorrow.'

After that they went forward to Finncairn of the watch-tower on sharp-peaked Slieve Fuad, and Deirdre stayed after them in the valley, and sleep fell on her there.

When Naoise saw that Deirdre was left after them, he turned back as she was rising out of her sleep, and he said, 'What made you wait after us, Queen?' 'Sleep that was on me,' said Deirdre; 'and I saw a vision in it.' 'What vision was that?' said Naoise. 'It was,' she said, 'Fair-Haired Iollan that I saw without his head on him, and Rough-Red Buinne with his head on him; and it is without help of Rough-Red Buinne you were, and it is with the help of Fair-Haired Iollan you were.' And she made this complaint:

'It is a sad vision has been shown to me, of my four tall, fair, bright companions; the head of each has been taken from him, and no help to be had one from another.'

But when Naoise heard this he reproached her, and said, 'O fair, beautiful woman, nothing does your mouth speak but evil. Do not let the sharpness and the great misfortune that come from it fall on your friends.' And Deirdre answered him with kind, gentle words, and it is what she said: 'It would be better to me to see harm come on any other person than upon any one of you three, with whom I have travelled over the seas and over the wide plains; but when I look on you, it is only Buinne I can see safe and whole, and I know by that his life will be longest among you; and indeed it is I that am sorrowful tonight.'

After that they came forward to the high willows, and it was then Deirdre said, 'I see a cloud in the air, and it is a cloud of blood; and I would give you a good advice, sons of Usnach,' she said. 'What is that advice?' said Naoise. 'To go to Dundealgan where Cuchulain is, until Fergus has done with the feast, and to be under the protection of Cuchulain, for fear of the treachery of Conchubar.' 'Since there is no fear on us, we will not follow that advice,' said Naoise. And Deirdre complained, and it is what she said: 'O Naoise, look at the cloud I see above us in the air; I see a cloud over green Macha, cold and deep red like blood. I am startled by the cloud that I see here in the air; a thin, dreadful cloud that is like a clot of blood. I give a right advice to the beautiful sons of Usnach not to go to Emain tonight, because of the danger that is over them.'

'We will go to Dundealgan, where the Hound of the Smith is; we will come tomorrow from the south along with the Hound, Cuchulain.'

But Naoise said in his anger to Deirdre, 'Since there is no fear on us, we will not follow your advice.' And Deirdre turned to the grandsons of Rogh, and it is what she said: 'It is seldom until now, Naoise, that yourself and myself were not of the one mind. And I say to you, Naoise, that you would not have gone against me like this, the day Manannan gave me the cup in the time of his great victory.'

After that they went on to Emain Macha. 'Sons of Usnach,' said Deirdre, 'I have a sign by which you will know if Conchubar is going to do treachery on you.' 'What sign is that?' said Naoise. 'If you are let come into the house where Conchubar is, and the nobles of Ulster, then Conchubar is not going to do treachery on you. But if it is in the House of the Red Branch you are put, then he is going to do treachery on you.'

After that they came to Emain Macha, and they took the handwood and struck the door, and the doorkeeper asked who was there. They told him that it was the sons of Usnach, and Deirdre, and the two sons of Fergus were there.

When Conchubar heard that, he called his stewards and serving men to him, and he asked them how was the House of the Red

Branch for food and for drink. They said that if all the seven armies of Ulster would come there, they would find what would satisfy them. 'If that is so,' said Conchubar, 'bring the sons of Usnach into it.'

It was then Deirdre said, 'It would have been better for you to follow my advice, and never to have come to Emain, and it would be right for you to leave it, even at this time.' 'We will not,' said Fair-Haired Iollan, 'for it is not fear or cowardliness was ever seen on us, but we will go to the house.' So they went on to the House of the Red Branch, and the stewards and the serving-men with them, and well-tasting food was served to them, and pleasant drinks, till they were all glad and merry, except only Deirdre and the sons of Usnach; for they did not use much food or drink, because of the length and the greatness of their journey from Dun Borach to Emain Macha. Then Naoise said, 'Give the chessboard to us till we go playing.' So they gave them the chessboard and they began to play.

It was just at that time Conchubar was asking, 'Who will I send that will bring me word of Deirdre, and that will tell me if she has the same appearance and the same shape she had before, for if she has, there is not a woman in the world has a more beautiful shape or appearance than she has, and I will bring her out with edge of blade and point of sword in spite of the Sons of Usnach, good though they be. But if not, let Naoise have her for himself.' 'I myself will go there,' said Levarcham, 'and I will bring you word of that.' And it is how it was, Deirdre was dearer to her than any other person in the world; for it was often she went through the world looking for Deirdre and bringing news to her and from her. So Levarcham went over to the House of the Red Branch, and near it she saw a great troop of armed men, and she spoke to them, but they made her no answer, and she knew by that it was none of the men of Ulster were in it, but men from some strange country that Conchubar's messengers had brought to Emain.

And then she went in where Naoise and Deirdre were, and it is how she found them, the polished chessboard between them, and they playing on it; and she gave them fond kisses, and she said:

'You are not doing well to be playing; and it is to bring Conchubar word if Deirdre has the same shape and appearance she used to have that he sent me here now; and there is grief on me for the deed that will be done in Emain tonight, treachery that will be done, and the killing of kindred, and the three bright candles of the Gael to be quenched, and Emain will not be the better of it to the end of life and time,' and she made this complaint sadly and wearily:

'My heart is heavy for the treachery that is being done in Emain this night; on account of this treachery, Emain will never be at peace from this out.

'The three that are most king-like today under the sun; the three best of all that live on the earth, it is grief to me tonight they to die for the sake of any woman. Naoise and Ainnle whose deeds are known, and Ardan, their brother; treachery is to be done on the young, bright-faced three, it is not I that am not sorrowful tonight.'

When she had made this complaint, Levarcham said to the sons of Usnach and to the children of Fergus to shut close the doors and the windows of the house and to do bravery. 'And oh, sons of Fergus,' she said, 'defend your charge and your care bravely till Fergus comes, and you will have praise and a blessing for it.' And she cried with many tears, and she went back to where Conchubar was, and he asked news of Deirdre of her. And Levercham said, 'It is good news and bad news I have for you.' 'What news is that?' said Conchubar. 'It is the good news,' she said, 'the three sons of Usnach to have come to you and to be over there, and they are the three that are bravest and mightiest in form and in looks and in countenance, of all in the world; and Ireland will be yours from this out, since the sons of Usnach are with you; and the news that is worst with me is, the woman that was best of the women of the world in form and in looks, going out of Emain, is without the form and without the appearance she used to have.'

When Conchubar heard that, much of his jealousy went backward, and he was drinking and making merry for a while, until he thought on Deirdre again the second time, and on that he asked, 'Who will I get to bring me word of Deirdre?' But he did not find any one would go there. And then he said to Gelban, the merry, pleasant son of the king of Lochlann:[2] 'Go over and bring me word if Deirdre has the same shape and the same appearance she used to have, for if she has, there is not on the ridge of the world or on the waves of the earth, a woman more beautiful than herself.'

So Gelban went to the House of the Red Branch, and he found the doors and the windows of the fort shut, and fear came on him. And it is what he said: 'It is not an easy road for any one that would get to the sons of Usnach, for I think there is very great anger on them.' And after that he found a window that was left open by forgetfulness in the house, and he was looking in. Then Deirdre saw him through the window, and when she saw him looking at her, she went into a red blaze of blushes, and Naoise knew that someone was looking at her from the window, and she told him that she saw a young man looking in at them. It is how Naoise was at that time, with a man of the chessmen in his hand, and he made a fair throw over his shoulder at the young man, that put the eye out of his head. The young man went back to where Conchubar was. 'You were merry and pleasant going out,' said Conchubar, 'but you are sad and cheerless coming back.' And then Gelban told him the story from beginning to end. 'I see well,' said Conchubar, 'the man that made that throw will be king of the world, unless he has his life shortened. And what appearance is there on Deirdre?' he said. 'It is this,' said Gelban, 'although Naoise put out my eye, I would have wished to stay there looking at her with the other eye, but for the haste you put on me; for there is not in the world a woman is better of shape or of form than herself.'

When Conchubar heard that, he was filled with jealousy and with envy, and he bade the men of his army that were with him, and that had been drinking at the feast, to go and attack the place where the sons of Usnach were. So they went forward to the House of the Red Branch, and they gave three great shouts around it, and they put fires and red flames to it. When the sons of Usnach heard the shouts, they asked who those men were that were about the house. 'Conchubar and the men of Ulster,' they all said together. 'It is the pledge of Fergus you would break?' said Fair-Haired Iollan. 'On my word,' said Conchubar, 'there will be sorrow on the sons of Usnach, Deirdre to be with them.' 'That is true,' said Deirdre, 'Fergus had deceived you.' 'By my oath,' said Rough-Red Buinne, 'if he betrayed, we will not betray.' It was then Buinne went out and killed three fifths of the fighting men outside, and put great disturbance on the rest; and Conchubar asked who was there, and who was doing destruction on his men like that. 'It is I, myself, Rough-Red Buinne, son of Fergus,' said he. 'I will give you a good gift if you will leave off,' said Conchubar. 'What gift is that?' said Rough-Red Buinne. 'A hundred of land,' said Conchubar. 'What besides?' said Rough-Red Buinne. 'My own friendship and my counsel,' said Conchubar. 'I will take that,' said Rough-Red Buinne. It was a good mountain that was given him as a reward, but it turned barren in the same night, and no green grew on it again for ever, and it used to be called the Mountain of the Share of Buinne.

Deirdre heard what they were saying. 'By my word,' she said, 'Rough-Red Buinne has forsaken you, and in my opinion, it is like the father the son is.' 'I give my word,' says Fair-Haired Iollan, 'that is not so with me; as long as this narrow, straight sword stays in my hand, I will not forsake the sons of Usnach.'

After that, Fair-Haired Iollan went out, and made three courses around the house, and killed three fifths of heroes outside, and he came in again where Naoise was, and he playing chess, and Ainnle with him. So Iollan went out the second time, and made three other courses round the fort, and he brought a lighted torch with him on the lawn, and he went destroying the hosts, so that they dared not come to attack the house. And he was a good son, Fair-Haired Iollan, for he never refused any person on the ridge of the world anything that he had, and he never took wages from any person but only Fergus.

It was then Conchubar said: 'What place is my own son, Fiacra the Fair?' 'I am here, High Prince,' said Fiacra. 'By my word,' said Conchubar, 'It is on the one night yourself and Iollan were born, and as it is the arms of his father he has with him, let you take my arms with you, that is, my shield, the Ochain, my two spears, and my great sword, the Gorm Glas, the Blue Green – and do bravery and great deeds with them.'

Then Fiacra took Conchubar's arms, and he and Fair-Haired Iollan attacked one another, and they made a stout fight, one against the other. But however it was, Fair-Haired Iollan put down Fiacra, so that he made him lie under the shelter of his shield, till it roared for the greatness of the strait he was in; for it was the way with the Ochain, the shield of Conchubar, to roar when the person on whom it would be was in danger; and the three chief waves of Ireland, the Wave of Tuagh, the Wave of Cliodna, and the Wave of Rudraige roared in answer to it.

It was at that time Conall Cearnach was at Dun Sobairce, and he heard the Wave of Tuagh. 'True it is,' said Conall, 'Conchubar is in some danger, and it is not right for me to be here listening to him.'

Conall rose up on that, and he put his arms and his armour on him, and came forward to where Conchubar was at Emain Macha, and he found the fight going on on the lawn, and Fiacra, the son of Conchubar, greatly pressed by Fair-Haired Iollan, and neither the king of Ulster nor any other person dared to go between them. But Conall went aside, behind Fair-Haired Iollan and thrust his sword through him. 'Who is it has wounded me behind my back?' said Fair-Haired Iollan. 'Whoever did it, by my hand of valour, he would have got a fair fight, face to face, from myself.' 'Who are you yourself?' said Conall. 'I am Iollan, son of Fergus, and are you yourself Conall?' 'It is I,' said Conall. 'It is evil and it is heavy the work you have done,' said Iollan, 'and the sons of Usnach under my protection.' 'Is that true?' said Conall. 'It is true, indeed,' said Iollan. 'By my hand of valour,' said Conall, 'Conchubar will not get his own son alive from me to avenge it,' and he gave a stroke of the sword to Fiacra, so that he struck his head off, and he left them so. The clouds of death came upon Fair-Haired Iollan then, and he threw his arms towards the fortress, and called out to Naoise to do bravery, and after that he died.

It is then Conchubar himself came out and nineteen hundred

men with him, and Conall said to him: 'Go up now to the doorway of the fort, and see where your sister's children are lying on a bed of trouble.' And when Conchubar saw them he said: 'You are not sister's children to me; it is not the deed of sister's children you have done me, but you have done harm to me with treachery in the sight of all the men of Ireland.' And it is what Ainnle said to him: 'Although we took well-shaped, soft-handed Deirdre from you, yet we did a little kindness to you at another time, and this is the time to remember it. That day your ship was breaking up on the sea, and it full of gold and silver, we gave you up our own ship, and ourselves went swimming to the harbour.' But Conchubar said: 'If you did fifty good deeds to me, surely this would be my thanks; I would not give you peace, and you in distress, but every great want I could put on you.'

And then Ardan said: 'We did another little kindness to you, and this is the time to remember it; the day the speckled horse failed you on the green of Dundealgan, it was we gave you the grey horse that would bring you fast on your road.'

But Conchubar said: 'If you had done fifty good deeds to me, surely this would be my thanks; I would not give you peace, and you in distress, but every great want I could put on you.'

And then Naoise said: 'We did you another good deed, and this is the time to remember it; we have put you under many benefits; it is strong our right is to your protection.

'The time when Murcael, son of Brian, fought the seven battles at Beinn Etair, we brought you, without fail, the heads of the sons of the king of the South-East.'

But Conchubar said: 'If you had done me fifty good deeds, surely this is my thanks; I would not give you peace in your distress, but every great want I could put upon you.

'Your death is not a death to me now, young sons of Usnach, since he that was innocent fell by you, the third best of the horsemen of Ireland.'

Then Deirdre said: 'Rise up, Naoise, take your sword, good son of a king, mind yourself well, for it is not long that life will be left in your fair body.'

It is then all Conchubar's men came about the house, and they put fires and burning to it. Ardan went out then, and his men, and put out the fires and killed three hundred men. And Ainnle went out in the third part of the night, and he killed three hundred, and did slaughter and destruction on them.

And Naoise went out in the last quarter of the night, and drove away all the army from the house.

He came into the house after that, and it is then Deirdre rose up and said to him: 'By my word, it is well you won your way; and do bravery and valour from this out, and it was bad advice you took when you ever trusted Conchubar.'

As for the sons of Usnach, after that they made a good protection with their shields, and they put Deirdre in the middle and linked the shields around her, and they gave three leaps out over the walls of Emain, and they killed three hundred men in that sally.

When Conchubar saw that, he went to Cathbad, the Druid, and said to him: 'Go, Cathbad, to the sons of Usnach, and work enchantment on them; for unless they are hindered they will destroy the men of Ulster for ever if they go away in spite of them; and I give the word of a true hero, they will get no harm from me, but let them only make agreement with me.' When Cathbad heard that, he agreed, believing him, and he went to the end of his arts and his knowledge to hinder the sons of Usnach, and he worked enchantment on them, so that he put the likeness of a dark sea about them, with hindering waves. And when Naoise saw the waves rising he put up Deirdre on his shoulder, and it is how the sons of Usnach were, swimming on the ground as they were going out of Emain; yet the men of Ulster did not dare to come near them until their swords had fallen from their hands. But after their swords fell from their hands, the sons of Usnach were taken. And when they were taken, Conchubar asked of the children of Durthacht to kill them. But the children of Durthacht said they would not do that. There was a young man with Conchubar whose name was Maine, and his surname Rough-Hand, son of the king of the fair Norwegians, and it is Naoise had killed his father and his two brothers; Athrac and Triathrach were their names. And he said he himself would kill the sons of Usnach. 'If that is so,' said Ardan, 'kill me the first, for I am younger than my brothers, so that I will not see my brothers killed.' 'Let him not be killed but myself,' said Ainnle. 'Let that not be done,' said Naoise, 'for I have a sword that Manannan, son of Lir, gave me, and the stroke of it leaves nothing after it, track nor trace; and strike the three of us together, and we will die at the one time.' 'That is well,' said they all, 'and let you lay down your heads,' they said. They did that, and Maine gave a strong quick blow of the sword on the three necks together on the block, and struck the three heads off them with one stroke; and the men of Ulster gave three loud sorrowful shouts, and cried aloud about them there.

As for Deirdre, she cried pitifully, wearily, and tore her fair hair, and she was talking on the sons of Usnach and on Alban, and it is what she said:

'A blessing eastward to Alban from me; good is the sight of her bays and valleys, pleasant was it to sit on the slopes of her hills, where the sons of Usnach used to be hunting.

'One day, when the nobles of Scotland were drinking with the sons of Usnach, to whom they owed their affection, Naoise gave a kiss secretly to the daughter of the lord of Duntreon. He sent her a frightened deer, wild, and a fawn at its foot; and he went to visit her coming home from the host of Inverness. When myself heard that, my head filled full of jealousy; I put my boat on the waves, it was the same to me to live or to die. They followed me swimming, Ainnle and Ardan, that never said a lie; they turned me back again, two that would give battle to a hundred; Naoise gave me his true word, he swore three times with his arms as witness, he would never put vexation on me again, until he would go from me to the hosts of the dead.

'Och! if she knew tonight, Naoise to be under a covering of clay, it is she would cry her fill, and it is I would cry along with her.'

After she had made this complaint, seeing they were all taken up with one another, Deirdre came forward on the lawn, and she was running round and round, up and down, from one to another, and Cuchulain met her, and she told him the story from first to last, how it had happened to the sons of Usnach. It is sorrowful Cuchulain was for that, for there was not in the world a man was dearer to him than Naoise. And he asked who killed him. 'Maine Rough-Hand,' said Deirdre. Then Cuchulain went away, sad and sorrowful, to Dundealgan.

After that Deirdre lay down by the grave, and they were digging earth from it, and she made this lament after the sons of Usnach:

'Long is the day without the sons of Usnach; it was never wearisome to be in their company; sons of a king that entertained exiles; three lions of the Hill of the Cave.

'Three darlings of the women of Britain; three hawks of Slieve Cuilenn; sons of a king served by valour, to whom warriors did obedience. The three mighty bears; three lions of the fort of Conrach; three sons of a king who thought well of their praise; three nurslings of the men of Ulster.

'Three heroes not good at homage; their fall is a cause of sorrow; three sons of the sister of a king; three props of the army of Cuailgne.

'Three dragons of Dun Monad, the three valiant men from the Red Branch; I myself will not be living after them, the three that broke hard battles.

'Three that were brought up by Aoife, to whom lands were under tribute; three pillars in the breach of battle; three pupils that were with Scathach.

'Three pupils that were with Uathach; three champions that were lasting in might; three shining sons of Usnach; it is weariness to be without them.

'The High King of Ulster, my first betrothed, I forsook for love of Naoise; short my life will be after him; I will make keening at their burial.

'That I would live after Naoise let no one think on the earth; I will not go on living after Ainnle and after Ardan.

'After them I myself will not live; three that would leap through the midst of battle; since my beloved is gone from me I will cry my fill over his grave.

'O young man, digging the new grave, do not make the grave narrow; I will be along with them in the grave, making lamentation and ochones!

'Many the hardship I met with along with the three heroes; I suffered want of house, want of fire, it is myself that used not to be troubled.

'Their three shields and their spears made a bed for me often. O young man, put their three swords close over their grave.

'Their three hounds, their three hawks, will be from this time without huntsmen; three helpers of every battle; three pupils of Conall Cearnach.

'The three leashes of those three hounds have brought a sigh from my heart; it is I had the care of them, the sight of them is a cause of grief.

'I was never one day alone to the day of the making of this grave, though it is often that myself and yourselves were in loneliness.

'My sight is gone from me with looking at the grave of Naoise; it is short till my life will leave me, and those who would have keened me do not live.

'Since it is through me they were betrayed I will be tired out with sorrow; it is a pity I was not in the earth before the sons of Usnach were killed.

'Sorrowful was my journey with Fergus, betraying me to the Red Branch; we were deceived all together with his sweet, flowery words. I left the delights of Ulster for the three heroes that were bravest; my life will not be long, I myself am alone after them.

'I am Deirdre without gladness, and I at the end of my life; since it is grief to be without them, I myself will not be long after them.'

After that complaint Deirdre loosed out her hair, and threw herself on the body of Naoise before it was put in the grave and gave three kisses to him, and when her mouth touched his blood, the colour of burning sods came into her cheeks, and she rose up like one that had lost her wits, and she went on through the night till she came to where the waves were breaking on the strand. And a fisherman was there and his wife, and they brought her into their cabin and sheltered her, and she neither smiled nor laughed, nor took food, drink, or sleep, nor raised her head from her knees, but crying always after the sons of Usnach.

But when she could not be found at Emain, Conchubar sent Levarcham to look for her, and to bring her back to his place, that he might make her his wife. And Levarcham found her in the fisherman's cabin, and she bade her come back to Emain, where she would have protection and riches and all that she would ask. And she gave her this message she brought from Conchubar: 'Come up to my house, O branch with the dark eye-lashes, and there need be no fear on your fair face, of hatred or of jealousy or of reproach.' And Deirdre said: 'I will not go up to his house, for it is not land or earth or food I am wanting, or gold or silver or horses, but leave to go to the grave where the sons of Usnach are lying, till I give the three honey kisses to their three white, beautiful bodies.' And she made this complaint:

'Make keening for the heroes that were killed on their coming to Ireland; stately they used to be, coming to the house, the three great sons of Usnach.

'The sons of Usnach fell in the fight like three branches that were growing straight and nice, and they destroyed in a heavy storm that left neither bud nor twig of them.

'Naoise, my gentle, well-learned comrade, make no delay in crying him with me; cry for Ardan that killed the wild boars, cry for Ainnle whose strength was great.

'It was Naoise that would kiss my lips, my first man and my first sweetheart; it was Ainnle would pour out my drink, and it was Ardan would lay my pillow.

'Though sweet to you is the mead that is drunk by the soft-living son of Ness, the food of the sons of Usnach was sweeter to me all through my lifetime.

'Whenever Naoise would go out to hunt through the woods or the wide plains, all the meat he would bring back was better to me than honey.

'Though sweet to you are the sounds of pipes and of trumpets, it is truly I say to the king, I have heard music that is sweeter.

'Delightful to Conchubar, the king, are pipes and trumpets; but the singing of the sons of Usnach was more delightful to me.

'It was Naoise had the deep sound of the waves in his voice; it was the song of Ardan that was good, and the voice of Ainnle towards their green dwelling-place.

'Their birth was beautiful and their blossoming, as they grew to the strength of manhood; sad is the end today, the sons of Usnach to be cut down.

'Dear were their pleasant words, dear their young, high strength; in their going through the plains of Ireland there was a welcome before the coming of their strength.

'Dear their grey eyes that were loved by women, many looked

on them as they went; when they went freely searching through the woods, their steps were pleasant on the dark mountain.

'I do not sleep at any time, and the colour is gone from my face; there is no sound can give me delight since the sons of Usnach do not come.

'I do not sleep through the night; my senses are scattered away from me, I do not care for food or drink. I have no welcome today for the pleasant drink of nobles, or ease, or comfort, or delight, or a great house, or the palace of a king.

'Do not break the strings of my heart as you took hold of my young youth, Conchubar; though my darling is dead, my love is strong to live. What is country to me, or land, or lordship? What are swift horses? What are jewels and gold? Och! it is I will be lying tonight on the strand like the beautiful sons of Usnach.'

So Levarcham went back to Conchubar to tell him what way Deirdre was, and that she would not come with her to Emain Macha.

And when she was gone, Deirdre went out on the stand, and she found a carpenter making an oar for a boat, and making a mast for it, clean and straight, to put up a sail to the wind. And when she saw him making it, she said: 'It is a sharp knife you have, to cut the oar so clean and so straight, and if you will give it to me,' she said, 'I will give you a ring of the best gold in Ireland for it, the ring that belonged to Naoise, and that was with him through the battle and through the fight; he thought much of it in his lifetime; it is pure gold, through and through.' So the carpenter took the ring in his hand, and the knife in the other hand, and he looked at them together, and he gave her the knife for the ring, and for her asking and her tears. Then Deirdre went close to the waves, and she said: 'Since the other is not with me now, I will spend no more of my lifetime without him.' And with that she drove the black knife into her side, but she drew it out again and threw it in the sea to her right hand, the way no one would be blamed for her death.

Then Conchubar came down to the strand and five hundred men along with him, to bring Deirdre away to Emain Macha, but all he found before him was her white body on the ground, and it without life. And it is what he said:

'A thousand deaths on the time I brought death on my sister's children; now I am myself without Deirdre, and they themselves are without life.

'They were my sister's children, the three brothers I vexed with blows, Naoise, and Ainnle, and Ardan; they have died along with Deirdre.'

And they took her white, beautiful body, and laid it in a grave, and a flagstone was raised over her grave, and over the grave of the sons of Usnach, and their names were written in Ogham,[3] and keening was made for their burial.

And as to Fergus, son of Rogh, he came on the day after the children of Usnach were killed, to Emain Macha. And when he found they had been killed and his pledge to them broken, he himself, and Cormac Conloingeas, Conchubar's own son, and Dubthach, the Beetle of Ulster, with their men, made an attack on Conchubar's house and men, and a great many were killed by them, and Emain Macha was burned and destroyed.

And after doing that, they went into Connacht, to Ailell and to Maeve at Cruachan, and they were made welcome there, and they took service with them and fought with them against Ulster because of the treachery that was done by Conchubar. And that is the way Fergus and the others came to be on the side of the men of Connacht in the war for the Brown Bull of Cuailgne.

And Cathbad laid a curse on Emain Macha, on account of that great wrong. And it is what he said, that none of the race of Conchubar should have the kingdom, to the end of life and time.

And that came true, for the most of Conchubar's sons died in his own lifetime, and when he was near his death, he bade the men of Ulster bring back Cormac Conloingeas out of Cruachan and give him the kingdom.

So they sent messengers to Cormac, and he set out and his three troops of men with him, and he left his blessing with Ailell and with Maeve, and he promised them a good return for all the kind treatment they had given him. And they crossed the river at Athluain, and there they saw a red woman at the edge of the ford, and she washing her chariot and her harness. And after that they met a young girl coming towards them, and a light green cloak about her, and a brooch of precious stones at her breast. And Cormac asked her was she coming with them, and she said she was not, and it would be better for himself to turn back, for the ruin of his life was come.

And he stopped for the night at the House of the Two Smiths on the hill of Bruighean Mor, the great dwelling-place.

But a troop of the men of Connacht came about the house in the night, for they were on the way home after destroying and robbing a district of Ulster, and they thought to make an end of Cormac before he would get to Emain.

And it chanced there was a great harper, Craiftine, living close by, and his wife, Sceanb, daughter of Scethern, a Druid of Connacht, loved Cormac Conloingeas, and three times she had gone to meet him at Athluain, and she planted three trees there – Grief, and Dark, and Dumbness.

And there was great hatred and jealousy of Cormac on Craiftine, so when he knew the men of Connacht were going to make an attack on him, he went outside the house with his harp, and played a soft sleepy tune to him, the way he had not the strength to rouse himself up, and himself and the most of his people were killed. And Amergin, that had gone with the message to him, made his grave and his mound, and the place is called Cluain Duma, the Lawn of the Mound.

## The Only Son of Aoife

The time Cuchulain came back from Alban, after he had learned the use of arms under Scathach, he left Aoife, the queen he had overcome in battle, with child.

And when he was leaving her, he told her what name to give the child, and he gave her a gold ring, and bade her keep it safe till the child grew to be a lad, and till his thumb would fill it; and he bade her to give it to him then, and to send him to Ireland, and he would know he was his son by that token. She promised to do so, and with that Cuchulain went back to Ireland.

It was not long after the child was born, word came to Aoife that Cuchulain had taken Emer to be his wife in Ireland. When she heard that, great jealousy came on her, and great anger, and her love for Cuchulain was turned to hatred; and she remembered her three champions that he had killed, and how he had overcome herself, and she determined in her mind that when her son would come to have the strength of a man, she would get her revenge through him. She told Conlaoch her son nothing of this, but brought him up like any king's son; and when he was come to sensible years, she put him under the teaching of Scathach, to be taught the use of arms and the art of war. He turned out as apt a scholar as his father, and it was not long before he had learnt all Scathach had to teach.

Then Aoife gave him the arms of a champion, and bade him go to Ireland, but first she laid three commands on him: the first never to give way to any living person, but to die sooner than be made turn back; the second, not to refuse a challenge from the greatest champion alive, but to fight him at all risks, even if he was sure to lose his life; the third, not to tell his name on any account, though he might be threatened with death for hiding it. She put him under *geasa*, that is, under bonds, not to do these things.

Then the young man, Conlaoch, set out, and it was not long before his ship brought him to Ireland, and the place he landed at was Baile's Strand, near Dundealgan.

It chanced that at that time Conchubar, the High King, was holding court there, for it was a convenient gathering-place for his chief men, and they were settling some business that belonged to the government of that district.

When word was brought to Conchubar that there was a ship come to the strand, and a young lad in it armed as if for fighting, and armed men with him, he sent one of the chief men of his household to ask his name, and on what business he was come.

The messenger's name was Cuinaire, and he went down to the strand, and when he saw the young man he said: 'A welcome to you, young hero from the east, with the merry face. It is likely, seeing you come armed as if for fighting, you are gone astray on your journey; but as you are come to Ireland, tell me your name

198

and what your deeds have been, and your victories in the eastern bounds of the world.'

'As to my name,' said Conlaoch, 'it is of no great account; but whatever it is, I am under bonds not to tell it to the stoutest man living.'

'It is best for you to tell it at the king's desire,' said Cuinaire, 'before you get your death through refusing it, as many a champion from Alban and from Britain has done before now.' 'If that is the order you put on us when we land here, it is I will break it,' said Conlaoch, 'and no one will obey it any longer from this out.'

So Cuinaire went back and told the king what the young lad had said. Then Conchubar said to his people: 'Who will go out into the field, and drag the name and the story out of this young man?' 'I will go,' said Conall, for his hand was never slow in fighting. And he went out, and found the lad angry and destroying, handling his arms, and they attacked one another with a great noise of swords and shouts, and they were gripped together, and fought for a while, and then Conall was overcome, and the great name and the praise that was on Conall, it was on the head of Conlaoch it was now.

Word was sent then to where Cuchulain was, in pleasant, bright-faced Dundealgan. And the messenger told him the whole story, and he said: 'Conall is lying humbled, and it is slow the help is in coming; it is a welcome there would be before the Hound.'[4]

Cuchulain rose up then and went to where Conlaoch was, and he still handling his arms. And Cuchulain asked him his name and said: 'It would be well for you, young hero of unknown name, to loosen yourself from this knot, and not to bring down my hand upon you, for it will be hard for you to escape death.' But Conlaoch said: 'If I put you down in the fight, the way I put down your comrade, there will be a great name on me; but if I draw back now, there will be mockery on me, and it will be said I was afraid of the fight. I will never give in to any man to tell the name, or to give an account of myself. But if I was not held with a command,' he said, 'there is no man in the world I would sooner give it to than to yourself, since I saw your face. But do not think, brave champion of Ireland, that I will let you take away the fame I have won, for nothing.'

With that they fought together, and it is seldom such a battle was seen, and all wondered that the young lad could stand so well against Cuchulain.

So they fought a long while, neither getting the better of the other, but at last Cuchulain was charged so hotly by the lad that he was forced to give way, and although he had fought so many good fights, and killed so many great champions, and understood the use of arms better than any man living, he was pressed very hard.

And he called for the Gae Bulg,[5] and his anger came on him, and the flames of the hero-light began to shine about his head, and by that sign Conlaoch knew him to be Cuchulain, his father. And just at that time he was aiming his spear at him, and when he knew it was Cuchulain, he threw his spear crooked that it might pass beside him. But Cuchulain threw his spear, the Gae Bulg, at him with all his might, and it struck the lad in the side and went into his body, so that he fell to the ground.

And Cuchulain said: 'Now, boy, tell your name and what you are, for it is short your life will be, for you will not live after that wound.'

And Conlaoch showed the ring that was on his hand, and he said: 'Come here where I am lying on the field, let my men from the east come round me. I am suffering for revenge. I am Conlaoch, son of the Hound, heir of dear Dundealgan; I was bound to this secret in Dun Scathach,[6] the secret in which I have found my grief.'

And Cuchulain said: 'It is a pity your mother not to be here to see you brought down. She might have stretched out her hand to stop the spear that wounded you.' And Conlaoch said: 'My curse be on my mother, for it was she put me under bonds; it was she sent me here to try my strength against yours.' And Cuchulain said: 'My curse be on your mother, the woman that is full of treachery; it is through her harmful thoughts these tears have been brought on us.' And Conlaoch said: 'My name was never forced from my mouth till now; I never gave an account of myself to any man under the sun. But, O Cuchulain of the sharp sword, it was a pity you not to know me the time I threw the slanting spear behind you in the fight.'

And then the sorrow of death came upon Conlaoch, and Cuchulain took his sword and put it through him, sooner than leave him in the pain and the punishment he was in.

And then great trouble and anguish came on Cuchulain, and he made this complaint:[7]

'It is a pity it is, O son of Aoife, that ever you came into the province of Ulster, that you ever met with the Hound of Cuailgne.

'If I and my fair Conlaoch were doing feats of war on the one side, the men of Ireland from sea to sea would not be equal to us together. It is no wonder I to be under grief when I see the shield and the arms of Conlaoch. A pity it is there is no one at all, a pity there are not hundreds of men on whom I could get satisfaction for his death.

'If it was the king himself had hurt your fair body, it is I would have shortened his days.

'It is well for the House of the Red Branch, and for the heads of its fair army of heroes, it was not they that killed my only son.

'It is well for Laegaire of Victories it is not from him you got your heavy pain.

'It is well for the heroes of Conall they did not join in the killing of you; it is well that travelling across the plain of Macha they did not fall in with me after such a fight.

'It is well for the tall, well-shaped Forbuide; well for Dubthach, your Black Beetle of Ulster.

'It is well for you, Cormac Conloingeas, your share of arms gave no help, that it is not from your weapons he got his wound, the hard-skinned shield or the blade.

'It is a pity it was not one on the plains of Munster, or in Leinster of the sharp blades, or at Cruachan of the rough fighters, that struck down my comely Conlaoch.

'It is a pity it was not in the country of the Cruithne, of the fierce Fians, you fell in a heavy quarrel, or in the country of the Greeks, or in some other place of the world, you died, and I could avenge you.

'Or in Spain, or in Sorcha, or in the country of the Saxons of the free armies; there would not then be this death in my heart.

'It is very well for the men of Alban it was not they that destroyed your fame; and it is well for the men of the Gall.

'Och! It is bad that it happened; my grief! it is on me is the misfortune, O Conlaoch of the Red Spear, I myself to have spilled your blood.

'I to be under defeat, without strength. It is a pity Aoife never taught you to know the power of my strength in the fight.

'It is no wonder I to be blinded after such a fight and such a defeat.

'It is no wonder I to be tired out, and without the sons of Usnach beside me.

'Without a son, without a brother, with none to come after me; without Conlaoch, without a name to keep my strength.

'To be without Naoise, without Ainnle, without Ardan; is it not with me is my fill of trouble?

'I am the father that killed his son, the fine green branch; there is no hand or shelter to help me.

'I am a raven that has no home; I am a boat going from wave to wave; I am a ship that has lost its rudder; I am the apple left on the tree; it is little I thought of falling from it; grief and sorrow will be with me from this time.'

Then Cuchulain stood up and faced all the men of Ulster. 'There is trouble on Cuchulain,' said Conchubar; 'he is after killing his own son, and if I and all my men were to go against him, by the end of the day he would destroy every man of us. Go now,' he said to Cathbad, the Druid, 'and bind him to go down to Baile's Strand, and to give three days fighting against the waves of the sea, rather than to kill us all.'

So Cathbad put an enchantment on him, and bound him to go down. And when he came to the strand, there was a great white stone before him, and he took his sword in his right hand, and he said: 'If I had the head of the woman that sent her son to his death, I would split it as I split this stone.' And he made four quarters of the stone.

Then he fought with the waves three days and three nights, till he fell from hunger and weakness, so that some men said he got his death there. But it was not there he got his death, but on the plain of Muirthemne.

# from *Gods and Fighting Men*

## The Fate of the Children of Lir

Now at the time when the Tuatha De Danann chose a king for themselves after the battle of Tailltin, and Lir heard the kingship was given to Bodb Dearg, it did not please him, and he left the gathering without leave and with no word to any one; for he thought it was he himself had a right to be made king. But if he went away himself, Bodb was given the kingship none the less, for not one of the five begrudged it to him but only Lir. And it is what they determined, to follow after Lir, and to burn down his house, and to attack himself with spear and sword, on account of his not giving obedience to the king they had chosen. 'We will not do that,' said Bodb Dearg, 'for that man would defend any place he is in; and besides that,' he said, 'I am none the less king over the Tuatha De Danann, although he does not submit to me.'

All went on like that for a good while, but at last a great misfortune came on Lir, for his wife died from him after a sickness of three nights. And that came very hard on Lir, and there was heaviness on his mind after her. And there was great talk of the death of that woman in her own time.

And the news of it was told all through Ireland, and it came to the house of Bodb, and the best of the Men of Dea were with him at that time. And Bodb said: 'If Lir had a mind for it,' he said, 'my help and my friendship would be good for him now, since his wife is not living to him. For I have here with me the three young girls of the best shape, and the best appearance, and the best name in all Ireland, Aobh, Aoife, and Ailbhe, the three daughters of Oilell of Aran, my own three nurslings.' The Men of Dea said then it was a good thought he had, and that what he said was true.

Messages and messengers were sent then from Bodb Dearg to the place Lir was, to say that if he had a mind to join with the Son of the Dagda[1] and to acknowledge his lordship, he would give him a foster-child of his foster-children. And Lir thought well of the offer, and he set out on the morrow with fifty chariots from Sidhe Fionnachaidh; and he went by every short way till he came to Bodb's dwelling-place at Loch Dearg, and there was a welcome before him there, and all the people were merry and pleasant before him, and he and his people got good attendance that night.

And the three daughters of Oilell of Aran were sitting on the one seat with Bodb Dearg's wife, the queen of the Tuatha De Danann, that was their foster-mother. And Bodb said: 'You may have your choice of the three young girls, Lir.' 'I cannot say,' said Lir, 'which one of them is my choice, but whichever of them is the eldest, she is the noblest, and it is best for me to take her.' 'If that is so,' said Bodb, 'it is Aobh is the eldest, and she will be given to you, if it is your wish.' 'It is my wish,' he said. And he took Aobh for his wife that night, and he stopped there for a fortnight, and then he brought her away to his own house, till he would make a great wedding-feast.

And in the course of time Aobh brought forth two children, a daughter and a son, Fionnuala and Aodh their names were. And after a while she was brought to bed again, and this time she gave birth to two sons, and they called them Fiachra and Conn. And she herself died at their birth. And that weighed very heavy on Lir, and only for the way his mind was set on his four children he would have gone near to die of grief.

The news came to Bodb Dearg's place, and all the people gave out three loud, high cries, keening their nursling. And after they had keened her it is what Bodb Dearg said: 'It is a fret to us our daughter to have died, for her own sake and for the sake of the good man we gave her to, for we are thankful for his friendship and his faithfulness. However,' he said, 'our friendship with one another will not be broken, for I will give him for a wife her sister Aoife.'

When Lir heard that, he came for the girl and married her, and brought her home to his house. And there was honour and affection with Aoife for her sister's children; and indeed no person at all could see those four children without giving them the heart's love.

And Bodb Dearg used often to be going to Lir's house for the sake of those children; and he used to bring them to his own place for a good length of time, and then he would let them go back to their own place again. And the Men of Dea were at that time using the Feast of Age in every hill of the Sidhe in turn; and when they came to Lir's hill those four children were their joy and delight, for the beauty of their appearance; and it is where they used to sleep, in beds in sight of their father Lir. And he used to rise up at the break of every morning, and to lie down among his children.

But it is what came of all this, that a fire of jealousy was kindled in Aoife, and she got to have a dislike and a hatred of her sister's children.

Then she let on to have a sickness, that lasted through nearly the length of a year. And the end of that time she did a deed of jealousy and cruel treachery against the children of Lir.

And one day she got her chariot yoked, and she took the four children in it, and they went forward towards the house of Bodb Dearg; but Fionnuala had no mind to go with her, for she knew by her she had some plan for their death or their destruction, and she had seen in a dream that there was treachery against them in Aoife's mind. But all the same she was not able to escape from what was before her.

And when they were on their way Aoife said to her people: 'Let you kill now,' she said, 'the four children of Lir, for whose sake their father has given up my love, and I will give you your own choice of a reward out of all the good things of the world.' 'We will not do that indeed,' said they; 'and it is a bad deed you have thought of, and harm will come to you out of it.'

And when they would not do as she bade them, she took out a sword herself to put an end to the children with; but she being a woman and with no good courage, and with no great strength in her mind, she was not able to do it.

They went on then west to Loch Dairbhreach, the Lake of the Oaks, and the horses were stopped there, and Aoife bade the children of Lir to go out and bathe in the lake, and they did as she bade them. And as soon as Aoife saw them out in the lake she struck them with a Druid rod, and put on them the shape of four swans, white and beautiful. And it is what she said: 'Out with you, children of the king, your luck is taken away from you for ever; it is sorrowful the story will be to your friends; it is with flocks of birds your cries will be heard for ever.'

And Fionnuala said: 'Witch, we know now what your name is, you have struck us down with no hope of relief; but although you put us from wave to wave, there are times when we will touch the land. We shall get help when we are seen; help, and all that is best for us; even though we have to sleep upon the lake, it is our minds will be going abroad early.'

And then the four children of Lir turned towards Aoife, and it is what Fionnuala said: 'It is a bad deed you have done, Aoife, and it is a bad fulfilling of friendship, you to destroy us without cause; and vengeance for it will come upon you, and you will fall in satisfaction for it, for your power for our destruction is not greater than the power of our friends to avenge it on you; and put some bounds now,' she said, 'to the time this enchantment is to stop on us.' 'I will do that,' said Aoife, 'and it is worse for you, you to have asked it of me. And the bounds set to your time are this, till the Woman from the South and the Man from the North will come together. And since you ask to hear it of me,' she said, 'no friends and no power that you have will be able to bring you out of these shapes you are in through the length of your lives, until you have been three hundred years on Loch Dairbhreach, and three hundred years on Sruth na Maoile between Ireland and Alban, and three hundred years at Irrus Domnann and Inis Gluaire; and these are to be your journeys from this out,' she said.

But then repentance came on Aoife, and she said: 'Since there is no other help for me to give you now, you may keep your own speech; and you will be singing sweet music of the Sidhe, that would put the men of the earth to sleep, and there will be no music in the world equal to it; and your own sense and your own nobility will stay with you, the way it will not weigh so heavy on you to be in the shape of birds. And go away out of my sight now, children of Lir,' she said, 'with your white faces, with your stammering Irish. It is a great curse on tender lads, they to be driven out on the rough wind. Nine hundred years to be on the water, it is a long time for any one to be in pain; it is I put this on you through treachery, it is best for you to do as I tell you now.

'Lir, that got victory with so many a good cast, his heart is a kernel of death in him now; the groaning of the great hero is a sickness to me, though it is I that have well earned his anger.'

And then the horses were caught for Aoife, and the chariot yoked for her, and she went on to the palace of Bodb Dearg, and there was a welcome before her from the chief people of the place. And the son of the Dagda asked her why she did not bring the children of Lir with her. 'I will tell you that,' she said. 'It is because Lir has no liking for you, and he will not trust you with his children, for fear you might keep them from him altogether.'

'I wonder at that,' said Bodb Dearg, 'for those children are dearer to me than my own children.' And he thought in his own mind it was deceit the woman was doing on him, and it is what he did, he sent messengers to the north to Sidhe Fionnachaidh. And Lir asked them what did they come for. 'On the head of your children,' said they. 'Are they not gone to you along with Aoife?' he said. 'They are not,' said they; 'and Aoife said it was yourself would not let them come.'

It is downhearted and sorrowful Lir was at that news, for he understood well it was Aoife had destroyed or made an end of his children. And early in the morning of the morrow his horses were caught, and he set out on the road to the south-west. And when he was as far as the shore of Loch Dairbhreach, the four children saw the horses coming towards them, and it is what Fionnuala said: 'A welcome to the troop of horses I see coming near to the lake; the people they are bringing are strong, there is sadness on them; it is us they are following, it is for us they are looking; let us move over to the shore, Aodh, Fiachra, and comely Conn. Those that are coming can be no others in the world but only Lir and his household.'

Then Lir came to the edge of the lake, and he took notice of the swans having the voice of living people, and he asked them why was it they had that voice.

'I will tell you that, Lir,' said Fionnuala. 'We are your own four children, that are after being destroyed by your wife, and by the sister of our own mother, through the dint of her jealousy.' 'Is there any way to put you into your own shapes again?' said Lir. 'There is no way,' said Fionnuala, 'for all the men of the world could not help us till we have gone through our time, and that will not be,' she said, 'till the end of nine hundred years.'

When Lir and his people heard that, they gave out three great heavy shouts of grief and sorrow and crying.

'Is there a mind with you,' said Lir, 'to come to us on the land, since you have your own sense and your memory yet?' 'We have not the power,' said Fionnuala, 'to live with any person at all from this time; but we have our own language, the Irish, and we have the power to sing sweet music, and it is enough to satisfy the whole race of men to be listening to that music. And let you stop here tonight,' she said, 'and we will be making music for you.'

So Lir and his people stopped there listening to the music of the swans, and they slept there quietly that night. And Lir rose up early on the morning of the morrow and he made this complaint:

'It is time to go from this place. I do not sleep though I am in my lying down. To be parted from my dear children, it is that is tormenting my heart.

'It is a bad net I put over you, bringing Aoife, daughter of Oilell of Aran, to the house. I would never have followed that advice if I had known what it would bring upon me.

'O Fionnuala, and comely Conn, O Aodh, O Fiachra of the beautiful arms; it is not ready I am to go away from you, from the border of the harbour where you are.'

Then Lir went on to the palace of Bodb Dearg, and there was a welcome before him there; and he got a reproach from Bodb Dearg for not bringing his children along with him. 'My grief!' said Lir. 'It is not I that would not bring my children along with me; it was Aoife there beyond, your own foster-child and the sister of their mother, that put them in the shape of four white swans on Loch Dairbhreach, in the sight of the whole of the men of Ireland; but they have their sense with them yet, and their reason, and their voice, and their Irish.'

Bodb Dearg gave a great start when he heard that, and he knew what Lir said was true, and he gave a very sharp reproach to Aoife, and he said: 'This treachery will be worse for yourself in the end, Aoife, than to the children of Lir. And what shape would you yourself think worst of being in?' he said.

'I would think worst of being a witch of the air,' she said. 'It is into that shape I will put you now,' said Bodb. And with that he struck her with a Druid wand, and she was turned into a witch of the air there and then, and she went away on the wind in that shape, and she is in it yet, and will be in it to the end of life and time.

As to Bodb Dearg and the Tuatha De Danann they came to the shore of Loch Dairbhreach, and they made their camp there to be listening to the music of the swans.

And the Sons of the Gael used to be coming no less than the Men of Dea to hear them from every part of Ireland, for there never was any music or any delight heard in Ireland to compare with that music of the swans. And they used to be telling stories, and to be talking with men of Ireland every day, and with their teachers and their fellow-pupils and their friends. And every night they used to sing very sweet music of the Sidhe; and everyone that heard that music would sleep sound and quiet whatever trouble or long sickness might be on him; for everyone that heard the music of the birds, it is happy and contented he would be after it.

These two gatherings now of the Tuatha De Danann and of the Sons of the Gael stopped there around Loch Dairbhreach through the length of three hundred years. And it is then Fionnuala said to her brothers: 'Do you know,' she said, 'we have spent all we have to spend of our time here, but this one night only.'

And there was great sorrow on the sons of Lir when they heard that, for they thought it the same as to be living people again, to be talking with their friends and their companions on Loch

Dairbhreach, in comparison with going on the cold, fretful sea of the Maoil in the north.

And they came on the morrow to speak with their father and with their foster-father, and they bade them farewell, and Fionnuala made this complaint:

'Farewell to you, Bodb Dearg, the man with whom all knowledge is in pledge. And farewell to our father along with you, Lir of the Hill of the White Field.

'The time is come, as I think, for us to part from you, O pleasant company; my grief it is not on a visit we are going to you.

'From this day out, O friends of our heart, our comrades, it is on the tormented course of the Maoil we will be, without the voice of any person near us.

'Three hundred years there, and three hundred years in the bay of the men of Domnann, it is a pity for the four comely children of Lir, the salt waves of the sea to be their covering by night.

'O three brothers, with the ruddy faces gone from you, let them all leave the lake now, the great troop that loved us, it is sorrowful our parting is.'

After that complaint they took to flight, lightly, airily, till they came to Sruth na Maoile between Ireland and Alban. And that was a grief to the men of Ireland, and they gave out an order no swan was to be killed from that out, whatever chance might be of killing one, all through Ireland.

It was a bad dwelling-place for the children of Lir they to be on Sruth na Maoile. When they saw the wide coast about them, they were filled with cold and with sorrow, and they thought nothing of all they had gone through before, in comparison to what they were going through on that sea.

Now one night while they were there a great storm came on them, and it is what Fionnuala said: 'My dear brothers,' she said, 'it is a pity for us not to be making ready for this night, for it is certain the storm will separate us from one another. And let us,' she said, 'settle on some place where we can meet afterwards, if we are driven from one another in the night.'

'Let us settle,' said the others, 'we meet one another at Carraig na Ron, the Rock of the Seals, for we all have knowledge of it.'

And when midnight came, the wind came on them with it, and the noise of the waves increased, and the lightning was flashing, and a rough storm came sweeping down, the way the children of Lir were scattered over the great sea, and the wideness of it set them astray, so that no one of them could know what way the others went. But after that storm a great quiet came on the sea, and Fionnuala was alone on Sruth na Maoile; and when she took notice that her brothers were wanting she was lamenting after them greatly, and she made this complaint:

'It is a pity for me to be alive in the state I am; it is frozen to my sides my wings are; it is little that the wind has not broken my heart in my body, with the loss of Aodh.

'To be three hundred years on Loch Dairbhreach without going into my own shape, it is worse to me the time I am on Sruth na Maoile.

'The three I loved, Och! the three I loved, that slept under the shelter of my feathers; till the dead come back to the living I will see them no more for ever.

'It is a pity I to stay after Fiachra, and after Aodh, and after comely Conn, and with no account of them; my grief I to be here to face every hardship this night.'

She stopped all night there upon the Rock of the Seals until the rising of the sun, looking out over the sea on every side till at last she saw Conn coming to her, his feathers wet through and his head hanging, and her heart gave him a great welcome; and then Fiachra came wet and perished and worn out, and he could not say a word they could understand with the dint of the cold and the hardship he had gone through. And Fionnuala put him under her wings, and she said: 'We would be well off now if Aodh would but come to us.'

It was not long after that, they saw Aodh coming, his head dry and his feathers beautiful, and Fionnuala gave him a great welcome, and she put him in under the feathers of her breast, and Fiachra under her right wing and Conn under her left wing, the way she could put her feathers over them all. 'And Och! my brothers,' she said, 'this was a bad night to us, and it is many of its like are before us from this out.'

They stayed there a long time after that, suffering cold and misery on the Maoil, till at last a night came on them they had never known the like of before, for frost and snow and wind and cold. And they were crying and lamenting the hardship of their life, and the cold of the night and the greatness of the snow and the hardness of the wind. And after they had suffered cold to the end of a year, a worse night again came on them, in the middle of winter. And they were on Carraig na Ron, and the water froze about them, and as they rested on the rock, their feet and their wings and their feathers froze to the rock, the way they were not able to move from it. And they made such a hard struggle to get away, that they left the skin of their feet and their feathers and the tops of their wings on the rock after them.

'My grief, children of Lir,' said Fionnuala, 'it is bad our state is now, for we cannot bear the salt water to touch us, and there are bonds on us not to leave it; and if the salt water goes into our sores,' she said, 'we will get our death.' And she made this complaint:

'It is keening we are tonight; without feathers to cover our bodies; it is cold the rough, uneven rocks are under our bare feet.

'It is bad our stepmother was to us the time she played enchantments on us, sending us out like swans upon the sea.

'Our washing place is on the ridge of the bay, in the foam of flying manes of the sea; our share of the ale feast is the salt water of the blue tide.

'One daughter and three sons; it is in the clefts of the rocks we are; it is on the hard rocks we are, it is a pity the way we are.'

However, they came on to the course of the Maoil again, and the salt water was sharp and rough and bitter to them, but if it was itself, they were not able to avoid it or to get shelter from it. And they were there by the shore under that hardship till such time as their feathers grew again, and their wings, and till their sores were entirely healed. And then they used to go every day to the shore of Ireland or of Alban, but they had to come back to Sruth na Maoile every night.

Now they came one day to the mouth of the Banna, to the north of Ireland, and they saw a troop of riders, beautiful, of the one colour, with well-trained pure white horses under them, and they travelling the road straight from the south-west.

'Do you know who those riders are, sons of Lir?' said Fionnuala.

'We do not,' they said; 'but it is likely they might be some troops of the Sons of Gael, or of the Tuatha De Danann.'

They moved over closer to the shore then, that they might know who they were, and when the riders saw them they came to meet them until they were able to hold talk together.

And the chief men among them were two sons of Bodb Dearg, Aodh Aithfhiosach, of the quick wits, and Fergus Fithchiollach, of the chess, and a third part of the Riders of the Sidhe along with them, and it was for the swans they had been looking for a long while before that, and when they came together they wished one another a kind and loving welcome.

And the children of Lir asked for news of all the Men of Dea, and above all of Lir, and Bodb Dearg and their people.

'They are well, and they are in the one place together,' said they, 'in your father's house at Sidhe Fionnachaidh, using the Feast of Age pleasantly and happily, and with no uneasiness on them, only for being without yourselves, and without knowledge of what happened you from the day you left Loch Dairbhreach.'

'That has not been the way with us,' said Fionnuala, 'for we have gone through great hardship and uneasiness and misery on the tides of the sea until this day.'

And she made this complaint:

'There is delight tonight with the household of Lir! Plenty of ale with them and of wine, although it is in a cold dwelling-place this night are the four children of the king.

'It is without a spot our bedclothes are, our bodies covered over with curved feathers; but it is often we were dressed in purple, and we drinking pleasant mead.

'It is what our food is and our drink, the white sand and the bitter water of the sea; it is often we drank mead of hazel-nuts from round four-lipped drinking cups.

'It is what our beds are, bare rocks out of the power of the waves; it is often there used to be spread out for us beds of the breast-feathers of birds.

'Though it is our work now be swimming through the frost and through the noise of the waves, it is often a company of the sons of kings were riding after us to the Hill of Bodb.

'It is what wasted my strength, to be going and coming over the current of the Maoil the way I never was used to, and never to be in the sunshine on the soft grass.

'Fiachra's bed and Conn's bed is to come under the cover of my wings on the sea. Aodh has his place under the feathers of my breast, the four of us side by side.

'The teaching of Manannan without deceit, the talk of Bodb Dearg on the pleasant ridge; the voice of Angus, his sweet kisses; it is by their side I used to be without grief.'

After that the riders went on to Lir's house, and they told the chief men of the Tuatha De Danann all the birds had gone through, and the state they were in. 'We have no power over them,' the chief men said, 'but we are glad they are living yet, for they will get help in the end of time.'

As to the children of Lir, they went back towards their old place in the Maoil, and they stopped there till the time they had to spend in it was spent. And then Fionnuala said: 'The time is come for us to leave this place. And it is to Irrus Domnann we must go now,' she said, 'after our three hundred years here. And indeed there will be no rest for us there, or any standing ground, or any shelter from the storms. But since it is time for us to go, let us set out on the cold wind, the way we will not go astray.'

So they set out in that way, and left Sruth na Maoile behind them, and went to the point of Irrus Domnann, and there they stopped, and it is a life of misery and a cold life they led there. And one time the sea froze about them that they could not move at all, and the brothers were lamenting, and Fionnuala was comforting them, for she knew there would be help come to them in the end.

And they stayed at Irrus Domnann till the time they had to spend there was spent. And then Fionnuala said: 'The time is come for us to go back to Sidhe Fionnachaidh, where our father is with his household and with all our own people.'

'It pleases us well to hear that,' they said.

So they set out flying through the air lightly till they came to Sidhe Fionnachaidh; and it is how they found the place, empty before them, and nothing in it but green hillocks and thickets of nettles, without a house, without a fire, without a hearthstone. And the four pressed close to one another then, and they gave out three sorrowful cries, and Fionnuala made this complaint:

'It is a wonder to me this place is, and it without a house, without a dwelling-place. To see it the way it is now, Ochone! it is bitterness to my heart.

'Without dogs, without hounds for hunting, without women, without great kings; we never knew it to be like this when our father was in it.

'Without horns, without cups, without drinking in the lighted house; without young men, without riders; the way it is tonight is a foretelling of sorrow.

'The people of the place to be as they are now, Ochone! it is grief to my heart! It is plain to my mind tonight the lord of the house is not living.

'Och, house where we used to see music and playing and the gathering of people! I think it a great change to see it lonely the way it is tonight.

'The greatness of the hardships we have gone through going from one wave to another of the sea, we never heard of the like of them coming on any other person.

'It is seldom this place had its part with grass and bushes; the man is not living that would know us, it would be a wonder to him to see us here.'

However, the children of Lir stopped that night in their father's place and their grandfather's, where they had been reared, and they were singing very sweet music of the Sidhe. And they rose up early on the morning of the morrow and went to the Inis Gluaire, and all the birds of the country gathered near them on Loch na-n Ean, the Lake of the Birds. And they used to go out to feed every day to the far parts of the country, to Inis Geadh and to Accuill, the place Donn, son of Miled, and his people that were drowned were buried, and to all the western islands of Connacht, and they used to go back to Inis Gluaire every night.

*

It was about that time it happened them to meet with a young man of good race, and his name was Aibric; and he often took notice of the birds, and their singing was sweet to him and he loved them greatly, and they loved him. And it is this young man that told the whole story of all that had happened them, and put it in order.

And the story he told of what happened them in the end is this.

It was after the faith of Christ and blessed Patrick came into Ireland, that Saint Mochaomhog came to Inis Gluaire. And the first night he came to the island, the children of Lir heard the voice of his bell, ringing near them. And the brothers started up with fright when they heard it. 'We do not know,' they said, 'what is that weak, unpleasing voice we hear.'

'That is the voice of the bell of Mochaomhog,' said Fionnuala; 'and it is through that bell,' she said, 'you will be set free from pain and from misery.'

They listened to that music of the bell till the matins were done, and then they began to sing the low, sweet music of the Sidhe.

And Mochaomhog was listening to them, and he prayed to God to show him who was singing that music, and it was showed to him that the children of Lir were singing it. And on the morning of the morrow he went forward to the Lake of the Birds, and he saw the swans before him on the lake, and he went down to them at the brink of the shore. 'Are you the children of Lir?' he said.

'We are indeed,' said they.

'I give thanks to God for that,' said he, 'for it is for your sakes I am come to this island beyond any other island, and let you come to land now,' he said 'and give your trust to me, that you may do good deeds and part from your sins.'

They came to the land after that, and they put trust in Mochoamhog, and he brought them to his own dwelling-place, and they used to be hearing Mass with him. And he got a good smith and bade him make chains of bright silver for them, and he put a chain between Aodh and Fionnuala, and a chain between Conn and Fiachra. And the four of them were raising his heart and gladdening his mind, and no danger and no distress that was on the swans before put any trouble on them now.

Now the king of Connacht at that time was Lairgren, son of Colman, son of Cobthach, and Deoch, daughter of Finghin, was his wife. And that was the coming together of the Man from the North and the Woman from the South, that Aoife had spoken of.

And the woman heard talk of the birds, and a great desire came on her to get them, and she bade Lairgren to bring them to her, and he said he would ask them of Mochaomhog.

And she gave her word she would not stop another night with him unless he would bring them to her. And she set out from the house there and then. And Lairgren sent messengers after her to bring her back, and they did not overtake her till she was at Cill Dun. She went back home with them then, and Lairgren sent messengers to ask the birds of Mochaomhog, and he did not get them.

There was great anger on Lairgren then, and he went himself to the place Mochaomhog was, and he asked was it true he had refused him the birds. 'It is true indeed,' said he. At that Lairgren rose up, and he took hold of the swans, and pulled them off the altar, two birds in each hand, to bring them away to Deoch. But no sooner had he laid his hand on them than their skins fell off, and what was in their place was three lean, withered old men and a thin withered old woman, without blood or flesh.

And Lairgren gave a great start at that, and he went out from the place. It is then Fionnuala said to Mochaomhog: 'Come and baptise us now, for it is short till our death comes; and it is certain you do not think worse of parting with us than we do of parting with you. And make our grave afterwards,' she said, 'and lay Conn at my right side and Fiachra on my left side, and Aodh before my face, between my two arms. And pray to the God of Heaven,' she said, 'that you may be able to baptise us.'

The children of Lir were baptised then, and they died and were buried as Fionnuala had desired; Fiachra and Conn one at each side of her, and Aodh before her face. And a stone was put over them, and their names were written in Ogham, and they were keened there, and heaven was gained for their souls.

And that is the fate of the children of Lir so far.

# The Coming of Finn

At the time Finn was born his father Cumhal, of the sons of Baiscne, Head of the Fianna of Ireland, had been killed in battle by the sons of Morna that were fighting with him for the leadership. And his mother, that was beautiful long-haired Muirne, daughter of Tadg, son of Nuada of the Tuatha De Danann and of Ethlinn, mother of Lugh of the Long Hand, did not dare to keep him with her; and two women, Bodhmall, the woman Druid, and Liath Luachra, came and brought him away to care for him.

It was to the woods of Slieve Bladhma they brought him, and they nursed him secretly, because of his father's enemies, the sons of Morna, and they kept him there a long time.

And Muirne, his mother, took another husband that was king of Carraighe; but at the end of six years she came to see Finn, going through every lonely place till she came to the wood, and there she found the little hunting cabin, and the boy asleep in it, and she lifted him up in her arms and kissed him, and she sang a little sleepy song to him; and then she said farewell to the women, and she went away again.

And the two women went on caring for him till he came to sensible years; and one day when he went out he saw a wild duck on the lake with her clutch, and he made a cast at her that cut the wings off her that she could not fly, and he brought her back to the cabin, and that was his first hunt.

And they gave him good training in running and leaping and swimming. One of them would run round a tree, and she having a thorn switch, and Finn after her with another switch, and each one trying to hit at the other; and they would leave him in a field, and hares along with him, and would bid him not to let the hares quit the field, but to keep before them whichever way they would go; and to teach him swimming they would throw him into the water and let him make his way out.

But after a while he went away with a troop of poets, to hide from the sons of Morna, and they hid him in the mountain of

Crotta Cliach; but there was a robber in Leinster at that time, Fiacuil, son of Codhna, and he came where the poets were in Fidh Gaible and killed them all. But he spared the child and brought him to his own house, that was in a cold marsh. But the two women, Bodhmall and Liath, came looking for him after a while, and Fiacuil gave him up to them, and they brought him back to the same place he was before.

He grew up there, straight and strong and fair-haired and beautiful. And one day he was out in Slieve Bladhma, and the two women along with him, and they saw before them a herd of the wild deer of the mountain. 'It is a pity,' said the old women, 'we not to be able to get a deer of those deer.' 'I will get one for you,' said Finn; and with that he followed after them, and caught two stags of them and brought them home to the hunting cabin. And after that he used to be hunting for them every day. But at last they said to him: 'It is best for you to leave us now, for the sons of Morna are watching again to kill you.'

So he went away then by himself, and never stopped till he came to Magh Lifé, and there he saw young lads swimming in a lake, and they called to him to swim against them. So he went into the lake, and he beat them at swimming. 'Fair he is and well shaped,' they said when they saw him swimming, and it was from that time he got the name of Finn, that is, Fair. But they got to be jealous of his strength, and he went away and left them.

He went on then till he came to Loch Lein, and he took service there with the King of Finntraigh; and there was no hunter like him, and the king said: 'If Cumhal had left a son, you would be that son.'

He went from that king after, and he went into Carraighe, and there he took service with the king, that had taken his mother Muirne for his wife. And one day they were playing chess together and he won seven games one after another. 'Who are you at all?' said the king then. 'I am a son of a countryman of the Luigne of Teamhair,' said Finn. 'That is not so,' said the king, 'but you are the son that Muirne my wife bore to Cumhal. And do not stop here any longer,' he said, 'that you may not be killed under my protection.'

From that he went into Connacht looking for his father's brother, Crimall, son of Trenmor; and as he was going on his way he heard the crying of a lone woman. He went to her, and looked at her, and tears of blood were on her face. 'Your face is red with blood, woman,' he said. 'I have reason for it,' said she, 'for my only son is after being killed by a great fighting man that came on us.' And Finn followed after the big champion and fought with him and killed him. And the man he killed was the same man that had given Cumhal his first wound in the battle where he got his death, and had brought away his treasure-bag with him.

Now as to that treasure-bag, it is of a crane skin it was made, that was one time the skin of Aoife, the beautiful sweetheart of Ilbrec, son of Manannan, that was put into the shape of a crane through jealousy. And it was in Manannan's house it used to be, and there were treasures kept in it, Manannan's shirt and his knife, and the belt and the smith's hook of Goibniu, and the shears of the King of Alban, and the helmet of the King of Lochlann, and a belt of the skin of a great fish, and the bones of Asal's pig that had been brought to Ireland by the sons of Tuireann. All those treasures would be in the bag at full tide, but at the ebbing of the tide it would be empty. And it went from Manannan to Lugh, son of Ethlinn, and after that to Cumhal, that was husband to Muirne, Ethlinn's daughter.

And Finn took the bag and brought it with him till he found Crimall, that was now an old man, living in a lonely place, and some of the old men of the Fianna were with him, and used to go hunting for him. And Finn gave him the bag, and told him his whole story.

And then he said farewell to Crimall, and went on to learn poetry from Finegas, a poet that was living at the Boinn, for the poets thought it was always on the brink of water poetry was revealed to them. And he did not give him his own name, but he took the name of Deimne. Seven years, now, Finegas had stopped at the Boinn, watching the salmon, for it was in the prophecy that he would eat the salmon of knowledge that would come there, and that he would have all knowledge after. And when at the last the salmon of knowledge came, he brought it to where Finn was, and bade him to roast it, but he bade him not to eat any of it. And when Finn brought him the salmon after a while he said: 'Did you eat any of it at all, boy?' 'I did not,' said Finn; 'but I burned my thumb putting down a blister that rose on the skin, and after that, I put my thumb in my mouth.' 'What is your name, boy?' said Finegas. 'Deimne,' said he. 'It is not, but it is Finn your name is, and it is to you and not to myself the salmon was given in the prophecy.' With that he gave Finn the whole of the salmon, and from that time Finn had the knowledge that came from the nuts of the nine hazels of wisdom that grow beside the well that is below the sea.

And besides the wisdom he got then, there was a second wisdom came to him another time, and this is the way it happened. There was a well of the moon belonging to Beag, son of Buan, of the Tuatha De Danann, and whoever would drink out of it would get wisdom, and after a second drink he would get the gift of foretelling. And the three daughters of Beag, son of Buan, had charge of the well, and they would not part with a vessel of it for anything less than red gold. And one day Finn chanced to be hunting in the rushes near the well, and the three women ran out to hinder him from coming to it, and one of them that had a vessel of water in her hand, threw it at him to stop him, and a share of the water went into his mouth. And from that out he had all the knowledge that the water of that well could give.

And he learned the three ways of poetry; and this is the poem he made to show he had got his learning well:

'It is the month of May is the pleasant time; its face is beautiful; the blackbird sings his full song, the living wood is his holding, the cuckoos are singing and ever singing; there is a welcome before the brightness of the summer.

'Summer is lessening the rivers, the swift horses are looking for the pool; the heath spreads out its long hair, the weak white bog-down grows. A wildness comes on the heart of the deer; the sad restless sea is asleep.

'Bees with their little strength carry a load reaped from the flowers; the cattle go up muddy to the mountains; the ant has a good full feast.

'The harp of the woods is playing music; there is colour on the hills, and a haze on the full lakes, and entire peace upon every sail.

'The corncrake is speaking, a loud-voiced poet; the high lonely waterfall is singing a welcome to the warm pool, the talking of the rushes has begun.

'The light swallows are darting; the loudness of music is around the hill; the fat soft mast is budding; there is grass on the trembling bogs.

'The bog is as dark as the feathers of the raven; the cuckoo makes a loud welcome; the speckled salmon is leaping; as strong is the leaping of the swift fighting man.

'The man is gaining; the girl is in her comely growing power; every wood is without fault from the top to the ground, and every wide good plain.

'It is pleasant is the colour of the time; rough winter is gone; every plentiful wood is white; summer is a joyful peace.

'A flock of birds pitches in the meadow; there are sounds in the green fields, there is in them a clear rushing stream.

'There is a hot desire on you for the racing of horses; twisted holly makes a leash for the hound; a bright spear has been shot into the earth, and the flag-flower is golden under it.

'A weak lasting little bird is singing at the top of his voice; the lark is singing clear tidings; May without fault, of beautiful colours.

'I have another story for you; the ox is lowing, the water is creeping in, the summer is gone. High and cold the wind, low the sun, cries are about us; the sea is quarrelling.

'The ferns are reddened and their shape is hidden; the cry of the wild goose is heard; the cold has caught the wings of the birds; it is the time of ice-frost, hard, unhappy.'

And after that, Finn being but a young lad yet, made himself ready and went up at Samhain[2] time to the gathering of the High King at Teamhair. And it was the law at that gathering, no one to raise a quarrel or bring out any grudge against another through the whole of the time it lasted. And the king and his chief men, and Goll, son of Morna, that was now Head of the Fianna, and Caoilte, son of Ronan, and Conan, son of Morna, of

the sharp words, were sitting at a feast in the great house of the
Middle Court; and the young lad came in and took his place
among them, and none of them knew who he was.

The High King looked at him then, and the horn of meetings
was brought to him, and he put it into the boy's hand, and asked
him who was he.

'I am Finn, son of Cumhal,' he said, 'son of the man that used
to be head over the Fianna, and king of Ireland; and I am come
now to get your friendship, and to give you my service.'

'You are son of a friend, boy,' said the king, 'and son of a man
I trusted.'

Then Finn rose up and made his agreement of service and of
faithfulness to the king; and the king took him by the hand and
put him sitting beside his own son, and they gave themselves to
drinking and to pleasure for a while.

Every year, now, at Samhain time, for nine years, there had
come a man of the Tuatha De Danann out of Sidhe Finnachaidh
in the north, and had burned up Teamhair. Aillen, son of Midhna,
his name was, and it is the way he used to come, playing music of
the Sidhe, and all the people that heard it would fall asleep. And
when they were all in their sleep, he would let a flame of fire out of
his mouth, and would blow the flame till all Teamhair was burned.

The king rose up at the feast after a while, and his smooth horn
in his hand, and it is what he said: 'If I could find among you,
men of Ireland, any man that would keep Teamhair till the
break of day tomorrow without being burned by Aillen, son of
Midhna, I would give him whatever inheritance is right for him
to have, whether it be much or little.'

But the men of Ireland made no answer, for they knew well
that at the sound of the sweet pitiful music made by that comely
man of the Sidhe, even women in their pains and men that were
wounded would fall asleep.

It is then Finn rose up and spoke to the King of Ireland. 'Who
will be your sureties that you will fulfil this?' he said. 'The kings
of the provinces of Ireland,' said the king, 'and Cithruadh with
his Druids.' So they gave their pledges, and Finn took in hand to
keep Teamhair safe till the breaking of day on the morrow.

Now there was a fighting man among the followers of the King of Ireland, Fiacha, son of Conga, that Cumhal, Finn's father, used to have a great liking for, and he said to Finn: 'Well, boy,' he said, 'what reward would you give me if I would bring you a deadly spear, that no false cast was ever made with?' 'What reward are you asking of me?' said Finn. 'Whatever your right hand wins at any time, the third of it to be mine,' said Fiacha, 'and a third of your trust and your friendship to be mine.' 'I will give you that,' said Finn. Then Fiacha brought him the spear, unknown to the sons of Morna or to any other person, and he said: 'When you will hear the music of the Sidhe, let you strip the covering off the head of the spear and put it to your forehead, and the power of the spear will not let sleep come upon you.'

Then Finn rose up before all the men of Ireland, and he made a round of the whole of Teamhair. And it was not long till he heard the sorrowful music, and he stripped the covering from the head of the spear, and he held the power of it to his forehead. And Aillen went on playing his little harp, till he had put every one in their sleep as he was used; and then he let a flame of fire out from his mouth to burn Teamhair. And Finn held up his fringed crimson cloak against the flame, and it fell down through the air and went into the ground, bringing the four-folded cloak with it deep into the earth.

And when Aillen saw his spells were destroyed, he went back to Sidhe Finnachaidh on the top of Slieve Fuad; but Finn followed after him there, and as Aillen was going in at the door he made a cast of the spear that went through his heart. And he struck his head off then, and brought it back to Teamhair, and fixed it on a crooked pole and left it there till the rising of the sun over the heights and invers of the country.

And Aillen's mother came to where his body was lying, and there was great grief on her, and she made this complaint:

> 'Ochone! Aillen is fallen, chief of the Sidhe of Beinn Boirche; the slow clouds of death are come on him. Och! he was pleasant, Och! he was kind. Aillen, son of Midhna of Slieve Fuad.
>
> 'Nine times he burned Teamhair. It is a great name he was always looking for, Ochone, Ochone, Aillen!'

And at the breaking of day, the king and all the men of Ireland came out upon the lawn at Teamhair where Finn was. 'King,' said Finn, 'there is the head of the man that burned Teamhair, and the pipe and the harp that made his music. And it is what I think,' he said, 'that Teamhair and all that is in it is saved.'

Then they all came together into the place of counsel, and it is what they agreed, the headship of the Fianna[3] of Ireland to be given to Finn. And the king said to Goll, son of Morna: 'Well, Goll,' he said, 'is it your choice to quit Ireland or to put your hand in Finn's hand?' 'By my word, I will give Finn my hand,' said Goll.

And when the charms that used to bring good luck had done their work, the chief men of the Fianna rose up and struck their hands in Finn's hand, and Goll, son of Morna, was the first to give him his hand the way there would be less shame on the rest for doing it.

And Finn kept the headship of the Fianna until the end; and the place he lived in was Almhuin of Leinster, where the white dun was made by Nuada of the Tuatha De Danann, that was as white as if all the lime in Ireland was put on it, and that got its name from the great herd of cattle that died fighting one time around the well, and that left their horns there, speckled horns and white.

And as to Finn himself, he was a king and a seer and a poet; a Druid and a knowledgeable man; and everything he said was sweet-sounding to his people. And a better fighting man than Finn never struck his hand into a king's hand, and whatever anyone ever said of him, he was three times better. And of his justice it used to be said, that if his enemy and his own son had come before him to be judged, it is a fair judgment he would have given between them. And as to his generosity it used to be said, he never denied any man as long as he had a mouth to eat with, and legs to bring away what he gave him; and he left no woman without her bride-price, and no man without his pay; and he never promised at night what he would not fulfil on the morrow, and he never promised in the day what he would not fulfil at night, and he never forsook his right-hand friend. And if he was quiet in peace he was angry in battle, and Oisin his son and Oscar his son's son followed him in that. There was a young man of Ulster came and claimed kinship with them one time, saying they were of the one blood. 'If that is so,' said Oisin, 'it is from the men of Ulster we took the madness and the angry heart we have in battle.' 'That is so indeed,' said Finn.

# Oisin and Patrick

## [ I ]

As to Oisin, it was a long time after he was brought away by Niamh that he came back again to Ireland. Some say it was hundreds of years he was in the Country of the Young,[4] and some say it was thousands of years he was in it; but whatever time it was, it seemed short to him.

And whatever happened him through the time he was away, it is a withered old man he was found after coming back to Ireland, and his white horse going away from him, and he lying on the ground.

And it was Saint Patrick had power at that time, and it was to him Oisin was brought; and he kept him in his house, and used to be teaching him and questioning him. And Oisin was no way pleased with the way Ireland was then, but he used to be talking of the old times, and fretting after the Fianna.

And Patrick bade him to tell what happened him the time he left Finn and the Fianna and went away with Niamh. And it is the story Oisin told: 'The time I went away with golden-haired Niamh, we turned our backs to the land, and our faces westward, and the sea was going away before us, and filling up in waves after us. And we saw wonderful things on our journey,' he said, 'cities and courts and duns and lime-white houses, and shining sunny-houses and palaces. And one time we saw beside us a hornless deer running hard, and an eager white red-eared hound following after it. And another time we saw a young girl on a horse and having a golden apple in her right hand, and she going over the tops of the waves; and there was following after her a young man riding a white horse, and having a crimson cloak and a gold-hilted sword in his right hand.'

'Follow on with your story, pleasant Oisin,' said Patrick, 'for you did not tell us yet what was the country you went to.'

'The country of the Young, the Country of Victory, it was,'

said Oisin. 'And O Patrick,' he said, 'there is no lie in that name; and if there are grandeurs in your Heaven the same as there are there, I would give my friendship to God.

'We turned our backs then to the dun,' he said, 'and the horse under us was quicker than the spring wind on the backs of the mountains. And it was not long till the sky darkened, and the wind rose in every part, and the sea was as if on fire, and there was nothing to be seen of the sun.

'But after we were looking at the clouds and the stars for a while the wind went down, and the storm, and the sun brightened. And we saw before us a very delightful country under full blossom, and smooth plains in it, and a king's dun that was very grand, and that had every colour in it, and sunny-houses beside it, and palaces of shining stones, made by skilled men. And we saw coming out to meet us three fifties of armed men, very lively and handsome. And I asked Niamh was this the Country of the Young, and she said it was. "And indeed, Oisin," she said. "I told you no lie about it, and you will see all I promised you before you for ever."

'And there came out after that a hundred beautiful young girls, having cloaks of silk worked with gold, and they gave me a welcome to their own country. And after that there came a great shining army, and with it a strong beautiful king, having a shirt of yellow silk and a golden cloak over it, and a very bright crown on his head. And there was following after him a young queen, and fifty young girls along with her.

'And when all were come to the one spot, the king took me by the hand, and he said out before them all: "A hundred thousand welcomes before you, Oisin, son of Finn. And as to this country you are come to," he said, "I will tell you news of it without a lie. It is long and lasting your life will be in it, and you yourself will be young for ever. And there is no delight the heart ever thought of," he said, "but it is here against your coming. And you can believe my words, Oisin," he said, "or I myself am the King of the Country of the Young, and this is its comely queen, and it was golden-headed Niamh our daughter that went over the sea looking for you to be her husband for ever." I gave thanks to him then, and I stooped myself down before the queen, and we went forward to the royal house, and all the high nobles came out to meet us, both men and women, and there was a great feast made there through the length of ten days and ten nights.

'And that is the way I married Niamh of the Golden Hair, and that is the way I went to the Country of the Young, although it is sorrowful to me to be telling it now, O Patrick from Rome,' said Oisin.

'Follow on with your story, Oisin of the destroying arms,' said Patrick, 'and tell me what way did you leave the Country of the Young, for it is long to me till I hear that; and tell us now had you any children by Niamh, and was it long you were in that place.'

'Two beautiful children I had by Niamh,' said Oisin, 'two young sons and a comely daughter. And Niamh gave the two sons the name of Finn and of Oscar, and the name I gave to the daughter was The Flower.

'And I did not feel the time passing, and it was a long time I stopped there,' he said, 'till the desire came on me to see Finn and my comrades again. And I asked leave of the king and of Niamh to go back to Ireland. "You will get leave from me," said Niamh; "but for all that," she said, "it is bad news you are giving me, for I am in dread you will never come back here again through the length of your days." But I bade her have no fear, since the white horse would bring me safe back again from Ireland. "Bear this in mind, Oisin," she said then, "if you once get off the horse while you are away, or if you once put your foot to ground, you will never come back here again. And O Oisin," she said, "I tell it to you now for the third time, if you once get down from the horse, you will be an old man, blind and withered, without liveliness, without mirth, without running, without leaping. And it is a grief to me, Oisin," she said, "you ever to go back to green Ireland; and it is not now as it used to be, and you will not see Finn and his people, for there is not now in the whole of Ireland but a Father of Orders and armies of saints; and here is my kiss for you, pleasant Oisin," she said, "for you will never come back any more to the Country of the Young."

'And that is my story, Patrick, and I have told you no lie in it,' said Oisin. 'And O Patrick,' he said, 'if I was the same the day I came here as I was that day, I would have made an end of all your clerks, and there would not be a head left on a neck after me.'

'Go on with your story,' said Patrick, 'and you will get the same good treatment from me you got from Finn, for the sound of your voice is pleasing to me.'

So Oisin went on with his story, and it is what he said: 'I have nothing to tell of my journey till I came back into green Ireland, and I looked about me then on all sides, but there were no tidings to be got of Finn. And it was not long till I saw a great troop of riders, men and women, coming towards me from the west. And when they came near they wished me good health; and there was wonder on them all when they looked at me, seeing me so unlike themselves, and so big and so tall.

'I asked them then did they hear if Finn was still living, or any other one of the Fianna, or what had happened them. "We often heard of Finn that lived long ago," said they, "and that there never was his equal for strength or bravery or a great name; and there is many a book written down," they said, "by the sweet poets of the Gael, about his doings and the doings of the Fianna, and it would be hard for us to tell you all of them. And we heard Finn had a son," they said, "that was beautiful and shining, and that there came a young girl looking for him, and he went away with her to the Country of the Young."

'And when I knew by their talk that Finn was not living or any of the Fianna, it is downhearted I was, and tired, and very sorrowful after them. And I made no delay, but I turned my face and went on to Almhuin of Leinster. And there was great wonder on me when I came there to see no sign at all of Finn's great dun, and his great hall, and nothing in the place where it was but weeds and nettles.'

And there was grief on Oisin then, and he said: 'Och, Patrick! Och, ochone, my grief! It is a bad journey that was to me; and to be without tidings of Finn or the Fianna has left me under pain through my lifetime.'

'Leave off fretting, Oisin,' said Patrick, 'and shed your tears to the God of grace. Finn and the Fianna are slack enough now, and they will get no help forever.' 'It is a great pity that would be,' said Oisin, 'Finn to be in pain for ever; and who was it gained the victory over him, when his own hand had made an end of so many a hard fighter?'

'It is God gained the victory over Finn,' said Patrick, 'and not the strong hand of an enemy; and as to the Fianna, they are condemned to hell along with him, and tormented for ever.'

'O Patrick,' said Oisin, 'show me the place where Finn and his people are, and there is not a hell or a heaven there but I will put it down. And if Oscar, my own son, is there,' he said, 'the hero that was bravest in heavy battles, there is not in hell or in the Heaven of God a troop so great that he could not destroy it.'

'Let us leave off quarrelling on each side now,' said Patrick; 'and go on, Oisin, with your story. What happened you after you knew the Fianna to be at an end?'

'I will tell you that, Patrick,' said Oisin. 'I was turning to go away, and I saw the stone trough that the Fianna used to be putting their hands in, and it full of water. And when I saw it I had such a wish and such a feeling for it that I forgot what I was told, and I got off the horse. And in the minute all the years came on me, and I was lying on the ground, and the horse took fright and went away and left me there, an old man, weak and spent, without sight, without shape, without comeliness, without strength or understanding, without respect.

'There, Patrick, is my story for you now,' said Oisin, 'and no lie in it, of all that happened me going away and coming back again from the Country of the Young.'

# [ II ]

OISIN IN PATRICK'S HOUSE

And Oisin stopped on with Saint Patrick, but he was not very well content with the way he was treated. And one time he said:

'They say I am getting food, but God knows I am not, or drink; and I Oisin, son of Finn, under a yoke, drawing stones.' 'It is my opinion you are getting enough,' said Saint Patrick then, 'and you getting a quarter of beef and a churn of butter and a griddle of bread every day.' 'I often saw a quarter of a blackbird bigger than your quarter of beef,' said Oisin, 'and a rowan berry as big as your churn of butter, and an ivy leaf as big as your griddle of bread.' Saint Patrick was vexed when he heard that, and he said to Oisin that he had told a lie.

There was great anger on Oisin then, and he went where there was a litter of pups, and he bade a serving-boy to nail up the hide of a freshly killed bullock to the wall, and to throw the pups against it one by one. And every one that he threw fell down from the hide till it came to the last, and he held on to it with his teeth and his nails. 'Rear that one,' said Oisin, 'and drown all the rest.'

Then he bade the boy to keep the pup in a dark place, and to care it well, and never to let it taste blood or see the daylight. And at the end of a year, Oisin was so well pleased with the pup, that he gave it the name of Bran Og, young Bran.

And one day he called to the serving-boy to come on a journey with him, and to bring the pup in a chain. And they set out and passed by Slieve-nam-ban, where the witches of the Sidhe do be spinning with their spinning-wheels; and then they turned eastward into Gleann-na-Smol. And Oisin raised a rock that was there, and he bade the lad take from under it three things, a great sounding horn of the Fianna, and a ball of iron they had for throwing, and a very sharp sword. And when Oisin saw those things, he took them in his hands, and he said: 'My thousand farewells to the day when you were put here!' He bade the lad to clean them well then; and when he had done that, he bade him to sound a blast on the horn. So the boy did that, and Oisin asked him did he see anything strange. 'I did not,' said the boy. 'Sound it again as loud as you can,' said Oisin. 'That is as hard as I can sound it, and I can see nothing yet,' said the boy when he had done that. Then Oisin took the horn himself, and he put it to his mouth, and blew three great blasts on it. 'What do you see now?' he said. 'I see three great clouds coming,' he said, 'and they are settling down in the valley; and the first cloud is a flight of very big birds, and the second cloud is a flight of birds that are bigger again, and the third flight is of the biggest and the blackest birds the world ever saw.' 'What is the dog doing?' said Oisin. 'The eyes are starting from his head, and there is not a rib of hair on him but is standing up.' 'Let him loose now,' said Oisin.

The dog rushed down to the valley then, and he made an attack on one of the birds, that was the biggest of all, and that had a shadow like a cloud. And they fought a very fierce fight, but at last Bran Og made an end of the big bird, and lapped its blood. But if he did, madness came on him, and he came rushing back towards Oisin, his jaws open and his eyes like fire. 'There is dread on me, Oisin,' said the boy, 'for the dog is making for us, mad and raging.' 'Take this iron ball and make a cast at him when he comes near,' said Oisin. 'I am in dread to do that,' said the boy. 'Put it in my hand, and turn it towards him,' said Oisin. The boy did that, and Oisin made a cast of the ball that went into the mouth and the throat of the dog, and choked him, and he fell down the slope, twisting and foaming.

Then they went where the great bird was left dead, and Oisin bade the lad to cut a quarter off it with the sword, and he did so. And then he bade him cut open the body, and in it he found a rowan berry, the biggest he had ever seen, and an ivy leaf that was bigger than the biggest griddle.

So Oisin turned back then, and went to where Saint Patrick was, and he showed him the quarter of the bird that was bigger than any quarter of a bullock, and the rowan berry that was bigger than a churning of butter, and the leaf. 'And you know now, Patrick of the Bells,' he said, 'that I told no lie; and it is what kept us all through our lifetime,' he said, 'truth that was in our hearts, and strength in our arms, and fulfilment in our tongues.'

'You told no lie indeed,' said Patrick.

And when Oisin had no sight left at all, he used every night to put up one of the serving-men on his shoulders, and to bring him out to see how were the cattle doing. And one night the servants had no mind to go, and they agreed together to tell him it was a very bad night.

And it is what the first of them said: 'It is outside there is a heavy sound with the heavy water dropping from the tops of trees; the sound of the waves is not to be heard for the loud splashing of the rain.' And then the next one said: 'The trees of the wood are shivering, and the birch is turning black; the snow is killing the birds; that is the story outside.' And the third said: 'It is to the east they have turned their face, the white snow and the dark rain; it is what is making the plain so cold is the snow that is dripping and getting hard.'

But there was a serving-girl in the house, and she said: 'Rise up, Oisin, and go out to the white-headed cows, since the cold wind is plucking the trees from the hills.'

Oisin went out then, and the serving-man on his shoulders; but it is what the serving-man did, he brought a vessel of water and a birch broom with him, and he was dashing water in Oisin's face, the way he would think it was rain. But when they came to the pen where the cattle were, Oisin found the night was quiet, and after that he asked no more news of the weather from the servants.

## [ III ]

### THE ARGUMENTS

And Saint Patrick took in hand to convert Oisin, and to bring him to baptism; but it was no easy work he had to do, and everything he would say, Oisin would have an answer for it. And it is the way they used to be talking and arguing with one another, as it was put down afterwards by the poets of Ireland:

PATRICK. Oisin, it is long your sleep is. Rise up and listen to the Psalm. Your strength and your readiness are gone from

234

you, though you used to be going into rough fights and battles.

OISIN. My readiness and my strength are gone from me since Finn has no armies living; I have no liking for clerks, their music is not sweet to me after his.

PATRICK. You never heard music so good from the beginning of the world to this day; it is well you would serve an army on a hill, you that are old and silly and grey.

OISIN. I used to serve an army on a hill, Patrick of the closed-up mind; it is a pity you to be faulting me; there was never shame put on me till now.

I have heard music was sweeter than your music, however much you are praising your clerks: the song of the blackbird in Leiter Laoi, and the sound of the Dord Fiann; the very sweet thrush of the Valley of the Shadow, or the sound of the boats striking the strand. The cry of the hounds was better to me than the noise of your schools, Patrick.

Little Nut, little Nut of my heart, the little dwarf that was with Finn, when he would make tunes and songs he would put us all into deep sleep.

The twelve hounds that belonged to Finn, the time they would be let loose facing out from the Siuir, their cry was sweeter than harps and than pipes.

I have a little story about Finn; we were but fifteen men; we took the King of the Saxons of the feats, and we won a battle against the King of Greece.

We fought nine battles in Spain, and nine times twenty battles in Ireland: from Lochlann and from the eastern world there was a share of gold coming to Finn.

My grief! I to be stopping after him, and without delight in games or in music; to be withering away after my comrades; my grief it is to be living. I and the clerks of the Mass books are two that can never agree.

If Finn and the Fianna were living, I would leave the clerks and the bells; I would follow the deer through the valleys, I would like to be close on his track.

Ask Heaven of God, Patrick, for Finn of the Fianna and his race; make prayers for the great man; you never heard of his like.

PATRICK. I will not ask Heaven for Finn, man of good wit that my anger is rising against, since his delight was to be living in valleys with the noise of hunts.

OISIN. If you had been in company with the Fianna, Patrick of the joyless clerks and of the bells, you would not be attending on schools or giving heed to God.

PATRICK. I would not part from the Son of God for all that have lived east or west; O Oisin, O shaking poet, there will harm come on you in satisfaction for the priests.

OISIN. It was a delight to Finn the cry of his hounds on the mountains, the wild dogs leaving their harbours, the pride of his armies, those were his delights.

PATRICK. There was many a thing Finn took delight in, and there is not much heed given to it after him; Finn and his hounds are not living now, and you yourself will not always be living, Oisin.

OISIN. There is a greater story of Finn than of us, or of any that have lived in our time; all that are gone and all that are living, Finn was better to give out gold than themselves.

PATRICK. All the gold you and Finn used to be giving out, it is little it does for you now; he is in Hell in bonds because he did treachery and oppression.

OISIN. It is little I believe of your truth, man from Rome with the white books, Finn the open-handed head of the Fianna to be in the hands of devils or demons.

PATRICK. Finn is in bonds in Hell, the pleasant man that gave out gold; in satisfaction for his disrespect to God, he is under grief in the house of pain.

OISIN. If the sons of Morna were within it, or the strong men of the sons of Baiscne, they would take Finn out of it, or they would have the house for themselves.

PATRICK. If the five provinces of Ireland were within it, or the strong seven battalions of the Fianna, they would not be able to bring Finn out of it, however great their strength might be.

OISIN. If Faolan and Goll were living, and brown-haired Diarmuid and brave Oscar, Finn of the Fianna could not be held in any house that was made by God or devils.

PATRICK. If Faolan and Goll were living, and all the Fianna that ever were, they could not bring out Finn from the house where he is in pain.

OISIN. What did Finn do against God but to be attending on schools and on armies? Giving gold through a great part of his time, and for another while trying his hounds.

PATRICK. In payment for thinking of his hounds and for serving the schools of the poets, and because he gave no heed to God, Finn of the Fianna is held down.

OISIN. You say, Patrick of the Psalms, that the Fianna could not take out Finn, or the five provinces of Ireland along with them.

I have a little story about Finn. We were but fifteen men when we took the King of Britain of the feasts by the strength of our spears and our own strength.

We took Magnus the great, the son of the King of Lochlann of the speckled ships; we came back no way sorry or tired, we put our rent on far places.

O Patrick, the story is pitiful, the King of the Fianna to be under locks; a heart without envy, without hatred, a heart hard in earning victory.

It is an injustice, God to be unwilling to give food and riches; Finn never refused strong or poor, although cold Hell is now his dwelling-place.

It is what Finn had a mind for, to be listening to the sound of Druim Dearg; to sleep at the stream of Ess Ruadh, to be hunting the deer of Gallimh of the bays.

The cries of the blackbird of Leiter Laoi, the wave of Rudraighe beating the strand, the bellowing of the ox of Magh Maoin, the lowing of the calf of Gleann da Mhail.

The noise of the hunt on Slieve Crot, the sound of the fawns round Slieve Cua, the scream of the sea-gulls there beyond on Iorrus, the screech of the crows over the battle.

The waves vexing the breasts of the boats, the howling of the hounds at Druim Lis; the voice of Bran on Cnoc-an-Air, the outcry of the streams about Slieve Mis.

The call of Oscar going to the hunt; the voice of the hounds on the road of the Fianna, to be listening to them and to the poets, that was always his desire.

A desire of the desires of Oscar was to listen to the striking of shields; to be hacking at bones in a battle, it is what he had a mind for always.

We went westward one time to hunt at Formaid of the Fianna, to see the first running of our hounds.

It was Finn was holding Bran, and it is with myself Sceolan was; Diarmuid of the Women had Fearan, and Oscar had lucky Adhnuall.

Conan the Bald had Searc; Caoilte, son of Ronan, had Daol; Lugaidh's Son and Goll were holding Fuaim and Fothran.

That was the first day we loosed out a share of our hounds to a hunting; and Och! Patrick, of all that were in it, there is not one left living but myself.

O Patrick, it is a pity the way I am now, a spent old man without sway, without quickness, without strength, going to Mass at the altar.

Without the great deer of Slieve Luchra; without the hares of Slieve Cuilinn; without going into fights with Finn; without listening to the poets.

Without battles, without taking of spoils; without playing at nimble feats; without going courting or hunting, two trades that were my delight.

PATRICK. Leave off, old man, leave your foolishness; let what you have done be enough for you from this out. Think on the pains that are before you; the Fianna are gone, and you yourself will be going.

OISIN. If I go, may yourself not be left after me, Patrick of the hindering heart; if Conan, the least of the Fianna, were living, your buzzing would not be left long to you.

Or if this was the day I gave ten hundred cows to the headless woman that came to the Valley of the Two Oxen; the birds of the air brought away the ring I gave her, I never knew where she went herself from me.

PATRICK. That is little to trouble you, Oisin; it was but for a while she was with you; it is better for you to be as you are than to be among them again.

OISIN. O Son of Calphurn of the friendly talk, it is a pity for him that gives respect to clerks and bells; I and Caoilte my friend, we were not poor when we were together.

The music that put Finn to his sleep was the cackling of the ducks from the lake of the Three Narrows; the scolding talk of the blackbird of Doire an Cairn, the bellowing of the ox from the Valley of the Berries.

The whistle of the eagle from the Valley of Victories, or from the rough branches of the ridge by the stream; the grouse of the heather of Cruachan; the call of the otter of Druim-re-Coir.

The song of the blackbird of Doire an Cairn indeed I never heard sweeter music, if I could be under its nest.

My grief that I ever took baptism; it is little credit I got by it, being without food, without drink, doing fasting and praying.

PATRICK. In my opinion it did not harm you, old man; you will get nine score cakes of bread, wine and meat to put a taste on it; it is bad talk you are giving.

OISIN. This mouth that is talking with you, may it never confess to a priest, if I would not sooner have the leavings of Finn's house than a share of your own meals.

PATRICK. He got but what he gathered from the banks, or whatever he could kill on the rough hills; he got hell at the last because of his unbelief.

OISIN. That was not the way with us at all, but our fill of wine and of meat; justice and a right beginning at the feasts, sweet drinks and everyone drinking them.

It is fretting after Diarmuid and Goll I am, and after Fergus of the True Lips, the time you will not let me be speaking of them, O new Patrick from Rome.

PATRICK. We would give you leave to be speaking of them, but first you should give heed to God. Since you are now at the end of your days, leave your foolishness, weak old man.

OISIN. O Patrick, tell me as a secret, since it is you have the best knowledge, will my dog or my hound be let in with me to the court of the King of Grace?

PATRICK. Old man in your foolishness that I cannot put any bounds to, your dog or your hound will not be let in with you to the court of the King of Power.

OISIN. If I had acquaintance with God, and my hound to be at hand, I would make whoever gave food to myself give a share to my hound as well.

One strong champion that was with the Fianna of Ireland would be better than the Lord of Piety, and than you yourself, Patrick.

PATRICK. O Oisin of the sharp blades, it is mad words you are saying. God is better for one day than the whole of the Fianna of Ireland.

OISIN. Although I am now without sway and my life is spent to the end, do not put abuse, Patrick, on the great men of the sons of Baiscne.

If I had Conan with me, the man that used to be running down the Fianna, it is he would break your head within among your clerks and your priests.

PATRICK. It is a silly thing, old man, to be talking always of the Fianna; remember your end is come, and take the Son of God to help you.

OISIN. I used to sleep out on the mountain under the grey dew; I was never used to go to bed without food, while there was a deer on the hill beyond.

PATRICK. You are astray at the end of your life between the straight way and the crooked. Keep out from the crooked path of pains, and the angels of God will come beneath your head.

OISIN. If myself and open-handed Fergus and Diarmuid were together now on this spot, we would go in every path we ever went in, and ask no leave of the priests.

PATRICK. Leave off, Oisin; do not be speaking against the priests that are telling the word of God in every place. Unless you leave off your daring talk, it is great pain you will have in the end.

OISIN. When myself and the leader of the Fianna were looking for a boar in a valley, it was worse to me not to see it than all your clerks to be without their heads.

PATRICK. It is pitiful seeing you without sense; that is worse to you than your blindness; if you were to get sight within you, it is great your desire would be for Heaven.

OISIN. It is little good it would be to me to be sitting in that city, without Caoilte, without Oscar, without my father being with me.

The leap of the buck would be better to me, or the sight of badgers between two valleys, than all your mouth is promising me, and all the delights I could get in Heaven.

PATRICK. Your thoughts are foolish, they will come to nothing; your pleasure and your mirth are gone. Unless you will take my advice tonight, you will not get leave on this side or that.

OISIN. If myself and the Fianna were on the top of a hill today drawing our spear-heads, we would have our choice of being here or there in spite of books and priests and bells.

PATRICK. You were like the smoke of a wisp, or like a stream in a valley, or like a whirling wind on the top of a hill, every tribe of you that ever lived.

OISIN. If I was in company with the people of strong arms, the way I was at Bearna da Coill, I would sooner be looking at them than at this troop of the crooked croziers.

If I had Scolb Sceine with me, or Oscar, that was smart in battles, I would not be without meat tonight at the sound of the bell of the seven tolls.

PATRICK. Oisin, since your wits are gone from you be glad at what I say; it is certain to me you will leave the Fianna and that you will receive the God of the stars.

OISIN. There is wonder on me at your hasty talk, priest that has travelled in every part, to say that I would part from the Fianna, a generous people, never niggardly.

PATRICK. If you saw the people of God, the way they are settled at feasts, every good thing is more plentiful with them than with Finn's people, however great their name was.

Finn and the Fianna are lying now very sorrowful on the flag-stone of pain; take the Son of God in their place; make your repentance and do not lose Heaven.

OISIN. I do not believe your talk now, O Patrick of the crooked staves, Finn and the Fianna to be there within, unless they find pleasure being in it.

PATRICK: Make right repentance now, before you know when your end is coming; God is better for one hour than the whole of the Fianna of Ireland.

OISIN. That is a daring answer to make to me, Patrick of the crooked crozier; your crozier would be in little bits if I had Oscar with me now.

If my son Oscar and God were hand to hand on the Hill of the Fianna, if I saw my son put down, I would say that God was a strong man.

How could it be that God or his priests could be better men than Finn, the King of the Fianna, a generous man without crookedness.

If there was a place above or below better than the Heaven of God, it is there Finn would go, and all that are with him of his people.

You say that a generous man never goes to the hell of pain; there was not one among the Fianna that was not generous to all.

Ask of God, Patrick, does He remember when the Fianna were alive, or has He seen east or west any man better than themselves in their fighting.

The Fianna used not to be saying treachery; we never had the name of telling lies. By truth and the strength of our hands we came safe out of every battle.

There never sat a priest in a church, though you think it sweet to be singing psalms, was better to his word than the Fianna, or more generous than Finn himself.

If my comrades were living tonight, I would take no pleasure in your crooning in the church; as they are not living now, the rough voice of the bells has deafened me.

Och! in the place of battles and heavy fights, where I used to have my place and to take my pleasure, the crozier of Patrick being carried; and his clerks at their quarrelling.

Och! slothful, cheerless Conan, it is great abuse I used to be giving you; why do you not come to see me now? you would get leave for making fun and reviling through the whole of the niggardly clerks.

Och! where are the strong men gone that they do not come together to help me! O Oscar of the sharp sword of victory, come and free your father from his bonds!

Where is the strong son of Lugaidh? Och! Diarmuid of all the women! Och! Caoilte, son of Ronan, think of our love, and travel to me!

PATRICK. Stop your talk, you withered, witless old man; it is my King that made the Heavens, it is He that gives blossom to the trees, it is He made the moon and the sun, the fields and the grass.

OISIN. It was not in shaping fields and grass that my king took his delight, but in overthrowing fighting men, and defending countries, and bringing his name into every part.

In courting, in playing, in hunting, in baring his banner at the first of a fight; in playing at chess, at swimming, in looking around him at the drinking-hall.

O Patrick, where was your God when the two came over the sea that brought away the queen of Lochlann of the Ships? Where was He when Dearg came, the son of the King of Lochlann of the golden shields? Why did not the King of Heaven protect them from the blows of the big man?

Or when Tailc, son of Treon, came, the man that did great slaughter on the Fianna; it was not by God that champion fell, but by Oscar, in the sight of all.

Many a battle and many a victory was gained by the Fianna of Ireland; I never heard any great deed was done by the King of Saints, or that He ever reddened His hand.

It would be a great shame for God not to take the locks of pain off Finn; if God Himself were in bonds, my king would fight for His sake.

Finn left no one in pain or in danger without freeing him by silver or gold, or by fighting till he got the victory.

For the strength of your love, Patrick, do not forsake the great men; bring in the Fianna unknown to the King of Heaven.

It is a good claim I have on your God, to be among his clerks the way I am; without food, without clothing, without music, without giving rewards to poets.

Without the cry of the hounds or the horns, without guarding coasts, without courting generous women; for all that I have suffered by the want of food, I forgive the King of Heaven in my will.

OISIN said: My story is sorrowful. The sound of your voice is not pleasant to me. I will cry my fill, but not for God, but because Finn and the Fianna are not living.

## [ IV ]

OISIN'S LAMENT

And Oisin used to be making laments, and sometimes he would be making praises of the old times and of Finn; and these are some of them that are remembered yet:

I saw the household of Finn, it was not the household of a soft race; I had a vision of that man yesterday.

I saw the household of the High King, he with the brown, sweet-voiced son; I never saw a better man.

I saw the household of Finn; no one saw it as I saw it; I saw Finn with the sword, Mac an Luin. Och! it was sorrowful to see it.

I cannot tell out every harm that is on my head; free us from our trouble for ever; I have seen the household of Finn.

It is a week from yesterday I last saw Finn; I never saw a braver man. A King of heavy blows; my law, my adviser, my sense and my wisdom, prince and poet, braver than kings, King of the Fianna, brave in all countries; golden salmon of the sea, clean hawk of the air, rightly taught, avoiding lies; strong in his doings, a right judge, ready in courage, a high messenger in bravery and in music.

His skin lime-white, his hair golden; ready to work, gentle to women. His great green vessels full of rough sharp wine, it is rich the king was, the head of his people.

Seven sides Finn's house had, and seven score shields on every side. Fifty fighting men he had about him having woollen cloaks; ten bright drinking-cups in his hall; ten blue vessels, ten golden horns.

It is a good household Finn had, without grudging, without

lust, without vain boasting, without chattering, without any slur on any one of the Fianna.

Finn never refused any man; he never put away anyone that came to his house. If the brown leaves falling in the woods were gold, if the white waves were silver, Finn would have given away the whole of it.

Blackbird of Doire an Chairn, your voice is sweet; I never heard on any height of the world music was sweeter than your voice, and you at the foot of your nest.

The music is sweetest in the world, it is a pity not to be listening to it for a while, O son of Calphurn of the sweet bells, and you would overtake your nones again.

If you knew the story of the bird the way I know it, you would be crying lasting tears, and you would give no heed to your God for a while.

In the country of Lochlann of the blue streams, Finn, son of Cumhal, of the red-gold cups, found that bird you hear now; I will tell you its story truly.

Doire an Chairn, that wood there to the west, where the Fianna used to be delaying, it is there they put the blackbird, in the beauty of the pleasant trees.

The stag of the heather of quiet Cruachan, the sorrowful croak from the ridge of the Two Lakes; the voice of the eagle of the Valley of the Shapes, the voice of the cuckoo on the Hill of Brambles.

The voice of the hounds in the pleasant valley; the scream of the eagle on the edge of the wood; the early outcry of the hounds going over the Strand of the Red Stones.

The time Finn lived and the Fianna, it was sweet to them to be listening to the whistle of the blackbird; the voice of the bells would not have been sweet to them.

There was no one of the Fianna without his fine silken shirt and his soft coat, without bright armour, without shining stones on his head, two spears in his hand, and a shield that brought victory.

If you were to search the world you would not find a harder man, best of blood, best in battle; no one got the upper hand of him. When he went out trying his white hound, which of us could be put beside Finn?

One time we went hunting on Slieve-nam-ban; the sun was beautiful overhead, the voice of the hounds went east and west, from hill to hill. Finn and Bran sat for a while on the hill, every man was jealous for the hunt. We let out three thousand hounds from their golden chains; every hound of them brought down two deer.

Patrick of the true crozier, did you ever see, east or west, a greater hunt than that hunt of Finn and the Fianna? O son of Calphurn of the bells, that day was better to me than to be listening to your lamentations in the church.

There is no strength in my hands tonight, there is no power within me; it is no wonder I to be sorrowful, being thrown down in the sorrow of old age.

Everything is a grief to me beyond any other man on the face of the earth, to be dragging stones along to the church and the hill of the priests.

I have a little story of our people. One time Finn had a mind to make a dun on the bald hill of Cuailgne, and he put it on the Fianna of Ireland to bring stones for building it; a third on the sons of Morna, a third on myself, and a third on the sons of Baiscne.

I gave an answer to Finn, son of Cumhal; I said I would be under his sway no longer, and that I would obey him no more.

When Finn heard that, he was silent a long time, the man without a lie, without fear. And he said to me then: 'You yourself will be dragging stones before your death comes to you.'

I rose up then with anger on me, and there followed me the fourth of the brave battalions of the Fianna. I gave my own judgments, there were many of the Fianna with me.

Now my strength is gone from me, I that was adviser to the Fianna; my whole body is tired tonight, my hands, my feet, and my head, tired, tired, tired.

It is bad the way I am after Finn of the Fianna; since he is gone away, every good is behind me.

Without great people, without mannerly ways; it is sorrowful I am after our king that is gone.

I am a shaking tree, my leaves gone from me; an empty nut, a horse without a bridle; a people without a dwelling-place, I Oisin, son of Finn.

It is long the clouds are over me tonight! It is long last night was; although this day is long, yesterday was longer again to me; every day that comes is long to me!

That is not the way I used to be, without fighting, without battles, without learning feats, without young girls, without music, without harps, without bruising bones, without great deeds; without increase of learning, without generosity, without drinking at feasts, without courting, without hunting, the two trades I was used to; without going out to battle Ochone! the want of them is sorrowful to me.

No hunting of deer or stag, it is not like that I would wish to be; no leashes for our hounds, no hounds; it is long the clouds are over me tonight!

Without rising up to do bravery as we were used, without playing as we had a mind; without swimming of our fighting men in the lake; it is long the clouds are over me tonight!

There is no one at all in the world the way I am: it is a pity the way I am; an old man dragging stones; it is long the clouds are over me tonight!

I am the last of the Fianna, great Oisin, son of Finn, listening to the voice of bells; it is long the clouds are over me tonight!

# ESSAYS ON IRISH CULTURE

# from 'Ireland, Real and Ideal'

The Gaelic League, which has come into being during the lull in
politics, is a popular movement for the revival of the Irish
language. A society for its preservation had been in existence for
some time, and had done good literary work. But as a spoken
language Irish was dying away. England had tried to stamp it
out in the penal days; and in our own days, after the Famine, the
people themselves grew so eager to learn the language that would
fit them for breadwinning across the sea that they were ready to
risk the loss of their own. Old people tell how they were forced to
speak English in their school days. 'I used to have a card tied
round my neck,' an Aran man says, 'when I was going home
from school, and if I spoke one word of Irish there was to be a
mark put on it, and I'd get a beating from the master next day.
But often my father wouldn't like to put it on to get me the
beating, and anyway boys like to do what they're told not to do,
and we talked Irish all the more.' But what parents and hedge
schoolmasters had failed in doing the 'National' school system
stepped in and did. There is no danger now of any child growing
up ignorant of English, the people are too well aware of its value
in the battle of life. But the child in learning it has too often lost
his own language, and with it lost the keen edge of his intelligence.
In Irish-speaking districts he begins his school days thinking in
Irish. He is set to learn a comparatively strange language by
symbols that to him have no meaning, and that are explained in
that unfamiliar language. The author of *Day Dreams of a Schoolmaster* tells us of his early trials in having to learn Latin from a
grammar in which some of the rules were given in Latin. 'The
round shot of this Latin grammar,' he says, 'had been, I believe,
tied to our legs to prevent our intellectually straying ... The
hour at length arrived in which it was considered wise to attach
another round shot to our other leg. This was done in the shape
of a Greek grammar written entirely in Latin. This extra weight

answered the purpose effectually: we were all brought to an immediate standstill.' And in the same way the Irish-thinking child set to learn English through Irish on his arrival at school has round shot attached to him at once, with the inevitable result of dulling his power of learning anything at all.

I have been on an island where, with the exception of a few coastguards, the only inhabitant who did not know Irish was the National schoolmaster. He complained of the slowness of the children in learning, and said it was the result of intermarriages. On a neighbouring island I found the master teaching in Irish, out of humanity and common sense and with no encouragement from the National Board, and I did not hear any complaints of the children's want of intelligence from him. Under the system I have described the native language began to die away rapidly. Dignity and power of expression were to a great extent lost with the tongue that, like all other tongues, expressed the spirit of the race. It went out of fashion. Priests ceased to preach in it and peasants to pray in it. It was not understood that the really uncultured Irishman is the man who has lost the Gaelic tradition and culture and has not yet gained the tradition and culture of England. Sometimes even emigrants affected to look down on the language of their childhood. A man who returned some time ago from Australia tells me how he once greeted two Clare men in Irish, and they professed not to understand him; but a servant girl who was standing by turned on them and gave them a rating and said, 'You don't know your own language, and you don't know English,' and then they went away ashamed! But the people soon began to regret what they were losing, though they did not know the true extent of their loss in the loss of the widened horizon and intellectual training of a bilingual people.

But again the hour had come, and the man came to blow the smouldering turf to a flame. Even in England the name of Dr Douglas Hyde is known through his beautiful translations of *The Love Songs of Connacht*: and on the Continent it is well known as that of a scholar, a poet, a man of letters. He had devoted himself to finding and preserving what fragments of folklore, poetry, and tradition might have remained among the people from the time of their literary greatness; for it must be remembered that we had a lyric poetry before Chaucer, and a literature that is now the mine at which scholars in France and Germany are eagerly working. Though he found much that had remained, he was shocked at the swiftness with which the language and its traditions were passing away. He saw that if it was to be saved it must be saved by the people themselves. The Gaelic League, founded in 1893, of which he is president, rests upon this basis. It aims, not at getting rid of English, but at 'keeping Irish spoken where it is spoken still'. Forty-three branches have now been founded. A bilingual weekly paper, *Fainne an Lae* (*The Dawn of Day*), is published, and has a large circulation. Sets of *Simple Lessons in Irish* are selling by the thousand. A yearly festival, the 'Oire-achtas', has been founded and is held in Dublin. This year Highland delegates attended it, and the first telegram in Gaelic crossed the Atlantic, bringing a greeting from America. For Ireland in America has come into the movement. New York has joined, Boston has joined, San Francisco has joined, Washington has endowed a Celtic chair in its Catholic University with £10,000. No rich endowments have been made in Ireland yet, the movement has rested upon those whose pence are precious. I notice in the report of the Galway branch that it began with meetings of working-men only. Then the National teachers were asked to join, and then the priests came in. The Bishop of Galway, the Bishop of Raphoe, Cardinal Logue, support the League strongly, and plead 'to have the tongue in which Columba and Adamnan spoke and preached taught in our schools side by side with the language of Shakespeare and Newman'. When a movement begins among the people and is then taken up by the priests, we may be sure the elements of success have been recognised in it.

Little incidents mark the turn of the tide. An old Limerick farmer tells me that in his youth 'all the farmers of Munster, the aristocracy of Ireland were able to read and write Irish'. Then came the generation that began to forget it, and 'Now,' he says, 'my son is vexed that it was not taught to him, and is learning it himself in Limerick.' Some time ago, in a village on the Galway coast, an old woman used to appear regularly every week at the dispensary, with a description of some new illness she was developing. It was found that this was her realistic way of interpreting for her neighbours, who 'had no English', and so could not themselves explain their symptoms. The other day I noticed in a newspaper report that there had been a new doctor appointed to this dispensary district, and that the members of the Gaelic League had brought the weight of opinion to bear on the choice, and that an Irish-speaking doctor had been appointed.

The Christian Brothers now teach Irish in their schools, but the National Board is not yet awake to the strength of feeling in this matter, although, owing to the impulse given by the League, teachers of Irish have been appointed in two of the training colleges for teachers. And inspectors have been given leave, if they wish, to conduct examinations in Irish; but as all but two or three of these inspectors are ignorant of the language, this act of grace is not likely to be worn out by usage. Irish is now taught in about seventy National schools, as against seven in 1884; but, as the Galway head-inspector reports, 'Its teaching as an extra is so hampered by regulations that but little can be done while these regulations remain in force.' And it may only be taught at all in the higher forms, so that children must be from three to five years at school with 'the round shot tied to the leg' before they are allowed to learn it at all. The Chief Commissioner of National Education has many anxious eyes upon him, and there is even a question of which policy would serve best, 'to have a torchlight procession in his honour, or to break his windows'. But I am not in favour of window-breaking, for the Chief Commissioner is not only a Galway man, but is himself a scholar and a master of so many languages that he will not grudge his young fellow-countrymen the advantage of two.

I have heard that some years ago, owing to the spread of German, the Czech language had so nearly died out in Bohemia that one of a small company of learned men gathered together to discuss the possibility of its revival glanced up and said, 'If that ceiling were to fall, the Bohemian language would be at an end.' But not only that language but its literature have now come to

vigorous life again. Our Gaelic movement, which is being sympa-
thetically watched by the countries bordering encroaching Germany, has not been born such a weakling, for Gaelic is still
spoken as a living language by over half a million of our race.
Nationalist MPs in neglecting it lost a great opportunity. Had
they been able to carry on those stormy Home Rule debates in
their native tongue at Westminster, they would soon not only
have been allowed but implored to carry their oratory to College
Green. It is still remembered in this county how O'Connell,
himself no advocate of Irish, baffled the Government reporters at
an open-air meeting by delivering his speech in that tongue.
Even a few years ago a local board of guardians proposed and
passed a resolution in Irish in favour of some Land League
measure, which would never have been sanctioned by their
chairman, a worthy Unionist peer, if he had had any idea what it
was all about. And in an Irish-speaking parish on the sea coast,
the priest, obliged to read the Pope's rescript against boycotting,
read it in English, that it might not be understood by those of his
congregation most in need of it. But the Irish tongue never
reached Parliament. Mr O'Brien would have none of it in those
days, or spare it a corner in *United Ireland*. But he afterwards
learned it while in gaol, and is now making up for his early errors
by support of the League and the gift of a silver cup for competi-
tion. Mr Healy is also said to have learned it in gaol from
another member of the Land League, teaching him French in
return. 'But,' says his fellow-prisoner, 'if he knows as little Irish
now as I do French, there isn't much between us.'

# The Felons of Our Land

> What spirits these so forsaken and so jaded:
> White plumes stained and apparel that is rent:
> Wild eyes dim with ideals that have faded:
> Weary feet wearily resting in ascent?
> Heroes and patriots, a company benighted,
> Looking back drearily they see along the plain
> Many a bright beacon that liberty had lighted
> Dying out slowly in the wind and in the rain.
>
> — Lord Bowen

## [ I ]

For a century past, to go back no further, the song-writers of
England have been singing of victory, the song-writers of Ireland only of defeat. Nelson and Wellington and Clive and their
days of triumph have been set in lasting verse by English poets,
not the generals driven back by Washington, or Hicks or Herbert Stewart or Majuba Hill. Gordon, dead and defeated, has
never passed into popular song, but the conqueror of Omdur-
man has already had the hall mark of success stamped upon
him by the unofficial laureate of the Empire. And yet it is not
a material victory that most needs interpretation in song. The
newspaper placard that tells of it is enough to stir the blood, to
swell the pride, of the passer-by. The song-writer, the poet,
would find a better mission were he to tell of the meaning of
failure, of the gain that may lie in the wake of a lost battle. If
he himself possessed the faith that is the evidence of things
unseen, he would strive to give spiritual vision to trembling
and discouraged men. He would strive for the power of the
man of God in the little hill city besieged by the Syrian host,
when he comforted his trembling and discouraged servant with
the assurance that 'they that be with us are more than they

254

that be with them', and opened his eyes to see the mountainsides alight with chariots and horses of fire.

Whether with such a purpose, or whether through the nature formed by generations of loss, it is not of conquerors or of victories our poets have written and our people have sung through the last hundred years, but of defeat and of prison and of death. This feeling, or instinct, has been thus expressed:

> They say the British Empire owes much to Irish hands,
> That Irish valour fixed her flag o'er many conquered lands,
> And ask if Erin takes no pride in these her gallant sons,
> Her Wolseleys and her Lawrences, her Wolfes and Wellingtons.

> Ah! these were of the Empire, we yield them to her fame,
> And ne'er in Erin's orisons is heard their alien name;
> But those for whom her heart beats high and benedictions swell,
> They died upon the scaffold and they pined within the cell.

Another song, more distinctively of the people, is the one from which I have taken the name of this paper:

> Let cowards sneer and tyrants frown,
>     Oh little do we care:
> A felon's cap's the noblest crown
>     An Irish head can wear!
> And though they sleep in dungeons deep
>     Or flee outlawed and banned,
> We love them yet, we can't forget
>     The felons of our land.

Felony is given in Johnson's dictionary as 'a crime denounced capital *by the law*', and this is how it, or perhaps I should use the word coined for Ireland, 'treason-felony', is defined in Ireland also – a crime in the eyes of the law, not in the eyes of the people. A thief is shunned, a murder prompted by brutality or personal malice is vehemently denounced, a sheepstealer's crime is visited on the third and fourth generations; but a 'felon' has come to mean one who has gone to death or to prison for the sake of a principle or a cause. In consequence, the prison rather lends a halo than leaves a taint. In a country that is not a reading country, 'Speeches from the Dock', the last public words of political prisoners, is in its forty-eighth edition. The chief ornament of many a cottage is the warrant for the arrest of a son of the house framed and hung up as a sort of diploma of honour. I remember an election to a dispensary district before which one candidate sent round certificates of his medical skill, the other merely a statement that several members of his family had been prosecuted by the government. And it was the latter who won the appointment. I have known the hillsides blaze with bonfires when prisoners were released, not because they were believed to be innocent, but because they were believed to be guilty. It has been so all through the century. I find among Under-Secretary Gregory's papers a letter written by Colonel Barry from Limerick in 1816 in connection with some executions that were taking place at that disturbed time.

> The Sheriff has requested that I would remark to you the propriety of appealing to Government to forbid the Bodies of all such people, or indeed any part of their clothing, being given up to their familys, who consider that these people have died as Martyrs in the cause of their country, and instead of holding them out as examples to avoid, cry them up as characters to be imitated. The anxiety to get the corps of the execution is very curious, it is carried to such length by the different Branches of the family as to cause very great Battles, indeed the last execution that took place here there was very nearly being a Battle, and there were as I understand upwards of a thousand people clearing for action when the Mayor threatened to turn out the main guard if they did not disperse . . . Not even a shoe should be given to the family, for all the cloths the deceased had on are considered as relicks.

Then, as in later years, the act of the government executioner seems often to have been a swift act of canonisation.

## [ II ]

Irish history, having been forbidden in the national schools, has lifted up its voice in the streets, and has sung the memory of each new movement, and of the men who guided it, into the memory of each new generation. At little Catholic bookshops, at little sweet and china shops in country towns, one finds the cheap ballad books, in gaudy paper covers, red, yellow, and green, that hold these summaries of a sad history. The 'Harp of Tara', the 'Green Flag of Ireland', the 'Rising of the Moon', are some of them. And at fairs and markets the favourite ballads are sold singly or in broadsheets by the singers at a yet lower price. Sometimes it is a movement that is celebrated, the '98 rebellion above all. The well-known 'Who Fears to Speak of Ninety-eight', the contribution of Trinity College to national song, has lately taken new youth in a translation into Irish, but a more general favourite is the simple and picturesque 'Rising of the Moon':

> Oh! then tell me, Shawn O'Ferrall,
>   Where the gathering is to be –
> In the old spot by the river
>   Right well known to you and me.
> One word more – for signal token
>   Whistle up the marching tune,
> With your pike upon your shoulder
>   By the rising of the moon.

* * *

> Well they fought for poor old Ireland,
>   And full bitter was their fate
> (Oh! what glorious pride and sorrow
>   Fill the name of ninety-eight!)
> Yet, thank God, e'en still are beating
>   Hearts in manhood's burning noon,
> Who would follow in their footsteps
>   At the rising of the moon!

The Union and 'The Fate of the Forties' (the forty shilling freeholders evicted when they ceased to be of political use) and the famine and other disastrous events are touched on. But for the most part the ballads are written to keep in honour the names of the 'felons' themselves, 'the men who loved the cause that never dies'.

In a little packet of papers in my possession marked as 'proved to have been found in Lord Edward Fitzgerald's apartment in Leinster House', probably at the time of his arrest, there is a card, 'Sacred to the memory of William Orr', the inscription carefully written and surrounded with emblems of Erin and of Liberty and of Death, painted possibly by Lord Edward's own hand. Orr, the writing explains, was 'offered up at Carrickfergus on Saturday, 14th October 1797, an awful sacrifice to Irish freedom on the altar of British tyranny'. Orr in '97, Lord Edward himself and Wolfe Tone in '98, began the long procession that has passed into a century of Irish song through the qualifying prison gate.

A street ballad that has now found its way into songbooks touches with some precision as to facts, though without much regard to sequence, on the felons of some fifty years. It was composed by a Dublin street singer, and, in spite of the stilted words of one who has learned a style from newspapers and from mob oratory, there is something touching in the conscientious attention to detail where it concerns those whose names might be slipping out of memory, and in the return to Mitchel's name without any detail, as if the tears in the voice of the singer would not allow the fate of the living convict he had known to be dwelt upon.

> By Memory inspired,
> And love of country fired,
> The deeds of them I love to dwell upon –
> And the patriotic glow
> Of my spirit must bestow
> A tribute to O'Connell that is gone, boys, gone.
> Here's a memory to the friends that are gone.
>
> In October '97 –
> May his soul find rest in heaven –
> William Orr to execution was led on;
> The jury, drunk, agreed

That Irish was his creed;
For perjury and threats drove them on, boys, on.
　Here's the memory of John Mitchel that is gone.

　　We saw a nation's tears
　　Shed for John and Henry Sheares,
Betrayed by Judas, Captain Armstrong;
　　We may forgive, but yet
　　We never can forget
The poisoning of Maguire that is gone, boys, gone.
　Our high Star and true Apostle that is gone!

　　How did Lord Edward die?
　　Like a man, without a sigh;
But he left his handiwork on Major Swan!
　　But Sirr, with steel-clad breast,
　　And coward heart at best,
Left us cause to mourn Lord Edward that is gone, boys, gone.
　Here's the memory of our friends that are gone!

　　September, eighteen-three,
　　Closed this cruel history,
When Emmett's blood the scaffold flowed upon –
　　Oh, had their spirits been wise,
　　They might then realise
Their freedom – but we drink to Mitchel that is gone, boys, gone.
　Here's the memory of the friends that are gone!

Lord Edward, Emmett, O'Connell, Wolfe Tone, have had their story so often told that it is unnecessary to touch on it. The Sheares, Henry and John, were sons of a member of the Irish parliament. The elder was educated at Trinity College, and both brothers were called to the Irish bar. They threw in their lot with the United Irishmen, and were executed in '98. Sir Jonah Barrington, who had been at Trinity with John Sheares, did his utmost for them with Lord Clare, but was only promised a respite of one hour, and this promise came too late. 'I hastened to Newgate,' he says, 'and arrived at the very moment that the executioner was holding up the head of my old college friend, and saying, "Here is the head of a traitor!" They had been hanged side by side, holding each other's hands.'

Wolfe Tone, in spite of the romance that must always hang about Lord Edward's name, is looked on, as founder of the United Irishmen, as the more direct representative of the rebellion. One song by him is in the ballad books, and there is not, I think, one in which his name is not found. In many later movements men's thoughts have turned to him. Kickham, the poet–felon, sent to imprisonment in 1866, cries:

> Oh, Knowledge is a wondrous power,
>     And stronger than the wind,
> And thrones shall fall and despots bow
>     Before the might of mind.
>
> The poet and the orator
>     The heart of man can sway,
> And would to the kind heavens
>     That Wolfe Tone were here today!

Davis,[1] though he died young, before his 'Young Ireland' friends had found their way to the dock, to which he himself was inevitably tending, wrote while he lived of him and of other felons who had come before his time:

> Sure 'twas for this Lord Edward died, and Wolfe Tone sank
>     serene,
> Because they could not bear to leave the red above the green.
> And 'twas for this that Owen fought, and Sarsfield nobly bled,
> Because their eyes were hot to see the green above the red!

His verses on 'Tone's Grave' are usually found on the broadsheets, for that grave has been for the last hundred years a place of pilgrimage. No tomb has yet been built there, for others feel, as Davis felt, that the time has not yet come, but stones have often been laid on his grave to mark it, and have as often been carried away by the pilgrims as relics. Davis's verses begin and end thus:

In Bodenstown churchyard there is a green grave,
And wildly along it the winter winds rave;
Small shelter, I ween, are the ruined walls there
When the storm sweeps down on the plains of Kildare.

\* \* \*

In Bodenstown churchyard there is a green grave,
And freely around it let winter winds rave.
Far better they suit him – the ruin and gloom –
Till Ireland, a nation, can build him a tomb.

O'Connell's influence was growing weak, and men were becoming hardened and embittered by the terrible scenes of the famine, when, in 1848, John Mitchel – the 'friend' whose name the poor street singer comes back upon, but cannot dwell upon – came out from, or in advance of, the Young Ireland group and openly preached revolution. His arrest took place in March, his trial in May. He was convicted of the newly baptised crime, 'treason-felony', and was condemned to fourteen years' transportation. Then he was hurried off in a police van to the war sloop that was waiting for him with fires lighted and steam up. His *Jail Journal*, a book of extraordinary power, begins with the entry: 'May 27, 1848. On this day, about four o'clock in the afternoon, I, John Mitchel, was kidnapped and carried off from Dublin in chains as a convicted felon.' He was first sent to Bermuda, and in the next year with a batch of convicts to the Cape. But insurrection had broken out there also. The colonists had been promised that their country should never be made a penal settlement without their consent. This promise had been broken though by means of an 'Order in Council'. The colonists took the law into their own hands and refused to allow the convicts to land, though they were 'ready to make an exception in the case of Mr Mitchel'; but he was not allowed to land alone. For five months the battle with the Mother Country raged, and the convicts lay tossing in Simon's Bay. At last HM's Government gave in, and the *Neptune*, with her live cargo, was sent on to Van Diemen's Land. On the first voyage the *Essays of Macaulay*, then a cabinet minister, fell into Mitchel's hands, and the young convict slings his pebbles with a will at the head of the big Philistine. It happened that I first came across the *Jail Journal* in 1887, at the time of the Jubilee, when England was celebrating in the name of the Queen her own fifty years' fatness. Such sentences as these came as a commentary on each day's papers.

> He (Macaulay) has the right omniscient tone and air, and the true knack of administering reverential flattery to British civilisation, British prowess, honour, enlightenment, and all that, especially to the great nineteenth century and its astounding civilisation, that is, to his readers. It is altogether a new thing in the history of mankind, this triumphant glorification of a current century upon being the century it is. No former age, before or after, ever took any pride in itself, and sneered at the wisdom of its ancestors; and the new phenomenon indicates, I believe, not higher wisdom, but deeper stupidity. The nineteenth century is come, but not gone; and what now if it should be hereafter memorable among centuries for something quite other than its wondrous enlightenment? . . . What the mass of mankind understand by the word good is, of course, pudding, and praise, and profit, comfort, power, luxury, supply of vulgar wants – all, in short, which Bacon included under the word *commoda*; and to minister to mankind in these things is, according to the great English teacher, the highest aim – the only aim and end of true philosophy and wisdom. O Plato! O Jesu! . . . They did actually imagine – those ancient wise men – that it is true wisdom to raise our thoughts and aspirations above what the mass of mankind calls good – to regard truth, fortitude, honesty, purity, as the great objects of human effort and *not* the supply of vulgar wants.

These words were not spoken by any living preacher, but by a convicted felon who had not lived to see the jubilee –

> So we drink to John Mitchel that is gone, boys, gone:
> Here's the memory of the friends that are gone.

The Fenian outbreak – it can hardly be called 'rising' – of 1867 would not perhaps have found a large place in national song but for the Manchester triple execution. As it is, the songs connected with that tragedy are perhaps the most numerous and popular of all. The outbreak came in 1867, and was easily put down. As in '98, the chief leaders had already been arrested, and the whole plan fell into disorder. Some of the principal organisers escaped; two of them, Kelly and Deasy, were arrested at Manchester. On September 18 they were placed in the dock, and were remanded and sent back to the borough gaol, handcuffed and locked into separate compartments of a prison van, with a strong escort of police. About halfway on the road to Salford the van was attacked by a body of men, some armed, who shot down one of the horses and so brought it to a full stop. They tried to break the door open, but it was locked. The lock was blown open by a pistol shot, and Sergeant Brett, who was inside, and who had bravely refused to give up the keys, was shot dead, whether by this shot or by a deliberate one was the point disputed at the trial. The prisoners were snatched out, helped, handcuffed as they were, over the wall, and made their escape. The police rallied, and, helped by the mob, seized some of the rescuers who had stayed on the spot to cover the flight of the prisoners. The Irish quarter of Manchester was searched, and before morning sixty Irishmen were in prison.

The final trial of the rescuers took place on October 28. By this time five men had been pitched upon as ringleaders, Allen, Larkin, O'Brien, Maguire and Condon. All were found guilty and condemned to death. The last two were afterwards released, Maguire, curiously enough, on the intercession of the whole body of press representatives who had attended the trial, Condon, it was believed, because he was an American citizen. The other three were hanged publicly at Manchester on November 23.

The excitement caused in Ireland was extraordinary. It was believed that these men were put to death, not because they were guilty of murder, for this was not proved, and each one to the end protested his innocence, but because, as has often happened in other countries in a moment of passion and panic, the mob had demanded a victim, and the lot had fallen not on one but on three. They were all men of good character, working for their bread. O'Brien was the son of an evicted farmer; Larkin, the grandson of a farmer flogged and transported in '98; Allen, for whose fate most pity was felt, had been brought up a carpenter, was only nineteen, and was soon to have been married. He, like the others, had not asked for mercy or denied his share in the rescue, but only in the death of Sergeant Brett. In his last letter to his family he said, 'I am dying an honourable death. I am dying for Ireland, dying for the land that gave me birth, dying for the island of saints and dying for liberty. Every generation of our countrymen has suffered, and where is the Irish heart could stand by unmoved? I should like to know what trouble, what passion, what mischief could separate the true Irish heart from its own native isle.' On the next Sunday the chapels were filled with prayers for the soul of the victims. Their bodies had been buried in quicklime but immense funeral processions were held, and are still held in their memory.

Their fate gave the touch of pathos that had been wanting to the Fenian movement. After sentence of death had been pronounced on them, and before they left the dock, they had cried out together, 'God Save Ireland!' The song founded on these words has become the national anthem of the greater part of Ireland.

> Never till the latest day
> Shall the memory pass away
> Of the gallant lives thus given for our land;
> But on the cause must go,
> Amidst joy or weal or woe,
> Till we've made our isle a nation free and grand –
>
> God save Ireland, say we proudly,
> God save Ireland, say we all;
> If upon the scaffold high
> Or the battle-field we die,
> Oh, what matter when for Erin dear we fall?

Many other songs have been written and are sung in their honour – 'The Martyrs', 'Martyrs' Day', 'The Martyred Three', and the one that, to take the test of the broadsheets, is most popular, the 'Smashing of the Van'.

> One cold November morning in 1867,
> These martyrs to their country's cause a sacrifice were given.
> God save Ireland! was the cry, all through the crowd it ran;
> The Lord have mercy on the boys that helped to smash the van.

Our ballad singers, in their summaries of history, are never afraid of names, but daringly string them together in a sort of rhymed 'Calendar of Worthies', as:

Now to begin to name them, I'll continue in a direct line,
There's John Mitchel, Thomas Francis Maher, and also William
    Smith O'Brien,
John Martin and O'Donoghue, Erin sorely feels their loss,
For to complete their number I will include O'Donovan Ross.

There is a redeeming intensity and continuity of purpose through even such doggerel verses as these; they are not without dignity if looked on as roughly hammered links in an unequally wrought chain.

Parnell, when in Kilmainham Jail, was sung at fairs and markets all through the country, and in the first burst of sorrow for his loss many verses were written, but none that have taken, or are likely to take, a real hold on the country, and this, although the first that were printed in *United Ireland* after his death were written by the first of our poets, Yeats. The split in the party, or the influence of priests, or perhaps the strange belief held by many that he is still alive, has laid a silencing finger on the singers' lips. And some have looked elsewhere for words to associate with his grave:

Oh, I have dreamed a dreary dream,
    Beyond the Isle of Skye:
I saw a dead man win a fight,
    And I thought that man was I.

But Davis's beautiful 'Lament for Owen Roe' best expresses the despair that has been felt by every new peasant generation, as one leader after another has been struck down:

We thought you would not die, we were sure you would not go
And leave us in our utmost need to Cromwell's cruel blow.
Sheep without a shepherd, when the snow shuts out the sky.
Oh, why did you leave us, Owen? Why did you die?

Soft as woman's was your voice, O'Neil, bright was your eye.
Oh, why did you leave us, Owen, why did you die?
Your troubles are all over, you're at rest with God on high;
But we're slaves and we're orphans, Owen. Why did you die?

## [ III ]

Few of our ballads can take rank with those of Davis at his best,
but there are some of them, those written by the felons themselves,
that stand outside criticism, sweat-drops of the worker, blood-
drops of the fighter shed as he passed along the hard highway. As
some old lines say:

> And he was also in the war,
> He who this rhyme did write;
> Till evening fought he with the sword,
> And sang the song at night.[2]

Such are those of Doheny, who was hunted over bogs and
mountains for many weeks in '48, after Smith O'Brien's rising, in
which he had taken part. He has told of these wanderings in his
book, *On a Felon's Track*, and also in one of his ballads, written
while 'on his keeping' on the Kerry mountains, and addressed to
Ireland, 'Acushla gal machree':

> I've given thee my youth and prime
> And manhood's waning years,
> I've blest thee in the sunniest time
> And shed for thee my tears;
> And, mother, though thou'st cast away
> The child who'd die for thee,
> My fondest wish is still to pray
> For Cushla gal machree.
>
> I've tracked for thee the mountain sides
> And slept within the brake,
> More lonely than the swan that glides
> On Lua's fairy lake;

The rich have spurned me from their door
    Because I'd set thee free,
Yet do I love thee more and more
    Acushla gal machree!

Another felon ballad writer was Kickham, from whose 'Rory of the Hill' I have already quoted. His 'Patrick Sheehan', well known in country places, is still an obstacle in the path of the recruiting sergeant:

Bereft of home, and kith and kin,
    With plenty all around,
I starved within my cabin
    And slept upon the ground;
But cruel as my lot was
    I ne'er did hardship know
Till I joined the English army
    Far away from Aherlow.

'Rouse up there,' says the Corporal,
    'You lazy Hirish hound –
Why, don't you hear, you sleeping dog,
    The call "to arms" sound?'
Alas! I had been dreaming
    Of days long, long ago:
I woke before Sebastopol
    And not in Aherlow.

\* \* \*

Then, Irish youths, dear countrymen,
    Take heed of what I say,
For if you join the English ranks
    You'll surely rue the day.
And whenever you are tempted
    A soldiering to go,
Remember poor blind Sheehan
    Of the glen of Aherlow.

# [ IV ]

To the spiritual mind the spiritual truth underlying each development of Christianity is always manifest. But there is a significant contrast in the outward form in which religion appears to the peasant of England and the peasant of Ireland. In England (I quote again from the *Jail Journal*) 'is there not our venerable Church, our beautiful liturgy?' There is a *department* for all that, with the excellent Archbishop of Canterbury at the head of it. To the English peasant the well-furnished village church, the pulpit cushion, the gilt-edged Bible, the cosy rectory, represent respectability, comfort, peace, a settled life. In Ireland the peasant has always before his eyes, on his own cottage walls or in his whitewashed chapel, the cross, the spear, the crown of thorns, that tell of what once seemed earthly failure, that tell that He to whom he kneels was led to a felon's death.

In England the poet of today must, if he will gain a hearing, write of the visible and material things that appeal to a people who have made 'The Roast Beef of Old England' a fetish, and whose characteristic song is:

We don't want to fight, but by Jingo if we do,
We've got the ships, we've got the men, *we've got the money too.*

In Ireland he is in touch with a people whose thoughts have long been dwelling on an idea; whose heroes have been the failures, the men 'who went out to battle and who always fell', who went out to a battle that was already lost – men who, whatever may have been their mistakes or faults, had an aim quite apart from personal greed or gain.

Some of us are inclined to reproach our younger poets with a departure from the old tradition because they no longer write patriotic and memorial ballads. But in singing of 'the dim wisdoms old and deep that God gives unto man in sleep', they have not departed from it, they have only travelled a little further on the road that leads from things seen to things unseen. And a poet is not to be shaped and trained like a yew tree and set in a hedgerow, to guard even the most hallowed ashes. He must be left to his own growth, like the tree that clings to its own hillside, that sends down its roots to find hidden waters, that sends out its branches to the winds and to the stars.

# Our Irish Theatre

## The Fight with the Castle

In the summer of 1909 I went one day from London to Ayot St Lawrence, a Hertfordshire village, to consult Mr Bernard Shaw on some matters connected with our Theatre. When I was leaving, he gave me a little book, *The Shewing-up of Blanco Posnet*, which had just been printed, although not published. It had, however, been already rejected by the Censor, as all readers of the newspapers know; and from that quiet cottage the fiery challenge-giving answers had been sent out. I read the play as I went back in the train, and when at St Pancras Mr Yeats met me to talk over the business that had taken me away, I showed him the little book that had been given the black ball, and I said, 'Hypocrites.'

A little time afterwards Mr Shaw offered us the play for the Abbey, for the Censor has no jurisdiction in Ireland – an accidental freedom. We accepted it and put it in rehearsal that we might produce it in Horse Show week. We were without a regular stage manager at that time, and thought to have it produced by one of the members of the Company. But very soon the player who had taken it in charge found the work too heavy and troublesome, and withdrew from the stage management, though not from taking a part. I had a letter one morning telling me this, and I left by the next train for Dublin. As I left, I sent a wire to a London actor – a friend – asking if he could come over and help us out of this knot. Meanwhile, that evening, and before his answer came, I held a rehearsal, the first I had ever taken quite alone. I thought out positions during the night, and next morning, when I had another rehearsal, I began to find an extraordinary interest and excitement in the work. I saw that Blanco's sermon, coming as it did after bustling action, was in danger of seeming monotonous. I broke it up by making him deliver the first part standing up on the Sheriff's bench, then bringing him down to sit on the table and speak some of the words into the face of Elder

Posnet. After that I sent him with a leap on to the table for the last phrases. I was very much pleased with the effect of this action, and by the time a telegram told me my London friend could come, I was confident enough to do without him. We were very proud and pleased when the whole production was taken to London later by the Stage Society. I have produced plays since then, my own and a few others. It is tiring work; one spends so much of one's own vitality.

That is what took me away from home to Dublin in that summer time, when cities are out of season. Mr Yeats had stayed on at Coole at his work, and my letters to him, and letters after that to my son and to Mr Shaw, will tell what happened through those hot days, and of the battle with Dublin Castle, which had taken upon itself to make the writ of the London Censor run at the Abbey.

I received while in Dublin, the following letter from a permanent official in Dublin Castle:

DEAR LADY GREGORY:

'I am directed by the Lord Lieutenant to state that His Excellency's attention has been called to an announcement in the Public Press that a play entitled *The Shewing-up of Blanco Posnet* is about to be performed in the Abbey Theatre.

'This play was written for production in a London theatre, and its performance was disallowed by the Authority which in England is charged with the Censorship of stage plays. The play does not deal with an Irish subject, and it is not an Irish play in any other sense than that its author was born in Ireland. It is now proposed to produce this play in the Abbey Theatre, which was founded for the express purpose of encouraging dramatic art in Ireland, and of fostering a dramatic school growing out of the life of the country.

'The play in question does not seem well adapted to promote these laudable objects or to belong to the class of plays originally intended to be performed in the Abbey Theatre, as described in the evidence on the hearing of the application for the Patent.

'However this may be, the fact of the proposed performance

having been brought to the notice of the Lord Lieutenant, His Excellency cannot evade the responsibility cast upon him of considering whether the play conforms in other respects to the conditions of the Patent.

'His Excellency, after the most careful consideration, has arrived at the conclusion that in its original form the play is not in accordance either with the assurances given by those interested when the Patent was applied for, or with the conditions and restrictions contained in the Patent as granted by the Crown.

'As you are the holder of the Patent in trust for the generous founder of the Theatre, His Excellency feels bound to call your attention, and also the attention of those with whom you are associated, to the terms of the Patent and to the serious consequences which the production of the play in its original form might entail . . .'

I tell what followed in letters written to Coole.

'Thursday, August 12th. At the Theatre this morning the Secretary told me Whitney & Moore (our solicitors) had telephoned that they had a hint there would be interference with the production of *Blanco Posnet* by the Castle, and would like to see me.

'I went to see Dr Moore. He said a Castle Official, whose name he would not give, had called the day before yesterday and said, "As a friend of Sir Benjamin Whitney, I have come to tell you that if this play is produced it will be a very expensive thing for Miss Horniman." Dr Moore took this to mean the Patent would be forfeited. I talked the matter over with him and asked if he would get further information from his friend as to what method they meant to adopt, for I would not risk the immediate forfeiture of the Patent, but would not mind a threat of refusal to give a new Patent, as by that time – 1910 – perhaps neither the present Lord Lieutenant nor the present Censor would be in office.

'Dr Moore said he would go and see his friend, and at a quarter past two I had a message on the telephone from him that I had better see the Castle Official or that he wished to see me (I didn't hear very well) before 3 o'clock. I went to the Castle and saw the Official. He said, "Well." I said, "Are you going to cut off our heads?" He said, "This is a very serious business; I think you are very ill-advised to think of putting on this play. May I ask how it came about?" I said, "Mr Shaw offered it and we accepted it." He said, "You have put us in a most difficult and disagreeable position by putting on a play to which the English Censor objected." I answered, "We do not take his view of it, and we think it hypocrisy objecting to a fallen woman in homespun on the stage, when a fallen woman in satin has been the theme of such a great number of plays that have been passed." He said, "It is not that the Censor objected to; it is the use of certain expressions which may be considered blasphemous. Could not they be left out?" "Then there would be no play. The subject of the play is a man, a horse-thief, shaking his fist at Heaven, and finding afterwards that Heaven is too strong for him. If there were no defiance, there could be no victory. It is the same theme that Milton has taken in Satan's defiance in *Paradise Lost*. I consider it a deeply religious play, and one that could hurt no man, woman or child. If it had been written by some religious leader, or even by a dramatist considered 'safe', nonconformists would admire and approve of it." He said, "We have nothing to do with that, the fact for us is that the Censor has banned it." I said, "Yes, and passed *The Merry Widow*, which is to be performed here the same week, and which I have heard is objectionable, and *The Devil*, which I saw in London." He said, "We would not have interfered, but what can we do when we see such paragraphs as these?" handing me a cutting from the *Irish Times* headed, "Have we a Censor?" I replied, "We have not written or authorised it, as you might see by its being incorrect. I am sole Patentee of the Theatre." He said, "Dublin society will call out against us if we let it go on." "Lord Iveagh has taken six places." "For that play?" "Yes, for that play, and I believe Dublin society is likely to follow Lord Iveagh." He went on, "Archbishop Walsh may object." I was silent. He said, "It is very hard on the Lord Lieutenant. You should have had more consideration for him." I replied, "We did not know or remember that the power rested

with him, but it *is* hard on him, for he can't please everybody."
He said, "Will you not give it up?" "What will you do if we go
on?" "Either take no notice or take the Patent from you at
once." I said, "If you decide to forfeit our Patent, we will not
give a public performance; but if we give no performance to be
judged by, we shall rest under the slur of having tried to produce
something bad and injurious." "We must not provoke Public
opinion." "We provoked Nationalist public opinion in *The Playboy*, and you did not interfere." "Aye," said he, "exactly so, that
was quite different; that had not been banned by the Censor." I
said, "Time has justified us, for we have since produced *The
Playboy* in Dublin and on tour with success, and it will justify us
in the case of this play." "But *Blanco Posnet* is very inferior to *The
Playboy*." I said, "Even so, Bernard Shaw has an intellectual
position above that of Mr Synge, though he is not above him in
imaginative power. He is recognised as an intellectual force, and
his work cannot be despised." "Lord Aberdeen will have to
decide." "I should like him to know," I said, "that from a
business point of view the refusal to allow this play, already
announced, to be given would do us a serious injury." He said,
"No advertisements have been published." "Yes," I said, "the
posters have been out some days, and there is a good deal of
booking already from England as well as here. We are just
beginning to pay our way as a Theatre. We should be able to do
so if we get about a dozen more stalls regularly. The people who
would take our stalls will be frightened off by your action. The
continuance of our Theatre at all may depend on what you do
now. We are giving a great deal of employment, spending in
Dublin over £1500 a year, and our Company bears the highest
possible character." He said, "I know that well." I said, "I know
Lord Aberdeen is friendly to our Theatre, though he does not
come to it, not liking the colour of our carpets." He said, "He is a
supporter of the drama. He was one of Sir Henry Irving's pall-
bearers." "When shall we know the decision?" "In a day or two,
perhaps tomorrow. You can produce it in Cork, Galway or
Waterford. It is only in Dublin the Lord Lieutenant has power."
He read from time to time a few lines from the Patent or Act of

Parliament before him, "just to get them into your head". The last words he read were, "There must be no profane representation of sacred personages"; "and that," he said, "applies to Blanco Posnet's representations of the Deity." I told him of the Censor's note on *The Playboy*, "The expression 'Khaki cut-throats' must be cut out, together with any others that may be considered derogatory to His Majesty's Forces," and he laughed. Then I said, "How can we think much of the opinion of a man like that?" He said, "I believe he was a bank manager." We then said goodbye.

'Friday, 5 o'c. Dr Moore sent for me at 4 o'clock. I went with W. B. Yeats, who had arrived. The Crown Solicitor at the Castle, Sir B. Whitney's "friend", had called and told him the Lord Lieutenant was "entirely opposed to the play being proceeded with and would use every power the law gave him to stop it", and that, "it would be much better for us to lay the play aside".

'We decided to go on with the performance and let the Patent be forfeited, and if we must die, die gloriously. Yeats was for this course, and I agreed. Then I thought it right to let the Permanent Official know my change of intention, and, after some unsuccessful attempts on the telephone, W.B.Y. and I went to see him at the Castle. He was very smiling and amiable this time, and implored us, as we had understood him to do through the telephone, to save the Lord Lieutenant from his delicate position. "You defy us, you advertise it under our very nose, at the time everyone is making a fight with the Censor."[1] He threatened to take away our Patent before the play came on at all, if we persisted in the intention. I said that would give us a fine case. Yeats said we intended to do *Oedipus*, that this also was a censored play, although so unobjectionable to religious minds that it had been performed in the Catholic University of Notre Dame, and that we should be prevented if we announced it now. He replied, "leave that till the time comes, and you needn't draw our attention to it." We said the *Irish Times* might again draw his attention to it. He proposed our having a private performance only. I said, "I had a letter from Mr Shaw objecting to that course." He moaned, and said, "it is very hard upon us. Can you suggest no way out of it?" We answered, "None, except our being left alone." "Oh, Lady Gregory," he said, "appeal to your own common sense." When I mentioned Shaw's letter, he said, "All Shaw wants is to use the Lord Lieutenant as a whip to lay upon the Censor." Yeats said, "Shaw would use him in that way whatever happens." "I know he will," said the Official. At last he asked if we could get Mr Shaw to take out the passages he had already offered to take out for the Censor. We agreed to ask him to do this, as we felt the Castle was beaten, as the play even then would still be the one forbidden in England.'

This is the letter I had received from Mr Shaw:

'10 Adelphi Terrace, W. C. 12th August, 1909

'Your news is almost too good to be true. If the Lord Lieutenant would only forbid an Irish play without reading it, and after it had been declared entirely guiltless and admirable by the leading high class journal on the side of his own party [the *Nation*], forbid it at the command of an official of the King's household in London, then the green flag would indeed wave over Abbey Street, and we should have questions in Parliament and all manner of reverberating advertisement and nationalist sympathy for the Theatre.

'I gather from your second telegram that the play has perhaps been submitted for approval. If so, that will be the worse for us, as the Castle can then say they forbade it on its demerits without the slightest reference to the Lord Chamberlain.

'In any case, do not threaten them with a contraband performance. Threaten that we shall be suppressed; that we shall be made martyrs of; that we shall suffer as much and as publicly as possible. Tell them that they can depend on me to burn with a brighter blaze and louder yells than all Foxe's martyrs.'

Mr Shaw telegraphed his answer to the demand for cuts:

'The *Nation* article gives particulars of cuts demanded, which I refused as they would have destroyed the religious significance of the play. The line about moral relations is dispensable as they are mentioned in several other places; so it can be cut if the Castle is silly enough to object to such relations being called immoral, but I will cut nothing else. It is an insult to the Lord Lieutenant to ignore him and refer me to the requirements of a subordinate English Official. I will be no party to any such indelicacy. Please say I said so, if necessary.'

I give in the Appendix the *Nation* article to which he refers. My next letter home says:

'August 14. Having received the telegram from Shaw and the *Nation* article, we went to the Castle to see the Official, but only found his secretary, who offered to speak to him through a telephone, but the telephone was wheezy, and after long trying, all we could arrive at was that he wanted to know if we had seen Sir H. Beerbohm Tree's evidence, in which he said there were passages in *Blanco* that would be better out. Then he proposed our going to see him at his house, as he has gout and rheumatism and couldn't come to us.

'We drove to his house. He began on Tree, but Yeats told him Tree was the chief representative of the commercial theatre we are opposed to. He then proposed our giving a private performance, and we again told him Shaw had forbidden that. I read him the telegram refusing cuts, but he seemed to have forgotten that he had asked for cuts, and repeated his appeal to spare the Lord Lieutenant. I showed him the *Nation* article, and he read it and said, "But the *Book of Job* is not by the same author as *Blanco Posnet*." Yeats said, "Then if you could, you would censor the Deity?" "Just so," said he. He asked if we could make no concession. We said, "no", but that if they decided to take away the Patent, we should put off the production till the beginning of our season, end of September, and produce it with *Oedipus*; then they would have to suppress both together. He brightened up and said, if we could put it off, things would be much easier, as the Commission would not be sitting then or the Public be so much interested in the question. I said, "Of course we should have to announce at once that it was in consequence of the threatened action of the Castle we had postponed it." "Oh, you really don't mean that! You would let all the bulls loose. It would be much better not to say anything at all, or to say the rehearsals took longer than you expected." "The public announcement will be more to our own advantage." "Oh, that is dreadful!" I said, "We did not give in one quarter of an inch to Nationalist Ireland at *The Playboy* time, and we certainly cannot give in one quarter of an inch to the Castle."

'"We must think of Archbishop Walsh!" I said. "The Archbishop would be slow to move, for if he orders his flock to keep away from our play, he can't let them attend many of the Censor's plays, and the same thing applies to the Lord Lieutenant." The Official said, "I know that." We said, "We did not give in to the Church when Cardinal Logue denounced the *Countess Cathleen*. We played it under police protection." "I never heard of that. Why did he object?" Yeats said, "For exactly the same objection as is made to the present one, speeches made by demons in the play."

'Yeats spoke very seriously then about the principle involved; pointing out that we were trying to create a model on which a great national theatre may be founded in the future, that if we accepted the English Censor's ruling in Ireland, he might forbid a play like Wills's *Robert Emmet*, which Irving was about to act, and was made to give up for political reasons. He said, "You want, in fact, to have liberty to produce all plays refused by the Censor." I said, "We have produced none in the past and not only that, we have refused plays that we thought would hurt Catholic religious feeling. We refused, for instance, to produce Synge's *Tinker's Wedding*, much as we uphold his work, because a drunken priest made ridiculous appears in it. That very play was directly after Synge's death asked for by Tree, whom you have been holding up to us, for production in London." He said, "I am very sorry attention was drawn to the play. If no attention had been drawn to it by the papers, we should be all right. It is so wrong to produce it while the Commission is actually sitting and the whole question *sub judice*. We are in close official relation with the English officials of whom the Lord Chamberlain is one; that is the whole question." We said, "We see no way out of it. We are determined to produce the play. We cannot accept the

Censor's decision as applying to Ireland and you must make up your mind what course to take, but we ask to be let known as soon as possible because if we are to be suppressed, we must find places for our players, who will be thrown out of work." He threw up his hands and exclaimed, "Oh, my dear lady, but do not speak of such a thing as possible!" "Why," I asked, "what else have you been threatening all the time?" He said, "Well, the Lord Lieutenant will be here on Tuesday and will decide. He has not given his attention to the matter up to this" (this does not bear out the Crown Solicitor's story); "Perhaps you had better stay to see him." I told him that I wanted to get home, but would stay if absolutely necessary. He said, "Oh, yes, stay and you will probably see Lady Aberdeen also."'

Mr Shaw's next letter was from Kerry where he was motoring. In it he said: "I saw an *Irish Times* today with *Blanco* announced for production; so I presume the Castle has not put its foot down. The officials made an appalling technical blunder in acting as agents of the Lord Chamberlain in Ireland; and I worded my telegram in such a way as to make it clear that I knew the value of that indiscretion.

'I daresay the telegram reached the Castle before it reached you.'

Meanwhile on August 15th I had written to the Castle:

'I am obliged to go home tomorrow, so if you have any news for us, will you very kindly let us have it at Coole.

'We are, as you know, arranging to produce *Blanco* on Wednesday, 25th, as advertised and booked for, unless you serve us with a "Threatening notice", in which case we shall probably postpone it till September 30th and produce it with the already promised *Oedipus*.

'I am very sorry to have given you so much trouble and worry, and, as we told you, we had no idea the responsibility would fall on any shoulders but our own; but I think we have fully explained to you the reasons that make it necessary for us now to carry the matter through.'

I received the following answer:

'I am sorry you have been obliged to return to Galway. His Excellency, who arrived this morning, regrets that he has missed you and desires me to say that if you wished an interview with him on Thursday, he would be glad to receive you at the Viceregal Lodge.

'He will give the subject which has been discussed between us his earliest attention.'

I received by the same post a long and very kind letter from the Lord Lieutenant, written with his own hand. I am sorry that it was marked 'Private', and so I cannot give it here. I may, however, quote the words that brought us back to Dublin. 'It would seem that some further personal conference might be very desirable and therefore I hope that it may be possible for you to revisit Dublin on the earliest available day. I shall, of course, be most happy to have an opportunity for a talk with Mr Yeats.'

So my next letter home says: 'Friday, 20th. We arrived at the Broadstone yesterday at 2.15, and were met by the Official's secretary, who asked us to go to the Viceregal Lodge. Arrived there, another secretary came and asked me to go and see the Lord Lieutenant alone, saying Mr Yeats could go in later.'

Alas! I must be discreet and that conversation with the King's representative must not be given to the world, at least by me. I can only mention external things: Mr Yeats, until he joined the conference, being kept by the secretary, whether from poetical or political reasons, to the non-committal subject of Spring flowers; my grieved but necessary contumacy; our joint and immovable contumacy; the courtesy shown to us and, I think, also by us; the kindly offers of a cup of tea; the consuming desire for that tea after the dust of the railway journey all across Ireland; our heroic refusal, lest its acceptance should in any way, even if it did not weaken our resolve, compromise our principles ... His Excellency's gracious nature has kept no malice and he has since then publicly taken occasion to show friendship for our Theatre. I felt it was a business forced upon him, who had used his high office above all for reconcilement, as it was upon me, who lived under a peaceful star for some half a hundred years. I think it was a relief to both of us when at last he asked us to go on to the Castle and see again 'a very experienced Official'.

I may now quote again from my letters: 'We found the Official rather in a temper. He had been trying to hear Lord Aberdeen's account of the interview through the telephone and could not. We gave our account, he rather threatening in tone, repeating a good deal of what he had said before. He said we should be as much attacked as they, whatever happened, and that men connected with two newspapers had told him they were only waiting for an opportunity of attacking not only the Lord Lieutenant but the Abbey, if the play is allowed; so we should also catch it. I said, "*Après vous*." He said Mr Yeats had stated in the Patent Enquiry, the Abbey was for the production of romantic work. I quoted Parnell, "Who shall set bounds to the march of a Nation?" We told him our Secretary reported, "Very heavy booking, first class people, *a great many from the Castle*."

'He said he would see the Lord Lieutenant on his way home. We went to Dame Street Post Office and wired to Mr Shaw: "Have seen Viceroy. Deleted immoral relations, refused other cuts. He is writing to King, who supports Censor."'

Then, as holder of the Patent, I took counsel's opinion on certain legal points, of which the most vital was this:

'Should counsel be of opinion that the Crown will serve notice requiring the play to be discontinued, then counsel will please say what penalty he thinks querist would expose herself to by disregarding the notice of the Crown and continuing the representation?'

The answer to this question was:

'If the theatre ceases to be licensed, as pointed out above, and any performance for gain takes place there, the penalty under the 26. Geo. III. cap 57, sec. (2) *is £300 for each offence*, to be recovered in a "*qui tam*" action; one half of the £300 going to the Rotunda Hospital, the other half to the informer who sues.'

Mr Yeats and I were just going to a rehearsal at the Abbey on the evening of August 21st when we received a letter from the Castle, telling us that a formal legal document, forbidding the performance of the play, would reach us immediately. The matter had now become a very grave one. We knew that we should, if we went on and this threat were carried out, lose not only the Patent but that the few hundred pounds that we had been able to save and with which we could have supported our players till they found other work, would be forfeited. This thought of the players made us waver, and very sadly we agreed that we must give up the fight. We did not say a word of this at the Abbey but went on rehearsing as usual. When we had left the Theatre and were walking through the lamp-lighted streets, we found that during those two or three hours our minds had come to the same decision, that we had given our word, that at all risks we must keep it or it would never be trusted again; that we must in no case go back, but must go on at any cost.

We wrote a statement in which we told of the pressure put upon us and the objections made, but of these last we said: 'there is nothing to change our conviction that so far from containing offence for any sincere and honest mind, Mr Shaw's play is a high and weighty argument upon the working of the Spirit of God in man's heart, or to show that it is not a befitting thing for us to set upon our stage the work of an Irishman, who is also the most famous of living dramatists, after that work has been silenced in London by what we believe an unjust decision.

'One thing,' we continued, 'is plain enough, an issue that swallows up all else and makes the merit of Mr Shaw's play a secondary thing. If our Patent is in danger, it is because the decisions of the English Censor are being brought into Ireland, and because the Lord Lieutenant is about to revive, on what we consider a frivolous pretext, a right not exercised for a hundred and fifty years to forbid at the Lord Chamberlain's pleasure, any play produced in any Dublin theatre, all these theatres holding their Patents from him.

'We are not concerned with the question of the English Censorship now being fought out in London, but we are very certain that the conditions of the two countries are different, and that we must not, by accepting the English Censor's ruling, give away anything of the liberty of the Irish Theatre of the future. Neither can we accept without protest the revival of the Lord Lieutenant's claim at the bidding of the Censor or otherwise. The Lord Lieutenant is definitely a political personage, holding office from the party in power, and what would sooner or later grow into a political Censorship cannot be lightly accepted.'

Having sent this out for publication, we went on with our rehearsals.

In rehearsal I came to think that there was a passage that would really seem irreverent and give offence to the genuinely religious minds we respect. It was where Blanco said: 'Yah! What about the croup? I guess He made the croup when He was thinking of one thing; and then He made the child when He was thinking of something else; and the croup got past Him and killed the child. Some of us will have to find out how to kill the croup, I guess. I think I'll turn doctor just on the chance of getting back on Him by doing something He couldn't do.'

I wrote to Mr Shaw about this, and he answered in this very interesting letter:

'Parknasilla, 19 August, 1909

'I have just arrived and found all your letters waiting for me. I am naturally much entertained by your encounters and Yeats's with the Castle. I leave that building cheerfully in your hands.

'But observe the final irony of the situation. The English Censorship being too stupid to see the real blasphemy, makes a fool of itself. But you, being clever enough to put your finger on it at once, immediately proceed to delete what Redford's blunders spared.

'To me, of course, the whole purpose of the play lies in the problem, "What about the croup?" When Lady —, in her most superior manner, told me, "He is the God of Love," I said, "He is also the God of Cancer and Epilepsy." That does not present any difficulty to me. All this problem of the origin of evil, the mystery of pain, and so forth, does not puzzle me. My doctrine is that God proceeds by the method of "Trial and error", just like a workman perfecting an aeroplane; he has to make hands for himself and brains for himself in order that his will may be done.

He has tried lots of machines – the diphtheria bacillus, the tiger, the cockroach; and he cannot extirpate them, except by making something that can shoot them, or walk on them, or, cleverer still, devise vaccines and anti-toxins to prey on them. To me the sole hope of human salvation lies in teaching Man to regard himself as an experiment in the realisation of God, to regard his hands as God's hands, his brain as God's brain, his purpose as God's purpose. He must regard God as a helpless longing, which *longed* him into existence by its desperate need for an executive organ. You will find it all in *Man and Super Man*, as you will find it all behind *Blanco Posnet*. Take it out of my play, and the play becomes nothing but the old cry of despair – Shakespeare's, "As flies to wanton boys, so we are to the Gods; they kill us for their sport" – the most frightful blasphemy ever uttered.'

Mr Shaw enclosed with this the passage rewritten, as it now appears in the published play.

We put on *Blanco* on the date announced, the 25th August. We were anxious to the last, for counsel were of the opinion that if we were stopped, it would be on the Clause in the Patent against 'Any representation which should be deemed or construed immoral', and that if Archbishop Walsh or Archbishop Peacocke or especially the Head of the Lord Lieutenant's own Church, the Moderator of the Presbyterian Assembly, should say anything which might be 'deemed and construed' to condemn the play, the threats made would be carried out. There were fears of a riot also, for newspapers and their posters had kept up the excitement, and there was an immense audience. It is a pity we had not thought in time of putting up our prices. Guineas were offered even for standing room in the wings.

The play began, and till near the end it was received in perfect silence. Perhaps the audience were waiting for the wicked bits to begin. Then, at the end, there was a tremendous burst of cheering, and we knew we had won. Some stranger outside asked what was going on in the Theatre. 'They are defying the Lord Lieutenant' was the answer; and when the crowd heard the cheering, they took it up and it went far out through the streets.

There were no protests made on any side. And the play, though still forbidden in England, is still played by us, and always with success. And even if the protests hoped for had been made and we had suffered, does not Nietzsche say, 'A good battle justifies every cause'?

# from 'Laughter in Ireland'

I find in our Irish country people, who are after all the real
nation, the underlying melancholy, the tragic dignity, the poetic
imagination I find in the Gaelic writers, old and new. And these
songs of sadness are the ones most cared for. I lent a little book of
Gaelic verse by *An Craoibhin* (i.e. Douglas Hyde) to a young
farmer, and when I asked him a little later which he liked best,
he turned the leaves over, passing by those that were of love and
satire, and put his finger on a lament for one who died young.

> *Nois ann san uaig fuair o ta tu sinte*
> *Go saorig Dia tu*
> *Is buaidearta, bronac, boct ata mo samointe*
> *Is bronac me inniv.*

> Now that you are stretched in the cold grave
> May God set you free
> It is vexed and sorry and pitiful are my thoughts
> It is sorrowful I am today.

In the earliest epics as of Finn and Cuchulain there is but the
rarest glimpse of humour. Towards the end of the great war for
the Bull of Cuailgne, Maeve of Connacht makes a plan to take
Conchubar, King of Ulster, alive. 'Let us make a pen before him of
all the army standing around on three sides, and thirty hundred
men ready to shut the mouth of it on him when he comes in.'
And the Ulster historian writing this down comments, 'Conchubar and his thirty hundred of the best men in Ulster to be taken
alive! That is one of the most laughable things that was said in
the whole course of the war!' And when Maeve had made her
pen Conchubar 'never so much as looked for an opening' but
went straight through, cutting a gap for himself and killed eight
hundred men, so making it but a bitter joke in the end. But this
poverty of humour may be common to the early times of the

world. The laughter of the gods was caused for the most part by the misery of mortals, and in the *Morte D'Arthur*, Launcelot and King Arthur and it may be Galahad, himself, roar with laughter at the very feeble puns of Dinadin.

In looking through the Gaelic poetry, one sees it is the elegy rather than the epithalamium that holds the sway. Listen to the lament of Deirdre over the Sons of Usnach:

'That I would live after Naoise let no one think on the earth; I will not go on living after Ainnle and after Ardan;

'O young man digging the new grave, do not make the grave narrow; I will be along with them in it making lamentations and Ochones!

'Their three hounds, their three hawks will be from this time without huntsmen; three helpers of every battle, three helpers of Conall Cearnach.

'I am Deirdre without gladness and I at the end of my life; since it is grief to be without them I myself will not be long after them.'

And here is Emer's lament over Cuchulain:

'Och head, ochone O head; you gave death to great heroes, to many hundreds; my head will lay in the same grave; the one stone will be made for both of us.

'Dear the king, dear the king that never gave a refusal to any, thirty days it is tonight since my body lay by your body.

'I am glad, I am glad, Cuchulain of Muirthemne, I never brought red shame on your face for any unfaithfulness against you. I am carried away like a branch on the stream, I will not bind up my hair today; from this day I have nothing to say that is better than Ochone!'

One of Mr Yeats's poems most popular in Ireland has a refrain:

'Come away O human child, to the woods and waters wild, with a faery hand in hand; for the world's more full of weeping than you can understand.'

Raftery, the Connacht poet, calls to nature itself as fellow mourner in his lament for a Galway landlord!

'There's no dew or grass on Cluain Leathen; the cuckoo is not to be seen on the furze; the leaves are withering and the trees complaining of the cold. There is no sun or moon in the air or in the sky or no light in the stars coming down, with the stretching of O'Kelly in the grave!'

An Irish priest in Göttingen writes a sorrowful lament for Ireland:

> My thoughts alas are without strength;
> My Spirit is journeying towards death;
> My eyes are as a frozen sea;
> My tears my daily food;
> There is nothing in my life but only misery;
> My poor heart is torn;
> And my thoughts are sharp wounds within me,
> Mourning the miserable state of Ireland.
>
> I do not know of anything under the sky
> That is friendly or favourable to the Gael
> But only the sea that our need brings us to
> Or the wind that blows to the harbour
> The ship that is bearing us away from Ireland;
> And there is reason that these are reconciled with us
> For we increase the sea with our tears
> And the wandering wind with our sighs.

In looking through the whole mass of the Gaelic poetry of Connacht one finds collections of religious songs, of love songs, and some of these heartbroken enough, patriotic songs. There are even some drinking songs, but no comic songs. I thought I had found one in a collection that had been written down for me in Aran. It is a lament of a girl for her beautiful comb that had been carried away by her lover, on her refusing to marry till she had 'taken a little more out of her youth'. With that he had stolen the comb, and the mother gives her wise advice as to how to get it back: 'He will go the road tomorrow and let you welcome him; settle down a wooden chair in the middle of the house; snap the hat from him and so not give him any ease till you get back the beautiful comb that was high on the back of your head!' I thought this was made for laughter, but an Aran man told me,

'No, it is a very serious song. It is meant to praise the girl and to tell what a loss she had in the comb.' And then he showed me the song that makes most merriment in Aran. It is the day-dream of an old woman, of all she will buy when she has gathered a harvest of the Carrageen moss, once in request for invalids but now used chiefly for glazing in the linen factories of Belfast.

'If I had two cars and a little boat of my own, I would go pulling the Carrageen; I would dry it in the sun; I would bring a boat of it to Galway; it would go away in the train to pay the rent to Robinson, and what is over would be my own.

'It is long I am hearing talk of the Carrageen, and I never knew what it was; if I spent the last spring-tide with it I would buy a gown and a long cloak and a wide little shawl; that and a dress-cap with frills on every side like feathers.'

But what causes the laughter is that the purpose can never be carried out; it is the mordant laughter at the day-dream, at the impossible building of Babel:

'This is what the Cailleach said and she over a hundred years old!'

As to folk-tales, some time ago I spent some afternoons in a Galway workhouse listening to stories told by the old men. We sat in a gravelled yard where only the leaves of a few young sycamores told that spring had come. Some of the old men sat on a bench against the whitewashed wall of a shed, in their rough frieze uniform and round grey caps, and others stood around pressing closer and closer as their interest in the story grew. The incongruous caused them to laugh and applaud, as when in the Perseus and Andromeda story, the rescue of the Princess from the dragon, leading to the marriage of hero and Princess, ends with the couplet:

> And if they didn't live happy that we may;
> Put down the kettle and boil the tea.

And there is laughter at a harshly humorous story, one of them told of a man that used to be in Ballinasloe lunatic asylum, and

that was not very mad, just a little mad, and he used to be raking about the gate, and there was a clock over the gate; and one day the doctor was going out and he took the watch out and looked up and said to himself: 'That clock is not right.' 'If it was right it wouldn't be here,' said the man that was raking.

But it was fantasy, imagination, rather than humour that was the keynote. The stories that they showed delight in were of quite visionary things; of swans that turn into kings' daughters, and of castles with crowns over the doors; and lovers' flights on the backs of eagles; and music-loving water witches, and journeys to the other world; and sleeps that last for seven hundred years. Fancy and fantasy for delight; harsh satire for humour; poetry and tragedy filling our whole literature; how did we ever get the name of being a humorous people?

We all of us contain I suppose a double personality: 'The spirit warring against the flesh.' Ireland contains as a country what each of us feels in himself, tragedy and comedy, idealism and common sense, the knight errant and the squire erred, the Don Quixote and the Sancho Panza. Sometimes one is up and the other down, one is more visible than the other. Now when the Gaelic poets wrote or sang it was for a disheartened Gaelic-speaking audience, and the poet as well as the writer requires hearers, and can no more do without these than the rush without water to the roots. He does not live by himself, he is speaking all the time to an audience that gives back something, if but the desire to go on creating. And in the Gaelic audience there was as we have seen no incitement to compose comic songs. It is a gloomy thing to make a joke that is not called for or understood. I think of Goldsmith's most pathetic picture of that

> Poor well remembered guest
> Who may not rudely be dismissed;
> Yet hath outstayed his welcome while
> And brings the jest without the smile.

Our players still shiver at the recollection of an English provincial audience in which *Spreading the News* was played through without a single laugh.

But with the beginning of the nineteenth century, the time of the legislative Union, an English and English-speaking audience was called in. They didn't want to hear of the lament for Owen Roe O'Neill or the Fate of the Children of Usnach. They wanted, and got what they wanted, Mickey Free, Handy Andy, the butt, the blunderer, the inferior, who to them symbolise Ireland, whose mistakes would make them feel comfortably superior, over which they would comfortably laugh. The poets writing in English at that time held out, Mangan and Davis and O'Mahony; like Raftery and Sweeny and the other Gaelic poets they went on unchanged; they would not make sport for the Philistines or show the Helots' drunken mirth. I think of the Knight of the Sorrowful Figure brought suddenly into that insolent court which entertained him with the design of playing some mocking trick, of getting the laugh that pleased their vanity. I think of the song,

> The world wears on to sundown and love is lost and won
> But he recks not of loss or gain, the King of Ireland's son;
> He follows on forever when all your chase is done,
> He follows after shadows, the King of Ireland's son.

I think of Don Quixote, his courtesy, his ideality, and I see the high kinship. I hear him call out in his last battle: 'Dulcinea is the most beautiful woman of the world, and I the most unfortunate knight on earth, and it is not fit that my weakness should discredit this truth!' And this even though he had said in a quieter moment: 'God knows whether there be a Dulcinea in the world or not.' I think of the very servants making sport of him, for the delight of the court, throwing a lather of soap into his face and eyes; dressing up as devils to frighten him; befooling him with a serenade, dressing up a bearded damsel in distress; emptying a sackful of cats into his room whose scratches cost him five days in his bed. I think of the jests played in my own country by Britons looking for a buffoon, and I don't wonder at the old Donegal woman who said bitterly, when gracious Queen Alexandra came to smile away wrongs, 'She is but wearing green for a mockery.'

But the breaking of the knight errant's heart had but little effect upon his squire. When Sancho was threatened with the soapsuds his master said, 'Let him alone, for neither he nor I understand jesting'; but he said, 'No, no, let them jibe and let them curry this beard and if they find there anything that offends against cleanliness let them shear me crosswise.' So the Duchess ordered Sancho to be near her, 'being mightily delighted with his conceits', and he was easily prevailed upon. He saw his market and his profit and he said, 'Let them come to play at bo-peep, ay, let them slight and backbite me; for they may come for wool and be sent back shorn.' And so when they left the court, the master went out of it trembling as if he had quicksilver in his veins and with the beginning of that heartbreak that killed him; the man with four hundred gold crowns in his pocket.

I have been reading *Harry Lorrequer*. A natural instinct had kept me from Lever[1] until now. Yet he had been a pleasant acquaintance of my father, Dudley Persse, and told a story that once out hunting he, my father, had jumped over a high wall with such a drop beyond it that he and his horse had clean disappeared from sight. 'What's on the other side, Dudley?' Lord Clanricarde called out, and the answer that came was, 'I am, thank God.'

But now reading this novel, and looking through *Charles O'Malley*, I see how its humour has set the pace. I see it artificial, superficial, meant for another audience and another market than our own, with its rough practical jokes, its situations turning over and over again on drunkenness as when its tipsy priest is persuaded by a sentry to call out the imaginary password 'To hell with the Pope', or the doctor, after a carouse, leads a wandering horse home by the hair of its mane believing it to be another strayed reveller he is leading by the hair of the head; the acceptance of the view of the stage manager of a show wanting to replace some escaped Indians (North America Indians by the way) who have made off because they think they would die happy if they 'could have a roast child for supper'! The unlucky harvesters found to take their place are

> bare-legged and lanky with hay ropes fastening their old grey coats around them; their uncouth appearance, their wild looks, their violent gesture, above all their strange and gutteral language,

for they were all speaking Irish, attracted the attention of the manager; it was scarcely necessary to alter anything about them, they were ready made to his hand, and in many respects better savages than their prototypes.

That is what has called the tune, that and the 'tare-an-ages' of Micky Free, his love songs in place of

> I thought O my love you were so
> As the moon is, or sun on a fountain
> And I thought after that you were snow,
> The cold snow on the top of the mountain;
>
> And I thought after that you were more
> Like God's lamp shining to find me;
> Or the bright star of knowledge before
> And the star of knowledge behind me.

That is one of the love songs of the people, but Lever has replaced it with

> Oh Mary Brady, ye are my darlin'
> Ye are my lookin' glass from night till morning
> I'd rayther have ye without one farden
> Nor Shusey Gallagher and her house and garden.

All that humour is forced in form, is a bit brutal at heart and forced humour is vulgar; the real humour must come 'like Dian's kiss, unasked unsought' even when there is a touch of bitter aloes on the laughing lip. Nothing in those tales or in their long line of successors arises from character, from the roots of human nature. No wonder Lever was given the British consulship at Trieste '£600 a year and nothing to do' wrote Lord Derby to him, 'and I don't know any man who can do it better'. And no wonder Lever grumbled afterwards and said it was not enough for him 'after all he had done'.

For it was Lover[2] first and then Lever who found and showed the market for the practical joking, the ridicule of dependants, the horse play, the detachable jokes that might be applied to any artificially created buffoon. It was the English, the Protestant,

humour of ascendancy. From that time a certain kind of facetious-
ness was expected whenever the Irish voice was heard. I remember a story of an artist in India who sent to an illustrated paper
some sketches of scenery. They were accepted but when he saw
the reproductions, the foreground of each was stocked with palm
trees; he was indignant and complained, 'There are no palm trees
in that district.' 'That does not matter,' said the editor, 'when
there is a picture of India the British public demand palm trees.'
In like manner, Ireland was not to be represented to the British
public without what it demanded, if not palm trees, then at least
potatoes, poteen and pigs. The stage Irishman came next; he
must not appear without a sprig of shillelagh, and a dudeen
stuck in his high crowned hat. Then the carmen came in, and the
boatmen that attend on tourists, each with a profitable joke. And
English jest books kept set up in type the 'Well Pat' of the
questioner.

* * *

There was a picture long ago in some paper, *Punch* or another,
in which a painter's canvas had been left on an easel in the
neighbourhood of a jungle, and the lion was looking at it, for it
represented a lion hunt, and saying, 'You'll see the other side of
the story when we have a painter of our own!' I remember
another of a baby in its cradle seeing the nursemaid drinking its
milk and thinking, 'I'll tell of you when I'm able to speak!' One
remembers also what was said in a leading article of the *Times* in
the Famine days: 'The Irish are crossing the Atlantic with a
vengeance.' That is often quoted at meetings of the Clan na Gael,
the Ancient Order, the Knights of Columbus, and the like, to
emphasise the tragedy of that emigration, that flight. But laughter
is more shattering than resolutions, a better weapon than hate, at
least when it is used without the contempt or scorn that may hurt
what is eternal in us, if it does but batter down the walls built by
custom and prejudice, acquiesced in by languor or convenience,
that are the barriers between soul and soul. But the creator of
laughter needs the detachment, the freedom from illusions, of a

wife who has obtained her divorce and is able to discuss with her present husband the weak points, the clumsiness, of her first.

I once sent to Mr Forster, 'Buckshot' Forster as he was called, at that Land League time when he was our Chief Secretary, a caricature of himself in some Irish paper. He wrote back, 'The English caricature their friends, the French their enemies; I wonder if this is the Irish way also?' I think it is so. As to the English way, I remember once at my own table in London, at a time when Lord Randolph Churchill was just on the threshold of his career, and was looked on by serious people as a noisy empty young man, witty Lord Morris said: 'Believe me, he will rise to the top. He has twice been caricatured in *Punch*.' But as to Ireland, a caricature of Mr Yeats by Max Beerbohm was sent to one of the Nationalist papers at the start of our theatre, and Mr Manning, the editor of it, was sad because he was a friend of Yeats and was unwilling to put it in, and when he did put it in at last, he had reduced it to the size of a penny stamp. And that was the way with Synge's *Playboy*, a fantastic caricature; the Irish societies did not like it; they thought Synge must be an enemy, they would have liked to reduce it to the size of a halfpenny stamp. Yet Synge loved his country even in their way, having once led a charge against the Dublin police. And when he woke from chloroform after an operation the first words that could be distinguished were 'Those damned English can't even swear without vulgarity.'

In a folk-history play of mine, *The Canavans*, I give a dispute between the Mayor of Scartana and two washerwomen of the people. He is trying to bring them to loyalty to Queen Elizabeth and threatens that 'the next day you'll be late with the washing I'll indict you for default of appearance'. Tag and rag from the riverside to be correcting the Mayor on the bench. But they call out, 'We are well able to revenge ourselves. Whatever may be done in this district, it's the telling of the story is with us.' For our people have long memories and keep history a living thing. At a Connacht *Feis* I heard a schoolmaster give out with great vigour a long poem in Irish. Someone asked him, as another master stood up to follow, what the poems were about, and he said,

'Both are called "Thoughts on Ireland". My one tells how the Sassanachs baffled us entirely, and the one he's giving tells how the Sassanachs murdered us a while ago.' An English friend who carries on a business near the coast told me that on one of his first days there he had gone to some races nearby and been followed through the crowd by a club-footed man shaking a stick at him and shouting, 'Elizabethian!' As to that long-hated Queen, her story as told on our countryside is not just that in the schoolbooks, and has its own grim laughter.

* * *

It was a town called Calais brought her to her death, and she [Queen Elizabeth] lay chained to the floor three days and three nights. The Archbishop was trying to urge her to eat, but she said, 'You would not ask me to do it if you knew the way I am,' for nobody could see the chains. After her death they waked her for six days in Whitehall, and there were six ladies sitting beside the body every night. Three coffins were about it, the one nearest the body of lead, and then a wooden one, and a leaden one on the outside. And the last night there came a bellow that broke the three coffins open, and tore the velvet, and there came out a stench that killed the most of the ladies and a million of the people of London with the plague. Queen Victoria was more honourable than that. It would be hard to beat Queen Elizabeth.

As to jokes, to show their serious nature in Ireland, the greatest number of them it seems to me are made in Court or during trials or by the lawyers or the witnesses or the judge, perhaps even by the prisoner. Some poor man at my door told me the other day: 'There was a man going to be hanged one time in Galway, and the wife went to see him the night before, and all she said was, "Where will I sow the flax this year?" He was vexed at that and he said, "Is that all you are come to say to me?" "Is it that you are in a sulk because you are going to be hanged in the morning?" says the wife.' There is something of Molière's Martha in like circumstances in her 'If you had but cut the scallops before you were hanged, that would be something.' And he went on to tell me, 'As to Curran, he was a judge, and there was a boy brought before him for stealing gooseberries, and he gave him three months in gaol. "And now," says he, "it is likely you will say out your curses on gooseberries." "I will, and on *Currans*," says the boy. Wasn't he a smart boy to think of that? There was another smart lad was brought into Court as a witness and before he was let take the oath they asked him did he know where would he go if he broke it. "I do," says he. "Where is that?" says the judge. "In the same place where the lawyers go," says he. For there was a man went to heaven one time and he asked was there ever a lawyer in it, and there was not one to be found.'

If, as some think, there is humour less harsh than that of the satirists, more natural than that of the novelists, finding its expressions in the comedies of our Irish theatre today, it is because the laughter is at ourselves, for ourselves, rather than for the markets of 'the big world'. Is not Sancho's own humour at its wildest when he has but the Sorrowful Knight as listener?

# PLAYS

# Kathleen ni Houlihan

PERSONS IN THE PLAY

PETER GILLANE
MICHAEL GILLANE, his son, going to be married
PATRICK GILLANE, a lad of twelve, Michael's brother
BRIDGET GILLANE, Peter's wife
DELIA CAHEL, engaged to Michael
THE POOR OLD WOMAN
NEIGHBOURS

SCENE. *Interior of a cottage close to Killala,[1] in 1978.* BRIDGET *is standing at a table undoing a parcel.* PETER *is sitting at one side of the fire,* PATRICK *at the other.*

PETER. What is that sound I hear?

PATRICK. I don't hear anything. (*He listens.*) I hear it now. It's like cheering. (*He goes to the window and looks out.*) I wonder what they are cheering about. I don't see anybody.

PETER. It might be a hurling.

PATRICK. There's no hurling today. It must be down in the town the cheering is.

BRIDGET. I suppose the boys must be having some sport of their own. Come over here, Peter, and look at Michael's wedding clothes.

PETER (*shifts his chair to table*). Those are grand clothes, indeed.

BRIDGET. You hadn't clothes like that when you married me, and no coat to put on of a Sunday more than any other day.

PETER. That is true, indeed. We never thought a son of our own would be wearing a suit of that sort for his wedding, or have so good a place to bring a wife to.

PATRICK. (*who is still at the window*). There's an old woman coming down the road. I don't know is it here she is coming.

BRIDGET. It will be a neighbour coming to hear about Michael's wedding. Can you see who it is?

PATRICK. I think it is a stranger, but she's not coming to the house. She's turned into the gap that goes down where Maurteen and his sons are shearing sheep. (*He turns towards* BRIDGET.) Do you remember what Winny of the Cross-Roads was saying the other night about the strange woman that goes through the country whatever time there's war or trouble coming?

BRIDGET. Don't be bothering us about Winny's talk, but go and open the door for your brother. I hear him coming up the path.

PETER. I hope he has brought Delia's fortune[2] with him safe, for fear the people might go back on the bargain and I after making it. Trouble enough I had making it.

(PATRICK *opens the door and* MICHAEL *comes in.*)

BRIDGET. What kept you, Michael? We were looking out for you this long time.

MICHAEL. I went round by the priest's house to bid him be ready to marry us tomorrow.

BRIDGET. Did he say anything?

MICHAEL. He said it was a very nice match, and that he was never better pleased to marry any two in his parish than myself and Delia Cahel.

PETER. Have you got the fortune, Michael?

MICHAEL. Here it is.

(MICHAEL *puts bag on table and goes over and leans against chimney-jamb.* BRIDGET, *who has been all this time examining the clothes, pulling the seams and trying the lining of the pockets, etc., puts the clothes on the dresser.*)

PETER (*getting up and taking the bag in his hand and turning out the money*). Yes, I made the bargain well for you, Michael. Old John Cahel would sooner have kept a share of this a while longer. 'Let me keep the half of it until the first boy is born,' says he. 'You will not,' says I. 'Whether there is or is not a boy, the whole hundred pounds must be in Michael's hands before he brings your daughter to the house.' The wife spoke to him then, and he gave in at the end.

BRIDGET. You seem well pleased to be handling the money, Peter.

PETER. Indeed, I wish I had had the luck to get a hundred pounds, or twenty pounds itself, with the wife I married.

BRIDGET. Well, if I didn't bring much I didn't get much. What had you the day I married you but a flock of hens and you feeding them, and a few lambs and you driving them to the market at Ballina? (*She is vexed and bangs a jug on the dresser.*) If I brought no fortune I worked it out in my bones, laying down the baby, Michael that is standing there now, on a stook[3] of straw, while I dug the potatoes, and never asking big dresses or anything but to be working.

PETER. That is true, indeed. (*He pats her arm.*)

BRIDGET. Leave me alone now till I ready the house for the woman that is to come into it.

PETER. You are the best woman in Ireland, but money is good, too. (*He begins handling the money again and sits down.*) I never thought to see so much money within my four walls. We can do great things now we have it. We can take the ten acres of land we have the chance of since Jamsie Dempsey died, and stock it. We will go to the fair at Ballina to buy the stock. Did Delia ask any of the money for her own use, Michael?

MICHAEL. She did not, indeed. She did not seem to take much notice of it, or to look at it at all.

BRIDGET. That's no wonder. Why would she look at it when she had yourself to look at, a fine, strong young man? It is proud she must be to get you; a good steady boy that will make use of the money, and not be running through it or spending it on drink like another.

PETER. It's likely Michael himself was not thinking much of the fortune either, but of what sort the girl was to look at.

MICHAEL (*coming over towards the table*). Well, you would like a nice comely girl to be beside you, and to go walking with you. The fortune only lasts for a while, but the woman will be there always.

303

PATRICK (*turning round from the window*). They are cheering again down in the town. Maybe they are landing horses from Enniscrone. They do be cheering when the horses take the water well.

MICHAEL. There are no horses in it. Where would they be going and no fair at hand? Go down to the town, Patrick, and see what is going on.

PATRICK (*opens the door to go out, but stops for a moment on the threshold*). Will Delia remember, do you think, to bring the greyhound pup she promised me when she would be coming to the house?

MICHAEL. She will surely.

(PATRICK *goes out, leaving the door open*.)

PETER. It will be Patrick's turn next to be looking for a fortune, but he won't find it so easy to get it and he with no place of his own.

BRIDGET. I do be thinking sometimes, now things are going so well with us, and the Cahels such a good back to us in the district, and Delia's own uncle a priest, we might be put in the way of making Patrick a priest some day, and he so good at his books.

PETER. Time enough, time enough. You have always your head full of plans, Bridget.

BRIDGET. We will be well able to give him learning, and not to send him tramping the country like a poor scholar that lives on charity.

MICHAEL. They're not done cheering yet.

(*He goes over to the door and stands there for a moment, putting up his hand to shade his eyes*.)

BRIDGET. Do you see anything?

MICHAEL. I see an old woman coming up the path.

BRIDGET. Who is it, I wonder? It must be the strange woman Patrick saw a while ago.

MICHAEL. I don't think it's one of the neighbours anyway, but she has her cloak over her face.

BRIDGET. It might be some poor woman heard we were making ready for the wedding and came to look for her share.

304

PETER. I may as well put the money out of sight. There is no use leaving it out for every stranger to look at.

(*He goes over to a large box in the corner, opens it and puts the bag in and fumbles at the lock.*)

MICHAEL. There she is, father! (*An* OLD WOMAN *passes the window slowly. She looks at Michael as she passes.*) I'd sooner a stranger not to come to the house the night before my wedding.

BRIDGET. Open the door, Michael; don't keep the poor woman waiting.

(*The* OLD WOMAN *comes in.* MICHAEL *stands aside to make way for her.*)

OLD WOMAN. God save all here!

PETER. God save you kindly!

OLD WOMAN You have good shelter here.

PETER. You are welcome to whatever shelter we have.

BRIDGET. Sit down there by the fire and welcome.

OLD WOMAN (*warming her hands*). There is a hard wind outside.

(MICHAEL *watches her curiously from the door.* PETER *comes over to the table.*)

PETER. Have you travelled far today?

OLD WOMAN I have travelled far, very far; there are few have travelled so far as myself, and there's many a one that doesn't make me welcome. There was one that had strong sons I thought were friends of mine, but they were shearing their sheep, and they wouldn't listen to me.

PETER. It's a pity indeed for any person to have no place of their own.

OLD WOMAN. That's true for you indeed, and it's long I'm on the roads since I first went wandering.

BRIDGET. It is a wonder you are not worn out with so much wandering.

OLD WOMAN. Sometimes my feet are tired and my hands are quiet, but there is no quiet in my heart. When the people see me quiet, they think old age has come on me and that all the stir has gone out of me. But when the trouble is on me I must be talking to my friends.

BRIDGET. What was it put you wandering?

OLD WOMAN. Too many strangers in the house.

BRIDGET. Indeed you look as if you'd had your share of trouble.

OLD WOMAN. I have had trouble indeed.

BRIDGET. What was it put the trouble on you?

OLD WOMAN. My land that was taken from me.

PETER. Was it much land they took from you?

OLD WOMAN. My four beautiful green fields.

PETER (*aside to* BRIDGET). Do you think could she be the widow Casey that was put out of her holding at Kilglass a while ago?

BRIDGET. She is not. I saw the widow Casey one time at the market in Ballina, a stout fresh woman.

PETER (*to* OLD WOMAN). Did you hear a noise of cheering, and you coming up the hill?

OLD WOMAN. I thought I heard the noise I used to hear when my friends came to visit me. (*She begins singing half to herself.*)

> I will go cry with the woman,
> For yellow-haired Donough is dead,
> With a hempen rope for a neckcloth,
> And a white cloth on his head,—

MICHAEL (*coming from the door*). What is it that you are singing, ma'am?

OLD WOMAN. Singing I am about a man I knew one time, yellow-haired Donough that was hanged in Galway. (*She goes on singing, much louder.*)

> I am come to cry with you, woman,
> My hair is unwound and unbound;
> I remember him ploughing his field,
> Turning up the red side of the ground,
> And building his barn on the hill
> With the good mortared stone;
> O! we'd have pulled down the gallows
> Had it happened in Enniscrone!

MICHAEL. What was it brought him to his death?

OLD WOMAN. He died for love of me: many a man has died for love of me.

PETER (*aside to* BRIDGET). Her trouble has put her wits astray.

MICHAEL. Is it long since that song was made? Is it long since he got his death?

OLD WOMAN. Not long, not long. But there were others that died for love of me a long time ago.

MICHAEL. Were they neighbours of your own, ma'am?

OLD WOMAN. Come here beside me and I'll tell you about them. (MICHAEL *sits down beside her on the hearth.*) There was a red man of the O'Donnells from the north, and a man of the O'Sullivans from the south, and there was one Brian that lost his life at Clontarf by the sea, and there were a great many in the west, some that died hundreds of years ago, and there are some that will die tomorrow.

MICHAEL. Is it in the west that men will die tomorrow?

OLD WOMAN. Come nearer, nearer to me.

BRIDGET. Is she right, do you think? Or is she a woman from beyond the world?

PETER. She doesn't know well what she's talking about, with the want and the trouble she has gone through.

BRIDGET. The poor thing, we should treat her well.

PETER. Give her a drink of milk and a bit of the oaten cake.

BRIDGET. Maybe we should give her something along with that, to bring her on her way. A few pence or a shilling itself, and we with so much money in the house.

PETER. Indeed I'd not begrudge it to her if we had it to spare, but if we go running through what we have, we'll soon have to break the hundred pounds, and that would be a pity.

BRIDGET. Shame on you, Peter. Give her the shilling and your blessing with it, or our own luck will go from us.

(PETER *goes to the box and takes out a shilling.*)

BRIDGET (*to the* OLD WOMAN). Will you have a drink of milk, ma'am?

OLD WOMAN. It is not food or drink that I want.

PETER (*offering the shilling*). Here is something for you.

OLD WOMAN. This is not what I want. It is not silver I want.

PETER. What is it you would be asking for?

OLD WOMAN. If anyone would give me help he must give me himself, he must give me all.

(PETER *goes over to the table staring at the shilling in his hand in a bewildered way, and stands whispering to* BRIDGET.)

MICHAEL. Have you no one to care for you in your age, ma'am?

OLD WOMAN. I have not. With all the lovers that brought me their love I never set out the bed for any.

MICHAEL. Are you lonely going the roads, ma'am?

OLD WOMAN. I have my thoughts and I have my hopes.

MICHAEL. What hopes have you to hold to?

OLD WOMAN. The hope of getting my beautiful fields back again; the hope of putting the strangers out of my house.

MICHAEL. What way will you do that, ma'am?

OLD WOMAN. I have good friends that will help me. They are gathering to help me now. I am not afraid. If they are put down today they will get the upper hand tomorrow. (*She gets up.*) I must be going to meet my friends. They are coming to help me and I must be there to welcome them. I must call the neighbours together to welcome them.

MICHAEL. I will go with you.

BRIDGET. It is not her friends you have to go and welcome, Michael; it is the girl coming into the house you have to welcome. You have plenty to do; it is food and drink you have to bring to the house. The woman that is coming home is not coming with empty hands; you would not have an empty house before her. (*To the* OLD WOMAN.) Maybe you don't know, ma'am, that my son is going to be married tomorrow.

OLD WOMAN. It is not a man going to his marriage that I look to for help.

PETER (*to* BRIDGET). Who is she, do you think, at all?

BRIDGET. You did not tell us your name yet, ma'am.

OLD WOMAN. Some call me the Poor Old Woman, and there

308

are some that call me Kathleen, the daughter of Houlihan.

PETER. I think I knew someone of that name, once. Who was it, I wonder? It must have been someone I knew when I was a boy. No, no; I remember, I heard it in a song.

OLD WOMAN (*who is standing in the doorway*). They are wondering that there were songs made for me; there have been many songs made for me. I heard one on the wind this morning. (*Sings*)

> Do not make a great keening
> When the graves have been dug tomorrow.
> Do not call the white-scarfed riders
> To the burying that shall be tomorrow.
> Do not spread food to call strangers
> To the wakes that shall be tomorrow;
> Do not give money for prayers
> For the dead that shall die to-morrow . . .

They will have no need of prayers, they will have no need of prayers.

MICHAEL. I do not know what that song means, but tell me something I can do for you.

PETER. Come over to me, Michael.

MICHAEL. Hush, father, listen to her.

OLD WOMAN. It is a hard service they take that help me. Many that are red-cheeked now will be pale-cheeked; many that have been free to walk the hills and the bogs and the rushes will be sent to walk hard streets in far countries; many a good plan will be broken; many that have gathered money will not stay to spend it; many a child will be born and there will be no father at its christening to give it a name. They that have red cheeks will have pale cheeks for my sake, and for all that, they will think they are well paid.

(*She goes out; her voice is heard outside singing.*)

> They shall be remembered for ever,
> They shall be alive for ever,
> They shall be speaking for ever,
> The people shall hear them for ever.

BRIDGET (*to* PETER). Look at him, Peter; he has the look of a man that has got the touch.[4] (*Raising her voice.*) Look here, Michael, at the wedding clothes. Such grand clothes as these are! You have a right to fit them on now; it would be a pity tomorrow if they did not fit. The boys would be laughing at you. Take them, Michael, and go into the room and fit them on. (*She puts them on his arm.*)

MICHAEL. What wedding are you talking of? What clothes will I be wearing tomorrow?

BRIDGET. These are the clothes you are going to wear when you marry Delia Cahel tomorrow.

MICHAEL. I had forgotten that.

> (*He looks at the clothes and turns towards the inner room, but stops at the sound of cheering outside.*)

PETER. There is the shouting come to our own door. What is it has happened?

> (NEIGHBOURS *come crowding in,* PATRICK *and* DELIA *with them.*)

PATRICK. There are ships in the Bay; the French are landing at Killala!

> (PETER *takes his pipe from his mouth and his hat off, and stands up. The clothes slip from* MICHAEL'*s arm.*)

DELIA. Michael! (*He takes no notice.*) Michael! (*He turns towards her.*) Why do you look at me like a stranger?

> (*She drops his arm.* BRIDGET *goes over towards her.*)

PATRICK. The boys are all hurrying down the hillside to join the French.

DELIA. Michael won't be going to join the French.

BRIDGET (*to* PETER). Tell him not to go, Peter.

PETER. It's no use. He doesn't hear a word we're saying.

BRIDGET. Try and coax him over to the fire.

DELIA. Michael, Michael! You won't leave me! You won't join the French, and we going to be married!

> (*She puts her arms about him, he turns towards her as if about to yield.*)

OLD WOMAN'*s voice outside.*

They shall be speaking for ever,
The people shall hear them for ever.

(MICHAEL *breaks away from* DELIA, *stands for a second at the door, then rushes out, following the* OLD WOMAN'*s voice.* BRIDGET *takes* DELIA, *who is crying silently, into her arms.*)

PETER (*to* PATRICK, *laying a hand on his arm*). Did you see an old woman going down the path?

PATRICK. I did not, but I saw a young girl, and she had the walk of a queen.

# Spreading the News

PERSONS IN THE PLAY

  BARTLEY FALLON
  MRS FALLON
  JACK SMITH
  SHAWN EARLY
  TIM CASEY
  JAMES RYAN
  MRS TARPEY
  MRS TULLY
  *A Policeman* (JO MULDOON)
  A REMOVABLE MAGISTRATE[1]

SCENE. *The outskirts of a Fair. An Apple Stall.* MRS TARPEY *sitting at it.* MAGISTRATE *and* POLICEMAN *enter.*

MAGISTRATE. So that is the Fair Green. Cattle and sheep and mud. No system. What a repulsive sight!

POLICEMAN. That is so, indeed.

MAGISTRATE. I suppose there is a good deal of disorder in this place?

POLICEMAN. There is.

MAGISTRATE. Common assault?

POLICEMAN. It's common enough.

MAGISTRATE. Agrarian crime, no doubt?

POLICEMAN. That is so.

MAGISTRATE. Boycotting? Maiming of cattle? Firing into houses?

POLICEMAN. There was one time, and there might be again.

MAGISTRATE. That is bad. Does it go any farther than that?

POLICEMAN. Far enough, indeed.

MAGISTRATE. Homicide, then! This district has been shamefully neglected! I will change all that. When I was in the Andaman Islands,[2] my system never failed. Yes, yes, I will change all that. What has that woman on her stall?

POLICEMAN. Apples mostly – and sweets.

MAGISTRATE. Just see if there are any unlicensed goods underneath – spirits or the like. We had evasions of the salt tax in the Andaman Islands.

POLICEMAN (*sniffing cautiously and upsetting a heap of apples*). I see no spirits here – or salt.

MAGISTRATE (to MRS TARPEY). Do you know this town well, my good woman?

MRS TARPEY (*holding out some apples*). A penny the half-dozen, your honour.

POLICEMAN (*shouting*). The gentleman is asking do you know the town! He's the new magistrate!

MRS TARPEY (*rising and ducking*). Do I know the town? I do, to be sure.

MAGISTRATE (*shouting*). What is its chief business?

MRS TARPEY. Business, is it? What business would the people here have but to be minding one another's business?

MAGISTRATE. I mean what trade have they?

MRS TARPEY. Not a trade. No trade at all but to be talking.

MAGISTRATE. I shall learn nothing here.

(JAMES RYAN *comes in, pipe in mouth. Seeing* MAGISTRATE, *he retreats quickly, taking pipe from mouth.*)

MAGISTRATE. The smoke from that man's pipe had a greenish look; he may be growing unlicensed tobacco at home. I wish I had brought my telescope to this district. Come to the post-office, I will telegraph for it. I found it very useful in the Andaman Islands.

(MAGISTRATE *and* POLICEMAN *go out left.*)

MRS TARPEY. Bad luck to Jo Muldoon, knocking my apples this way and that way. (*Begins arranging them.*) Showing off he was to the new magistrate.

(*Enter* BARTLEY FALLON *and* MRS FALLON.)

BARTLEY. Indeed it's a poor country and a scarce country to be living in. But I'm thinking if I went to America it's long ago the day I'd be dead!

Mrs Fallon. So you might, indeed.

(*She puts her basket on a barrel and begins putting parcels in it, taking them from under her cloak.*)

Bartley. And it's a great expense for a poor man to be buried in America.

Mrs Fallon. Never fear, Bartley Fallon, but I'll give you a good burying the day you'll die.

Bartley. Maybe it's yourself will be buried in the graveyard of Cloonmara before me, Mary Fallon, and I myself that will be dying unbeknownst some night, and no one a-near me. And the cat itself may be gone straying through the country, and the mice squealing over the quilt.

Mrs Fallon. Leave off talking of dying. It might be twenty years you'll be living yet.

Bartley (*with a deep sigh*). I'm thinking if I'll be living at the end of twenty years, it's a very old man I'll be then!

Mrs Tarpey (*turns and sees them*). Good morrow, Bartley Fallon; good morrow, Mrs Fallon. Well, Bartley, you'll find no cause for complaining today; they are all saying it was a good fair.

Bartley (*raising his voice*). It was not a good fair, Mrs Tarpey. It was a scattered sort of a fair. If we didn't expect more, we got less. That's the way with me always; whatever I have to sell goes down and whatever I have to buy goes up. If there's ever any misfortune coming to this world, it's on myself it pitches, like a flock of crows on seed potatoes.

Mrs Fallon. Leave off talking of misfortunes, and listen to Jack Smith that is coming the way, and he singing. (*Voice of* Jack Smith *heard singing:*)

> I thought, my first love,
> There'd be but one house between you and me,
> And I thought I would find
> Yourself coaxing my child on your knee.
> Over the tide
> I would leap with the leap of a swan,
> Till I came to the side
> Of the wife of the Red-haired man!

(JACK SMITH *comes in; he is a red-haired man, and is carrying a hayfork.*)

MRS TARPEY. That should be a good song if I had my hearing.

MRS FALLON (*shouting*). It's 'The Red-haired Man's Wife'.

MRS TARPEY. I know it well. That's the song that has a skin on it!

(*She turns her back to them and goes on arranging her apples.*)

MRS FALLON. Where's herself, Jack Smith?

JACK SMITH. She was delayed with her washing; bleaching the clothes on the hedge she is, and she daren't leave them, with all the tinkers[3] that do be passing to the fair. It isn't to the fair I came myself, but up to the Five Acre Meadow I'm going, where I have a contract for the hay. We'll get a share of it into tramps[4] today.

(*He lays down hayfork and lights his pipe.*)

BARTLEY. You will not get into tramps today. The rain will be down on it by evening, and on myself too. It's seldom I ever started on a journey but the rain would come down on me before I'd find any place of shelter.

JACK SMITH. If it didn't itself, Bartley, it is my belief you would carry a leaky pail on your head in place of a hat, the way you'd not be without some cause of complaining.

(*A voice is heard, 'Go on, now, go on out o' that. Go on I say.'*)

JACK SMITH. Look at that young mare of Pat Ryan's that is backing into Shaughnessy's bullocks with the dint of the crowd! Don't be daunted, Pat, I'll give you a hand with her.

(*He goes out, leaving his hayfork.*)

MRS FALLON. It's time for ourselves to be going home. I have all I bought put in the basket. Look at there, Jack Smith's hayfork he left after him! He'll be wanting it. (*Calls.*) Jack Smith! Jack Smith! – He's gone through the crowd – hurry after him, Bartley, he'll be wanting it.

BARTLEY. I'll do that. This is no safe place to be leaving it. (*He takes up fork awkwardly and upsets the basket.*) Look at that now! If there is any basket in the fair upset, it must be our own basket!

(*He goes out to right.*)

MRS FALLON. Get out of that! It is your own fault, it is. Talk of misfortunes and misfortunes will come. Glory be! Look at my new egg-cups rolling in every part – and my two pound of sugar with the paper broke—

MRS TARPEY (*turning from stall*). God help us, Mrs Fallon, what happened your basket?

MRS FALLON. It's himself that knocked it down, bad manners to him. (*Putting things up.*) My grand sugar that's destroyed, and he'll not drink his tea without it. I had best go back to the shop for more, much good may it do him!

(*Enter* TIM CASEY.)

TIM CASEY. Where is Bartley Fallon, Mrs Fallon? I want a word with him before he'll leave the fair. I was afraid he might have gone home by this, for he's a temperate man.

MRS FALLON. I wish he did go home! It'd be best for me if he went home straight from the fair green, or if he never came with me at all? Where is he, is it? He's gone up the road (*jerks elbow*) following Jack Smith with a hayfork.

(*She goes out to left.*)

TIM CASEY. Following Jack Smith with a hayfork! Did ever anyone hear the like of that. (*Shouts.*) Did you hear that news, Mrs Tarpey?

MRS TARPEY. I heard no news at all.

TIM CASEY. Some dispute I suppose it was that rose between Jack Smith and Bartley Fallon, and it seems Jack made off, and Bartley is following him with a hayfork!

MRS TARPEY. Is he now? Well, that was quick work! It's not ten minutes since the two of them were here, Bartley going home and Jack going to the Five Acre Meadow; and I had my apples to settle up, that Jo Muldoon of the police had scattered, and when I looked round again Jack Smith was gone, and Bartley Fallon was gone, and Mrs Fallon's basket upset, and all in it strewed upon the ground – the tea here – the two pound of sugar there – the egg-cups there – Look, now, what a great hardship the deafness puts upon me, that I didn't hear the commincement of the fight! Wait till I tell James Ryan that I see below; he is a neighbour of Bartley's, it would be a pity if he wouldn't hear the news!

(*She goes out. Enter* SHAWN EARLY *and* MRS TULLY.)

TIM CASEY. Listen, Shawn Early! Listen, Mrs Tully, to the

news! Jack Smith and Bartley Fallon had a falling out, and Jack knocked Mrs Fallon's basket into the road, and Bartley made an attack on him with a hayfork, and away with Jack, and Bartley after him. Look at the sugar here yet on the road!

SHAWN EARLY. Do you tell me so? Well, that's a queer thing, and Bartley Fallon so quiet a man!

MRS TULLY. I wouldn't wonder at all. I would never think well of a man that would have that sort of a mouldering look. It's likely he has overtaken Jack by this.

(*Enter* JAMES RYAN *and* MRS TARPEY.)

JAMES RYAN. That is great news Mrs Tarpey was telling me! I suppose that's what brought the police and the magistrate up this way. I was wondering to see them in it a while ago.

SHAWN EARLY. The police after them? Bartley Fallon must have injured Jack so. They wouldn't meddle in a fight that was only for show!

MRS TULLY. Why wouldn't he injure him? There was many a man killed with no more of a weapon than a hayfork.

JAMES RYAN. Wait till I run north as far as Kelly's bar to spread the news!

(*He goes out.*)

TIM CASEY. I'll go tell Jack Smith's first cousin that is standing there south of the church after selling his lambs.

(*Goes out.*)

MRS TULLY. I'll go telling a few of the neighbours I see beyond to the west.

(*Goes out.*)

SHAWN EARLY. I'll give word of it beyond at the east of the green.

(*Is going out when* MRS TARPEY *seizes hold of him.*)

MRS TARPEY. Stop a minute, Shawn Early, and tell me did you see red Jack Smith's wife, Kitty Keary, in any place?

SHAWN EARLY. I did. At her own house she was, drying clothes on the hedge as I passed.

MRS TARPEY. What did you say she was doing?

SHAWN EARLY (*breaking away*). Laying out a sheet on the hedge.

(*He goes.*)

MRS TARPEY. Laying out a sheet for the dead! The Lord have mercy on us! Jack Smith dead, and his wife laying out a sheet for his burying! (*Calls out.*) Why didn't you tell me that before, Shawn Early? Isn't the deafness the great hardship? Half the world might be dead without me knowing of it or getting word of it at all! (*She sits down and rocks herself.*) O my poor Jack Smith! To be going to his work so nice and so hearty, and to be left stretched on the ground in the full light of the day!

(*Enter* TIM CASEY.)

TIM CASEY. What is it, Mrs Tarpey? What happened since?

MRS TARPEY. O my poor Jack Smith!

TIM CASEY. Did Bartley overtake him?

MRS TARPEY. O the poor man!

TIM CASEY. Is it killed he is?

MRS TARPEY. Stretched in the Five Acre Meadow!

TIM CASEY. The Lord have mercy on us! Is that a fact?

MRS TARPEY. Without the rites of the Church or a ha'porth!⁵

TIM CASEY. Who was telling you?

MRS TARPEY. And the wife laying out a sheet for his corpse. (*Sits up and wipes her eyes.*) I suppose they'll wake him the same as another?

(*Enter* MRS TULLY, SHAWN EARLY *and* JAMES RYAN.)

MRS TULLY. There is great talk about this work in every quarter of the fair.

MRS TARPEY. Ochone! cold and dead. And myself maybe the last he was speaking to!

JAMES RYAN. The Lord save us! Is it dead he is?

TIM CASEY. Dead surely, and the wife getting provision for the wake.

SHAWN EARLY. Well, now, hadn't Bartley Fallon great venom in him?

MRS TULLY. You may be sure he had some cause. Why would he have made an end of him if he had not? (*To* MRS TARPEY, *raising her voice.*) What was it rose the dispute at all, Mrs Tarpey?

MRS TARPEY. Not a one of me knows. The last I saw of them, Jack Smith was standing there, and Bartley Fallon was standing there, quiet and easy, and he listening to 'The Red-haired Man's Wife'.

MRS TULLY. Do you hear that, Tim Casey? Do you hear that, Shawn Early and James Ryan? Bartley Fallon was here this morning listening to red Jack Smith's wife, Kitty Keary that was! Listening to her and whispering with her! It was she started the fight so!

SHAWN EARLY. She must have followed him from her own house. It is likely some person roused him.

TIM CASEY. I never knew, before, Bartley Fallon was great with Jack Smith's wife.

MRS TULLY. How would you know it? Sure it's not in the streets they would be calling it. If Mrs Fallon didn't know of it, and if I that have the next house to them didn't know of it, and if Jack Smith himself didn't know of it, it is not likely you would know of it, Tim Casey.

SHAWN EARLY. Let Bartley Fallon take charge of her from this out so, and let him provide for her. It is little pity she will get from any person in this parish.

TIM CASEY. How can he take charge of her? Sure he has a wife of his own. Sure you don't think he'd turn souper[6] and marry her in a Protestant church?

JAMES RYAN. It would be easy for him to marry her if he brought her to America.

SHAWN EARLY. With or without Kitty Keary, believe me it is for America he's making at this minute. I saw the new magistrate and Jo Muldoon of the police going into the post-office as I came up – there was hurry on them – you may be sure it was to telegraph they went, the way he'll be stopped in the docks at Queenstown!

MRS TULLY. It's likely Kitty Keary is gone with him, and not minding a sheet or a wake at all. The poor man, to be deserted by his own wife, and the breath hardly gone out yet from his body that is lying bloody in the field!

(*Enter* MRS FALLON.)

MRS FALLON. What is it the whole of the town is talking about? And what is it you yourselves are talking about? Is it about my man Bartley Fallon you are talking? Is it lies about him you are telling, saying that he went killing Jack Smith? My grief that ever he came into this place at all!

JAMES RYAN. Be easy now, Mrs Fallon. Sure there is no one at all in the whole fair but is sorry for you!

MRS FALLON. Sorry for me, is it? Why would anyone be sorry for me? Let you be sorry for yourselves, and that there may be shame on you for ever and at the day of judgment, for the words you are saying and the lies you are telling to take away the character of my poor man, and to take the good name off of him, and to drive him to destruction! That is what you are doing!

SHAWN EARLY. Take comfort now, Mrs Fallon. The police are not so smart as they think. Sure he might give them the slip yet, the same as Lynchehaun.

MRS TULLY. If they do get him, and if they do put a rope around his neck, there is no one can say he does not deserve it!

MRS FALLON. Is that what you are saying, Bridget Tully, and is that what you think? I tell you it's too much talk you have, making yourself out to be such a great one, and to be running down every respectable person! A rope, is it? It isn't much of a rope was needed to tie up your own furniture the day you came into Martin Tully's house, and you never bringing as much as a blanket, or a penny, or a suit of clothes with you and I myself bringing seventy pounds and two feather beds. And now you are stiffer[7] than a woman would have a hundred pounds! It is too much talk the whole of you have. A rope is it? I tell you the whole of this town is full of liars and schemers that would hang you up for half a glass of whiskey. (*Turning to go.*) People they are you wouldn't believe as much as daylight from without you'd get up to have a look at it yourself. Killing Jack Smith indeed! Where are you at all, Bartley, till I bring you out of this? My nice quiet little man! My decent comrade! He that is as kind and as harmless as an innocent beast of the field! He'll be doing no harm at all if he'll shed the blood of some of you after this day's work! That much would be no harm at all. (*Calls out.*) Bartley! Bartley Fallon! Where are you? (*Going out.*) Did anyone see Bartley Fallon?

(*All turn to look after her.*)

JAMES RYAN. It is hard for her to believe any such a thing, God help her!

(*Enter* BARTLEY FALLON *from right, carrying hayfork.*)

BARTLEY. It is what I often said to myself, if there is ever any misfortune coming to this world it is on myself it is sure to come!

(*All turn round and face him.*)

BARTLEY. To be going about with this fork and to find no one to take it, and no place to leave it down, and I wanting to be gone out of this – Is that you, Shawn Early? (*Holds out fork.*) It's well I met you. You have no call to be leaving the fair for a while the way I have, and how can I go till I'm rid of this fork? Will you take it and keep it until such time as Jack Smith—

SHAWN EARLY (*backing*). I will not take it, Bartley Fallon, I'm very thankful to you!

BARTLEY (*turning to apple stall*). Look at it now, Mrs Tarpey, it was here I got it; let me thrust it in under the stall. It will lie there safe enough, and no one will take notice of it until such time as Jack Smith—

MRS TARPEY. Take your fork out of that! Is it to put trouble on me and to destroy me you want? putting it there for the police to be rooting it out maybe.

(*Thrusts him back.*)

BARTLEY. That is a very unneighbourly thing for you to do, Mrs Tarpey. Hadn't I enough care on me with that fork before this, running up and down with it like the swinging of a clock, and afeard to lay it down in any place! I wish I never touched it or meddled with it at all!

JAMES RYAN. It is a pity, indeed, you ever did.

BARTLEY. Will you yourself take it, James Ryan? You were always a neighbourly man.

JAMES RYAN (*backing*). There is many a thing I would do for you, Bartley Fallon, but I won't do that!

SHAWN EARLY. I tell you there is no man will give you any help or any encouragement for this day's work. If it was something agrarian now—

BARTLEY. If no one at all will take it, maybe it's best to give it up to the police.

TIM CASEY. There'd be a welcome for it with them surely!

(*Laughter.*)

MRS TULLY. And it is to the police Kitty Keary herself will be brought.

MRS TARPEY (*rocking to and fro*). I wonder now who will take the expense of the wake for poor Jack Smith?

BARTLEY. The wake for Jack Smith!

TIM CASEY. Why wouldn't he get a wake as well as another? Would you begrudge him that much?

BARTLEY. Red Jack Smith dead! Who was telling you?

SHAWN EARLY. The whole town knows of it by this.

BARTLEY. Do they say what way did he die?

JAMES RYAN. You don't know that yourself, I suppose, Bartley Fallon? You don't know he was followed and that he was laid dead with the stab of a hayfork?

BARTLEY. The stab of a hayfork!

SHAWN EARLY. You don't know, I suppose, that the body was found in the Five Acre Meadow?

BARTLEY. The Five Acre Meadow!

TIM CASEY. It is likely you don't know that the police are after the man that did it?

BARTLEY. The man that did it!

MRS TULLY. You don't know, maybe, that he was made away with for the sake of Kitty Keary, his wife?

BARTLEY. Kitty Keary, his wife!

(*Sits down bewildered.*)

MRS TULLY. And what have you to say now, Bartley Fallon?

BARTLEY (*crossing himself*). I to bring that fork here, and to find that news before me! It is much if I can ever stir from this place at all, or reach as far as the road!

TIM CASEY. Look, boys, at the new magistrate, and Jo Muldoon along with him! It's best for us to quit this.

SHAWN EARLY. That is so. It is best not to be mixed in this business at all.

JAMES RYAN. Bad as he is, I wouldn't like to be an informer against any man.

(*All hurry away except* MRS TARPEY, *who remains behind her stall. Enter* MAGISTRATE *and* POLICEMAN.)

MAGISTRATE. I knew the district was in a bad state, but I did not expect to be confronted with a murder at the first fair I came to.

POLICEMAN. I am sure you did not, indeed.

MAGISTRATE. It was well I had not gone home. I caught a few words here and there that roused my suspicions.

POLICEMAN. So they would, too.

MAGISTRATE. You heard the same story from everyone you asked?

POLICEMAN. The same story – or if it was not altogether the same, anyway it was no less than the first story.

MAGISTRATE. What is that man doing? He is sitting alone with a hayfork. He has a guilty look. The murder was done with a hayfork!

POLICEMAN (*in a whisper*). That's the very man they say did the act; Bartley Fallon himself!

MAGISTRATE. He must have found escape difficult – he is trying to brazen it out. A convict in the Andaman Islands tried the same game, but he could not escape my system! Stand aside – Don't go far – have the handcuffs ready. (*He walks up to* BARTLEY, *folds his arms, and stands before him.*) Here, my man, do you know anything of John Smith?

BARTLEY. Of John Smith! Who is he, now?

POLICEMAN. Jack Smith, sir – Red Jack Smith!

MAGISTRATE (*coming a step nearer and tapping him on the shoulder*). Where is Jack Smith?

BARTLEY (*with a deep sigh, and shaking his head slowly*). Where is he, indeed?

MAGISTRATE. What have you to tell?

BARTLEY. It is where he was this morning, standing in this spot, singing his share of songs – no, but lighting his pipe – scraping a match on the sole of his shoes—

MAGISTRATE. I ask you, for the third time, where is he?

BARTLEY. I wouldn't like to say that. It is a great mystery, and it is hard to say of any man, did he earn hatred or love.

MAGISTRATE. Tell me all you know.

BARTLEY. All that I know – Well, there are the three estates; there is Limbo, and there is Purgatory, and there is—

MAGISTRATE. Nonsense! This is trifling! Get to the point.

BARTLEY. Maybe you don't hold with the clergy so? That is the teaching of the clergy. Maybe you hold with the old people. It is what they do be saying, that the shadow goes wandering, and the soul is tired, and the body is taking a rest – The shadow! (*Starts up.*) I was nearly sure I saw Jack Smith not ten minutes ago at the corner of the forge, and I lost him again – Was it his ghost I saw, do you think?

MAGISTRATE (*to* POLICEMAN). Conscience-struck! He will confess all now!

BARTLEY. His ghost to come before me! It is likely it was on account of the fork! I to have it and he to have no way to defend himself the time he met with his death!

MAGISTRATE (*to* POLICEMAN). I must note down his words. (*Takes out notebook.*) (*To* BARTLEY.) I warn you that your words are being noted.

BARTLEY. If I had ha' run faster in the beginning, this terror would not be on me at the latter end! Maybe he will cast it up against me at the day of judgment – I wouldn't wonder at all at that.

MAGISTRATE (*writing*). At the day of judgment—

BARTLEY. It was soon for his ghost to appear to me – is it coming after me always by day it will be, and stripping the clothes off in the night time? – I wouldn't wonder at all at that, being as I am an unfortunate man!

MAGISTRATE (*sternly*). Tell me this truly. What was the motive of this crime?

BARTLEY. The motive, is it?

MAGISTRATE. Yes; the motive; the cause.

BARTLEY. I'd sooner not say that.

MAGISTRATE. You had better tell me truly. Was it money?

BARTLEY. Not at all! What did poor Jack Smith ever have in his pockets unless it might be his hands that would be in them?

MAGISTRATE. Any dispute about land?

BARTLEY (*indignantly*). Not at all! He never was a grabber or grabbed from anyone!

MAGISTRATE. You will find it better for you if you tell me at once.

BARTLEY. I tell you I wouldn't for the whole world wish to say what it was — it is a thing I would not like to be talking about.

MAGISTRATE. There is no use in hiding it. It will be discovered in the end.

BARTLEY. Well, I suppose it will, seeing that mostly everybody knows it before. Whisper here now. I will tell no lie; where would be the use? (*Puts his hand to his mouth, and* MAGISTRATE *stoops*.) Don't be putting the blame on the parish, for such a thing was never done in the parish before — it was done for the sake of Kitty Keary, Jack Smith's wife.

MAGISTRATE (*to* POLICEMAN). Put on the handcuffs. We have been saved some trouble. I knew he would confess if taken in the right way.

(POLICEMAN *puts on handcuffs*.)

BARTLEY. Handcuffs now! Glory be! I always said, if there was ever any misfortune coming to this place it was on myself it would fall. I to be in handcuffs! There's no wonder at all in that.

(*Enter* MRS FALLON, *followed by the rest. She is looking back at them as she speaks*.)

MRS FALLON. Telling lies the whole of the people of this town are; telling lies, telling lies as fast as a dog will trot! Speaking against my poor respectable man! Saying he made an end of Jack Smith! My decent comrade! There is no better man and no kinder man in the whole of the five parishes! It's little annoyance he ever gave to anyone! (*Turns and sees him*.) What in the earthly world do I see before me? Bartley Fallon in charge of the police! Handcuffs on him! O Bartley, what did you do at all at all?

BARTLEY. O Mary, there has a great misfortune come upon me! It is what I always said, that if there is ever any misfortune—

MRS FALLON. What did he do at all, or is it bewitched I am?

MAGISTRATE. This man has been arrested on a charge of murder.

MRS FALLON. Whose charge is that? Don't believe them! They are all liars in this place! Give me back my man!

MAGISTRATE. It is natural you should take his part, but you have no cause of complaint against your neighbours. He has been arrested for the murder of John Smith, on his own confession.

MRS FALLON. The saints of heaven protect us! And what did he want killing Jack Smith?

MAGISTRATE. It is best you should know all. He did it on account of a love affair with the murdered man's wife.

MRS FALLON (*sitting down*). With Jack Smith's wife! With Kitty Keary! – Ochone, the traitor!

THE CROWD. A great shame, indeed. He is a traitor indeed.

MRS TULLY. To America he was bringing her, Mrs Fallon.

BARTLEY. What are you saying, Mary? I tell you—

MRS FALLON. Don't say a word! I won't listen to any word you'll say! (*Stops her ears.*) O, isn't he the treacherous villain? Ohone go deo!

BARTLEY. Be quiet till I speak! Listen to what I say!

MRS FALLON. Sitting beside me on the ass car coming to the town, so quiet and so respectable, and treachery like that in his heart!

BARTLEY. Is it your wits you have lost or is it I myself that have lost my wits?

MRS FALLON. And it's hard I earned you, slaving – and you grumbling, and sighing, and coughing, and discontented, and the priest wore out anointing you, with all the times you threatened to die!

BARTLEY. Let you be quiet till I tell you!

MRS FALLON. You to bring such a disgrace into the parish. A thing that was never heard of before!

BARTLEY. Will you shut your mouth and hear me speaking?

MRS FALLON. And if it was for any sort of a fine handsome woman, but for a little fistful of a woman like Kitty Keary, that's not four feet high hardly, and not three teeth in her head unless she got new ones! May God reward you, Bartley Fallon, for the black treachery in your heart and the wickedness in your mind, and the red blood of poor Jack Smith that is wet upon your hand!

(*Voice of* JACK SMITH *heard singing.*)

> The sea shall be dry,
>    The earth under mourning and ban!

> Then loud shall he cry
> For the wife of the red-haired man!

BARTLEY. It's Jack Smith's voice — I never knew a ghost to sing before —. It is after myself and the fork he is coming! (*Goes back. Enter* JACK SMITH) Let one of you give him the fork and I will be clear of him now and for eternity!

MRS TARPEY. The Lord have mercy on us! Red Jack Smith! The man that was going to be waked!

JAMES RYAN. Is it back from the grave you are come?

SHAWN EARLY. Is it alive you are, or is it dead you are?

TIM CASEY. Is it yourself at all that's in it?

MRS TULLY. Is it letting on you were to be dead?

MRS FALLON. Dead or alive, let you stop Kitty Keary, your wife, from bringing my man away with her to America!

JACK SMITH. It is what I think, the wits are gone astray on the whole of you. What would my wife want bringing Bartley Fallon to America?

MRS FALLON. To leave yourself, and to get quit of you she wants, Jack Smith, and to bring him away from myself. That's what the two of them had settled together.

JACK SMITH. I'll break the head of any man that says that! Who is it says it? (*To* TIM CASEY.) Was it you said it? (*To* SHAWN EARLY.) Was it you?

ALL TOGETHER (*backing and shaking their heads*). It wasn't I said it!

JACK SMITH. Tell me the name of any man that said it!

ALL TOGETHER (*pointing to* BARTLEY). It was *him* that said it!

JACK SMITH. Let me at him till I break his head!

(BARTLEY *backs in terror. Neighbours hold* JACK SMITH *back.*)

JACK SMITH (*trying to free himself*). Let me at him! Isn't he the pleasant sort of a scarecrow for any woman to be crossing the ocean with! It's back from the docks of New York he'd be turned (*trying to rush at him again*), with a lie in his mouth and treachery in his heart, and another man's wife by his side, and he passing her off as his own! Let me at him can't you.

(*Makes another rush, but is held back.*)

MAGISTRATE (*pointing to* JACK SMITH). Policeman, put the handcuffs on this man. I see it all now. A case of false impersonation, a conspiracy to defeat the ends of justice. There was a case in the Andaman Islands, a murderer of the Mopsa tribe, a religious enthusiast—

POLICEMAN. So he might be, too.

MAGISTRATE. We must take both these men to the scene of the murder. We must confront them with the body of the real Jack Smith.

JACK SMITH. I'll break the head of any man that will find my dead body!

MAGISTRATE. I'll call more help from the barracks. (*Blows* POLICEMAN'*s whistle.*)

BARTLEY. It is what I am thinking, if myself and Jack Smith are put together in the one cell for the night, the handcuffs will be taken off him, and his hands will be free, and murder will be done that time surely!

MAGISTRATE. Come on! (*They turn to the right.*)

*Curtain.*

*The earliest printings of this play left the last word to* MRS TARPEY: 'The two of them in charge now, and a great troop of people going by from the fair. Come up here the whole of you! It would be a pity you to be passing, and I not to be spreading the news!'

# Hyacinth Halvey

## PERSONS IN THE PLAY

HACINTH HALVEY
JAMES QUIRKE, *a butcher*
FARDY FARRELL, *a telegraph boy*
SERGEANT CARDEN
MRS DELANE, *Postmistress at Cloon*
MISS JOYCE, *the Priest's Housekeeper*

SCENE: *Outside the Post Office at the little town of Cloon.*[1] MRS DELANE *at Post Office door.* MR QUIRKE *sitting on a chair at butcher's door. A dead sheep hanging beside it, and a thrush in a cage above.* FARDY FARRELL *playing on mouth organ. Train whistle heard.*

MRS DELANE. There is the four o'clock train, Mr Quirke.

MR QUIRKE. Is it now, Mrs Delane, and I not long after rising? It makes a man drowsy to be doing the half of his work in the night time. Going about the country, looking for little stags of sheep, striving to knock a few shillings together. That contract for the soldiers gives me a great deal to attend to.

MRS DELANE. I suppose so. It's hard enough on myself to be down ready for the mail car in the morning, sorting letters in the half dark. It's often I haven't time to look who are the letters from – or the cards.

MR QUIRKE. It would be a pity you not to know any little news might be knocking about. If you did not have information of what is going on who should have it? Was it you, ma'am, was telling me that the new Sub-Sanitary Inspector would be arriving today?

MRS DELANE. Today it is he is coming, and it's likely he was in that train. There was a card about him to Sergeant Carden this morning.

329

Mr Quirke. A young chap from Carrow they were saying he was.

Mrs Delane. So he is, one Hyacinth Halvey; and indeed if all that is said of him is true, or if a quarter of it is true, he will be a credit to this town.

Mr Quirke. Is that so?

Mrs Delane. Testimonials he has by the score. To Father Gregan they were sent. Registered they were coming and going. Would you believe me telling you that they weighed up to three pounds?

Mr Quirke. There must be great bulk in them indeed.

Mrs Delane. It is no wonder he to get the job. He must have a great character so many persons to write for him as what there did.

Fardy. It would be a great thing to have a character like that.

Mrs Delane. Indeed I am thinking it will be long before you will get the like of it, Fardy Farrell.

Fardy. If I had the like of that character it is not here carrying messages I would be. It's in Noonan's Hotel I would be, driving cars.

Mr Quirke. Here is the priest's housekeeper coming.

Mrs Delane. So she is; and there is the Sergeant a little while after her.

(*Enter* Miss Joyce.)

Mrs Delane. Good-evening to you, Miss Joyce. What way is his Reverence today? Did he get any ease from the cough?

Miss Joyce. He did not indeed, Mrs Delane. He has it sticking to him yet. Smothering he is in the night time. The most thing he comes short in is the voice.

Mrs Delane. I am sorry, now, to hear that. He should mind himself well.

Miss Joyce. It's easy to say let him mind himself. What do you say to him going to the meeting tonight? (Sergeant *comes in.*) It's for his Reverence's *Freeman* I am come, Mrs Delane.

Mrs Delane. Here it is ready. I was just throwing an eye on it to see was there any news. Good-evening, Sergeant.

SERGEANT (*holding up a placard*). I brought this notice, Mrs Delane, the announcement of the meeting to be held tonight in the Courthouse. You might put it up here convenient to the window. I hope you are coming to it yourself?

MRS DELANE. I will come, and welcome. I would do more than that for you, Sergeant.

SERGEANT. And you, Mr Quirke.

MR QUIRKE. I'll come, to be sure. I forget what's this the meeting is about.

SERGEANT. The Department of Agriculture is sending round a lecturer in furtherance of the moral development of the rural classes. (*Reads.*) 'A lecture will be given this evening in Cloon Courthouse, illustrated by magic lantern slides –' Those will not be in it; I am informed they were all broken in the first journey, the railway company taking them to be eggs. The subject of the lecture is 'The Building of Character'.

MRS DELANE. Very nice, indeed. I knew a girl lost her character, and she washed her feet in a blessed well after, and it dried up on the minute.

SERGEANT. The arrangements have all been left to me, the Archdeacon being away. He knows I have a good intellect for things of the sort. But the loss of those slides puts a man out. The thing people will not see it is not likely it is the thing they will believe. I saw what they call tableaux – standing pictures, you know – one time in Dundrum—

MRS DELANE. Miss Joyce was saying Father Gregan is supporting you.

SERGEANT. I am accepting his assistance. No bigotry about me when there is a question of the welfare of any fellow-creatures. Orange and green will stand together tonight. I myself and the station-master on the one side; your parish priest in the chair.

MISS JOYCE. If his Reverence would mind me he would not quit the house tonight. He is no more fit to go speak at a meeting than (*pointing to the one hanging outside* QUIRKE'*s door*) that sheep.

SERGEANT. I am willing to take the responsibility. He will have no speaking to do at all, unless it might be to bid them give the lecturer a hearing. The loss of those slides now is a great annoyance to me – and no time for anything. The lecturer will be coming by the next train.

MISS JOYCE. Who is this coming up the street, Mrs Delane?

MRS DELANE. I wouldn't doubt it to be the new Sub-Sanitary Inspector. Was I telling you of the weight of the testimonials he got, Miss Joyce?

MISS JOYCE. Sure I heard the curate reading them to his Reverence. He must be a wonder for principles.

MRS DELANE. Indeed it is what I was saying to myself, he must be a very saintly young man.

(*Enter* HYACINTH HALVEY. *He carries a small bag and a large brown paper parcel. He stops and nods bashfully.*)

HYACINTH. Good-evening to you. I was bid to come to the post office—

SERGEANT. I suppose you are Hyacinth Halvey? I had a letter about you from the Resident Magistrate.

HYACINTH. I heard he was writing. It was my mother got a friend he deals with to ask him.

SERGEANT. He gives you a very high character.

HYACINTH. It is very kind of him indeed, and he not knowing me at all. But indeed all the neighbours were very friendly. Anything anyone could do to help me they did it.

MRS DELANE. I'll engage it is the testimonials you have in your parcel? I know the wrapping paper, but they grew in bulk since I handled them.

HYACINTH. Indeed I was getting them to the last. There was not one refused me. It is what my mother was saying, a good character is no burden.

FARDY. I would believe that indeed.

SERGEANT. Let us have a look at the testimonials. (HYACINTH HALVEY *opens parcel, and a large number of envelopes fall out.*)

SERGEANT (*opening and reading one by one*). 'He possesses the fire of the Gael, the strength of the Norman, the vigour of the Dane, the stolidity of the Saxon'—

HYACINTH. It was the Chairman of the Poor Law Guardians wrote that.

SERGEANT. 'A magnificent example to old and young'—

HYACINTH. That was the Secretary of the De Wet Hurling Club—

SERGEANT. 'A shining example of the value conferred by an eminently careful and high-class education'—

HYACINTH. That was the National Schoolmaster.

SERGEANT. 'Devoted to the highest ideals of his Mother-land to such an extent as is compatible with a hitherto non-parliamentary career'—

HYACINTH. That was the Member for Carrow.

SERGEANT. 'A splendid exponent of the purity of the race'—

HYACINTH. The Editor of the *Carrow Champion*.

SERGEANT. 'Admirably adapted for the efficient discharge of all possible duties that may in future be laid upon him'—

HYACINTH. The new Station-master.

SERGEANT. 'A champion of every cause that can legitimately benefit his fellow-creatures' – Why, look here, my man, you are the very one to come to our assistance tonight.

HYACINTH. I would be glad to do that. What way can I do it?

SERGEANT. You are a newcomer – your example would carry weight – you must stand up as a living proof of the beneficial effect of a high character, moral fibre, temperance – there is something about it here I am sure – (*Looks.*) I am sure I saw 'unparalleled temperance' in some place—

HYACINTH. It was my mother's cousin wrote that – I am no drinker, but I haven't the pledge taken[2]—

SERGEANT. You might take it for the purpose.

MR QUIRKE (*eagerly*). Here is an anti-treating button.[3] I was made a present of it by one of my customers – I'll give it to you (*sticks it in* HYACINTH's *coat*) and welcome.

SERGEANT. That is it. You can wear the button on the platform – or a bit of blue ribbon – hundreds will follow your example – I know the boys from the Workhouse will—

HYACINTH. I am in no way wishful to be an example—

SERGEANT. I will read extracts from the testimonials. 'There he is,' I will say, 'an example of one in early life who by his own unaided efforts and his high character has obtained a profitable situation' – (*Slaps his side.*) I know what I'll do. I'll engage a few corner-boys from Noonan's bar, just as they are, greasy and sodden, to stand in a group – there will be the contrast – The sight will deter others from a similar fate – That's the way to do a tableau – I knew I could turn out a success.

HYACINTH. I wouldn't like to be a contrast—

SERGEANT (*puts testimonials in his pocket*). I will go now and engage those lads – sixpence each, and well worth it – Nothing like an example for the rural classes.

(*Goes off,* HYACINTH *feebly trying to detain him.*)

MRS DELANE. A very nice man indeed. A little high up in himself, may be. I'm not one that blames the police. Sure they have their own bread to earn like every other one. And indeed it is often they will let a thing pass.

MR QUIRKE (*gloomily*). Sometimes they will, and more times they will not.

MISS JOYCE. And where will you be finding a lodging, Mr Halvey?

HYACINTH. I was going to ask that myself, ma'am. I don't know the town.

MISS JOYCE. I know of a good lodging, but it is only a very good man would be taken into it.

MRS DELANE. Sure there could be no objection there to Mr Halvey. There is no appearance on him but what is good, and the Sergeant after taking him up the way he is doing.

MISS JOYCE. You will be near to the Sergeant in the lodging I speak of. The house is convenient to the barracks.

HYACINTH (*doubtfully*). To the barracks?

MISS JOYCE. Alongside of it and the barrack yard behind. And that's not all. It is opposite to the priest's house.

HYACINTH. Opposite, is it?

MISS JOYCE. A very respectable place, indeed, and a very clean room you will get. I know it well. The curate can see into it from his window.

HYACINTH. Can he now?

FARDY. There was a good many, I am thinking, went into that lodging and left it after.

MISS JOYCE (*sharply*). It is a lodging you will never be let into or let stop in, Fardy. If they did go they were a good riddance.

FARDY. John Hart, the plumber, left it—

MISS JOYCE. If he did it was because he dared not pass the police coming in, as he used, with a rabbit he was after snaring in his hand.

FARDY. The schoolmaster himself left it.

MISS JOYCE. He needn't have left it if he hadn't taken to card-playing. What way could you say your prayers, and shadows shuffling and dealing before you on the blind?

HYACINTH. I think maybe I'd best look around a bit before I'll settle in a lodging—

MISS JOYCE. Not at all. *You* won't be wanting to pull down the blind.

MRS DELANE. It is not likely *you* will be snaring rabbits.

MISS JOYCE. Or bringing in a bottle and taking an odd glass the way James Kelly did.

MRS DELANE. Or writing threatening notices, and the police taking a view of you from the rear.

MISS JOYCE. Or going to roadside dances, or running after good-for-nothing young girls—

HYACINTH. I give you my word I'm not so harmless as you think.

MRS DELANE. Would you be putting a lie on these, Mr Halvey? (*Touching testimonials.*) I know well the way *you* will be spending the evenings, writing letters to your relations—

MISS JOYCE. Learning O'Growney's exercises—

MRS DELANE. Sticking post cards in an album for the convent bazaar.

MISS JOYCE. Reading the *Catholic Young Man*—

MRS DELANE. Playing the melodies on a melodeon—

MISS JOYCE. Looking at the pictures in the *Lives of the Saints*. I'll hurry on and engage the room for you.

HYACINTH. Wait. Wait a minute—

MISS JOYCE. No trouble at all. I told you it was just opposite.

(*Goes.*)

MR QUIRKE. I suppose I must go upstairs and ready myself for the meeting. If it wasn't for the contract I have for the soldiers' barracks and the Sergeant's good word, I wouldn't go anear it

(*Goes into shop.*)

Mrs Delane. I should be making myself ready too. I must be in good time to see you being made an example of, Mr Halvey. It is I myself was the first to say it; you will be a credit to the town.

(*Goes.*)

Hyacinth (*in a tone of agony*). I wish I had never seen Cloon.

Fardy. What is on you?

Hyacinth. I wish I had never left Carrow. I wish I had been drowned the first day I thought of·it, and I'd be better off.

Fardy. What is it ails you?

Hyacinth. I wouldn't for the best pound ever I had be in this place today.

Fardy. I don't know what you are talking about.

Hyacinth. To have left Carrow, if it was a poor place, where I had my comrades, and an odd spree, and a game of cards – and a coursing match coming on, and I promised a new greyhound from the city of Cork. I'll die in this place, the way I am. I'll be too much closed in.

Fardy. Sure it mightn't be as bad as what you think.

Hyacinth. Will you tell me, I ask you, what way can I undo it?

Fardy. What is it you are wanting to undo?

Hyacinth. Will you tell me what way can I get rid of my character?

Fardy. To get rid of it, is it?

Hyacinth. That is what I said. Aren't you after hearing the great character they are after putting on me?

Fardy. That is a good thing to have.

Hyacinth. It is not. It's the worst in the world. If I hadn't it, I wouldn't be like a prize mangold at a show with every person praising me.

Fardy. If I had it, I wouldn't be like a head in a barrel, with every person making hits at me.

Hyacinth. If I hadn't it, I wouldn't be shoved into a room with all the clergy watching me and the police in the back-yard.

FARDY. If I had it, I wouldn't be but a message-carrier now, and a clapper scaring birds in the summer time.

HYACINTH. If I hadn't it, I wouldn't be wearing this button and brought up for an example at the meeting.

FARDY (*whistles*). Maybe you're not, so, what those papers make you out to be?

HYACINTH. How would I be what they make me out to be? Was there ever any person of that sort since the world was a world, unless it might be Saint Antony of Padua looking down from the chapel wall? If it is like that I was, isn't it in Mount Melleray I would be, or with the Friars at Esker? Why would I be living in the world at all, or doing the world's work?

FARDY (*taking up parcel*). Who would think, now, there would be so much lies in a small place like Carrow?

HYACINTH. It was my mother's cousin did it. He said I was not reared for labouring – he gave me a new suit and bid me never to come back again. I daren't go back to face him – the neighbours knew my mother had a long family – bad luck to them the day they gave me these. (*Tears letters and scatters them.*) I'm done with testimonials. They won't be here to bear witness against me.

FARDY. The Sergeant thought them to be great. Sure he has the samples of them in his pocket. There's not one in the town but will know before morning that you are the next thing to an earthly saint.

HYACINTH (*stamping*). I'll stop their mouths. I'll show them I can be a terror for badness. I'll do some injury. I'll commit some crime. The first thing I'll do I'll go and get drunk. If I never did it be-fore I'll do it now. I'll get drunk – then I'll make an assault – I tell you I'd think as little of taking a life as of blowing out a candle.

FARDY. If you get drunk you are done for. Sure that will be held up after as an excuse for any breaking of the law.

HYACINTH. I will break the law. Drunk or sober I'll break it. I'll do something that will have no excuse. What would you say is the worst crime that any man can do?

FARDY. I don't know. I heard the Sergeant saying one time it was to obstruct the police in the discharge of their duty—

HYACINTH. That won't do. It's a patriot I would be then, worse than before, with my picture in the weeklies. It's a red crime I must commit that will make all respectable people quit minding me. What can I do? Search your mind now.

FARDY. It's what I heard the old people saying there could be no worse crime than to steal a sheep—

HYACINTH. I'll steal a sheep – or a cow – or a horse – if that will leave me the way I was before.

FARDY. It's maybe in gaol it will leave you.

HYACINTH. I don't care – I'll confess – I'll tell why I did it – I give you my word I would as soon be picking oakum or breaking stones as to be perched in the daylight the same as that bird, and all the town chirruping to me or bidding me chirrup—

FARDY. There is reason in that, now.

HYACINTH. Help me, will you?

FARDY. Well, if it is to steal a sheep you want, you haven't far to go.

HYACINTH (*looking round wildly*). Where is it? I see no sheep.

FARDY. Look around you?

HYACINTH. I see no living thing but that thrush—

FARDY. Did I say it was living? What is that hanging on Quirke's rack?

HYACINTH. It's (*fingers it*) a sheep, sure enough—

FARDY. Well, what ails you that you can't bring it away?

HYACINTH. It's a dead one—

FARDY. What matter if it is?

HYACINTH. If it was living I could drive it before me—

FARDY. You could. Is it to your own lodging you would drive it? Sure everyone would take it to be a pet you brought from Carrow?

HYACINTH. I suppose they might.

FARDY. Miss Joyce sending in for news of it and it bleating behind the bed.

HYACINTH (*distracted*). Stop! stop!

MRS DELANE (*from upper window*). Fardy! Are you there, Fardy Farrell?

FARDY. I am, ma'am.

338

MRS DELANE. Look and tell me is that the telegraph I hear ticking?

FARDY (*looking in at door*). It is, ma'am.

MRS DELANE. Then botheration to it, and I not dressed or undressed. Wouldn't you say, now, it's to annoy me it is calling me down. I'm coming! I'm coming! (*Disappears.*)

FARDY. Hurry on, now! hurry! She'll be coming out on you. If you are going to do it, do it, and if you are not, let it alone.

HYACINTH. I'll do it! I'll do it!

FARDY (*lifting the sheep on his back*). I'll give you a hand with it.

HYACINTH (*goes a step or two and turns round*). You told me no place where I could hide it.

FARDY. You needn't go far. There is the church beyond at the side of the Square. Go round to the ditch behind the wall – there's nettles in it.

HYACINTH. That'll do.

FARDY. She's coming out – run! run!

HYACINTH (*runs a step or two*). It's slipping!

FARDY. Hoist it up! I'll give it a hoist! (HALVEY *runs out.*)

MRS DELANE (*calling out*). What are you doing Fardy Farrell? Is it idling you are?

FARDY. Waiting I am, ma'am, for the message—

MRS DELANE. Never mind the message yet. Who said it was ready? (*Going to door.*) Go ask for the loan of – no, but ask news of – Here, now go bring that bag of Mr Halvey's to the lodging Miss Joyce has taken—

FARDY. I will, ma'am. (*Takes bag and goes out.*)

MRS DELANE (*coming out with a telegram in her hand*). Nobody here? (*Looks round and calls cautiously.*) Mr Quirke! Mr Quirke! James Quirke!

MR QUIRKE (*looking out of his upper window with soap-suddy face*). What is it, Mrs Delane?

MRS DELANE (*beckoning*). Come down here till I tell you.

MR QUIRKE. I cannot do that. I'm not fully shaved.

MRS DELANE. You'd come if you knew the news I have.

MR QUIRKE. Tell it to me now. I'm not so supple as I was.

MRS DELANE. Whisper now, have you an enemy in any place?

MR QUIRKE. It's likely I may have. A man in business—

MRS DELANE. I was thinking you had one.

MR QUIRKE. Why would you think that at this time more than any other time?

MRS DELANE. If you could know what is in this envelope you would know that, James Quirke.

MR QUIRKE. Is that so? And what, now, is there in it?

MRS DELANE. Who do you think now is it addressed to?

MR QUIRKE. How would I know that, and I not seeing it?

MRS DELANE. That is true. Well, it is a message from Dublin Castle to the Sergeant of Police!

MR QUIRKE. To Sergeant Carden, is it?

MRS DELANE. It is. And it concerns yourself.

MR QUIRKE. Myself, is it? What accusation can they be bringing against me? I'm a peaceable man.

MRS DELANE. Wait till you hear.

MR QUIRKE. Maybe they think I was in that moonlighting case—

MRS DELANE. That is not it—

MR QUIRKE. I was not in it – I was but in the neighbouring field – cutting up a dead cow, that those never had a hand in—

MRS DELANE. You're out of it—

MR QUIRKE. They had their faces blackened. There is no man can say I recognised them.

MRS DELANE. That's not what they're saying—

MR QUIRKE. I'll swear I did not hear their voices or know them if I did hear them.

MRS DELANE. I tell you it has nothing to do with that. It might be better for you if it had.

MR QUIRKE. What is it, so?

MRS DELANE. It is an order to the Sergeant bidding him immediately to seize all suspicious meat in your house. There is an officer coming down. There are complaints from the Shannon Fort Barracks.

MR QUIRKE. I'll engage it was that pork.

MRS DELANE. What ailed it for them to find fault?

MR QUIRKE. People are so hard to please nowadays, and I recommended them to salt it.

MRS DELANE. They had a right to have minded your advice.

MR QUIRKE. There was nothing on that pig at all but that it went mad on poor O'Grady that owned it.

MRS DELANE. So I heard, and went killing all before it.

MR QUIRKE. Sure it's only in the brain madness can be. I heard the doctor saying that.

MRS DELANE. He should know.

MR QUIRKE. I give you my word I cut the head off it. I went to the loss of it, throwing it to the eels in the river. If they had salted the meat, as I advised them, what harm would it have done to any person on earth?

MRS DELANE. I hope no harm will come on poor Mrs Quirke and the family.

MR QUIRKE. Maybe it wasn't that but some other thing—

MRS DELANE. Here is Fardy. I must send the message to the Sergeant. Well, Mr Quirke, I'm glad I had the time to give you a warning.

MR QUIRKE. I'm obliged to you, indeed. You were always very neighbourly, Mrs Delane. Don't be too quick now sending the message. There is just one article I would like to put away out of the house before the Sergeant will come. (*Enter* FARDY.)

MRS DELANE. Here now, Fardy – that's not the way you're going to the barracks. Anyone would think you were scaring birds yet. Put on your uniform. (*Fardy goes into office.*) You have this message to bring to the Sergeant of Police. Get your cap now, it's under the counter.

(FARDY *reappears, and she gives him telegram.*)

FARDY. I'll bring it to the station. It's there he was going.

MRS DELANE. You will not, but to the barracks. It can wait for him there.

(FARDY *goes off.* MR QUIRKE *has appeared at door.*)

MR QUIRKE. It was indeed a very neighbourly act, Mrs Delane, and I'm obliged to you. There is just *one* article to put out of the way. The Sergeant may look about him then and welcome. It's well I cleared the premises on yesterday. A consignment to Birmingham I sent. The Lord be praised isn't England a terrible country with all it consumes?

341

Mrs Delane. Indeed you always treat the neighbours very decent, Mr Quirke, not asking them to buy from you.

Mr Quirke. Just one article. (*Turns to rack.*) That sheep I brought in last night. It was for a charity indeed I bought it from the widow woman at Kiltartan Cross. Where would the poor make a profit out of their dead meat without me? Where now is it? Well, now, I could have swore that that sheep was hanging there on the rack when I went in—

Mrs Delane. You must have put it in some other place.

Mr Quirke (*going in and searching and coming out*). I did not; there is no other place for me to put it. Is it gone blind I am, or is it not in it, it is?

Mrs Delane. It's not there now anyway.

Mr Quirke. Didn't you take notice of it there yourself this morning?

Mrs Delane. I have it in my mind that I did; but it's not there now.

Mr Quirke. There was no one here could bring it away?

Mrs Delane. Is it me myself you suspect of taking it, James Quirke?

Mr Quirke. Where is it at all? It is certain it was not of itself it walked away. It was dead, and very dead, the time I bought it.

Mrs Delane. I have a pleasant neighbour indeed that accuses me that I took his sheep. I wonder, indeed, you to say a thing like that! I to steal your sheep or your rack or anything that belongs to you or to your trade! Thank you, James Quirke. I am much obliged to you indeed.

Mr Quirke. Ah, be quiet woman; be quiet—

Mrs Delane. And let me tell you, James Quirke, that I would sooner starve and see everyone belonging to me starve than to eat the size of a thimble of any joint that ever was on your rack or that ever will be on it, whatever the soldiers may eat that have no other thing to get, or the English that devour all sorts, or the poor ravenous people that's down by the sea! (*She turns to go into shop.*)

Mr Quirke (*stopping her*). Don't be talking foolishness, woman. Who said you took my meat? Give heed to me now.

There must be some other message has come. The Sergeant must have got some other message.

MRS DELANE (*sulkily*). If there is any way for a message to come that is quicker than to come by the wires, tell me what it is and I'll be obliged to you.

MR QUIRKE. The Sergeant was up here making an excuse he was sticking up that notice. What was he doing here, I ask you?

MRS DELANE. How would I know what brought him?

MR QUIRKE. It is what he did; he made as if to go away – he turned back again and I shaving – he brought away the sheep – he will have it for evidence against me—

MRS DELANE (*interested*). That might be so.

MR QUIRKE. I would sooner it to have been any other beast nearly ever I had upon the rack.

MRS DELANE. Is that so?

MR QUIRKE. I bade the Widow Early to kill it a fortnight ago – but she would not, she was that covetous!

MRS DELANE. What was on it?

MR QUIRKE. How would I know what was on it? Whatever was on it, it was the will of God put it upon it – wasted it was, and shivering and refusing its share.

MRS DELANE. The poor thing.

MR QUIRKE. Gone all to nothing – wore away like a flock of thread. It did not weigh as much as a lamb of two months.

MRS DELANE. It is likely the Inspector will bring it to Dublin?

MR QUIRKE. The ribs of it streaky with the dint of patent medicines—

MRS DELANE. I wonder is it to the Petty Sessions you'll be brought or is it to the Assizes?

MR QUIRKE. I'll speak up to them. I'll make my defence. What can the Army expect at fivepence a pound?

MRS DELANE. It is likely there will be no bail allowed?

MR QUIRKE. Would they be wanting me to give them good quality meat out of my own pocket? Is it to encourage them to fight the poor Indians and Africans they would have me? It's the Anti-Enlisting Societies should pay the fine for me.

MRS DELANE. It's not a fine will be put on you, I'm afraid.

It's five years in gaol you will be apt to be getting. Well, I'll try and be a good neighbour to poor Mrs Quirke.

(MR QUIRKE, *who has been stamping up and down, sits down and weeps.* HALVEY *comes in and stands on one side.*)

MR QUIRKE. Hadn't I heart-scalding enough before, striving to rear five weak children?

MRS DELANE. I suppose they will be sent to the Industrial Schools?

MR QUIRKE. My poor wife—

MRS DELANE. I'm afraid the workhouse—

MR QUIRKE. And she out in an ass-car at this minute helping me to follow my trade.

MRS DELANE. I hope they will not arrest her along with you.

MR QUIRKE. I'll give myself up to justice. I'll plead guilty! I'll be recommended to mercy!

MRS DELANE. It might be best for you.

MR QUIRKE. Who would think so great a misfortune could come upon a family through the bringing away of one sheep!

HYACINTH (*coming forward*). Let you make yourself easy.

MR QUIRKE. Easy! It's easy to say let you make yourself easy.

HYACINTH. I can tell you where it is.

MR QUIRKE. Where what is?

HYACINTH. The sheep you are fretting after.

MR QUIRKE. What do you know about it?

HYACINTH. I know everything about it.

MR QUIRKE. I suppose the Sergeant told you?

HYACINTH. He told me nothing.

MR QUIRKE. I suppose the whole town knows it, so?

HYACINTH. No one knows it, as yet.

MR QUIRKE. And the Sergeant didn't see it?

HYACINTH. No one saw it or brought it away but myself.

MR QUIRKE. Where did you put it at all?

HYACINTH. In the ditch behind the church wall. In among the nettles it is. Look at the way they have me stung. (*Holds out hands.*)

MR QUIRKE. In the ditch! The best hiding place in the town.

HYACINTH. I never thought it would bring such great trouble upon you. You can't say anyway I did not tell you.

Mr Quirke. You yourself that brought it away and that hid it! I suppose it was coming in the train you got information about the message to the police.

Hyacinth. What now do you say to me?

Mr Quirke. Say! I say I am as glad to hear what you said as if it was the Lord telling me I'd be in heaven this minute.

Hyacinth. What are you going to do to me?

Mr Quirke. Do, is it? (*Grasps his hand.*) Any earthly thing you would wish me to do. I will do it.

Hyacinth. I suppose you will tell—

Mr Quirke. Tell! It's I that will tell when all is quiet. It is I will give you the good name through the town!

Hyacinth. I don't well understand.

Mr Quirke (*embracing him*). The man that preserved me!

Hyacinth. That preserved you?

Mr Quirke. That kept me from ruin!

Hyacinth. From ruin?

Mr Quirke. That saved me from disgrace!

Hyacinth (*to* Mrs Delane). What is he saying at all?

Mr Quirke. From the Inspector!

Hyacinth. What is he talking about?

Mr Quirke. From the magistrates!

Hyacinth. He is making some mistake.

Mr Quirke. From the Winter Assizes!

Hyacinth. Is he out of his wits?

Mr Quirke. Five years in gaol!

Hyacinth. Hasn't he the queer talk?

Mr Quirke. The loss of the contract!

Hyacinth. Are my own wits gone astray?

Mr Quirke. What way can I repay you?

Hyacinth (*shouting*). I tell you I took the sheep—

Mr Quirke. You did, God reward you!

Hyacinth. I stole away with it—

Mr Quirke. The blessing of the poor on you!

Hyacinth. I put it out of sight—

Mr Quirke. The blessing of my five children—

Hyacinth. I may as well say nothing—

MRS DELANE. Let you be quiet now, Quirke. Here's the Sergeant coming to search the shop—

(SERGEANT *comes in:* QUIRKE *leaves go of* HALVEY, *who arranges his hat, etc.*)

SERGEANT. The Department to blazes!

MRS DELANE. What is it is putting you out?

SERGEANT. To go to the train to meet the lecturer, and there to get a message through the guard that he was unavoidably detained in the South, holding an inquest on the remains of a drake.

MRS DELANE. The lecturer, is it?

SERGEANT. To be sure. What else would I be talking of? The lecturer has failed me, and where am I to go looking for a person that I would think fitting to take his place?

MRS DELANE. And that's all? And you didn't get any message but the one?

SERGEANT. Is that all? I am surprised at you, Mrs Delane. Isn't it enough to upset a man, within three quarters of an hour of the time the meeting? Where, I would ask you, am I to find a man that has education enough and wit enough and character enough to put up speaking on the platform on the minute?

MR QUIRKE (*jumps up*). It is I myself will tell you that.

SERGEANT. You!

MR QUIRKE (*slapping* HALVEY *on the back*). Look at here, Sergeant. There is not one word was said in all those papers about this young man before you but it is true. And there could be no good thing said of him that would be too good for him.

SERGEANT. It might not be a bad idea.

MR QUIRKE. Whatever the paper said about him, Sergeant, I can say more again. It has come to my knowledge – by chance – that since he came to this town that young man has saved a whole family from destruction.

SERGEANT. That is much to his credit – helping the rural classes—

MR QUIRKE. A family and a long family, big and little, like sods of turf – and they depending on a— on one that might be on his way to dark trouble at this minute if it was not for his

346

assistance. Believe me, he is the most sensible man, and the wittiest, and the kindest, and the best helper of the poor that ever stood before you in this square. Is not that so, Mrs Delane?

MRS DELANE. It is true indeed. Where he gets his wisdom and his wit and his information from I don't know, unless it might be that he is gifted from above.

SERGEANT. Well, Mrs Delane, I think we have settled that question. Mr Halvey, you will be the speaker at the meeting. The lecturer sent these notes – you can lengthen them into a speech. You can call to the people of Cloon to stand out, to begin the building of their character. I saw a lecturer do it one time at Dundrum. 'Come up here,' he said. 'Dare to be a Daniel,' he said—

HYACINTH. I can't – I won't—

SERGEANT (*looking at papers and thrusting them into his hand*). You will find it quite easy. I will conduct you to the platform – these papers before you and a glass of water – That's settled. (*Turns to go.*) Follow me on to the Courthouse in half an hour – I must go to the barracks first – I heard there was a telegram – (*Calls back as he goes*) Don't be late, Mrs Delane. Mind, Quirke, you promised to come.

MRS DELANE. Well, it's time for me to make an end of settling myself – and indeed, Mr Quirke, you'd best do the same.

MR QUIRKE (*rubbing his cheek*). I suppose so. I had best keep on good terms with him for the present. (*Turns.*) Well, now, I had a great escape this day.

(*Both go in as* FARDY *reappears whistling.*)

HYACINTH (*sitting down*). I don't know in the world what has come upon the world that the half of the people of it should be cracked!

FARDY. Weren't you found out yet?

HYACINTH. Found out, is it? I don't know what you mean by being found out.

FARDY. Didn't he miss the sheep?

HYACINTH. He did, and I told him it was I took it – and what happened I declare to goodness I don't know – Will you look at these? (*Holds out notes.*)

FARDY. Papers! Are they more testimonials?

HYACINTH. They are what is worse. (*Gives a hoarse laugh.*) Will you come and see me on the platform – these in my hand – and I speaking – giving out advice. (FARDY *whistles*.) Why didn't you tell me, the time you advised me to steal a sheep, that in this town it would qualify a man to go preaching, and the priest in the chair looking on.

FARDY. The time I took a few apples that had fallen off a stall, they did not ask me to hold a meeting. They welted me well.

HYACINTH (*looking round*). I would take apples if I could see them. I wish I had broke my neck before I left Carrow and I'd be better off! I wish I had got six months the time I was caught setting snares – I wish I had robbed a church.

FARDY. Would a Protestant church do?

HYACINTH. I suppose it wouldn't be so great a sin.

FARDY. It's likely the Sergeant would think worse of it – Anyway, if you want to rob one, it's the Protestant church is the handiest.

HYACINTH (*getting up*). Show me what way to do it?

FARDY (*pointing*). I was going around it a few minutes ago, to see might there be e'er a dog scenting the sheep, and I noticed the window being out.

HYACINTH. Out, out and out?

FARDY. It was, where they are putting coloured glass in it for the distiller—

HYACINTH. What good does that do me?

FARDY. Every good. You could go in by that window if you had some person to give you a hoist. Whatever riches there is to get in it then, you'll get them.

HYACINTH. I don't want riches. I'll give you all I will find if you come and hoist me.

FARDY. Here is Miss Joyce coming to bring you to your lodging. Sure I brought your bag to it, the time you were away with the sheep—

HYACINTH. Run! Run!

(*They go off. Enter* MISS JOYCE.)

MISS JOYCE. Are you here, Mrs Delane? Where, can you tell me, is Mr Halvey?

MRS DELANE (*coming out dressed*). It's likely he is gone on to the Courthouse. Did you hear he is to be in the chair and to make an address to the meeting?

MISS JOYCE. He is getting on fast. His Reverence says he will be a good help in the parish. Who would think, now, there would be such a godly young man in a little place like Carrow!

(*Enter* SERGEANT *in a hurry, with telegram.*)

SERGEANT. What time did this telegram arrive, Mrs Delane?

MRS DELANE. I couldn't be rightly sure, Sergeant. But sure it's marked on it, unless the clock I have is gone wrong.

SERGEANT. It is marked on it. And I have the time I got it marked on my own watch.

MRS DELANE. Well, now, I wonder none of the police would have followed you with it from the barracks – and they with so little to do—

SERGEANT (*looking in at* QUIRKE'S *shop*). Well, I am sorry to do what I have to do, but duty is duty.

(*He ransacks shop.* MRS DELANE *looks on.* MR QUIRKE *puts his head out of window.*)

MR QUIRKE. What is that going on inside? (*No answer.*) Is there anyone inside, I ask. (*No answer.*) It must be that dog of Tannian's – wait till I get at him.

MRS DELANE. It is Sergeant Carden, Mr Quirke. He would seem to be looking for something—

(MR QUIRKE *appears in shop.* SERGEANT *comes out, makes another dive, taking up sacks, etc.*)

MR QUIRKE. I'm greatly afraid I am just out of meat, Sergeant – and I'm sorry now to disoblige you, and you not being in the habit of dealing with me—

SERGEANT. I should think not, indeed.

MR QUIRKE. Looking for a tender little bit of lamb, I suppose you are, for Mrs Carden and the youngsters?

SERGEANT. I am not.

MR QUIRKE. If I had it now, I'd be proud to offer it to you, and make no charge. I'll be killing a good kid tomorrow. Mrs Carden might fancy a bit of it—

SERGEANT. I have had orders to search your establishment for unwholesome meat, and I am come here to do it.

MR QUIRKE (*sitting down with a smile*). Is that so? Well, isn't it a wonder the schemers does be in the world.

SERGEANT. It is not the first time there have been complaints.

MR QUIRKE. I suppose not. Well, it is on their own head it will fall at the last!

SERGEANT. I have found nothing so far.

MR QUIRKE. I suppose not, indeed. What is there you could find, and it not in it?

SERGEANT. Have you no meat at all upon the premises?

MR QUIRKE. I have, indeed, a nice barrel of bacon.

SERGEANT. What way did it die?

MR QUIRKE. It would be hard for me to say that. American it is. How would I know what way they do be killing the pigs out there? Machinery, I suppose, they have – steam hammers—

SERGEANT. Is there nothing else here at all?

MR QUIRKE. I give you my word, there is no meat living or dead in this place, but yourself and myself and that bird above in the cage.

SERGEANT. Well, I must tell the Inspector I could find nothing. But mind yourself for the future.

MR QUIRKE. Thank you, Sergeant. I will do that. (*Enter* FARDY. *He stops short.*)

SERGEANT. It was you delayed that message to me, I suppose? You'd best mend your ways or I'll have something to say to you. (*Seizes and shakes him.*)

FARDY. That's the way everyone does be faulting me. (*Whimpers.*)

(*The* SERGEANT *gives him another shake. A half-crown falls out of his pocket.*)

MISS JOYCE (*picking it up*). A half-a-crown! Where, now, did you get that much, Fardy?

FARDY. Where did I get it, is it!

MISS JOYCE. I'll engage it was in no honest way you got it.

FARDY. I picked it up in the street—

MISS JOYCE. If you did, why didn't you bring it to the Sergeant or to his Reverence?

MRS DELANE. And some poor person, may be, being at the loss of it.

MISS JOYCE. I'd best bring it to his Reverence. Come with me, Fardy, till he will question you about it.

FARDY. It was not altogether in the street I found it—

MISS JOYCE. There, now! I knew you got it in no good way! Tell me, now.

FARDY. It was playing pitch and toss I won it—

MISS JOYCE. And who would play for half-crowns with the like of you, Fardy Farrell? Who was it, now?

FARDY. It was – a stranger—

MISS JOYCE. Do you hear that? A stranger! Did you see e'er a stranger in this town, Mrs Delane, or Sergeant Carden, or Mr Quirke?

MR QUIRKE. Not a one.

SERGEANT. There was no stranger here.

MRS DELANE. There could not be one here without me knowing it.

FARDY. I tell you there was.

MISS JOYCE. Come on, then, and tell who was he to his Reverence.

SERGEANT (taking other arm). Or to the bench.

FARDY. I did get it, I tell you, from a stranger.

SERGEANT. Where is he, so?

FARDY. He's in some place – not far away.

SERGEANT. Bring me to him.

FARDY. He'll be coming here.

SERGEANT. Tell me the truth and it will be better for you.

FARDY (weeping). Let me go and I will.

SERGEANT (letting go). Now – who did you get it from?

FARDY. From that young chap came today, Mr Halvey.

ALL. Mr Halvey!

MR QUIRKE (indignantly). What are you saying, you young ruffian you? Hyacinth Halvey to be playing pitch and toss with the like of you!

FARDY. I didn't say that.

MISS JOYCE. You did say it. You said it now.

MR QUIRKE. Hyacinth Halvey! The best man that ever came into this town

MISS JOYCE. It's my belief the half-crown is a bad one. May be it's to pass it off it was given to him. There were tinkers in the town at the time of the fair. Give it here to me. (*Bites it.*) No, indeed, it's sound enough. Here, Sergeant, it's best for you take it.

(*Gives it to* SERGEANT, *who examines it.*)

SERGEANT. Can it be? Can it be what I think it to be?

MR QUIRKE. What is it? What do you take it to be?

SERGEANT. It is, it is. I know it. I know this half-crown—

MR QUIRKE. That is a queer thing, now.

SERGEANT. I know it well. I have been handling it in the church for the last twelvemonth—

MR QUIRKE. Is that so?

SERGEANT. It is the nest-egg half-crown we hand round in the collection plate every Sunday morning. I know it by the dint on the Queen's temples and the crooked scratch under her nose.

MR QUIRKE (*examining it*). So there is, too.

SERGEANT. This is a bad business. It has been stolen from the church.

ALL. O! O! O!

SERGEANT (*seizing* FARDY). You have robbed the church!

FARDY (*terrified*). I tell you I never did!

SERGEANT. I have the proof of it.

FARDY. Say what you like! I never put a foot in it!

SERGEANT. How did you get this, so?

MISS JOYCE. I suppose from the *stranger*?

MRS DELANE. I suppose it was Hyacinth Halvey gave it to you, now.

FARDY. It was so.

SERGEANT. I suppose it was he robbed the church?

FARDY (*sobs*). You will not believe me if I say it.

MR QUIRKE. O! the young vagabond! Let me get at him!

MRS DELANE. Here he is himself now!

(HYACINTH *comes in.* FARDY *releases himself and creeps behind him.*)

MRS DELANE. It is time you to come, Mr Halvey, and shut the mouth of this young schemer.

MISS JOYCE. I would like you to hear what he says of you, Mr Halvey. Pitch and toss, he says.

MR QUIRKE. Robbery, he says.

MRS DELANE. Robbery of a church.

SERGEANT. He has had a bad name long enough. Let him go to a reformatory now.

FARDY (*clinging to* HYACINTH). Save me, save me! I'm a poor boy trying to knock out a way of living; I'll be destroyed if I go to a reformatory. (*Kneels and clings to* HYACINTH's *knees*.)

HYACINTH. I'll save you easy enough.

FARDY. Don't let me be gaoled!

HYACINTH. I am going to tell them.

FARDY. I'm a poor orphan—

HYACINTH. Will you let me speak?

FARDY. I'll get no more chance in the world—

HYACINTH. Sure I'm trying to free you—

FARDY. It will be tasked to me always.

HYACINTH. Be quiet, can't you.

FARDY. Don't you desert me!

HYACINTH. Will you be silent?

FARDY. Take it on yourself.

HYACINTH. I will if you'll let me.

FARDY. Tell them you did it.

HYACINTH. I am going to do that.

FARDY. Tell them it was you got in at the window.

HYACINTH. I will! I will!

FARDY. Say it was you robbed the box.

HYACINTH. I'll say it! I'll say it!

FARDY. It being open!

HYACINTH. Let me tell, let me tell.

FARDY. Of all that was in it.

HYACINTH. I'll tell them that.

FARDY. And gave it to me.

HYACINTH (*putting hand on his mouth and dragging him up*). Will you stop and let me speak?

SERGEANT. We can't be wasting time. Give him here to me.

HYACINTH. I can't do that. He must be let alone.

SERGEANT (*seizing him*). He'll be let alone in the lock-up.

HYACINTH. He must not be brought there.

SERGEANT. I'll let no man get him off.

HYACINTH. I will get him off.

SERGEANT. You will not!

HYACINTH. I will.

SERGEANT. Do you think to buy him off?

HYACINTH. I will buy him off with my own confession.

SERGEANT. And what will that be?

HYACINTH. It was I robbed the church.

SERGEANT. That is likely indeed!

HYACINTH. Let him go, and take me. I tell you I did it.

SERGEANT. It would take witnesses to prove that.

HYACINTH (*pointing to* FARDY). He will be witness.

FARDY. O! Mr Halvey, I would not wish to do that. Get me off and I will say nothing.

HYACINTH. Sure you must. You will be put on oath in the court.

FARDY. I will not! I will not! All the world knows I don't understand the nature of an oath!

MR QUIRKE (*coming forward*). Is it blind ye all are?

MRS DELANE. What are you talking about?

MR QUIRKE. Is it fools ye all are?

MISS JOYCE. Speak for yourself.

MR QUIRKE. Is it idiots ye all are?

SERGEANT. Mind who you're talking to.

MR QUIRKE (*seizing* HYACINTH'*s hands*). Can't you see? Can't you hear? Where are your wits? Was ever such a thing seen in this town?

MRS DELANE. Say out what you have to say.

MR QUIRKE. A walking saint he is!

MRS DELANE. Maybe so.

MR QUIRKE. The preserver of the poor! Talk of the holy martyrs! They are nothing at all to what he is! Will you look at him! To save that poor boy he is going! To take the blame on himself he is going! To say he himself did the robbery he is going! Before the magistrate he is going! To gaol he is going! Taking the blame on his own head! Putting the sin on his own shoulders! Letting on to have done a robbery! Telling a lie – that it may be forgiven him – to his own injury! Doing all that I tell you to save the character of a miserable slack lad, that rose in poverty.

(*Murmur of admiration from* ALL.)

MR QUIRKE. Now, what do you say?

SERGEANT (*pressing his hand*). Mr Halvey, you have given us all a lesson. To please you, I will make no information against the boy. (*Shakes him and helps him up.*) I will put back the half-crown in the poor-box next Sunday. (*To* FARDY.) What have you to say to your benefactor?

FARDY. I'm obliged to you, Mr Halvey. You behaved very decent indeed. I'll never let a word be said against you if I live to be a hundred years.

SERGEANT (*wiping eyes with a blue handkerchief*). I will tell it at the meeting. It will be a great encouragement to them to build up their character. I'll tell it to the priest and he taking the chair—

HYACINTH. O stop, will you—

MR QUIRKE. The chair. It's in the chair he himself should be. It's in a chair we will put him now. It's to chair him through the streets we will. Sure he'll be an example and a blessing to the whole of the town. (*Seizes* HALVEY *and seats him in chair.*) Now, Sergeant, give a hand. Here, Fardy.

(*They all lift the chair with* HALVEY *in it, wildly protesting.*)

MR QUIRKE. Come along now to the Courthouse. Three cheers for Hyacinth Halvey! Hip! hip! hoora!

(*Cheers heard in the distance as the curtain drops.*)

*Curtain.*

# The Gaol Gate

PERSONS IN THE PLAY

MARY CAHEL, *an old woman*
MARY CUSHIN, *her daughter-in-law*
THE GATEKEEPER

SCENE. *Outside the gate of Galway Gaol. Two countrywomen, one in a long dark cloak, the other with a shawl over her head, have just come in. It is just before dawn.*

MARY CAHEL. I am thinking we are come to our journey's end, and that this should be the gate of the gaol.

MARY CUSHIN. It is certain it could be no other place. There was surely never in the world such a terrible great height of a wall.

MARY CAHEL. He that was used to the mountain to be closed up inside of that! What call had he to go moonlighting¹ or to bring himself into danger at all?

MARY CUSHIN. It is no wonder a man to grow faint-hearted and he shut away from the light. I never would wonder at all at anything he might be driven to say.

MARY CAHEL. There were good men were gaoled before him never gave in to anyone at all. It is what I am thinking, Mary, he might not have done what they say.

MARY CUSHIN. Sure you heard what the neighbours were calling the time their own boys were brought away. 'It is Denis Cahel,' they were saying, 'that informed against them in the gaol.'

MARY CAHEL. There is nothing that is bad or is wicked but a woman will put it out of her mouth, and she seeing them that belong to her brought away from her sight and her home.

MARY CUSHIN. Terry Fury's mother was saying it, and Pat Ruane's mother and his wife. They came out calling it after me, 'It was Denis swore against them in the gaol!' The sergeant was boasting, they were telling me, the day he came searching Daire-caol, it was he himself got his confession with drink he had brought him in the gaol.

MARY CAHEL. They might have done that, the ruffians, and the boy have no blame on him at all. Why should it be cast up against him, and his wits being out of him with drink?

MARY CUSHIN. If he did give their names up itself, there was maybe no wrong in it at all. Sure it's known to all the village it was Terry that fired the shot.

MARY CAHEL. Stop your mouth now and don't be talking. You haven't any sense worth while. Let the sergeant do his own business with no help from the neighbours at all.

MARY CUSHIN. It was Pat Ruane that tempted them on account of some vengeance of his own. Every creature knows my poor Denis never handled a gun in his life.

MARY CAHEL (*taking from under her cloak a long blue envelope*). I wish we could know what is in the letter they are after sending us through the post. Isn't it a great pity for the two of us to be without learning at all?

MARY CUSHIN. There are some of the neighbours have learning, and you bade me not bring it anear them. It would maybe have told us what way he is or what time he will be quitting the gaol.

MARY CAHEL. There is wonder on me, Mary Cushin, that you would not be content with what I say. It might be they put down in the letter that Denis informed on the rest.

MARY CUSHIN. I suppose it is all we have to do so, to stop here for the opening of the door. It's a terrible long road from Slieve Echtge we were travelling the whole of the night.

MARY CAHEL. There was no other thing for us to do but to come and to give him a warning. What way would he be facing the neighbours, and he to come back to Daire-caol?

MARY CUSHIN. It is likely they will let him go free, Mary,

before many days will be out. What call have they to be keeping him? It is certain they promised him his life.

MARY CAHEL. If they promised him his life, Mary Cushin, he must live it in some other place. Let him never see Daire-caol again, or Daroda or Druimdarod.

MARY CUSHIN. O, Mary, what place will we bring him to, and we driven from the place that we know? What person that is sent among strangers can have one day's comfort on earth?

MARY CAHEL. It is only among strangers, I am thinking, he could be hiding his story at all. It is best for him to go to America, where the people are as thick as grass.

MARY CUSHIN. What way could he go to America and he having no means in his hand? There's himself and myself to make the voyage and the little one-een² at home.

MARY CAHEL. I would sooner to sell the holding³ than to ask for the price paid for blood. There'll be money enough for the two of you to settle your debts and to go.

MARY CUSHIN. And what would yourself be doing and we to go over the sea? It is not among the neighbours you would wish to be ending your days.

MARY CAHEL. I am thinking there is no one would know me in the workhouse at Oughterard. I wonder could I go in there, and I not to give them my name?

MARY CUSHIN. Ah, don't be talking foolishness. What way could I bring the child? Sure he's hardly out of the cradle; he'd be lost out there in the States.

MARY CAHEL. I could bring him into the workhouse, I to give him some other name. You could send for him when you'd be settled or have some place of your own.

MARY CUSHIN. It is very cold at the dawn. It is time for them to open the door. I wish I had brought a potato or a bit of a cake or of bread.

MARY CAHEL. I'm in dread of it being opened and not knowing what will we hear. The night that Denis was taken he had a great cold and a cough.

MARY CUSHIN. I think I hear some person coming. There's a

sound like the rattling of keys. God and His Mother protect us! I'm in dread of being found here at all!

(*The gate is opened, and the* GATEKEEPER *is seen with a lantern in his hand.*)

GATEKEEPER. What are you doing here, women? It's no place to be spending the night time.

MARY CAHEL. It is to speak with my son I am asking, that is gaoled these eight weeks and a day.

GATEKEEPER. If you have no order to visit him it's as good for you to go away home.

MARY CAHEL. I got this letter ere yesterday. It might be it is giving me leave.

GATEKEEPER. If that's so he should be under the doctor, or in the hospital ward.

MARY CAHEL. It's no wonder if he's down with the hardship, for he had a great cough and a cold.

GATEKEEPER. Give me here the letter to read it. Sure it never was opened at all.

MARY CAHEL. Myself and this woman have no learning. We were loth to trust any other one.

GATEKEEPER. It was posted in Galway the twentieth, and this is the last of the month.

MARY CAHEL. We never thought to call at the post office. It was chance brought it to us in the end.

GATEKEEPER (*having read letter*). You poor unfortunate women, don't you know Denis Cahel is dead? You'd a right to come this time yesterday if you wished any last word at all.

MARY CAHEL (*kneeling down*). God and His Mother protect us and have mercy on Denis's soul!

MARY CUSHIN. What is the man after saying? Sure it cannot be Denis is dead?

GATEKEEPER. Dead since the dawn of yesterday, and another man now in his cell. I'll go see who has charge of his clothing if you're wanting to bring it away.

(*He goes in. The dawn has begun to break.*)

MARY CAHEL. There is lasting kindness in Heaven when no kindness is found upon earth. There will surely be mercy found for him, and not the hard judgment of men! But my boy that was best in the world, that never rose a hair of my head, to have died with his name under blemish, and left a great shame on his child! Better for him have killed the whole world than to give any witness at all! Have you no word to say, Mary Cushin? Am I left here to keen him alone?

MARY CUSHIN (*who has sunk on to the step before the door, rocking herself and keening*). Oh, Denis, my heart is broken you to have died with the hard word upon you! My grief you to be alone now that spent so many nights in company!

What way will I be going back through Gort and through Kilbecanty? The people will not be coming out keening you, they will say no prayer for the rest of your soul!

What way will I be the Sunday and I going up the hill to the Mass? Every woman with her own comrade, and Mary Cushin to be walking her lone!

What way will I be the Monday and the neighbours turning their heads from the house? The turf[4] Denis cut lying on the bog, and no well-wisher to bring it to the hearth!

What way will I be in the night time, and none but the dog calling after you? Two women to be mixing a cake, and not a man in the house to break it!

What way will I sow the field, and no man to drive the furrow? The sheaf to be scattered before springtime that was brought together at the harvest!

I would not begrudge you, Denis, and you leaving praises after you. The neighbours keening along with me would be better to me than an estate.

But my grief your name to be blackened in the time of the blackening of the rushes! Your name never to rise up again in the growing time of the year! (*She ceases keening and turns towards the old woman.*) But tell me, Mary, do you think would they give us the body of Denis? I would lay him out with myself only; I would hire some man to dig the grave.

(*The* GATEKEEPER *opens the gate and hands out some clothes.*)

GATEKEEPER. There now is all he brought in with him; the flannels and the shirt and the shoes. It is little they are worth altogether; those mountainy boys do be poor.

MARY CUSHIN. They had a right to give him time to ready himself the day they brought him to the magistrates. He to be wearing his Sunday coat, they would see he was a decent boy. Tell me where will they bury him, the way I can follow after him through the street? There is no other one to show respect to him but Mary Cahel, his mother, and myself.

GATEKEEPER. That is not to be done. He is buried since yesterday in the field that is belonging to the gaol.

MARY CUSHIN. It is a great hardship that to have been done, and not one of his own there to follow after him at all.

GATEKEEPER. Those that break the law must be made an example of. Why would they be laid out like a well behaved man? A long rope and a short burying, that is the order for a man that is hanged.

MARY CUSHIN. A man that was hanged! O Denis, was it they that made an end of you and not the great God at all? His curse and my own curse upon them that did not let you die on the pillow! The curse of God be fulfilled that was on them before they were born! My curse upon them that brought harm on you, and on Terry Fury that fired the shot!

MARY CAHEL (*standing up*). And the other boys, did they hang them along with him, Terry Fury and Pat Ruane that were brought from Daire-caol?

GATEKEEPER. They did not, but set them free twelve hours ago. It is likely you may have passed them in the night time.

MARY CUSHIN. Set free is it, and Denis made an end of? What justice is there in the world at all?

GATEKEEPER. He was taken near the house. They knew his foot-mark. There was no witness given against the rest worth while.

MARY CAHEL. Then the sergeant was lying and the people were lying when they said Denis Cahel had informed in the gaol?

GATEKEEPER. I have no time to be stopping here talking. The judge got no evidence and the law set them free.

(*He goes in and shuts gate after him.*)

MARY CAHEL (*holding out her hands*). Are there any people in the streets at all till I call on them to come hither? Did they ever hear in Galway such a thing to be done, a man to die for his neighbour?

Tell it out in the streets for the people to hear, Denis Cahel from Slieve Echtge is dead. It was Denis Cahel from Daire-caol that died in the place of his neighbour!

It is he was young and comely and strong, the best reaper and the best hurler. It was not a little thing for him to die, and he protecting his neighbour!

Gather up, Mary Cushin, the clothes for your child; they'll be wanted by this one and that one. The boys crossing the sea in the springtime will be craving a thread for a memory.

One word to the judge and Denis was free, they offered him all sorts of riches. They brought him drink in the gaol, and gold, to swear away the life of his neighbour!

Pat Ruane was no good friend to him at all, but a foolish, wild companion; it was Terry Fury knocked a gap in the wall and sent in the calves to our meadow.

Denis would not speak, he shut his mouth, he would never be an informer. It is no lies he would have said at all giving witness against Terry Fury.

I will go through Gort and Kilbecanty and Druim-da-rod and Daroda; I will call to the people and the singers at the fairs to make a great praise for Denis!

The child he left in the house that is shook, it is great will be his boast in his father! All Ireland will have a welcome before him, and all the people in Boston.

I to stoop on a stick through half a hundred years, I will never be tired with praising! Come hither, Mary Cushin, till we'll shout it through the roads, Denis Cahel died for his neighbour!

(*She goes off to the left,* MARY CUSHIN *following her.*)

*Curtain.*

# *The Rising of the Moon*

PERSONS IN THE PLAY

SERGEANT
POLICEMAN X
POLICEMAN B
A RAGGED MAN

SCENE. *Side of a quay in a seaport town. Some posts and chains. A large barrel. Enter three policemen. Moonlight.*

(SERGEANT, *who is older than the others, crosses the stage to right and looks down steps. The others put down a pastepot and unroll a bundle of placards.*)

POLICEMAN B. I think this would be a good place to put up a notice. (*He points to barrel.*)

POLICEMAN X. Better ask him. (*Calls to* SERGEANT.) Will this be a good place for a placard?

(*No answer.*)

POLICEMAN B. Will we put up a notice here on the barrel?

(*No answer.*)

SERGEANT. There's a flight of steps here that leads to the water. This is a place that should be minded well. If he got down here, his friends might have a boat to meet him; they might send it in here from outside.

POLICEMAN B. Would the barrel be a good place to put a notice up?

SERGEANT. It might; you can put it there.

(*They paste the notice up.*)

SERGEANT (*reading it*). Dark hair – dark eyes, smooth face, height five feet five – there's not much to take hold of in that – It's a pity I had no chance of seeing him before he broke out of gaol. They say he's a wonder, that it's he makes all the plans for the whole organisation. There isn't another man in Ireland would have broken gaol the way he did. He must have some friends among the gaolers.

POLICEMAN B. A hundred pounds is little enough for the government to offer for him. You may be sure any man in the force that takes him will get promotion.

SERGEANT. I'll mind this place myself. I wouldn't wonder at all if he came this way. He might come slipping along there (*points to side of quay*), and his friends might be waiting for him there (*points down steps*), and once he got away it's little chance we'd have of finding him; it's maybe under a load of kelp he'd be in a fishing boat, and not one to help a married man that wants it to the reward.

POLICEMAN X. And if we get him itself, nothing but abuse on our heads for it from the people, and maybe from our own relations.

SERGEANT. Well, we have to do our duty in the force. Haven't we the whole country depending on us to keep law and order? It's those that are down would be up and those that are up would be down, if it wasn't for us. Well, hurry on, you have plenty of other places to placard yet, and come back here then to me. You can take the lantern. Don't be too long now. It's very lonesome here with nothing but the moon.

POLICEMAN B. It's a pity we can't stop with you. The government should have brought more police into the town, with *him* in gaol, and at assize time too. Well, good luck to your watch.

(*They go out.*)

SERGEANT (*walks up and down once or twice and looks at placard*). A hundred pounds and promotion sure. There must be a great deal of spending in a hundred pounds. It's a pity some honest man not to be better of that.

(A RAGGED MAN *appears at left and tries to slip past.* SERGEANT *suddenly turns.*)

SERGEANT. Where are you going?

MAN. I'm a poor ballad-singer, your honour. I thought to sell some of these (*holds out bundle of ballads*) to the sailors.

(*He goes on.*)

SERGEANT. Stop! Didn't I tell you to stop? You can't go on there.

MAN. Oh, very well. It's a hard thing to be poor. All the world's against the poor!

SERGEANT. Who are you?

MAN. You'd be as wise as myself if I told you, but I don't mind. I'm one Jimmy Walsh, a ballad-singer.

SERGEANT. Jimmy Walsh? I don't know that name.

MAN. Ah, sure, they know it well enough in Ennis. Were you ever in Ennis, sergeant?

SERGEANT. What brought you here?

MAN. Sure, it's to the assizes I came, thinking I might make a few shillings here or there. It's in the one train with the judges I came.

SERGEANT. Well, if you came so far, you may as well go farther, for you'll walk out of this.

MAN. I will, I will; I'll just go on where I was going.

(*Goes towards steps.*)

SERGEANT. Come back from those steps; no one has leave to pass down them tonight.

MAN. I'll just sit on the top of the steps till I see will some sailor buy a ballad off me that would give me my supper. They do be late going back to the ship. It's often I saw them in Cork carried down the quay in a hand-cart.

SERGEANT. Move on, I tell you. I won't have anyone lingering about the quay tonight.

MAN. Well, I'll go. It's the poor have the hard life! Maybe yourself might like one, sergeant. Here's a good sheet now. (*Turns one over.*) 'Content and a pipe' – that's not much. 'The Peeler and the goat' – you wouldn't like that. 'Johnny Hart' – that's a lovely song.

SERGEANT. Move on.

MAN. Ah, wait till you hear it. (*Sings:*)

There was a rich farmer's daughter lived near the town of Ross;
She courted a Highland soldier, his name was Johnny Hart;

Says the mother to her daughter, 'I'll go distracted mad
If you marry that Highland soldier dressed up in Highland
    plaid.'

SERGEANT. Stop that noise.

(MAN *wraps up his ballads and shuffles towards the steps.*)

SERGEANT. Where are you going?

MAN. Sure you told me to be going, and I am going.

SERGEANT. Don't be a fool. I didn't tell you to go that way; I
told you to go back to the town.

MAN. Back to the town, is it?

SERGEANT (*taking him by the shoulder and shoving him before him*).
Here, I'll show you the way. Be off with you. What are you
stopping for?

MAN (*who has been keeping his eye on the notice, points to it*). I think
I know what you're waiting for, sergeant.

SERGEANT. What's that to you?

MAN. And I know well the man you're waiting for – I know
him well – I'll be going.

(*He shuffles on.*)

SERGEANT. You know him? Come back here. What sort is he?

MAN. Come back is it, sergeant? Do you want to have me
killed?

SERGEANT. Why do you say that?

MAN. Never mind. I'm going. I wouldn't be in your shoes if
the reward was ten times as much. (*Goes on off stage to left.*) Not if
it was ten times as much.

SERGEANT (*rushing after him*). Come back here, come back.
(*Drags him back.*) What sort is he? Where did you see him?

MAN. I saw him in my own place, in the County Clare. I tell
you you wouldn't like to be looking at him. You'd be afraid to be
in the one place with him. There isn't a weapon he doesn't know
the use of, and as to strength, his muscles are as hard as that
board (*slaps barrel*).

SERGEANT. Is he as bad as that?

MAN. He is then.

SERGEANT. Do you tell me so?

MAN. There was a poor man in our place, a sergeant from Ballyvaughan. – It was with a lump of stone he did it.

SERGEANT. I never heard of that.

MAN. And you wouldn't, sergeant. It's not everything that happens gets into the papers. And there was a policeman in plain clothes, too . . . It is in Limerick he was . . . It was after the time of the attack on the police barrack at Kilmallock . . . Moonlight . . . just like this . . . waterside . . . Nothing was known for certain.

SERGEANT. Do you say so? It's a terrible county to belong to.

MAN. That's so, indeed! You might be standing there, looking out that way, thinking you saw him coming up this side of the quay (*points*), and he might be coming up this other side (*points*), and he'd be on you before you knew where you were.

SERGEANT. It's a whole troop of police they ought to put here to stop a man like that.

MAN. But if you'd like me to stop with you, I could be looking down this side. I could be sitting up here on this barrel.

SERGEANT. And you know him well, too?

MAN. I'd know him a mile off, sergeant.

SERGEANT. But you wouldn't want to share the reward?

MAN. Is it a poor man like me, that has to be going the roads and singing in fairs, to have the name on him that he took a reward? But you don't want me. I'll be safer in the town.

SERGEANT. Well, you can stop.

MAN (*getting up on barrel*). All right, sergeant. I wonder, now, you're not tired out, sergeant, walking up and down the way you are.

SERGEANT. If I'm tired I'm used to it.

MAN. You might have hard work before you tonight yet. Take it easy while you can. There's plenty of room up here on the barrel, and you see farther when you're higher up.

SERGEANT. Maybe so. (*Gets up beside him on barrel, facing right. They sit back to back, looking different ways.*) You made me feel a bit queer with the way you talked.

MAN. Give me a match, sergeant (*he gives it and man lights pipe*); take a draw yourself? It'll quiet you. Wait now till I give you a

367

light, but you needn't turn round. Don't take your eye off the quay for the life of you.

SEARGEANT. Never fear, I won't. (*Lights pipe. They both smoke.*) Indeed it's a hard thing to be in the force, out at night and no thanks for it, for all the danger we're in. And it's little we get but abuse from the people, and no choice but to obey our orders, and never asked when a man is sent into danger, if you are a married man with a family.

MAN (*sings*) –

As through the hills I walked to view the hills and shamrock
    plain,
I stood awhile where nature smiles to view the rocks and
    streams,
On a matron fair I fixed my eyes beneath a fertile vale,
And she sang her song it was on the wrong of poor old
    Granuaile.[1]

SERGEANT. Stop that; that's no song to be singing in these times.

MAN. Ah, sergeant, I was only singing to keep my heart up. It sinks when I think of him. To think of us two sitting here, and he creeping up the quay, maybe, to get to us.

SERGEANT. Are you keeping a good lookout?

MAN. I am; and for no reward too. Amn't I the foolish man? But when I saw a man in trouble, I never could help trying to get him out of it. What's that? Did something hit me?

    (*Rubs his heart.*)

SERGEANT (*patting him on the shoulder*). You will get your reward in heaven.

MAN. I know that, I know that, sergeant, but life is precious.

SERGEANT. Well, you can sing if it gives you more courage.

MAN (*sings*) –

Her head was bare, her hands and feet with iron bands were
    bound,
Her pensive strain and plaintive wail mingles with the
    evening gale,

And the song she sang with mournful air, I am old
   Granuaile.
Her lips so sweet that monarchs kissed . . .

SERGEANT. That's not it . . . 'Her gown she wore was stained
with gore.' . . . That's it – you missed that.

MAN. You're right, sergeant, so it is; I missed it. (*Repeats
line.*) But to think of a man like you knowing a song like
that.

SERGEANT. There's many a thing a man might know and
might not have any wish for.

MAN. Now, I daresay, sergeant, in your youth, you used to be
sitting up on a wall, the way you are sitting up on this barrel
now, and the other lads beside you, and you singing
'Granuaile'? . . .

SERGEANT. I did then.

MAN. And the 'Shan Van Vocht'? . . .[2]

SERGEANT. I did then.

MAN. And the 'Green on the Cape'?

SERGEANT. That was one of them.

MAN. And maybe the man you are watching for tonight used
to be sitting on the wall, when he was young, and singing those
same songs . . . It's a queer world . . .

SERGEANT. Whisht! . . . I think I see something coming . . .
It's only a dog.

MAN. And isn't it a queer world? . . . Maybe it's one of the
boys you used to be singing with that time you will be arresting
today or tomorrow, and sending into the dock . . .

SERGEANT. That's true indeed.

MAN. And maybe one night, after you had been singing, if the
other boys had told you some plan they had, some plan to free
the country, you might have joined with them . . . and maybe it
is you might be in trouble now.

SERGEANT. Well, who knows but I might? I had a great spirit
in those days.

MAN. It's a queer world, sergeant, and it's little any mother
knows when she sees her child creeping on the floor what might

369

happen to it before it has gone through its life, or who will be who in the end.

SERGEANT. That's a queer thought now, and a true thought. Wait now till I think it out . . . If it wasn't for the sense I have, and for my wife and family, and for me joining the force the time I did, it might be myself now would be after breaking gaol and hiding in the dark, and it might be him that's hiding in the dark and that got out of gaol would be sitting up here where I am on this barrel . . . And it might be myself would be creeping up trying to make my escape from himself, and it might be himself would be keeping the law, and myself would be breaking it, and myself would be trying to put a bullet in his head, or to take up a lump of stone the way you said he did . . . no, that myself did . . . Oh! (*Gasps. After a pause*) What's that? (*Grasps man's arm.*)

MAN (*jumps off barrel and listens, looking out over water*). It's nothing, sergeant.

SERGEANT. I thought it might be a boat. I had a notion there might be friends of his coming about the quays with a boat.

MAN. Sergeant, I am thinking it was with the people you were, and not with the law you were, when you were a young man.

SERGEANT. Well, if I was foolish then, that time's gone.

MAN. Maybe, sergeant, it comes into your head sometimes, in spite of your belt and your tunic, that it might have been as well for you to have followed Granuaile.

SERGEANT. It's no business of yours what I think.

MAN. Maybe, sergeant, you'll be on the side of the country yet.

SERGEANT (*gets off barrel*). Don't talk to me like that. I have my duties and I know them. (*Looks round.*) That was a boat; I hear the oars.

(*Goes to the steps and looks down.*)

MAN (*sings*) –

> O, then, tell me, Shawn O'Farrell,
>     Where the gathering is to be.
> In the old spot by the river
>     Right well known to you and me!

SERGEANT. Stop that! Stop that, I tell you!

MAN (*sings louder*)

> One word more, for signal token,
>     Whistle up the marching tune,
> With your pike upon your shoulder,
>     At the Rising of the Moon.

SERGEANT. If you don't stop that, I'll arrest you.

(*A whistle from below answers, repeating the air.*)

SERGEANT. That's a signal. (*Stands between him and steps.*) You must not pass this way ... Step farther back ... Who are you? You are no ballad-singer.

MAN. You needn't ask who I am; that placard will tell you.

(*Points to placard.*)

SERGEANT. You are the man I am looking for.

MAN (*takes off hat and wig.* SERGEANT *seizes them*). I am. There's a hundred pounds on my head. There is a friend of mine below in a boat. He knows a safe place to bring me to.

SERGEANT (*looking still at hat and wig*). It's a pity! It's a pity! You deceived me. You deceived me well.

MAN. I am a friend of Granuaile. There is a hundred pounds on my head.

SERGEANT. It's a pity, it's a pity!

MAN. Will you let me pass, or must I make you let me?

SERGEANT. I am in the force. I will not let you pass.

MAN. I thought to do it with my tongue. (*Puts hand in breast.*) What is that?

(*Voice of* POLICEMAN X *outside*). Here, this is where we left him.

SERGEANT. It's my comrades coming.

MAN. You won't betray me ... the friend of Granuaile. (*Slips behind barrel.*)

(*Voice of* POLICEMAN B). That was the last of the placards.

POLICEMAN X (*as they come in*). If he makes his escape it won't be unknown he'll make it.

(SERGEANT *puts hat and wig behind his back.*)

POLICEMAN B. Did anyone come this way?

SERGEANT (*after a pause*). No one.

POLICEMAN B. No one at all?

SERGEANT. No one at all.

POLICEMAN B. We had no orders to go back to the station; we can stop along with you.

SERGEANT. I don't want you. There is nothing for you to do here.

POLICEMAN B. You bade us to come back here and keep watch with you.

SERGEANT. I'd sooner be alone. Would any man come this way and you making all that talk? It is better the place to be quiet.

POLICEMAN B. Well, we'll leave you the lantern anyhow.

(*Hands it to him.*)

SERGEANT. I don't want it. Bring it with you.

POLICEMAN B. You might want it. There are clouds coming up and you have the darkness of the night before you yet. I'll leave it over here on the barrel. (*Goes to barrel.*)

SERGEANT. Bring with you I tell you. No more talk.

POLICEMAN B. Well, I thought it might be a comfort to you. I often think when I have it in my hand and can be flashing it about into every dark corner (*doing so*) that it's the same as being beside the fire at home, and the bits of bogwood blazing up now and again.

(*Flashes it about, now on the barrel, now on* SERGEANT.)

SERGEANT (*furious*). Be off the two of you, yourselves and your lantern!

(*They go out.* MAN *comes from behind barrel. He and* SERGEANT *stand looking at one another.*)

SERGEANT. What are you waiting for?

MAN. For my hat, of course, and my wig. You wouldn't wish me to get my death of cold?

(SERGEANT *gives them.*)

MAN (*going towards steps*). Well, goodnight, comrade, and thank you. You did me a good turn tonight, and I'm obliged to you. Maybe I'll be able to do as much for you when the small rise up and the big fall down . . . when we all change places at the Rising (*waves his hand and disappears*) of the Moon.

SERGEANT (*turning his back to audience and reading placard*). A hundred pounds reward! A hundred pounds! (*Turns towards audience.*) I wonder, now, am I as great a fool as I think I am?

*Curtain.*

# The Workhouse Ward

## Persons in the Play

MIKE MCINERNEY  
MICHAEL MISKELL  } *paupers*  
MRS DONOHUE, *a countrywoman*

SCENE. *A ward in Cloon Workhouse. The two old men in their beds.*

MICHAEL MISKELL. Isn't it a hard case, Mike McInerney, myself and yourself to be left here in the bed, and it the feast day of Saint Colman,[1] and the rest of the ward attending on the Mass.

MIKE MCINERNEY. Is it sitting up by the hearth you are wishful to be, Michael Miskell, with cold in the shoulders and with speckled shins? Let you rise up so, and you well able to do it, not like myself that has pains the same as tin-tacks within in my inside.

MICHAEL MISKELL. If you have pains within in your inside there is no one can see it or know of it the way they can see my own knees that are swelled up with the rheumatism, and my hands that are twisted in ridges the same as an old cabbage stalk. It is easy to be talking about soreness and about pains, and they maybe not to be in it at all.

MIKE MCINERNEY. To open me to analyse me you would know what sort of a pain and a soreness I have in my heart and in my chest. But I'm not one like yourself to be cursing and praying and tormenting the time the nuns are at hand, thinking to get a bigger share than myself of nourishment and of the milk.

MICHAEL MISKELL. That's the way you do be picking at me and faulting me. I had a share and a good share in my early time, and it's well you know that, and the both of us reared in Skehanagh.

MIKE MCINERNEY. You may say that, indeed, we are both of us reared in Skehanagh. Little wonder you to have good nourishment the time we were both rising, and you bringing away my rabbits out of the snare.

MICHAEL MISKELL. And you didn't bring away my own eels, I suppose, I was after spearing in the Turlough? Selling them to the nuns in the convent you did, and letting on they to be your own. For you were always a cheater and a schemer, grabbing every earthly thing for your own profit.

MIKE MCINERNEY. And you were no grabber yourself, I suppose, till your land and all you had grabbed wore away from you!

MICHAEL MISKELL. If I lost it itself, it was through the crosses I met with and I going through the world. I never was a rambler and a cardplayer like yourself, Mike McInerney, that ran through all and lavished it unknown to your mother!

MIKE MCINERNEY. Lavished it, is it? And if I did was it you yourself led me to lavish it or some other one? It is on my own floor I would be today and in the face of my family, but for the misfortune I had to be put with a bad next door neighbour that was yourself. What way did my means go from me is it? Spending on fencing, spending on walls, making up gates, putting up doors, that would keep your hens and your ducks from coming in through starvation on my floor, and every four footed beast you had from preying and trespassing on my oats and my mangolds[2] and my little lock[3] of hay!

MICHAEL MISKELL. O to listen to you! And I striving to please you and to be kind to you and to close my ears to the abuse you would be calling and letting out of your mouth. To trespass on your crops is it? It's little temptation there was for my poor beasts to ask to cross the mering.[4] My God Almighty! What had you but a little corner of a field!

MIKE MCINERNEY. And what do you say to my garden that

your two pigs had destroyed on me the year of the big tree being knocked, and they making gaps in the wall.

MICHAEL MISKELL. Ah, there does be a great deal of gaps knocked in a twelvemonth. Why wouldn't they be knocked by the thunder, the same as the tree, or some storm that came up from the west?

MIKE McINERNEY. It was the west wind, I suppose, that devoured my green cabbage? And that rooted up my Champion potatoes? And that ate the gooseberries themselves from off the bush?

MICHAEL MISKELL. What are you saying? The two quietest pigs ever I had, no way wicked and well ringed. They were not ten minutes in it. It would be hard for them eat strawberries in that time, let alone gooseberries that's full of thorns.

MIKE McINERNEY. They were not quiet, but very ravenous pigs you had that time, as active as a fox they were, killing my young ducks. Once they had blood tasted you couldn't stop them.

MICHAEL MISKELL. And what happened myself the fair day of Esserkelly, the time I was passing your door? Two brazened dogs that rushed out and took a piece of me. I never was the better of it or of the start I got, but wasting from then till now!

MIKE McINERNEY. Thinking you were a wild beast they did, that had made his escape out of the travelling show, with the red eyes of you and the ugly face of you, and the two crooked legs of you that wouldn't hardly stop a pig in a gap. Sure any dog that had any life in it at all would be roused and stirred seeing the like of you going the road!

MICHAEL MISKELL. I did well taking out a summons against you that time. It is a great wonder you not to have been bound over through your lifetime, but the laws of England is queer.

MIKE McINERNEY. What ailed me that I did not summons yourself after you stealing away the clutch of eggs I had in the barrel, and I away in Ardrahan searching out a clocking hen.

MICHAEL MISKELL. To steal your eggs is it? Is that what you are saying now? (*Holds up his hands.*) The Lord is in heaven, and Peter and the saints, and yourself that was in Ardrahan that day put a hand on them as soon as myself! Isn't it a bad story for me to be wearing out my days beside you the same as a spancelled[5] goat. Chained I am and tethered I am to a man that is ransacking his mind for lies!

MIKE MCINERNEY. If it is a bad story for you, Michael Miskell, it is a worse story again for myself. A Miskell to be next and near me through the whole of the four quarters of the year. I never heard there to be any great name on the Miskells as there was on my own race and name.

MICHAEL MISKELL. You didn't, is it? Well, you could hear it if you had but ears to hear it. Go across to Lisheen Crannagh and down to the sea and to Newtown Lynch and the mills of Duras and you'll find a Miskell, and as far as Dublin!

MIKE MCINERNEY. What signifies Crannagh and the mills of Duras? Look at all my own generations that are buried at the Seven Churches. And how many generations of the Miskells are buried in it? Answer me that!

MICHAEL MISKELL. I tell you but for the wheat that was to be sowed there would be more side cars and more common cars at my father's funeral (God rest his soul!) than at any funeral ever left your own door. And as to my mother, she was a Cuffe from Claregalway, and it's she had the purer blood!

MIKE MCINERNEY. And what do you say to the banshee?[6] Isn't she apt to have knowledge of the ancient race? Was ever she heard to screech or to cry for the Miskells? Or the Cuffes from Claregalway? She was not, but for the six families, the Hyneses, the Foxes, the Faheys, the Dooleys, the McInerneys. It is of the nature of the McInerneys she is I am thinking, crying them the same as a king's children.

MICHAEL MISKELL. It is a pity the banshee not to be crying for yourself at this minute, and giving you a warning to quit your lies and your chat and your arguing and your contrary ways; for there is no one under the rising sun could stand you. I tell you you are not behaving as in the presence of the Lord!

MIKE MCINERNEY. Is it wishful for my death you are? Let it come and meet me now and welcome so long as it will part me from yourself! And I say, and I would kiss the book on it, I to have one request only to be granted, and I leaving it in my will, it is what I would request, nine furrows of the field, nine ridges of the hills, nine waves of the ocean to be put between your grave and my own grave the time we will be laid in the ground!

MICHAEL MISKELL. Amen to that! Nine ridges, is it? No, but let the whole ridge of the world separate us till the Day of Judgment! I would not be laid anear you at the Seven Churches, I to get Ireland without a divide!

MIKE MCINERNEY. And after that again! I'd sooner than ten pound in my hand, I to know that my shadow and my ghost will not be knocking about with your shadow and your ghost, and the both of us waiting our time. I'd sooner be delayed in Purgatory! Now, have you anything to say?

MICHAEL MISKELL. I have everything to say, if I had but the time to say it!

MIKE MCINERNEY (*sitting up*). Let me up out of this till I'll choke you!

MICHAEL MISKELL. You scolding pauper you!

MIKE MCINERNEY (*shaking his fist at him*). Wait a while!

MICHAEL MISKELL (*shaking his fist*). Wait a while yourself!

(MRS DONOHOE *comes in with a parcel. She is a countrywoman with a frilled cap and a shawl. She stands still a minute. The two old men lie down and compose themselves.*)

MRS DONOHOE. They bade me come up here by the stair. I never was in this place at all. I don't know am I right. Which now of the two of ye is Mike McInerney?

MIKE MCINERNEY. Who is it is calling me by my name?

MRS DONOHOE. Sure amn't I your sister, Honor McInerney that was, that is now Honor Donohoe.

MIKE MCINERNEY. So you are, I believe. I didn't know you till you pushed anear me. It is time indeed for you to come see me, and I in this place five year or more. Thinking me to be no credit to you, I suppose, among that tribe of the Donohoes. I

377

wonder they to give you leave to come ask am I living yet or dead?

MRS DONOHOE. Ah, sure, I buried the whole string of them. Himself was the last to go. (*Wipes her eyes.*) The Lord be praised he got a fine natural death. Sure we must go through our crosses. And he got a lovely funeral; it would delight you to hear the priest reading the Mass. My poor John Donohoe! A nice clean man, you couldn't but be fond of him. Very severe on the tobacco he was, but he wouldn't touch the drink.

MIKE MCINERNEY. And is it in Curranroe you are living yet?

MRS DONOHOE. It is so. He left all to myself. But it is a lonesome thing the head of a house to have died!

MIKE MCINERNEY. I hope that he has left you a nice way of living?

MRS DONOHOE. Fair enough, fair enough. A wide lovely house I have; a few acres of grass land ... the grass does be very sweet that grows among the stones. And as to the sea, there is something from it every day of the year, a handful of periwinkles to make kitchen, or cockles maybe. There is many a thing in the sea is not decent, but cockles is fit to put before the Lord!

MIKE MCINERNEY. You have all that! And you without ere a man in the house?

MRS DONOHOE. It is what I am thinking, yourself might come and keep me company. It is no credit to me a brother of my own to be in this place at all.

MIKE MCINERNEY. I'll go with you! Let me out of this! It is the name of the McInerneys will be rising on every side!

MRS DONOHOE. I don't know. I was ignorant of you being kept to the bed.

MIKE MCINERNEY. I am not kept to it, but maybe an odd time when there is a colic rises up within me. My stomach always gets better the time there is a change in the moon. I'd like well to draw anear you. My heavy blessing on you, Honor Donohoe, for the hand you have held out to me this day.

MRS DONOHOE. Sure you could be keeping the fire in, and stirring the pot with the bit of Indian meal for the hens, and milking the goat and taking the tacklings off the donkey at the door; and maybe putting out the cabbage plants in their time. For when the old man died the garden died.

MIKE MCINERNEY. I could to be sure, and be cutting the potatoes for seed. What luck could there be in a place and a man not to be in it? Is that now a suit of clothes you have brought with you?

MRS DONOHOE. It is so, the way you will be tasty coming in among the neighbours at Curranroe.

MIKE MCINERNEY. My joy you are! It is well you earned me! Let me up out of this! (*He sits up and spreads out the clothes and tries on coat.*) That now is a good frieze coat . . . and a hat in the fashion . . . (*He puts on hat.*)

MICHAEL MISKELL (*alarmed*). And is it going out of this you are, Mike McInerney?

MIKE MCINERNEY. Don't you hear I am going? To Curranroe I am going. Going I am to a place where I will get every good thing!

MICHAEL MISKELL. And is it to leave me here after you you will?

MIKE MCINERNEY (*in a rising chant*). Every good thing! The goat and the kid are there, the sheep and the lamb are there, the cow does be running and she coming to be milked! Ploughing and seed sowing, blossom at Christmas time, the cuckoo speaking through the dark days of the year! Ah, what are you talking about? Wheat high in hedges, no talk about the rent! Salmon in the rivers as plenty as turf! Spending and getting and nothing scarce! Sport and pleasure, and music on the strings! Age will go from me and I will be young again. Geese and turkeys for the hundreds and drink for the whole world!

MICHAEL MISKELL. Ah, Mike, is it truth you are saying, you to go from me and to leave me with rude people and with townspeople, and with people of every parish in the union,[7] and they having no respect for me or no wish for me at all!

MIKE MCINERNEY. Whist now and I'll leave you . . . my pipe (*hands it over*); and I'll engage it is Honor Donohoe won't refuse to be sending you a few ounces of tobacco an odd time, and neighbours coming to the fair in November or in the month of May.

MICHAEL MISKELL. Ah, what signifies tobacco? All that I am craving is the talk. There to be no one at all to say out to whatever thought might be rising in my innate mind! To be lying here and no conversible person in it would be the abomination of misery!

MIKE McINERNEY. Look now, Honor ... It is what I often heard said, two to be better than one ... Sure if you had an old trouser was full of holes ... or a skirt ... wouldn't you put another in under it that might be as tattered as itself, and the two of them together would make some sort of a decent show?

MRS DONOHOE. Ah, what are you saying? There is no holes in that suit I brought you now, but as sound it is as the day I spun it for himself.

MIKE McINERNEY. It is what I am thinking, Honor ... I do be weak an odd time ... any load I would carry, it preys upon my side ... and this man does be weak an odd time with the swelling in his knees ... but the two of us together it's not likely it is at the one time we would fail. Bring the both of us with you, Honor, and the height of the castle of luck on you, and the both of us together will make one good hardy man!

MRS DONOHOE. I'd like my job! Is it queer in the head you are grown asking me to bring in a stranger off the road?

MICHAEL MISKELL. I am not, ma'am, but an old neighbour I am. If I had forecasted this asking I would have asked it myself. Michael Miskell I am, that was in the next house to you in Skehanagh!

MRS DONOHUE. For pity's sake! Michael Miskell is it? That's worse again. Yourself and Mike that never left fighting and scolding and attacking one another! Sparring at one another like two young pups you were, and threatening one another after like two grown dogs!

MIKE McINERNEY. All the quarrelling was ever in the place it was myself did it. Sure his anger rises fast and goes away like the wind. Bring him out with myself now, Honor Donohoe, and God bless you.

Mrs Donohoe. Well, then, I will not bring him out, and I will not bring yourself out, and you not to learn better sense. Are you making yourself ready to come?

Mike McInerney. I am thinking, maybe ... it is a mean thing for a man that is shivering into seventy years to go changing from place to place.

Mrs Donohue. Well, take your luck or leave it. All I asked was to save you from the hurt and the harm of the year.

Mike McInerney. Bring the both of us with you or I will not stir out of this.

Mrs Donohoe. Give me back my fine suit so (*begins gathering up the clothes*), till I'll go look for a man of my own!

Mike McInerney. Let you go so, as you are so unnatural and so disobliging, and look for some man of your own, God help him! For I will not go with you at all!

Mrs Dònohoe. It is too much time I lost with you, and dark night waiting to overtake me on the road. Let the two of you stop together, and the back of my hand to you. It is I will leave you there the same as God left the Jews!

(*She goes out. The old men lie down and are silent for a moment.*)

Michael Miskell. Maybe the house is not so wide as what she says.

Mike McInerney. Why wouldn't it be wide?

Michael Miskell. Ah, there does be a good deal of middling poor houses down by the sea.

Mike McInerney. What would you know about wide houses? Whatever sort of a house you had yourself it was too wide for the provision you had into it.

Michael Miskell. Whatever provision I had in my house it was wholesome provision and natural provision. Herself and her periwinkles! Periwinkles is a hungry sort of food.

Mike McInerney. Stop your impudence and your chat or it will be the worse for you. I'd bear with my own father and mother as long as any man would, but if they'd vex me I would give them the length of a rope as soon as another!

Michael Miskell. I would never ask at all to go eating periwinkles.

MIKE MCINERNEY (*sitting up*). Have you anyone to fight me?

MICHAEL MISKELL (*whimpering*). I have not, only the Lord!

MIKE MCINERNEY. Let you leave putting insults on me so, and death picking at you!

MICHAEL MISKELL. Sure I am saying nothing at all to displease you. It is why I wouldn't go eating periwinkles, I'm in dread I might swallow the pin.

MIKE MCINERNEY. Who in the world wide is asking you to eat them? You're as tricky as a fish in the full tide!

MICHAEL MISKELL. Tricky is it! Oh, my curse and the curse of the four and twenty men upon you!

MIKE MCINERNEY. That the worm may chew you from skin to marrow bone! (*Seizes his pillow.*)

MICHAEL MISKELL (*seizing his own pillow*). I'll leave my death on you, you scheming vagabone!

MIKE MCINERNEY. By cripes! I'll pull out your pin feathers! (*Throwing pillow.*)

MICHAEL MISKELL (*throwing pillow*). You tyrant! You big bully you!

MIKE MCINERNEY (*throwing pillow and seizing mug*). Take this so, you stobbing[8] ruffian you!

> (*They throw all within their reach at one another, mugs, prayer books, pipes, etc.*)

*Curtain.*

# *Grania*

## Persons in the Play

GRANIA
FINN
DIARMUID
TWO YOUNG MEN

## Act I

SCENE. *The scene is laid at Almhuin¹ in Ireland. Time, evening. Inside a richly decorated tent; a fire in brazier centre, a high candlestick on each side; a table with round loaves and wine. An opening at each side of tent.* FINN *is leading in* GRANIA; *she is wearing a golden dress and jewels. Music and joyous shouts are heard outside.*

FINN. My five hundred welcomes to you, Grania, coming into Almhuin.

GRANIA. I thank you, Finn.

FINN. Who would be welcome if it was not the King of Ireland's daughter, that will be my wife tomorrow?

GRANIA. Your people that were outside and on the road lighted all the district with fires as I came.

FINN. We would have been better prepared if your coming was not so sudden at the last. You did not come too soon, that is a thing that could not happen. But the big house of Almhuin will not be set out fit for you till tomorrow, and it is in the tents of our captains you and your company must be sheltered tonight.

GRANIA. It was my father, before going to Lochlann, said he must leave me in a husband's care.

FINN. Who would protect you if I would not?

GRANIA. I am sure of that. Are you not the best of all the world's big men?

383

FINN. They told me you could have made great marriages, not coming to me?

GRANIA. My father was for the King of Foreign, but I said I would take my own road.

FINN. He has great riches and a great name.

GRANIA. I would have been afraid going to him, hearing talk of him as so dark and wild looking, and his shield tusked with the tusks of a boar.

FINN. You were not in dread coming to me, and you so delicate and so cherished?

GRANIA. I had an old veneration for you, hearing all my lifetime that you are so gentle to women and to dogs and to little children, and you wrestling with the powers of the world and being so hard in war.

FINN. It would be strange any person not to be gentle with you.

GRANIA. And another thing. I had no wish to go travelling forth and hither to strange countries and by strange seas. I have no mind for going through crosses. I would sooner pass my life at Almhuin, where I ever and always heard there are wide white halls and long tables, and poets and fine company.

FINN. Your father has a good house.

GRANIA. There was little to listen to but my father planning the wars in Lochlann. There was no pleasant stir in it, unless what there might be in myself.

FINN. It may be you will tire of Almhuin itself after a while.

GRANIA. There will be good company. I have heard talk of the men and the captains of the Fenians, of Oisin and Oscar and Goll, that came to meet me a while ago.

FINN. The man you will think most of is not with them today, that is my own kinsman, Diarmuid.

GRANIA. I heard of him often. They say him to be the best lover of women in the whole world, and the most daring in the war.

FINN. He has a good name from gentle and simple, from the big man and from the poor. Those even that have no call to him, cannot but love him.

GRANIA. It was he fought seven days and seven nights with the terrible wild ox upon the mountains.

384

FINN. Any time I am tired or fretted, all he could do for me he would not think it enough.

GRANIA. Where is he at this time, that he did not come to meet me with the rest?

FINN. I sent him to a far lonesome hill where I have a secret store of treasures and of jewels. It is right there should be a good man to guard them upon the road. It is for you he is bringing them, he will be here within a short while.

GRANIA. It is likely it is a man of that sort a woman would find it easy to love.

FINN. Did you ever give a thought to any man in the way of love?

GRANIA. I did – at least I think I did – but that was a long time ago.

FINN. Who was he? Did he belong to your own place?

GRANIA. I do not know. I never heard his name – but I saw him.

FINN. Did you speak to him?

GRANIA. No, he was but as if a shadow, that came for a moment and was gone.

FINN. Tell me all the story.

GRANIA. They had been hunting – there were a great many strangers. I was bade keep away from the hall. I was looking from a high window – then there was a great outcry in the yard – the hounds were fighting, the hounds the strange men had brought with them. One of them made as if to attack a little dog I owned at the time – I screamed out at the hounds. Then a young man ran out and beat them away, and he held up my little dog to me, laughing, and his cap fell off from his head.

FINN. Did they not tell you his name?

GRANIA. I was shy to ask them, and I never saw him again. But my thoughts went with him for a good while, and sometimes he came through my dreams. – Is that now what you would call love?

FINN. Indeed, I think it is little at all you know of it.

GRANIA. I heard often in the stories of people that were in pain and under locks[2] through love. But I think they are but foolishness. There was one of a lover was made go through a fire for his sweetheart's sake, and came out shivering. And one that climbed to his darling's window by one golden thread of her hair.

FINN. There are many such tales and there are more in the making, for it is likely the tearing and vexing of love will be known so long as men are hot-blooded and women have a coaxing way.

GRANIA. I asked the old people what love was, and they gave me no good news of it at all. Three sharp blasts of the wind they said it was, a white blast of delight and a grey blast of discontent and a third blast of jealousy that is red.

FINN. That red blast is the wickedest of the three.

GRANIA. I would never think jealousy to be so bad a smart.

FINN. It is a bad thing for whoever knows it. If love is to lie down on a bed of stinging nettles, jealousy is to waken upon a wasp's nest.

GRANIA. But the old people say more again about love. They say there is no good thing to be gained without hardship and pain, such as a child to be born, or a long day's battle won. And I think it might be a pleasing thing to have a lover that would go through fire for your sake.

FINN. I knew enough of the heat of love in my time, and I am very glad to have done with it now, and to be safe from its torments and its whip and its scourge.

GRANIA. It being so bad a thing, why, I wonder, do so many go under its sway? That should be a good master that has so many servants and is so well obeyed.

FINN. We do not take it up of ourselves but it sweeps us away before it, and asks no leave. When that blast comes upon us, we are but feathers whirled before it with the dust.

GRANIA. It is a good thing surely, that I will never know an unhappy, unquiet love, but only love for you that will be by my side forever. (*A loud peal of laughter is heard outside.*) What is that laughter? There is in it some mocking sound.

FINN (*going to the door*). It is not laughter now – it is a merry outcry as if around some very welcome friend. It is Diarmuid that is come back.

(DIARMUID *comes in.* GRANIA *shrinks back from him.*)

DIARMUID. I am here, Finn, my master.

FINN. What way are you, Diarmuid? There is some wound upon your arm.

DIARMUID. It is a wound I was given on the road. But all you sent me for is safe.

FINN. I knew you would mind them well. But was that hurt cared and eased?

DIARMUID. It is nothing to signify. I drove the robbers off. All is safe. They are bringing the bags in here.

(*Two fair-haired young men come in two or three times laying bags on the floor during the next sentences.*)

I will stop here and mind them through the night time. I would sooner keep charge until you will open them for the wedding on the morrow. I will sit there by the hearth. They are jewels would be coveted by the witches of the lakes, or the sea-women sporting among the golden ribs and the wreckage of the ships of Greece.

FINN. It is to a woman worthy of them they are to be given.

DIARMUID. I am sure of that, indeed, and she being worthy to wed with you.

FINN. Come here, Grania, until I make you acquainted with the branch and the blossom of our young men.

GRANIA (*coming forward*). It is – who is it?

(*She gives a little cry and goes back a step as* DIARMUID *takes off his cap.*)

FINN. What is it ails you, Grania, that you are turned to be so wild and so shy?

GRANIA. It is that – that – he is wounded.

FINN. You have lost your talk on the road, Diarmuid, you, that were always so ready to string words and praises for comely young women.

DIARMUID. I had no time to wash away the dust and the sweat. I did not know Grania was in the place. You should have forewarned me.

FINN. He thinks you are vexed because he is not settled out in handsome clothes.

GRANIA. It is strange – it is all strange to me – I will get used to meeting strangers. Another time – in a very short while – my voice will be more steady – my heart will leave starting.

FINN. You will get courage knowing you are a queen. Where, Diarmuid, is the crown I bade you bring? It is not the high crown of pearls from the far Indies I want, but the thin golden crown shaped like the rising sun, that I thought of late would be never used, and that I had been keeping till I met with my own queen and my bride.

DIARMUID. It is wrapped about with tanned marten skins and bound with purple thongs.

FINN (*unwrapping it*). Come to me, Grania. (*He puts the crown on her head.*) Courage will come into your heart now, with this sign and token of your estate.

GRANIA. I am tired. It is weighty on my head – it is time for me to be with myself only. I have seen too much company since morning.

FINN. That is so, and I am much to blame, not taking better thought for you. Come to your women, they will bring you to your tent that is close at hand. You have travelled a long strange road, and tomorrow is your wedding day.

GRANIA. Tomorrow? Could it not be put off for a while? This is but May, and no great luck in the moon. There is more luck in the last moon of July – or the first new moon after it. Put it off until that time.

FINN. That cannot be. Your father looked to me to put you in your right place without delay. You must be my wife tomorrow.

GRANIA. Must it be tomorrow?

FINN. All the armies are gathered together for that, and the feasts are ready. You yourself will be ready when you have taken your sleep through the night time.

GRANIA. Sleep – sleep – yes, I will go sleep if I can.

FINN. Diarmuid is tired as well as you.

DIARMUID. I have no desire to sleep. I will sit and watch here till the dawn.

(*He sits down by the hearth, pulling cloak over his head. GRANIA turns back to look at him from the door as FINN takes her out. After a moment FINN comes back and sits near fire.*)

FINN. Tell me, Diarmuid, is it right that a man past the mering of age should give any thought to love?

DIARMUID. It is right for a man with a great burden of care upon him to have a place of his own where he can let it fall from him. And what is a home or a house without a wife and companion at the hearth?

FINN. That is so, and that is what I had in mind at the time this marriage was settled and pressed on, for the good of Ireland and my own good. But as to love, that is another thing.

DIARMUID. It is another thing, sure enough.

FINN. I thought myself on the far side of it and of its trouble and its joy. But now this young girl has come to me, so fearless, so mannerly, so plain and simple in her talk, it seems to me I would wed with her, and she not a king's daughter but a poor girl carrying the bag. (DIARMUID *nods, but is silent.*) It is not the one way with you and me, Diarmuid, for many women have offered you their beauty and themselves; but as for myself, there is no one I ever gave my heart to but was swept from me in some hard way. And this is come like good wine to the mouth that was filled for a long while with grey mist and rain. And indeed, indeed my heart leaps up with her. Is not that natural, Diarmuid, and she so well reared and so young?

DIARMUID. It is natural, indeed.

FINN. Would you not say her to be well shaped and of good blood and wise?

DIARMUID. She is all that, indeed.

FINN. It is not often I have known you to be so begrudging of praise.

DIARMUND. What call have I to be praising her? I could tell you no more than you knew before, through your own heart and through your eyes.

FINN. But, tell me this, now. Is she that is so airy and beautiful any sort of a fitting wife for me?

DIARMUID. You are brave and she will put her pride in you. You are the best of all, and she is a woman would only join with the best.

FINN. With all that, I would be well pleased if I could change my years for yours, Diarmuid. I would give you in their place all the riches I have ever won.

DIARMUID. Such a woman will be a right head for Almhuin. She is used to a king's house, she will be open-handed, and open-hearted along with that.

FINN. I think, indeed, she will be a right wife for me, and loyal. And it is well that is so, for if ever any man should come between her thoughts and mine I would not leave him living, but would give him the sorrow of death.

DIARMUID. There is no good lover in Ireland but would do the same, and his wife or his sweetheart failing him.

FINN. Yet, in the end there are but few do it; for the thought of men that have passed their midday is mixed with caution and with wisdom and the work they have in hand, or weakness is gaining on their limbs. And as for youngsters, they do not know how to love, because there is always some tomorrow's love possible in the shadow of the love of today. It is only the old it goes through and through entirely, because they know all the last honey of the summer time has come to its ferment in their cup, and that there is no new summer coming to meet them for ever. And so (*he gets up and stirs fire*) they think to carry that cup through life and death and even beyond the grave. But can I bring this young girl to be satisfied with that one love?

DIARMUID. There is no one among the men of Ireland can stand against your will. It should be easy for you to keep a woman faithful.

FINN. Yet the storytellers make out that love is the disturber; that where it is on the road it is hard to be sure of any woman at all or any friend.

DIARMUND. It is I can give you out an answer to that. My master, you are sure of me.

FINN. I am sure of you, indeed, and it is many a time you put your life in danger for my sake.

DIARMUID (*standing up*). I am your son and your servant always, and your friend. And now, at this marriage time, I will ask one asking.

FINN. Who would get his desire and you not to get it?

DIARMUID. I am tired of courts and of sports and of wars where we gain the day always. I want some hard service to put my hand to. There are the dark men of Foreign, their King has laid it down he will come and master Ireland. Let me go out now and put him down in his own country.

FINN. I will give you leave, but not till after the wedding moon.

DIARMUID. No, but let me go now, this very night, at the brink of dawn.

FINN. No, but stop near me. You are more to me than any of my comrades or my friends.

DIARMUID. It is a strange thing, the first asking I have made, you have refused me.

FINN. Go then and take your own way, and my blessing go with you.

DIARMUID. I thank you for that leave.

FINN. But you will be tired out before morning. You have been on the road these three days, you got no sleep last night.

DIARMUID. I am drowsy enough and tired, but I will go.

FINN. Lie down over there upon the otter skins. I will sit here by the fire and keep a watch in your place.

DIARMUID. Make a promise then, to wake me at the first whitening of the dawn.

FINN. I will do that.

(DIARMUID *lies down on skins and sleeps.* FINN *looks at him a moment and covers him, then puts out candles and sits down where* DIARMUID *had been sitting, pulling his cloak over his head. Silence a moment,* GRANIA *comes in.*)

GRANIA (*in a low voice*). Diarmuid! (*No answer.*) Diarmuid! (*She comes nearer to* FINN *and speaks a little louder.*) Diarmuid, help me! (FINN *slightly moves.*) Give me your help now. I cannot wed with Finn. I cannot go to him as his wife. I do not know what has happened – half an hour ago I was content to go to him. You came in – I knew you – it was you I saw that day at Tara³ – my heart started like a deer a while ago. There is something gone astray – the thought of Finn is different. What way could I live beside him and my heart, as I am thinking, gone from him? What name might I be calling out in my sleep? (*She goes close to*

FINN *and puts her hand on his shoulder*.) Have you no way to help me, Diarmuid? It would be a terrible thing, a wedded woman not to be loyal – to call out another man's name in her sleep. (FINN *gets up and goes back into shadow*.) Oh, do not turn away from me! Do not leave me to the marriage I am in dread of. You will not help me? Is it you, Diarmuid, are failing me, you that came to my help that other time. Is it to fail me you will now? And is it my fault if this strange thing has come upon me, and that there is as if no one in all the world but you? You are angry with me and vexed, and it is a bad day, the day I came into this place. But I am not ashamed. Was it my fault at all? I will light now this candle, I will dare to show you my face. You will see in that I am not come to you as a light woman that turns this way and that way, but that I have given you the love I never gave to any man and never will give to any other! (*She lights candle and holds it up*.)

FINN (*sternly*). Grania!

GRANIA. Oh! It is Finn! And where then is Diarmuid?

FINN. There he is before you. It is the boy lying down and rising with me has betrayed me.

DIARMUID (*moving and starting up*). What is it? What has happened? Is that Grania?

FINN. You were looking for her to come. She was ready and willing. You are well fitted to rear traitors to one another.

DIARMUID. You are out of your wits. I had no thought she was coming here. What brought her?

FINN. Did she come giving you her love unasked? I thought she was a king's daughter.

DIARMUID. She is, and well worthy!

FINN. What was her mother then? Was she some woman of the camp? (*Pushes her from him*.)

DIARMUID (*putting his arm round her*). I will not let any man say that. (*Half draws sword*.)

FINN. My life is a little thing beside what you have taken!

DIARMUID. You are talking folly. You never found a lie after me in any sort of way. But the time courage was put in your heart there was madness furrowed in your brain!

FINN. Was it every whole minute of your life you were false to me?

DIARMUID. You would not have said that, the day I freed you from the three Kings of the Island of the Floods.

FINN. It is quickly you have been changed by a false woman's flattering words!

GRANIA. It is not his fault! It is mine! It is on me the blame is entirely! It is best for me to go out a shamed woman. But I will not go knocking at my father's door! I will find some quick way to quiet my heart for ever. Forgive me, Finn, and I have more cause yet to ask you to forgive me, Diarmuid. And if there were hundreds brought together this day for my wedding, it is likely there will be at my burying but the plover and the hares of the bog! (*Goes towards door.*)

DIARMUID (*seizing her*). I will not let you go out this way. I will not fail you!

FINN. There is all your talk of faith to me gone down the wind!

DIARMUID. I will not forsake her, but I will keep my faith with you. I give my word that if I bring her out of this, it is as your queen I will bring her and show respect to her, till such time as your anger will have cooled and that you will let her go her own road. It is not as a wife I will bring her, but I will keep my word to you, Finn.

FINN. Do you give me your oath to that?

DIARMUID. I do give it.

FINN. It is the woman will make you break that swearing. Grania is no pitiful hag with the hair matted wild to her knees.

DIARMUID. It will not be broken. Let my own heart break and be torn by wild dogs before that promise will be broken at all.

FINN. The moon is coming now to the full, and before its lessening you will have lied to me.

DIARMUID (*taking up a loaf*). Look at this cake of bread. I will send you its like, white and round and unbroken at every moon of the year, full moon and harvest moon, while I am along with her, as a sign my own oath is in the same way clean and whole and unbroken.

FINN. It is the woman will make you break that swearing. There will be another telling bye and bye.

DIARMUID (*taking* GRANIA's hands). There is this league between us, Grania. I will bring you with me and I will keep you safe from every danger. But understand well, it is not as a wife I will bring you, but I will keep my faith with Finn.

GRANIA. Do as is pleasing to you. I have made an end of askings.

DIARMUID. Come out with me now, till I put you in some place of safety.

FINN. You will find no safety in any place or in any Connacht corner north or west. And out in the big world itself, there is no one will give my enemy so much as shelter from the rain.

DIARMUID. I know well I have earned enemies in the big world because I fought with all its best men for your sake.

GRANIA. Oh, take me, take me away out of this! For it is hard treatment is falling upon me!

DIARMUID. And I tell you, Grania, but that I am bound to Finn by my word I have given him, and by kindnesses past counting and out of measure, it would be better to me than the riches of the whole world, you to have given me your love!

GRANIA. I have given it to you indeed. (*She puts up her face to be kissed.*)

DIARMUID (*kissing her forehead*). That is the first kiss and it will be the last.

FINN. You will give up your life as the charge for that kiss!

GRANIA. Come out! Come out! The very blood of my heart is rising against him!

FINN. I will not let you go! Let our wedding be here and now, and I will call in as my witnesses to that word Goll and Oisin and Oscar and the captains of the armies of the Fenians!

(FINN *goes to door, blows horn, then turns towards* GRANIA *as if to seize her, sways and falls.*)

GRANIA. Oh, is it death!

DIARMUID. It is but a weakness that took hold of him, with the scorching of his jealousy and its flame.

GRANIA. Come away before he will rise up and follow us. My father's horses are in the field outside.

DIARMUID. Come out then to the hunting – for it is a long

hunting it will be, and it is little comfort we will have from this out. For that is a man driven by anger, and that will not fail from our track so long as the three of us are in the living world.

(*The sound of many horns and shouts is heard at Right.* DIARMUID *opens door at Left.* GRANIA *goes out quickly. He follows with bowed head.*)

*Curtain.*

## Act II

### (*Seven Years After*)

SCENE. *Interior of a rough tent. The door opens on a wood outside. A bed strewn with rushes.* DIARMUID *lying on it asleep.* GRANIA *is moving about and singing.*

GRANIA.

> Sleep a little, a little little;
> Green the wild rushes under my dear.
> Sleep here quiet, easy and quiet,
> Safe in the wild wood, nothing to fear.

(*She stirs fire and puts some round cakes she has been making, to bake over it. Then comes to* DIARMUID *and puts her hand on him as she sings:*)

> Waken darling, darling waken!
> Wild ducks are flying, daylight is kind;
> Whirr of wild wings high in the branches.
> Hazel the hound stands snuffing the wind!

DIARMUID (*awaking and taking her hand*). There is a new light in your eyes – there is a new blush in your cheeks – there is a new pride stirring in your thoughts. The white sun of Heaven should be well pleased shining on you. Are you well content, Grania, my wife?

GRANIA. I am well content indeed with my comrade and my man.

DIARMUID. And did you love me ever and always, Grania?

GRANIA. Did I not tell you long ago, my heart went down to you the day I looked from the high window, and I in my young youth at Tara.

DIARMUID. It was a long waiting we had for our marriage time.

GRANIA. It was a long waiting, surely.

DIARMUID. Let us put it out of mind and not be remembering it at all. This last moon has made up for all those seven years.

GRANIA. It was a troublesome time indeed and a very troublesome life. In all that time we never stopped in any place so long as in the shades and the shelters of this wood.

DIARMUID. It seems to me only one day we have been in it. I would not be sorry in this place, there to be the length of a year in the day.

GRANIA. The young leaves on the beach trees have unfolded since we came.

DIARMUID. I did not take notice of their growth. Oh, my dear, you are as beautiful as the blossoming of the wild furze on the hill.

GRANIA. It was not love that brought you to wed me in the end.

DIARMUID. It was, surely, and no other thing. What is there but love can twist a man's life, as sally rods are twisted for a gad?

GRANIA. No, it was jealousy, jealousy of the King of Foreign, that wild dark man, that broke the hedge between us and levelled the wall.

DIARMUID (*starting up*). Do not bring him back to mind! It was rage that cracked me, when I saw him put his arms about you as if to bring you away.

GRANIA. Was it my fault? I was but gathering a sheaf of rushes for our two beds, and I saw him coming alongside of the stream to the pool. I knew him by the tusks on his shield and the bristled boar-skin cloak.

DIARMUID. What was it ailed you not to call to me?

GRANIA. You were far away – you would not have heard me – it is he himself would have heard my call. And I was no way afraid – I hid myself up in the branches of the big red sally by the pool.

DIARMUID. That was a foolish place to go hiding.

GRANIA. I thought myself safe and well hidden on the branch that goes over the stream. What way could I know he would stop at that very place, to wash the otter blood from his spear, and the blood from his hands, and the sweat?

DIARMUID. If I had been near, it is his own blood would have splashed away in the pool.

GRANIA. He stopped then to throw the water on his face – it was my own face he saw in the pool. He looked up of a sudden – he gave a great delighted laugh.

DIARMUID. My lasting grief that I was not there, and my hand gripping his throat.

GRANIA. He bent the branch – he lifted me from it – he not to have caught me in his arms I would have fallen in the stream.

DIARMUID. That itself might have been better than his hand to have rested on you at all!

GRANIA. Then you were there – within one minute. You should likely have heard the great shout he gave out and the laugh?

DIARMUID. I lifted my hand to strike at him, and it was as if struck down. It is grief to my heart that he escaped me! I would have crushed him and destroyed him and broken his carcase against the rocks.

GRANIA. It was I myself struck your hand down. I was well pleased seeing you in that rage of anger.

DIARMUID. If I had known that, it is likely I would have killed you in his place.

GRANIA. But you did not kill me.

DIARMUID. What was it happened? I was as if blind – you were in my arms not his, – my lips were on the lips he had nearly touched, that I myself had never touched in all those seven years.

GRANIA. It was a long, long kiss.

DIARMUID. That moment was like the whole of life in a single day, and yet it was but a second of time. And when I looked around he was gone, and there was no trace of him and he had made away and I could not kill him.

GRANIA. What matter? You should forgive him, seeing it was he brought us together at the last. You should help him to win another kingdom for that good deed. There is nothing will come between us now. You are entirely my own.

DIARMUID. I am belonging to you, indeed, now and forever. I will bring you away from this rambling life, to a place will be all our own. We will do away with this trade of wandering, we will go on to that bare shore between Burren and the big sea. There will be no trace of our footsteps on the hard flagstones.

GRANIA. We were in that craggy place before and we were forced to quit it. To live on the wind and on the air you cannot. The wind is not able to support anybody.

DIARMUID. We will get a currach[4] this time. We will go out over the waves to an island. The sea and the strand are wholesome. We shall sleep well, and the tide beating its watch around us.

GRANIA. Even out in those far Aran Islands we would be threatened and driven as happened in the time past.

DIARMUID. But beyond Aran, far out in the west, there is another island that is seen but once in every seven years.

GRANIA. Is that a real place at all? Or is it only in the nurses' tales?

DIARMUID. Who knows? There is no good lover but has seen it at some time through his sleep. It is hid under a light mist, away from the track of traders and kings and robbers. The harbour is well fenced to keep out loud creaking ships. Some fisherman to break through the mist at some time, he will bring back news of a place where there is better love and a better life than in any lovely corner of the world that is known. (*She turns away.*) And will you come there with me, Grania?

GRANIA. I am willing to go from this. We cannot stop always in the darkness of the woods – but I am thinking it should be very strange there and very lonesome.

DIARMUID. The sea-women will rise up giving out news of the Country-under-Wave,[5] and the birds will have talk as in the old days. And maybe some that are beyond the world will come to keep us company, seeing we are fitted to be among them by our unchanging love.

GRANIA. We are going a long time without seeing any of the

people of the world, unless it might be herds and fowlers, and robbers that are hiding in the wood.

DIARMUID. It is enough for us having one another. I would sooner be talking with you than the world wide.

GRANIA. It is likely some day you will be craving to be back with the Fenians.

DIARMUID. I was fretting after them for a while. But now they are slipping out of mind. It would seem as if some soul-brother of my own were calling to me from outside the world. It may be they have need of my strength to help them in their hurling and their wars.

GRANIA. I have not had the full of my life yet, for it is scared and hiding I have spent the best of my years that are past. And no one coming to give us news or knowledge, and no friendly thing at all at hand, unless it might be Hazel the hound, or that I might throw out a handful of meal to the birds to bring me company. I would wish to bring you back now to some busy peopled place.

DIARMUID. You never asked to be brought to such a place in all our time upon the road. And are you not better pleased now than when we dragged lonely-hearted and sore-footed through the days?

GRANIA. I am better pleased, surely – and it is by reason of that I would wish my happiness to be seen, and not to be hidden under the branches and twigs of trees.

DIARMUID. If I am content here, why would not you be content?

GRANIA. It is time for you to have attendance again, and good company about you. We are the same here as if settled in the clay, clogged with the body and providing for its hunger and its needs, and the readying of the dinner of today and the providing of the dinner for tomorrow. It is at the head of long tables we should be, listening to the old men with their jokes and flatteries, and the young men making their plans that will change the entire world.

DIARMUID. That is all over for me now, and cast away like the husk from the nut.

GRANIA. They will be forgetting us altogether.

DIARMUID. No, but they will put us into songs, till the world will wonder at the luck of those two lovers that carried love entire and unbroken out beyond the rim of sight.

GRANIA. That may be. And some night at the supper the men will turn their heads hearing that song and will say, 'Is Diarmuid living yet?' or 'Grania must be withered now and a great trouble to those that are about her.' And they will turn to the women that are smiling beside them, and that have delicate hands, and little blushes in their cheeks, and that are maybe but my own age all the same, but have kept their young looks, being merry and well cared. And Grania and Diarmuid will be no more than a memory and a name.

DIARMUID (*taking her hand*). These white hands were always willing hands, and where, I wonder, was this discontent born? A little while ago it was the woods you wanted, and now it is the palaces you want.

GRANIA. It is not my mind that changes, it is life that changes about me. If I was content to be in hiding a while ago, now I am proud and have a right to be proud. And it is hard to nourish pride in a house having two in it only.

DIARMUID. I take pride in you here, the same as I would in any other place.

GRANIA. Listen to me. You are driving me to excuses and to words that are not entirely true. But here, now, is truth for you. All the years we were with ourselves only, you kept apart from me as if I was a shadow-shape or a hag of the valley. And it was not till you saw another man craving my love, that the like love was born in yourself. And I will go no more wearing out my time in lonely places, where the martens and hares and badgers run from my path, but it is to thronged places I will go, where it is not through the eyes of wild startled beasts you will be looking at me, but through the eyes of kings' sons that will be saying: 'It is no wonder Diarmuid to have gone through his crosses for such a wife!' And I will overhear their sweethearts saying: 'I would give the riches of the world, Diarmuid to be my own comrade.' And our love will be kept kindled for ever, that would be spent and consumed in desolate places, like the rushlight in a cabin by the bog. For it is certain it is by the respect of others we partly judge even those we know through and through.

DIARMUID (*getting up and speaking gravely*). There is no going back for us, Grania, and you know that well yourself.

GRANIA. We will go to my father's house – he is grown old, he will not refuse me – we will call to your people and to my people – we will bring together an army of our own.

DIARMUID. That is enough of arguing. There is no sense or no reason in what you are saying.

GRANIA. It is a bad time you have chosen to give up your mannerly ways. You did not speak that way the day you found me in the hand of the King of Foreign. You would maybe be better pleased if I had gone with him at that time.

DIARMUID. You are but saying that to vex and to annoy me. You are talking like an innocent or a fool.

GRANIA. He made me great promises. A great place and power and great riches.

DIARMUID. I can win you riches in plenty if that is what you are coveting in your mind.

GRANIA. I cared little for his talk of riches – but – when he put his arms about me and kissed me—

DIARMUID. You let him leave a kiss upon your mouth?

GRANIA. It as if frightened me – it seemed strange to me – there came as if a trembling in my limbs. I said: 'I am this long time going with the third best man of the Fenians, and he never came as near as that to me.'

DIARMUID (*flinging her from him*). Go then your own way, and I would be well pleased never to have met you, and I was no better than a fool, thinking any woman at all could give love would last longer than the froth upon the stream!

(*The sound of a rattle is heard outside.*)

GRANIA. What is that? Who is it?

(FINN *disguised as a beggar is seen at door.*)

DIARMUID. It is but a beggar or a leper.

FINN. Is this a house is sheltering a handsome young woman and a lathy tall young man, that are not belonging to this district, and having no follower but a hound?

DIARMUID. Who are you? Keep back from the door!

FINN. I am no leper if I am a beggar. And my name is well earned that is Half-Man – for there is left to me but one arm by the wolves, and one side of my face by the crows that came picking at me on the ridge where I was left for dead. And beyond that again, one of the feet rotted from me, where I got it hurted one time through a wound was given me by treachery in the heel.

DIARMUID. Take off that mask till I see your face.

FINN. I will and welcome, if you have a mind to see it, but it is not right a lovely young lady to get a view of a bare gnawed skull, and that is what this caul covers. It is by reason of that I go sounding the rattle, to scare children from the path before me, and women carrying child.

DIARMUID. If it is alms you are seeking it is a bare place to come, for we carry neither gold or silver, there being no market in the woods.

FINN. Not at all, not at all – I am asking nothing at all. Believe me, the man that sent me is a good payer of wages.

DIARMUID. What call had he to send you here? We own nothing for any man to covet.

FINN. With a message he sent me, a message. You to be the man and the young woman I am searching after, I have to give a message and get a message. That is all the business I have to do. I will get fair play, never fear, from the man that sent me.

DIARMUID. Tell me who is that man, till I know is he enemy or friend.

FINN. You to see him you would not forget him. A man he is, giving out gold from his hand the same as withered leaves, and having on his shield the likeness of the rising sun.

GRANIA. That can surely be no other than Finn. What did he want sending you?

FINN. I will tell you that, and it is little I know why would he want it. You would not say him to be a man would be in need of bread.

GRANIA. Tell out now what you have to tell.

FINN. Wouldn't you say it to be a strange thing, a man having that much gold in his hand, and the sun in gold on his shield, to be as hungry after bread as a strayed cur dog would have nothing to eat or to fall back on, and would be yelping after his meal.

DIARMUID. Give out the message.

FINN. It is what he bade me say: 'Tell that young woman,' he said, 'and that youngster with her,' he said, 'that on every first night of the round moon these seven years, there used to be a round cake of bread laid upon my road. And the moon was at her strength yesterday,' he said, 'and it has failed me to find on any path that cake of bread.'

DIARMUID. It is Finn that sent him! It is Finn is calling me to account because I have forgotten my promise to him, and my faith.

GRANIA. He has come upon our track. We must go our road again. It is often we escaped him before this. I am no way afraid.

DIARMUID. It is not fear that is on me, it is shame. Shame because Finn thought me a man would hold to my word, and I have not held to it. I am as if torn and broken with the thought and the memory of Finn.

GRANIA. It is time to put away that memory. It is long enough you gave in to his orders.

DIARMUID. I did that with my own consent. Nothing he put upon me was hard. He trusted me and he could trust me, and now he will never put trust in me again.

GRANIA. It may not be Finn will be getting his commands done, and our friends gathering to our help. Let him learn that time, not to thrust his hand between the wedges and the splint.

FINN (*who has been sitting crouched over fire*). Have you the message ready and the bread I was bade bring back to the champion that met me on the path?

GRANIA (*taking up one of the cakes*). It is best send it to him and gain the time to make our escape.

DIARMUID. No, no more lying. I will tell no more lies to my master and my friend!

(DIARMUID *takes cake from* GRANIA *and flings it down, then throws himself on the bed and covers his face with his hands.*

GRANIA *takes up cake, breaks it again and again, and gives it to* FINN.)

GRANIA. That is the answer to his message. Say to him that as that bread is broken and torn, so is the promise given by the man that did right in breaking it. Tell Finn, the time you meet him, it was the woman herself gave that to you, and bade you leave it in his hand as a message and as a sign!

FINN. Take care now. Is that a right message you are sending, and one that you will not repent?

GRANIA. It is a right message for that man to get. And give heed to what I say now. If you have one eye is blind, let it be turned to the place where we are, and that he might ask news of. And if you have one seeing eye, cast it upon me, and tell Finn you saw a woman no way sad or afraid, but as airy and high-minded as a mountain filly would be challenging the winds of March!

FINN. I can tell him that, surely, and you not giving it out to me at all.

GRANIA. And another thing. Tell him there is no woman but would be proud, and that oath being broken for her sake. And tell him she is better pleased than if she was a queen of the queens of the world, that she, a travelling woman going out under the weather, can turn her back on him this day as she did in the time that is past. Go now, and give that message if you dare to give it, and keep those words red scorched in your mind.

FINN. I will bring that message, sure enough, and there will be no fear on me giving it out. For all the world knows Finn never took revenge on a fool, or a messenger, or a hound. But it would be well for them that send it to bear in mind that he is a hard man – a hard man – a hard man, surely. As hard as a barren stepmother's slap, or a highway gander's gob.[6]

GRANIA. Go, go on your road. Or will you take food and drink before you go?

FINN. Not at all, I will eat in no man's house or in any place at all, unless in the bats' feeding time and the owls', the way the terror of my face will not be seen. I will be going now, going my road. But, let you mind yourself. Finn does be very wicked the time he does be mad vexed. And he is a man well used to get the mastery, and any that think to go daring him, or to go against him, he will make split marrow of their bones.

DIARMUID (*looking up*). There might kindness grow in him yet. It is not big men, the like of him, keep up enmity and a grudge forever.

FINN. Who can know, who can know? Finn has a long memory. There is Grania he doted down on, and that was robbed from him, and he never threw an eye on any woman since and never will, but going as if crazed, and ransacking the whole country after her. As restless as the moon of Heaven he is, and at some times as wasted and as pale.

GRANIA. It is time for him to leave thinking about her.

FINN. A great memory he has and great patience, and a strong fit of the jealous, that is the worst thing ever came from the skies. How well he never forgave and never will forgive Diarmuid O'Duibhne, that he reared on his knee and nourished with every marrow-bone, and that stole away his wife from him, and is dead.

GRANIA. That is no true story. Diarmuid is not dead, but living!

FINN. That's my hearing of the thing. And if he is on the earth yet, what is he doing? Would you call that living? Screening himself behind bushes, running before the rustling of a wren on the nest. In dread to face his master or the old companions that he had.

GRANIA. There is no man but must go through trouble at some time; and many a good man has been a stranger and an exile through a great share of his lifetime.

FINN. I am no friend to Diarmuid O'Duibhne. But he to be my friend, I would think it a great slur upon him it being said a man that had so great a name was satisfied and content, killing hares and conies for the supper, casting at cranes for sport, or for feathers to stuff a pillow for his sweetheart's head, the time there is an army of the men of Foreign in Ireland.

GRANIA. I can tell you it will not be long till he will be seen going out against them, and going against some that are not foreign, and he having an army of his own.

FINN. It is best for him make no delay so, where they are doing every whole thing to drag the country down.

DIARMUID (*standing up*). I will go out and fight. I will delay no minute.

GRANIA. No, but do as I tell you. Gather your friends till you can make your own stand. Where is the use of one man only, however good he may be?

FINN. A queer thing indeed, no queerer. Diarmuid, that was the third best man of the whole of the armies of the Fenians, to be plucking and sorting pigeon's feathers to settle out a pillow and a bed.

DIARMUID. I will go as I am, by myself. There is no man living would let his name lie under reproach as my name is under it.

GRANIA (*to* FINN). Go quick – you have brought messages – bring another message for me, now, to the High King's house at Tara.

DIARMUID. I will wait for no man's help. I will go.

GRANIA. Is it that you will leave me? It is certain Finn has tracked us – we have stopped too long in the one place. If Finn is there his strength will be there. Do not leave me here alone to the power and the treachery of Finn! It is in at this door he may be coming before the fall of night.

DIARMUID. I will stop here. I will not leave you under Finn's power for any satisfaction to myself. (*To* FINN) Go, as you are bidden, and bring help from the King at Tara.

FINN. Very good, very good. That now is the message of a wise housekeeping husband.

DIARMUID. I give my word it needs more courage at some times to be careful than to be forward and daring, and that is the way with me now.

FINN. Maybe so, maybe so. And there is no wonder at all a common man to be tame and timid, when Diarmuid, grandson of Duibhne has a faint miserable heart.

DIARMUID. That is the wicked lie of some old enemy.

FINN (*going to door*). Very likely, very likely; but maybe it would be better for Grania I was speaking of, to have stopped with the old man that made much of her, in place of going with the young man that belittles her.

GRANIA. That is a slander and no true word.

FINN (*at door*). Ha! Ha! Ha! It is a story makes great sport among gentle and simple in every place. It is great laughing is given out when the story is heard, that the King of Foreign put his arms about Grania's neck that is as white as a hound's tooth, and that Diarmuid saw him do it – and that the King of Foreign is living yet, and goes boasting on his road! (*Goes out.*)

DIARMUID (*fastening on sword*). Give that to me. (*Points to spear.*)

GRANIA (*throwing it from her*). Oh, stop with me, my darling, and my love, do not go from me now or forsake me! And to stay in the lonely woods forever or in any far desolate place, you will never hear a cross word or an angry word from me again. And it is for you I will wear my jewels and my golden dress. For you are my share of life, and you are the east and the west to me, and all the long ago and all that is before me! And there is nothing will come between us or part us, and there will be no name but yours upon my lips, and no name but my own spoken by your lips, and the two of us well contented forever!

FINN (*comes back and looks in at door*). It is what they were saying a while ago, the King of Foreign is grunting and sighing, grunting and sighing, around and about the big red sally tree beside the stream! (*He disappears.* DIARMUID *rushes out.*)

*Curtain.*

## Act III

(*Afternoon of the same day*)

SCENE. *In the same tent.* GRANIA *has put on her golden dress and jewels, and is plaiting gold into her hair. Horns and music suddenly heard, not very near. She goes startled to door, and falls back as* FINN *comes in. He is dressed as if for war and has his banner in his hand. He looks older and more worn than in the First Act.*

FINN. I have overtaken you at last, Grania.

GRANIA. Finn! It is Finn! (*She goes a step back and takes up a spear.*)

FINN. It would be no great load upon you to bid me welcome.

GRANIA. What is it has brought you here?

FINN. Foolishness brought me here, and nature.

GRANIA. It is foolishness for a man not to stop and mind his own estate.

FINN. A wild bird of a hawk I had, that went out of my hand. I am entitled to it by honest law.

GRANIA. I know your meaning well. But hearken now and put yourself in a better mind. It is a heavy punishment you put upon us these many years, and it is short till we'll all be in the grave, and it is as good for you leave us to go our own road.

FINN. A queer long way I would have walked for no profit. Diarmuid is gone out from you. There is nothing to hinder me from bringing you away.

GRANIA. There is such a thing.

FINN. Is it your own weak hand on that spear?

GRANIA (*throwing it down*). No, but your own pride, if it has not gone from you and left you snapping and angry, like any moon-crazed dog.

FINN. If there is madness within me, it is you yourself have a right to answer for it. But for all that, it is truth you are speaking, and I will not bring you away, without you will come with me of your own will.

GRANIA. That will be when the rivers run backward.

FINN. No, but when the tide is at the turn. I tell you, my love that was allotted and foreshadowed before the making of the world will drag you in spite of yourself, as the moon above drags the waves, and they grumbling through the pebbles as they come, and making their own little moaning of discontent.

GRANIA. You have failed up to this to drag or to lead me to you.

FINN. There is great space for rememberings and regrettings in the days and the nights of seven years.

GRANIA. I and Diarmuid stopped close to one another all that time, and being as we were without hearth or frolic, or welcome or the faces of friends.

FINN. Many a day goes by, and nothing has happened in it worth while. And then there comes a day that is as if the ring of life, and that holds all the joy and the pain of life between its two darknesses. And I am thinking that day has come, and that it will put you on the road to myself and Almhuin.

GRANIA. You think I will give in to you because I am poor in the world. But there is grief in my heart I not to have strength to drive that spear through you, and be quit of your talk forever.

FINN. Would you think better of me if I had been satisfied to put this crown on some other woman's head, and it having rested upon your own for one moment of time? (*Takes crown from under his cloak and holds it up.*)

GRANIA. It would have been best. I would be well pleased to see you do it yet.

FINN. But I would not do that to gain the whole world entirely. And I to have my youth seven times over, it is after you I would come searching those seven times. And I have my life spent and wasted following you, and I have kissed the sign of your foot in every place all through Ireland.

GRANIA. I have no forgiveness for you that have been a red enemy to my darling and my man. I have too long a memory of all the unkindness you have done.

FINN. It is your fault if I did them. Every time the thought of kindness came to me, the thought of you came with it, and put like a ring of iron around my heart.

GRANIA. It is turned to iron indeed. And listen to me now, Finn, and believe what I say. You to have hunted us through crags and bushes, and sent us out in the height of hailstones and of rain, I might overlook it and give you pardon. But it is the malice you showed, putting a hedge between myself and Diarmuid that I never will forgive, but will keep it against you for ever. For it is you left my life barren, and it was you came between us two through all the years.

FINN. I did right doing that. There is no man but would keep the woman he is to wed for himself only.

GRANIA. It was your shadow was between us through all that time, and if I carry hatred towards you, I leave it on your own head. And it is little I would have thought of hardships, and we two being lovers and alone. But that is not the way it was. For the time he would come in, sweaty and sorefooted from the hunting, or would be dull and drowsy from the nights of watching at the door, I would be down-hearted and crabbed maybe; or if I was kind itself, it would be like a woman would be humouring a youngster, and her mind on some other track. But we to have a settled home and children to be fondling, that would not have been the way with us, and the day would have been short, and we showing them off to one another, and laying down there was no one worthy to have called them into the world but only our two selves.

FINN. You are saying what is not true, and what you have no right to say. But you know well and you cannot deny it, you are man and wife to one another this day.

GRANIA. And if we are, it is not the same as a marriage on that day we left Almhuin would have been. It was you put him under a promise and a bond that was against nature, and he was a fool to make it, and a worse fool to keep it. And what are any words at all put against the love of a young woman and a young man? It was you turned my life to weariness, and my heart to bitterness, and put me under the laughter and the scorn of all. For there was not a poor man's house where we lodged, but I could see wonder and mockery and pity in the eyes of the woman of the house, where she saw that poor as she was, and ugly maybe and ragged, a king's daughter was thought less of than herself. Because if Diarmuid never left his watch upon my threshold, he never came across it, or never gave me the joy and pride of a wife! And it was you did that on me, and I leave it on your own head; and if there is any hatred to be found in the world, and it to be squeezed into one cup only, it would not be so black and so bitter as my own hatred for you!

FINN. That hatred is as if crushed out of the great bulk of my love for you, that is heaped from the earth to the skies.

GRANIA. I am not asking it or in need of it. Why would I listen to a story I have heard often and too often.

FINN. But you will listen, and you will give heed to it. You came of your own free will to Almhuin to be my wife. And my heart went out to you there and then, and I thought there would be the one house between us, and that it was my child I would see reared on your knee. And that was known to every one of my people and of my armies, and you were willing it should be known. And after that, was it a little thing that all Ireland could laugh at the story that I, Finn, was so spent, and withered, and loathsome in a woman's eyes, that she would not stop with me in a life that was full and easy, but ran out from me to travel the roads, the same as any beggar having seven bags. And I am not like a man of the mean people, that can hide his grief and his heart-break, bringing it to some district where he is not known, but I must live under that wrong and that insult in full sight of all, and among mockery and malicious whisperings in the mouth of those maybe that are shouting me!

GRANIA. I have a great wrong done to you, surely, but it brings me no nearer to you now. And our life is settled, and let us each go our own course.

FINN. Is it not a great wonder the candle you lighted not to have been quenched in all that time? But the light in your grey eyes is my desire forever, and I am pulled here and there over hills and through hollows. For my life was as if cut in two halves on that night that put me to and fro; and the half that was full and flowing was put behind me, and it has been all on the ebb since then. But you and I together could have changed the world entirely, and put a curb upon the spring-tide, and bound the seven elements with our strength. And now, that is not the way I am, but dragging there and hither, my feet wounded with thorns, the tracks of tears down my cheeks; not taking rest on the brink of any thick wood, because you yourself might be in it, and not stopping on the near side of any lake or inver because you might be on the far side; as wakeful as a herd in lambing time, my companions stealing away from me, being tired with the one corn-crake cry upon my lips always, that is, Grania. And it is no wonder the people to hate you, and but for dread of me they would many a time have killed you.

GRANIA. If I did you wrong, did I do no wrong against Diarmuid? And all the time we were together he never cast it up against me that it was I brought him away from his comrades, or, as he could have done, that I asked him without waiting for his asking. He never put reproaches on me, as you are reproaching me, now that I am alone and without any friend at hand.

FINN. Diarmuid has no harm in his heart, and he would find it hard to do anything was not mannerly, and befitting a man reared in king's houses, if he is no good lover itself.

GRANIA. Diarmuid that gave all up for love is the best lover of the whole world.

FINN. No, for his love is not worth a reed of straw beside mine.

GRANIA. His love knows no weakening at all. He would begrudge me to walk the road! Listen to this now. The King of Foreign had put his arms about me – he had left but one kiss on my mouth – and for that much Diarmuid is gone out at this time to take his life!

FINN. Diarmuid to be a good lover, it is my own life he would have shortened. If he had any great love for you, it is I myself he would not have left living.

GRANIA. You are belittling Diarmuid, and I will judge you by your own words. You boast that you are a better lover. Then why are you wasting talk here, and you having let him go out of your hand today?

FINN. He is not gone out of reach of my hand.

GRANIA. He is! He is safe and gone from you. Would I have been so daring in talk, and I not certain of that?

FINN. It is hard for any man to escape the thing was laid down for him, and that he has earned.

GRANIA. It is no friend of yours he went out fighting. It is that foreign king. He will be well able to put him down.

FINN. It is not a man weakened with love that goes out to win in a fight. It is a foreign hand will do judgment upon him, but it was I myself sent him out to that judgment.

GRANIA. That is not true! It is a boast and a bragging you are making to threaten me. You would never dare to do it. He is of your own blood.

FINN. You are beautiful and I am old and scarred. But if it was different, and I to be what I was, straight as a flag-flower, and yellow-haired, and you what the common people call out that hate you, wide and low-born, a hedgehog, an ugly thing, I would kill any man at all that would come between us, because you are my share of the world and because I love you.

GRANIA. You are speaking lies — I know it is a lie and that it was not you sent him out to that fight. It was not you, it was that sharp-tongued beggar, that spiteful crippled man.

FINN. There is no man only a lover, can be a beggar, and not ashamed.

GRANIA. It was not you — you were not that cripple.

FINN. This is the hand where you put the broken bread.

GRANIA. It was you sent Diarmuid out! It was you came between us! It was you parted us! It was your voice he obeyed and listened to, the time he had no ears for me! Are you between us always? — I will go out after him, I will call him back — I will tell him your treachery — he will make an end of it and of you. He will know you through and through this time. It will fail you to come between us again.

(*A heavy shout is heard.*)

FINN. Hush, and listen! (*Goes to the door.*)

GRANIA. What is it? Let me find Diarmuid—

FINN (*holding her back*). It is Diarmuid is coming in.

(DIARMUID's *body is carried in by two fair-haired* YOUNG MEN. *They lay it on the bed and take off their caps.* FINN *looks at him, takes his hand, then lays it down and turns away.*)

Death and the judgment of death have overtaken him.

GRANIA (*bending over him*). Oh, Diarmuid, you are not dead! You cannot be dead! It is not in this hour you could die, and all well between us, and all done away with that had parted us!

FINN. He is dead indeed. Look at that wound in his neck. He is bleeding and destroyed with blood.

GRANIA. Come back to me, come back, my heart's darling, my one love of the men of the world! Come back, if but for one moment of time. Come back, and listen to all I have to tell. And it is well we have the world earned, and is it not a hard thing, a young man to die because of any woman at all casting an eye on him, and making him her choice, and bringing her own bad luck upon him, that was marked down for her maybe in the time before the world. And it is hunger I gave you through my love, and it is a pity it is around you it was cast, and it is a pity now, you to be loosed out of it. And it would have been better for you, some girl of the ducks and ashes, hard reared and rough, to have settled out your pillow, and not myself that brought ill-will upon you, and the readying of your grave!

FINN. Where is the use of calling to him and making an outcry? He can hear no word at all, or understand anything you say. And he has brought with him a good memory of happiness and of love; and some of the world's great men bringing with them but empty thoughts of a life that was blasted and barren.

GRANIA. Ochone, my grief! For all is at an end, and you are clean wheat ground and bruised and broken between two hard stones, the luckless love of a woman, and the love turned to anger of a friend.

FINN (*putting his hand on her arm*). That is enough. A red death is a clean death, and the thing that is done cannot be undone, and the story is ended, and there is no other word to say.

GRANIA (*pushing him away*). You stood between us long enough and he living, but you cannot come between us and he dead! And I own him from this time any way, and I am glad and could nearly laugh, knowing your power is spent and run out, and that it will fail you to come meddling any more between us that are lovers now to the end!

FINN. Your bitter words are no matter. There is no one to give heed to them.

GRANIA. It is well I will keen him, and I never will quit his grave till such time as the one flagstone will cover the two of us from the envious eyes of the women of Ireland and from your own. And a woman to lose her comrade, she loses with him her crown! And let you go to some other place, Finn, for you have nothing to say to him at all, and no other hand will be laid on him from this out but my own!

FINN (*bending over him*). He is not dead – his lips are stirring – there is a little blush in his face—

GRANIA (*stooping*). Oh, Diarmuid, are you come back to me? (*He moves.*) Speak to me now. Lift now your lips to my own – hush! He is going to speak. Oh, Diarmuid, my darling, give me one word!

DIARMUID (*turns his head slightly and looks at* FINN). Is that you, my master, Finn? I did not know you were dead along with me.

GRANIA. You are not dead, you are living – my arms are about you. This is my kiss upon your cheek. (*Kisses him.*)

DIARMUID (*not noticing her*). The King of Foreign is dead. I struck him down by the sally tree – as he was falling he struck at me, and the life went out of me. But what way did you meet with your death, my master Finn?

GRANIA. You are living I say – turn towards me. I am Grania, your wife.

DIARMUID (*still speaking to* FINN). It is a very friendly thing you to have met me here, and it is Ireland and the world should be lonesome after you this day!

GRANIA. Speak to him, Finn. Tell him he is astray. Tell him he is living. Bring the wits back to him.

FINN. Diarmuid, you are not dead, you are in the living world.

GRANIA. Come back, now, come back to life! Finn thought he had sent you to your death, but it failed him – he is treacherous – he is no friend to you. You will know that now. Come back, and leave thinking of him! !

DIARMUID (*still speaking to* FINN). There was some word I had to say meeting you – it is gone – I had it in my mind a while ago.

GRANIA. Do you not see me? It is I myself am here – Grania!

DIARMUID. Some wrong I did you, some thing past forgiving. Is it to forgive me you are waiting here for me, and to tell me you are keeping no anger against me after all?

FINN. Come back now, and put out your strength, and take a good grip of life, and I will give you full forgiveness for all you have done against me. And I will have done with anger, and with jealousy that has been my bedfellow this long time, and I will meddle with you no more, unless in the way of kindness.

DIARMUID. Kindness – you were always kind surely, and I a little lad at your knee. Who at all would be kind to me and you not being kind?

FINN. I will turn back altogether, I will leave you Grania your wife, and all that might come between us from this time.

DIARMUID. What could there be would come between us two? That would be a strange thing indeed.

FINN. I will go, for the madness is as if gone from me; and you are my son and my darling, and it is beyond the power of any woman to put us asunder, or to turn you against me any more.

DIARMUID. That would be a very foolish man would give up his dear master and his friend for any woman at all. (*He laughs.*)

GRANIA. He is laughing – the sense is maybe coming back to him.

DIARMUID. It would be a very foolish thing, any woman at all to have leave to come between yourself and myself. I cannot but laugh at that.

FINN. Rouse yourself up now, and show kindness to the wife that is there at your side.

DIARMUID. There is some noise of the stream where I died. It is in my ears yet – but I remember – I am remembering now – there was something I begrudged you, the time our bodies were heavy about us. Something I brought away from you, and kept from you. What wildness came upon me to make me begrudge it? What was it I brought away from you? Was not Hazel my own hound? (*He dies.*)

FINN. Lift up your head, open your eyes, do not die from me! Come back to me, Diarmuid, now!

GRANIA. He will say no word to either one of us again for ever. (*She goes to wall, leaning her head against it, her hands working.*)

FINN. Are you gone indeed, Diarmuid, that I myself sent to your death? And I would be well pleased it was I, Finn, was this day making clay, and you yourself holding up your head among the armies. It is a bad story for me you to be dead, and it is in your place I would be well satisfied to be this day; and you had not lived out your time. But as to me, I am tired of all around me, and all the weight of the years is come upon me, and there will be no more joy in anything happens from this day out forever. And it is as if all the friends ever I had went to nothing, losing you. (*After a moment's silence he turns to the* YOUNG MEN.) Bring him out now, slaves of Britain, to his comrades and his friends, and the armies that are gathering outside, till they will wake him and mourn him and give him burial, for it is a king is lost from them this day. And if you have no mind to keen him, let you raise a keen for the men of your own country he left dumb in the dust, and a foolish smile on their face. For he was a good man to put down his enemies and the enemies of Ireland, and it is living he would be this day if it was not for his great comeliness and the way he had, that sent every woman stammering after him and coveting him; and it was love of a woman brought him down in the end, and sent him astray in the world. And what at all is love, but lies on the lips and drunkenness, and a bad companion on the road?

(*The body is carried out. The bearers begin to keen. The keen is taken up by the armies outside.* FINN *sits down, his head bowed in his hand.* GRANIA *begins fastening up her hair and as if preparing for a journey.*)

FINN. You are doing well going out to keen after him.

GRANIA. It is not with him I am going. It is not with Diarmuid I am going out. It is an empty thing to be crying the loss of a comrade that banished me from his thoughts, for the sake of any friend at all. It is with you I will go to Almhuin. Diarmuid is no more to me than a sod that has been quenched with the rain.

FINN. I will meddle no more with what belongs to him. You are the dead man's wife.

GRANIA. All the wide earth to come between Diarmuid and myself, it would put us no farther away from one another than what we are. And as for the love I had for him, it is dead now, and turned to be as cold as the snow is out beyond the path of the sun.

FINN. It is the trouble of the day that is preying on you.

GRANIA. He had no love for me at any time. It is easy to know it now. I knew it all the while, but I would not give in to believe it. His desire was all the time with you yourself and Almhuin. He let on to be taken up with me, and it was but letting on. Why would I fret after him that so soon forgot his wife, and left her in a wretched way?

FINN. You are not judging him right. You are distracted with the weight of your loss.

GRANIA. Does any man at all speak lies at the very brink of death, or hold any secret in his heart? It was at that time he had done with deceit, and he showed where his thought was, and had no word at all for me that had left the whole world for his sake, and that went wearing out my youth, pushing here and there as far as the course of the stars of Heaven. And my thousand curses upon death not to have taken him at daybreak, and I believing his words! It is then I would have waked him well, and would have cried my seven generations after him! And I have lost all on this side of the world, losing that trust and faith I had, and finding him to think of me no more than of a flock of stares would cast their shadow on his path. And I to die with this scald upon my heart, it is hard thistles would spring up out of my grave.

FINN. Quiet yourself, for this is grief gone wild and that is beyond all measure.

GRANIA. I to have known that much yesterday I would have left him and would have gone with that King that clutched at me. And I would have said words to Diarmuid would have left a burn and a sting.

FINN. I will call in women to cry with you and to be comforting you.

GRANIA. You are craving to get rid of me now, and to put me away out of your thoughts, the same as Diarmuid did. But I will not go! I will hold you to your word, I will take my revenge on him! He will think to keep your mind filled with himself and to keep me from you, — he will be coming back showing himself as a ghost about Almhuin. He will think to come whispering to you, and you alone in the night time. But he will find me there before him! He will shrink away lonesome and baffled! I will have my turn that time. It is I will be between him and yourself, and will keep him outside of that lodging forever!

FINN. I gave him my promise I would leave you to him from this out, and I will keep it to him dead, the same as if he was still living.

GRANIA. How well he kept his own promise to you! I will go to Almhuin in spite of you; you will be ashamed to turn me back in the sight of the people, and they having seen your feet grown hard in following and chasing me through the years. It is women are said to change, and they do not, but it is men that change and turn as often as the wheel of the moon. You filled all Ireland with your outcry wanting me, and now, when I am come into your hand, your love is rusted and worn out. It is a pity I that had two men, and three men, killing one another for me an hour ago, to be left as I am, and no one having any use for me at all!

FINN. It is the hardness of trouble is about my heart, and is bringing me down with its weight. And it seems to me to be left alone with December and the bareness of the boughs; and the fret will be on me to the end.

GRANIA. Is it not a strange thing, you, that saw the scores and the hundreds stretched dead, that at the sight of one young man only, you give in to the drowning of age. It is little I will give heed from this out to words or to coaxings, and I have no love to give to any man forever. But Diarmuid that belittled me will not see me beating my hands beside his grave, showing off to the cranes in the willows, and twisting a mournful cry. It is the thing I will give him to take notice of, a woman that cared nothing at all for his treachery.

FINN. Wait till the months of mourning are at an end, and till your big passion is cold, and do then what you may think fit, and settle out your life, as it is likely there will be another thought in your mind that time. But I am putting no reproach on you, for it is on myself the great blame should be, and from this out I have no more to say to love or friendship or anything but the hard business of the day.

GRANIA. I will not wait. I will give my thoughts no leave to repent. I will give no time to those two slaves to tell out the way I was scorned!

FINN. The men of the armies will laugh and mock at you, seeing you settle out a new wedding in the shadow of your comrade's wake.

GRANIA. There is many a woman lost her lord, and took another, and won great praise in the latter end, and great honour. And why should I be always a widow that went so long a maid? Give me now the crown, till I go out before them, as you offered it often enough. (*She puts it on her head.*) I am going, I am going out now, to show myself before them all, and my hand linked in your own. It is well I brought my golden dress.

FINN. Wait till the darkness of the night, or the dusk of the evening itself.

GRANIA. No, no. Diarmuid might not see me at that time. He might be gone to some other place. He is surely here now, in this room where he parted from the body – he is lingering there by the hearth. Let him see now what I am doing, and that there is no fear on me, or no wavering of the mind. Open the door now for me!

> (FINN *opens door and they go to the opening, she taking his hand.*
> *There is a mocking laugh heard. She falls back and crouches down.*
> FINN *tries to raise her.*)

FINN. I thought to leave you and to go from you, and I cannot do it. For we three have been these seven years as if alone in the world; and it was the cruelty and the malice of love made its sport with us, when we thought it was our own way we were taking, driving us here and there, knocking you in between us, like the ball between two goals, and the hurlers being out of sight and beyond the boundaries of the world. And all the three of us have been as if worsted in that play. And now there are but the two of us left, and whether we love or hate one another, it is certain I can never feel love or hatred for any other woman from this out, or you yourself for any other man. And so as to yourself and myself, Grania, we must battle it out to the end.

> (FINN *raises her up. A louder peal of laughter is heard.*)

GRANIA (*going towards the door*). It is but the armies that are laughing! I thought I heard Diarmuid's laugh.

FINN. It is his friends in the armies gave out that mocking laugh.

GRANIA. And is it not a poor thing, strong men of the sort to be mocking at a woman has gone through sharp anguish, and the breaking of love, on this day? Open the door again for me. I am no way daunted or afraid. Let them laugh their fill and welcome, and laugh you, Finn, along with them if you have a mind. And what way would it serve me, their praise and their affection to be mine? For there is not since an hour ago any sound would matter at all, or be more to me than the squeaking of bats in the rafters, or the screaming of wild geese overhead!

(*She opens the door herself. FINN puts his arm about her. There is another great peal of laughter, but it stops suddenly as she goes out.*)

*Curtain.*

# POEMS

# A Woman's Sonnets

## [ I ]

If the past year were offered me again,
And choice of good and ill before me set
Would I accept the pleasure with the pain
Or dare to wish that we had never met?
Ah! could I bear those happy hours to miss
When love began, unthought of and unspoke –
That summer day when by a sudden kiss
We knew each other's secret and awoke?
Ah no! not even to escape the pain,
Debate and anguish that I underwent
Flying from thee and my own self in vain
With trouble wasted, till my strength all spent
   I knew at last that thou or love or fate
    Had conquered and repentance was too late.

## [ II ]

Ah, my own dear one do not leave me yet!
Let me a little longer hold thy hand.
It is too soon to ask me to forget
Too soon I should from happiness be banned.
The future holds no hope of good for me,
The past I only wish to shut away
But while thou'rt with me and thy face I see
The sun shines on me, it is always day.
And time and fate bring near our parting hour
Which well I know thy love will not outlast –
But then perchance I may have gained more power
More strength and will to bury my dead past
   Ah! try to love me still a moment's space
    'Tis all I ask thee dear, this little grace.

## [ III ]

Where is the pride for which I once was blamed?
The pride which made me hold my head so high?
Who would believe it, seeing me so tamed
As at thy feet I subject, pleading lie –
Pleading for love which now is all my life –
Begging a word that memory may keep,
Asking a sign to still my inward strife,
Petitioning a touch to smooth my sleep –
Bowing my head to kiss the very ground
On which the feet of him I love have trod,
Controlled and guided by that voice whose sound
Is dearer to me than the voice of God.
    And knowing all the time that some dark day
    Indifferent and cold thou'lt turn away.

## [ IV ]

Should e'er that drear day come in which the world
Shall know the secret which so close I hold,
Should taunts and jeers at my bowed head be hurled,
And all my love and all my shame be told,
I could not, as some women use to do
Fling jests and gold and live the scandal down –
I could not, knowing all the story true
Hold up my head and brave the talk of town –
I have no courage for such tricks and ways,
No wish to flaunt a once dishonoured name –
Have still such memory of early days
And such great dread of that deserved shame
    That when it comes, with one all hopeless cry,
    For pardon from my wronged ones, I must die.

## [ V ]

Whate'er the cost may be I say farewell
I will not see thee, speak to thee again.
If some on earth must know the pangs of Hell
Mine be the torture, mine be all the pain.
What if my life grow blank and void and dead,
If my last hope of love be dashed away –
Better than risk dishonour on the head
Of her in whose arms as a babe I lay.
I have no right to bring such grief as this
Into the lives that linked are with mine,
No right to vex the dead in new found bliss,
With knowledge of my sin and great decline.
   Their peace I seek, and though my soul be rent
   With the hard conflict, I will not relent.

## [ VI ]

What have I lost? The faith I had that right
Must surely prove itself than ill more strong.
For all my prayers and efforts had no might
To save me, when the trial came, from wrong.
And lost the days when with untroubled eyes
Scorning deceit, I could hold up my head.
I lead a double life – myself despise
And fear each day to have my secret read.
No longer will the loved and lost I mourn
Come in my sleep to breathe a blessed word.
Tossing I lie, and restless and forlorn,
And their dear memory pierces like a sword.
   In thy dear presence only have I rest.
   To thee alone naught needs to be confessed.

## [ VII ]

What have I gained? A little charity?
I never more may dare to fling a stone
Or say of any weakness I may see
That I more strength and wisdom would have shown –
And I have learned in love lore to be wise:
And knowledge of the evil and the good
Have had one moment's glimpse of Paradise
And know the flavour of forbidden food.
But this, if it be gold has much alloy,
And I would gladly all the past undo
Were it not for the thought that brings me joy
That I once made some happiness for you –
    That sometimes in a dark and troubled hour
    I had, like Jesse's son, a soothing power.


## [ VIII ]

Thou needst not on me any pityance lay
If I have sinned the judgment has begun.
The joy I knew lasted but one short day,
The clouds descended with the setting sun.
Thou wert my all dear, and too soon I knew
How small a part I could be in thy life –
That all a woman may endure or do
Counts little to her hero in the strife.
Ah dearest, thou wert not at all to blame
Thou hast so many worlds within thy ken.
I staked my all upon a losing game
Knowing thy nature and the ways of men.
    Knowing that one chill day I must repent
    With open eyes to love and death I went.

## [ IX ]

I think the day draws near when I could stay
Within thy presence with no thought of ill –
And having put all earthliness away
Could listen to thy accents and be still.
And feel no sudden throbbing of the heart
No foolish rising of unbidden tears
Seeing thee come and go – and meet or part
Without this waste of gladness and of fears.
Only have patience for a little space.
I am not yet so wise to see unmoved
Another woman put into my place
Or loved as I was for a moment loved
   Be not so cruel as to let me see
   The love-light in thine eyes if not for me!

## [ X ]

Love, e'er I go, forgive me any wrong
I may to thee unwittingly have wrought.
Although my heart, my life to thee belong
I may have vexed thee by some random thought:
One sin against thee I would fain atone
The crime of having loved thee yet unwooed,
The blame, the guiltiness are mine alone –
The woman tempted thee from right and good.
Forgive me also, e'er thy pity cease
That I denied thee, vexed thee with delay,
Sought my own soul to save, sought my own peace,
And having gained thy love yet said thee nay.
  But now for pardon now for grace I plead.
  Forgive me dearest! I thy pity need –

## [ X ]

Wild words I write, wild words of love and pain
To lay within thy hand before we part.
For now that we may never meet again
I would make bare to thee my inmost heart.
For when I speak you answer with a jest
Or laugh and break the sentence with a kiss
And so my love is never half confessed
Nor have I told thee what has been my bliss.
And when the darkness and the clouds prevail
And I begin to know what I have lost
I would not vex thee with so sad a tale
Or tell how all too dear my love has cost.
   But now the time has come when I must go
   The tumults and the joy I fain would show.

## [ XII ]

The hour has come to part! and it is best
The severing stroke should fall in one short day
Rather than fitful fever spoil my rest,
Watching each gradual sign of love's decay.
Go forth dear! thou hast much to do on earth;
In life's campaign there waits thee a great part –
Much to be won and conquered of more worth
Than this poor victory of a woman's heart –
For me, the light is dimmed, the dream has past –
I seek not gladness, yet may find content
Fulfilling each small duty, reach at last
Some goal of peace before my youth is spent.
   But come whatever may, come weal or woe
   I love thee, bless thee where so e'er thou go!

## 'Alas! a woman may not love!'

Alas! a woman may not love!
For why should she bestow in vain
The riches of that treasure-trove
To win but a receipt of pain
For never will the gainer pay
In full the love she gives away –
Be it a brother – soon some other
Sweet maiden passing holds his eye
And in his thought she stands for naught
His second self in days gone by –
Be it a husband – ah! how soon
The rainbow-coloured honeymoon
Fades in dull tints of common life
With misty cares and clouds of strife –
Be it her sons – some few short years
They cling to her in smiles and tears
But childhood passes fast and then
The boys look on themselves as men
And learn too quickly to despise
The love lore in their mother's eyes –
Or if – ah me! she chance to find
One led to her by wayward fate
In whom she learns a kindred mind
Found by her own too late – too late –
Ah pity her – for if she yield
What from remorse her soul can shield –
Or if she conquer, the sore strife
May yet have cost her half her life –
The wound that ne'er can be laid bare
May be the sorest scar to wear –
The grief that brings no right to weep
May be the one to banish sleep –
Perchance not so in heaven above –
But here, a woman may not love –

# JOURNALS

# from *Volume I* (*1916–1925*)

## 1919

Yesterday, Sunday afternoon, there was a sudden tumult and we in the reading room lifted the blinds and saw a surging, boohing mob threatening to break into the Hotel. I went to an open window upstairs to see better. There had been a meeting to protest against the seizure of St Enda's School by the Military, and some Police Inspectors who were taking notes had been chased by the mob and had taken refuge in the Hall here. The mob boohed at them, the Management was afraid, I think, to let them out by a back entrance lest the Hotel should be broken into. The mob looked very threatening for a while.

Then, a man in black, I do not think he was a priest, stood up on something, I think on one of the tree standards in the middle of the street, and said in a very clear voice: 'Fellow-citizens, the Military seized without notice the house belonging to Mrs Pearse at Rathmines. We have met to protest against it and some Police who came to interfere have taken shelter in the Gresham Hotel. The people of Dublin are not an undisciplined mob as they were in 1913. They are now organised. We make no war on private property. We are not going to attack the Gresham Hotel. I ask you to sing the Soldier's Song and to go home and leave the police to take care of themselves.'

There was a little cheering, very little singing, and a great many went quietly away. The rest stayed, pressing near the door, and boohing whenever they caught sight of the police-men or boohing when another came. I was afraid the Military would arrive and there would be trouble, but after a while a young man in a sort of uniform got up just under the window where I was and said: 'Fellow Republicans,' (great cheering) 'you know me as one of yourselves. I ask you to go home now and leave the police to themselves.' And after that they went away quietly enough. (This was the first time I heard the word 'Republican' used.)

16 MARCH

I went to the almost empty matinée at the Abbey. The bills were there for Monday with *Kathleen ni Houlihan* and *Minerals*, but Millington said casually that Miss Walker has to go to Manchester after all and so can't play Kathleen till Wednesday, and *Rising* is to be played in its stead. A bad moment to make a change, when we are already weak with the loss of players. I left a card for Robinson asking him to come round, and told him I would rather myself play Kathleen than let it drop (after all what is wanted but a hag and a voice?). He said it was 'splendid' of me, and we arranged a rehearsal for today but my heart sinks now; remembering the words will be the chief difficulty, and I could joyfully welcome Maire Walker should she return, yet if all goes well I shall be glad to have done it.

In the evening I set out again for the Abbey, but when the tram reached O'Connell Bridge, at about eight o'clock, there were immense crowds blocking the street and I went on to the pillar. I asked a newspaper-seller what was going on and he said excitedly: 'The Countess is coming back!' I got into another tram seeing it would be difficult to get to the Abbey and perhaps impossible to get anywhere, and we set out but very soon came to a stop.

Then a band was heard and then came a waggonette and pair and I saw Madame Markievicz standing and waving a bouquet, yellow, white and with long green sprays (I had noticed a man carrying it through the streets earlier and had thought regretfully that we have no actress now to whom it could possibly be on its way as a tribute). There was a large, long procession following the waggonette – we were still held up – and there was cheering when it came to the bridge. Madame Gonne followed in another waggonette, but was not cheered. We must have been over half an hour there, the long procession moving all the time, and then a procession of helmeted police passed us but there was no disturbance or rioting.

17 MARCH

Yesterday morning to the Abbey and rehearsed *Kathleen ni Houlihan* feeling very nervous about it, and wishing Maire Walker would suddenly appear and do still wish it – though I think I would be disappointed afterwards if she did.

18 MARCH

To the Abbey, and ran through *Kathleen* with Shields, my heart sinking more and more at the thought of the stage.

\* \* \*

On to the Abbey, and my face was painted with grease paint – white with black under the eyes and red inside the lids – dreadful! Luckily my own hair is grey enough without a wig. And I had got a slight cold so I was a little hoarse and felt miserable. When I went on to the stage it was a shock to find the auditorium was black darkness, I thought for a moment the curtain was still down and hesitated. But I got through all right, only once Shields had to prompt me. He was kneeling beside me so it didn't matter. Seaghan was behind the fireplace, book in hand, but didn't have to use it. There were few stalls, but as I guessed from the applause and saw afterwards, the pit and gallery were full. Of course the patriotic bits were applauded, especially 'They are gathering to meet me now', and I had two curtains all to myself. I wish tonight were over for all that. The actors seemed pleased, and Mrs Martin (Charwoman) came and hugged me with enthusiasm. Home very tired and hungry, and the fire out, and had stale bread with butter and a glass of milk.

19 MARCH

Working at *John Bull* at the Abbey under difficulties, not having all the cast, some at their work and some yet to find. Yeats came and took me to lunch and showed me a cutting from the *Morning*

*Post* about his new book *Wild Swans at Coole*, saying the poem about R. was 'certainly the most distinguished of the many proud laments for the fallen'.

At 7, I set out again for the theatre in pouring rain (as in the morning when I had a long wait and then had to go on top of tram till there was a place). I was even more nervous than the first night but got through without prompts and had my own two curtains. But the audience was not so large or so patriotic as the St Patrick's night one, Millington thought there was 'more thrill' in my performance then. And Yeats came up to the gallery afterwards and said coldly it was 'very nice, but if I had rehearsed you it would have been much better'. Ruth, however, said she had never known so much could be put into Kathleen's part. Madame Gonne – a former Kathleen – was there, and Iseult and Mrs Groen and Mrs Stephens all together.

## 27 SEPTEMBER

I went to see Mrs Childers, Erskine is in Ireland, looking for a Dublin house where they will settle. She gave me an account of the gun-running (looking so delicate and fragile – she is kept in bed). It was Mary Spring Rice's idea and they got a yacht and Darrell Figgis went over and bought the guns in Liege, and they waited for them off Dover. 'The British Navy was all about and I went downstairs with 2 sailors and we packed away the bunks and fittings to make room for the guns ... Then the tug came and they were transferred to us. When one bundle was being lowered to us the sailors who held it said: "this is ammunition – it will explode if it touches anything". We went on up the Welsh coast and lay outside Milford Haven, afraid of Custom House officers. Then for Holyhead and across to Ireland and sailed about the bay and outside Howth till the boat came when Erskine said, "I am going to do it." It was just the hour when the tide was highest. We saw someone run up to a height and wave to us as a signal – it was a young officer whose name I cannot tell ... Then we saw the Volunteers coming down and when they saw us they broke into a run. The guns that had taken 6 hours to get on board were unloaded in a few minutes. As we left there were cheers for "the lady at the helm" – it had been put into my hand.

'Some members of the government thanked us when we came back to London, they said it was the best thing that could have been done, to show the South could take up arms as well as Ulster.'

## 1920

### 28 SEPTEMBER

Yesterday evening I came home. I had been told that Feeney's house in Kinvara had been burned in the night – the Sunday night – and we passed by the ruined walls in the town. A little farther, at the crossroads, there was another ruin, McMerney's the smith. His house had also been burned down in the night by soldiers and police. He and his family had found shelter in the cart shed. It seemed so silent, we had always heard the hammer in the smithy and seen the glow of the fire. And he was such a good smith – I remember how Robert used to send his hunters to him. 'One of his sons was said to be secretary to a Sinn Fein Committee.' Today Malachi Quinn came to ask for sand for the building up of Burke's house at Ballymacwiff – burnt also by military and police. They had gone to look for one of the sons and he was not there. Then they told Burke to take whatever money he had out of the house, and then set fire to it. First I said I must ask Margaret's leave for the sand and wrote to her. Then I tore up the letter and gave leave. There were children in the house, Malachi has taken two of them to his. They say Gort would have been burnt on Saturday by drunken soldiers arriving from Ennistymon, but three of the old police restrained them.

### 30 SEPTEMBER

I was quite ill, could not sleep or eat after the homecoming – the desolation of that burnt forge, and all one hears. Edward

Martyn's beautiful little village hall burnt down. C. Griffin says on Monday night two lorries of military came into Gort 'firing and shouting – and the people brought out their furniture from their houses expecting the burnings to begin'. 'Black and Tans and police and military' burned Burke's house, 'an officer with them. But are there any *gentlemen* among them?' Griffin takes their part, says it brought tears to his eyes when five bodies of policemen were carried through Gort, one only 25. Terrible on both sides, but it was in Clare they had been shot. Police they say were fired at near Ardrahan, but not wounded or killed – that was the excuse for the Sunday burnings.

1 OCTOBER

No post today.

Peter Glynn told me today, 'There did two car loads of the Black and Tans come into Gort late yesterday evening – they were a holy fright shouting and firing. They broke into houses and searched them, and they searched the people in the street, women and girls too that were coming out from the chapel, that they came running down the street in dread of their life. Then they went into Spelman's to drink and got drunk there. It is terrible to let them do that. Look at McMerney's they burned all the bedding in the house and every bit of money he had. And at Burke's the same way, burnt all in the house, and nine acres of oats. They would have burned the hay but didn't see it. Mr Martyn's beautiful hall they didn't leave a stone of, and at Ardrahan the same way as at Burke's they kept the boys running up and down the road for near an hour and a half and they all but naked while they were chasing them up and down, and girls the same way. It is a holy crime – it is worse than Belgium. What call have they coming to Gort that is such a quiet little town? Jack Hehir that went into Gort in the evening with a message from his wife that is sick was stopped near the town and made put his hands up and was searched.'

Marian has just brought me back a book 'Chez Swan' that I had sent to go back to Mudies.

There was a 'regiment of soldiers with their bayonets standing at the Post office door and no one could go in – and the shutters up as on Sundays. They were said to be searching the letters inside'. Tim is trembling. 'There is no one is safe.'

## 2 OCTOBER

No letters yet, J. says the military opened all the letters that came in yesterday, that time they were in the Post Office. The Black and Tans left last night. 'They searched a good many houses and found nothing, but any pictures they saw that had anything to do with Sinn Fein they tore and broke them. Young Hayes was trying to slip away from them but they fired and hit him in the thigh. They went singing about the streets "Irishmen come into the Parlour" and "Who fears to speak of Easter Week". There were not three people in Gort went to bed last night, but sitting up through the night-time keeping the lights quenched. Carr X. that is a policeman's son was the Captain over the Black and Tans, a tall young fellow. He was wearing a white cloth over his face and holes cut in it for the eyes. Prospect was searched twice. But Stephens says it would have been worse but for Carr X. being in it, he has friends he would not wish to face in the town.

'The reason for Burke's house being burned was that he had driven cattle in Druimhasna, and the police say they felt (heard) shots there one night. There are others living near say there were no shots fired. It was 7 o'clock in the night time they burned the house, and the wheat and the oats. A slated house and as well furnished as any house you could see. The boy they were looking for was in it, and they covered him with their revolvers, eight of them, holding them to his head and his body, but the Captain said, "We can do enough harm without killing him," and they began the burning.'

Mike says the military had stopped the mail car yesterday and opened most of the letters; mine opened was one from Galway telling, 'At 12.30 last night the Post Office, which is a nest of Sinn Feiners, was riddled with bullets, also my grocer's shop (2nd attack on him) Heaney our bacon merchant and others.'

M.J. says the Black and Tans fired 12 shots at Hayes but only one hit, in the shoulder, and that they broke all the pictures and furniture at F.'s.

Glynn says, 'They stole a piece of tweed from B.'s shop, and a gold necklace and a watch from a house in Church Street. Carr, their officer, made them put back the tweed, and the watch and the necklace they brought away. They drank in every bar and went about drunk in the evening shouting and singing. Savages they were. And after they had left the town police got drunk and went drunk about the town with their revolvers – a holy terror.'

## 4 OCTOBER

Shaughnessy and Cahel of the Volunteers here about land, but only wanted to know details, acreage etc . . . I asked about the Black and Tans, if it was true they drank, they said yes; 'They arrived drunk and drank in most of the bars while they were there. They stole in Gort many things – a bicycle and such like and would have done more but we have a good D.I., who kept them back.'

## 5 OCTOBER

John took my letter to McMerney's. They told him the attacking party had come about midnight and had begun by firing into the kitchen through the windows but that they thanked God there was no one there. Then they broke in and dragged the boys out, ordered them all out, and poured oil about, and set fire to the house. One of the soldiers had told the wife to go back and save her money and clothes and she was going in, but a policeman dragged her back. They had saved nothing at all.

## 24 OCTOBER

A rather trying day at Coole, to meet Frank, and try to insist on good terms for the workmen, as the Committee have written to them to 'bring £200' to Gort (which they are not inclined to do until they know what is to be had for it). F. grew grumpy after lunch attacked me for having spent money (my own, earned!) on planting instead of 'keeping it for Richard to spend'. But Richard may love trees too – and they can't be grown in a minute. Then M.Q. came and was quite abusive at 'the old tenants' not getting the land which they had refused to offer for! Rain came on and a long drive back here. Poor Grandmama! ... but the chicks delighted because I brought apples.

We were at church, Mrs Scovell and Stanley, the two children and I, a congregation of five. A strange Litany astonished me, then Mrs S. sent a copy across. I tried to join and indeed might have, but that it was so manifest that the crime of murder and superstition and other sins prayed against were set down as those of Ireland, that it seemed almost an exoneration of 'those appointed for the government of this land'.

I am reading Garibaldi's *Defence of the Roman Republic*, very comforting, because so many a praise of Italy's fighters and martyrs taken from its contents could stand as justly for ours. 'Men who would have been called to make her laws and lead her armies and write her songs and history when their day came, but that they judged it becoming to die there in order that her day should come.' I go on saying daily the prayers for the Lord Mayor to Him 'with whom do live the spirits of just men made perfect, after they are delivered from their earthly prisons'.

30 OCTOBER

Quiet days. The chicks picking blackberries and harnessing the go-cart to Tommy and digging shell fish out of the sand.

I have sent off *Aristotle's Bellows* to be typed, probably the last play I shall write. I am face to face with my memories, or whatever I have gathered from my life.

Yesterday *Punch* had a caricature of 'the Irish Volunteer army' that degraded type that helped the bitterness in the land war and before. I felt the Lord Mayor had not given his life in vain if even to contradict that, for his portrait must be also in those Dublin papers; it is, they say in all the American ones. Reading Garibaldi still, with envy.

## 31 OCTOBER

J.D. from Coole – The Black and Tans have been several times at Gort, shooting and destroying. Three policemen have been shot or shot at near Castle Daly. Then Doctor Foley came. He was very excited, and said houses at Ardrahan had been burnt down last night and that the Black and Tans are spreading terror and ruin. He could not speak explicitly before the children . . . but I saw him for a few minutes alone and he said that at Clarenbridge they had got drunk and had assaulted a widow. And a man there – Casey – had come to him yesterday saying, 'Don't let your Misses walk on the road, they are out for drink and women,' and said he and his son had been dragged from their houses, put against the wall and while held there his two daughters were assaulted. Foley thinks the attempt succeeded to violate them. I begged him to get the facts and write them down, that I may send them to Massingham. He says even Unionists are shocked at Greenwood's falsehoods in the House of Commons. A bad night.

Today I wrote to G.B.S., begging him to come over to Coole and examine into these Black and Tan horrors.

I wrote to Margaret saying the workmen ought to be given their houses and an acre or two, – and that if she did not feel the same way I would use the Crannagh £300.

The chicks so good at lessons, spurred by fear of the Italian governess, Catherine reading her page off, hardly needing a prompt.

## 5 NOVEMBER

A. writes, 'The milk girl says a young woman was shot yesterday at Kiltartan by a lorry of passing military – it seems dreadful – they are very careless with guns.'

Then Ellen told me it was Malachi Quinn's young wife who had been shot dead with her child in her arms.

Ellen says her mother's house near Athenry was broken into by military the other night, she was made get out of bed, but she was not assaulted. Poor Malachi Quinn; he had trouble enough to bear, and was sad last week when he came to see me . . .

Foley said it is dangerous now to be on the road, and it was dangerous to stay in the house at night.

When I pray 'God save Ireland' the words come thrusting through 'Gott strafe England' in spite of my desire not to give in to hatred.

## 5 NOVEMBER

We came back from Burren, late, for rain had kept us back. J. had been the two nights at Malachi's house – says the little children said, 'Mamma's asleep.' Malachi was in Gort when it happened, they sent for him. Marian had been there also, says, 'You could take up the three little children in your arms together,' and there was another coming. There were 89 cars at the funeral. 'Burning would be too good for the Black and Tans,' J. says. Tim says they have been firing continually as they pass, his sick daughter cannot sleep, 'the day they killed Mrs Quinn they had fired at Donoghue's house as they passed and killed some fowl' – 'It is to show their authority,' Tim says. They say now that it was not done by them, but the dying woman herself was the witness, told her mother and the priest that she had been shot by the Black and Tans. 'They fired at Callinan's house as they passed on, and broke the windows. The old police in Gort are ashamed of them. They stopped a man the other day turning up the road and robbed him of £50, he had just sold calves and was bringing it home.'

'Malachi cannot stand alone – he has to be led "linked" – They were so happy, they had just got in the harvest, just dug the potatoes and threshed the corn and were ready for the winter.'

## 6 NOVEMBER

A letter from poor Malachi in answer to mine: 'My God it is too cruel!'

J. says Father Considine had never preached a better sermon since before the War than he did on Sunday, praising the young men of the parish for not having joined in any of the attacks on police, and begging them to keep patient; the police came down the road after and thanked him.

The next day a Holy day (All Saints) and pig fair. 'There were a great many people in Gort and on the road. The Black and Tans came dashing out and began to fire shots from Lally's down so that the houses shook. Swift, that was bringing up water from the river in a tin can, said he could hear the bullets singing over his head as they passed. An ambush! in a big open country like that!'

## 8 NOVEMBER

I asked the Archdeacon after church about the Black and Tans. He began by saying there was a hill or at least a slight incline near Malachi's house which might have helped an ambush, and that there was no robbery or drinking while they were in Gort, and praised the Auxiliaries who have been there and he had chatted with through the evening says also that if Gort doesn't kill it makes bullets, and that men from Lough Cutra and Gort were at the Castledaly police ambush. Then I told him I had heard of things stolen; 'O, yes, when they raided a house they often carried things off, they looked on it as loot.' 'And if they found drink, they thought they were serving their cause by taking it – drinking.' Mr Johnson put in, 'There are bad lads among the Black and Tans'; and the Archdeacon said, 'The police are drinking too'; just as I had heard.

'They were Black and Tans in the lorries on Monday. They had come out from Galway for the day and when they were leaving Gort they began firing in the street.'

As we set out for church I asked J.D. how long he had Ford's field for. He said till April. I said Ford had asked for it again and I had promised to write to Mrs Gregory. He burst out: 'Isn't my money as good as another's,' excitedly, and I said nothing till we were at the White gate coming back, and then asked him if Mrs

Gregory had not told him how angry she was at his having deceived her in saying Ford didn't want to keep it on – as he did. He blustered, but confessed she had. I said I did not know if it would be let again, that I thought we might want it for ourselves. He said, 'if you want it for yourselves I'll say nothing – but if anyone else gets it – I'll . . .' I said, 'What will you do?' He said, 'I'll fight my battle.' I said, 'Then it is a threat' – that was all. I am very sorry – an ugly revelation of character and just when I was doing my best to help him. No letter from Margaret. Poor John.

### 9 NOVEMBER

L.R. writes about a possible Fund to help the homeless we may play for 'though probably by that time we will be among those asking for charity. All the theatres are hard hit but we are especially so, and I think it's because the military now often go to a concert and hold up the whole audience to search them, and our audience is more Sinn Fein than most audiences so it naturally doesn't want that.'

A. writes, 'After the wedding (a Black and Tan officer to a widow) the Black and Tans formed an arch of revolvers for the Bride and Groom to walk under and then fired (blank) cartridges. Being Saturday all the Market was filled and the old women stampeded in terror. Later the wedding motor ran into a lorry and the bride fainted.'

Malachi Quinn came to see me looking dreadfully worn and changed and his nerves broken, he could hardly speak when he came in. There had been aeroplanes flying very low over the place all day and as he came from Raheen one had swooped and fired 3 shots over him. He believes they shot her on purpose – they came so close. He was so fond of his wife 'she could play every musical instrument'. It is true the messenger sent for a doctor was shot from another lorry, wounded in the leg.

R.D. came to tea – she says the Black and Tans are a bad lot but thinks them justified in flogging (the Archdeacon said 'scourging') because they say they had found a paper with sixteen names signing it, on the guard of a train, saying a convoy of soldiers was going to Galway and that the boys there would know how to be ready for them.

I am troubled by another talk with J.D., who still keeps to his threat of not allowing Ford back into the field he got from him by his misstatements, 'It is not ye I threaten, it is Ford.' I have not told Margaret.

15 NOVEMBER

Una [Pope-Hennessy] writes about Terence McSwiney: 'You could not see the face of that man in his coffin, looking like the face of a starved child of 10, without feeling the most awful moral wrong had been done – It overwhelmed you.'

18 NOVEMBER

A. writes from Galway that there had been a raid in the University, and some students who had not saluted the flag there were made to do so. The paper says 'forced to uncover while the National Anthem was sung'.

The children were in the wood cutting sticks and heard a great many shots – 4 – close together. Swift told them it was the Black and Tans.

I was so angry at the official report of Eileen Quinn's shooting – beginning 'the enquiry was open to all but few chose to attend it'. I had heard none but the family and the witnesses were allowed to it and I asked the Archdeacon after church if he had heard it and he said, 'No, no one was allowed in but the witnesses. I sat outside with –' I forget whom.

20 NOVEMBER

Dr Foley here yesterday. He says the family of the girls violated by the Black and Tans wish it hushed up. There has been another case of the same sort in Clare – but there also it is to be kept quiet. Peterswell has been undergoing its reprisals. A man

Foley had long known – an old Land Leaguer – had come to the dispensary to have his back treated – 'I think there was hardly a worse scourging given to our Lord – the whole back black and blue with bruises and the Blood drawn in some places.'

Other men there were beaten 'one thrown on a dung heap – a Black and Tan put one foot on his face to press it into the dung, and another on his stomach. And then he and others treated the same way were thrown into the village well to wash themselves.

'There is an old man of 70 living at the side of the mountain. He had come down to the village and went into Hayes' public house. He had 18/6 in his pocket – a Black and Tan came in and called "Hands up". He put up his hands and the Black and Tan took the 18/6 out of his pocket and walked out with it.'

I am told 'no one but witnesses were allowed into the Quinn enquiry. The President of the Court looked like a gentleman and was well mannered but after the first he had nothing to say, an officer with a dark countenance and a Scotch accent took it all into his hands and the other seemed afraid of him. The Arch-deacon sat outside on a bench, with Father Considine. The Head Constable was in the house while Mrs Quinn was still alive, but asked for no statement from her. It is their custom to ask that even when told a patient wasn't fit for it.'

I was just sitting down to write this when 'Mr Nevinson' was announced and came in, with a Doctor Watson. He is writing for the *Daily Herald*. They had just come from Scariff where those four young men were shot in trying to escape the day before yesterday. He is certain they were not trying to escape – the shooting was on a bridge, where they would certainly not have been – he is sure they were shot in cold blood. They stayed the night – pleasant visitors as we talked of many other things – and it is a great relief to my mind that these horrors are being made known by so competent a writer. He said, 'Those "Nation" articles of yours have been of the greatest use.' I said, 'They are not known to be mine,' and he said, 'Oh, no, but *I* know.' Foley told me some of what he had said to me had been recognised by a friend of his. He said I was welcome to tell all he told me, that it ought to be made known. But he thinks if the Black and Tans hear I am doing this, revenge and loot may bring them here.

## 22 NOVEMBER

With the chicks to the garden and to church with Anne. When they were out after lunch, I began to compose a letter about getting compensation (!) for poor Malachi Quinn. He had been on Saturday evening to ask me to help towards this. I had consulted the Archdeacon after church, and he did not think it possible because it was not 'malicious injury' and said 'the bullet if fired in the air might have come perpendicularly down and struck her' (I said it was odd if the fowl at Mrs Donohues next door had also been perpendicularly struck). After I had written a draft of this I went out, going at 4 o'clock into the hut wood. Presently I saw 5 or 6 dogs of sorts running through the bushes, then lads 6 or 8, big and small one carrying a great bunch of rabbits strung on a stick over his shoulder. I called to them and they stopped a moment, did not answer, and went on. I turned back to meet them at the gate, but they turned up another path though still keeping in sight, and standing, and then moving as I came near. I called to them to come back, that it was cowardly to run away – that if they were doing no harm they must not be afraid. However, I had to give up the chase. Then I met the children, coming from Shanwalla wood, where they had seen boys catching rabbits – the same I think, for they had yellow terriers and one black and white. I felt terribly upset – it seemed like what we had heard of the French Revolution as it began, and lately in Russia, the peasants making themselves free of the woods. I felt so helpless; the police are out of the running, and the Volunteers are being chased by the Black and Tans. It seemed as if I must give in and consent to give up Coole.

I grew more tranquil reading to the children, and looking at their treasures, dogwood and furze, and knowing that having found they can be happy and occupied in woods and fields, they will never fall into the separation from the earth that makes the country an intolerable prison to the town bred.

### 30 NOVEMBER

Yesterday fine and peaceful. I wrote out extracts from my Diary for the *Nation* – for we still need an enquiry. Today tells of the fires at Liverpool – Consequent I should think on Griffith's arrest. Well, we were brought up to revere Moses and the Ten Plagues of Egypt. Worked through Sir A. Lyall's letters. Today I am typing the H. James fragment to send to J. Quinn.

### 3 DECEMBER

Whispers on the countryside tell of anxiety, Marian tells me, about the two Shanaglish boys who were taken away and have not been heard of. And the men who took them – military or Black and Tans – came back with them to Coen's in Gort, and bought a rope.

Writing 'Memories and Meditations' for I feel as H. James did as the War went on – page 402, Vol. II, of his letters. And I also am 'in time of War'; and see on page 418: 'If you have got something to do stick to it tight and do it with faith and force; some things will, no doubt eventually be redeemed.'

### 4 DECEMBER

J. says it is feared there was 'bad work', that the two Loughnane boys from Shanaglish were done away with. 'A man MacGill, took notice where a lorry had turned on the road, where it was narrow – and had knocked down a part of the wall, and he wondered to see it broken, and looked behind it, and there were two boys lying, their heads near one another, and dark clothes on them. He went home and it was three days before he could rise from the bed. He told others and when some went to look there after, the bodies were gone and no word of them.'

## 5 DECEMBER

In Henry James's appeal for Belgian refugees, *Times Supplement*, June 23; he writes,

> ... people surprised by sudden ruffians, murderers or thieves in the dead of night, and marched out terrified and half clad, snatching at the few scant household goods nearest at hand, into a darkness mitigated but by the flaring incendiary torches – this has been the experience stamped on our scores and scores of thousands whose testimony to utter dismay and despoilment, silence alone, the silence of vain uncontrollable wonderment, has for the most part been able to express.

Is not this just what I have been hearing of from the crossroads, from Maree, Peterwell?

The mason R. here, says the Black and Tans came back to Shanaglish after two days, looking for the Loughnanes, 'said they had escaped, and everyone believes they were done away with'. It is drink that urges them. He saw the lorries leaving Gort the day Mrs Quinn was shot; the T.'s in their car firing, and two of them were lying back 'lifeless as if drunk'.

## 6 DECEMBER

J. says 'there was news brought to him last night that the bodies of those two Loughnane boys were found, near Murty Sheehan's crossroads, in a pond that is back from it towards Ballindoreen. It is said they had no clothes on them, and had the appearance of being choked. It looks very bad, but those Black and Tans can do what they like, and no check on them. Look how the Head Constable was afraid to take a deposition from Mrs Quinn before she died, and he in the house.'

*The Connacht Tribune* has an advertisement of 'German toys in great variety at lower prices' – to be had from – Belfast. Going to the woods with J., he says, 'At my dinner hour I met two boys from Shanaglish. It is true about the Loughnanes. Friends had gone to the place they were found, and saw the bodies and they knew them, although they could not be sure what way they met their death. The flesh was as if torn off the bones. God help the poor mother! There is one sister but no boy left in the house.'

The Abbey has lost £500 in the last quarter – chiefly in the last month, since Curfew came in, and the raids became incessant. We must close till Christmas, and after it, until better times come.

## 7 DECEMBER

Marian hears the two Loughnane boys could not be recognised – that 'the bodies looked as if they had been dragged after the lorries. When the men in the lorry came to Coen's shop for the rope they took a bottle of whiskey too, and when he asked for payment all they did was to point a revolver at him. The bodies were brought home last night. When they passed through Gort at 6 o'c. the dead bells were ringing. God help the poor mother, that is a widow!

'Father C. has sent a notice that any sick calls in the night time are to be sent to the other priest, for he himself will be fired at if he goes out. He knows why they are threatening him, and will tell it bye and bye.'

A letter from Lady Greenwood, very kind has

> gone fully into the Quinn case with my husband, who did, as you say, most sincerely deplore it, and is as anxious as I am that the application for a grant will be sympathetically received. I do not think I am raising false hopes if I say that I expect to be able to write again shortly to tell you that the grant is to be made to the bereaved husband.

## 7 DECEMBER

J. says 'the two funerals passed last night going to Shanaglish. I don't know was the mother there, but the sister went to see the bodies after they were found. She could not recognise one of them, but when she saw the other she called out that it was her youngest brother. It is not known for certain how they came by their death. There are some say they were burned. For Murphy went out into the pond after they were found to bring them in, and when he took a hold of the hand of one of them it came off in his hand. They are giving out that they had to do with the Castle Daly murder, but it's strange that if they knew it was boys scared off, they burned the houses that were near.' M. says, 'It is said when they were taken they gave impudence to the Black and Tans.

'It will never be known what way they died. There is no one dare ask a question. But the work they are doing will never be forgotten in Ireland.'

## 8 DECEMBER

M., having been at Mass, says lorries packed with military are passing. 'Those boys were winnowing at their mother's house when they were taken, they had been looked for before but had been away, but came back. It is said that the mother came to Gort barracks and asked where they were, and was told they were safe in prison. Another whisper is that the police or soldiers came back a day or two after they had taken them and said they had escaped, asked if they had come home.' S. doesn't know how they met with their death but says those 'Black and Tans are a terrible class – one of the old police in Gort said to me the other day, as I went to draw my pension, pointing at one of them, "That is what we have to put up with now!" The standard reduced, little chaps of 5ft 6 – and with no character. There are two in Gort that were sent up from Kilcolgan where they were suspected of having stolen £120. Filling their pockets from the people in the name of Law and Order.'

M.J. says 'that Plumber that comes here told me he heard one of them say he was put in Gaol for 7 years for killing his wife, but had only served two of them.'

## 9 DECEMBER

Malachi Quinn here, I read him Lady Greenwood's letter and he was grateful. He says Burke's house that had been burned down and been rebuilt by the neighbours has been raided again in the night by the Black and Tans. He hears they threatened to burn it again, but that the Ardrahan old police have said that if that is done by the 'Castle Police' they will all in a body resign.

He knew the Loughnane boys – 'One of them may have been a bit in it, but the other was as innocent as myself. It is said they were hanged, and that Gill saw them hanging when he went in over the stile, but that he went back on it and was afraid to say it.'

Tim and G. working in the garden tell of it. Tim says, 'It would break your heart to see that funeral, the two hearses and the poor mother between them. She came from her house but she could not recognise her sons. She had come to the barracks before that looking for tidings of them, and some say she got none, and some say she was told they were at Renmore barracks; and the next day she got tidings they were found. Some say that one of them was bayoneted through the heart. Such a thing could hardly happen in savage lands out in Turkey.' J. says, 'There was an enquiry at the barracks yesterday, and we heard nothing since. It is hard to know what happened. There is no one dare trace or tell.'

The *Independent* gives Mr Henry's 'printed reply' in Parliament, that 'he was informed they escaped from custody and had not since been heard of'.

J. says, 'They say they dragged the eldest boy out and beat him – and the other took his part and they beat him too and the mother looking on.'

10 DECEMBER

Today's *Independent* reports, 'The sister gave evidence of making enquiries at Leneboy barrack, where she said she was told by the Commanding Officer that her brothers had escaped.'

The Commissioner of Oaths witnessing my signature said 'the soldiers had sent to Mrs Loughnane's house a couple of days after they had taken the boys, to say they had escaped, and asked if they had gone home – just a bluff.'

Gort Hall (S. Colman's) raided last night, and one prisoner taken – he had a letter in Irish in his pocket.

M. says, 'The B & Ts went into French's house and took a pair of brown boots and some books. Then they went into C. who is employed by the Post Office and were taking his bicycle, but he said, "I will lay my complaint at the barracks if you take government property," and when they saw it was a red bicycle they left it. He and French complained about it and they were sent for to the barracks, and the officer brought out Black and Tans and said, "Tell me if you recognise them," but though they knew them well they would not say it, knowing if they did their house would be burned in the night.'

## 16 DECEMBER

I asked J. if it was true about the Ashtown tenants being forced to work, and he said, 'Yes, there were notices put up saying if they did not their houses would be burned down. Co. coming later to see me about the rates, says the same thing. J. said, 'Is Lord A. in the army? He must have the great influence to make them do that for him.' C. says, 'What are they at all at all, taking away and murdering the two sons of a widow? There are some of them leaving Drumhasna now and coming to Ballylee. There have provisions been sent there today. It is likely it is to bring prisoners to him; they will find more facilities there, to bring them over the bridge and drown them in the river. For Drumhasna is as Cromwell said, without a tree for hanging or water for drowning. A bad class – for it is not drink that urges them it is cruelty.' Mr Edmunds motoring us to Galway says with pride that 15 officers of the Guards have volunteered to come as privates among them. I say if they come to stay it would be an improvement to have at least gentlemen.

## 26 DECEMBER

Mr Johnson says they are overpowered with work at the Bank – all the people are bringing in their money to put in deposit, to save it from the Black and Tans, since the robbing in Kinvara of £200 from Flattery about a week ago.

J. says, 'The poorest creature has some fireside to come in to. But God help the boys on the run.'

Father Considine preached yesterday advising the people to keep no money in their houses, 'and don't be telling me you must keep enough to run the house. If it's taken you'll get no satisfaction.' The Wren-boys have been here – 4 sets of them – not very well up in their lines about the Wren but all singing 'The Soldier's Song'.

Margaret back from church says Miss Daly told Captain Turner what I had said about leaving out 'God Save the King', on the ground that it turns our mind to politics when it should be turned to religion. And he said, 'If you do that is very simple. I would order it on again!'

A. writes that Dillon said in joke to a countryman coming to his shop, 'Have you brought me a turkey?' and he said, 'If you want turkeys it's to Leneboy barrack you must go – it's there they'll have the queer Christmas dinner!' M. says, 'Why wouldn't they, going into houses and taking sucking pigs and whiskey and everything they take a fancy to, and walking off with it.'

## 31 DECEMBER

Mr J. came to tea – he says £200 was taken from Lydon at Duras, and the rush to lodge money at the Bank goes on – £2,000 having been brought 'from the mountains' by one man, but probably others had joined with him to get the higher interest – 5 per cent. Yeats writes in consternation at the idea of B & Ts going to Ballylee and wants 'the name of the Commanding officer in Gort for George's solicitor to write to'!

## 1921

### 1 JANUARY

A clouded night; but today I am more tranquil. I have had a talk with Margaret – she says that Coole takes £800 a year to keep up and brings in nothing so that we cannot keep it and her London home and she and the children could not stay here all the year round. So after discussions I agreed to her plan of trying to let it for 7(9) years, to Richard coming of age and he can decide then about keeping it. Burren will be kept for the summer and River Court be the home for the rest of the year, there is a good day school for A., and C. I shall be glad if this can be carried out. It is quite different from an irrevocable selling of the place. And I am thankful that even Catherine is now 7 years old and they all know the happiness of the country life and could return to it, as I have done with content. So I think this may bring a better understanding. For myself I may buy a little home – Beach House at Burren – that is to be with the children for the summer holidays. M. talks again of giving up Coole . . . But for my sunset it doesn't much matter – I shall just work anywhere while mind and energy last – and after that – what does the last phase matter, except to be in no one's way.

### 5 JANUARY

The piper here – had been ill in the workhouse at Portumna, but was well treated except in tea – 'Did you hear talk ever of the fair-haired tea?' – but he had complained to the doctor, and he had ordered the nurses to 'put a colour on it' next day.

'The Black and Tans are queer hawks, you wouldn't like to be under them any hours at all. The less of them is the best. But I was in a herd's house – a well-off house near dad Ffrench's and they came in and searched the house and brought the man away. In the night time we heard a great beating and hammering at the door and I knew what they were by the nature of their talk. I lay shivering, stretched in my little bed, but they heard me moving and did no harm. They asked me who was I and I said a poor dark man and they asked did I carry a gun and I said I did not. They had brought a great many bottles of whiskey from some house in Ahascragh and they put them on the table and were drinking them, and they asked me did I like whiskey and I said I did not, but I'd take a little, for I was shaking with fear of them. And they filled out the full of a tea cup and put it on the dresser and told me not to let the cat get at it, and they went away.

'Up in Roscommon where there was a land dispute they shot the cattle that were put upon the land. And they put something in whatever they shot them with that left them no use for eating but they had to be burned . . . In two or three places in Roscommon they did that.' Frank says D. goes out shooting under police protection lest the B & Ts could see him when he is near the road and fire. F. advises him to carry a Union Jack as they could not fire on that.

14 JANUARY

On Monday I had a long talk with Margaret. By her showing we cannot keep the woods – she thought not the house – that all must go—land and rates so high. We went through and through. I asked how much she thought she ought to give to keep the house going. She said, nothing, that it would be only for the Christmas holidays. I awoke in the night and thought it over and over – taking it to the 'Higher Court'. I could not and cannot see it right to abandon it, if it be possible to keep it – a place of rest and security for the children in the midst of a changing world. I thought and thought and decided that if I could sell some things I might keep it; Yeats portrait by A. John – and my writing table, and the books given me by authors. I talked again to her next day and we walked out to see how much we could cut off and what we could keep. We planned out keeping Nut Wood, Pond field, Shanwalla, to Lake farm gate – tillage fields and the strip of trees beyond them and plantations. This would make a little demesne about 350 acres, wooded and romantic and beautiful, tho' any who know the old woods would miss the extent. This she thinks – even this – would come to £300 a year in rates and taxes. Then what makes it the more desirable I thought that perhaps the 300 acres woodland we sell might be taken for forestry and so be kept as woods – a great advantage instead of selling them to farmers or timber merchants who would cut them down and turn in cattle. I should be quite satisfied could this be done and would try hard to attain the £300 a year by selling things and try to do the rest out of my income – under £500 a year outside my uncertain earnings! I would be sorry not to keep the place so many have loved, I told M. that Anne would be the one to miss it most and to this she agreed.

If this plan is impossible – then House, Gardens – back lawn, field, Shanwalla she thought £150 rates and taxes.

She is against my selling the writing table – but doesn't grudge the books. I feel more peaceful having a clear understanding. I have written to Robinson to try and find out about Forestry purchase probabilities.

DUBLIN, 25 FEBRUARY

*The Revolutionist* at the Abbey with a large audience all much interested in the play . . .

Mrs MacSwiney was there, I went to meet her in the Green Room, such a charming face and manner – 'a sweet girl' she would have been called a while ago. I told her with what pride we gave this play for the first time, that we felt we were laying a wreath upon the grave.

SUNDAY, 27 FEBRUARY

Splendid audiences. Yesterday's matinée the stalls were not full, but so many people were standing in the Pit that I sent for Robinson, and we brought all we could find places for to the front. Last night all places full, many turned away at the door. We had already decided to play it again next week, and R.

announced this from the stage. I feel so happy that we have been able to keep the Abbey going if only for this one week, the production of a national play of fine quality by one who has literally given his life to save the lives of others. For by his death and endurance he has made it unnecessary for any other prisoners to protest through hunger strike; he has done it once for all. It is strange to see the change in political thought now; the audience (in spite of Robinson's request in the programmes for no applause during acts) cheering the revolutionist who stands up against the priest's denunciation, denounces his meddling in return. They applauded also fine sentences: 'Life is a divine adventure; he will go farthest who has most faith.'

2 MARCH. COOLE

Came home yesterday *via* Galway. I went to tea with Sarah Purser on Sunday, she is much pleased because I had written of her good work in getting up the Hone–Yeats exhibition which had been Hugh's first acquaintance with their work. And this I had done without any hint from her or others, but just from finding from the old catalogues what she had done. She told me of a French newspaper paragraph telling of a bequest to the Louvre, carried out by the executors, though not in legal form. She, anxious as we must be about the country, hears that the extreme Sinn Feiners now declare they will fight it out this time, even if the rest of Dublin is burnt down.

Monday morning at the Abbey they were rehearsing *Aristotle*; very cheerily.

In Galway I found the chicks well and merry, and liking school, so will leave them on. (I went to see Mr Cruise about Malachi Quinn's compensation – so very small – but he says there is no use in trying to get it increased.) I said the interest on £300 would not even pay a servant to take the wife's place in housework, but he said the father of a boy shot by mistake had only been given £150.

I said the policemen's families were given much larger compensation which seemed hardly fair, but he gave the, I think, inadequate reason that the County Court Judges fixed these. He asked what policy I would propose? I said I was no politician, I have no taste for politics, and besides this I had to keep out of them, because I could do my work better about Hugh's pictures, and especially in the Abbey which I think so important. He said, 'Yes, that is of great importance.' Then presently he said, 'I once sent a play there and it was refused!' He told me the plot, a dispute about a right of way, but I didn't remember it. We did talk politics a little, or rather a possible settlement. He says the government cannot give in because Egypt and India would then think they had but to murder policemen to get their self government. I said the present troubles were doing as much to injure the government in India and Egypt as anything else could do, and he assented. I told him that I had said to the Volunteers that I would prefer a republic, but were I in authority would accept Dominion Home Rule because the Dominions will one day be republics. He blames S.F. for rejecting the present Home Rule Bill, says if they would accept it the government would give them almost anything they want; and blamed people for objecting to it who had not read it. I said I had not read it, but that it was so strongly objected to by the three provinces that I did not see how De Valera could, if he would, accept it and keep self respect. I told him what A.E. said, that the Prime Minister is not master in the Cabinet. Then he asked if De Valera would be master enough to carry a settlement against Michael Collins. (Of course one feels that he may have to shed Collins and Lloyd George and Bonar Law, before any settlement can come.) We parted in the room cordially enough, but on the steps he renewed an offer to send me back to Coole in his own car. I had refused, making excuses, but when he pressed it I said, 'The real truth is I would lose my character if I went home in a police car.' He seemed hurt, but I explained I had all through kept free from official surroundings, I was working with Nationalists, and they have so often been deserted or betrayed. I told him of G. Wyndham's offer of £5, and how Lady Aberdeen had asked me to dine at the V.L., offering not to have my name put in the papers ('people often dine with us whose names are not sent to the papers') but I had refused on this ground. He defended his B & Ts – yet read me a letter from the Schoolmaster at Kilchreest begging for protection, as he was threatened night and day, and ordered to leave within a week. I was surprised and said, 'Is he a Unionist?' But he said, 'No, the threats are from the Forces of the Crown.' (I heard afterwards he had spoken at a farmer's meeting in favour of the division of ranches.)

All quiet here, but J.D. says, 'A lady has been staying at Lally's Hotel who went about, to Shanaglish, and to M. Quinn's and other places – and the police arrested her a couple of days ago and took her away.' He thought it might have been Mrs Watts; but she had left the day after she was here.

I asked again about Mrs Quinn's house at Caheraboneen. He says the young men were stripped naked, thrown down, a heavy stone put on their backs to keep them from moving, and then flogged. 'They will never be the better of it. And there is no one knows what it was for.' They had taken her money before burning the house.

COOLE, TUESDAY, 22 MARCH

All well here.

Old Niland today says, 'Bartley Hynes that was living up the road from Kinvara to Galway had his house burned, and the furniture and the hay and corn, by the Black and Tans. And there is a woman, an O'Donnell, over in Peterswell, and she having but the one son, and they pulled him out of the bed and brought him abroad in the street and shot him, and they brought her out that she'd seen him shot. And she took the son in her arms and he died in her arms. About twelve days ago that happened. They didn't give no reason at all for what they done.

'At Stanton's house, up from Kinvara, they took £20 worth of a pig and threw it into the lorry and brought it away; and fowl they took and they burned the house, a fortnight before Patrick's day. It's for robbery they are out and for killing. They were firing in Gort four nights ago, about forty shots around the street, and a bullet went by Pat Lally's ear as he came out of his own gate where he was watching ewes. They are like wild animals that came from some place, or savages out from some island.

'Look at the way the rates are gone up, that the less man that will have land will be the best man in the end. What way can they pay them? It was in the prophecy of Columcille that a man would pay twice but he wouldn't pay the third time; and that he'd shoot his cow in the door before he'd give it up to them.

'In Cromwell's time there wasn't half as much done because they hadn't the way of doing it. What was Cromwell's army only walking Ireland? But now with their lorries there's not one of them has to walk half a mile.

'And what can the Sinn Feiners do? It's as good to be standing on the ground firing stones at the moon as to be trying to knock rights out of the government, unless that America might come at them. And if America would stir and go out against them, sure the Japanese are watching themselves.'

Mona Gough writes in answer to my letter that Lady Carson 'has promised she will speak to Sir Edward herself about the matter of the pictures, and told me to send a message to you that she would do what she could. The Baby is a most delightful child, *very* like Sir Edward!'

## 24 MARCH

Power says, 'The name of the Black and Tans will go from generations down the same as Cromwell. Out in Shanaglish they burned a picture of the Redeemer – "Is this another Sinn Feiner?" says one of them and he pulled it down and threw it into the fire.'

Peter says, 'The town is filled up with police and Black and Tans these last days. In dread they are something might happen at Easter, and they have a notice put up that if anything is done the town of Gort will blaze.

'But there might come some change, for in England gentle and simple would seem to be wishing for peace.

'There was a schoolmaster in Kilchreest brought out from his house and beaten because he was teaching Irish to the children.'

## 7 APRIL

Robinson's wire about the matinée is cheering. I've written to Sara Allgood.

Yesterday Regan, Hanlon, Donohoe, down again, abusing Malachi Quinn – wanting I know not what. Regan I think afraid of his sons being arrested.

But Tim says Malachi was 'beaten with a hurl' and that his door was broken down as well as his windows, and that he knows who the doers were. I preach to both sides the wickedness and folly of this private quarrel over a month's grazing, when the great battle is going on in the country.

## 20 JUNE

Old cracked Mary in her rags says, 'They are terrible in Gort and out beyond, and firing down the second next boreen near Kelly's, and out in the borders of the town, and if they got any person lonesome down the road what would they care about them?

'I was out gathering a faggot for the fire and two of them came up to me, soldiers, having black gaiters and guns at their shoulders. "Have you any money," they said. "I have not," I said, "I haven't one penny if you gave me Ireland." "I wonder you wouldn't have some ha'pence to give us," they said. But when they saw I had nothing they went away.'

Young H. and F. hunting through the fields, yesterday and knocking down walls. No law to appeal to. 'The men who could have been called to make her laws and lead her armies in prison or dead,' as in Italy, in Trevelyan's *Defence of Roman Republic*.

## SATURDAY, 17 SEPTEMBER

I got up at 6 a.m. and left by early train for home. The papers more cheering, De V. having sent a rather cloudy 'surprised' telegram to L.G., who will probably find another cloud in which to meet him. I had only just come back when P.C., now Commandant of Volunteers, came to ask for a subscription 'to buy arms'. I said I had seen in the appeal they sent round that it was wanted also for reparations, and that I didn't think they would need arms, there would be peace. He said he thought so too 'but if we do want them'. I asked if money could be applied to restoration at the giver's wish, and he said certainly, and I gave £1 to show my goodwill, but said I could not approve of killings on one side or the other, or indeed of capital punishment at all, remembering Shelley . . . 'Whether death is good or evil, a punishment or a reward, or whether it be wholly indifferent, no man can take upon himself to assert; and so it seems to me that while we live in that unfathomed ignorance it is too terrible a responsibility for any man to take on himself, the sending of another out of the life we know, unless it may be in the certainty of thus saving other lives.' Yet this 'unless' leads one very far, and I am not certain that I was quite honest, for I do think if war can ever be justified these surprises and ambushes called murder were justified to break the government by England that has been destroying both body and soul, and my heart goes out to those who have taken that responsibility and have risked their own lives – or lost them, while I have been but 'the hurler sitting on the wall'.

### TUESDAY, 4 OCTOBER

Sunday was a wet day so I stayed in the house glad of the rest, and Keller came to talk about the Coole avenues. The agreement only gives us a right of way by Gort avenue, not reserving it for sole use, and we have no power to stop blocking of middle avenue. The agreement must have been very carelessly drawn. It is a pity.

Keller is disturbed at the prospect of a new government, thinks land business will be no more, and 'doesn't know what line to take'. He had lunched at the Wicklow Hotel the other day, and seen a young man at one of the tables, on whose words all the others were hanging, and who when going and presented with

the bill took out a handful of notes and threw one to the waiter
with a great air. He asked who it was; 'Michael Collins'. I said to
Dolan he seemed to be Dublin's 'fancy man', and he said, 'That
is the way with the hunted men.' I had asked if our new actors
were Sinn Fein and he said, 'Is not everyone Sinn Fein now?'

Yesterday, Monday, I tried to see the Lord Mayor about the
statement re Hugh's pictures but he was presiding at a Corpora-
tion meeting and made an appointment for today. I came back
to the Abbey and read plays, none good. And at dress rehearsal
of *Lord Mayor* we had five priests in, not allowed to see real
performances, and I brought them to the Green room where the
players were having tea and the barmbrack I had brought from
home. They were delighted with *Lord Mayor*, not so enthusiastic
about *A Serious Thing*.

This Tuesday morning, I got to the Mansion House at 11 o'c.,
and saw the Lord Mayor and read him my statement. He
suggested my sending it to Lloyd George myself, but I told him I
had been working almost single-handed all this time, and it was
time for others to take the matter up; that the pictures should be
of more importance to him, as they are the property of the
Municipality (or should be) than to me. And he said he would
consult the Dail Eireann Cabinet and let me know on Thursday.

Then I said I had very much on my mind those unfortunate
interned prisoners kept shut up untried, winter coming on, and
that they must feel it all the more at this time of excitement. He
said at once, 'That is just what I have had in my mind for some
days.' I said I saw in the papers that the leaders will not *ask* for
their release as an act of grace, and I thought perhaps some
outsiders might be of use in doing so. He thought this possible. I
asked if representative names, perhaps of Bishops, on a petition or
letter to the papers would be of use. He said, 'No, not Bishops.' I
said, 'I meant Protestant ones.' 'No,' he said. 'We have done very
well without the Church all this time and we don't want to bring
them in now.' I asked if Horace Plunkett's people could be of any
use as he is a little sore at being left out. And he has secretaries
and organisation. And I said that when Conscription was threatened I had myself got a few writers to sign a letter against it for

the English papers. He said, 'I would do it straight off, but that now the Cabinet is sitting I would do nothing without consulting them.' I said that was just my own feeling, we must do nothing without their authority. This also he will let me know on Thursday.

Keller said he had asked Hogan, just out from a meeting of the Dail, what he thought would be the future of the country. He said he believed that within three or four years of independence 'there would not be a ballad heard, all thoughts would be turned to economics'. He thought also there would be less individual liberty than in England, that Ireland would be more on the American model.

## 6 OCTOBER

Today Thursday, I went to Mansion House at 11 o'c., and the Lord Mayor brought in Alderman Cosgrave, Minister of Home Affairs, who said my letter about the pictures had been considered by the Cabinet; that they think it better not to take up the matter until the Peace Treaty is being made in detail, and have sent it to the Minister of Fine Arts to keep till then. He asked if I thought this satisfactory, and I said Yes, if it is remembered at the proper time, and that I advised their pressing for the Government Bill (Macpherson's) to be got through, as simply legalising the Codicil. It will avoid future legal difficulties.

Then the Lord Mayor said we were to do nothing yet about Prisoners' release; he will let me know when the time comes. I suppose they have some reason for this. I told him I had thought of either a meeting at the Abbey to pass a resolution, or a letter signed by all our playwrights, Yeats, G.B.S., Robinson &c. But he said 'Wait' so I shall get home.

I said as I was going that I had never seen De Valera and would much like to see him, even from the window, when he comes as expected at 3 o'c. The Lord Mayor said, 'God help you!' I asked, 'Why?' and he said, 'I oughtn't to have said that,' and murmured something about idols. I said I didn't make an idol of him, but I had been fighting his battles, and he said, 'Oh,

I know that.' But then he called out, 'Here he is coming in!' and hurried me to the doorway he would pass through to the Cabinet meeting, and said as he came, 'Lady Gregory – President De Valera.' I said I was just going to his old constituency, West Clare, and he said he had never had time to go there since just after his first election, and I said there were many very proud of having had him as a representative. The Lord Mayor said, 'Lady Gregory was just wishing to see you,' and I said, 'You have been so often in my prayers I wanted to see what you looked like.' And indeed I liked his face, good, honest, with something in it of Lincoln.

I I DECEMBER

At church today, and said the General Thanksgiving with a full heart. The Archdeacon stopped me to ask if it was true De Valera had come to lunch with me last Sunday, and when I said No, he said he would have no objection to meet him himself, and thinks he must have seen him at Blackrock school in his boyhood, and supposes he will resign and be made Premier instead of President. Quite a change from his old 'Rebellion is as the sin of witchcraft' days.

J. says the prisoners back from internment are against the continuance of war, especially those from Derrybrian, who 'got fierce treatment, were often dragged from their beds and flogged by the Black and Tans, because it was thought they gave shelter to the Clare boys. And so they might give them bed and a bit of breakfast, and they'd make off for the day then.'

We had arrived early at church and while waiting I read as is my habit the Tate and Brady psalms; my favourite

> The trees of God without the care
> Or art of man with sap are fed;
> The mountain cedar looks as fair
> As those in royal gardens bred.

But going farther where in the plagues of Egypt:

> From fields to villages and towns
> Commissioned vengeance flew

my mind went back to last winter and the reprisals.

Meanwhile Father C. at Kiltartan had said very little about the peace, just that he thought it likely it would be all right. But had in his sermon given 'a terrible dressing' to four of the young men of the parish who, though he had been given the use of the fields by the coursing committee for the coursing match he has been getting up, was sent in by these a bill for £35. The four denounced being unpopular, the congregation enjoyed the sermon. Marian is astonished to hear that Insurance with other departments of government will be in Irish hands, says, 'Isn't that a good thing?' I say, 'Yes, very good, and they are good men who are making plans for all, though I don't suppose they will please everybody'; and she says, 'How can they? There was a little boy asked by the Bishop at the Catechising "Can God do everything?" and he said, "No," and the Bishop said, "What is it he cannot do?" and the little chap said, "He can't please the farmers."'

## 26 DECEMBER

The adjournment of the Dail gives one breathing time and hope! and Christmas has passed peacefully. I miss the workhouse children now it is closed, after so many years. Robert used to come with me to give them toys and the old men their tobacco, and last year I had Richard and Anne with me. Our Christmas tree here, Guy and Olive staying in the house, Bagots, officers, M.F.H., etc. Today the wrenboys came, knowing but few lines about the wren. Some sang the Soldiers Song, and two of the groups gave a song about Kevin Barry being hanged in Mountjoy gaol for Ireland's sake.

1922

SUNDAY, 8 JANUARY

I was getting ready for church when Anne came up to say the telegraph boy was coming and was calling out that the Treaty is ratified. I ran down and got L.R.'s telegram. Such a relief! The little boy had fallen off his bicycle with excitement on the avenue and had shouted the news to the maids coming from Mass and they had cheered. He said, 'This is the first time I ever was sent with a message, and I brought the best message that ever was brought!' and I gave him a shilling in addition to his apples. Mine had been the only message to Gort; and had been given out, everyone delighted except the poor Bagots who foresee the vanishing of officers. We met a motor lorry leaving Gort in charge of one soldier and I said to Guy, 'There is the army in retreat!' And we went to the Barracks after church (where I had said the General Thanksgiving with a full heart) and got Richard's gun and cartridges back again.

SUNDAY, 29 JANUARY

Church today very empty but for a new group of police come from some distant part. Bagot at the door said Black and Tans were expected today, but their motor had been stolen at Kilchreest. He also heard Mr Cruise had been fired at near Galway (I think not true).

The first Sunday for years there was no 'God save the King'. We had the Royal Family prayers, but these I used sincerely, putting in place of Royalties the new government of Ireland.

EASTER SUNDAY

Conservative Evening. John Dillon and Professor Henry came to lunch. Dillon looks impressive in his old age; an El Greco type, and talked all the time, stayed till 4.30, very interesting all he said.

* * *

'It was the executions after the Rising that led to it all. If the leaders had been kept in prison until after the war a settlement could have been made and accepted. I was shut up in Gt George's Street for three days by the Sinn Feiners, and the first day I got out — told me there were going to be executions, and we went together to the Viceregal Lodge and found Wimborne there, and Lady Wimborne, holding a rifle and ready to leave. He promised to do his best and said, "I have been disgracefully treated, I was told nothing, I have no power." Then we went to General Maxwell, and I protested against the executions and he said, "Mr Dillon, these men have shot English soldiers, and I have come to Dublin first to put down the Rebellion and then to punish the offenders." "But the Rebellion is over now." "Yes and I am going to punish the offenders, four of them are to be shot tomorrow morning. I am going to ensure that there will be no treason whispered, even whispered in Ireland for a hundred years." "You have been trying to do that for years." "Well, I am going to do it now. There will not be a whisper."

'I went back to Wimborne and he promised to do his best. Next day I heard the four men had been shot in the morning and I went to him. He was very angry said, "I dined with General Maxwell last night and he promised that only two should be killed." Then I went over to Westminister and when I saw Asquith he said, "I am going over to Ireland." "What on earth are you going for?" He said the wires had been cut and he was going to see what was going on. It is well he did go, for the military were having their way, they had made a list of fifty for execution. Then it was cut down to 35, but Asquith stopped them. It was to please the military leave had been given for these. I saw Lloyd George about it too, and I said, "Maxwell is a brute." "No," he said, "he is not that, he is an ass."

'Redmond's speech was the great misfortune, promising the help of Ireland for the Empire. That is a word that is hated in Ireland. It has always been so; there has been actual joy at any defeat of it.'

I told of my old nurse and the cheering she remembered hearing for the landing of the French in '98, and he said, 'There was an uncle of mine who laid down his head and cried when he heard of the victory at Waterloo.'

13 MAY

Yesterday a nice motor drive with Guy to Ballylee and to Burren, sea and mountains beautiful. I went to bed tired, and at 11 o'c. Mike knocked at the door. 'There's men downstairs knocking at the hall door. I think they are raiders.' I told him I would follow him down, put on dressing gown and veil over my hair. He said they had called out to him to open the door. He said he hadn't the key. 'Where is it?' 'Upstairs in Lady Gregory's room' (it being in the door all the time). When I came to the door they were knocking again. I went to it and said, 'Who is there?' 'Open or it will be the worse for you' – a young unpleasant bullying voice. I knew one would not gain anything by speaking to such men, so stood at the foot of the stairs. They kicked the door then and I expected every moment they would break in the unshuttered window and come in. I prayed for help though without much hope, and stood still. After a while the knocking ceased, I thought they had gone to look for another door and whispered to Mike to come up to the playroom by the back stairs as we could see from there. But the door on back stairs was locked, and the moonlight was now so bright on front staircase I didn't like to show myself on it. We could see nothing or hear nothing. Once I saw a red light and thought they were coming back with helpers. But no one came, and I could see no one from any window, and at 1 o'c. went back to bed and Mike to his. It did shake the nerves. Yet at the worst moment I felt it was right somehow I should know what others had suffered in like cases, and that I might be glad later to have known it. (February 1924. Yes it has given me more sympathy and understanding, for now that I am alone again in the house, so long after, I constantly feel a slight nervousness when I have gone to bed, a feeling that there may again come a knock at the door. And this although of those two men one is in gaol (for a more serious crime) and the other in the Civic Guards – something like Pharaoh's butler and baker!)

1 AUGUST

Cold and showery. Yesterday Yeats and G. came to lunch and for the afternoon. She had just come back from Dublin. She had met at Gogartys several members of the Dail. Michael Collins himself had come in near midnight in his uniform of Commander in Chief, with shining buttons – had walked there alone though his life is threatened. All seemed in good spirits and very confident that within two months the country will be quiet. They are a little anxious about Cork, there are good fighters in it, Kerry men, and it is feared they will not fight there but will get out and go through the country. Yeats thought all the news good. I think two months a long time and think this new outburst of burning country houses a bad sign. On the way to Ballinasloe with Dr Walsh (the priest who had been at Tillyra) they had to pull down walls sometimes and take the motor through the fields. They said there was a train running to Gort today.

This morning I was told that Kiltartan bridge was blown up the night before last by three bombs and is 'the greatest shipwreck ever was seen'. The train that was coming was signalled to go back, and we are more than ever cut away. And X. says he believes the Irregulars are hiding in our woods. Ten of them came through the place on Sunday night, before the blowing up of the bridge and were joined by others, not all from a distance, on the road. A girl of the Donoghues showed John her milkpans, quite black from the dust shaken down from the roof by the explosion.

2 AUGUST

A post this afternoon. The Dalys and Mr Johnson here for tea say Captain H. is back in Gort, he was found marooned on an island and rescued. The troops in Gort are not allowed into public houses now. They are very well behaved and vigilant, examine strangers. And the little children in Crow Lane play 'Put up your hands! You have to be identified!' Lough Cutra is none the worse for its two sets of occupants, the Free Staters were very careful, their officers locked most of the rooms lest they should use them. Captain Lennard when there used to say, 'I like living in a lordly hall, but I'd like to see a lordly table!' However they killed five sheep and commandeered milk and butter, and from the garden cucumbers and tomatoes.

Now Z. tells me there is serious danger of the Ballylee bridge being blown up. I said I would go over and tell Yeats; then remembered Mrs B. is coming to tea so I have written a note to the C.O. in Gort and will ask her to leave it at the Barracks, I must not send one of the men. One is told over and over, 'The government is confident,' but we seem far from peace here.


20 AUGUST. EVENING

Before church I was told there had been trees cut again, blocking the road to Ennis. And at the gate Mr B. told me he had just heard the bridge at Ballylee had been blown up last night, so I was in anxiety all through the service. After it John said Yeats had gone to Coole, and had left a message that though the bridge was destroyed they were all safe.

Mr B. said that last Sunday as they went home from church they had without knowing it driven over a mine near Kilbecanty. They are told there were Irregulars behind the wall and in a shed with a machine-gun and holding the wire, ready to explode the mine when the Free State troops were on it on their way to Mass; this is their revenge because of some having been arrested as they came out of chapel. However the F.S. men didn't go to Kilbecanty that day.

I found Yeats here. He said all were safe, and not a pane of glass broken. He said, 'Last night about 12 o'c. there was a knock at the door, I went down. There was a man, not in uniform. He said, "What room do you sleep in?" I pointed up to it and he said, "That's all right, you will be safe there. Stay in the house." I said, "Are you going to blow up the bridge?" "Yes." "I suppose you will give me time to bring the children up into our room?" "Yes, there will be plenty of time, the explosion won't be for an hour and a half. There will be three explosions, I'll warn you when they are coming." We got the children and maids upstairs, opened the windows that the glass might not be broken, and waited, put cotton wool in our ears and the children's. Then we saw men running away and one came to the door again and called out it was coming, and went away saying, "Good night; thanks." The explosions were not very loud, I had expected much worse remembering the air raids. Anne said, "Glynn (the carpenter) is making a great noise up in the workshop" and Mary said, "yes, he makes a great noise when he lets his hammer fall." The miller had come to look at the bridge in the morning and said, 'It's a pity, it's a pity, it took a long time to make all that worked stone. They won't find many to help them in their work.'

## 23 AUGUST

They say there was fighting at Gortnacorna, and the Chevy woods were searched, and Irregulars driven towards Peterswell, and eleven taken there; one or two wounded and brought to Gort Workhouse-Barrack, 'and two of your own tenants among them.'

John brings back from the Post Office news of Michael Collins's death, shot at Bandon – 'You have bad news to bring to Coole, her ladyship will be in a great way' – And indeed it was a great blow – my hopes had been so much in him and he had been so good about Hugh's pictures. I was stunned, I could not stay in the house but went and sat in the garden for a long time – found at last a little comfort in Mulcahy's fine call to the army:

Stand calmly by your posts. Then bravely and undaunted do
  your work.
Let no cruel act of reprisal blemish your bright honour.
Every dark hour that Michael Collins met since 1916 seemed
  but to steel that bright strength of his and temper his gay
  bravery.

You are left each inheritors of that strength and of that bravery. To each of you falls his unfinished work.'

## 28 AUGUST

The morning of Michael Collins's funeral. I have been reading over Housman's poem:

They carry back bright to the coiner the mintage of man –
The lads that will die in their glory and never be old. (A long
    list now!)

Then I hear 'The Republicans are glad. K. was glad telling of it, and T.S. said, "Isn't this a great victory!" but four of the Free State men and their Captain that were in the house were in a great way and they said, "The next time we go out we'll shoot to kill!" And one F. a great republican said, "I'd sooner have the British back again." The Republicans think that if they got their Republic they would have no more rent, rates or taxes to pay. They are sure of that. Miskell's farm has been taken from him, or the most of it, two hundred acres, walled around, and he forbidden to put any more stock on it. He complained about his turf being cut, and they drove away fifty of his cattle then. Some say it is because one day the Republicans went into his house and asked breakfast, and the wife gave the worst breakfast they ever got in any place, and they said it would be a dear breakfast to them. Skim milk they got.'

And A. writes that in Galway on the very evening of Collins's death (but they may not have known of it) there were sarcastic notices put up in Galway calling for recruits and signed 'Michael Collins. God Save the King'. 'And when those boys were taken near this one of them called out, "Up De Valera", and one of the Free Staters said to another, "Will I shoot him?" And after that there was quiet.'

## 2 DECEMBER

G. Yeats had heard at Gogarty's the government could no longer refuse to release Miss McSwiney when a resolution asking for it was sent from Cork by Michael Collins's sisters and Mrs Mulcahy. And that a big offensive is threatened for the 6th December (ratifying of the Treaty). Also that they will not state the crime of the four men executed, because then revolvers would be carried as before by those who have no criminal charge against them. Two of those executed were criminal looters, one had been a spy in the government offices and had betrayed the planned journey, the road to be taken by Michael Collins; the fourth was the man who had shot (when robbing a public house) Cosgrave's uncle dead. She hears also that St Helena has actually been borrowed for the prisoners. Little Anne Yeats welcomed me. She had shouted the other day, 'Sacred Heart! The cat's eating the canary!' and the maids rushed in just in time to save it from the cat's mouth. But Anne is especially indignant because she says the cat had already had its tea.

## 1923

### 15 APRIL

I dined with the Yeatses on Thursday. The door was cautiously opened on the chain and a voice asked, 'Who is there.' I laughed and said, 'A friend,' and a Guard in uniform let me in. I had a little talk with him on my usual line – where is the quarrel? and he agreed. Yeats had been threatened, owing to a conversation with Mrs McBride, when he had refused to interfere for Miss MacSwiney, and has told her he will have no more political conversations with her. But now both she and Iseult have been arrested and lodged in Kilmainham.

At Mullingar on the way up, I went to the waiting-room and found it guarded and a soldier evidently wounded lying on a bench. But Dublin is quieter though there is some firing most nights, and there is real hope of peace. Yeats says that the five names in favour of peace in the captured document were of the military, and the six against it politicians.

At the Abbey I found an armed guard; there has been one ever since the theatres were threatened if they kept open. And in the Green room I found one of them giving finishing touches to the costume of Tony Quinn, who is a Black and Tan in the play, and showing him how to hold his revolver. The *Shadow of a Gunman* was an immense success, beautifully acted, all the political points taken up with delight by a big audience. Sean O'Casey, the author, only saw it from the side wings the first night but had to appear to make his bow. I brought him into the stalls the other two nights and have had some talk with him. Last night there was an immense audience, the largest I think since the first night of *Blanco Posnet*. Many, to my grief, had to be turned away from the door. Two seats had been kept for Yeats and me, but I put Casey in one of them and sat in the orchestra for the first act, and put Yeats in the orchestra for the second. I had brought Casey round to the door before the play to share my joy in seeing the crowd surging in (Dermod O'Brien caught in the queue) and he introduced me to two officers, one a Colonel. (Yeats has wanted me to go with them to a *ball* given by the army, 'good names being wanted'!)

Casey told me he is a labourer, and as we talked of masons said he had 'carried the hod'. He said, 'I was among books as a child, but I was sixteen before I learned to read or write. My father loved books, he had a big library, I remember the look of the books high up on shelves.' I asked why his father had not taught him and he said, 'He died when I was three years old, through those same books. There was a little ladder in the room to get to the shelves, and one day when he was standing on it, it broke and he fell and was killed.' I said, 'I often go up the ladder in our library at home,' and he begged me to be careful. He is learning what he can about Art, has bought books on Whistler and Raphael, and takes *The Studio*. All this was as we watched the crowd. I forget how I came to mention the Bible, and he asked, 'Do you like it?' I said, 'Yes, I read it constantly, even for the beauty of the language.' He said he admires that beauty, he was brought up as a Protestant but has lost belief in religious forms. Then, in talking of our war here, we came to Plato's *Republic*, his dream-city, whether on earth or in heaven not far away from the city of God. And then we went in to the play. He says he sent us a play four years ago *Frost and Flowers* and it was returned, but marked 'Not far from being a good play'. He has sent others, and says how grateful he was to me because when we had to refuse the Labour one, 'The Crimson in the Tri-Colour', I had said, 'I believe there is something in you' and 'Your strong point is characterisation'. And I had wanted to pull that play together and put it on to give him experience, but Yeats was down on it. Perrin says he has offered him a pass sometimes when he happened to come in, but he refused and said, 'No one ought to come into the Abbey Theatre without paying for it.' He said, 'All the thought in Ireland for years past has come through the Abbey. You have no idea what an education it has been to the country.' That, and the fine audience on this our last week, put me in great spirits.

17 SEPTEMBER

An afternoon with Lady Ardilaun at St Annes. She will give help to the Abbey if we need it. She is a lonely figure in her wealth; childless and feeling the old life shattered around her. Macroom Castle, her childhood home burned, and a desecration she feels more, the Free State soldiers in it have put a roof over a part, 'So I have not even my ruins.' She laments for Ashford also, now a Barrack, and for the loss of Society and 'those nice young officers who used to write their names in our book'; and she speaks with violent despair over government and its opponents – 'Our class is gone, and who is there to replace it?' Yet she has stood her ground, taken a house in Dublin for the winter and brings friends to the Abbey on Saturday afternoons and has given several concerts, or musical afternoons. She is 'grande dame' all through, and her welcome touched me, she took my hands and kissed me. Her lovely garden is, she says, the one thing that keeps her there. When she spoke with despair of the country I said it was from outside our help must come, a spiritual influence to do away with rancour, and she said, 'Oh yes, there must be forgiveness. Monks must go through the country and preach.' Today an Anglican brother, Father Fitzgerald, has been here and wants to found a community for the brotherhood to which he belongs. Yeats told him of Father Stephen Brown who has at his own expense founded a library of Catholic theology in Westmoreland St; thinks they might help each other. Yeats talked of his long belief that the reign of democracy is over for the present, and in reaction there will be violent government from above, as now in Russia, and is beginning here. It is the thought of this force coming into the world that he is expressing in his Leda poem, not yet quite complete. He sat up till 3 o'c. this morning working over it, and read it to me as complete at midday, and then half an hour later I heard him at it again.

I NOVEMBER

I have sold the rabbits to Bernard Cunningham (who was in old days brought before me as a poacher!). He has been very steady and hardworking since his release from gaol.

EVENING. Near 8 o'c. when the children had been roasting chestnuts and I was reading *The Castaways* to them in the library, Marian came up looking rather frightened, and said there were men at the door wanting to see me, would not give their names. I went down and opened the hall door. There were three young men, I could only see one, the spokesman, clearly, the light falling on him, but I didn't recognise him, may have seen him before, but I have no gift for remembering faces. He asked if I had sold the rabbits to Cunningham. I. 'Yes.' He. 'What money did he give?' I. 'That is between him and me.' 'Did not Murty O'Loughlin get the rabbits for twenty years?' I. 'For a good many years certainly.' He. 'Why didn't he get them now?' I. 'He did not ask for them either this year or last year. I had no offer from him or anyone last year.' He. 'He should have them.' I. 'He did not ask for them. He has his old age pension now, I don't suppose he wanted them.' He. 'He could not take them last year because there was no law or order in the country. There will be trouble if Cunningham gets them.' I. 'Do you mean that you will cause trouble?' Another. 'We are here for the sake of quietness.'

1st. 'It is likely Cunningham will not be allowed to have them. There will be trouble.' I. 'I suppose you mean by that you will cause trouble but I hope you will think again before you do anything that will break the law of God.' He. 'You must take back the agreement.' I. 'That would be a dishonourable thing to do. I will not do what is dishonourable.'

Then he harped on Murty's twenty years, and I said I had no reason to believe he wanted them. And I begged them again to keep the peace, to follow the law of Christ. 'Do unto others as you would they should do unto you'. He. 'Do you know Cunningham used to take your rabbits?' I. 'Yes, he was brought before me once or twice, or came to ask forgiveness.' He. 'Do you know that he was in gaol?' I. 'Yes. It was I who got him out.' He. 'You did! He was convicted!' I. 'Yes, but he was young and foolish, he had been long enough in gaol, others had led him on. And since he came back I have heard nothing but good of him.'

Then the speaker put his hand in his pocket, fumbled, and brought out a cigarette which he tipsily offered to another. I laughed and said, 'I thought it might have been a revolver.' The other said, 'Oh no,' and I said Goodnight, the spokesman saying as he turned to go, 'There will be trouble and the responsibility will be on you.' I only remembered afterwards that Murty could not have taken up the business without losing his pension. But it makes me sad and anxious.

I came back and read to the children, and they knew nothing of it. They were young men, and Marian thinks as I do that the one who spoke had been drinking.

The children are watching the stars. Anne has twice seen falling stars. Ellen tells them that if they can see seven stars at the same time, for seven nights one after another, they will have whatever they wish.

I began today typing my old journals, chiefly about the fight for the pictures.

## 1924

### 5 MARCH

I felt very downhearted last night, that violence going on, we need the teaching of Christ again and his example, so blurred it seems now. Today old Niland comes for firing, tells me there were seven men who attacked Houston. One, as I thought, was the man who had been fined. He has been arrested.

Poor old Padraig, his pension has been cut down this week (or so he said), a shilling from his wife's, a shilling from his. After his glass of wine his indignation rose. 'The English will be back again, and this beggarly government put out, and I'll be glad of it. If I was a scholar to write to the English papers I would put them out.' He is certain the English will be back again. I said No, but he is confident, 'It is in Columcille's prophecy. There was a Lord one time was with O'Brien at Dromoland and O'Brien promised him whatever he would ask, and he said, "Give me the house of Dromoland and the lands." So he agreed to that. But then he said he had some request to make, and the Lord said he would give it, and he said, "Give me the house and the land of Dromoland back again," and he had to give it. That will be the way with the English. They gave up Ireland but they have their two eyes fixed on it till they will get it back again.'

### 8 MARCH

Dublin. Yesterday I came up by early train. At Athenry there were about fifteen soldiers, fully equipped, tin plates, knapsacks. I asked Daly where they were bound for, but he said they were to be 'demobbed'. At Athlone eight or nine young men tumbled in, with little trunks and boxes. One who sat next me was from Mayo, a nice freshfaced boy. They were going he said to Manchester, had got a message that there was work for them there, but did not know what it would be. Another who got in was a young lad, ghastly, looking as if in the last stages of consumption, coughing, spitting, speechless. I meant to change into another carriage, for I had to sit with my eyes shut. But at Mullingar I got out my tea bottle and gave him hot tea that revived him wonderfully, and a clean handkerchief. And then I stayed. He had come from Castlebar was going to a sanatorium near Dublin, 'was doing no good at home'. Poor lad. It cannot save him. I waited with him at Broadstone till a pleasant-looking messenger from the Sanatorium came and took him in a cab. Then to 82 Merrion Square, opened my basket in the hall and had my tea and sandwich. Then to the Baggot St Hospital to see Houston. He looked better than I expected for he was walking about, though his broken jaw was bandaged, and the wounds on his face had been stitched and had plaster over them. He says he was driving home from church when eight men got over the wall inside Lough Cutra and ordered him to stop, firing a shot over his head. They asked what he meant by having D. fined for three rabbits. He said it was his duty, and they asked if he would pay the fine as he was poor. He refused. 'And then I remember nothing until I heard them say, "Shove him into the trap," and I was put into it and drove home, half dazed. They must have struck a blow from behind that broke the jaw and stunned me.' He did not tell me, as his brother told J. that these men had first while he was at church, raided his house and taken away 83 cartridges, left from the deer shoot. A very sad and horrible thing, so many coming against one man.

In the evening to the Abbey with W.B.Y. *Juno and the Paycock* a long queue at the door, the theatre crowded, many turned away, so it will be run on next week. A wonderful and terrible play of futility, of irony, humour, tragedy. When I went round to the Green room I saw O'Casey and had a little talk with him. He is very happy. I asked him to come to tea after the next day matinée as I had brought up a barmbrack for the players, but he said, 'No I can't come, I'll be at work till the afternoon, and I'm working with cement, and that takes such a long time to get off.' 'But after that?' 'Then I have to cook my dinner. I have but one room and I cook for myself since my mother died.' He is of course happy at the great success of the play and I said, 'You must feel now that we were right in not putting on that first one you sent in *The Crimson in the Tricolour*. I was inclined to put it on because some of it was so good and I thought you might learn by seeing it on the stage, though some was very poor, but Mr Yeats was firm.' He said, 'You were right not to put it on. I can't read it myself now. But I will tell you that was a bitter disappointment for I not only thought at the time it was the best thing I had written, but I thought that no one in the world had ever written anything so fine.' Then he said, 'You had it typed for me, and I don't know how you could have read it as I sent it in with the bad writing and the poor paper. But at that time it was hard for me to afford even the paper it was written on.' And he said, 'I owe a great deal to you and Mr Yeats and Mr Robinson, but to you above all. You gave me encouragement. And it was you who said to me upstairs in the office – I could show you the very spot where you stood – "Mr. O'Casey, your gift is characterisation." And so I threw over my theories and worked at characters, and this is the result.'

Yeats hadn't seen the play before, and thought it very fine, reminding him of Tolstoi. He said when he talked of that imperfect first play, 'Casey was bad in writing of the vices of the rich which he knows nothing about, but he thoroughly understands the vices of the poor.' But that full house, the packed pit and gallery, the fine play, the call of the mother for the putting away of hatred – 'Give us Thine own eternal love!' – made me say to Yeats, 'This is one of the evenings at the Abbey that makes me glad to have been born.'

9 MARCH

I took cakes to the Abbey and after the performance gave tea in the Green room. An American, Mr Jewell, had come to see *Juno*, is writing for USA magazines, so I asked him to tea, and having only the Company themselves was glad of an outsider. They were a little constrained, but I suggested their singing to show what they can do, as in the play they had to turn their songs into a part of the comedy. So Dolan, Will Shields, Nolan, sang. Then

Sara Allgood, very charming – 'I know who I love' and 'Oh, had I wist!' And by that time Yeats had arrived, and he had to read them one or two scraps of verse in his book of plays, there being no volume of his poems there. And then with prompting he repeated 'Wandering Angus'. So my barmbrack was the centre of a House of Melody.

I came back there for the evening performance – such a queue! and so many had to be turned away, but we are running on next week and I hope they will come then. Casey was with me watching them and being persuaded to come and meet the Americans on Yeats's Monday evening. Miss Bushell came to ask if she might sell my stall there was such a demand and I said Yes, certainly. Then Jack Yeats and his wife came, could get no seat; so we went round to the stage door and when the orchestra stopped we went down and took their chairs. When the mother whose son has been killed – 'Leader of an ambush where my neighbour's Free State soldier son was killed' – cries out, 'Mother of Jesus put away from us this murderous hatred and give us thine own eternal love,' I whispered to Casey, 'That is the prayer we must all use, it is the only thing that will save us, the teaching of Christ.' He said, 'Of humanity.' But what would that be without the Divine atom?

The *Observer* critic (Griffith) had come over from London for the night. Such a good moment for him to see the Abbey!

II MARCH

No more news of the mutiny yesterday, and by the papers it doesn't look serious, though the President and other Ministers have given up their intention of dining on Wednesday at 'the Round Table', a dinner club formed by their wives.

I had heard nothing said about my *Story Brought by Brigit* since I had read it to Yeats and L.R., but Yeats asked on Sunday when it was to be put in rehearsal, said it must certainly be put on, and before the end of Lent. So I went to consult L.R. and he is for putting it on the week before Holy Week. We tried to think out cast, but could not fill it, I am anxious to read it to the

Company before deciding anything, to see how they like it. Yeats says they are getting Sara Allgood here for their entertainment for the Drama League to recite 'The Old Woman Remembers', which he thinks very fine. After this my pride was cast down, for he gave me the typed article on his visit to Sweden in which he describes me as 'An old woman sinking into the infirmities of age' – (not even fighting against them!). However L.R. agreed with me that this description would send down my market value, and be considered to mean I had gone silly, so he has consented to take it out, but confesses he had already sent a copy to the Dail, and will have to write about it and may not be in time.

We made £87 profit on last week's bill, and Casey will get over £15.

He came last night, Yeats's 'Monday', also A.E. and Mr Jewell and A. Duncan; and Gogarty dropped in late. It is supposed to be for men only, and might be better so. Anyhow the talk was rather 'scattered', the mutiny, Hashish, whether Darrell Figgis did or did not write 'the Return of the Hero'. Casey, sheltering by me, interested me most. Yeats explained that the long debates and delay of the Fishery Bill in the Senate had all been caused by the incompetence of the Minister for Fisheries, who had given wrong statistics. Casey asked if he had been dismissed, and could not understand why not, when a labourer found incompetent would be turned out of his job. Someone said he had given good service before the Treaty, and he, Casey, said, 'Nothing can be done until this government is out and we have a government with no one in it that has ever fired a gun. We can abuse them then.' They say the occupation of the four Courts, the real beginning of trouble was the result of a quarrel about the appointment of a Chief of Staff. No one can see how Republicans can join a government, or rather come into the Dail, until the watering of the oath. He believes if they ever do form a government, they will be found just as quiet as the others. And here as in the country the conviction seems to be that nothing towards a reconciliation can come until this government is out, between the memory of the executions and the harshness of their speeches.

When Gogarty came in he did not find a congenial audience

and talk flagged. I got him to talk of his escape from his kidnappers by plunging into the Liffey, for Jewell's benefit – a little 'story' for him. When the others were talking of Hashish, Casey told me he had been all but shot in the Rising. He had taken no part in it, but a shot had been fired from some house he was in or near, and the soldiers had dragged him out and were actually raising their rifles to fire at him – 'I felt in a daze, just from instinct I said a prayer, was certain death was there. But someone fired a shot that just missed their Captain, and they ran to see where it came from, and I ran for my life through the fields and escaped.' He thinks the Rising was 'a terrible mistake and we lost such fine men. We should have won freedom by degrees with them. And Parnell's death was a great misfortune, he would have got Home Rule, that would have been a step.'

He is studying pictures now, has bought some books but knows so little about painting he wishes lectures could be given, 'And if the employers cared for us workers they would sometimes arrange for an afternoon at the Galleries, or an evening at the Abbey for their men.'

It was an interesting evening, I enjoyed hearing different views after what Yeats calls in another part of his article 'the laborious solitary life'. He is very kind, and would ask politicians and officers to meet me but thinks I don't care to meet them, and that is true enough. It is the creators that I like best to meet.

EVENING. Today I went into the National Gallery to see Stephens; the men there so civil and kind, remembering Hugh. Stephens is still working at the epic tales, says he can find nothing of worth that I have not used. He is now beginning on another tale, not in my Saga, and finds the difference not having my clear outline to work on. He also is astonished by the power of Casey's play. And Yeats (in spite of my 'sinking') had told him the *Brigit* is the finest thing I have done – 'a great play'. I worked all the morning on *Brigit*, putting in a verse to be sung before the curtain goes up and giving more words to Sara Allgood. L.R. took me to dine with him at the Metropole, and on to the Abbey not so full as on Friday and Saturday, but Perrin said £30 in the house, and we began with £19 last week. And I signed a cheque of over £17 for Casey. The evening papers give Mulcahy's statement telling that some resignations from the army have taken place here and there, about twenty in Dublin, and there are threats that many officers will resign 'If the terms contained in the government letter are carried out, and set themselves up in arms against the government'. And that he is only anxious about Co. Cork.

There was an immense meeting in College Green as I passed in the tram coming back late, in support of the Anti-Treaty candidate.

## 8 JUNE

He [O'Casey] grieves for his Mother. She was 89, died in 1919. He had lived all his life with her, the others of her children had died or gone away. 'She had a strong sense of humour, could always see the humorous side of human life. I did everything for her, she did not like to have anyone else about her. I had written a little story. Maunsel promised me £15 for it, and after it was published I wanted the money and went three times for it but could never get it. Then when my mother was so ill I had to go again to press for it, and I did get it, but when I came back she was gone.

'I made arrangements for the funeral, but when the day came the undertaker said that if I did not pay at once he would take it back again and there would be no funeral. It had to be put off until I could get change for the cheque. I thought I should have to go to the Bank, but I went to the Rector and he cashed it. I felt the treatment of the undertaker very bitterly, he was a Labour man, I a Labour man, and I had helped him and worked in that movement, worked for them all, and that is how I was treated.

'We formed at one time a workers' union, we were to carry on work ourselves without employers, we were to earn big money. George Russell gave £50 towards it. We did well for a week or two, there was one of us worked from 8 o'c. in the morning till 7 o'c. at night. But after a little work fell off; one would read the papers and not work more than a couple of hours. I saw it was a hopeless business. I had done my best to help. I have helped strikers and revolution according to what were then my lights. I was a Socialist then.'

Now his desire and hope is rather to lead the workers into a better life, in interest in reading, in drama especially. The Abbey Theatre has done so much he has a great belief in Drama.

His eyesight has always been weak, a sort of film over the eyes. A doctor advised him not to read but he said, 'Then I should be ignorant,' and he refused an operation because there was a thousandth chance he might go blind and so remain ignorant. He had been sent to a National school as a child for a few months but learned little more than his letters. Then one day when he was fourteen he listened to his brother and a friend as they talked of William of Orange, trying to make out the date of the Battle of the Boyne, 'And I thought to myself, Why cannot I tell them that?

'I determined to learn to read. There were a lot of old Primers lying about and I learned from them, and then I went through a grammar and learned the rules. The first book I ever read was Merle D'Aubigné's *History of the Reformation*.' (I said here I had never heard that mentioned since I was a child. There was a copy then at Roxborough.) 'It was hard to understand, at least the long notes were. And many of them were in German, I thought of learning German to read them. But the second book I read was harder still, Locke on the Human Understanding. But when I got a few pennies together I would buy a book here and there from the stalls, Dickens because he was cheap, and some of the Waverley novels. But one day for a shilling I bought the Globe edition of Shakespeare, and that began a new life. I read it over and over and learned a great deal of it by heart.'

## 27 AUGUST

Burren. Yesterday I came back here for a couple of days, Guy bringing me. Old Niland came again, and had 5/- the week before, but he looked so tired I sent for bread and butter and a couple of glasses of port and put half a crown in my pocket and promised him some firing *before* he told me a little story: 'There was a poor woman had nothing in the house, nothing for herself and her children, and she went to ask charity from four women that were in rich houses. And she came back empty and when she was sitting in the house and had nothing to give the children there was a man came in and he asked her what ailed her. And when she told him he said, "Go open that chest you have in the room." And she said there was nothing in it. But when she opened it she found it was full of every sort of thing. And the man said, "From this day you will never be in want, but as to those four women that refused you, before a twelve-month they will come begging to your door." And so they did before the twelve-month was over. But as to her, she had full and plenty from that out, and she had three daughters in America that helped her. For the man who came to tell her that was an angel from God.'

## 22 OCTOBER

Dublin. Came here yesterday by early train for the 'urgent and important' Carnegie meeting. Yeats met me at Broadstone and took me to 82 M.Sq. I went in to 84 after a little to see A.E. about the meeting. We had had a visit from Father Finlay in the morning, who told him of having sent in his letter of resignation to the Carnegie Committee because of the article published by the Secretary L.R. in *Tomorrow* – 'could not continue association with him'. Dermod O'Brien had also been in and told him L.R. intended anyhow to resign in June, doesn't find enough time for his own work, so they inclined to think he might solve the matter by resigning now. A.E. hated the story, and also one in the same number about black men and white women written (not in her own name) by Mrs C., the wife of a Professor in Trinity. A.E. is unwilling to face 'a fight with two churches', for the Provost, by Father Finlay's account, is as indignant with the story as he is. A.E. wouldn't object to the fight if it was on a good ground, but doesn't feel we should fight on this. I came back and told Yeats. He was furious at the idea of letting L.R. resign. And G.Y. said he had only intended it vaguely hadn't decided even for June. Then McGreevy came in, said he has no intention at all of resigning. He and Yeats went in to see A.E. and had rather a row. Yeats came back excited and said he had said too much.

I went to the Abbey, saw a part of the play, and went round and saw the actors, in good spirits. This morning to A.E. again, and with him to the Carnegie meeting. The Provost read Father Finlay's letter and said he had obtained a copy of *Tomorrow*, thought that story very offensive, also Yeats's Leda – 'so unlike his early poems'. Also another story in the same number 'one must speak plainly – it is about the intercourse of white women with black men'. He had written to Dunfermline calling attention to L.R.'s story, and Colonel Mitchell had answered they would take no action until they knew what view the Dublin Committee took of it. Then there was discussion. He asked us all in turn to give an opinion. When it came to me I said we all had the Carnegie scheme at heart and must do anything possible to keep it up – 'but I do not think it a possible thing to dismiss the Secretary who has helped our work for over nine years so well, and that with a slur on his character'. The Provost said, 'There is no question of dismissing him,' crossly, and would give no hint of what action should be taken beyond asking Father Finlay to reconsider his decision. We all agreed to that, but feeling sure he would not. Mr O'Donnell was L.R.'s chief champion. He said, 'I was brought up in County Kerry, among Catholics, I am a Catholic, an Irish speaker. I never knew a Protestant until I was grown up and came to Dublin. My sisters are pious Catholics, I read them that story and they thought it a beautiful story, could see no harm in it. There is no doubt an obsession with that idea among many Irish country girls, I have three times heard a priest preach against it.' The Provost listened with suspicious toleration and some surprise. After endless talk a resolution was proposed by the Provost asking Father F. to reconsider his intention of resigning and saying, 'We consider the article unfortunate and deplorable.' I asked this to be amended to 'the publication of the article', saying that was all that concerned us, we had nothing to do with what our Secretary writes, but objected to an article that might give offence being published. He would not at first alter it, put it to the vote, and it was passed by one vote, but he consented to put an amendment making the alteration. A.E., who had approved of the alteration, now could not make up his mind which side to take, and the Provost said it was not necessary for him to vote, and he didn't. But then the numbers were equal, and after a little A.E. voted for the amendment. (He could not make up his mind, all hung on him, then he seemed confused and asked what the amendment was. I said (quoting the Provost) 'the milder form', and then he said, 'I am for the milder form'). The Provost very cross, spoke again against the paper, and 'especially that horrible story about the blacks'. I said, 'That is said to have come from Trinity.' 'Impossible,' he said. Someone whispered to him it was a Professor's wife. He looked at the paper and said triumphantly, 'There is no such name among our professors.' 'It is signed in her maiden name,' said someone. He jumped up and went away evidently intending to have the writer's blood. But she is said to have gone away with Liam O'Flaherty, so he will find only the unoffending husband, who is writing a history of ancient Ireland. I kept them from cursing the article itself, because I fancy the Provost means to ask for L.R.'s resignation at the next meeting, perhaps threatening his own, and I didn't want to let the meeting commit itself against the story. Cosgrave had been prepared to prosecute the paper but sent it on to O'Higgins, Minister of Justice, and he refused saying, 'The prosecution would merely represent the moral attitude of a certain people and place and time.' Very good.

Very tired after all this, had some tea (it was 2 o'c. when I returned) and stayed in. Willie much delighted with the account but wished he had been there; he would have begun by an attack on the Provost for having written to Dunfermline before consulting the Dublin Committee.

30 NOVEMBER

Yesterday wet. Worked at *Bourgeois* and wrote letters. Then to Abbey matinée, good stalls; the play went well. Lady Ardilaun had a party there and took me back to tea at 42 Stephens Green, a pleasant change, the house full of beautiful flowers. And it was like a change of plays at the Abbey, from my intercourse with what I may call progressives, Jack and the others last night, and the actors in the Green room, all living in a world that is alive, and these in a decaying one. A sort of *ancien régime* party, a lament for banished society. Mrs Plunkett, the Bishop's wife, talked of the burned houses, 'and if they rebuild them they will be burned again. And if they are not burned who will want to live in them with no society? And all we are paying in postage! And the posts so slow in coming . . .' Lady A. herself very good and bright, loving our theatre and gathering what scraps of surviving friends she can yet angry with the people – 'all bad'. But in practice she is kind and if she lived in the country I am sure would help them. She says there is no chance of any young men of our class getting employment in the future. Some relative of hers had given up a foreign appointment and come back, and knows languages and is very well fitted to be a consul or foreign representative. But he could get nothing from the government and one of the questions asked was 'What did you do in the war? – The war against England?' But an old gentleman whose name I forget (I think Stoney) was louder in his regrets; had been to the Castle, now occupied by lawyers, on some business, and recalled with grief the nights when the ballroom was filled with company. 'If you gave a dance then you had only to send a note to the Barracks asking forty or fifty or whatever number of officers you wanted. Now who is there for our daughters to dance with?' (true enough that). 'And the Governor General gets £37,000 a year and what is there to show for it? The Cadogans had only £20,000 and entertained so splendidly.' I said I had only been once to the V.R. Lodge in those days, to see Lord Aberdeen about *Blanco Posnet*. 'Oh Aberdeen, he wasn't much. But the Cadogans! Now the town is peopled with ghosts, it is sad to see the empty houses as you walk about Fitwilliam Square. The Arnotts' the only house that exists in Merrion Square!'

## 1925

### 6 JANUARY

Darling Richard's birthday, his 16th. Thank God he has come safe so far. He looked so happy last night, the drawing-room lighted up, the card table near the fire, he and Anne and Catherine, Margaret, Olive, Mrs Scovell, Guy. I, sitting near them, could see Robert's shadowy portrait on the wall and I felt he would approve. But what a birthday it would have been could he have been here – that is the heartbreak.

I gave Richard today my husband's little revolver to practise with at marks and he is pleased.

### 8 JANUARY

The birthday went so happily, no outside guests to be had, yet we never had a merrier evening. The bonfire lighted well, and Richard and Anne raced after each other with lighted wisps gigantic fireflies tearing about. And they all dressed up for dinner, had ransacked the camphor chests. I was but 'A Spanish grandmother' with high comb and mantle and diamonds and Margaret hadn't time to dress at all when she had costumed the others. Mrs Scovell came down in a 'Du Maurier', and I was sitting with her in the drawing-room when 'Miss Persse of Roxboro' was announced and a young lady came in with ringlets, with my old Paris purple brocade (worn as I see in a photograph at Fanny Trench's wedding and she is a grandmother!) and a fan; a very sweet thoughtful face and gentle manner. I was puzzled for a minute and only when the profile was turned I knew it was Richard! The gentle manner continued till towards the end of dinner when he suddenly seized and ate an apple in schoolboy fashion. Then a very tall officer in scarlet – Olive! and a cornet in ditto Anne – and a drummer in the little uniform Mrs Chatteris had given Anne and that now fits Catherine. Guy had a Highland costume, also from the camphor boxes; and swords

were in all directions. We had the maids up after dinner to see
them, and Mrs Scovell played and they danced, Guy a sword
dance. Richard said it was the pleasantest birthday he had ever
had. (They had gone to the woods for a bit for woodcock) and
Guy thought it the pleasantest birthday he had ever known. So
they have been happy indoors and out, Richard bringing in a
woodcock this morning and Anne a rabbit. But now Margaret
has a cold and is in bed.

## 12 JANUARY

Yesterday, Sunday, so very few in church, only four in the
sittings, Guy opposite in his gallery, Rita and George Daly and
the Mitchells, Richard with me (the other chicks had colds).
Daphne and Mr Newbold here; Guy to lunch and take them
back to Lough Cutra for the night. Margaret and Olive went
also. I read *Dr Doolittle* to the chicks and got them to bed earlier
than usual. Today they are on the lake with their guns.

# From *Volume II* (1925–1932)

## 1925

### 23 AUGUST

Casey arrived yesterday. His play, the *Plough and the Stars*, had come in the morning with a letter from L.R. saying he and W.B.Y. like it. I slipped away after dinner and read the first Act to myself, and finding it so good I took it to the library and read it to Jack and his wife (and the author) and they liked it, a fine opening but tragic. He has been working at it for thirteen months and is tired and glad of a rest, his delight in the country as great as ever, for he still lives in his tenement room.

### 2 SEPTEMBER

Dolan writes objecting to the *Plough and the Stars* – 'At any time I would think twice before having anything to do with it. The language is – to use an Abbey phrase – beyond the beyonds. The song at the end of the second Act sung by the "girl-of-the-streets" is impossible.'

I have usually consulted the players about phrases that might give offence, they knowing the mind of the audience better than I, and would do so now, but it must wait for Yeats and Robinson.

### 4 SEPTEMBER

Some apples taken from the garden last night. Happily I had brought a good many in, not quite ripe, for cooking. I am writing to the Civic Guard at last – asking them to come out these moonlight nights.

Sent back plays, with suggestions for improving them. Began going through my letters to Quinn, to see if any may come in for Memoir.

## 24 SEPTEMBER. THURSDAY. DUBLIN

Yeats and I came up on Monday, I to the Russell Hotel. Very tired next morning and rain pouring. I read a play and accepted it (the *Black Bull*).

Then the Directors' meeting, Dr O'Brien making his objections to the play; I, chief spokesman (by request) telling him Blythe had made no condition whatever in giving the subsidy and certainly no hint of appointing a Censor. I told him of our old fights, about *Countess Cathleen* (with the Catholic Church) *Blanco Posnet* with the government; Lord Aberdeen's efforts to get passages left out of the play (as now played in England) and my refusal – (though then there was a real threat of closing the Theatre). Yeats also spoke in the same sense. O'Brien sat up in his chair reiterating at intervals, 'That song is objectionable.' (We had from the first decided that must go, but left it as a bone for him to gnaw at.) 'And that word bitch' &c. We told him cuts are usually made in rehearsal, by producers and players, but that we had at the beginning told Casey the Clitheroe parts must be rewritten etc. and at last got him to confess, 'I had mistaken my position' (of Censor). But he wants to see a rehearsal a little later. I then proposed (already arranged) – that now we are four Directors we had better bring a rule of majority voting or we might come to a deadlock, two and two; and we passed that resolution. Chairman to have a casting vote. It was a long meeting. I wished some artist could have looked in. Yeats and I so animated, L.R. so amused, G.O'B. sitting upright and without change of expression repeating his parrot cry, 'That song must be left out!'

Then back to hotel, and Casey here for tea, and then a long talk, very little about his play, for though I told him of O'Brien I didn't tell him of Dolan having made the trouble. He doesn't object to any cuts we make and is re-writing Mrs Clitheroe. He says Jim Larkin is now selling coal to his workers at ninepence less than the dealers, and at a profit which goes to the fund. The Republicans are joining him. Father O'Flanagan (as I had seen in the papers) was on his platform last Sunday, and I had been rather astonished at Larkin hailing him as 'One of the Lord's anointed'. Casey thinks he will be put out of the Church. We talked of Communism for he said, 'I am a Communist,' but it is always hard to get a clear definition and he hopes he will not be alive when it comes – in 30 years or so but 'I see the terrible conditions in which the workers live – we must try to change that at any cost'. He had been ill with a cold, kept in bed for a day and had heard a terrible fight going on between a husband and wife, and the beating of one of their children.

* * *

I went with W.B.Y. and George to see the film, *Wanderer of the Wasteland*, the first in colour I have seen, a very great improvement on the black and white, less tiring to the eyes, it seemed less jerky, and the desert scenes wonderful. When they perfect some invention of giving the words as well, the theatres may tremble. Then back to Merrion Square, and after dinner George went out and Willie read me pages from his proofs of his new book – (*A Vision*) I had already read some pages on the way up. The introduction very witty and fanciful, then some chapters quite unintelligible to me, with figures and circles. Then the chapters in the different divisions, very interesting, for he has made them critical essays on writers dead or living – not only writers – personalities. He had told me my division, 24, was 'a very good one', but I don't know that I like being classed as a 'certain friend' (as well as with Galsworthy) with Queen Victoria!! So do we appear to our friends. But I don't think she could have written *Seven Short Plays*. He went on last night reading some fine chapters – one of 'The Great Year'. I exclaimed at one sentence – one should do things 'not because we ought but because we can', and said how fine that is, and he said, 'That is one of the dictated sentences written by G.'s hand.' He gave me his new edition of the early poems &c just arrived – the ones he had altered at Coole.

## 25 SEPTEMBER

Directors meeting easy, O'Brien like a lamb, though after it he held back Perrin to say, 'I think Mr Robinson has now given up that song.' And he is in disgrace with Robinson, having told him he had taken *The White Blackbird* to the Kingstown Club and consulted various people – 'legal men' – as to whether the end is improper!!

## 1926

### SUNDAY. 14 FEBRUARY, 1926. RUSSELL HOTEL, DUBLIN

On Friday I left for Dublin to see the *Plough and Stars*. And I packed up things for London not having had any answer from W.B.Y. as to whether the government had yet been there about the Boundary. I thought they might have been and that if so I had better go on there.

I got the post and papers in Gort and when the train had started opened the *Independent* and saw a heading right across the page 'Riotous Scenes at the Abbey. Attempt to stop O'Casey's play'; and an account of wild women especially having raised a disturbance, blown whistles &c, prevented second Act from being heard and had then clambered on to the stage – a young man had struck Miss Delany on the face &c &c. Then the police had been sent for, and quiet apparently restored for the rest of the play to be given. It is so lucky I had set out and not seen this, when at Coole, too late to take the train.

At Athenry I got the *Irish Times* which gave a fuller account. Yeats had spoken from the stage but the clamour had drowned his speech, but the reporters had got some of it. The train was very crowded, groups of men getting in at each station. I thought at first there must be a fair going on, but they were going up for the football, England v. Ireland next day.

Yeats met me at the station and gave his account of the row, thought of inviting the disturbers to a debate as we had done in *Playboy* riots. But I was against that, in *Playboy* time our opponents were men. They had a definite objective, they thought the country people were being injured by Synge's representation of them. These disturbers were almost all women who have made demonstrations on Poppy Day and at elections and meetings; have made a habit of it, of the excitement. Mrs Skeffington who leads them lost her husband in 1916, but he was not a fighter but a pacifist, killed by order of an insane British officer.

We found the Abbey crowded, many being turned away. Yeats said that last night he had been there by accident, for he does not often go to more than one performance. Robinson had not come that evening, and when the disturbance began and he wanted to call for Police, he found it was Perrin's night off and the telephone had been closed up. But at last the Civic Guards came and carried the women off the stage and the play went on without interruption to the end. At the end of the second Act a good many people had thought it was not to be resumed and had gone, and the disturbers had seized their places and kept up the noise from there, while some climbed on to the stage, breaking two lamps and tearing a piece out of the curtain, and attacked the actresses. The papers said Miss Delany had been struck on the face by a young man. But the actors say he came next morning, very indignant at the accusation, said he had thrown something at Sean Barlow and it had accidentally hit Miss Craig. Miss Richards says she herself threw a shoe at one of the intruders and it missed its aim and one of them took it up and threw it at Yeats, but it then also missed its aim. I went round to see them in the Green room and they were very cheerful. There was no attempt at disturbance though one man said from the Gallery in the public House scene, 'This is an insult to the memory of Pearse,' and walked out. Someone else cried out when the two men of the Citizen Army came into the pub holding one the flag of the Republic, the other of the Citizen army, the Plough and Stars flag – (it was designed by A.E.). 'Those flags were never in a public house!' And it is natural they might object to that, though they don't know that scenes can't be re-arranged for every episode – the flags had to be shown and that scene was the most convenient. And their bearers did but take a modest glass at the bar, and carried them out again with decency and order.

I thought the play very fine indeed. And the next day at the matinée, when though the House was full and overflowing there was no danger of riot and I could listen without distraction, it seemed to me a very wonderful play – 'the forgiveness of sins' as real literature is supposed to be. These quarrelling drinking women have tenderness and courage showing all through, as have the men. At intervals in the public house scene one hears from the meeting being held outside fragments of a speech of Pearse's (spoken in Stephenson's fine voice) with extraordinary effect. One feels those who heard it were forced to obey its call, not to be afraid to fight even in the face of defeat. One honours and understands their emotion. Lionel Johnson's lines to Ireland came into my mind:

> For thy dead is grief on thee?
> Can it be thou dost repent
> That they went, thy chivalry
> Those sad ways magnificent?

And then comes what all nations have seen, the suffering that falls through war and especially civil war on the women, the poor, the wretched homes and families of the slums. An overpowering play, I felt at the end of it as if I should never care to look at another; all others would seem so shadowy to the mind after this. I saw it again in the evening, but too tired then to feel much emotion. The immense audience all applauding, and Casey was called at the end with the Players and cheered.

The morning's excitement had been an attempt to kidnap Barry Fitzgerald 'Fluter', the chief actor in the play. A motor with armed men had come to his house and demanded to see him. But he was not there; someone said he now lived elsewhere, but when I spoke of it he told me he had not gone home that night, had some little suspicion in his mind. I said if taken he would now be wandering in the Wicklow mountains like some man who has lately been carried off.

It was thought safer for the Players to stay in the theatre between matinée and evening performance. So there was a meal made ready for them. And G. Yeats brought Rummel who had been giving a concert and he played for the actors in the auditorium, Chopin – several pieces. During Beethoven's Moonlight Sonata, Yeats fell asleep and awakening said he had dreamed there was a storm going on; and when he awoke and saw Rummel playing his last chords he thought, 'They can't have noticed it!' The players were delighted. Rummel had arrived on Saturday morning for his concert. There was a great crush in the boat and he could not get a cabin until he happened to say he was coming over to play, and then he was given a cabin at once – he thought from respect for music – but found they thought he was one of the English football team!

Yeats had failed to get me any information as to the government visit to England re Boundary, when the Lane pictures were to be pressed for, and I had packed clothes for London intending to go on there if they had done so. And as he had still no information – had asked Brown to write and ask Cosgrave what was happening – I went yesterday morning to government buildings and saw Blythe. He says the visit to London was put off by the British government on account of Locarno business. That it will certainly take place within the next three weeks, and before St Patrick's Day. That he is the Minister to be sent over, as the questions are chiefly financial and that his hope is that in settling some outstanding financial question about the Boundary, he may offer to give up some claim if the pictures are restored to us. This is hopeful. But I am going back to Coole, not wanting to see London helpers until our own government has moved.

MONDAY, 15 FEBRUARY

Donaghy came in as I was writing and we had a long talk – he is full of ideas and plans, hopes to have some of his poems published soon; to take his degree in June, and then go to London, try his hand at literature, perhaps acting. He is working at the translation of *Prometheus*. He was wearing a heavy Ulster and I asked if he would not take it off, but he said No, there was a large rent in his coat, gained in 'the celebrations' last night of the football victory.

He had been at the Abbey the night of the riot, had seen the first attack on the stage, a woman climbing up on it, and then the ferocious face of Sean Barlow, almost petrified with astonishment at *his* stage being invaded, and who had then stepped forward and flung the invader off it. He had met Holloway in the hall in a state of fury – 'an abominable play'.

'I See nothing abominable in it.' H. 'Then you have a dirty mind.' D. 'No I haven't.' H. 'Well you have a filthy mind. There are no street walkers in Dublin.' D. 'I was accosted by one only last night.' H. 'There were none in Dublin till the Tommies brought them over!' Then H. said to a man coming down from the Gallery, 'That play should be put off the stage!' But he answered, 'No it should not. I've just been talking to Dan Breen' (a new censor!). Donaghy stayed till 4 o'c. I had been writing letters about Hugh's pictures to Carson, Healy and T. P. O'Connor, and one to Blythe asking him to let me know when the date of his going over is fixed. I hope to go then and make a great effort to get the matter settled. Yeats says the N.G. (London) has written to our N.G. asking for the return of pictures lent us about forty years ago – thinks this is to keep a claim on the Lane pictures if they are returned on loan.

I ran round to see the Yeats children and W. showed me the *Observer* account of the riot. Then to the Café, where I had O'Casey and Donaghy to tea. Casey in good spirits after his reception last night. One of the objections made was the rebel flag having been carried into a public House, but two old IRA men have since told him they themselves had brought the flag in to pubs. He reminded some of the men who objected to a street walker having been put on, how often they had received food and shelter from these women when being hunted by the Black and Tans. He stayed talking till near 8 o'c., has his mind full of plays, too full perhaps, but his eyes have been very troublesome again. He has a difficulty in typing what he has written. His doctor says he must get a better lodging where he can have his food cooked for him for he is indolent about doing it himself and is letting down his strength. One of the accusations of the interrupters had been that he did not make the Tommies offensive enough. But he says they were usually quite civil until they were frightened and turned cruel. They would come into the house and say, 'Mother give us some tea,' or whatever they wanted.

And some of the girls who came on the stage had taunted him, 'You, – having supper with *Birkenhead*!' He couldn't think what that meant. It was that they had seen in some paper he had been invited to the St Patrick's Day banquet in London – He had refused – 'If I went to London I'd head for Augustus John and Bernard Shaw, not for that company'. Then to the Abbey. Eugene O'Neill's little clever sailor play, and Chesterton's *Magic* (these given by the Drama League) slight and dull. I went to the gallery, it being a Drama League production and 'fashionable' Dublin in the stalls. But Yeats came up and sat with me, and Rummel came up to say his farewell, indignant at having been kept from seeing *Plough and Stars* by a dreadful dinner of 10 courses given at the Russell by some well meaning ladies.

COOLE, TUESDAY. 16 FEBRUARY

Glad to leave Dublin yesterday. I had found so little sleep in the hotel that, opening my eyes after what had seemed a minute's doze I found we were at Ballinasloe, and at Athenry, still sleepier, I neglected to look after my luggage and it was taken on to Galway in spite of labels. All well here, and I am the better for that day or two of companionship and excitement.

Irene S. had come on Sunday, had seen me through the hotel window, is very much pleased because the *Independent* has printed her little article on Winkles and sent her £1.11; says it is all owing to me, I had given her my usual advice, to use what is close at hand, to write first of the harvest of the sea that is at her door.

I found here a letter from Millington giving an account of the riot and of his impression of the play, written on Friday (he didn't know I was coming up) very interesting. He had seen the play on Monday . . . 'I lay awake, heard every hour strike up to 3 in the morning, thinking of the way O'Casey had bludgeoned me, and protesting that it wasn't fair. I thought of the handling of the turns in the play which to me seems almost genius and the wonderful stage pictures he provides – the man has an uncanny sense of stage effect.' Then about the next night, 'the women started to get busy. Rosie, they would have it, was an insult to the men who died in Easter week. The players carried on bravely but things got worse and the newspaper reports are fairly accurate. Only of course no one heard the speech made by Mr Yeats. He came on, held up his hand in the customary fashion and looked – well, what an archangel should look like – but his remarks were drowned in insults about pensions – "take the play to London" – "we don't want it here – "&c. The disturbers nearly all women – the one male combatant got a puck on the jaw from Will Shields which knocked most of the animosity and all of the fight out of him. I felt bursting to hit someone myself, was wedged in on the balcony. The players were splendid. I liked them all before but now nothing could be too good for them. I couldn't help thinking of your advice when Robinson was starting his career: Granville Barker: "He must be taught to put his name as producer on the programme." Lady Gregory: "He must be taught boxing so that he can put people out of the Theatre."'

## SUNDAY EVENING, 8 MAY

Yesterday I saw A.E. and asked him to put a paragraph in the *Statesman* about the pictures, emphasising the necessity of sending back especially those fine ones that are being exhibited at the Tate, and that young Dublin artists have been deprived of the benefit of seeing. I was at both performances of *Plough and Stars*, both went well with crowded audiences, but in the evening some 'Smell bombs' were let off at the beginning of the performance. Perrin and the CID searched under the seats in the gallery and found small bottles there full of the stuff, especially under the one Miss Barry, poor Kevin's sister had sat in — she had left early. They were not thrown this time but they think stamped on or left to be trodden on and broken, however all were taken and there was no further demonstration. An immense audience (which Mrs Sheehy-Skeffington gives out is composed of CID men 'of both sexes'!)

## TUESDAY, 11 MAY

I went to see Molly Childers, but Mrs Osgood was there so no chance of a quiet talk. She looked pulled down and was affectionate, asked if I would go and stay with her but I could not do that. This split among Republicans must dishearten her, poor thing. She asked about *Plough and Stars* and her eyes filled with tears when I quoted

> Can you wonder that they went
> Those sad ways magnificent?

Little Michael has been taken to an ear doctor. I've been telling Anne about Puss in Boots, but Michael has just come in looking very lively to say, 'I didn't mind it a bit!'

## 2 SEPTEMBER

Nursing Home Dublin. I came to Dublin on Friday, to go through the pamphlet. But Yeats was away. And a lump had developed a week or so ago, where the old one had been. And though I had determined not to have anything done that would keep me from home while the holidays last, I went to Slattery, and he said it must come out, the sooner the better. I said, not till end of September. But then I thought it best to give in. And so on Monday evening I came in here (àfter two Acts of Murray's *Autumn Fire* at the Abbey). And next morning at quarter to eleven (after preparations from 6 o'c. on) I was laid on the table, no chloroform, just the local anaesthetic — it lasted about 20 minutes. I had not much pain, though feeling the knife working about made me feel queer. But I fixed my mind upon a river, the river at Roxborough, imagined it as it flows from the mountains through the flat land from Kilchreest – then under the road bridge, then under the Volunteer memorial bridge; through the deerpark, then deepens; sallys and bulrushes on one side, coots and wild fowl making their nests there – on the other, the green lawns; past the house, past the long line of buildings, stables, kennels, dairy, the garden walls; then, narrow and deep here, it turned the old millwheel supplying water also for the steam engine that helped the sawmills work. Then the division the parting of the waters, the otters' cave, the bed of soft mud which we children used to make the little vessels that never went through the baking without cracks; the dip of the stream under-ground, rising later to join its sunlit branch; a rushing current again, passing by Ravahasey, Caherlinney, Poll na Sionnach Eserkelly, Castleboy, bridges again and then through thickets of laurel, beside a forsaken garden – (A sting of pain here from the knife, but I only make a face and hear a voice say, 'Put in another drop') – And then by a sloping field of daffodils – and so at last to the high road where it went out of our demesne. (Some pain again) and for a moment I think of the river that has bounded my second phase of life rising in the park at Coole, flowing under the high poplars on its steep bank, vanishing under rocks that nature has made a bridge; then flowing on again till it widens into the lake. But before I had come to its disappearance under the rocks at Inchy only to appear again as it mixes into Galway Bay, the Surgeon told me the knife had done its work. And presently the flow of warm blood was stopped with straps and bandages, and I was given praise for courage and told I was 'very good' and there was but a slight feeling of faintness and then I was carried upstairs.

Nights not very good. I have pain when I lie on the left side where I have always turned to for sleep. But the days pass pleasantly enough. Yeats very good, sat with me through that dreadful hour before I was taken downstairs, and for happier hours since then. Today he is full of the Coinage Committee, they have chosen their artists and subjects for designs.

And Lennox R. came in, had worked at the rehearsals of his *Big House* to be produced next week.

4 SEPTEMBER

Saturday. Sitting up, and Slattery has been here and says I may go home on Tuesday. So kind, and his fee much less than I expected, a relief my poor cheque book having been 'under the knife' of late. A nice letter from Margaret, and such a nice one from Frank, offering to help the expense of operation! That happily not needed; May will come down and stay a while with me at Coole.

Yeats was to have had the pamphlet yesterday for us to go through; and to have heard third Act of *Sancho* today. But alas, had some proofs that kept him from the first, and is afraid he would let me off too easily because of my invalid state if he doesn't like *Sancho*, so puts it off till he is at Ballylee.

Slattery has been talking much of Kerry, of its beauty and the wonderful salmon fishing which would bring tens of thousands into the country if preserved and advertised and the hotels made more comfortable.

May very glad to come to Coole, hadn't been in the country for seven years.

I had gone to see Molly Childers before being laid up, she looked very pretty, and not so sad, though depressed about Ireland. Is with de Valera 'because he is trying to do what is the right thing, the abolition of the oath', but she is a Republican still, and I think feels out of things. Bobby and Mrs Osgood came to *Autumn Fire* the evening I was there, and it went very well. Sir John Simon, from the Viceregal Lodge, came and talked to me, doesn't seem very happy about the Lane pictures. Oh! I am so anxious to get the pamphlet out. I told him who Bobby was, and he came and shook hands with him and said what friends he and his father had been. He said to me he had drawn up the suggested appeal for mercy sent from England – 'Yet,' he said, 'what could be done? And he was not an Irishman – there was not that excuse.' I left before the third Act, having to come here.

Next morning those dreadful preparations, much worse than the knife.

MONDAY, 6 SEPTEMBER

I suppose it is cancer. Thank God, if so, that it is only now it has come when I have I think done my work. I think kind Slattery was sorry to have to tell me.

1927

SUNDAY, 20 MARCH

Liverpool since then, calm crossings and a good journey. Mr (Alderman) Harford met me, and two interviewers and photographers, and I was taken to the Art Gallery – some fine old pictures, and bad modern ones, though good Rossettis. Then to the Library, a kind Director gave us tea and showed his treasures. Then a short rest, and dressed and went down, to the reception room; Joe Devlin had arrived, and he and I shook hands with a good many arrivals. Then the Archbishop appeared stood on the raised floor, and each guest half kneeled and kissed his hand. Dinner at last. I was next him, with a very different Prelate on my other side, Dr Downey, who lectures on philosophy and loves literature. A long dinner, long speeches – the Archbishop giving the lead in praising Ireland's morality, 'a country where immoral newspapers are seized at the ports, where girls are safe, where there is no birth control, where there is now a Catholic government, where the Catholic colleges will increase', &c &c. Devlin spoke very well, none of the others except Father Downey who came last and spoke on literature, Yeats, Shaw, G. Moore, and, to my great pleasure, with enthusiasm of my *Story Brought by Brigit*. There were songs and recitations between the speeches, there had not been a St Patrick's dinner since 1913 and it seemed as if nothing had been learned or forgotten meanwhile – 'The Dear Little Shamrock' &c, and the old and vulgar somebody's 'Old Sheebeen'.

Then at the end of my speech – as short as I could make it, just telling of the rise of intellectual efforts after the Land League broke down, the split and Parnell's death. I gave credit to Hyde, spoke of the Gaelic League, Abbey Theatre, and then, with some fire, of Hugh's pictures, and hope this may lead to some help there.

Next morning Alderman Harford who came to take me to the station said he and Devlin and some of the others had sat up till 3 o'c. talking and had been furious at the Catholic nature of the speeches: 'The Archbishop holding up a Catholic government just when we want Ulster to come in.'

MONDAY, 18 JULY

Poor Mme Markievicz also gone. Her funeral on Sunday was made a Republican demonstration. I knew her in her Castle days when she was rather a jealous meddler in the Abbey and Hugh's Gallery. But her energy found a better scope when she took up the Labour movement, and then a more violent outlet in 1916 when she fought, with the Boy Scouts she had trained, against the English troops, and was imprisoned. I remember one evening late, when I was coming from some hard hours' work at the Abbey. I felt tired and jaded in the tram. And then she got in, tired and jaded also from some drilling of her 'Fianna', and I felt drawn to her. There was something gallant about her. We were each working for what we believed would help Ireland, and we talked together. Once later I saw her, I again having some work at the Abbey, going there, and all traffic was stopped because of a procession coming down O'Connell Street. I asked a little boy what it was and he said, 'It's the *Countess*.' And then I saw her standing up in a waggonette, cheered as she passed, for she was on her way home from England where she had been in prison. That was the last time I saw her.

## 20 OCTOBER

Today Mr Reed of the Land Commission and Mr Donovan of the Forestry Department came and formally took over Coole, took possession. It no longer belongs to anyone of our family or name. I am thankful to have been able to keep back a sale for these years past, for giving it into the hands of the Forestry people makes the maintenance and improvement of the woods secure, and will give employment and be for the good and dignity of the country. As to the house, I will stay and keep it as the children's home as long as I keep strength enough and can earn money enough. It had a good name before I came here, its owners were of good, even of high, repute; and that has been continued, has increased, in Robert's time and mine. Perhaps some day one of the children may care enough for it to come back; they have been happy here.

## 21 NOVEMBER

I was tired yesterday but in the afternoon went to see Molly Childers and stayed a long time. Poor thing, her spine trouble is I am afraid increasing and may need an operation later. But she is happy about her boys, Erskine at Cambridge (with wife and baby!) and Bobby is soon going there. She is anxious to write her husband's Life or compile it from his letters – he had written such beautiful ones during the war. He had also kept a diary during it, two volumes. But one has disappeared, she is afraid taken in a raid. For her house was raided again after Kevin O'Higgins' death. Two CID came into her bedroom, she was in bed with her little grandson in her arms. They were looking for Bobby – on suspicion. She has had all letters and papers taken away to safety. She is Sinn Fein, would rather have kept Fianna Fail out of the Dail. But when I talked of the pictures and the hope of the new Gallery being begun, she begged me to see de Valera in case he will support it. She will telephone him (hadn't his number there) and let me know. I shall be glad to see him if it helps.

Then I went to 82 Merrion Square, had tea with Michael and Anne and told stories and played and romped with them till bedtime. And then, later to the Abbey to see *O'Flaherty V. C.* I had never seen it acted. It was very well done (Jack Dwan's Co.). Theatre crowded. I paid for my seat 3/9, the first time I had ever paid at an Abbey performance (I as Patentee being responsible to see 'that there are no wild beasts on the stage, and no men or women hung from the flies'!). But I was glad to see so big an audience of unfashionable people for *O'Flaherty* and a harmless play called *Cupid and the Styx*, in which Paul Farrell gave a very fine performance.

22 NOVEMBER

* * *

This morning a note from Molly Childers saying de Valera would be glad to see me at 12 o'c. I had some difficulty finding the Office, 'Fianna Fail' — some repairs going on outside, and inside I was sent up a narrow staircase, and then told he was a flight lower. He was in a very small dingy room, just one small table and a couple of chairs. He did not remember Lord Mayor O'Neill's hurried introduction, but 'knew my face'. He looked older and darker, and depressed but was interested about the Gallery only he says there is little money to be had, and so much wanted for relief of unemployment. I said this would be spent chiefly on employment but he says a good deal of steel &c would he thinks have to be imported. But he will help if he can — he will consult on that matter, and Labour being for us that should be all right. I gave him the pamphlet and promised him Hugh's *Life*. I said I am glad his party had come into the Dail and he said, 'But we have left a large section — some of them our best people — outside. Sinn Fein will not come in.' That seems to pain him. He looked worn and sad. I told him he had often been in my prayers in the old troubles. There were several men waiting outside the door to see him. It touched me, these poor even squalid surroundings, such a contrast to government buildings, those large airy rooms and the solid mahogany furniture. I am glad to have seen him, but feel troubled, and the words are in my mind – 'We thought it had been he that would have redeemed Israel.'

### 31 DECEMBER

We had seven sets of Wrenboys, not much good, and for the first time for years there was no song about Kevin Barry nor any patriotic song.

## 1928

### 1 JANUARY

Alone this morning, all at Lough Cutra, but came back bye and bye. The ground so slippery last night John thought it would be dangerous for a horse today and I am glad of the quiet morning at home.

The year that is past was troublesome in its first half – 'Eviction' and an auction hanging over me. But this (by no interference of mine, I had assented and even helped) has passed. The sale of the woods and house has been completed. I hope to be able to keep it as long as the children need a home. All land troubles are at an end. I don't know how my money will hold out. I have written some of my articles about the house and its contents and am going on with the political portraits in the breakfast room slowly, with atmosphere; they are easy to scamp but difficult to get into a meditation, a setting. That is one of my tasks for this year; and to keep the house peaceful, and as comfortable for children and guests as means and my remaining energy will allow.

The Lane pictures still to be won.

Love the solution of life, of living in Heaven while on earth – I seem to grasp it sometimes; it would set everything right if I could feel to all as I do to, say – Richard.

Ireland is I think happier than a year ago; the politicians less harsh though that terrible murder of K. O'Higgins stirred up the old bitterness. The country, the neighbourhood, tranquil; the Civic Guard have almost done away with those small robberies and personal attacks that had outlasted the Treaty and the Civil War. I have seen a great deal of history in my 75 – nearly 76 years.

A few days ago an ex-policeman from near Ballyturin came to ask me to write on his behalf for compensation or a gratuity from an English Association. I did not know him, and his face was indicative of drink, but as I could not say that to him I was relieved when I found that the signature to be of any use should be that of 'a prominent Loyalist'.

I told him I was not one and he seemed surprised. I advised him to go to Rita Daly.

## 23 JULY

Yesterday Richard motored me with Anne to Ardrahan church where the service is being held while ours is being painted. I think it is fifty years or more since I was last there, and the few – very few – faces were new. In my early days, except for the incumbent's family, the congregation was entirely of my near relations and their households; Clan Morris my first cousin and his wife (a more distant cousin), and their children; Walter Shawe-Taylor and his wife, my sister; their children. Richard and Anne were amused when I told them I had been a bridesmaid in that church, to Florence Bingham, dressed in white embroidered muslin with a wreath of violets. I had been ill, and had a moment's faintness when kneeling in the aisle, and was brought very indignantly back to liveliness by hearing a whisper that the bridegroom had been known to admire me and perhaps I coveted him from the bride! A simpler wedding in that little church had been that of my sister Adelaide to the Rev J. Lane, our parents not allowing it to take place at our own little church in the Roxborough demesne. An unhappy marriage, yet that clash of opposing temperaments in wife and husband brought forth him of whom Augustus John has said, 'He was one of those rare ones who, singlehanded, are able to enrich and dignify an entire nation.' And outside, in the green burial plot, is the grave of his cousin and fellow-worker, John Shawe-Taylor, who brought together the Conference that under George Wyndham and Dunraven led to the peaceable and friendly settlement of the thorny Land quarrel. In dedicating a play, *The Image*, to these two, my sisters' sons (as I did in a later printing 'to their dear memory'), I wrote, 'So we must say "God love you" to the Image Makers, for do we not live by the shining of those scattered fragments of their dream.'

Anne and Richard motored to Limerick in the afternoon, thinking to have a game of tennis at the Burkes, were surprised at the crowds in the streets.

And no wonder, for Monday's paper says it was the Diamond Jubilee of the Arch-Confraternity of the Holy Family – 'Upwards of 30,000 people visited the city. Bannerets were carried and half a dozen bands played. His Eminence Cardinal van Rassam was there, six Irish Bishops and one from USA. The Dutch National Anthem was played.'

A contrast to our morning's handful of people in the little Ardrahan church! Yet as I had just written, influences have gone out from it that have helped to the peace and the imaginative culture of Ireland.

I had Raftery's children to the garden for a long gooseberry picking, and I picked a basketful for the postman's children.

## 1929

TUESDAY, 5 FEBRUARY

Last Monday, with what terror and sinking of heart, having left my poor little Catherine at the Alexandra College, I think with hardly less apprehension (I have seen her but once since and then a light form of Flu took her but she is better now).

I was so tired I slept a good deal, and would have slept longer had I not been awakened at 7 o'c. – the operation not to be till

10.30. Those hours were the worst. Then an hour downstairs – three minutes of transit, then the table – Of course the needles hurt – not a great deal. But the effect wonderful! I could *hear* the flesh being cut, without feeling it. And I did not faint though very tired.

I tried to keep my mind on the new plantings in the woods, and the happiness the little trees must feel when their roots, dry and packed together from their journey, are spread out in that soft damp leafmould where the clearings have been made, and their branches loosened from the packing. But when a second little avenue of stabs began being made by kind wise Slattery on the old scar, it was rather the spade that came to mind.

19 MARCH. TUESDAY

Yesterday evening at Lough Cutra I went down to the wireless room to hear the St Patrick's day programme, chosen by James Stephens. Chilcott worked the machine, not very skilfully, and the bagpipes and what followed seemed a long way off. Then of a sudden a beautiful voice came as it were into the room – Sara Allgood's – so clear, so rich. She gave the lament from *Gaol Gate*, and then 'Wandering Angus' and some other folksongs – all beautiful. And another fine voice – two – (one of them, Donovan's), spoke very finely the dialogue between Usheen and Padraig, or part of it from *Gods and Fighting Men*. And the whole wound up with Sally again – my translation of Pearse's lines.

> I am Ireland
> Older than the Hag of Beara.

> Great my pride
> I gave birth to great Cuchulain.

> Great my shame
> My own children killed their mother.

> I am Ireland
> Lonelier than the Hag of Beara

11 MAY

I wrote an evening or two ago, 'Reading Anatole France's definition of criticism – "Adventures among masterpieces" has made me restless, I am not sure why. It is not that I have the impulse that led me to Shakespeare and Dante and Morte D'Arthur – and to the Irish Epics, opening these last to many through translation and arrangement. It is the feeling as it were of having passed beyond childbearing. I have turned my mind steadily from play-writing that was in these late years my means of expression –. The little essays were easy, almost a copyist's work from what I see before me, the Library, the pottery figures. I write a diary, and type copies of it and correct them, and feel I am like the rubber band of the sawmill engine in my childhood, going round and round, getting no farther. Scholars and poets have taken up the Irish translations, Robin Flower with his scholarship, his form; Stephens with his elfish and lovely genius. My delving is no longer needed, the experts have taken it in hand. I suppose in my 78th year I should be content to sit still and meditate on the life that is past and the unseen life to come. My bodily strength is lessening, the morning uprising less buoyant, the evening reading has its danger signals up against small type (I who could read, and still can, the smallest print by moonlight!), I do not grumble or complain. I have had a full life, a happy life, apart from its two great griefs. I have served my country, my darlings and my friends. If I were certain all work is over I think I should be even happy to sit still. But I do not feel certain. I believe I could take work in some fourth declension, some yet untried sphere, some new discovery of beauty or of truth – perhaps it is but the feeling that led that other ancient lady in her hundredth year to climb an apple tree (and met her death thereby!) And although I am still in that long fight on Hugh's behalf in Ireland, I believe the torches are alight, that the unworthy British barrier will fall to ashes without need of me now.'

## 1930

### 29 JANUARY

F.G.'s *Nation* has waked up this week – anger at the attacks on Fianna Fail's coolness towards the Papal Envoy. They were at the Cathedral Service – but their names were put in small print. (And I, who had *not* been at the evening reception feel equally aggrieved because my name – even in small print – is printed as having been there!)

And he gives the Declaration of Independence read at the first Dail – stirring enough – though it was not found possible to keep it intact . . .

'We ordain that the elected Representatives of the Irish people alone have power to make laws binding on the people of Ireland, and that the Irish Parliament is the only Parliament to which that people will give its allegiance' . . .

It is logical, it would be admired coming from another nation but – as to us – 'He follows after shadows the King of Ireland's son'!

I myself wish full independence could have been given, even though greater material loss had come to us – to my class. For that breaking would have been followed by a remaking – in which the whole country, even Ulster – might have worked out, free from bitterness, its salvation.

### 15 MARCH

This my birthday, my 78th! The last of the Roxborough generation. And although that cold caught in Dublin has turned to a cough, I am wonderfully well, took that three hours walk among the woods the other day; sleep well, eat very little, no meat – porridge and a slice of bread for breakfast, vegetables or broth or an occasional egg for lunch, 1.30. Tea at 6.30 bread and butter, jam, perhaps cake; a glass of milk and some biscuits at night. I keep strength, and my mind clear (I think!) A wire in the afternoon 'Love and good wishes all and—from Leixlip'.

Stephen Aldridge, my brother's tutor of I suppose over sixty years ago or more – yes, more – writes, 'I feel sure you retain your former charm of manner and appearance, notwithstanding the passage of the years'! He has never seen me since then!

## 18 OCTOBER

'What was the Mistress talking about?' A. once asked Mrs Moon my mother's maid. 'Praising herself mostly,' was the answer. And I'm afraid I'm getting into this. Yet why should I let the good be 'interred with my bones'? And I feel ashamed and useless now, remembering all the work I did so easily in my time. But I don't want to give in to idleness, and am trying to get what I had written about the old Bridge at Roxborough into shape.

And let me boast that the *Daily Telegraph*, writing on the new religious Drama Society says 'Lady Gregory's modern fantasy, the *Travelling Man*, was easily the most moving of the four (miracle and morality) plays.'

## MONDAY, 20 OCTOBER

I've sent *Volunteer Bridge* to be typed. I had begun it long ago and lack energy to finish. But no creative work yet. I am 'past childbearing' I suppose. And no wonder at seventy-eight. Yet the thought irks me.

1931

I APRIL

I have been reading Joyce's *Portrait of the Artist as a Young Man* – his first book, I think. Rather terrible – it gives the cruelties of the School – Clongowes? – and the horror of Dublin sensuality – but with here & there a passage of beauty – like a birds sudden song . . . 'His thinking was a dusk of doubt & self-mistrust, lit up at moments by the lightnings of intuition, but lightnings of so clear a splendour that in those moments the world perished about his feet as if it had been fireconsumed; & thereafter his tongue grew heavy & he met the eyes of others with unanswering eyes for he felt that the spirit of beauty had folded him round like a mantle & that in reverie at least he had been acquainted with nobility. But, when this brief pride of silence upheld him no longer, he was glad to find himself still in the midst of common lives, passing on his way amid the squalor and noise & sloth of the city fearlessly and with a light heart.'

Such a handsome petulant boy he was long ago – heading from A.E.['s] room with 'It is what I expected. You are no use to me.'

17 APRIL

A card from Charlotte Shaw from Venice with picture – St Marks. Made me almost sick with longing for the peace & beauty there – though it would be sad without a Capello long passed away. But I must not grumble – for from my own windows here I have glimpses through woods of the lake – and beyond that the tranquil blue range of the hills. Hobbling about with this rheumatic pain. I suppose one of 'Dobson's Three Warnings'!

Reading again last ev. Vincent Benets's *John Brown's Body* & being, as ever moved by it – and feeling such a desire that our own late war could be so finely told of in the same way – in verse – in prose – with passion – with humour. I suddenly thought how finely James Stephens could do that. And so I have, on the bare chance – written to him, enclosing a note to Hatchards asking them to forward it to him (I hope he will post it!). And I've written telling him this. I think his imagination would catch fire in the reading. It always excites mine – the two dominant races – landed gentry North & South. And the Rising. And the executions – the Black and Tans. And alas, Michael Collins's death. Erskine Childers' death – terrible tragedies both – as are John Brown's at the beginning & Lincoln's at the end of that other struggle.

[Glued in at the foot of the page is the following press-cutting.]

'I propose that we take *service* as our touchstone, and reject all other touchstones; and that without bothering our heads about sorting out, segregation, and labelling Irishmen and Irishwomen according to their opinions, we agree to accept as fellow-Nationalists all who specifically or virtually recognise this Irish nation as an entity and, being part of it, owe it and give it their service.'

– Padraic Pearse

20 APRIL

Gr. pain still – and a 'cure' that did me good at first 'Sloans Lotion' seems to have turned against me & brings more pain than profit.

21 APRIL

Now after a day of pain, reading *The Dynasts* that idea of a history, a drama – in verse & prose comes even more strongly to me. Sarsfield, Wolfe Tone & the rest watching the sleepers in Dublin – seeing signs they will awaken – call to them in dreams – to Pearse, McNeill and McDonagh.

24 APRIL

Determined to make an effort, no longer to give in to idleness, I arranged this book & the typing paper – and sat down to begin copying. But after one or two lines the machine stopped – tho' Mr Warren had touched it up a few days ago – & pronounced it workable! So I am back at the writing table. But what to write – Age has come on me, this troublesome rheumatic pain makes walking a difficulty, though I can get about the gardens. I have still the idea of a possible great play or poem garnished history of our shaking off (to some extent) the British govt – that is what I hope Stephens may do. I'm reading again with this in mind *The Dynasts* – it seems less good than when I read it to Sean O'Casey – but those shadowy forms might – (our martyrs) well appear & inspire the 1916 Rising – whispering in dream to Pearse (asleep in his newspaper office) to McDonagh, as I last saw him, going to Limerick for his weekend – a gun in his hand. Perhaps if I could write out suggestions some one or two of our young poets & writers might take it up.

23 NOVEMBER

*Agony.* These pains sometimes very hard to bear. But what can one do? Such waste of time when I can't write – or even as I had intended to go thru' MSS. Yeats was here such a mercy – and he is so kind – tho' I hide my suffering as far as I can. And he is working so well & seems content. Lough Cutra comes in very often. Anne's hunting has begun. Oh pain! I must try & get a sleep on the sofa bye & bye.

1932

14 FEBRUARY

Not much change. The night pain less severe, I manage the pillows better! I think. The pain during the days increased, especially if I sit at table – writing or at meals it is torture – and there seems no remedy. I have to lie on the sofa a good deal in the breakfast-room. And the weather is bad – snow as a change from rain. I had never been shut from the open air so long. My idleness frets me. I can write nothing but a few letters – those with difficulty – & I cannot attempt arranging MSS – tho' that should be done to save trouble later – or rather settle what should be destroyed and what typed. Yeats so kind – tho' I am a poor companion – tho' I can still read to him in the evenings – Shirley now – We have exhausted Trollope – or all the vols I have. I do not desire the extension of life. I have had my day – and had not rested when there was work to be done that I could do. I do not like to think of a deserted Coole & will stay here while strength permits, or till the pressure of Celbridge is too strong for my weakness.

## 18 FEBRUARY

Alone now. Yeats in Dublin for this week – to vote in the election, & get some typing done. Anne has been here for 2 nights – gone to MFH headquarters now. The voting for the elections yesterday. I sent subscription – £2 – but of course couldn't get to Kiltartan to vote – & did not mind, for if Cosgrave wins back we shall go on placidly as before – And if it is De V— there may be trouble with England – over the oath – & trouble. But that wd not last. 'The noise of the Captains & the shouting' will give way to practical matters – & both sides want to serve Ireland – & will find what is practicable when in office –

# NOTES

## *Autobiography*

### from *Seventy Years*

Lady Gregory's autobiography was discovered by accident among family papers some forty years after her death.\* Her unwillingness to publish it herself may be attributed to ambivalence about revealing her private life as well as concern that she might offend her contemporaries. Our selection, comprising the first two chapters and a portion of Chapter 19, describes her life at Roxborough, the early years of her marriage and her initial collaboration with W. B. Yeats. Square brackets indicate portions of the text deleted by Lady Gregory but restored by the original editors at Colin Smythe Ltd.

#### THE FIRST DECADES

1. See Glossary.
2. Hamilton Rowan (1751–1834), a member of the United Irishmen; tried and sentenced for sedition in 1794, but escaped and was eventually pardoned.
3. *Lalla Rookh*, a romantic poem (1817) by Thomas Moore (1779–1852) set in Persia.
4. See Glossary.
5. 'For the original Cave of Adullam see I *Samuel* 22:1' (note to original edition).
6. Charles James Lever (1806–72), an Irish novelist noted for his humorous army tales.
7. 'Probably Baron Oranmore . . .' (note to original edition).

---

\* Colin Smythe, Foreword, *Seventy Years*, pp. v–xl.

8. 'From another Persse who was ruined by the long struggle against the richer and more powerful elder branch . . .' (note to original edition).
9. Refers to law dissolving special status of the Anglican Church in Ireland.
10. A collection of patriotic songs from the *Nation*, which first appeared in 1843.
11. Edward Dowden (1843–1913), literary critic and Professor of English at Trinity College, Dublin, who was against the use of Irish subject matter for poetry and was publically challenged by Yeats in 1886.

## MARRIAGE

1. Daniel O'Connell (1775–1847), legendary Irish political leader responsible for Catholic Emancipation in 1829.
2. A movement to dissolve the Act of Union (1800) with England and restore a separate Irish parliament.
3. 'Whatever men do'.
4. The English public school attended by Sir William and his son, Robert.
5. 'Shadows of men'.
6. 'Long-winded'.
7. 'Little gifts preserve friendship'.
8. Irish for 'a hundred thousand welcomes'.

## THE CHANGING IRELAND

1. Lady Enid Layard, a close friend.
2. Arthur Symons (1865–1945), English poet and critic; encouraged Yeats's interest in French symbolists.
3. Irish response to English celebration of Queen Victoria's fiftieth year on the throne in 1897; Maud Gonne made a speech that inflamed the crowd gathered in Dublin.
4. A cromlech is a megalithic tomb marked by standing stones supporting a large capstone; traditionally associated with the beds of Diarmuid and Grania. For druid, see Glossary.

5. Standish James O'Grady (1846–1928), sometimes referred to as the father of the Irish Literary Revival; wrote *History of Ireland: Heroic Period* (1878–80), *Early Bardic Literature of Ireland* (1879) and *The Coming of Cuchulain* (1894).

6. 'Elizabeth Coxhead, in her book *Lady Gregory: A Literary Portrait*, points out that this date is incorrect, as it can be seen from Yeats's letters to Lady Gregory of November 1897 that the project was then already under way . . .' (note in original edition).

7. W. E. H. Lecky (1838–1903), an Irish historian noted for his *History of England in the Eighteenth Century*, in which he responded to J. A. Froude's denigration of Irish culture.

8. The English.

9. Irish for 'baby' or small child.

## Folklore and Translations from the Irish

*Visions and Beliefs in the West of Ireland*, Lady Gregory's most important book of folklore, was first published in 1920. It contains stories collected for the most part in Galway, Clare and the Aran Islands during the 1890s and the early years of the next century. The titles of the chapters from which these selections are taken ('Seers and Healers', 'Herbs, Charms and Wise Women', 'Banshees and Warnings', and so forth) are Lady Gregory's.

Originally published in 1903, *Poets and Dreamers* contains 'studies and translations from the Irish'. In the essay 'West Irish Ballads' Lady Gregory first published her most famous translation, 'The Grief of a Girl's Heart', from the Irish song 'Donall Og'. This poem, and her translation of 'Donncha Ban' ('Fair-haired Donough'), which she drew on in *Kathleen ni Houlihan*, were also published in *The Kiltartan Poetry Book*. An earlier version of the essay on Raftery was published in 1901, and of 'West Irish Ballads' in 1902.

*A Book of Saints and Wonders* was first published in 1906. The material reprinted here comes from various sources: the stories about Brigit combine traditional matter and stories Lady Gregory collected herself. Lady Gregory's translation of the early Irish poem 'The Old Woman of Beare' is based on that of Kuno Meyer.

*The Kiltartan Poetry Book* was first published in 1919. Although many of the poems and songs are not necessarily linked with Galway, Lady Gregory collected these versions of them there and translated them into the Irish–English that came to be called 'Kiltartanese'.

*The Kiltartan History Book* was first published in 1909; a revised edition appeared in 1926. 'I have given this book its name,' Lady Gregory wrote in a note to the second edition, 'because it is in this Barony of Kiltartan that I have heard the greater number of the stories, from beggars, pipers, travelling men, at my own door; or by the roadside or in the Workhouse, though others I have been given on the north of Galway Bay, in Connemara, or on its southern shore.' The stories, she says, might better be called 'Myths in the Making'. They are, quite literally, 'the Book of the People'.

Because the date of publication has no necessary connection with the date material was collected or translated, the chronology of most of Lady Gregory's folkloric material is problematic. Although some parts of *Poets and Dreamers* predate some parts of *Visions and Beliefs*, most of the stories in the latter volume date from the 1890s and are thus among the first Lady Gregory collected. The revised edition of *The Kiltartan History Book* includes stories about the Black and Tan Terror that are among the last she collected.

## from *Visions and Beliefs*

1. Michael Davitt (1846–1906) founded the Land League in 1879. John Dillon (1851–1927) worked with him in the campaign to regulate rents in favour of the tenant farmers. For Parnell, see Glossary.
2. See Glossary.
3. Churl or lout.
4. It was believed that supernatural forces were particularly active on May eve.

5. A fort.
6. Speckled
7. 'Slanlus' is plantain; 'garblus' is dandelion.
8. Thin, stony soil.
9. A stick.
10. Priest, from the Irish *sagart*.
11. A cloak of rough woollen cloth.

## from *Poets and Dreamers*

1. Not a bit of sight.
2. An eighteenth-century agrarian movement that mobilized small farmers and labourers to protest tithes, high rents and other economic abuses. Members concealed their identity behind white masks or sheets, hence the name.
3. See Glossary.
4. See Glossary.
5. See Glossary.
6. 'O'Neill' is probably Hugh O'Neill, Earl of Tyrone, who led the Irish armies during the late Elizabethan wars. 'William' is William of Orange, who defeated King James II and his Irish allies at the Battle of the Boyne in 1690. 'Sarsfield' is Patrick Sarsfield, an outstanding Irish commander in the Williamite Wars (1688–91).
7. An early nineteenth-century agrarian movement that was more consciously nationalist than the Whiteboys; advocated violence against landlords and their agents.
8. Poor, landless men.
9. Potatoes.
10. See Glossary.
11. See Glossary.
12. See Glossary.
13. See Glossary.
14. Owen Roe O'Sullivan (1748–84), a legendary Kerry poet.
15. A public house (frequently unlicensed) where liquor is sold.
16. Site of a pre-Norman Galway fishing village. 'Claddagh' (*cladagh* in modern Irish) means shore.

17. Irish for 'lame'.
18. Whiskey, literally 'water of life', *visce* in modern Irish.
19. Festival.
20. 'Pleasant Little Branch' (also *Craoibhin Aoibhinn*), the Irish signature adopted by Douglas Hyde.
21. See Glossary.
22. Illegally distilled whiskey.
23. Standard form is *cailleach*. See Glossary.
24. An Irish person who looks to English standards.
25. 'Young Donall'.

## from *A Book of Saints and Wonders*

1. Richard Fitzgilbert de Clare, Earl of Pembroke (*c.* 1130–1176); in 1170 the first Norman lord to invade Ireland (at the behest of Diarmud MacMurrough, King of Leinster).
2. From the Irish *lios*, a ring fort or fairy mound.
3. The month of May; May eve was a Celtic festival.
4. See Glossary.
5. An avatar of Lugh, a principal deity of the Tuatha Dé Danann; Cuchulain (the Hound) is his son.

## from *The Kiltartan Poetry Book*

1. See note 6 to *Poets and Dreamers*, above.

## from *The Kiltartan History Book*

1. Standard spelling, Oisín. See Glossary.
2. Daniel O'Connell. See note 1 to 'Marriage' in *Seventy Years*, above.
3. Irish for 'even so', 'if that's the case'.

# Irish Saga and Romance

The first two selections, 'Fate of the Sons of Usnach' and 'The Only Son of Aoife', are taken from *Cuchulain of Muirthemne* (1902). These are among the most poignant stories associated with *Táin Bó Cuailnge* (*The Táin*), the saga of Cuchulain's defence of Ulster against the marauding armies of Queen Maeve of Connacht. The earliest redactions of *The Tain* date from the eighth century. In her own notes to the stories, Lady Gregory lists among the 'authorities' used for 'Fate of the Sons of Usnach' the Text and Translations published by the Society for the Preservation of the Irish Language; Hyde's *Literary History of Ireland*; Eugene O'Curry's *Manners and Customs of Ancient Ireland* and *Lectures on the Manuscript Materials of Ancient Irish History*; and works by Cameron, Carmichael, de Jubainville, O'Flanagan, Stokes, Windisch, and others. For 'The Only Son of Aoife' she lists Charlotte Brooke's *Reliques of Irish Poetry*, Jeremiah Curtin's *Folk Tales*, and Geoffrey Keating's *History of Ireland*. The complete list can be found in *Cuchulain of Muirthemne*.

The next three selections, 'The Fate of the Children of Lir', the chapter 'The Coming of Finn' from 'Finn, Son of Cumhal' and 'Oisin and Patrick' were published in *Gods and Fighting Men* (1904). This medieval romance cycle, centred on Fionn mac Cumhail (Finn MacCool), was part of the oral tradition well into the twentieth century, when Joyce adopted it for *Finnegans Wake*. In her own notes to the stories, Lady Gregory lists as her authorities for 'Fate of the Children of Lir', Eugene O'Curry's *Atlantis*; for 'The Coming of Finn', Kuno Meyer's *Four Songs of Summer and Winter*, Standish Hayes O'Grady's *Silva Gaedelica*, Curtin's *Tales* and *Proceedings of the Ossianic Society*; and for 'Oisin and Patrick', Curtin's *Tales*, *Kilkenny Archaeological Journal* and *Proceedings of the Ossianic Society*. She also thanks John MacNeil, whose edition of *Duanaire Finn* she read in proof.

## from *Cuchulain of Muirthemne*

1. The stronghold of Conchubar; literally 'the twins of Macha'. The name refers to a pregnant woman forced to race the King's horses to save her husband's life. She won the race, giving birth to twins at the finish line, and thereupon cursed the men of Ulster unto nine generations. See *The Táin*, translated by Thomas Kinsella (Oxford: Oxford University Press), pp. 6–8.
2. See Glossary.
3. See Glossary.
4. Literally the 'hound' or watchdog of Cuailnge.
5. Cuchulain's ultimate weapon; sometimes described as a multi-pronged spear that disembowelled its victim.
6. The fort of Scathach.
7. What follows is Cuchulain's keen for his son.

## from *Gods and Fighting Men*

1. 'Good God', god of the earth, who possessed a marvellous cauldron from which no one went away hungry and a living harp whose music assured the proper progression of the seasons.
2. Harvest festival; comparable to Halloween.
3. See Glossary.
4. Tir na nÓg.

# *Essays on Irish Culture*

'Ireland, Real and Ideal' was published in 1898 in *Nineteenth Century*. Included here is the third of four sections.

'The Felons of Our Land' was published in the *Cornhill Magazine* (May 1900).

'The Fight with the Castle' was first published in *Our Irish Theatre* (1913). More information about this 1909 episode – the unabridged records from Lady Gregory's unpublished journals, the letter from the Viceroy, and the complete correspondence with Shaw – may be found in Dan H. Laurence's and Nicholas Grene's *Shaw, Lady Gregory and the Abbey: A Correspondence and a Record* (Gerrards Cross, Bucks.: Colin Smythe Ltd, 1993).

'Laughter in Ireland', a lecture published here (in shortened form) for the first time, is dated January 1916 in the typed manuscript copy in the Rare Book and Manuscript Library of Columbia University. Lady Gregory's punctuation has been silently amended.

## The Felons of Our Land

1. Thomas Davis (1818–45), journalist, poet, one of the founders of the *Nation* and a leader of the Young Ireland movement.
2. The 'old lines' are not very old. As James Pethica discovered, they were inscribed by Wilfred Blunt in Lady Gregory's copy of his book *The Wind and the Whirlwind* (London, 1883). See James Pethica, 'A Dialogue of Self and Service; Lady Gregory's Emergence as an Irish Writer and Partnership with W. B. Yeats', p. 106.

## Our Irish Theatre

### THE FIGHT WITH THE CASTLE

1. In the summer of 1909 the Joint Select Committee of the House of Lords and the House of Commons on the Stage Plays (Censorship) was holding hearings.

## from 'Laughter in Ireland'

1. For Lever, see n. 6 for 'The First Decades', *Seventy Years*.
2. Samuel Lover (1797–1868), folklorist and writer, author of *Rory O'More* and *Handy Andy*, among other works.

# Plays

For the casts of first performances, see the Colin Smythe edition of the *Collected Plays*.

> Perhaps I ought to have written nothing but these short comedies, but desire for experiment is like fire in the blood, and I had had from the beginning a vision of historical plays being sent by us through all the counties of Ireland. For to have a real success and to come into the life of the country, one must touch a real and eternal emotion, and history comes only next to religion in our country. And although the realism of our young writers is taking the place of fantasy and romance in the cities, I still hope to see a little season given up every year to plays on history and in sequence at the Abbey, and I think schools and colleges may ask to have them sent and played in their halls, as a part of the day's lesson. – *Our Irish Theatre*, p. 57.

## Kathleen ni Houlihan

*Kathleen ni Houlihan* was composed by Lady Gregory and Yeats at Coole in September, October and the early weeks of November 1901 and first produced by William and Frank Fay's Irish National Dramatic Company at St Teresa's Hall, Dublin, on 2 April 1902. Maud Gonne played the title role. In addition to the manuscript evidence, comments by Lady Gregory and Yeats attest to her co-authorship of the play. Yeats told Lennox Robinson 'more than once' that Lady Gregory's share in *Kathleen ni Houlihan* was so large that 'the authorship of the play should be ascribed to her'.\* In *Our Irish Theatre* Lady Gregory writes,

---

\* Robinson, unpublished biography of Lady Gregory, Berg Collection. Cited by James Pethica, 'A Dialogue of Self and Service: Lady Gregory's Emergence as an Irish Writer and Partnership with W. B. Yeats' (D. Phil. thesis, Oxford University, 1987), p. 204.

Later in the year we wrote together *Kathleen ni Houlihan* and to that Yeats wrote an introductory letter addressed to me: 'One night I had a dream almost as distinct as a vision, of a cottage where there was well-being and firelight and talk of a marriage, and into the midst of that cottage there came an old woman in a long cloak. She was Ireland herself, that Kathleen ni Houlihan for whom so many songs have been sung and for whose sake so many have gone to their death. I thought if I could write this out as a little play, I could make others see my dream as I had seen it, but I could not get down from that high window of dramatic verse, and in spite of all you had done for me, I had not the country speech. One has to live among the people, like you, of whom an old man said in my hearing, "She has been a serving maid among us," before one can think the thoughts of the people and speak their tongue. We turned my dream into the little play, *Kathleen ni Houlihan*, and when we gave it to the little theatre in Dublin and found that working people liked it, you helped me to put my other dramatic fables into speech' (*Our Irish Theatre*, pp. 53–4).

1. The Mayo port where a French military force landed under General Joseph Humbert to support the abortive Irish Rising of 1798.
2. Dowry.
3. A pile of straw.
4. Affected by the supernatural.

## Spreading the News

This play was first performed on the opening night of the Abbey Theatre, 27 December 1904.
1. One who is not elected but serves by appointment.
2. Indian islands in the Bay of Bengal.
3. See Glossary.
4. Stacks of hay.
5. A halfpenny's worth (of whiskey).
6. One who converted to Protestantism in exchange for food from proselytizing members of the Anglican Church.
7. Prouder.

*Lady Gregory's note:*

The idea of this play first came to me as a tragedy. I kept seeing as in a picture people sitting by the roadside, and a girl passing to the market, gay and fearless. And then I saw her passing by the same place at evening, her head hanging, the heads of others turned from her, because of some sudden story that had risen out of a chance word, and had snatched away her good name.

But comedy and not tragedy was wanted at our theatre to put beside the high poetic work, *The King's Threshold*, *The Shadowy Waters*, *On Baile's Strand*, *The Well of the Saints*; and I let laughter have its way with the little play. I was delayed in beginning it for a while, because I could only think of Bartley Fallon as dull-witted or silly or ignorant, and the handcuffs seemed too harsh a punishment. But one day by the sea at Duras a melancholy man who was telling me of the crosses he had gone through at home said – 'But I'm thinking if I went to America, it's long ago today I'd be dead. And it's a great expense for a poor man to be buried in America.' Bartley was born at that moment, and, far from harshness, I felt I was providing him with a happy old age in giving him the lasting glory of that great and crowning day of misfortune.

It has been acted very often by other companies as well as our own, and the Boers have done me the honour of translating and pirating it.

– *Collected Plays: The Comedies*, p. 253

## Hyacinth Halvey

This play was first performed at the Abbey Theatre in February 1906.

1. Fictional Galway town associated with Gort.
2. Solemn promise not to drink alcohol.
3. A temperance badge.

*Lady Gregory's notes:*

I was pointed out one evening a well-brushed, well-dressed man in the stalls, and was told gossip about him, perhaps not all true, which made me wonder if that appearance and behaviour as of extreme respectability might not now and again be felt a burden.

After a while he translated himself in my mind into Hyacinth; and as one must set one's original a little way off to get a translation rather than a tracing, he found himself in Cloon, where, as in other parts of our country, 'character' is built up or destroyed by a password or an emotion, rather than by experience and deliberation.

The idea was more of a universal one than I knew at the first, and I have had but uneasy appreciation from some apparently blameless friends.

*– Collected Plays: The Comedies*, p. 255

To come back to play-writing, I find in a letter to Mr Yeats. 'You will be amused to hear that although, or perhaps because, I had evolved out of myself "Mr Quirke" as a conscious philanthropist, an old man from the workhouse told me two days ago that he had been a butcher of Quirke's sort and was quite vainglorious about it, telling me how many staggery sheep and the like he had killed, that would, if left to die, have been useless or harmful. "But I often stuck a beast and it kicking yet and life in it, so that it could do no harm to a Christian or a dog or an animal." And later: Yet another "Mr Quirke" has been to see me. He says there are no sick pigs now, because they are all sent off to . . . no, I mustn't give the address. Has not a purgatory been imagined where writers find themselves surrounded by the characters they have created?'

*– Our Irish Theatre*, p. 59

## The Gaol Gate

This play, inspired in part by Wilfrid Scawen Blunt's incarceration during the Land War in 1887–8, was first performed at the Abbey in October 1906.

1. Taking aggressive action against the landlords or the police.
2. Affectionate diminutive for little one, child.
3. Rights as tenant.
4. Peat, used as fuel.

*Lady Gregory's notes:*

I was told a story someone had heard, of a man who had gone to welcome his brother coming out of gaol, and heard he had died there before the gates had been opened for him.

I was going to Galway, and at the Gort station I met two cloaked and shawled countrywomen from the slopes of Slieve Echtge, who were obliged to go and see some law official in Galway because of some money left them by a kinsman in Australia. They had never been in a train or to any place farther than a few miles from their own village, and they felt astray and terrified 'like blind beasts in a bog' they said, and I took care of them through the day.

An agent was fired at on the road from Athenry, and some men were taken up on suspicion. One of them was a young carpenter from my old home, and in a little time a rumour was put about that he had informed against the others in Galway gaol. When the prisoners were taken across the bridge to the court-house he was hooted by the crowd. But at the trial it was found that he had not informed, that no evidence had been given at all; and bonfires were lighted for him as he went home.

These three incidents coming within a few months wove themselves into this little play, and within three days it had written itself, or been written. I like it better than any in the volume, and I have never changed a word of it.

*– Collected Plays: The Tragedies*, pp. 281–2

In a lecture I gave last year on play-writing I said I had been forced to write comedy because it was wanted for our theatre, to put on at the end of the verse plays, but that I think tragedy is easier. For, I said, tragedy shows humanity in the grip of circumstance, of fate, of what our people call 'the thing will happen', 'the Woman in the Stars that does all'. There is a woman in the stars they say, who is always hurting herself in one way or other, and according to what she is doing at the hour of your birth, so will it happen to you in your lifetime, whether she is hanging herself or drowning herself or burning herself in the fire. 'And,' said an old man who was telling me this, 'I am thinking she was doing a great deal of acting at the time I myself made my start in the world.' Well, you put your actor in the grip of this woman, in the claws of the cat. Once in that grip you know what the end must be. You may let your hero kick or struggle, but he is in the claws all the time, it is a mere question as to how nearly you will let him escape, and when you will allow the pounce. Fate itself is the protagonist, your actor cannot carry much character, it is out of place. You do not want to know the character of a wrestler you see trying his strength at a show.

In writing a little tragedy, *The Gaol Gate*, I made the scenario in three lines, 'He is an informer; he is dead; he is hanged.' I wrote that play very quickly. My two poor women were in the clutch of the Woman in the Stars ... I knew what I was going to do and I was able to keep within those three lines. But in comedy it is different. Character comes in, and why it is so I cannot explain, but as soon as one creates a character, he begins to put out little feet of his own and take his own way.

I had been meditating for a long time past on the mass of advice that is given one by friends and well-wishers and relations, advice that would be excellent if the giver were not ignorant so often of the one essential in the case, the one thing that matters. But there is usually something out of sight, of which the adviser is unaware, it may be something half mischievously hidden from him, it may be that 'secret of the heart with God' that is called religion. In the whole course of our work at the theatre we have been I may say drenched with advice by friendly people who for years gave us the reasons why we did not succeed ... All their advice, or at least some of it, might have been good if we had wanted to make money, to make a common place of amusement. Our advisers did not see that what we wanted was to create for Ireland a theatre with a base of realism, with an apex of beauty.

— *Collected Plays: The Comedies*, pp. 261–2

## The Rising of the Moon

This play was first performed at the Abbey Theatre in March 1907.

1. See Glossary.
2. See Glossary.

*Lady Gregory's notes:*

When I was a child and came with my elders to Galway for their salmon fishing in the river that rushes past the gaol, I used to look with awe at the window where men were hung, and the dark, closed gate. I used to wonder if ever a prisoner might by some means climb the high, buttressed wall and slip away in the darkness by the canal to the quays and find friends to hide him under a load of kelp in a fishing boat, as happens to my ballad-singing man. The play was considered offensive to some extreme Nationalists before it was acted, because it showed the police in too favourable a light, and a Unionist paper attacked it after it was acted because the policeman was represented 'as a coward and a traitor'; but after the Belfast police strike that same paper praised its 'insight into Irish character'. After all these ups and downs it passes unchallenged on both sides of the Irish Sea.

– *Collected Plays: The Comedies*, p. 257

Last night I read Hallie Flanagan's wonderful account of the Moscow Theatre. It seems the expression of the revolution of the people, a mass enthusiasm for the change. I had heard they had played *Rising of the Moon* under the name 'Those shall be up who are Down', and these plays with so many actors seem as if the title could be used for all. A victory for the workers, the enthusiasm born of it.

– *The Journals. Volume II, 21 February 1925 – 9 May 1932*
(11 December 1928)

Tomas O'Concannon, once Gaelic League Organiser, greeted me and sat beside me and I told him he was in part responsible for the play. He was astonished but I reminded him of an evening when he had come to Coole, very late, his bicycle having broken down. Hyde was with us, and others, but we had a room made ready for him. And he had told us of a policeman who had helped him to mend the bicycle and who seemed to have National sympathies under his tunic. Tomas, when I said this, started – said he remembered all perfectly – it was close to Kinvara that talk with the policeman had taken place.

– *The Journals. Volume II, 21 February 1925 – 9 May 1932*
(23 April 1929)

I may look on *The Rising of the Moon* as an historical play, as my history goes, for the scene is laid in the historical time of the rising of the Fenians in the sixties. But the real fight in the play goes on in the sergeant's own mind, and so its human side makes it go as well in Oxford or London or Chicago as in Ireland itself. But Dublin Castle finds in it some smell of rebellion and has put us under punishment for its sins. When we came back from America last March, we had promised to give a performance on our first day in Dublin and *The Rising of the Moon* was one of the plays announced. But the stage costumes had not yet arrived, and we sent out to hire some from a depot from which the cast uniforms of the Constabulary may be lent out to the companies performing at the theatres – the Royal, the Gaiety, and the Queens. But our messenger came back emptyhanded. An order had been issued by the authorities that 'no clothes were to be lent to the Abbey because *The Rising of the Moon* was derogatory to His Majesty's forces'. So we changed the bill and put on the *Workhouse Ward*, in which happily a quilt and blanket cover any deficiency of clothes.

– *Our Irish Theatre*, p. 60

## The Workhouse Ward

This play, based on *The Poorhouse*, a translation of *Teach Na mBocht* (written with Douglas Hyde), was first performed at the Abbey Theatre in April 1908.

1. A Galway saint associated with healing.
2. Beets.
3. A small quantity.

4. See Glossary.
5. Tethered in one place.
6. See Glossary.
7. An ecclesiastical unit.
8. Stumpy, a sliver.

*Lady Gregory's notes:*

As to *The Poorhouse*, the idea came from a visit to Gort Workhouse one day when I heard that the wife of an old man, who had been long there, maimed by something, a knife I think, that she had thrown at him in a quarrel, had herself now been brought into the hospital. I wondered how they would meet, as enemies or as friends, and I thought it likely they would be glad to end their days together for old sake's sake.

I intended to write the full dialogue myself, but Mr Yeats thought a new Gaelic play more useful for the moment, and rather sadly I laid that part of the work upon Dr Hyde. It was all for the best in the end, for the little play, when we put it on at the Abbey, did not go very well. It seemed to ravel out into loose ends, and we did not repeat it; nor did the Gaelic players like it as well as *The Marriage* and *The Lost Saint*. After a while, when the Fays had left us, I wanted a play that would be useful to them, and with Dr Hyde's full leave I re-wrote the *Poorhouse* as *The Workhouse Ward*. I had more skill by that time, and it was a complete re-writing, for the two old men in the first play had been talking at an imaginary audience of other old men in the ward. When this was done away with the dialogue became of necessity more closely knit, more direct and personal, to the great advantage of the play, although it was rejected as 'too local' by the players for whom I had written it. The success of this set me to cutting down the number of parts in later plays until I wrote *Grania* with only three persons in it, and *The Bogie Men* with only two. I may have gone too far, and have, I think, given up an intention I at one time had of writing a play for a man and a scarecrow only, but one has to go on with experiment or interest in creation fades, at least so it is with me . . .

– *Our Irish Theatre*, pp. 55–7

I sometimes think the two scolding paupers are a symbol of
ourselves in Ireland –
  – 'it is better to be quarrelling than to be lonesome.'
                                  – *Collected Plays: The Comedies*, p. 260


## Grania

This is probably Lady Gregory's best three-act play. It was
published in *Irish Folk History Plays*, first series, in 1912, but never
produced at the Abbey Theatre.

1. Stronghold of Fionn mac Cumhail; the Hill of Allen near
   Kildare.
2. Under penalties, bound.
3. See Glossary.
4. See Glossary.
5. Presumably Tír na nÓg, the Country of the Young.
6. As hard as the beak of a gander on the road. 'Gob' means
   'mouth'.

*Lady Gregory's note:*

I think I turned to Grania because so many have written
about sad, lovely Deirdre, who when overtaken by sorrow
made no good battle at the last. Grania had more power of
will, and for good or evil twice took the shaping of her life
into her own hands. The riddle she asks us through the ages
is, 'Why did I, having left great grey-haired Finn for comely
Diarmuid, turn back to Finn in the end, when he had
consented to Diarmuid's death?' And a question tempts one
more than the beaten path of authorised history. If I have
held but lightly to the legend, it is not because I do not
know it, for in *Gods and Fighting Men* I have put together
and rejected many versions. For the present play I have
taken but enough of the fable on which to set, as on a sod of
grass, the three lovers, one of whom had to die. I suppose it
is that 'fascination of things difficult' that has tempted me to
write a three-act play with only three characters. Yet where
Love itself, with its shadow Jealousy, is the true protagonist
I could not feel that more were needed. When I told Mr

Yeats I had but these three persons in the play, he said incredulously, 'They must have a great deal to talk about.' And so they have, for the talk of lovers is inexhaustible, being of themselves and one another.

As to the Fianna, the Fenians, I have heard their story many a time from my neighbours, old men who have drifted into workhouses, seaweed gatherers on the Burren Coast, turf-cutters on Slieve Echtge, and the like. For though the tales that have gathered around that mysterious race are thought by many to come from the earliest days, even before the coming of the Aryan Celt, the people of the West have a very long memory. And these tales are far better remembered than those of the Red Branch, and this, it is suggested, is part proof of their having belonged to the aboriginal race. Cuchulain's bravery and Deirdre's beauty 'that brought the Sons of Usnach to their death' find their way, indeed, into the folk-poetry of all the provinces; but the characters of the Fianna, Grania's fickleness, and Conan's bitter tongue, and Oisin's gentleness to his friends and his keen wit in the arguments with St Patrick, and Goll's strength, and Oscar's high bravery, and Finn's wisdom, that was beyond that of earth, are as well known as the characteristics of any noticeable man of modern times.

An old man I talked with on the beach beyond Kinvara told me, 'They were very strong in those days, and six or seven feet high. I was digging the potato garden one day about forty years ago, and down in the dyke the spade struck against something, and it was the bones of a man's foot, and it was three feet long. I brought away one bone of it myself, and the man that was along with me, but we buried it after. It was the foot of one of those men. They had every one six or seven dogs, and first they would set two of the dogs to fight, and then they'd fight themselves. And they'd go to all countries in curraghs that were as strong as steamers; to Spain they went in their curraghs. They went across from this hill of Burren to Connemara one time, and the sea opened to let them pass. There are no men like them now; the Connemara men are the best, but even with them, if there was a crowd of them together, and you to throw a stick over their heads, it would hardly hit one, they are mostly all the one height, and no one a few inches taller than another.'

Another man says, 'They were all strong men in those times; and one time Finn and his men went over to Granagh to fight the men there, and it was the time of the harvest, and what they fought with was sheaves, and every one that got a blow of a sheaf got his death. There is one of them buried now in Fardy Whelan's hill, and there's two head-stones, and my father often measured the grave, and he said it is seven yards long.'

On Slieve Echtge I was told, 'Oisin and Finn took the lead for strength, and Samson, too, he had great strength.' 'I would rather hear about the Irish strong men,' said I. 'Well, and Samson was of the Irish race, all the world was Irish in those times, and he killed the Philistines, and the eyes were picked out of him after. He was said to be the strongest, but I think myself Finn MacCumhail was stronger.' And again, 'It was before the flood those strong men lived here, Finn and Oisin and the others, and they lived longer than people do now, three or four hundred years.

'Giants they were; Conan was twelve feet high, and he was the smallest. But ever since, people are getting smaller and smaller, and will till they come to the end; but they are wittier and more crafty than they were in the old days, for the giants were innocent though they were so strong.'

I hear sometimes of 'a small race and dark, and that carried the bag', and that was probably the aboriginal one. 'There was a low-sized race came, that worked the land of Ireland a long time; they had their time like the others.' And, 'Finn was the last of the giants, the tall strong men. It was after that the Lochlannachs came to the country. They were very small, but they were more crafty than the giants, and they used to be humbugging them. One time they got a sack and filled it with sand, and gave it to one of the Fianna to put on his back to try him. But he lifted it up, and all he said was, "It is grain sowed in February it is."' Another says, 'An old man that was mending the wall of the house used to be telling stories about the strong men of the old time; very small they, were, about three feet high, but they were very strong for all that.'

Grania is often spoken of as belonging to that small race, as if her story had come from a very early time. 'She was very small, only four feet. She was the heiress of the princes of Ireland, and that is why they were after her.' 'They say Diarmuid and Grania were very small. They made the big cromlechs, there's a slab on the one near Crusheen, sixteen men couldn't lift, but they had *their own way* of doing it.' And again, 'Diarmuid and Grania were very small and very thick.' Another says, 'Grania was low-sized; and people now are handsomer than the people of the old time, but they haven't such good talk.'

I do not know if it is because of Grania's breach of faith, that I never hear her spoken of with sympathy, and her name does not come into the songs as Deirdre's does. A blind piper told me, 'Some say Grania was handsome, and some say she was ugly, there's a saying in Irish for that.' And an old basket-maker was scornful and said, 'Many would tell you Grania slept under the cromlechs, but I don't believe that, and she a king's daughter. And I don't believe she was handsome either. If she was, why would she have run away?'

An old woman says, 'Finn had more wisdom than all the men in the world, but he wasn't wise enough to put a bar on Grania. It was huts with big stones Grania made, that are called cromlechs now; they made them when they went away into the wilderness.'

And again I was told at Moycullen, near Lough Corrib, 'As they were passing a stream, the water splashed on Grania, and she said, "Diarmuid was never so near to me as that."'

*– Collected Plays: The Tragedies*, p. 286

# Poems

The twelve sonnets printed here were given by Lady Gregory to Wilfrid Scawen Blunt in the summer of 1883 at the end of their affair, which had begun a year earlier. With Lady Gregory's approval, they were printed – 'improved' by Blunt – under the title 'A Woman's Sonnets' in his *Love Lyrics and Songs of Proteus* (Kelmscott Press, 1892). See James Pethica's edition of the sequence in *Lady Gregory, Fifty Years After* (edited by Ann Saddlemyer and Colin Smythe), which prints Lady Gregory's originals opposite Blunt's revised versions.

'Alas! a woman may not love!', published here for the first

time, was written in April 1886 on board ship, while Sir William and Lady Gregory were returning to Europe from India and Ceylon. The poem was transcribed from the manuscript in the Berg Collection by James Pethica.

Poems by Lady Gregory written to Blunt, when he was imprisoned in Galway Gaol in the winter of 1888 for protesting the evictions of tenants, have been published in 'The Imprisonment of Wilfrid Scawen Blunt in Galway: Cause and Consequence' by James Mitchell (*The Journal of the Galway Archaeological and Historical Society* 46, 2 [1994], pp. 65–110). Lady Gregory is also the original author of 'The Eviction', a poem revised and published by Blunt (Kelmscott Press, 1892). Because no holograph manuscript of the poem has ever come to light, it cannot be known which lines are Lady Gregory's and which Blunt's.

# *Journals*

## 1919

GRESHAM HOTEL, 3 FEBRUARY *St Edna's School*: Irish-language school founded by Patrick Pearse, one of the leaders of the 1916 Rising.

16 MARCH *Lennox Robinson*: Lennox Robinson (1886–1958) was manager of the Abbey Theatre (1910–23) and one of its new playwrights.

*Madame Markievicz*: Constance Gore-Booth Markievicz (see Glossary), the only woman among the leaders of the Rising, was arrested, released and rearrested several times after the Rising. In 1918 she was interned in Holloway Prison in connection with the so-called 'German Plot'. Her cell-mates were *Maud Gonne* (see Glossary), Kathleen Clarke and (later) Hanna Sheehy-Skeffington. She was released on 10 March.

19 MARCH *R.* is Robert Gregory. The reference is to Yeats's 'In Memory of Major Robert Gregory'.

27 SEPTEMBER Mary Alden Osgood *Childers* (Molly), wife of Erskine Childers, was a close friend of Lady Gregory, who visited her often in Dublin. Here Childers is describing the Howth gun-running (the guns were landed at Howth on 26 July 1914 and given to the Irish Volunteers).


## 1920

28 SEPTEMBER *Margaret* Gregory is Lady Gregory's daughter-in-law, the widow of her son Robert. In 1928 Margaret married Lady Gregory's neighbour, Guy Gough of Lough Cutra.

30 SEPTEMBER *Edward Martyn*: see Glossary.
   *Black and Tans*: see Glossary.

1 OCTOBER *Marian* McGuinness was Lady Gregory's housekeeper for many years. She is mentioned often in the *Journals* and in Anne Gregory's *Me and Nu*.

2 OCTOBER *Sinn Feiners*: members of Sinn Féin (see Glossary).

24 OCTOBER *Frank* is Lady Gregory's brother Frank Persse, who acted as her agent at Coole.
   *M.Q.* is Malachi Quinn (see 5 November and following entries).

30 OCTOBER The *Lord Mayor* is Terence MacSwiney (1879–1920), Lord Mayor of Cork, who died on a hunger-strike in Brixton Prison. He had been active in the Volunteers and was elected to the first Dáil Éireann; he was arrested under the Defence of the Realm Act. The Abbey produced his play *The Revolutionist*.

31 OCTOBER *H. W. Massingham* was editor of the *Nation*, which published extracts from Lady Gregory's journals.
   *G.B.S.* is George Bernard Shaw, the playwright and good friend of Lady Gregory.

*Sir Hamar Greenwood* was Chief Secretary for Ireland, 1920–22.

5 NOVEMBER *A.* is Lady Gregory's widowed sister Arabella, who lived in Galway.

20 NOVEMBER *H.W. Nevinson*, progressive English journalist, author and social activist.

22 NOVEMBER The *Volunteers*, originally the army founded by Eoin MacNeill in 1913, had been redesignated the Army of the Irish Republic in 1919.

30 NOVEMBER Arthur *Griffith* (see Glossary) was at this time acting President of Dáil Éireann, while de Valera was in America.
  *John Quinn*, American lawyer and patron of the arts, especially in Ireland, was a close friend with whom Lady Gregory had a brief romance in 1912.

26 DECEMBER The *Wren-boys* go from house to house on St Stephen's Day singing a traditional song about 'The wren, the wren, the king of all birds' and asking for coins: 'I have a little box under my arm, / A tuppence or penny'll do it no harm'.

1921

DUBLIN, 25 FEBRUARY *The Revolutionist*: See note for 30 October 1920.

2 MARCH. COOLE *Sarah Purser*: Irish portrait-painter.
  *A.E.*: Pseudonym of George Russell (see Glossary).
  *Michael Collins* was at this time a member of Dáil Éireann and Minister for Finance (see Glossary).

TUESDAY, 4 OCTOBER *Horace Plunkett*: (1854–1932) One of the originators of the Co-operative Movement and of the Irish Agricultural Organization Society.

26 DECEMBER Hanged for his part in a Republican attack in November 1920 when only eighteen, *Kevin Barry* was commemorated in the ballad that became famous immediately.

## 1922

EASTER SUNDAY *John Dillon*: (1851–1927) Former member of the Irish Parliamentary Party, defeated by de Valera in 1918.

*John Redmond*: (1856–1918) Former leader of the Irish Parliamentary Party.

1 AUGUST *G.*: George (Bertha Georgiana) Yeats (1893–1968), W.B.'s wife.

*Oliver Gogarty*: (1878–1957) Writer, physician, friend of Joyce and Yeats as well as of Lady Gregory.

*Irregulars*: Soldiers of the anti-Treaty party.

## 1924

11 MARCH The Army 'mutiny' involved a struggle between the government and the republican leaders of the Free State army over the role of the Army Council and the interpretation of the Treaty.

22 OCTOBER The story by Lennox Robinson is 'The Madonna of Slieve Dun'.

## 1926

14 FEBRUARY. RUSSELL HOTEL, DUBLIN *Hanna Sheehy-Skeffington*: Widow of Francis Sheehy-Skeffington, who had been shot during the Rising while trying to prevent looting.

11 MAY *Mrs Osgood* is the mother of Molly Childers. Erskine Childers, a Republican during the Civil War, was executed by the Provisional Government in 1922.

4 SEPTEMBER *Bobby* Childers: Son of Molly and Erskine Childers (see note for 27 September 1919).

## 1927

21 NOVEMBER *O'Flaherty, V. C.*: Play by Bernard Shaw, set in Ireland.

## 1930

29 JANUARY *F.G.* is Frank Gallagher (1898–1962), journalist, writer, Fianna Fáil politician, and author of a book Lady Gregory much admired – *Days of Fear* (1928), an account of his 1920 hunger-strike.

18 OCTOBER Lady Gregory's mother, Frances Persse, was called 'the Mistress' even by her children.

## 1931

17 APRIL *James Stephens*: (1880–1950) Irish poet and novelist.

21 APRIL *The Dynasts*: Visionary historical work by Thomas Hardy.

## 1932

14 FEBRUARY *Celbridge*: Celbridge Abbey, in Co. Kildare, bought by Guy and Margaret Gregory Gough.

# GUIDE TO PRONUNCIATION OF
# IRISH NAMES

*This is a selection from the guide to the pronunciation of Irish names provided by Lady Gregory in* Cuchulain of Muirthemne *and* Gods and Fighting Men.

| | |
|---|---|
| Ailbhe | Alva |
| Almhuin | All-oon, or Alvin |
| Aobh | Aev, or Eev |
| Aodh | Ae (rhyming to *day*) |
| Aoife | Eefa |
| Beltaine | Bal-tinna |
| Bladhma | Bly-ma |
| Bodb Dearg | Bove Darrig |
| Caoilte | Cweeltia |
| Conchubar | Conachoor |
| Cuailgne | Cooley |
| Cuchulain | Cuhoolin, or Cu-hullin |
| Cliodna | Cleevna |
| Cumhal | Coo-al |
| Dun | Doon |
| Eimher | Aevir |
| Fionnchad | Finn-ăch-a |
| Loch Dairbhreach | Loch Darvragh |
| Lugh | Loo |
| Manannan | Mānănuan |
| Midhna | Mee-na |
| Mochaomhog | Mo-cweev-ōg |
| Muirthemne | Mur-hev-na |
| Rudraighe | Rury |
| Samhain | Sow-in |
| Sidhe | Shee |
| Slieve Echtge | Sleev Acht-ga |
| Tadg | Teig |
| Teamhair | T'yower or Tavvir (Tara) |
| Tuatha de Danaan | Too-ă-hă-dae Donnan |

# GLOSSARY: WORDS, PLACES, PERSONS, ALLUSIONS

**banshee** From the Irish *bean sidhe*, a female spirit who wails at the approaching death of an Irish person.

**Black and Tans** A special police force recruited to suppress Irish revolutionary activities in 1920–21. The name, based on their mismatched uniforms, derives from a Co. Limerick hunt, the Scarteen Black and Tans.

**cailleach** Nun; also old woman or proverbial hag, associated with the sovereignty of Ireland.

**Michael Collins** 1890–1922. Minister of Home Affairs (1918) and Minister for Finance (1919–22); Chairman of the Provisional Government and member of the delegation that signed the 1921 Treaty creating the Irish Free State; Commander of the government forces in the Civil War; killed in an ambush by unidentified parties.

**Columcille** Also known as Columba; a sixth-century poet, prophet and missionary who founded the monastic settlement on Iona.

**Conchubar** The Ulster king to whom Cuchulain owed allegiance.

**Cuchulain** Hero of the pre-Christian Ulster saga *The Táin* (*Táin Bó Cuailnge*).

**curragh/currach** A small boat made of a wicker framework and covered with skins or hides.

**Dáil Éireann** The Irish Parliament.

**Deirdre** Betrothed to Conchubar, High King of Ireland, but loves Naoise, one of the three sons of Usnach; flees with him and his two brothers; all are eventually betrayed and die. Their story is associated with *The Táin*.

**Éamon de Valera** 1882–1975. Commander of forces at Boland's Mills during the Easter Rising; President of the first Dáil Éireann (1919); resigned in opposition to the Treaty (1921); imprisoned by Free State troops (1923–4); established Fianna Fáil Party (1926); President of the Executive Council (1932–7); Taoiseach

(Prime Minister) (1937–48, 1951–4, 1957–9); President of the Republic (1959–72).

**Diarmuid** Known as the third best man of the Fianna. Beloved by Grania, who persuades him to go away with her on the eve of her marriage to Fionn. Diarmuid is finally slain by a magical boar on Ben Bulben in Sligo, and Grania returns to Fionn.

**Druids** Ancient priestly caste associated with magic and human sacrifice.

**dun** Fort.

**Easter Rising** Dublin-based insurrection in 1916 led by Thomas Clarke, Patrick Pearse, and others.

**Fenians** Popular name for the Irish Republican Brotherhood (IRB), founded in 1858 with the purpose of achieving independence through armed struggle. The name is derived from the Fianna, listed below.

**Fianna** Followers of Fionn mac Cumhail.

**Fionn mac Cumhail** Finn MacCool: legendary warrior of medieval Ireland.

**Firbolg** A legendary people of Ireland who supposedly preceded the Tuatha Dé Danann.

**forth** Probably fort; Irish *ráth* or *lios*.

**Granuaile** A traditional name for Ireland, popularized by nineteenth-century broadside ballads; linked to Gráinne Umhaill (Grace O'Malley, a sixteenth-century Mayo rebel).

**Maud Gonne** 1866–1953. Nationalist and feminist; supported tenant farmers in Land War; founded Inghinidhe na hÉireann (Daughters of Erin), 1900; married Major John MacBride (1903); separated (1905); interned in 1918 in connection with the so-called 'German Plot'; secretary of Women's Prisoners' Defence League (1922); active on behalf of poor school children; loved by Yeats and an inspiration of many of his poems.

**Arthur Griffith** 1871–1922. Editor of the *United Irishman* and *Sinn Féin*; attacked artistic policy of Abbey Theatre, especially in disputes involving Synge's *Playboy of the Western World*; Vice-President of Sinn Féin; in 1921 led the Irish delegates during Treaty negotiations; elected President of the Dáil (1922).

**Kathleen ni Houlihan** A traditional name for Ireland; the first known reference is to 'Caitilin ni Uallachain' by the eighteenth-century Gaelic poet William dall Heffernan. Later translated by James Clarence Mangan as 'Kathleen-Ny-Houlihan' (Kathleen, the daughter of Houlihan).

**keen** From the Irish *caoineadh*, a lament for the dead.

**Land War** 1879–82. Struggle to extend property rights of tenants, marked by evictions and violence.

**Lochlann** The country of the Fomors, a legendary tribe that came to prehistoric Ireland.

**Manannan mac Lir** God of the sea.

**Constance Markievicz** 1868–1927. Born Constance Gore-Booth of Lissadell, Co Sligo; married Count Casimir Markievicz (1900); joined Sinn Féin (1909); became an officer in the Irish Citizen Army and a leader in the Easter Rising; Sinn Féin MP (1918), and first woman elected to the House of Commons; Minister for Labour (1919–21); supported Republicans in the Civil War.

**Edward Martyn** 1859–1923. Lady Gregory's neighbour in Tullira Castle, Co. Galway; one of the founders of the Irish Literary Theatre (1899), which produced his plays *The Heather Field* and *Maeve*; President of Sinn Féin (1906–8).

**mering** Boundary, outer limit.

**ochone** Cry of misfortune or sorrow.

**ogham** The earliest writing in Ireland (*c.* AD 300); the alphabet consists of small strokes corresponding to letters in the Old Irish language; used in commemorative stone inscriptions.

**Oisín** Heroic son of Fionn mac Cumhail and the last survivor of the Fianna; journeys with Niamh to Tír na nÓg where he remains for 300 years before returning to Ireland to confront St Patrick.

**Oscar** Warrior son of Oisín.

**Charles Stewart Parnell** 1846–91. Leader of the Irish Parliamentary Party who secured Gladstone's support for Home Rule (1885); fell from power after he was cited as co-respondent in the O'Shea divorce case; died in 1891 after a futile bid for re-election; mythologized as 'the lost leader' of Ireland.

**George Russell** 1867–1935. Known as 'A.E.'; poet, painter, mystic, agrarian reformer; edited the *Irish Homestead* and the *Irish*

*Statesman*; friend of Lady Gregory and Yeats, and a major figure in the Irish Literary Revival.

**Sassanach** The English.

**Shan Van Vocht** From the Irish *Seanbhean Bhocht*, the Poor Old Woman, a traditional name for Ireland popularized by nineteenth-century broadside ballads.

**sidhe** Irish for fairy folk or spirits; pronounced *shee*.

**Sinn Féin** Irish for 'we ourselves'; a broad-based nationalist movement that worked for Irish independence and published the influential newspaper of the same name; reorganized by Éamon de Valera in 1917 to become the main national political party.

**Tara** Hill in Co. Meath regarded as the centre of ancient Ireland and the seat of the high king.

**Tuatha Dé Danann** The tribe of Danu, one of the legendary prehistoric tribes that colonized Ireland; associated with the *sidhe* who inhabit the underworld.

**tinkers** Travelling people viewed with suspicion by Irish farmers.

**Tír na nÓg** Legendary country of the eternally young. Also spelt Tir-Nan-Oge.

**United Irishmen** Political organization that crossed sectarian lines; founded in 1791 in Dublin and Belfast; responsible for 1798 Rising.

# BRIEF CHRONOLOGY OF MODERN IRISH HISTORY

1798 Rising of the United Irishmen
     Landing of the French at Killala Bay, Mayo
     Death of Wolfe Tone
1800 Act of Union between Britain and Ireland
1803 Rising and execution of Robert Emmet
1829 Catholic Emancipation Act
1831 National School System established
1842 Founding of the *Nation*, edited by Thomas Davis
1846–8 The Great Famine
1848 Arrest and transportation of Young Irelanders John
     Mitchel and William Smith O'Brien
1852 Birth of Isabella Augusta Persse at Roxborough, Co.
     Galway
1859 Founding of Fenian Brotherhood
1867 Execution of 'Manchester Martyrs'
1875 Charles Stewart Parnell elected to Parliament
1880 Augusta Persse married to Sir William Gregory of Coole
     Park
1881 Birth of Robert Gregory
1891 Death of Parnell
1892 Death of Sir William Gregory
1893 Founding of Gaelic League, with Douglas Hyde as first
     President
1894 Lady Gregory meets W. B. Yeats for the first time
1902 *Kathleen ni Houlihan* produced by the Irish National
     Theatre, directed by Willie and Frank Fay
1904 Opening of Abbey Theatre, with Lady Gregory's *Spread-
     ing the News* and Yeats's *On Baile's Strand*
1905 Sinn Féin established
1916 Easter Rising
1918 Death of Robert Gregory
1919 First Dáil Éireann; Eamon de Valera elected President

1919–21  Anglo-Irish War
1921  Truce
1922  Treaty establishing the Irish Free State; William Cosgrave succeeds Arthur Griffith as President
1922–3  Civil War
1932  Fianna Fáil victory in general election
Death of Lady Gregory
1938  Douglas Hyde elected President of Ireland

# BIBLIOGRAPHY

## *Works by Lady Gregory*

### The Coole Edition of Lady Gregory's Works

Published by Colin Smythe Ltd, Gerrards Cross, Buckinghamshire.

1. *Visions and Beliefs in the West of Ireland*, with two essays by W.B. Yeats and a foreword by Elizabeth Coxhead, 1970.
2. *Cuchulain of Muirthemne*, with preface by W. B. Yeats, foreword by Daniel J. Murphy, 1970.
3. *Gods and Fighting Men*, with preface by W. B. Yeats, foreword by Daniel J. Murphy, 1970.
4. *Our Irish Theatre*, foreword by Roger McHugh, 1972.
5–8. *The Collected Plays*, edited and introduced by Ann Saddlemyer, 1971.

*The Comedies* (*Twenty-Five, Spreading the News, Hyacinth Halvey, The Rising of the Moon, The Jackdaw, The Workhouse Ward, The Bogie Men, Coats, Damer's Gold, Hanrahan's Oath, The Wrens, On the Racecourse, Michelin, The Meadow Gate, The Dispensary, The Shoelace, The Lighted Window, A Losing Game*).

*The Tragedies* (*The Gaol Gate, Grania, Kincora, Dervorgilla, Mc-Donough's Wife*).

*The Tragic-Comedies* (*The Image, The Canavans, The White Cockade, The Deliverer*).

*The Wonder and Supernatural Plays* (*Colman and Guaire, The Travelling Man, The Full Moon, Shanwalla, The Golden Apple, The Jester, The Dragon, Aristotle's Bellows, The Story Brought by Brigit, Dave*).

*Translations and Adaptations* (*Teja, The Doctor in Spite of Himself, The Rogueries of Scapin, The Miser, The Would-be Gentleman, Mirandolina, Sancho's Master*).

*Collaborations* (with Douglas Hyde) *The Poorhouse*; (with W. B. Yeats) *The Unicorn from the Stars, Heads or Harps*.

559

9. *The Kiltartan Books* (*The Kiltartan Poetry Book*, *The Kiltartan History Book*, *The Kiltartan Wonder Book*), foreword by Padraic Colum, 1972.

10. *Sir Hugh Lane: His Life and Legacy* (*Hugh Lane's Life and Achievement*, *Case for the Return of Hugh Lane's Pictures to Dublin*, and other material concerning the Lane Bequest), foreword by James White, 1973.

11. *Poets and Dreamers* (including Lady Gregory's translations of nine plays by Douglas Hyde), foreword by T. R. Henn, 1974.

12. *A Book of Saints and Wonders*, foreword by Edward Malins, 1972.

13. *Seventy Years, 1852–1922*, edited and with a foreword by Colin Smythe, 1974 (also published 1976 by Macmillan, New York).

14. *The Journals. Volume I, 10 October 1916–24 February 1925*, edited and with a foreword by Daniel J. Murphy, 1978.

15. *The Journals. Volume II, 21 February 1925–9 May 1932*, edited by Daniel J. Murphy, essay 'The Death of Lady Gregory' by W.B. Yeats, afterword by Colin Smythe, 1987.

16. *The Lectures*, foreword by A. Norman Jeffares, in preparation.

17–18. *The Shorter Writings*, in preparation.

19. *Sir William Gregory, An Autobiography*, foreword by Edward McCourt, 1995.

20. *Mr Gregory's Letter-Box 1813–1835*, foreword by Jon Stallworthy, 1981.

21. *A Bibliography of Lady Gregory's Writings, General Index*, etc., in preparation.

22. *Lady Gregory's Diaries 1892–1902*, edited by James Pethica, in preparation.

## Select Works about Lady Gregory

Ayling, Ronald, 'Lady Gregory and Sean O'Casey: An Unlikely Friendship Revisited', in *Lady Gregory, Fifty Years After*, eds. Ann Saddlemyer and Colin Smythe (Gerrards Cross, Buckinghamshire: Colin Smythe Ltd, 1987), pp. 163–78.

Coxhead, Elizabeth, *Lady Gregory: A Literary Portrait* (London: Macmillan, 1961).

Dunleavy, Gareth W., 'The Pattern of Three Threads: The Hyde–Gregory Friendship' in *Lady Gregory, Fifty Years After*, pp. 131–42.

Fitzgerald, Mary, 'Four French Comedies: Lady Gregory's Translations of Molière' in *Lady Gregory, Fifty Years After*, pp. 277–90.
 —'"Perfection of the Life": Lady Gregory's Autobiographical Writings' in *Lady Gregory, Fifty Years After*, pp. 45–55.
 —'Sean O'Casey and Lady Gregory: The Record of a Friendship' in *Sean O'Casey Centenary Essays*, eds. David Krause and Robert G. Lowery (Totowa, New Jersey: Barnes & Noble, 1980), pp. 67–99.

Frazier, Adrian, *Behind the Scenes: Yeats, Horniman, and the Struggle for the Abbey Theatre* (Berkeley, California: University of California Press, 1990).

Gillin, Edward, '"Our Incorrigible Genius": Irish Comic Strategy in Lady Gregory's *Spreading the News*', *Colby Library Quarterly* 23, 4 (1987), pp. 168–72.

Gregory, Anne, *Me and Nu: Childhood at Coole* (Gerrards Cross, Buckinghamshire: Colin Smythe Ltd, 1970).

Hawkins, Maureen S. G., 'Ascendancy Nationalism, Feminist Nationalism and Stagecraft in Lady Gregory's Revision of *Kincora*' in *Irish Writers and Politics*, eds. Okifumi Komesu and Masaru Sekine (Gerrards Cross, Buckinghamshire: Colin Smythe Ltd, 1989), pp. 94–108.

Jenkins, Brian, 'The Marriage' in *Lady Gregory, Fifty Years After*, pp. 70–84.
 —*Sir William Gregory of Coole: A Biography* (Gerrards Cross, Buckinghamshire: Colin Smythe Ltd, 1986).

Kelly, John, '"Friendship is the only house I have": Lady Gregory and W. B. Yeats' in *Lady Gregory, Fifty Years After*, pp. 179–257.

Knapp, James, 'Irish Primitivism and Imperial Discourse: Lady Gregory's Peasantry' in *Macropolitics of Nineteenth-century Literature:*

*Nationalism, Exoticism, Imperialism*, eds. Jonathan Arac and Harriet Ritvo (Philadelphia: University of Pennsylvania Press, 1991), pp. 286–301.

Kohfeldt, Mary Lou, *Lady Gregory: The Woman Behind the Irish Renaissance* (New York: Atheneum, 1985; London: André Deutsch, 1985).
— 'The Cloud of Witnesses' in *Lady Gregory, Fifty Years After*, pp. 56–69.

Laurence, Dan H., ed., 'Note on Lady Gregory's Plays: by Bernard Shaw' in *Lady Gregory, Fifty Years After*, pp. 274–6.

Laurence, Dan H. and Grene, Nicholas, eds., *Shaw, Lady Gregory and the Abbey: A Correspondence and a Record* (Gerrards Cross, Buckinghamshire: Colin Smythe Ltd, 1993).

Longford Elizabeth, 'Lady Gregory and Wilfrid Scawen Blunt' in *Lady Gregory, Fifty Years After*, pp. 85–97.

McDiarmid, Lucy, 'Augusta Gregory, Bernard Shaw, and the Shewing-Up of Dublin Castle', *Publications of the Modern Language Association* (Special Topic: Literature and Censorship), 109, 1 (January 1994), pp. 26–44.
— 'The Demotic Lady Gregory' in *High and Low Moderns: Literature and Culture 1889–1939*, eds. Maria DiBattista and Lucy McDiarmid (New York: Oxford University Press), in preparation.

Malone, Andrew E., 'Lady Gregory, 1852–1932' in *Lady Gregory, Fifty Years After*, pp. 35–44.

Mikhail, E. H., ed., *Lady Gregory: Interviews and Recollections* (London: Macmillan, 1977).

Murphy, Daniel J., 'Lady Gregory, Co-Author and Sometimes Author of the Plays of W. B. Yeats' in *Modern Irish Literature: Essays in Honor of William York Tindall*, eds. Raymond J. Porter and James D. Brophy (New Rochelle: Iona College Press, 1972), pp. 43–52.
— '"Dear John Quinn"' in *Lady Gregory, Fifty Years After*, pp. 123–30.

Murphy, Maureen, 'Lady Gregory and the Gaelic League' in *Lady Gregory, Fifty Years After*, pp. 143–62.

—'Lady Gregory: "The Book of the People"', *Colby Quarterly* xxvii, 1 (March 1991), pp. 40–47.

Pethica, James, 'A Dialogue of Self and Service: Lady Gregory's Emergence as an Irish Writer and Partnership with W. B. Yeats', D. Phil. thesis (Oxford University, 1987).

—'Patronage and Creative Exchange: Yeats, Lady Gregory and the Economy of Indebtedness' in *Yeats and Women*, ed. Deirdre Toomey (London: Macmillan, 1992), pp. 60–94.

—'"Our Kathleen": Yeats's Collaboration with Lady Gregory in the Writing of *Cathleen ni Houlihan*' in *Yeats Annual 6*, ed. Warwick Gould (London: Macmillan, 1988), pp. 3–31.

—'Recontextualizing the Lyric Moment: Yeats's "The Happy Townland" and the Unpublished Play "The Country of the Young"' in *Yeats Annual 10*, ed. Warwick Gould (London: Macmillan, 1993), pp. 65–91.

Pethica, James, ed., 'A Woman's Sonnets, by Lady Gregory' in *Lady Gregory, Fifty Years After*, pp. 98–122.

Pihl, Lis, 'Literary Links: Lady Gregory, Francis Hackett and Signe Toksvig', *Irish University Review* 21, 2 (Autumn/Winter 1991), pp. 245–67.

Saddlemyer, Ann, 'Augusta Gregory, Irish Nationalist: "After all, what is wanted but a hag and a voice?"' in *Myth and Reality in Irish Literature*, ed. J. Ronsley (Waterloo, Ontario: Wilfrid Laurier University Press, 1977), pp. 29–40.

—'The Glory of the World and the Peasant Mirror' in *Lady Gregory, Fifty Years After*, pp. 306–21.

—'Image-maker for Ireland: Augusta, Lady Gregory' in *The World of W. B. Yeats*, revised edition, eds. Robin Skelton and Ann Saddlemyer (Seattle: University of Washington Press, 1967), pp. 161–8.

—*In Defence of Lady Gregory, Playwright* (Dublin: Dolmen Press, 1966).

Smythe, Colin, *A Guide to Coole Park, Home of Lady Gregory*, revised edition; foreword by Anne Gregory (Gerrards Cross, Buckingham-shire: Colin Smythe Ltd, 1983).

—'Lady Gregory's Contributions to Periodicals: A Checklist' in *Lady Gregory, Fifty Years After*, pp. 322–45.

Thuente, Mary Helen, 'Lady Gregory and "The Book of the People"', *Eire-Ireland*, 115 (Spring 1980), pp. 86–99.

Waters, Maureen, *The Comic Irishman* (Albany, New York: State University of New York Press, 1984).

—'Lady Gregory's *Grania*: A Feminist Voice', *Irish University Review* 25, 1 (Spring 1995), pp. 11–24.

Welch, Robert, 'A Language for Healing' in *Lady Gregory, Fifty Years After*, pp. 258–73.

Young, Lorna, 'In Retrospect: Lady Gregory's Plays Fifty Years Later' in *Lady Gregory, Fifty Years After*, pp. 291–306.

# INDEX